The Dark Side of Democracy

This book presents a new theory of ethnic cleansing based on the most terrible cases – colonial genocides, Armenia, the Nazi Holocaust, Cambodia, Yugoslavia, and Rwanda – and cases of lesser violence – early modern Europe, contemporary India, and Indonesia. Murderous cleansing is modern – it is "the dark side of democracy." It results where the *demos* (democracy) is confused with the *ethnos* (the ethnic group). Danger arises where two rival ethnonational movements each claims "its own" state over the same territory. Conflict escalates where either the weaker side fights rather than submit because of aid from outside or the stronger side believes it can deploy sudden, overwhelming force. But the state must also be factionalized and radicalized by external pressures like wars. Premeditation is rare, since perpetrators feel "forced" into escalation when their milder plans are frustrated. Escalation is not simply the work of "evil elites" or "primitive peoples." It results from complex interactions among leaders, militants, and "core constituencies" of ethnonationalism. Understanding this complex process helps us devise policies to avoid ethnic cleansing in the future.

Michael Mann is a professor of sociology at the University of California, Los Angeles. He is author of *The Sources of Social Power* (Cambridge, 1986, 1993) and *Fascists* (Cambridge, 2004).

The Dark Side of Democracy

Explaining Ethnic Cleansing

_____

MICHAEL MANN

University of California, Los Angeles

CAMBRIDGE
UNIVERSITY PRESS

PUBLISHED BY THE PRESS SYNDICATE OF THE UNIVERSITY OF CAMBRIDGE
The Pitt Building, Trumpington Street, Cambridge, United Kingdom

CAMBRIDGE UNIVERSITY PRESS
The Edinburgh Building, Cambridge CB2 2RU, UK
40 West 20th Street, New York, NY 10011-4211, USA
477 Williamstown Road, Port Melbourne, VIC 3207, Australia
Ruiz de Alarcón 13, 28014 Madrid, Spain
Dock House, The Waterfront, Cape Town 8001, South Africa

http://www.cambridge.org

First published 2005

Printed in the United States of America

Typeface Sabon 10/12 pt.   *System* LaTeX 2_ε [TB]

A catalog record for this book is available from the British Library.

Library of Congress Cataloging in Publication Data
Mann, Michael, 1942–
The dark side of democracy : explaining ethnic cleansing / Michael Mann.
p. cm.
Includes bibliographical references and index.
ISBN 0-521-83130-X – ISBN 0-521-53854-8 (pb.)
1. Political atrocities. 2. Genocide. 3. State-sponsored terrorism. 4. Ethnicity – Political
aspects. 5. Democracy – Moral and ethical aspects. I. Title.
HV6322.M36 2004
304.6'63 – dc22

2004045626

ISBN 0 521 83130 x hardback
ISBN 0 521 53854 8 paperback

Contents

Preface   *page* ix

1   The Argument   1

2   Ethnic Cleansing in Former Times   34

3   Two Versions of "We, the People"   55

4   Genocidal Democracies in the New World   70

5   Armenia, I: Into the Danger Zone   111

6   Armenia, II: Genocide   140

7   Nazis, I: Radicalization   180

8   Nazis, II: Fifteen Hundred Perpetrators   212

9   Nazis, III: Genocidal Careers   240

10 Germany's Allies and Auxiliaries   279

11 Communist Cleansing: Stalin, Mao, Pol Pot   318

12 Yugoslavia, I: Into the Danger Zone   353

13 Yugoslavia, II: Murderous Cleansing   382

14 Rwanda, I: Into the Danger Zone   428

15 Rwanda, II: Genocide   449

16 Counterfactual Cases: India and Indonesia   474

17 Combating Ethnic Cleansing in the World Today   502

Works Cited   531
Index   559

Preface

Since my previous work had neglected the extremes of human behavior, I had not thought much about good and evil. Like most people, I had tended to keep them in entirely separate categories from each other as well as from ordinary life. Having studied ethnic cleansing, I am now not so sure. Though I am not attempting here to morally blur good and evil, in the real world they are connected. Evil does not arrive from outside of our civilization, from a separate realm we are tempted to call "primitive." Evil is generated by civilization itself.

Consider the words of three prominent historical figures. We tend to think of President Thomas Jefferson as embodying Enlightened reason. Indeed, it was in the name of the advance of civilization that he declared that the "barbarities" of the native American Indians "justified extermination." A century later, President Theodore Roosevelt, a decent modern man, agreed, saying of the Indians, "extermination was as ultimately beneficial as it was inevitable." Forty years on, a third leader said, "It is the curse of greatness that it must step over dead bodies to create new life." This was SS Chief Heinrich Himmler, who is rightly considered as the personification of evil. Yet he and his colleague Adolf Hitler said they were only following in the Americans' footsteps. As I will argue here, murderous ethnic cleansing has been a central problem of our civilization, our modernity, our conceptions of progress, and our attempts to introduce democracy. It is our dark side. As we will see, perpetrators of ethnic cleansing do not descend among us as a separate species of evildoers. They are created by conflicts central to modernity that involve unexpected escalations and frustrations during which individuals are forced into a series of more particular moral choices. Some eventually choose paths that they know will produce terrible results. We can denounce them, but it is just as important to understand why they did it. And the rest of us (including myself) can breathe a sigh of relief that we ourselves have not been forced into such choices, for many of us would also fail them. The proposition underlying this book is that murderous ethnic cleansing comes from our civilization and from people, most of whom have been not unlike ourselves.

In trying to understand them, I owe debts to many. This is mainly a work of secondary analysis, depending on the primary work of others. My research is at the dismal end of a terrible subject matter, focusing on perpetrators, not on heroic resisters or even dignified victims. I can only admire many of my sources – the fortitude of survivors who bore witness to the horrors they experienced, the bystanders who carefully described what they saw, those who contributed to independent reports and judicial courts of inquiry, and those scholars who have dedicated their careers to comprehending what happened.

I have received much stimulation over the last few years from the Sawyer Seminars on Mass Violence held at the Center for Advanced Study in the Behavioral Sciences in Palo Alto, California. My thanks go to Norman Naimark, Ron Suny, Stephen Steadman, and Bob Zajonc, my co-organizers, to Doug McAdam, the director of the Center, and to all the Seminar's students and visiting speakers. They have all contributed intellectually to this book.

I owe a more particular debt to Hilmar Kaiser for inspiring me with his brilliant yet passionate scholarship on the Armenian genocide. I also thank Raymond Kévorkian for his kindness in giving me his major unpublished manuscript and Ödul Bozkurt for her translations from the Turkish. For help on the Nazi genocides I thank Ian Kershaw and Michael Burleigh for authoritative research guidance, Christopher Browning and George Browder for criticisms of an earlier manuscript, and Martin Tahany for German translations and Peter Stamatov for Magyar translations. Mark Lupher provided helpful criticisms of an earlier draft on Communist cleansings. Aleksandra Milicevic often corrected my outsider's ignorance of the Balkans, and I was privileged to discuss with Scott Straus his remarkable research in Rwanda. Patricia Ahmed helped me collect materials on India and Indonesia. I also thank David Laitin for his vigorous and helpful criticisms of my central arguments, though I fear my amendments will still not have satisfied him. UCLA provided me with generous research funds and talented students (I have named four of them here). As always, John Hall has given general intellectual encouragement, while Nicky and Louise Hart and Gareth and Laura Mann kept me sane amid such a disturbing research project.

Los Angeles, December 2003

1

The Argument

74-year-old Batisha Hoxha was sitting in her kitchen with her 77-year-old husband, Izet, staying warm by the stove. They had heard explosions but did not realize that Serbian troops had already entered the town. The next thing she knew, five or six soldiers had burst through the front door and were demanding "Where are your children?"

The soldiers began beating Izet, "so hard that he fell to the floor," she said. While they were kicking him, the soldiers demanded money and information on the whereabouts of the couple's sons. Then, while Izet was still on the floor looking up at them, they killed him. "They shot him three times in the chest," recalled Batisha. With her husband dying before her, the soldiers pulled the wedding ring off her finger.

"I can still feel the pain," she said. They fired shots . . . and finally they kicked Batisha and a 10-year-old boy who was staying with them and told them to get out.

"I was not even outside the gate when they burned it." . . . Her husband's body was in the flames. In that moment she was paralyzed. She was standing on the street in the rain with no house, no husband, no possessions but the clothes she was wearing. Finally, strangers passed in a tractor and bundled her into their wagon. Batisha's daughter later found her in a refugee camp in northern Albania.

Looking tenderly at her one photograph of herself and Izet, Batisha murmurs: "Nobody understands what we have seen and what we have suffered. Only God knows."[1]

This is how murderous ethnic cleansing was wreaked on one household in the village of Belanica in Kosovo in the very last year of the 20th century. The perpetrators were Serbs, using murder and mayhem to terrify the local Albanians into flight. Then the land could be occupied by Serbs, as was "our historic right," they said. Now the Kosovo boot is on the other foot. Since 1999 Albanians have been kicking out Serbs. Kosovo is now cleansed, not of Albanians but of almost all its Serbs.

Change the names of the people and places and the incident could have occurred almost anywhere in the world over the past few centuries – in

---

[1] We know too – thanks to *Los Angeles Times* reporter John Daniszewski, whose graphic report on Belanica appeared on April 25, 1999.

Australia, Indonesia, India, Russia, Germany, Ireland, the United States, Brazil. Ethnic cleansing is one of the main evils of modern times. We now know that the Holocaust of the Jews – though unique in important ways – is not unique as a case of genocide. The world's genocides remain thankfully few, but they are flanked by more numerous cases of less severe but nonetheless murderous cleansing.

This book offers an explanation of such terrible atrocities. For the sake of clarity, I lay it out up front now, in the form of eight general theses. These proceed from the very general to the particular, from the macro to the micro, successively adding parts of an overall explanation. I hope to prove these in the course of the book by examining in detail the very worst cases of cleansing, those that have involved mass murder.

1. My first thesis concerns the broad historical era in which murderous cleansing became common. *Murderous cleansing is modern, because it is the dark side of democracy.* Let me make clear at the outset that I do not claim that democracies routinely commit murderous cleansing. Very few have done so. Nor do I reject democracy as an ideal – I endorse that ideal. Yet democracy has always carried with it the possibility that the majority might tyrannize minorities, and this possibility carries more ominous consequences in certain types of multiethnic environments.

This thesis has two parts, concerning modernity and democracy. Ethnic cleansing is essentially modern. Though not unknown in previous history (and probably common among the very small groups who dominated prehistory), it became more frequent and deadly in modern times. The 20th-century death toll through ethnic conflict amounted to somewhere over 70 million, dwarfing that of previous centuries. Additionally, conventional warfare increasingly targeted entire peoples as the enemy. Whereas civilians accounted for less than 10 percent of deaths in World War I, they rocketed to over half in World War II and to somewhat above 80 percent in wars fought in the 1990s. Civil wars, mostly ethnic in nature, were now taking over from interstate wars as the main killers. Perhaps 20 million have died in them, though it is impossible to be precise (figures have been hazarded by Chesterman, 2001: 2; Fearon & Laitin, 2003; Gurr, 1993, 2000; Harff, 2003; Markusen & Kopf, 1995: 27–34).

Ethnic and religious conflicts continue to simmer as I write in 2003 – in Northern Ireland, the Basque Country, Cyprus, Bosnia, Kosovo, Macedonia, Algeria, Turkey, Israel, Iraq, Chechnya, Azerbaijan, Afghanistan, Pakistan, India, Sri Lanka, Kashmir, Burma, Tibet, Chinese Xinjiang, Fiji, the southern Philippines, various islands of Indonesia, Bolivia, Peru, Mexico, the Sudan, Somalia, Senegal, Uganda, Sierra Leone, Liberia, Nigeria, Congo, Rwanda, and Burundi. Over half of these cases involve substantial killing. As you read these words, one ethnic crisis probably will be exploding into violence on your television screen or newspaper, while several other explosions will not be deemed newsworthy. The 20th century was bad enough. Perhaps the 21st will be even worse.

The mayhem committed on September 11, 2001, and the "war against terrorism" that it triggered, have imprinted the horror of murderous ethnic and religious strife on the consciousness of the entire world. It has especially struck home in the prosperous countries of the North, shielded from such things over the past half-century. Neither the attack of September 11 nor the retaliatory attacks on Afghanistan and Iraq had as their intent ethnic cleansing, but they promptly became entwined with ethnic-religious conflicts involving cleansing between Israelis and Palestinians, Sunni and Shi'ite Muslims, Iraqis and Kurds, Russians and Chechens, Kashmiri Muslims and Hindus, and various Afghan tribes. In fact, some seem to be leading by the nose the foreign policies of the Great Powers.

Thus, unfortunately for us, murderous ethnic cleansing is not primitive or alien. It belongs to our own civilization and to us. Most say this is due to the rise of nationalism in the world, and this is true. But nationalism becomes very dangerous only when it is politicized, when it represents the perversion of modern aspirations to democracy in the nation-state. Democracy means rule by the people. But in modern times *the people* has come to mean two things. The first is what the Greeks meant by their word *demos*. This means the ordinary people, the mass of the population. So democracy is rule by the ordinary people, the masses. But in our civilization the people also means "nation" or another Greek term, *ethnos*, an ethnic group – a people that shares a common culture and sense of heritage, distinct from other peoples. But if the people is to rule in its own nation-state, and if the people is defined in ethnic terms, then its ethnic unity may outweigh the kind of citizen diversity that is central to democracy. If such a people is to rule, what is to happen to those of different ethnicity? Answers have often been unpleasant – especially when one ethnic group forms a majority, for then it can rule "democratically" but also tyrannically. As Wimmer (2002) argues, modernity is structured by ethnic and nationalist principles because the institutions of citizenship, democracy, and welfare are tied to ethnic and national forms of exclusion. I concede that some other features of modernity play more subsidiary roles in the upsurge of cleansing. We will see that some modern professional militaries have been tempted toward wars of annihilation of the enemy, while modern ideologies like fascism and communism have been similarly ruthless. But underlying all this is the notion that the enemy to be annihilated is a whole people.

I clarify this first thesis with some subtheses.

1a. Murderous ethnic cleansing is a hazard of the age of democracy since amid multiethnicity the ideal of rule by the people began to entwine the *demos* with the dominant *ethnos*, generating organic conceptions of the nation and the state that encouraged the cleansing of minorities. Later, socialist ideals of democracy also became perverted as the *demos* became entwined with the term *proletariat*, the working class, creating pressures to cleanse other classes. These have been the most general ways in which democratic ideals were transmuted into murderous cleansing.

1b. In modern colonies, settler democracies in certain contexts have been truly murderous, more so than more authoritarian colonial governments. The more settlers controlled colonial institutions, the more murderous the cleansing. This will be demonstrated in Chapter 4. It is the most direct relationship I have found between democratic regimes and mass murder.

1c. Regimes newly embarked upon democratization are more likely to commit murderous ethnic cleansing than are stable authoritarian regimes (Chua, 2004, also makes this argument). When authoritarian regimes weaken in multiethnic environments, *demos* and *ethnos* are most likely to become entwined. In contrast, stable authoritarian regimes in such contexts tend to govern by divide-and-rule. This leads them to seek to balance the demands of powerful groups, including ethnic ones. However, a few highly authoritarian regimes deviate. They mobilize majoritarian groups into a mass party-state mobilizing the people against "enemy" minorities. The Nazi and Communist regimes discussed in Chapters 7–11 were dictatorships, not democracies, though they did emerge out of would-be democratizing contexts, which they then exploited. They mobilized the people as *ethnos* or proletariat. They are partial exceptions to this subthesis.

1d. Stably institutionalized democracies are less likely than either democratizing or authoritarian regimes to commit murderous cleansing. They have entrenched not only elections and rule by the majority, but also constitutional guarantees for minorities. But their past was not so virtuous. Most of them committed sufficient ethnic cleansing to produce an essentially mono-ethnic citizen body in the present. In their past, cleansing and democratization proceeded hand in hand. Liberal democracies were built on top of ethnic cleansing, though outside of the colonies this took the form of institutionalized coercion, not mass murder.

1e. Regimes that are actually perpetrating murderous cleansing are never democratic, since that would be a contradiction in terms. These subtheses therefore apply beforehand, to the earlier phases of escalation of ethnic conflict. Indeed, as escalation proceeds, all perpetrating regimes become less and less democratic. The dark side of democracy is the perversion through time of either liberal or socialist ideals of democracy.

In view of these complex relations, we will not find any simple overall relationship in the world today between democracy and ethnic cleansing – as Fearon and Laitin (2003) confirm in their quantitative study of recent civil (mostly ethnic) wars. But mine is not a static comparative analysis. It is historical and dynamic: murderous cleansing has been moving across the world as it has modernized and democratized. Its past lay mainly among Europeans, who invented the democratic nation-state. The countries inhabited by Europeans are now safely democratic, but most have also been ethnically cleansed (as in thesis 1d). Now the epicenter of cleansing has moved into the South of the world. Unless humanity takes evasive action, it will continue to spread until democracies – hopefully, not ethnically cleansed ones – rule the world. Then it will ease. But if we wish to ease it more quickly from the world, we now have to face squarely up to the dark side of democracy.

2. *Ethnic hostility rises where ethnicity trumps class as the main form of social stratification, in the process capturing and channeling classlike sentiments toward ethnonationalism.* Cleansing was rare in the past because most big historic societies were class-divided. Aristocracies or other small oligarchies dominated them, and they rarely shared a common culture or ethnic identity with the common people. In fact they despised the people, often considering them barely human. The people did not exist across class lines – class trumped ethnicity.

Even the first modern societies were dominated by the politics of class. Liberal representative states first emerged as a way of compromising class conflict, giving them a plural sense of people and nation. They tolerated some ethnic diversity. But where the modern struggle for democracy involved a whole people struggling against rulers defined as foreign, an ethnic sense of the people arose, often capturing class resentments. The people was seen as a proletarian nation asserting fundamental democratic rights against upper-class imperial nations, which retorted that they were bringing civilization to their backward peoples. Today the Palestinian cause is decidedly proletarian in its tone, seeing its oppressor as an exploiting and colonial Israel – backed up by American imperialism – while Israelis and Americans claim they are defending civilization against primitive terrorists. The arguments are similar to those of class enemies of former times.

Ethnic differences entwine with other social differences – especially of class, region, and gender. Ethnonationalism is strongest where it can capture other senses of exploitation. The most serious defect of recent writing on ethnonationalism has been its almost complete neglect of class relations (as in Brubaker, 1996; Hutchinson, 1994; Smith, 2001). Others wrongly see class as materialistic, ethnicity as emotional (Connor, 1994: 144–64; Horowitz, 1985: 105–35). This simply inverts the defect of previous generations of writers who believed that class conflict dominated while ignoring ethnicity. Now the reverse is true, and not only among scholars. Our media are dominated by ethnic strife while largely ignoring class struggles. Yet in actuality these two types of conflict infuse each other. Palestinians, Dayaks, Hutus, and so on believe they are being materially exploited. Bolsheviks and Maoists believed that landlord and Kulak classes were exploiting the nation. To neglect either ethnicity or class is mistaken. Sometimes one or the other may come to dominate, but this will involve the capturing and channeling of the other. The same can be said of gender and regional sentiments.

Indeed, murderous cleansing does not occur among rival ethnic groups who are separate but equal. Mere difference is not enough to generate much conflict. It is not Christians against Muslims that causes problems, but contexts in which Muslims feel oppressed by Christians (or vice versa). If South Africa had actually lived up to its own apartheid claim to produce separate but equal development of the races, Africans would not have revolted. They revolted because apartheid was a sham, involving racial exploitation of Africans by whites. For serious ethnic conflict to develop, one ethnic group must be seen as exploiting the other. And in turn, the imperial oppressor will react in righteous outrage against the threat of having its "civilization" overwhelmed by "primitivism" – just as upper classes do when threatened with revolution.

3. *The danger zone of murderous cleansing is reached when (a) movements claiming to represent two fairly old ethnic groups both lay claim to their own state over all or part of the same territory and (b) this claim seems to them to have substantial legitimacy and some plausible chance of being implemented.* Almost all dangerous cases are bi-ethnic ones, where both groups are quite powerful and where rival claims to political sovereignty are laid on top of quite old senses of ethnic difference – though not on what are generally called *ancient hatreds*. Ethnic differences are worsened to serious hatreds, and to dangerous levels of cleansing, by persistent rival claims to political sovereignty. I characteristically identify four major sources of power in societies: ideological, economic, military, and political. Murderous ethnic conflict concerns primarily *political power relations*, though as it develops it also involves ideological, economic, and finally military power relations too. Mine is essentially a political explanation of ethnic cleansing.

4. *The brink of murderous cleansing is reached when one of two alternative scenarios plays out. (4a). The less powerful side is bolstered to fight rather than to submit* (for submission reduces the deadliness of the conflict) *by believing that aid will be forthcoming from outside* – usually from a neighboring state, perhaps its ethnic homeland state (as in Brubaker's, 1996, model). In this scenario both sides are laying political claim to the same territory, and both believe they have the resources to achieve it. This was so in the Yugoslav, Rwandan, Kashmiri, and Chechen cases, for example. The current U.S. war against terrorism aims at eliminating such outside support, labeling it *terrorism* (see Chapter 17). *(4b) The stronger side believes it has such overwhelming military power and ideological legitimacy that it can force through its own cleansed state at little physical or moral risk to itself.* This is so in colonial settler cases, as in the North American, Australian, and Circassian cases considered later. The Armenian and Jewish cases mixed these two scenarios together, since the dominant Turkish and German sides believed they had to strike first in order to prevent the weaker Armenian and Jewish sides from allying with far more threatening outsiders. All these terrible eventualities were produced by interaction between the two sides. We

cannot explain such escalation merely in terms of the actions or beliefs of the perpetrators. We need to examine the interactions between the perpetrator and victim groups – and usually with other groups as well. For few even bi-ethnic situations lead to murderous cleansing. One or both sides must first decide to fight rather than conciliate or manipulate, and that choice is unusual.

5. *Going over the brink into the perpetration of murderous cleansing occurs where the state exercising sovereignty over the contested territory has been factionalized and radicalized amid an unstable geopolitical environment that usually leads to war.* Out of such political and geopolitical crises radicals emerge calling for tougher treatment of perceived ethnic enemies. In fact, where ethnic conflict between rival groups is quite old, it is usually somewhat ritualized, cyclical, and manageable. Truly murderous cleansing, in contrast, is unexpected, originally unintended, emerging out of unrelated crises like war. Conversely, in cases where states and geopolitics remain stable, even severe ethnic tensions and violence tend to be cyclical and manageable at lesser levels of violence – as we see in Chapter 16 in present-day India. But where political institutions are unstable and affected by war, violence may lead to mass murder – as Harff's (2003) study of political cleansings across the world confirms.

There are different forms of political instability. Some states were fragmenting and factionalizing (like the Hutu state of Rwanda); others had been seized and were being newly consolidated, determinedly repressing dissidents and factionalism (like the Nazi state). In some brand-new states, consolidation was very uneven (as in the new Bosnian and Croatian states). But these were not stable and cohesive states, whether democratic or authoritarian. Nor were they often the failed states that political science researchers have shown are most likely to generate civil wars (the Congo at the beginning of the 21st century is an exception). Ethnic cleansings are in their most murderous phases usually directed by states, and this requires some state coherence and capacity.

6. *Murderous cleansing is rarely the initial intent of perpetrators.* It is rare to find evil geniuses plotting mass murder from the very beginning. Not even Hitler did so. Murderous cleansing typically emerges as a kind of Plan C, developed only after the first two responses to a perceived ethnic threat fail. Plan A typically envisages a carefully planned solution in terms of either compromise or straightforward repression. Plan B is a more radically repressive adaptation to the failure of Plan A, more hastily conceived amid rising violence and some political destabilization. When these both fail, some of the planners radicalize further. To understand the outcome, we must analyze the unintended consequences of a series of interactions yielding escalation. These successive Plans may contain both logical and more contingent escalations. The perpetrators may be ideologically determined from quite early on to rid themselves of the ethnic out-group, and when milder methods fail, they

almost logically seem to escalate with resolute determination to overcome all obstacles by more and more radical means. This was true of Hitler and his myrmidons: the Final Solution of the Jewish question seems much less of an accident than the logical escalation of an ideology ruthlessly overcoming all obstacles in its path. For the Young Turks, however, the final solution to the Armenian problem seems much more contingent, flowing out of what they saw as their suddenly desperate situation in 1915.

To downplay intentionality like this is morally uncomfortable, often involving me in arguing against those who speak in the name of the victims. Genocide of the Jews, the Armenians, the Tutsis, of some colonized native peoples, and of others was deliberately accomplished. The evidence is overwhelming. But surviving victims like to emphasize premeditation by their oppressors. This probably derives mostly from their need to find meaning in their sufferings. What could be worse than to regard such extreme suffering as accidental? In *King Lear*, Edgar says of his sufferings: "Like flies to wanton boys are we to the gods." I find that a tempting theory of human society, but I doubt many victims do. I am not actually arguing that murderous cleansing is accidental, only that it is far more complex and contingent than blame-centered theories allow. It is eventually perpetrated deliberately, but the route to deliberation is usually a circuitous one.

7. *There are three main levels of perpetrator: (a) radical elites running party-states; (b) bands of militants forming violent paramilitaries; and (c) core constituencies providing mass though not majority popular support.* Elites, militants, and core constituencies are all normally necessary for murderous cleansing to ensue. We cannot simply blame malevolent leaders or ethnic groups en masse. That would be to credit leaders with truly magical powers of manipulation or whole peoples with truly remarkable single-mindedness. Both assumptions are at odds with everything sociologists know about the nature of human societies. In all my cases particular elites, militants, and core constituencies are linked together in quite complex ways, forming social movements that (like other social movements) embody mundane power relations. Power is exercised in three distinct ways: top-down by elites, bottom-up by popular pressures, and coercively sideways by paramilitaries. These pressures interact and so generate mundane relations like those found in all social movements – especially of hierarchy, comradeship, and career. This has a big impact on perpetrators' motives, as we will see in a moment.

The notion of core constituencies reveals that murderous cleansing resonates more in environments favoring combinations of nationalism, statism, and violence. The main core constituencies are ethnic refugees and people from threatened border districts; those more dependent on the state for their subsistence and values; those living and working outside of the main sectors of the economy that generate class conflict (who are more likely to favor class over ethnonationalist models of conflict); those socialized into acceptance of physical violence as a way of solving social problems or achieving personal advancement – like soldiers, policemen, criminals, hooligans, and athletes; and those attracted to machismo ideology – young males striving to assert themselves in the world, often led by older males who were socialized as youths in an earlier phase of violence. So the main axes of stratification involved in cleansing movements are region, economic sector, gender, and age. Radical ethnonationalist movements tend to contain a normal class structure: leaders come from the upper and middle classes, the rank-and-file from lower down – with the real dirty work often performed by the working class. I explore all these groups' motivations, careers, and interactions.

8. Finally, *ordinary people are brought by normal social structures into committing murderous ethnic cleansing*, and their motives are much more mundane. To understand ethnic cleansing, we need a sociology of power more than a special psychology of perpetrators as disturbed or psychotic people – though some may be. As the psychologist Charny (1986: 144) observes, "the mass killers of humankind are largely everyday human beings – what we have called normal people according to currently accepted definitions by the mental health profession."

Placed in comparable situations and similar social constituencies, you or I might also commit murderous ethnic cleansing. No ethnic group or nation is invulnerable. Many Americans and Australians committed murderous cleansing in the past; some Jews and Armenians – the most victimized peoples of the 20th century – have perpetrated recent atrocities against Palestinians and Azeris (and, in turn, some of these victim groups are also perpetrators). There are no virtuous peoples. Religions tend to stress the presence in all humans of original sin, the human capacity for evil. Indeed, placed in the right circumstances and core constituencies, we are almost all capable of such evil – perhaps even of enjoying it. But original sin would be an insufficient explanation for this, since our capacity for evil becomes realized only in the circumstances explored in this book. In the case of cleansing, these circumstances are less primitive or ancient than modern. There is something in modernity releasing this particular evil on a mass scale.

Given the messiness and uniqueness of societies, my theses cannot be scientific laws. They do not even fit perfectly all my case studies. For example, Nazi genocide does not fit neatly into thesis 3, since Jews were not claiming sovereignty over any part of Germany. In Chapter 7 I offer a modified, indirect version of thesis 3 in which Jews seemed to German ethnonationalists to be implicated as conspirators in other groups' claims to political sovereignty (especially as so-called Judeo-Bolsheviks). In each case I investigate the extent to which my theses apply, pointing out necessary differences and modifications. Chapters 2 and 3 present a brief history of cleansing from ancient to modern times, showing how ethnic cleansing was originally quite rare but then became endemic in the world of the Europeans, at first in rather mild ways that remained subordinate to class conflict. Mass murder has been ubiquitous if uncommon throughout most of human history. But murder in order to remove ("cleanse") a people was rare in earlier centuries. Things became more dangerous with the rise of salvation religions and then with the rise of rule by the people. The empirical core of the book then consists of a series of studies of the worst outbursts of modern murderous cleansing. In all of them I go from the most general causes of danger zones to the events that precipitated going over the brink to the actual processes and perpetrators of murderous cleansing.

My analysis must also confront two difficulties of method. Murderous cleansing is fortunately rare. How can we generalize about such few cases? Might not the causes be unique to each case? To some extent this is true. Nazis and their hatred for Jews were unique. So is the situation of Tutsis and Hutus in Rwanda, living among each other across the country, unable to withdraw to their own core territories. All my cases have peculiarities that I must respect. Second, to consider only these cases would be to cover only cases that do escalate to mass murder, ignoring the more numerous cases where ethnic tensions get defused. This would be what social scientists call *sampling on the dependent variable*. So Chapter 16 examines contemporary India and Indonesia to see why diverse ethnic rivalries lead to varying degrees of violence. Finally, Chapter 17 reviews my theses and surveys trends in the world today.

DEFINING TERMS: ETHNICITY, NATION, ETHNIC CLEANSING

Ethnicity is not objective. Ethnic groups are normally defined as groups sharing a common culture and common descent. Yet culture is vague and descent usually fictitious. A common culture may refer to a relatively precise characteristic, like a shared religion or language. But it may merely refer to a claim to share a way of life – which cannot be precisely defined. Common descent is mythical for any group larger than a clan or a lineage (what I shall call a *micro-ethnicity*). The future use of DNA analysis will probably reveal that relatively immobile populations share substantial common heredity, but this will not be so for most large groups claiming ethnic commonality. People who define themselves as Serbs or Germans or Scots actually descend from many smaller descent groups who have moved around and intermarried with their neighbors. Claims to commonality among large groups actually aggregate together numerous descent groups. This book discusses these *macro-ethnicities* formed by social relations other than biology or kinship. None of the ethnic conflicts considered here are natural or primordial. They and their conflicts are socially created.

They are created in diverse ways. A common language is important in uniting Germans but not Serbs (their language is shared with Croats and Bosniaks). Religion is important for Serbs (their orthodox Christianity distinguishes them from Croats, Bosniaks, and Albanians) but not Germans (divided into Catholics and Protestants). Theories of civilization and race helped give Europeans a common sense of being civilized and then white, in contrast to their colonial subjects. Economic dominance or subordination can form identities, and so can military power. Imperial conquerors often create macro-ethnicities by allocating particular roles to groups they define as belonging to a single people or tribe. Finally, a shared political history as an independent state or province is of ubiquitous importance – as it is for Scots, not distinct in language or religion from the English but with a distinct political history. Given this diversity, it is safer to define ethnicities subjectively, in terms they themselves and/or their neighbors use.

An *ethnicity* is a group that defines itself or is defined by others as sharing common descent and culture. So *ethnic cleansing* is the removal by members of one such group of another such group from a locality they define as their own. A *nation* is such a group that also has political consciousness, claiming collective political rights in a given territory. A *nation-state* results where such a group has its own sovereign state. Not all self-conscious nations possess or desire nation-states. Some claim only local autonomy or entrenched rights within a broader multiethnic state.

Ethnic groups treat each other in many ways, most of which do not involve murder. Since the advent of global news media, the few cases involving mass murder have been imprinted upon our consciousness. But thankfully, they are rare. The continent of Africa figures mostly in the Western media only for really bad news. But there are only a few African cases of murderous ethnic cleansing – in a continent in which all states are multiethnic. Fearon and Laitin (1996) estimate all the cases of serious ethnic violence as less than 1 percent of all the multiethnic environments found in Africa. Table 1.1 identifies degrees of both violence and cleansing in ethnic relations. This enables us to distinguish murderous ethnic cleansing from nonmurderous cleansing, as well as from outbreaks of mass violence and killing whose purpose is not to ethnically cleanse. It concerns only the violent cleansing of civilians, excluding mass killings that are commonly legitimated by the rules of war.

Table 1.1 contains two dimensions: the extent to which a group is eliminated (cleansed) from a community and the extent to which violence is used to achieve it. Remember that since ethnic groups are culturally defined, they can be eliminated if their culture disappears, even if there is no physical removal of persons. People can change their cultural identity. But I shall not fly in the face of normal understandings of the term ethnic cleansing to include within it mere cultural elimination, except by placing inverted commas around the word cleansing in such cases – as I do in this table. But it is important to distinguish the various forms that cleansing and "cleansing" might take.

The terms found in Table 1.1 will be used through out this book. The first row of the table begins with policies that contain no significant violence. Row 1, column 1 contains the ideal way to handle ethnic differences,

TABLE 1.1 *Types of Violence and Cleansing in Intergroup Relations*

Types of Violence	Types of Cleansing		
	None	Partial	Total
1. None	1. Multiculturalism/toleration; 2. Consociational/confederalism	Partial abandoning of identity, e.g., through voluntary official language adoption	Voluntary assimilation
2. Institutional coercion	Discrimination	1. Official language restrictions; 2. Segregation	Cultural suppression
3. Policed repression	Selective policed repression	1. Policed partial repression of out-group's language and culture; 2. Policed out-group settlement/displacement	1. Policed total suppression of out-group's language and culture; 2. Population exchanges; 3. Policed deportations and pressured emigration
4. Violent repression	Generalized policed repression	1. Pogroms, communal riots, some forms of rape; 2. Violent settlement/displacement	1. Wild deportation and emigration; 2. Biological: sterilization, forced marriage, some forms of rape
5. Unpremeditated mass deaths	Mistaken war, civil war and revolutionary projects, fratricide	Callous war, civil war, and revolutionary projects	Ethnocide
6. Premeditated mass killing	Exemplary and civil war repression, systematic reprisals	1. Forced conversion; 2. Politicide; 3. Classicide →	Genocide

Note: Darker shading indicates the core of the zone of murderous cleansing discussed in this book; lighter shading indicates a borderline zone in which it may occasionally occur.

through equal treatment and respect for all ethnic groups – *multiculturalism*. Some multicultural states simply ignore ethnicity, treating all persons as equal regardless of their ethnicity. Their constitutions do not mention the rights of ethnic groups, while political parties and social movements (apart from cultural ones) do not organize around ethnicities. This is a common ideal in countries of ethnically plural immigration, like the United States or Australia. Since such immigrant groups cannot plausibly claim their own state, they present no threat to the existing state, and the constitution can safely ignore their ethnicity. Thus many people in the United States and Australia aspire to a culture that is multicultural but to a polity that is ethnically blind. Their politics would then concern class, region, gender, and so on more than ethnicity.

Things differ in the more potentially dangerous situation in which ethnic groups dominate distinct territories or can otherwise aspire to create their own states or regional autonomies. Multicultural ideals here have difficulty remaining ethnically blind in the political arena. They do not ignore ethnicity but explicitly build it into constitutions through collective guarantees for different ethnicities. This might be through *confederal* methods (ethnicities have a degree of regional control, as in contemporary Nigeria) or *consociational* methods (they are guaranteed power sharing at the center, as in Belgium). Such entrenchments are aimed at binding all major groups into the state. Here politics concerns ethnicity as well as class, region, gender, and so on, but hopefully they will be the politics of ethnic compromise. Affirmative action programs are a much milder, liberal version of this that guarantee protections at the individual level for out-groups. *Toleration* is the weaker and commoner version of recognizing the reality of multiculturalism. Toleration implies that we have feelings of hostility toward the out-group but are trying hard to suppress them. Unfortunately, these first policies are mostly ideal, not real-world, polities. Most ethnic relations are less tolerant than this.

The next two columns of row 1 include cases where ethnic groups weaken or disappear without violence, cleansed but by consent. This happened in the later phase of ethnic homogenization in Western Europe. By the mid-19th century in France or Britain, their states needed to apply little coercion to eliminate minority languages. Minorities accepted that their own regional language – say Breton or Welsh – was backward, depriving their children of success in modern society. Most immigrants to the United States or Australia similarly acquire English voluntarily, do not teach their children their own original language, and abandon many other ethnic cultural practices. Their descendants may retain only a sentimental sense of being Germans, Slovaks, or Welsh. So *voluntary assimilation* produces a cleansed society, not from hostile acts by the dominant group but by positive inducements. White immigrant groups in the United States or Australia lost most of their earlier ethnic identity as they pursued economic and status success and social conformity and became Americans or Australians. This is a pretty harmless and marginal form of cleansing, lamented only by those who value the preservation of traditional cultures. Indeed, the word cleansing (even inside its inverted commas) may be inappropriate here.

Row 2 contains the first escalation of violence, to *institutional coercion*. *Discrimination* is probably the most common policy of all. It limits the rights of the out-group but permits its members to retain their ethnic identity. Discrimination typically involves preferential hiring, redlining residential districts, negative cultural stereotyping, offensive interpersonal behavior, and police harassment. Most countries discriminate against some minorities. African Americans still suffer discrimination 150 years after the abolition of slavery and 50 years after the civil rights movement. Take, for example, the offense sardonically described in the United States as "driving while black," in which the cop pulls over a black man because he is driving "too good" a car. All such discrimination is to be deplored, but it is a lot better than what follows in the rest of this table.

Severe discrimination can restrict rights to acquire education, the vote, public office, or property. The dominant group may also compel out-groups to use its language as the official one of education and the public sphere. *Segregation* is geographical partial cleansing: the out-group is ghettoized in apartheid or enslaved conditions. This may be far more oppressive than the milder forms of total cleansing. After all, many slaves would like to run away from their oppression (which would produce a more cleansed society) but are prevented by force from doing so. Here ethnic and class politics continue alongside each other. Apartheid South Africa had almost normal class politics within its white community, and some traces of them within its African and colored communities, but race dominated politics as a whole.

The next column, "Cultural Suppression," involves total cleansing, though only through institutional coercion. Public institutions suppress the culture of the out-group, whose identity is thus forcibly assimilated into the dominant group. The group's language may be banned from schools or offices, its religion banned, its distinctive family names changed by law. Though this is coercive, it is usually legal and involves little physical force, except to put down scattered resistance to the policy (which the next row covers). Such suppression is not often viewed as ethnic cleansing, especially if it is successfully imposed. Then, after the passage of some time, it may not be generally remembered by either group as cleansing – as, for example, with the assimilation of Welsh people into a British identity largely defined by the English. Welsh people are generally proud of what Welshness they believe they have retained, not the probably larger cultural traits they have lost. Another example is the virtually total assimilation of Provencals or Acquitainians into French identity. Many members of the out-group may react to all these ill treatments by emigrating, as the Irish did in such large numbers. This is also a partly coerced, partly voluntary form of cleansing.

Physical violence begins in Row 3, containing *selective policed repression*. "Selective" means it is targeted at dissidents, usually protesters against row 2 policies. "Policed" means repression remains rather orderly, enforcing laws through routinized legitimate means – though this will typically also include some limited physical violence. The first column contains repression aimed specifically at protesters; the second escalates to an attempt to repress part of the out-group's identity. The latter also contains policed implantation of settlers from the dominant group, displacing the indigenous out-group from their homes, though not from the society as a whole. An example would be the settlement of Protestant Scots on Ulster farms from the 17th century on, forcibly displacing thousands of Irish Catholic farmers. The third column moves us to *policed total cultural suppression, population exchanges*, and *policed deportations and emigrations*, a wide variety of state-run cleansings, coercive but not usually very violent. The policies discussed so far normally involve a fairly stable state believing only that it is enforcing the rule of law.

Row 4 introduces serious physical violence. In the first column this remains routinized and orderly. *General policed repression* is aimed at groups harboring protesters, rioters, rebels, or terrorists, inflicting sanguinary official punishment in order to coerce the main part of the group to submit. If this is routine, states will employ specialized paramilitaries whose names become notorious to out-groups – like the Cossacks or the Black-and-Tans. The next two columns involve less controlled violence. Escalation to violent partial cleansing involves settlement/displacement, as in most European colonizations, and *pogroms* and communal riots, varied short-lived forms of violence, including rioting and looting, plus some murder and rape, with mixed motives: state agencies seek to displace political tensions onto out-groups; locals enjoy the looting, violence, and rape; ethnic cleansers try to induce terrorized flight. Pogroms typically induce some emigration. Common victims have been the Jewish, Armenian, and Chinese. The next escalation is to *wild deportation* and *emigration*, involving enough brutality to persuade members of the out-group to flee – as in the former Yugoslavia in recent years. Cleansing of a more racial form may involve distinctively *biological* policies. Here the out-group is denied reproduction by restrictive marriage or sexual policies, escalating perhaps to forcible sterilization or to rape where the intent is to make the woman unlikely to bear children carrying the identity of the out-group. Biological cleansing tends to center on females for obvious reasons: maternity is certain, paternity only presumed.

Row 5 escalates to the violence of mass deaths that were the unintended consequence of the dominant group's policies. The first column involves policy *mistakes*, often through submitting ethnic groups to labor conditions to which they were ill-adapted, or by revolutionaries seeking to achieve major social transformations with foolish policies – for example, the Great Leap Forward in China, which unintentionally killed millions. The implication is that once the mistake is realized, the policy will be abandoned, and so the out-group will not be wiped out. I do not wish to exonerate the perpetrators here, for the number of dead may be enormous. Most big mistakes border on the next category, labeled *callous* policies. These are not directly intended to kill the out-group, but the dominant group has such negative views of the out-group that it does not particularly care if this ensues. This is not quite true of the leadership of the Great Leap Forward, but its slowness in reacting to the disaster did reveal a relative lack of concern for the lives of the victims. Wars and civil wars loom large in the callous category, especially in the devastation inflicted on civilian populations through laying waste to the country or bombing cities. The limiting case is the very first colonization of Caribbean islands by the Spanish. By the time the colonialists collectively realized what their impact on the natives was, virtually all the natives were dead, which makes this strictly ethnocide.

Ethnocide refers to the unintended wiping out of a group and its culture. This will usually be extremely callous, and the dominant group may even welcome the elimination of the out-group. Ethnocide characterized the main thrust of many terrible encounters between colonial settlers and indigenous peoples, in which most deaths resulted from diseases carried from the dominant to the out-group, worsened by living on reservations and terrible labor conditions that were not intended to kill, but that did wear down the natives to near death. More of this in Chapter 4.

Finally, row 6 contains premeditated mass killing of civilians. *Exemplary repression* is how I style most of the more atrocious imperial conquest policies of history – for example, putting an entire city to the sword in order to cow other cities into submission. Recent military campaigns have involved indiscriminate bombing of cities, as in Dresden, Tokyo, and Hiroshima. The Romans sometimes *decimated*, killing every tenth person of a rebellious population. In the Balkans in the 1940s, the German army killed 50 local civilians for every German killed by guerrillas. Rebels and terrorists are usually capable of only smaller atrocities of this type, though September 11 was a very large one. Today, all exemplary repression could be theoretically prosecuted under international law as war crimes or crimes against humanity – though those who win wars are rarely prosecuted. Civil wars usually involve greater slaughter of civilians than do interstate wars.

Then come mass murders whose intent is partial cleansing. *Forced conversion* offers a stark choice: "convert or die," as Serbs were told by Croat Catholic Ustasha forces during World War II. In pogroms, Jews were often given such a choice. Some members of the out-group are killed, either because they resist or because perpetrators wish to show that the choice is for real. But most live, cleansed partially – of their religion but not their entire culture. *Politicide*, a recently coined term, refers to killing where the intended target is the entire leadership and potential leadership class of a more generally victimized and feared group (as defined by Harff & Gurr, 1988: 360). This may overlap with exemplary repression, though politicide has a more

cleansing intent. Wiping out leaders and intellectuals is intended to undermine the out-group's cultural identity, whereas cities cowed into submission
through exemplary repression may retain their identities. By killing all educated Poles, the Nazis intended to wipe out Polish cultural identity, just
as Burundian Tutsis intended to wipe out Hutu cultural identity in killing
educated Hutus.

I add my own coined term, *classicide*, to refer to the intended mass killing
of entire social classes. Since this may be more murderous than forced conversion or politicide, I have arrowed it in the table toward, but not in, the
genocide category. The Khmer Rouge were the worst perpetrators; Stalinists
and Maoists perpetrated short bursts. The victim classes were thought to
be irredeemable enemies. Classicide seems to be distinctive to leftists, since
only they are tempted to believe they can do without opposed ("exploiting") classes. Rightist regimes of capitalists and landlords always recognize
that they need workers and peasants to do the work for them. Thus the
mass slaughter by the Indonesian Army and Islamic paramilitaries of at least
500,000 Indonesian Communist sympathizers in 1965–6, though it disproportionately killed poor peasants, was targeted at a political rather than a
class enemy – at Communists, not peasants or workers. It was politicide, not
classicide. In Communist regimes like the Khmer Rouge, and under Stalinism
and Mao, it entwined with mistakes and callousness. All three types can be
prosecuted as war crimes or crimes against humanity.

Finally comes *genocide*, a term invented in 1944 by the Polish lawyer
Raphael Lemkin. The United Nations modified Lemkin's definition to say
that genocide is a criminal act intended to destroy an ethnic, national, or
religious group, which is targeted for destruction as such. This definition
is sometimes criticized because it includes both too much and too little. It
adds that "partial" destruction counts as genocide. Partial genocide makes
sense only in geographic terms. Settlers in California in 1851 attempting to
wipe out all the Indians from the Owens Valley embarked upon partial, in
the sense of local, genocide. The decision of Bosnian Serb commanders to
kill all the men and boys of Srebrenica in 1994 might be also so labeled,
since local women could not survive on their own as a viable community. But when killings are mixed in with forced deportations as in the nearby
cleansings of Prijedor, this seems not to be a local genocide. But, conversely,
genocide should cover more than just ethnic groups (Andreopoulos, 1994:
Part I). Genocide is intentional, aiming to wipe out an entire group, not only
physically but also culturally (destroying its churches, libraries, museums,
street names). Yet if only cultural cleansing occurs, I call this not genocide
but only cultural suppression. Genocide is typically committed by majorities
against minorities, whereas politicide is the reverse.

This book focuses on the worst, darkly shaded area of the table, which
I collectively label *murderous ethnic cleansing*. I have also colored three
adjacent cells in a lighter hue to acknowledge that these borderline zones

may also contain some murderous cleansing. I do not term many of these cells genocide, as some do (e.g., Jonassohn, 1998; Smith, 1997).

Making these distinctions reveals two paradoxical features of ethnic cleansing. On the one hand, most has been quite mild. Murderous cleansing is uncommon. Assimilation, backed up by milder institutional coercion, has dominated. On the other hand, most advanced countries today are ethnically cleansed since they are substantially mono-ethnic (i.e., at least 70 percent of the population considers itself to be of one ethnicity), whereas in the past they were far more multiethnic. So we have two main problems. Why did such cleansing occur? And why in only a few cases did it turn really nasty? These are the main historical questions that my book must answer.

RIVAL APPROACHES TO ETHNIC CLEANSING

I am not the first to have addressed these issues. I draw gratefully on a large body of literature in writing my case studies and in framing my theoretical approach. Let me briefly list the main theoretical dilemmas that have surfaced and indicate my position on each.

PRIMITIVE, ANCIENT, OR MODERN?

In stark contrast to my first thesis, stressing modernity, others see ethnic cleansing as a primitive throwback. To blame "primitive" peoples offers us psychological comfort, since we can view murderous Serbs or Hutus (and other African tribal hatreds) as far removed from we civilized moderns. Yet such primitives would have to include groups from all the continents, and people as modern in their time, and as culturally close to us, as 19th-century Americans and Australians and 20th-century Germans. I write this in Los Angeles, whose admirable Museum of Tolerance powerfully evokes the horrors of the far-off Nazi Final Solution yet completely ignores the genocide committed in Los Angeles itself by European settlers against the Chumash Indians. My historical chapters will demonstrate that ethnic cleansing has been a part of our modernity and civilization.

However, primitive may also have a more Freudian meaning. Below the layers of socialization, civility, the superego, and repression lie the murky reaches of aggressive instincts, the id, and perhaps even *thanatos*, the death wish. Remove or destabilize the top layers of socialization and human beings regress to primitive violence, said Freud in *Civilization and Its Discontents*. But this is misleading. In all my case studies the perpetrators formed social movements with their own institutions, ideologies, and socialization processes. Perpetrators were not autonomous individuals liberated from their superegos. When hatred and violence erupted, they were not so much freed from traditional socialization pressures as encouraged by new ones. Primitive theories are not very helpful.

The thesis of the primitive is modified somewhat by those who write of ancient hatreds spanning the centuries. They say, for example, that Serbs and Bosnian Muslims have been fighting each other since the Battle of Kosovo Field in 1389, making the Balkans "a region of pure memory" in which "each individual sensation and memory affects the grand movement of clashing peoples" to exert a "multiplier effect on violence" (Kaplan, 1993; cf. Vulliamy, 1994: 4). Though this is nonsense, Balkan conflicts have indeed flared up on several occasions over quite a long period. Smith (1986: chap. 2; 2000: chap. 2) has offered a general framework of what he calls *perennialism* for understanding it. He sees ethnic rivalries as old, but less continuous than perennial. He sees a minimal continuity in that ethnic groups have persistently shared a name, a myth of descent, a sense of history, a culture, a connection to a specific territory, and a sense of solidarity. But these have only intermittently surged forward into the historical record, especially precipitated by wars, border disputes, or diasporas. Thus modern nations can mobilize deep-rooted collective identities.

It depends how far back he is taking this idea. The rulers and ruled in most historical states until the past few centuries did not share the same culture and so could not share a common ethnic identity. Class usually trumped ethnicity until modern times. This pattern began to weaken as salvation religions emerged. Christianity, Islam, and other religions generated a religious culture shared across the classes. But the decisive shift came when modern democratic political ideals conferred citizenship on all, all social classes and both genders. Indeed, Smith's recent notion of *ethnosymbolism* seems to concede much of this. He says that modern nationalists have reinterpreted a real and popular living past with the aid of myths, memories, and traditions to make the nation more inclusive. Indeed they have, though how real this past was and what the balance is between memory and myth remains to be seen.

But why should ethnic groups hate each other? Are the reasons old or modern? Where citizenship was imposed upon older religious fault lines, things became more dangerous – as for Jews, for Muslims in the Balkans and the Caucasus, and for Christians in the Ottoman Empire. But, despite Smith, this history is more of a modern ethnic crescendo than a perennial recurrence – though, clearly, there can be exceptions. Jews of all classes suffered many centuries of intermittent oppression under the Roman Empire and Christendom. Their sense of a collective ethnic identity is probably the oldest of all. Still, some of today's worst ethnic rivalries do date back over a century or so. The Serb nationalist account of the Battle of Kosovo Field in 1389 is a modern invention, since the battle was actually fought between two armies we would today consider multiethnic, one giving allegiance to an Ottoman Sultan, the other to a Serb prince. Nineteenth-century Serb nationalists invented a Kosovo myth of an exclusively Serb army (in previous centuries it had been a myth of an exclusively Christian army), and Serb schoolchildren have now been taught this for over a century. So the myth does lie quite deep in contemporary Serb consciousness.

Of course, the age of an ethnic rivalry is not necessarily related to murderous proclivities. English–Scots and Danish–Swedish rivalries are also old, but they have been harmless for 200 years. And in my case studies serious ethnic cleansing had prior harbingers – disputes, violent incidents, perhaps pogroms, stretching erratically back over some time. Gurr (2000: 50–3) says that "virtually all" the "ethno-rebellions" occurring between 1986 and 1998 were preceded by significant and prolonged political agitation in which violence gradually accelerated. Harff (1998) emphasizes short-term escalation over a prior three-month period, though Bond (1998: 118) and Gurr (1998) refer to weeks, months, and even years. Yugoslav conflicts exploded spasmodically throughout the 20th century. Though age is relevant, we must explain more recent escalation.

PERPETRATORS: NATIONALIST MASSES OR AUTHORITARIAN ELITES?

My seventh thesis gives a multilayered account of the perpetrators as elites, militants, and core constituencies. But two much simpler views dominate – the perpetrators are whole ethnic groups or state elites. We routinely endorse the first view when in everyday speech we say that the Germans, the Serbs, and so on did this or that. Virtually all books on the ethnic wars in Yugoslavia intermittently describe the collective actors as the Serbs, the Croats, the Albanians, and so on, and even I may have slipped in a few such collective nouns without noticing. Popular accounts of ethnic cleansing often explicitly embrace this view, and a few scholars do too. Goldhagen (1996) says Germans as a whole embraced an ideology of "exterminist anti-Semitism" and had done so for half a century before the Holocaust. Oddly, his work is popular among Germans. But, as we see later, Goldhagen is not correct. Dadrian (1995: 121–7) says that the warrior values of the Turk combined with the intolerance of Islam to generate a Turkish cultural predisposition to massacre Christian Armenians. This is also false. Cigar (1995) makes his view of the Yugoslav ethnic wars clear with subheads like "The Serbs Sense of Superiority" and "The Serbs as a Threatened Nation." I label these views *nationalist* since it is nationalists who claim that the nation is a singular actor. The label is ironic, since Goldhagen, Dadrian, and Cigar are denouncing nationalism – but in ways that reproduce the categories of nationalist thought. Yet whole nations or ethnic groups *never* act collectively. The perpetrators are *some* Germans, *some* Serbs, *some* Hutus, coming disproportionately from core constituencies, particular regions, age groups, economic sectors, and so on, among which combinations of ethnonationalist values, statism, and approval of violence resonate most strongly. Ethnonationalists must first overcome dissidents in their own ethnic community, and in fact they often kill more people from their own ethnic group than from the out-group – a practice political scientists call *in-group policing* (Brubaker & Laitin, 1998: 433; Laitin, 1995). If ethnic groups do become more homogeneous as conflict escalates, this is precisely what we must explain.

The dangers of reifying nationalism are now so well known that some scholars have shifted to the opposite perspective, to what is called *constructivism*, seeing ethnicity and ethnic conflict as constructed by social movements, usually by elites, out of contingent events that might have gone otherwise, creating ethnic identities that are only partial and transient (Brubaker, 1996: chap. 1). Even if this were so, once an ethnic identity is socially constructed, it may engender deep and long-lasting sentiments such that it becomes institutionalized, even structural. Some ethnic identities lie quite deep and institutionalized; others are more contingent and precarious. My case studies must be aware of both and establish the depth of ethnic identities.

The most popular alternative to blaming the whole ethnic group has been to blame elites, especially state elites. It is said that atrocities happen when people are subjected to malign, manipulative leaders. Democracy and the people are seen as pacific, whereas leaders and elites are potentially more murderous. In *civil society* theory, democracy, peace, and tolerance are said to result when individuals are engaged in vibrant, dense social relations provided by voluntary institutions, which protect them from the manipulations of state elites (Putnam, 1993, 2000). This is naive. Radical ethnonationalists often succeed precisely because their civil society networks are denser and more mobilizing than those of their more moderate rivals. This was true of the Nazis (see my book *Fascists*, chap. 4; Hagtvet, 1980; Koshar, 1986), and we see later that it was also true of Serb, Croat, and Hutu nationalists. Civil society may be evil.

But ethnic cleansing has long been treated as a problem of states. Fein declared, "The victims of twentieth century premeditated genocide... were murdered in order to fulfill the state's design for a new order" (1984; cf. Horowitz, 1982; Smith, 1987). The modern state's weapons, transport, and administrative techniques have escalated the efficiency of mass, bureaucratic killing, says Baumann when analyzing the Holocaust (1989). Ethnic cleansing is a product of the most advanced stage of the modern state, reflecting its need for "order, transparency, and responsiveness," says Naimark (2001: 8). Human rights organizations invariably blame ethnic cleansing on state elites (as in the *Human Rights Watch* book of 1995; cf. Brown, 1996). The Yugoslav civil wars are often blamed on Milosevic and Serbian elites (Brown, 1996; Gagnon, 1997; Glenny, 1993). Fearon and Laitin (2000) say the dominant recent view has been that "large-scale ethnic violence is provoked by elites seeking to gain, maintain, or increase their hold on political power."

Democratic peace theory also argues that representative governments are pacific, rarely fighting wars, almost never against each other (Doyle, 1983;

for a critique see Barkawi & Laffey, 2001). It is rooted in the liberal belief that if the people's will is freely expressed, it will be pacific. Rummel says that the more authoritarian a state, the more likely it is to kill its own or other civilians: "Power kills; absolute Power kills absolutely," he repeats like a mantra (1994: 1, 12–27; 1998: 1). In a tautological sense he is right. Regimes that murder large numbers of their citizens cannot be considered democracies, since they are grossly infringing the civil liberties part of democracy. But for Rummel, it is the electoral part of democracy that guarantees social peace: perpetrating regimes got into power by authoritarian means, not free elections.

But there is a disturbing number of exceptions. European settlers from the 17th century on were more genocidal if they lived under constitutional than authoritarian governments. Perhaps settler democracies are better described as *ethnocracies*, democracy for one ethnic group, as Yiftachel (1999) has noted for the contemporary case of Israel. The Soviet Union and Tito's Yugoslavia usually damped down ethnic conflict, and their collapse led to ethnic wars as majority groups sought to found ethnocracies (Beissinger, 2002). Brass (1997) and Tambiah (1996) show that ethnic violence in the Indian subcontinent rose in periods of vigorous electoral politics and declined under martial law. "Majoritarian democracy" was the battle cry of the Hutu Power movement while committing genocide in 1994, while Northern Ireland Protestants and Sri Lankans denounce their Catholic and Tamil opponents for undermining (majoritarian) democracy. There is no simple relationship between authoritarian states and ethnic cleansing.

Like me, Snyder sees authoritarian regimes as better at damping down ethnic tensions than democracies unless democracies are already securely institutionalized. He also sees states newly embarked on democratization as the most vulnerable to ethnonationalism. He notes that though Human Rights Watch reports blame ethnic wars on authoritarian regimes, in actuality all their cases – Sri Lanka, India, South Africa, Lebanon, Israel, Romania, the former Yugoslavia, Russia, Armenia, and Azerbaijan – "had recently held openly contested elections where powerful opposition groups were more nationalist than the government" (2000: 267). Yet Snyder still blames the unraveling of transitions to democracy on malevolent, manipulative elites: "Democratization produces nationalism when powerful groups within the nation...want to avoid surrendering real political authority to the average citizen....Nationalist conflicts arise as a by-product of elites' efforts to persuade the people to accept divisive nationalist ideas" (2000: 32). This is too simple. Note that the worst perpetrating authoritarian regimes had a particular form. The Stalinist, Maoist, and Nazi regimes were *party-states*, dictatorships resting on a mobilized mass movement. Atrocities were often rather bottom-up as low-level militants settled scores against political and economic elites. Party-states figured in all my 20th-century cases. Apart from the colonial settler cases – which result from bottom-up pressures – it is always unpredictable combinations of top-down, bottom-up, and sideways-violent pressures that lead to the worst atrocities.

Political scientists have also noted that ethnic wars tend to occur where states weaken and factionalize. Transitions toward democracy upset states' normal repertoire of conflict management: the old state has collapsed; the new one is being formed (Beissinger, 1998, 2002; Gurr, 1993: 361–3; 2000: 36, 236). Some say that not strong but failed states see most mass killing, often of a very confused, anarchic kind (Esty et al., 1998; Fearon & Laitin, 2003; Posen, 1993). Yet this book investigates more deliberately targeted ethnic cleansing, which seems to involve governments continuing to exercise some degree of control. The Nazi, Young Turk, and Milosevic regimes were not failing. Factionalized and radicalizing states are more dangerous for ethnic cleansing than failed states. There *is* a relationship between democracy and murderous cleansing, but it is more complex and double-edged than many statist theorists acknowledge. In the end, murderous ethnic cleansing is almost always led by state elites. But, again, this is the *end process* of state disintegration, reconstitution, and radicalization. We must explain this process.

RATIONAL, EMOTIONAL, OR NORMATIVE PERPETRATORS?

The study of ethnic violence by political scientists has been increasingly dominated by *rational choice theory* (*rat. theory* for short). This theory suggests that human behavior results from rational individuals seeking to maximize their utility functions. It tends to stress economic motives, strives for parsimony by making a few simple assumptions about utility preferences, and seeks (perhaps only in its wildest fantasies) to fit human behavior into algebraic formulae.

Rat. theory is useful but limited. It works best with fairly utilitarian economistic disputes. Laitin (1998, 1999) shows that disputes over the official languages of states rarely escalate to serious violence, since they can be compromised by rational actors. Take the Russian minority living in Kazakhstan. Since Kazakh is the language of the country's public sector, a Russian might learn Kazakh to improve his job prospects. He need not abandon his ethnicity, since he can still speak Russian at home. Laitin identifies a *tipping point* or *cascade*. At first, a Russian would experience only a little payoff from learning Kazakh. If he does learn it, other Russians may reject him, while Kazakhs may still not accept him. But if one or more of these factors begins to change, the payoff for learning Kazakh increases and that for learning Russian declines until the expected returns for each language become the same. When they cross over, a tipping point is reached and a cascade begins, toward all Russians learning Kazakh, now the more useful language. But if Kazakhs still deny Russians jobs, Russians might cascade instead toward emigrating to Russia. This, observes Laitin, begins "as soon as a critical number of Russians believe that a critical number of Russians believe that a critical number of Russians will leave." But even pressured emigration is far short of mass killing. This language issue is a utilitarian one, relevant to jobs, and people can retain their ethnic identity by speaking more than one language.

But rival languages may be seen not as secular but as sacred, expressing the one true faith. Sudanese people do kill each other over whether Arabic or Christian languages are to predominate in their country. And serious violence did erupt in other post-Soviet countries, though not over the language issue. It turned on disputes over state border regions involving majority and minority ethnic populations. Rival ethnonationalist movements claimed their own state over the same piece of territory, with the minority helped by the new state next door (Beissinger, 2002: 287) – exactly as in my third and fourth ethnic theses. This is an emotional as well as a utilitarian matter, and it is not so amenable to rat. theory.

Rat. theorists do attempt to understand emotions. They focus on fear. Weingast (1989) says that persons told by ethnonationalists that they are targets for extermination might rationally decide to fight (or flee), even if the probability of extermination is extremely low. For should it actually happen, that would be curtains! So fear-driven preemptive violence might explain seemingly irrational violence. Thus Kalyvas (1999) has shown that in Algeria groups are massacred even if they seem rather harmless at present. Since they might conceivably threaten in the future, it is better to "get your retaliation in first." Rabushka and Shepsle (1972) say that as tensions rise, rival communities both come to fear extinction. Then their elites can engage in "competitive outbidding," outdoing each other in extreme ethnonationalism. This undercuts moderate rivals and mobilizes their community for violence. In turn, this realizes the worst fears of the other group, and so for both, the fear of extinction acquires a real basis that it did not initially have.

These are very real scenarios, though they may be unduly pessimistic. Why should moderate leaders be undercut? They can deliver peace, a desirable goal. Since wars and violence are costly, both sides should normally prefer diplomatic agreements. Fearon (1995) suggests three ways in which war and violence seem rational, though objectively they are not.

1. The *security dilemma* (Posen, 1993) means that each side's efforts to make itself more secure make its rival less secure. Escalation forces both communities to shelter behind their own men of violence. Fear and a sense of humiliation lead to enraged preemptive killing. This might account for the bizarre view of many killers that they are actually the victims. This dilemma means that the possession of overwhelming military superiority in a conflict situation leads to a first-strike incentive for aggression. I have incorporated this into my ethnic thesis 4b.

2. The *commitment problem* means that escalation results from reluctance to commit credibly to uphold agreements, which also makes the opponent

reluctant to commit. Durkheim long ago observed that "all that is in the contract is not contractual." For contracts to hold, he said, shared norms are necessary. Instrumental reason does not govern human actions. We must also study how norms, values, and social identities arise and help define our sense of our own interest. We commit to those we trust, but how does trust arise and how does it decline? Here we surely need a more social explanation than rat. theorists provide.

3. *Information failure* means that information is known by only one side. In saber-rattling bluffing, for example, the opponent does not know that it is a bluff and so arms himself unnecessarily, leading to further escalation. Sunstein (2000) believes this is very widespread. He draws on experimental and jury studies to note that prolonged discussion confined within a group tends to move it toward a more extreme version of its prior average opinion. In periods of ethnic tension, a group already may have somewhat negative views of the out-group. The more it confers only within itself, the more negative toward the out-group it becomes. But again this involves norms, values, and identities. How do people come to define themselves as belonging primarily to an ethnic group rather than having a cross-ethnic identity like class?

The problem is that all three processes also presuppose norms, values, and identity formation that rat. theorists do not specify. They tend to assume that ethnic group identities and rivalries already exist. Their actors are too stable. But the relevant collective actors are many, and some emerge in the process of escalation itself. Identities based on relationship to the state, class, occupation, region, generation, gender and so on weave in and out of ethnic identities, rechanneling ethnicity as they do so. Beissinger (2002) notes that as the Soviet Union collapsed, it unleashed an unexpected tidal wave of ethnonationalist hostilities, fueled by emotions and norms as well as interests. The participants astonished themselves, rapidly changing their priorities and political strategies. Crowds committed hate crimes of which they had not known they were capable. Ex-Soviet politicians jumped on an ethnonationalist bandwagon that they had hitherto despised.

Most importantly, murderous cleansing rarely seems rational. How could Germans come to fear Jews, 0.7 percent of the German population? Most perpetrating groups suffer more harm than they would have done had they compromised. Germany, Rwanda, and Yugoslavia are laid waste. Milosevic is on trial, a third of the Serb paramilitary leaders lie murdered, and the rest fear they are next for assassination or indictment. Shouldn't reason have led them down different paths?

The obvious response is, since when did reason govern human action? Max Weber (1978: I, 25) identified four main types of human action – instrumentally rational, habitual, affectual (i.e., emotional), and value-rational. *Instrumentally rational action*, as studied by rat. choice theorists, is obviously important in human affairs. But where power relations or ethnic identities are internalized, we may engage in *habitual action* unthinkingly, without rational calculation, if we are told by other members of the group that we are threatened. We then define our interests in terms of this group identification. Only within its blinkers do we instrumentally calculate our interests. In war we routinely obey an order to kill, even if we bear the victim no hate. Then, as ethnic hostilities escalate, *affectual action* arises. Love of one's own group and fear, hatred, and rage at the other may override instrumental concerns. Finally, we may engage in *value-rational action*, committing ourselves to certain goals whatever the costs. This is ideologically driven action. When people are willing to risk or inflict death in pursuit of their values, instrumental reason may be relegated to the back burner. Weber's distinctions seem very relevant to ethnic cleansing. All four types of action will enter into my list of perpetrator motives discussed later.

Rat. theory demands a level of rigor and simplicity not found in the real world. It sets us an admirable level of theoretical ambition: we should attempt to reconstruct the preferences of variable and changing actors, including values, traditions, and emotions as well as instrumental goals, amid broader and changing contexts of power. Indeed, my sixth thesis offers rational reconstruction of motives. I attempt to identify the successive plans of ethnic leaders, formally designating their original main goal as their Plan A, followed by their subsequent adaptations – Plan B, Plan C, and so on. This methodology will sometimes prove too schematic and too rationalistic, since intentions are often murky and fluid. But it will prove useful since murderous ethnic cleansing was never the initial solution devised by ethnonationalists, and we must be able to reconstruct the successive flow of their goals. But this also leads to more general questions of motive.

PERPETRATORS' MOTIVES: ORDINARY PEOPLE OR FANATICS?

Thousands of people assist in the worst murderous cleansings. One question above all others has seared the minds of the eyewitnesses: how can apparently ordinary people perpetrate murderous cleansing? A simple contrast has often been posed: were they ordinary people like you and I, placed in extraordinary circumstances, or were they ideological fanatics?

The most famous answer was given in Stanley Milgrams's experiments. He asked ordinary Americans to inflict what they believed to be severe electric shocks on experimental subjects who gave incorrect answers in IQ tests they administered. They were told that scientists were testing whether shock treatment might help improve IQ scores (and the experimenters wore white lab coats!). Sixty-five percent of these ordinary folk (there were no differences between men and women) complied when asked to inflict severe pain by pushing a lever in the room next to the victim. As they pushed, they could hear the victims' cries of pain coming through the wall. Thirty percent of them still did so if asked to administer the shock themselves by pushing the victim's hand down on a plate bearing an electric current. A few joined in the experiment with enthusiasm, seemingly enjoying administering pain. But most were deeply disturbed. At higher levels of shock, the subjects cried for the experimenter to stop. But despite their severe moral and physical discomfort, they continued administering pain – because they could not bring themselves to reject scientific authority. Milgram (1974: 10) commented, "Some subjects were totally convinced of the wrongness of what they were doing but could not bring themselves to make an open break with authority." But he was not as sadistic as this experiment seemed. The pain was not real but faked. The "victims" were his stooges, and no electric current was transmitted.

Milgram suggested that ordinary modern people can kill if an order comes from a legitimate scientific authority. More would comply with indirect killing (from the next room), so bureaucratic *desk-killing* would be easier than committing murder oneself. Not all subsequent research supported his conclusions. One study found that most subjects distinguished between mild pain and pain that might harm the victim. They refused to inflict the latter (Blau, 1993). But a study of California college students was even more worrying (to me, since I teach them). They were asked to play the roles of prisoners and wardens in a prison setting. The experiment had to be abandoned when the student-warders developed cruel and authoritarian tendencies (Haney et al., 1973). These experiments suggest that ordinary people are capable of cruel behavior if given license by legitimate institutions. No experiment can simulate actual murder, but we know from regular scandals that institutions like prisons, asylums, and orphanages have to be vigilant against abuse by the staff of their immense power over inmates.

Milgram's book is laced with references to the Final Solution. But the perpetrators there, as in other cases, were actually very varied. I distinguish nine common motives found among perpetrators.

1. *Ideological* killers believed in the righteousness of murderous cleansing. Found especially among the higher ranks of perpetrators, they pursued Weber's value rationality – murderous means supposedly justified by higher goals. Such an ideology might resonate in certain contexts (like war) or in core constituencies – like refugees who have already suffered at the hands of the out-group. The ideology might resonate in the practices and subcultures of certain professions. Doctors and biologists in the early 20th century found biomedical models of ethnicity and race particularly attractive. But the most common ideological motive is to self-righteously justify killing as self-defense. The killer protests that he is really the victim.

2. *Bigoted* killers are motivated by more mundane ideology. Especially rank-and-file perpetrators share the casual prejudices of their place and time and so engage in what Weber called *affectual* (emotional)

action. Jews, Muslims, and colonial natives evoked physical disgust from their killers. We all know bigoted people who in very different contexts might be led to condone mistreatment of disliked minorities – especially if feeling threatened by them.

3. *Violent* killers are drawn to murder itself. A few sadists experience it as emotionally pleasurable. Far more feel themselves driven to it, experiencing violence as a release or freedom from emotional anxiety. Jack Katz (1988) has described the "seductions" of violent crime in the United States. He says murder is usually a highly emotional action. Most commonly a sense of threat leads to an all-enveloping sense of personal humiliation, followed by a self-righteous rage to expunge it. "Rage," he says, "is livid with the awareness of humiliation." Ethnic hatreds may transpose this threat-humiliation-rage triad to a collective level: Hutus feel threatened and humiliated by Tutsi power, and they strike out, enraged at any Tutsi. A more triumphal emotion may be involved in wielding brute force, as any schoolyard reveals. Since weapons overcome class differences, they enable lower-class people to experience the joys of arbitrary power over prosperous groups (like Jews or Armenians or Tutsis). These are some of the worst features of ordinary human beings. But there are also core constituencies favoring violence as a legitimate solution to social problems – among soldiers, policemen, criminals, and experts in violent sports or football hooligans.

4. *Fearful* killers feel credibly threatened, fearing harm to life or limb, if they do not kill. These are physically coerced, sometimes reluctant killers. This motivation is instrumentally rational.

5. *Careerist* killers are employed in organizations involved in murderous cleansing. Their compliance with killing orders is perceived by them as materially advantageous, leading to greater career prospects – or to worse prospects if they do not assist killing. This is more common in the more bureaucratized murderous cleansings.

6. *Materialist* killers are lured by the prospect of direct economic gain by looting or taking the victims' jobs, businesses, or property. Some are freed from prison, provided that they kill. These are also highly instrumental motives.

7. *Disciplined* killers are caged within legitimate organizational authority, where noncompliance with orders is considered deviant. Less fear than the necessity of routine compliance with directives is at the forefront of their minds. People of all nationalities present, past, or future can be made conformists by pressure from above. They might become habitual killers in Weber's sense.

8. *Comradely* killers are caged into conformity by peer group pressure, especially by fear that the peer group might withdraw its emotional support. It evokes Weber's affectual action. It is partly how

Browning (1993) explained the mass murder committed by ordinary German policemen.

9. *Bureaucratic* killers are caged inside the bureaucracies of modernity. Their obedience is rather habitual, in Weber's sense, produced by institutionalized routines trapping them into what Arendt (1965) famously termed *the banality of evil* institutionalized in modern societies. This is where Milgram fits best. Ordinary modern people can murder, say Baumann (1989) and Katz (1993). Bartov (1996) agrees, tracing the origins of the trap to the "mechanized, rational and impersonal" killing machine of World War I.

So we have a rich panoply of potential killers – ideological, bigoted, violent, fearful, careerist, materialist, disciplined, comradely, and bureaucratic. The variety gives force to my eighth thesis, for it essentially makes ordinary people assist murderous cleansing. Some perpetrators murdered for what they claimed were idealistic, that is, ideological reasons. Some seemed to like violence or respect it as the best way to solve political problems. The murderous institutions were disciplined, comradely, career- or looting-friendly, and some were bureaucratic. Such large numbers of perpetrators must have included some fairly ordinary people. Since these are only ideal types, almost all perpetrators had mixed motives. And this list tends to "freeze" motives at the point of killing. Since few perpetrators initially intended to go out and kill people (thesis 5), their earlier motives must have differed. Thus I trace careers modifying motives and socializing them to the possibility of killing.

Nor should we abstract individuals from their environments. We are tempted toward an individualist approach in this unique area of human behavior partly because of the overwhelming import of the question of legal guilt. Are we to sentence, perhaps to death, this individual for acts personally committed? But we are also tempted toward individualism in trying to understand such behavior. Anyone who has pondered these cases has likely asked the question: "what would *I* have done in such circumstances if ordered to murder men, women, and children? How moral, how brave, would I have been?" And we then think perhaps of how cowardly, conformist, or ambitious we ourselves are – reflecting on our own more trivial failure to help some needy or persecuted person. Such ordinary human weaknesses were obviously important in assisting murderous cleansing.

Yet to answer the question "What would I have done?" we would have to place ourselves back in time as someone occupying a comparable position then. A professor like me placed in Germany in the 1930s would likely favor conservative nationalism and evince some sympathy for the Nazi cause. Students would be even more pro-Nazi, for the Nazis won the free national student elections in Germany in 1931. If I were then a professor of biology or medicine, I might be doused in scientific racism, amid which radical Nazism would resonate. As an actual professor of sociology who has written a book on fascism, I am uneasily aware of a predecessor. Professor Otto Ohlendorf's academic interest in fascism made him a Nazi. His rather self-righteous personality at first put him at odds with the Nazi leadership. But then he did his duty, agreeing to head one of the terrible *Einsatzgruppen* murder squads. His unit murdered 90,000 persons. He was executed at Nuremberg in 1951. Placed in other contexts, many of us might have been led quite close to murderous ethnic cleansing.

MY CAUSAL MODEL: THE SOURCES OF SOCIAL POWER

To explain murderous ethnic cleansing, we need an overall model of the power interactions involved. I employ the model of the four sources of social power used in my previous historical work (see Mann, 1986, 1993). I study ethnic cleansing as the outcome of four interrelated sets of power networks, all of which are necessary to its accomplishment, but one of which can be regarded as causally primary.

Ideological power refers to the mobilization of values, norms, and rituals in human societies. I do not imply that ideology is false, only that it surpasses experience and science alike, and so contains nontestable elements. Some use the term *culture* in roughly the sense that I use *ideology*, though I avoid it as too vague and multifarious a term. Ethnic conflict is very ideological. Benedict Anderson's (1983) well-known aphorism that "nations are imagined communities" indicates that it is not obvious from our direct life experience that complete strangers might share an identity with us as an ethnic group or nation. Such a bizarre conception has to be ideologically created, since it greatly surpasses our actual experience. We need a causal theory of in what particular circumstances and by what mechanisms culture/ideology helps to generate hate-filled ethnic identities. What did Germans really know of Jews that they might see them as a threat to their collective survival? How do perpetrators proceed to actual killing, overcoming the moral injunction "Thou shalt not kill"? How did some leaders and militants come to be driven by "value-rationality," to the detriment of all instrumental reason?

Ideologies are carried by communications networks in which some possess greater resources of knowledge and persuasion than others. They mobilize social movements and mass media – mass marches and meetings, the printed word, and the airwaves – all of which may acquire power over people. Yet people are not cultural dopes. They accept ideologies that make some plausible sense of their world, and they actively reinterpret them. Ideologies justifying ethnic cleansing are grounded in real, growing historical conflicts, though they must compete with alternative ideologies (liberal, socialist, etc.) that also usually offer plausible explanations. I will emphasize the close-run nature of their rivalry in most cases, at least in the early stages of escalation. Later in the process, control of the means of communication may provide greater ideological power to ethnonationalists. But this is part of a process that requires explanation.

Economic power is also important. All cases of cleansing involve material interests. Usually, members of an ethnic group come to believe they have a collective economic interest against an out-group. As in my second ethnic thesis, ethnicity can trump class. Class sentiments are displaced onto ethnic group relations. The oppressed group identifies the other as an imperial exploiting nation, considering itself an exploited proletarian nation (as did Hutus in Rwanda). The exploiter sees its imperial rule as bringing civilization to inferior ethnic groups. The defense of this imperium against revolutionary threats from below is what I will call *imperial revisionism* – so evident among Nazis, Serbs, and Tutsis.

Displacement of class sentiments also occurs in ethnic niche economies, where minorities occupy distinctive places in the division of labor – Jewish, Indian, or Chinese merchants, or Irish or Indian laborers. But, though this may generate discrimination and political protest, it rarely escalates to massive violence (Gurr, 2000: 229). Like the language issue, it is instrumental and can be compromised. The worst cases seem to occur where popular class resentments can be plausibly displaced onto capitalistic middlemen groups like Jews or Chinese, as Chua (2004) emphasizes. But ultimately most ethnic niches are too useful for upper classes to support their elimination. Thus Connor (1994: 144–64) and Horowitz (1985: 105–35) suggest that economic interests are rarely the main cause of ethnic conflict. Chua's (2004) attempts to trace genocide and murderous cleansing in Rwanda and Yugoslavia to market exploitation are rather far-fetched.

Yet this is not true where markets are limited by outright monopolies, either in highly statist economies or in exclusionary land ownership. A state dominated by one ethnicity may exclude other ethnic groups from owning land, getting jobs or obtaining business licenses. Control of the state becomes the most significant way to achieve material prosperity, intensifying ethnonationalists' drive to achieve their own state. In transitions from Communism and in developing countries, the state may control major industries and foreign aid, and may distribute their benefits according to ethnicity. Struggle over such a valuable state may lead to murderous cleansing of the loser. Land ownership is also inherently monopolistic. Unlike capital or labor, land is finite. Possession excludes others from its use. Possession by one ethnic group excludes others. In agrarian societies this is life-threatening. Thus colonial settlement produced especially murderous ethnic conflict over the possession of land. Seizing the land while requiring no native labor often brought ethnocide or genocide. Colonial cleansings are uniquely dominated by direct conflict over economic power resources.

More mundane economic conflict also figures once murderous cleansing is launched. Victims are stripped of valuables, houses, and clothes, adding mundane human greed to ethnic ferocity. Yet this requires preconditions. To benefit from looting our neighbors, we must be militarily stronger than they. Ideological and political sanctions also normally restrain us from looting our neighbors. We believe it morally wrong and expect punishment by the law.

We need to explain why ideological and political restraints crumble. Nor can greed account for the quickening of cleansing in the 20th century. Property and possessions were violently seized in all of history's wars, punitive raids, and communal riots. This is a historical constant. In fact, economic seizures are usually secondary in cleansing, and rarely important in its origins, appealing disproportionately to low-level perpetrators once the cleansing is underway.

Provided that groups do identify themselves and their economic interests in ethnic terms, ethnicity may trump class. But this requires that capitalists, workers, petty bourgeoisie, landlords, peasants, and others within an ethnic group come to view themselves as having economic interests in common. This is not an easy ideological task for ethnonationalists. Ethnicity or nation has not generally triumphed over class in modern times. Even in my cases, nationalists had to overcome liberals and socialists arguing that sectoral or class conflict was the primary material issue.

Military power is socially organized, concentrated lethal violence. This proves decisive in the later stages of the worst cases of ethnic cleansing. Armies, police forces, and irregular extrastate paramilitaries are the main agencies of military power. I will examine their funding, recruitment, and training. Who has access to guns or military training, and who favors violence as a way of solving social problems? Are there careers in violence that socialize people toward murder?

Most 20th-century cases of ethnic cleansing occurred during wars or during the chaotic transfer from war to peace (Melson, 1992: chap. 9; Naimark, 2001: 187). Conventional wars may be played according to rules governing mutual treatment of prisoners and civilians, yet rules have gaps – over civilian bombing and psychological torture today, and over siege warfare and living off the countryside in earlier centuries. Ideologically tinged wars reduce shared rules and may convert civilians into enemies. The Pacific Front in World War II saw racial atrocities against enemy soldiers and civilians; the Eastern Front saw atrocities between fascists and communists. Civil wars and wars of secession with a strong ethnic component are dangerous for ethnic groups trapped behind enemy lines. The lure toward murderous cleansing increases when it can be accomplished at low military cost, with little fear of retaliation (as in my thesis 4b). Military campaigns may generate tactical lures toward atrocities against civilians that were not originally intended. Prolonged siege warfare lures the besiegers to sack cities after capture. Guerrilla warfare lures guerrillas to kill civilians. An army superior in fixed resources facing a more mobile enemy may attack civilian settlements in order to force the enemy into more static defense, as General Sherman did against the Plains Indians. These are all features of military power that may produce murderous cleansing.

Political power is centralized, territorial regulation of social life. I argue that violence escalates most over rival claims to political sovereignty (cf. Horowitz, 1985; Wimmer, 2002). My theses find support from the quantitative data of the Minorities at Risk project. The variables best explaining ethnopolitical rebellion in the world in the late 1990s were political protest over the preceding five years, an unstable, divided, but repressive regime, territorial population concentration, extensive political organization, and support from foreign sympathizers. All but population concentration are essentially political variables. The results show that economic, cultural, and political discrimination may lead to ethnic protest but rarely escalates to the level of rebellion (Gurr, 2000: 234–6)

Political power is inherently territorial, authoritative, and monopolistic. Ideology is partially private and substantially voluntary, economic life involves market choices, and military power is normally institutionalized and kept away from our everyday life experiences. But we must submit routinely to regulation by a state, and we cannot choose which one – except by staying or leaving. Rival claims to sovereignty are the most difficult to compromise and the most likely to lead to murderous cleansing. Murderous cleansing is most likely to result where powerful groups within two ethnic groups aim at legitimate and achievable rival states "in the name of the people" over the same territory, and the weaker is aided from outside. It worsens in the presence of unstable, factionalized party-states. That is the main argument of this book, and it indicates that in explaining this particularly vicious area of human behavior, political power relations are ultimately decisive.

2

Ethnic Cleansing in Former Times

This chapter suggests that since in premodern states class usually trumped ethnicity (thesis 2), there was little ethnic cleansing (thesis 1). Though mass murders are obviously not new to human history, few earlier historical regimes intended to wipe out or expel whole civilian populations. Conquerors normally wanted people to rule over; they wanted to subordinate and enslave them, not remove them. Yet some disagree, declaring that murderous cleansing is equally ancient and modern, citing the notorious Assyrians or incidents like the Carthaginian destruction of Greek city-states and the Roman destruction of Numantia and Carthage (Chalk & Jonassohn, 1990; du Preez, 1994: 4–5; Freeman, 1995; Jonasson, 1998: chap. 17). Smith (1997) declares that "Genocide has existed in all periods of history," though he distinguishes different types – conquest, religious, colonial, and modern genocide – in different historical eras.

No age has had a monopoly on mass murder. Earlier ages may have been far more cruel than our own, more at ease, for example, with public torture and executions. We moderns prefer indirect, callous killing at a distance. We bomb from a safe height but are appalled by butchery with axes and swords (Collins, 1974: 421). In former times treatment of the lower classes, including common soldiers, was much crueler than it is today. Discipline was harsh and exemplary, floggings were routine, executions were common. The enemy's lower classes were treated even worse. Armies lived off the countryside; besiegers sacked, looted, and raped their way through a captured city. But in historic warfare, notes Smith (1997) people were killed for *where*, not *who* they were. Murder is not distinctively modern, but murder in order to cleanse particular identities is modern.

Even with cleansing, I must qualify this statement. Migrant conquerors who aim to settle and farm or herd the land themselves have strong economic motivations to displace the natives from the land and may engage in wild deportations, worsening to ethnocide if expelling them results in starvation. In a few cases this may have amounted to local genocide, as with some Hun, Mongol, and Anglo-Saxon incursions. If incursions were by pastoralists into settled land, the native death rate might have been high, since pastoralists need more extensive lands than farmers. Yet most ancient mass movements conventionally described as conquests were very different.

The Indo-Europeans (from whose language almost all European languages are descended) probably spread westward not through conquest at all, but through a centuries'-long process diffusing advanced neolithic farming. No one, concludes Renfrew (1992), may have actually moved more than a few miles. Most supposed conquerors of early history actually rose to power gradually. Dolukhanov (1994: 374) says that Middle Eastern Semites first appeared as migrant pastoralists living alongside sedentary agriculturalists. They adopted much of the agriculturalists' culture, entering their cities as laborers, mercenaries, and merchants. Eventually, they rose up and conquered them. Later they founded great empires – Akkadian, Hittite, and so on – ruling over, not eliminating, the agriculturalists.

We know most about more recent invaders, like the barbarians conquering the Roman Empire. The Visigothic conquerors of the Garonne Valley in southern France may have been typical. They constituted only one-sixth of the native population of the valley. Brown (1996: 57–62) says they were not perceived as "invaders from outer space" but as known neighbors, often previously engaged in defending the empire from other invaders. They recruited Roman renegades, poor people seeking to better themselves through violence. Except "for the occasional, chilling grand raid" (like Attila the Hun's), which might be quite devastating, they would set about "spoiling the meadows, cutting up the countryside and ruining the olive groves" as a way of forcing submission. Resisters were cut down, women were raped, and further deaths came from malnutrition and disease. The "aim was to inflict just enough damage to persuade the local leaders to think twice about offering further resistance: they would pay tribute or open their gates to a new overlord." The Goths didn't want to cleanse civilized peoples, they wanted to *be* civilized. King Theodoric, the Ostrogoth, summed it up: "An effective Goth wants to be like a Roman; only a poor Roman would want to be a Goth." He was describing *lateral assimilation*, confined within comparable social classes of the two peoples. Upper-class Goths become Romans; some lower-class Romans had become Goths. Mongols and Chinese did the same during weaker periods of the Chinese Empire. These barbarians practiced *exemplary repression* followed by *partial class assimilation*, not cleansing. This was probably the most common pattern where barbarians conquered more civilized peoples. And as they conquered, they assimilated more peoples into their culture and identity. By the time the heirs of Ghenghis Khan reached the Middle East, the conquering "Mongol" armies were mostly composed of Turkic soldiers picked up along the way. The ensuing Khanate was ethnically extremely mixed – and converted to Islam.

Since civilization was all about avoiding labor (it still is), barbarians wanted people to rule over, do the work, and create the surplus. If they killed them, they would have to do the labor themselves. At the extreme, they might kill or deport entire troublesome elites or defiant cities or local populations. Cities put to the sword might result in thousands of deaths, as in Numantia and the two Greek city-states mentioned earlier. They were made an example of. But conquerors assimilated elites who did submit. Since most empires and barbarians conquered their near neighbors, they did not regard them as aliens. The ferocity of ancient conquerors was intended to send an exemplary signal to other cities and regions to surrender; it did not commence more systematic elimination.

Most historic cities were very cosmopolitan, containing ethnic and religious tensions leading to riots. At the worst this might escalate to pogroms; wild, short-lived violence directed at a minority might also result from communal tensions and rulers' divide-and-rule strategies. Nero's scapegoating of Christians for the great fire of Rome and attacks on Jews in the European Middle Ages are obvious examples. Warfare occasionally strayed, as it still does, into ethnocide. Laying waste territory, burning crops and homes, and killing animals result in mass civilian deaths, callously regarded as an acceptable cost. Anger, revenge, panic, drunkenness, or paranoia shown by some rulers (Attila, Timur, or Ivan the Terrible seem obvious examples) might intensify the horrors. The extreme cases were deplored at the time. It is not true, as Smith (1997: 232) suggests, that such acts have produced "a sense of moral horror" only in modern times.

Rome had struggled for a century against Carthage. By the time Rome was getting the upper hand, feelings of revenge were strong. The policy of *Delenda est Carthago* – Carthage must be destroyed – was accomplished. It was razed to the ground, which was then supposedly salted to prevent crops ever growing there (probably apocryphal, given the amount of salt that would have been required). Mass Carthaginian deaths resulted. However, this treatment was exceptional, for the Roman conquerors tolerated Punic culture. It survived in Spain for at least three centuries and in North Africa and Sardinia for five centuries, to near the end of the Roman Empire. The Punic upper classes were almost immediately allowed some political autonomy and they began to assimilate, followed later by the lower classes (López Castro, 1995: 157–9, 210–19).

ETHNICITY IN EARLIER HISTORY

The overall explanation is not hard to find. As Ernest Gellner (1983) and I (1986) noted, most large states of history were the private possession of upper-class elites, whose cultures differed from the cultures of the masses. In Giddens's term, these were *class-divided* societies. Ethnic groups existed, but in large societies the elite of one or two of them ruled over the others. Thus mass cleansing of one people by or in the name of another was uncommon. This is more of a hazard of societies where whole peoples share the same collective identities and political claims. Whole peoples arose in two stages. The first came with the emergence of salvation religions preaching that people of all classes and regions had the same soul and the same capacity for salvation. This democratized the sacred but not the secular realm of society. Full macro-ethnicity emerged in the second phase, with aspirations for secular democracy, and with it the potential for serious ethnic cleansing. That mainly pins it down to modernity.

A sense of ethnicity has been very widespread in human history. The basic building blocks of all societies are locality and kinship, and if such ties remain intact over the generations, they generate a shared sense of ethnic community. Many of the clan and tribal groups studied by anthropologists were such tiny micro-ethnicities. Under the right conditions they might expand to form a smallish people. Larger states in early history were typically composed of many of these smallish ethnic groups. But were the larger units macro-ethnicities? Did the Akkadians, the Hittites, or the Assyrians share a sense of common identity transcending region and class?

Dolukhanov (1994) has summarized what archeologists know of ethnicity in the earliest Middle Eastern civilizations. The Neolithic revolution of around 8000 BC brought large and loose "sociocultural networks" of interaction connecting many small groups. There was little cultural closure or collective awareness amounting to ethnicity. Only with the emergence of smaller, tighter chiefdoms around 4000–3000 BC did some ethnic self-consciousness emerge. But when these chiefdoms became swallowed up by larger literate civilizations, ethnic boundaries weakened. The ruling elite, priestdom, and merchants might belong to distinct ethnic minorities, alien to the bulk of each local agricultural population. This was so of the Akkadian, Hittite, Assyrian, and Urartuan Empires, which were held together by military power – not by shared culture, still less by ethnic solidarity. Indeed, since most of the conquerors throughout the region spoke Semitic languages, the written form of one of them, Akkadian, became the *lingua franca* of elites across the entire Middle East, though it was not spoken by the masses anywhere. This was not an era in which ethnicity cemented states.

Social and geographic distance were obviously crucial: how far down and across could a shared sense of ethnic identity spread? The smaller the geographical space and the denser and more egalitarian the population within it, the easier the communication and the more likely a common ethnic sense. Let us consider the infrastructures of the four sources of social power.

1. *Ideological power* was transmitted mainly through language, literacy, and religion. The common folk of large-scale premodern societies did not speak the same common language, and they were illiterate. Elites might speak and write one or two common official languages, which were not usually native vernaculars. Greek, Latin, and Persian were, like Akkadian, unrelated to most of the empire's spoken languages.

Ancient religions varied. Some were class-bound. In Mesopotamia religious rituals were conducted in private for the benefit of elites in palaces and temples from which the common people were barred. Syncretic religions absorbed diverse local religions into a loose pantheon of gods at the official level. It is doubtful that much integration occurred at the popular level, though some cults might diffuse quite widely. Rulers tended to be tolerant of popular and local religions. When Alexander the Great arrived in Memphis, political expediency required that he pay homage to the Egyptian gods. In return, he was accepted as the new pharaoh. The Roman Emperor Augustus was supposedly disgusted at Egyptian sacrifices of animals, but there are stelae showing him performing sacrifices. As long as groups respected the official deities, they could follow whatever religion they liked. Since Christians would not do such obeisance, they were persecuted. Tolerance or syncretism was general across most empires before the rise of monotheistic salvation religions, while Islam remained quite tolerant and Hinduism syncretic. Religions reinforced multi-ethnicity, not macro-ethnicity. Some religious cultures even spanned multiple states, as in Sumer and Greece, and gave a sense of being ethnically Greek or Sumerian to people of most classes (perhaps not to slaves). But this was not very politically relevant. The city-states spent much time fighting each other, and the Greeks united against Persia only when they faced potential Persian hegemony. Otherwise, they were as likely to ally with as against Persia.

Were there no protonational religions in which religion might help cement a macro-ethnic identity? Judaism is usually identified as the main example. Yahweh did indeed become the god of all the Jews. His worship became the core of the Jewish sense of ethnic identity and of Jewish longings for political freedom. But archeologists and linguists believe this occurred much later than the biblical tradition asserts, after the collapse of the state of Israel and partly because the Persian rulers encouraged subject peoples to develop stable collective identities. Even then, it applied only to Palestine, one part of the land of Israel (Thompson, 1992: 422). Under the Romans the Jews did constitute an ethnic problem, having become unusually cohesive, resistant, and persecuted. The Armenians constituted a similar case in later history. But I doubt that there were many cases.

2. *Economic power* was also important. Most early subsistence economies were small-scale, integrating villages and manorial estates within walking distance. The rich could ride over longer distances; those near navigable water could take goods much further. Traders carried high-value goods over vast distances, but the bulk of the population had local economic horizons. Cities, especially capital cities, sent out denser networks into their hinterlands. Irrigation, especially systematic hydraulic economies, provided this for some large rural areas. Capitals and their hinterlands, unusual ecologies, highly effective imperial regimes, and close relations between merchants, artisans, and rulers might generate some integration, though merchants were usually cosmopolitan and transnational in their culture. Early modern European countries saw a stirring of national consciousness in the home counties surrounding the capital city – around London and Paris, for example. But across premodern societies we find few highly integrated economies capable

of generating macro-ethnic solidarities. In economic terms, these were class-divided societies.

3. *Military power* created most of the large states of history. Military service was where ordinary families most felt the weight of the state and where they might commit loyalty to the state. Yet most armies were formed from warrior castes or feudal levies, their allegiance more to their caste or lord than to the state, still less to the nation. Conscription might offer more macro-ethnic cement, especially where citizen-soldiers were the norm, though these usually had to be rich enough to provide their own weapons, armor, and horses. The Assyrian Empire was founded upon highly trained infantrymen recruited from peasants in the heartland of the empire. They probably shared some of the martial culture of their rulers and the spoils of war, generating a sense of being Assyrian across the classes. The empire would then resemble an ethnocracy, the rule of one ethnic group over diverse populations. Rome had something of this in its earlier republican days. But as Assyria and Rome expanded and became fully imperial, their armies were recruited from all the ethnic groups of the empire. It does not seem that their loyalty to the empire became an ethnic identity.

4. *Political power* is the final factor. Monarchies dominated, generating "ins" and "outs" at court and in assemblies, usually organized by region, detracting from macro-ethnicity across the realm. The Roman Senate constituted a partial and the Greek polis a major exception, an intense mobilizer of collective commitment among the citizenry of the individual city-state. In confederations of city-states, like those of Greece, Sumer, and Phoenicia, political infrastructures undercut potential ethnic identities by providing intenser local identities.

State administrations did seek to partially homogenize some of their subjects. The Chinese bureaucracy was renowned as an integrating device, though it was class-bound, bringing only the provincial gentry into an imperial Han identity. The extraordinary longevity and core territorial continuity of Chinese empires probably made them exceptional. After centuries of Chinese rule, ordinary peasants seem to have also considered themselves Chinese. Like many other conquerors, Greek and Roman elites often enforced intermarriages with conquered elites and carried off elite children to the capital and court for an education in Greek or Roman language and culture. Through such policies it is generally said that within a century of Roman rule it became impossible to tell the original ethnic identity of elites, especially among the less civilized conquered peoples. Roman soldiers were also married off to conquered women and settled in frontier areas. The disappearance of native elites was accompanied by Roman road building, urbanization, a degree of statist economic integration, and standardized military service and taxation. Thus a sense of being Roman spread quite widely among the population. From 212 AD citizenship became universal, though denuded of real content through the concomitant widening of class differences. Rulers and ruled were never part of the same ethnic community. As in almost all empires, this was a lateral, aristocratic culture.

THE ASSYRIAN CASE

Scholars who say that genocide was also found in the ancient world invariably point to the Assyrians. Smith (1997: 224) claims that "Assyria engaged in genocide almost annually" (cf. Bell-Fialkoff, 1996: 7; Rummel, 1994: 11), which makes us wonder how they could have had any subjects at all. Actually, the Assyrians made the mistake of mistreating the Jews, whose chronicles became sacred texts of the world's biggest religions. The books of Isaiah and Kings detail their atrocities, and their own bas-reliefs and inscriptions seem to confirm them. The successor Babylonian and Persian regimes were milder.

But in conquering and then in dealing with rebellions, the Assyrians behaved like other conquerors, if more systematically. Where a state submitted voluntarily at the prospect of having to face the Assyrian army, they were subjected to vassalage, indirect Assyrian rule. They retained political autonomy, usually under the same native ruler, but paid tribute. The people became one more among many within this multiethnic empire. If vassals rebelled but then submitted quickly, the ruler and his close allies might be killed, replaced with another local, and the level of tribute upped. The fiercer the resistance, the worse the repression. Sustained warfare or rebellion could result in the elimination of the whole ruling clan and the imposition of direct rule, incorporating the vassal state as a province within the Assyrian Empire proper. Most incorporated peoples nevertheless survived culturally for a long time. Persistent rebellions or arduous sieges would occasion exemplary repression amounting at the worst to politicide followed by deportations.

A five-year Babylonian rebellion culminated in a 15-month siege that ended in 689 BC when Sennacherib's Assyrian Army stormed Babylon. The streets were filled with corpses, the survivors were deported, the city was reduced to ruins. In other Babylonian cities, some leading rebels were tortured and killed by skinning them alive and cutting away their flesh. There was much looting and burning of crops, causing famine deaths. Motives of revenge figured, for Sennacherib had lost his son to Babylonian treachery. But such savagery was also realpolitik – to terrify and deter others. It worked. There were no more rebellions in Babylonian lands until 652, when some deportations were then considered sufficient punishment for the next rebellion, as they were after the next one in 627. On such occasions, the Assyrians also set up bas-reliefs and inscriptions publicly declaring the level of repression used and the reason for its use, proving the exemplary intent of their actions.

The Jewish King Hezekiah famously realized he had made a big mistake in joining one rebellion. His co-rebels had deserted him to make a deal with Sennacherib. Now isolated in Jerusalem, Hezekiah watched the Assyrian armies seize his other cities and arrive at the city gates. The Assyrian commander offered the Jews a choice, in Hebrew so that the defenders could understand: continue fighting and die or turn against Hezekiah:

Hearken not to Hezekiah: for thus saith the king of Assyria, Make an agreement with me by a present, and come out to me, and then eat ye every man of his own vine and every one of his fig tree, and drink ye every one the waters of his cistern; Until I come and take you away to a land like your own land, a land of corn and wine, a land of bread and vineyards, a land of olive oil and of honey, that ye may live and not die. (II Kings 18: 31–2)

He was offering them the traditional Assyrian choice for rebels: death or policed deportation.

The Assyrians specialized in deportations. Probably over a million people were deported altogether. Yet these involved relatively few deaths, unlike most modern deportations discussed in this book – from the Cherokee "vale of tears," to Chechens deported by the last tsars and Stalin, to the Jewish death marches of 1945. Assyrian bas-reliefs show soldiers driving on the deportees, but Assyrian officials along the route had to feed and house them. At their destination they were settled in family groups on farms or in urban occupations suitable to their skills, mostly with the same free or semifree statuses as the locals. The policy was instrumentally rational. Deportations eliminated troublesome states, not peoples. Elites and soldiers might be killed or enslaved, and the images and statues of the rebels' gods were smashed to destroy the ideology of their state. But people were valuable resources, and deportations helped rebuild Assyria. Constant warfare drained the population, especially in the main areas of fighting and recruitment. Preference was shown for deportees with economic skills to replenish skilled manpower. In time they might assimilate into the local population, but as Oded (1979: 86) says:

the Assyrian attitude to a person was based first and foremost on his political affiliation and the territory he lived in, and not on his ethnic-national identity, and that territorial unity rather than national purity determined the attitude of the Assyrian kings to conquered population.

Contrary to reputation, even the most militaristic ancient empire did not pursue ethnic cleansing (Becking, 1992: 61–93; Frame, 1992; Gallagher, 1999; Grayson, 1982; Yamada, 2000).

I have argued that macro-ethnicity and ethnic cleansing were rare in ancient times. Larger societies were ruled through class-bound lateral aristocratic assimilation. Conquered elites were assimilated into the cultural identity of the new rulers so that macro-ethnic identities were limited by class. There was massive violence, but it was almost never directed at cleansing whole peoples.

THE SALVATION RELIGIONS: NATIONS OF THE SOUL
(BUT NOT OF THE BODY)

This situation began to change with the emergence of salvation religions promising membership in the same religious community to all classes and regions. Monotheism tightened this: everyone had to worship the same God through similar rituals. States became "defender of the faith," "his most Catholic majesty," and so on. Christ preached salvation for all and supposedly favored the poor and oppressed over the rich and the rulers. Of course, churches and states subverted this message even in regard to souls, and in the secular realm there was no equality. States belonged not to the people, but to princes and aristocrats. Souls but not bodies were democratized and so could be ethnicized. Islam was more internally differentiated and more tolerant. In Hinduism class, status, and ethnic groups became subcastes, for the religion was syncretic, admitting local deities into the pantheon. Like Buddhism it preserved distance between the sacred and the secular, religion and the state. Christianity became the least tolerant of the world's salvation religions (Moore, 2000). It practiced more religious cleansing, killing people because of who rather than where they were (Smith, 1997: 233).

Yet the main minorities targeted for cleansing were not ethnic groups but Christian heretics, Muslims, lepers, and Jews. These were sometimes denounced for the impurity they supposedly presented to the body politic. Muslims were sometimes caricatured as dogs and wolves; Jews were depicted as pigs and as sacrificing Christian children. Most heresies had a regional base and, with some stretching of the term, might be considered ethnic. Yet all the targets could convert.

The Albigensians of southern France adopted the Cathar heresy in the late 12th and early 13th centuries. Regional and urban resentments were important. They were excommunicated, removed from the moral universe of obligations, and suppressed. When their stronghold of Beziers was stormed, chroniclers say that most of its 8,000 inhabitants were slaughtered – men, women, and children. After another stronghold was taken, chroniclers said that its lord and 400 knights were massacred. In a third case, the castle's chatelaine was stripped, humiliated, thrown down a hole, and buried alive. Most scholars believe the chroniclers exaggerated, but the atrocities especially shocked them since they breached the class-conscious rules of medieval warfare. Lords, knights, and a great lady were murdered. "Such a thing had never happened before," declared one. But, actually, most of the Cathar religious elite, the *perfecti*, were given a choice: confess or die. If they genuinely confessed their sin of heresy, they were forgiven; if not, they were burned at the stake (Barber, 2000; O'Shea, 2001). This was bad news for them but it was not genocide (as Smith, 1997: 231, and Jonassohn, 1998: 51, claim). It was callous warfare and forced conversion. Religion was viewed as belief. Change your beliefs and you were saved.

Though Jews were killed in pogroms, far more were forcibly converted, and far more converted "voluntarily" out of fear. Some states, usually under popular or church pressure, expelled the Jews during the late medieval period; this amounted to religious cleansing by forced deportation. This might indicate a belief that Jews could not be reformed, that their identity lay beyond mere belief – though also that they should not be killed. But though religion was the primary motive, Jews were also attacked for supposed economic extortion. Prohibited from owning land, most successful Jews were traders, entrepreneurs, and bankers, resented by most social classes. But the major persecutions occurred when Jews became caught up in broader political struggles (just as in the 20th century) like crusades against heresies and Muslims and in phases of resistance to tax gatherers and creditors. Both associations had a minimal level of plausibility. Jews had emigrated from the Muslim empires and had good relations with Islam. Jewish financiers were used by states for loans and tax extraction (Nirenberg, 1996; Roth, 1995: chaps. 2, 3).

This amounted to a "democratization of the soul" and obviously affected macro-ethnic identities. Salvation religions were religions of the book, encouraging mass literacy in vernacular languages, which boosted the sharing of culture across the classes and regions of each European state. This differed from Islam, since neither the Arabic nor Turkic languages that carried Islam were confined within states. Hastings (1997) claims this brought a sense of an English national identity in the late 14th century. He notes that by then a single native vernacular language dominated all but peripheral areas; and sufficient copies of the Bible had been translated into English to ensure that the Catholic religion was effectively Anglicized. This religious core of Englishness was reinforced by common customary law, a uniform borough and shire administration, royal domination of the Catholic Church, and emerging literate middling classes (like the pilgrims in Chaucer's *Canterbury Tales*). There were even negative views of foreigners. Hastings says Englishness was fully institutionalized in the 16th century, as Henry VIII achieved national religious independence, and nationalism was fully expressed in Shakespeare's history plays. Hastings believes England was the first nation in Europe, followed by Holland in the late 16th and early 17th centuries and France in the late 18th century (cf. Greenfeld, 1992, for a variant view of the early emergence of English nationalism).

But this neglects class divisions. Only 30 to 40 percent of the population was literate. Indeed, Peter Burke believes widening literacy widened the cultural divide. Medieval classes, he says, had shared in a popular culture consisting of festivals, carnivals, street theater, bear baiting, witch burning, ballads, drinking songs, and the like. Elites had joined in but also preserved the privacy of their own culture from the masses, whom they regarded with contempt as the "many-headed monster" and "the unstable fickle rabble." Guicciardini in *The Book of the Courtier* wrote, "to speak of the people is really to speak of a mad beast" (Burke, 1978: 27). But Burke says that written religion widened the cultural gulf between classes. Religion became more dogma-driven, more esoteric, more removed from popular rituals. This, he says, led gradually to the withdrawal of elites from the popular culture in which they had earlier participated. So it is doubtful whether English ethnicity was trumping class.

Gorski (2000) makes a stronger case for the 16th- and 17th-century Netherlands, claiming that all the elements of post–French Revolution nationalism were already present there. He identifies two nationalist myths. One saw the Dutch as a biblical chosen people, a new Israel, elected by God to defend the true faith; the other identified the Dutch as descendants of the ancient Batavian people resisting imperial tyranny. Then people, nation, sovereignty, and state became fused. Gorski believes the flood of nationalist pamphlets was by now so strong (among a people 80 percent literate) that almost all the Dutch must have been exposed to the myths. His account is plausible because of regional geopolitics. The Dutch embraced Lutheranism and especially Calvinism, with its leveling view of salvation and its emphasis on reading the Bible. But this exposed the Dutch to attacks from their powerful Catholic Spanish and Austrian overlords. Dutch elites needed to mobilize the people if they were to have any hope of victory, while the people needed the military and political organization of the elites. Equality of the soul cemented a cross-class national liberation struggle, perhaps the first one of modern times. As Gorski notes, English moves in a similar direction were aborted by the outbreak of the religious Civil War. The English defended themselves not against foreigners but each other. So religion weakened their sense of common national identity until the 18th century. Only when Protestantism solidified into one predominant orthodoxy could it nourish English/ British nationalism (Colley, 1992).

Hastings and Gorski are correct in arguing that modernist theories of the nation have seen too uniform and too late a move to nationalism. Political continuity, geopolitics, and social and geographic distance all made a difference. England and, to a lesser extent, Scotland had long existed as kingdoms with essentially the same borders under a fairly stable succession of kings. The two kingdoms were intermittently fighting each other, reinforcing their sense of distinctiveness from each other. The lowland core of Scotland was small, the southeastern and midland core of England not much bigger. The Dutch Republic was also small. For their middling classes to feel some basic identity with lords, clerics, and the land when under attack from outside, and for the combination to be called a sovereign people, was not implausible during the 16th and 17th centuries. Yet politics lagged. Princes rejected the notion that the middle classes might participate actively in the political community. The king in council ruled – sometimes with a parliament composed of the aristocracy, gentry, high churchmen, and merchant burgesses. These were gradual downward extensions of lateral aristocratic assimilation within the geographic cores of smaller European states. By the 16th century some might be considered national states, states making national appeals to their geographic and social cores. But they were not nation-states, and the bigger states remained aggregations through conquest or dynastic inheritance of territories with divergent traditions. French, Austrian, Spanish, and Russian elites faced two ways, into the dynastic center of the realm and into their own distinct historic province. Neither loyalty was national.

So over these centuries ethnic cleansing remained rare, unlike religious cleansing. Elites were still being assimilated, masses ignored – except when either strayed from religious orthodoxy. Yet in religious frontier zones protonational tinges appeared earlier. Armstrong (1982: chap. 2) sees the Islam–Christendom frontier as the main place where "nations existed before nationalism." Shallower fault lines also lay between the Western and Eastern and the Catholic and Protestant Christian Churches. Here cleansing went further. It appeared first in Spain

RELIGIOUS FRONTIER CLEANSING: SPAIN, GERMANY, IRELAND

The Iberian Peninsula had been uniquely multireligious in medieval Western Europe. All but a small northern enclave of the peninsula had been conquered by Islam in the 8th and 9th centuries, but the Islamic rulers tolerated religious minorities if they remained obedient and encouraged Jewish immigrants. There may have been more Jews in Spain than in the whole of the rest of Christian Europe. Then the Christian *reconquista* of the peninsula absorbed many Muslims (Moors) and Jews. In the Christian kingdom of Valencia, Moors remained a large majority. There were intermittent pogroms against Jews, and Moors were sometimes persecuted as fifth columnists at times of war against Islamic states. Yet the overall pattern was *convivencia*, "living together," marred by some institutional coercion embodying discrimination, language and cultural suppression, and intermittent pressure to convert. Even the *conversos* remained somewhat distinct, and they acquired considerable wealth and power. Many others remained Muslim or Jewish, directly protected and legally controlled by the monarch. In return, they paid him higher taxes.

In the late 15th century Spain moved toward unification. The crowns of Aragon and Castile, Ferdinand and Isabella, were joined in 1479. Yet their reign did not go smoothly. Ottoman Turkish pressure on Christian states of the Mediterranean was increasing, Spanish nobles resisted the monarchs, and all power actors struggled over access to the spoils of the new kingdom. One axis of conflict involved "old Christians" jealous of the power and wealth of the *conversos*. Roth (1995) sees a growing alliance against the *conversos* between old Christian aristocrats, lesser knights, and churchmen. The process of unification had increased the power of Spanish churchmen and lessened papal control. Catholicism expressed both Spanish unity and its means of defense. In 1481 the powers of the Inquisition of Aragon were extended to the whole kingdom in a bid to enhance doctrinal purity. Amid such factionalism, the monarchs launched their war against the last Moorish realm, Granada. It proved unexpectedly long, costly, and bitter, exacerbating tensions within the elite as well as hostility to Moors and other minorities. When Malaga was taken in 1487 after terrible fighting, the treatment of its Moorish population was unusually harsh, combining slaughter with enslavement.

Over the same period the Inquisition was intensifying. Over 90 percent of its investigations were directed at detecting heresy among the *conversos*. In 1491 its procedures were made public, and show trials became propaganda for church and state against heretics. It remains unclear whether evidence produced by the Inquisition against the *conversos* was real or not. But there were many convictions for the secret practice of Jewish rituals by *conversos*, for conspiracies between Jews and *conversos*, and of Jewish prophets preaching that the Messiah had come – and was the sultan! During the 1480s somewhere over 1,000 *conversos* were executed. Beset by the costs of war, the state also had an economic motive – expropriate the property of the guilty. *Conversos* who were already dead were posthumously condemned so that their property could be seized. The Inquisition also claimed that the remaining Jewish communities constituted an impurity in the realm, infecting the *conversos*, encouraging their backsliding. From 1483 Jewish communities in Jerez, Seville, and Zaragoza were charged with infecting their neighbors. These Jews were dispersed across Spain. In 1490 and 1491 there were scattered attacks on Jews led by young men drawn from the lesser nobility, the *caballeros*.

In January 1492 Granada finally surrendered and Spain became one and Catholic. On March 31, 1492, just after Columbus landed in the Americas, Ferdinand and Isabella issued an edict ordering all Jews to leave Spain within four months. This was so incongruent with most of their previous actions that it has never been easy to explain. It was not much premeditated. Jews wrote of a Catholic triumphalism surrounding the completion of the *reconquista*. Torquemada, the head of the Inquisition, aided by the religious military orders, was mounting pressure on the monarchs. The orders had for centuries spearheaded the struggle against Islam and had been prominent in Crusader atrocities. Some factions at court felt that a more Catholic and militant state was now possible. The monarchs seem to have been bowing to pressures rather than implementing their own policies.

The edict aimed not at forcing Jews out, but at forcing them to convert. It was expected that most would convert. If they stayed, they could still be milked for taxes. If they converted, the assimilation of *conversos* would no longer be undermined by the existence of separate Jewish communities. In the words of the edict, no longer would Jews "pervert faithful Christians from the holy Catholic faith." The monarchs said that local expulsions had failed to stop the "evils and harm which come to the Christians from participating with and conversation with the said Jews." There was no popular pressure or violence: this was the work of elites, not masses. Even among elites there was much dissent. Few emigrants lost their property, for they could sell it, and the traditional prohibition against Spaniards taking gold or silver out of the country was ignored in practice. Probably no more than 10,000 out of a total Spanish Jewish population of 80,000 left in the next two years. Most moved only to neighboring Portugal, from which they could still supervise their affairs. When Portugal enforced its own mass conversion of Jews in 1497, some Spanish Jews returned to Spain and formally converted there (Kamen, 1993a: 44; Roth, 1995: 285, 303–7). This was severe cleansing by a mixture of institutional assimilation and policed deportations.

Yet an Inquisition allowed to roam freely across the country could not be easily reined in. Escalation was erratic but cumulative. Jews, *conversos* and Moors alike, felt under pressure in the 1490s. Some resisted violently, causing further retaliation. Ineffective Moorish rebellions in Granada and Valencia led to forcible conversions and deportations from Spain. The Spanish policy spread to other Mediterranean states and increased the tension over the whole region. The Western Mediterranean constituted the threatened borders of Christendom. Islamic pressure from outside put pressure on all non-Christians within. Over the next two decades the emigration of Spanish Jews increased, eventually totaling somewhere between 40,000 and 100,000 (scholars agree neither about the number of the Jewish population nor about the number leaving). There was also emigration from Portugal, Provençe, and several Italian states. Most went east into the more tolerant Ottoman Empire. Many *conversos* were also emigrating, resettling right across Christendom, where they could be more anonymous. In 1502 the full policy was also applied to Moors still in Spain: leave or convert.

There were novel ethnic overtones. Even before 1492 Catholic extremists had been responding to the difficulties of proving heresy by advocating the simpler proof, blood – *limpieza de sangre*, "blood cleansing." Since tainted "Semite" blood might infect good Christians, all Jews should be expelled. This was true modern anti-Semitism, equating religion with race, rarely expressed in prior European history. Anyone of Jewish or Moorish ancestry should be forced out of Spain. Though this incurred much opposition and never became royal policy, private corporations did bar entry of those of impure blood to military and religious orders, and some cathedrals, universities, and guilds. Alongside this escalation occurred another. In 1576 the Inquisition expanded its activities by acquiring long-desired powers over converted Moors, the *Moriscos*. In royal edicts of 1609–10 all remaining *Moriscos* were expelled. Perhaps 300,000 of them suffered forcible deportation. There was armed but unavailing resistance in Valencia in which perhaps 10,000 *Moriscos* died. Spain was cleansed (my sources for this section are Dominguez Ortiz & Vincent, 1994; Edwards, 1999; Friedman, 1994; Kamen, 1993a, 1993b; Kriegel, 1994; Monter, 1994; Roth, 1995).

Ferdinand, Isabella, and their successors were no fanatics. Whatever their desire to pose as defenders of the faith, they were pragmatic politicians whose main focus was not on their Jewish or Moorish subjects. They yielded to pressures from important people for religious cleansing, probably because they found the fifth column argument sufficiently plausible to want to err on the side of security. So ended centuries of imperfect religious toleration in Spain. In the process, religious cleansing acquired national and even some racial overtones. Though many Spaniards had mixed blood (Ferdinand himself had Jewish blood on both sides of his family), a court faction argued successfully that new Jewish and Moorish converts could not be trusted. This was no holocaust, since the only deaths were incurred after rigorous (if often dubious) trials or during armed resistance. But it was total religious cleansing, becoming more ethnic as it proceeded. Within Europe it was exceptional. It did not reflect the dark side of democracy, as I shall argue were later cleansings. Spain was actually moving in the opposite direction, toward absolute monarchy, though the main cleansers were not the monarchs. But the notion that state and people should be unified in a single national creed was new, anticipating the Treaty of Westphalia by a century. In both ethnic and national senses, the expulsion of Jews and Moors was a unique bridge to modernity.

But in the early 16th century Western Christendom split apart. In France, Germany, and Ireland religious civil war resulted. The Thirty Years War of 1618–48 ravaged Germany and Bohemia. The Holy Roman Empire's population declined by 3–4 million, that is, by 15 to 20 percent (Parker, 1984; Rabb, 1964). Many more civilians than soldiers died, most from malnutrition and disease caused by callous warfare. There was a military tactical lure toward atrocities. Since states could not finance the scale of warfare required, the armies lived off the countryside under the principle that "war sustains war." The soldiers devastated crops, homes, villages, and small towns. They killed civilian men and raped women. Their callousness was helped by religious slurs. Protestants accused Catholics of idolatrous, "backward" "superstition" "in the work of the Devil"; Catholics saw Protestants as "bewitched" by heresy, practicing child murder, cannibalism, and promiscuous sex (Burke, 1978: 168–9). There was much forced conversion. When Protestant Bohemia was recaptured by the Catholic forces, the area was forcibly re-Catholicized, with 150,000 Protestants fleeing elsewhere. Many of the male refugees signed up as soldiers, impoverished and embittered. Class differences were muting: persons of all rank might be killed.

The worst atrocity was at Magdeburg, a Protestant stronghold city. When it was stormed by Catholic forces in 1631, perhaps 30,000 men, women, and children were put to the sword or died in fires set by the Catholic forces. The city remained depopulated for years. This was not entirely due to religious fanaticism. Sacking a town that resisted was within the conventional rules of war – which in such a class-bound period were drawn up with utter disregard for the lives of lower- and middle-class people. It was normal retaliation, and looting was the normal way to reward the soldiers. In long sieges like that of Magdeburg, the besiegers often suffered more privations in their trenches than the besieged did in their city. They wanted revenge and loot. Yet Magdeburg still shocked Europe; it was denounced in pamphlets and sermons, Catholic as well as Protestant, as wild and un-Christian. Such atrocities were rarely premeditated. Forced conversion or deportation were the worst premeditated policies in the wars of religion, though tactical lures produced worse. This was not ethnic but religious cleansing, and it was not premeditated, since conversion was considered the best solution.

The Thirty Years War was fought between multistate alliances with multiethnic armies. But it ended in a national solution. The 1648 Treaty of Westphalia stated *Cuius regio, eius religio:* the religion of the prince was to be the religion of his realm, and the prince could enforce it. No foreign state should now come to the aid of minorities. But with state power over religion now institutionalized, cleansing would be mainly through institutions, not weapons. A few martyrs were burned, a few sects scattered, but most converted or swore loyalty and accepted the institutional coercion of second-class citizenship. Most Protestant churches were now state-regulated as protonational churches. Though Catholicism was still a transnational faith, its states were now also bending the local church to their purposes. Cleansing was shifting from a religious to a national base, because the soul was becoming partly nationalized. Spain had been first, but then Western Europe had followed, and Eastern Europe saw divergence between the various national branches of the Orthodox Church.

However, religious cleansing might entwine with ethnic and national sentiments on the borders of European civilization, where more primitive peoples were detected. This was true in Lithuania in the east and in Ireland on the western frontier. I focus on the Irish case. Here religion reinforced the English state's attempt to subdue a country it regarded as backward and barbarous. The Gaelic Irish, especially in the west, lived in more impoverished conditions, were less literate, and used simpler (more savage) methods of warfare. The English could plausibly define the Irish as less civilized, as they also did Scottish Highlanders of the period.

Most of Ireland had been ruled by Anglo-Norman/English lords since 1250. But the settlers were few and the lords sought freedom from the English Crown. Many went native, and the Irish language revived. The Crown countered with coerced assimilation. The Statute of Kilkenny (1366) banned the Irish language, Irish surnames, and Irish sports. More settlers caused a direct confrontation over land (as in the colonies discussed in Chapter 4), and some Irish were deported to the west of the island. Yet English settlers were still few and many of them assimilated, speaking Gaelic and becoming known as the *Old English*, that is, formerly English. In the 16th century England and Scotland went Protestant, but the Gaelic Irish and most of the Old English settlers remained Catholic. The poet Edmund Spenser, a Crown official in Ireland, believed the solution was murderous cleansing: "Great force must be the instrument but famine must be the means for until Ireland be famished it cannot be subdued.... There can be no conformitie of government where there is no conformitie of religion.... There can be no sound agreement between twoe equall contraries viz: the English and Irish" (Hastings, 1997: 82–4). Callous war began, finally won by the English in 1607. Gaelic was now being pushed out of most of the public realm. More Protestant English and Scots settlers arrived, and more native Irish were forcibly deported westward.

The Civil War reopened the conflict, turning it less ethnic, more religious, and somewhat protonational in tone. It was also an imperial war, since it also brought the kingdoms of Scotland and Ireland finally under English dominance. Religious strife made the protonational resentments of the Scots and Irish upper classes more popular. Most Irish Protestants were relatively High Church and so supported the king, as did the Irish Catholic Church (both the Gaelic Irish and Old English factions). This alliance gave the king's party the upper hand in Ireland. The war had started with a Gaelic rising in which 4,000 Ulster Protestants had been massacred, with perhaps another 8,000 dying of hunger, fever, or exposure – including many women and children. Clifton (1999: 109) calls it "massacre by mismanagement," not premeditated, but the atrocity was to poison later events, since Protestant propagandists persuaded the English that hundreds of thousands of Protestants had died (Connolly, 1992: 16; Wheeler, 1999: 8–12).

The Civil War lasted longer in Ireland. But in 1649 Cromwell invaded at the head of his formidable Puritan New Model Army. He achieved the final conquest of Ireland with exemplary repression made more cruel by sentiments of revenge for the massacre of 1641 and contempt for a "barbarous" people full of "papist and savage superstitions." He declared that he would lead

the great work against the barbarous and bloodthirsty Irish, and the rest of their adherents and confederates, for the propagation of the Gospel of Christ, the establishment of truth and peace.

He summoned the city of Drogheda to surrender. When the garrison commander delayed, Cromwell ordered his canonry to breach the walls and personally led the storming. Sacking a city was conventional warfare at the time. Cromwell reported to Parliament what happened:

I forbade them to spare any that were in arms in the town, and, I think, that night they put to the sword about 2,000 men.... I am persuaded that this is a righteous judgement of God upon these barbarous wretches, who have imbrued their hands in so much innocent blood; and it will tend to prevent the effusion of blood for the future.... And now give me leave to say how it comes to pass that this work is wrought. It was set upon some of our hearts, That a great thing should be done, not by power or might, but by the Spirit of God. And is it not clear? That which caused your men to storm so courageously, it was the Spirit of God, who gave your men courage ... and therewith this happy success. And therefore it is good that God alone should have all the glory.

Hundreds more who surrendered were killed soon afterwards. Cromwell commented:

I believe we put to the sword the whole number of defendants, I do not think thirty of the whole number escaped with their lives. Those that did, are in safe custody for Barbados.

When the garrison commander at Wexford also stalled, Cromwell repeated the dose. The city was stormed with no quarter, and some fleeing civilians were also killed by soldiers seeming out of control. Cromwell made little attempt to rein them in. Cromwell again pinned the blame on God:

In His righteous justice, [he] brought a just judgement upon them, causing them to become a prey to the soldier, who in their piracies had made preys of so many families and [were] made with their bloods to answer the cruelties which they had exercised upon the lives of divers poor protestants.

In these two cities about 4,500 people were killed, comprising three-quarters of the garrisons and about 200–300 civilians. The Wexford garrison was Irish, but half of the Drogheda soldiers were English Protestant Royalists. This was broader than just a mixture of religious and ethnic cleansing. But when the garrison commander at Ross offered to surrender if liberty of conscience be allowed, Cromwell replied bluntly:

If by liberty of conscience, you mean the liberty to exercise the mass, I judge it best to use plain dealing and to let you know, where the parliament of England hath power, that will not be allowed of.

In Munster, Cromwell posted a rambling and venomously anti-Catholic proclamation. He said he did not intend to "extirpate the Catholic Religion," but only because "The word extirpate supposes a thing to be already rooted and established." The entire tone of the document suggests that he would eliminate Catholicism from Ireland by any means necessary (these quotes from Cromwell are from Abbot, 1939: II, 107, 126–7, 142, 201).

These were Cromwell's first battles in Ireland. He was sending the signal, surrender or die – Assyrian-style exemplary repression. It worked; the Irish finally surrendered. But this had also been extremely callous warfare, for about 15 percent of the Irish population, over 300,000 people, died in these two decades of warfare, mostly from malnutrition and disease.

In England the Civil War was fought in more gentlemanly fashion. There were a few massacres of garrisons refusing to surrender, but most civilians escaped direct harm, except where trapped in the plundering of stormed towns. Coster (1999) says slaughter was worst where resistance had been greatest, with Catholic and Irish soldiers showing greatest determination and so being most at risk. The cruelest general was reputed to be the most experienced – the Royalist Prince Rupert. Only 4 to 5 percent of England's population, about 180,000 people, died altogether. Even in his Scottish campaign, Cromwell showed courtesy to his opponents, giving quarter to the defeated and comfort to the wounded. Even when the Scottish Army invaded England and penetrated as far as Worcester, its final defeat did not bring savage reprisals. A handful of the leaders were executed and several hundred soldiers were transported to the New World. Yet in Ireland, religious fanaticism, ethnic contempt, and revenge for 1641 had perverted his fierce will to win. Catholics were finished off with a scorched earth campaign against guerrillas in Ulster. Locals were told to get out of the entire area or be shot. Some officers were worse than others. Sir Charles Coote was described by his Catholic enemies as "the thrice-cruel butcher and human blood-sucker"; Colonel Tothill ordered his men to slaughter all captured Irish. But the conservative Ireton (in command after Cromwell left Ireland), had Tothill court-martialed and cashiered. Ireton became alarmed by intermarriage between his soldiers and local Catholic women – by now there was a shortage of Catholic males in Ulster. So he ordered that any of the women whose conversion to Protestantism was not sincere should be expelled and their husbands reduced in rank (Wheeler, 1999). We see here the difference between Protestant radicals and moderates.

Cromwell's religious cleansing was also fueled by cleansing in the name of civilization against barbarism. But Drogheda was not like Magdeburg. Cromwell executed a garrison tardy in surrendering, but he did not kill its civilian population. This was well within the contemporary rules of conventional war (Clifton, 1999: 119). Each city was "correctly" summoned to surrender beforehand, and Cromwell did not target women or children. So this was not murderous cleansing aimed at a whole ethnic group. Rather, it was an attempt to wipe out armed resistance so that religious cleansing could proceed through milder institutional means.

It did so. The Act of Settlement of 1652 expropriated the owners of two-thirds of Irish land, supposedly for their participation in the 1641 massacre. Their lands passed to London merchants, Cromwell's soldiers, and Scottish settlers – all Protestants. In 1600 90 percent of Irish land had been held by Catholics; by 1685 this had fallen to 22 percent and by 1800 to only 5 percent. Until the 1770s anti-Catholic penal laws involved much discrimination, forcing Catholic heirs and would-be professionals to formally convert (Connolly, 1992: 145–7). But almost all the expropriated Irish stayed put as propertyless laborers. A few Catholic property owners were deported to the west coast, where they received lesser lands (Clifton, 1999: 123). The Irish language declined in the public sphere but held on in lower-class dialects. By the mid-19th century, Irish parents of all classes became eager for their children to learn the language of modernity and worldly success – English. Though about a quarter of the population of Ireland was of English or Scottish settler descent, Ireland was not quite a colony. As Connolly (1992: 111–22, 294–313) notes, Ireland was next door to England and Scotland, and its inhabitants were European in appearance, religion, and culture. There was mass movement in both directions across the narrow sea and much assimilation. Gaelic nomadic pastoralism was replaced by English tenurial practices. Attempts at mass conversion were halfhearted. There had been coercive assimilation among elites and severe discrimination among the masses. But the English did not commit mass cleansing. Ireland continued to contain two religious communities – as we see in the conflicts of today. Between 1969 and 2000 about 3,300 people were killed, though neither side was actually trying to remove the other.

Europe from the late 15th to the 17th centuries saw severer religious cleansing entwined with ethnic elements in religious frontier zones. In Spain ethnic antagonisms and cleansing increased; in Ireland they decreased. This was probably due mainly to differences between the severity of the frontier threat: the Islamic threat to Christian Mediterranean states remained strong during the major cleansing period (it began to ease only after the naval battle of Lepanto in 1572), while the Catholic Irish threat in the west steadily diminished. Farther east, across the frontiers of the warring Russian, Ottoman, and Persian Empires, murderous cleansing also spread between Christian, Sunni Muslim, and Shia Muslim communities (Lieven, 2000: 149). Ethnic-religious cleansing was stirring only where political and religious threats reinforced one another. Even then, most killing was not premeditated. It occurred where events spiraled out of control. Cleansing was systematic (especially in Spain), but murderous cleansing was not. Magdeburg and Drogheda resembled countless other sieges in earlier history more than the events of my later chapters.

There was no relationship between religious cleansing and regime form. In Spain the cleansing of Jews and Moors was pushed by secular and religious elites, though not by the monarchs themselves. In the wars of religion, Protestants generally pushed toward limited representative government, while Catholics favored greater monarchical powers, and both sides perpetrated atrocities equally. In England, Puritans favored the most representative form of government, with the lowest property franchise, and they were also the most fanatic in their hatred of papists, with the strongest desire to cleanse them from the land. Overrepresented in the army, they also had the military power to achieve it. But overall, this was not a phase of cleansing attributable to democratization – other than of the soul. It ended when almost all states became about 80 percent mono-religious.

This chapter has cut through a vast swathe of history during which I suggested that ethnic cleansing was uncommon since macro-ethnicity was also uncommon. Ethnicity rarely conquered either distance or class. But as salvation religions spread, religion began to cut across class and other boundarie, leading to protonational democratization and cleansing of souls. Yet secular matters remained dominated by class and other axes of stratification. And with religious cleansing achieved, things seemed to be improving in Europe.

3

Two Versions of "We, the People"

The notion that the people should rule was most famously stated thus:

We, the People of the United States, in Order to form a more perfect Union, establish Justice, insure domestic Tranquillity, provide for the common defence, promote the general Welfare, and secure the Blessings of Liberty to ourselves and our Posterity, do ordain and establish this CONSTITUTION for the United States of America.

"The people" described in the Preamble to the American Constitution now legitimates almost all modern states, and is seen unreservedly as a good and moral collectivity. Indeed, it may be the most benign form of rule humans have yet devised. But if the two meanings of "the people," *demos* and *ethnos,* become fused, problems result – for other ethnic groups living in the same territory. The privileges of citizens may involve discrimination against ethnic out-groups. At the extreme, the out-group may be excluded, cleansed, from the territory of the people.

Yet two rather different peoples may be distinguished, a *stratified* and an *organic* people. If the people is conceived of as diverse and stratified, then the state's main role is to mediate and conciliate among competing interest groups. This will tend to compromise differences, not try to eliminate or cleanse them. The stratified people came to dominate the Northwest of Europe. Yet if the people is conceived of as organic, as one and indivisible, as ethnic, then its purity may be maintained by the suppression of deviant minorities, and this may lead to cleansing. In Europe this danger began to loom more across its central and eastern regions.

Most views of liberalism stress individualism. Liberal democracies are said to be beneficent because their constitutions first and foremost protect individual human rights. But this was not actually how they were established, for the rights and regulation of groups have actually been more central for liberal democracy. The institutionalization of interest group struggle, and especially of class struggle, has ensured toleration and the restraint of cleansing by generating a stratified, not an organic, people. Nonetheless, liberal democracies *have* committed massive cleansing, sometimes amounting to genocide – but in colonial contexts where large social groups were defined as lying outside of the stratified people.

Of course, the people did not really "ordain and establish" the American Constitution. This was accomplished by 55 middle-aged white gentlemen of the highest rank and property, closeted together in private for two weeks in Philadelphia. They claimed to represent the people of the 13 colonies. But who was this people? The Founding Fathers did not mean to include women, slaves, and native Americans. Most of them did not want to include white men who lacked property, though they were pushed toward this by the revolutionary process surging around them. British politicians of the period defined the people by distinguishing it from *the populace* below. The populace comprised the lower orders, the crowd, the mob – out-groups who were definitely not a part of the people. "We, the people" comprised groups of propertied men who were termed at the time *interests* (gentlemen, merchants, manufacturers, artisans, etc.). These interests were acknowledged to be divisive, and it was important to conciliate their interests so that they would all share "a common stake in the nation." They recognized the citizen body as being internally stratified. Indeed, citizens' rights were at this time also stratified, since the people were entitled to "active" citizenship, while the populace enjoyed only "passive" citizenship. The populace did possess legal and civil rights, but not political rights.

Then moves toward the acquisition of full rights by all were also dominated by class. These were capitalist economies, now industrializing. Debates over the extension of the franchise were dominated by issues like these: Where should the property line be drawn? Should employees or servants (who many thought were incapable of forming independent judgments) have the vote, be jurors, or hold office? Should some classes have more votes than others? Could some of the more responsible members of a class be admitted first, so as to detach them from the rest of their class? It was recognized that these plural class and strata interests might be compromised, but they could not be eliminated. The people was not one and indivisible but plural and stratified. Indeed, the contending interests were institutionalized in political parties. Factional interest groups – ins and outs, Whigs and Tories – already existed, and the class conflicts of industrialism turned them into the "left versus right" and "religious versus secular" parties of the modern period. All accepted that their conflict could not be abolished or transcended, only compromised. And since the liberal state is mainly a mediator between interests, it is a limited state, enjoying few powers of its own. So both nationalism and statism were restrained by liberalism, and the development of class and nation were closely entwined.

Class was soon joined by age and gender. Should only household heads have full rights, and at what age could other men be said to be of independent mind? Then women of a certain age or class might be considered politically responsible before other women. This raises a second cause of restraint. Class, age, and gender all stratify, but they do not usually segregate people into different communities. These groups must necessarily live and work (and love and hate) among each other. Even during bouts of severe class conflict, workers and employers spent most of their waking hours cooperating with one another. People of different ages, and men and women, live and constitute families together. Though residential segregation may occur between classes, they are also routinely interdependent. Such interdependence restrains most potential antipathy between we, the people and out-groups defined by class, age, or gender.

The institutionalization of class conflict has been the main political accomplishment of the modern West, generating liberal and then social democratic states. Class, age, and gender remain as contending interests within the people, recognized as having legitimate conflicts that are institutionalized in multiparty systems. Since this form of polity does not try to eliminate exploitation, new oppressed groups will perennially rise up to make new demands. But class conflict amid liberal institutions is not settled by cleansing the land of one's opponents, still less by mass murder. However, a different outcome results if class is not compromised but repressed. A downward spiral of class conflict may lead to revolution, as it did across parts of Central and Eastern Europe (Mann, 1993: chaps. 16–18). Successful revolutionaries then made a distinctive claim to an organic "people as proletariat," as we see in Chapter 11.

Yet in Northwestern Europe two things were being accomplished by the late 18th century: religious conflict was declining (as we saw in the previous chapter), and liberal and class institutions were trumping ethnic solidarities. With religious homogeneity achieved within each state, ethnic conflict moderated and centered on the more secular issue of language. This made it less murderous. Although we cannot adhere to more than one salvation religion, we can speak more than one language, especially where it has no sacred status. I can learn a dominant official language in order to achieve material success in the public realm, retaining my maternal language in the private and emotional realm. Through this means, I may acquire more than one ethnic identity. Yet in the public sphere over a 500-year period, most European states sought monolingualism, and this did encourage a withering away of minority ethnic cultures. Over the long run Europe was cleansed, as local and regional languages and cultures have disappeared. The predominant means used have not been very violent, however. At most they have amounted to institutional coercion.

Nor did they transcend class. As in prior history, assimilation proceeded laterally, class by class, down from the aristocracy. Consider the cases of Wales. Coastal Wales had been conquered in the 12th and 13th centuries by Anglo-Norman lords. Plantations of English settler towns followed. The rulers periodically banned the Welsh language, limited intermarriage, and excluded the Welsh from office holding, but these actions were less persistent and less enforced than in Ireland. The kings were happy to use Welsh bowmen as their decisive weapon against the French king at Crecy and Agincourt.

After 1400 Wales was not regarded as a frontier society (unlike Ireland); after 1500 it was considered a loyal, even conservative, part of the kingdom. In 1509 the English burgesses of Conwy, one of the plantation towns in which English colonists had been settled, petitioned for more discrimination against the Welsh. They complained, "It is no more meete for a welshman to bears any office in Wales – than it is for a frinchman to be Officer in Calis [Calais], or a skotte in Barwicke [Berwick]." Unfortunately, the petition was sent to the Anglo-Welsh King Henry VII, whose accession culminated a long process of aristocratic lateral assimilation between English and Welsh lords. His son, Henry VIII, then absorbed Wales into England through his Act of Union in 1536, imposing one administration, one law, and one language. It said that no person who commanded only "the Welsh speech shall have or enjoy any manner of offices or fees within this realm." Yet the act provoked no organized opposition in Wales, for the gentry were pleased to be granted the same institutions as the English (Jenkins et al., 1997; Roberts, 1997; Smith 1997).

Perhaps 90 percent of the population spoke only Welsh (nearly 70 percent did so even in 1800). They were now officially disqualified from holding public office. But they had never held public office! As in England, 90 percent of the population did not count in politics. What mattered were the remaining 10 percent: the nobility, gentry, merchants, and guildsmen. English had already spread as the language of official documents, and most of this 10 percent had already learned English. They recognized that English was a high language, the language of rule, of the professions and of commerce. Most were keen to participate in that world, and so acquired English as a second language – as much of the world does today. Welsh speaking in public contexts declined, though not yet in private ones.

The institutional coercion involved in imposing the English language on Wales was partly national exploitation by the English, partly class betrayal by Welsh elites. Burke (1978: 270–2) sees an "upper class withdrawal" from popular culture occurring right across 16th- to 18th-century Europe. The Bohemian nobility withdrew from Czech to German, educated Norwegians withdrew to Danish, Finns to Swedish, and so on. But the Welsh-speaking gentry operated in a world in which bilingualism was the obvious strategy for advancement – and also the best way to provide protection for their retainers and dependents. Welsh pragmatism was matched by that of the English. In 1563 the Anglican Church recognized that to convert Welsh people to Protestantism required a Bible in Welsh, the only language understood by the masses. This project encouraged literacy in Welsh. Eventually, as middling and lower-class people were admitted to the public sphere in both England and Wales, English spread down to the lower classes. During the 19th century it made serious inroads into the Welsh language. Before then, assimilation was still lateral and elitist. Welsh, unlike Irish, was being voluntarily undermined from the top, class by class. This was becoming a stratified yet national state.

By the early 20th century, almost all Northwestern Europe had been linguistically cleansed, the last remnants by voluntary assimilation. Minorities in France had mostly accepted the Jacobin view, pleased to see their children educated in French, the language of modernity. Breton-speaking parents identified their language with backwardness and lack of opportunity. In public settings Welsh or Breton were subordinated to a British or French language and identity. Linguistic cleansing was completed, at first by force, then by institutional coercion, finally by voluntary assimilation. Indeed, though Ireland had been at first subjected to more ferocious cleansing, Irish parents joined in the last phase just as enthusiastically.

Only near the end, in the early 19th century in Britain and in the mid- to late 19th century elsewhere, did national identities spread out fully to the lowest classes. Eugene Weber's aptly titled book *Peasants into Frenchmen* (1976) has become a modern classic. In it he describes how most country-dwellers in France even in 1870 did not consider themselves members of the French nation. The regions around Paris, the home counties of France, did constitute a partial exception, since they were servicing the capital. But Weber concludes that most French men and women had much more local horizons. Peasants became Frenchmen only when state infrastructures actually penetrated their daily life, through military service, national education, and railways and motorized transport. I would also add national economic markets and production systems; national political infrastructures – routinized national parties, state institutions, and state services; and a national religion. But in 1864 Minister of Education Duruy asked his school inspectors to investigate the languages spoken right across the country. His ministry then drew up national maps of the departments' language skills. Across the departments of Brittany, Alsace-Lorraine, and almost the whole of the south, 40 percent or more of the population did not speak French, though they reported at that very time that the figure among schoolchildren aged 7 to 13 was down to half that level (the two maps are reproduced in de Certeau et al., 1975: 271–2). One inspector visiting the rural Lozère district in the south asked the children at a village school, "In what country is the Lozère situated?" None could answer. By the 1880s another school inspector found more knowledge, reporting, "they say they are in the Lozère, and when they cross the mountains they go *to* France" (Gibson, 1994: 178). They now knew where France was. But it was somewhere else.

Connor (1994: 221) notes the revealing responses given by European migrants to U.S. immigration officers between 1880 and 1910. When asked where they came from, they overwhelmingly identified themselves in terms of "locale, region, province and the like," not in terms of a country. But the most convincing evidence derives from a battery of statistics on intimate family practices. Susan Cott Watkins (1991) compared data for 1870 and 1960 across no less than 500 regions within 15 European countries. She collected data on rates of fertility, marriage, and illegitimacy. How often did people get married, how many children did they have, and were these legitimate? These are intimate practices indeed, resulting from millions of individual decisions taken by women and men in the privacy of their own relationships. But she found clear general trends. In 1870 differences were much greater within countries than between them. There was less of a French or a German family pattern than many varied local ones, some of which cut across national borders. But by 1960 the family had been substantially nationalized on all three issues. Now there was a French and a German and a British family norm regarding how many children one had, whether one married before children were born, and how frequently people got married. None of this had existed in 1870. The nation had been born very late – whether legitimately or illegitimately!

Virtually no states were mono-ethnic, since they had been formed as the ruling class in the core region defined itself as being of a single ethnicity, imposing rule over other regions and ethnic groups. Over several centuries they achieved a partly coerced, partly voluntary lateral aristocratic assimilation of peripheral ethnic groups, starting with aristocracies, then moving down the class structure. After 1688 in Britain all mainstream Protestant property owners were confirmed as political citizens – whether they spoke English, Welsh, or Scottish Gaelic. Bans against Irish Gaelic, dissenting Protestants, and Catholics were removed over the next 140 years. After the 1832 standardization of the franchise, all adult English, Welsh, Scottish, or Irish males who had freehold property to the value of £15 per annum were full political citizens, the people. They increasingly considered themselves "Britons" (Colley, 1992), but they also knew they had a second ethnicity, as English, Welsh, Scots, or Irish. Yet conflicts between these identities were now of much less significance than was class conflict.

Each country blended class and ethnicity in distinctive ways. Three had more multiethnicity. In Belgium the franchise was first dominated by a Flemish bourgeoisie speaking French in public, since they recognized it as the high language of modernity. Flemish and French elites mutually assimilated quite easily. The Flemish bourgeoisie had no desire to appeal downward to the Flemish masses, and French elites were happy to acquire Flemish high culture, which had historic caché. In Spain the dominant Castilian elite failed to greatly assimilate Catalan and Basque elites, but here both class and ethnic political movements endured. In the Third Spanish Republic of the 1930s there were separate Catalan and Basque nationalist parties of the left, center, and right. In multilingual Switzerland the central state was weak, most government being at the cantonal level. Since 18 of the 22 cantons were monolingual, Switzerland resembled a federation of tiny nation-states, each one dominated by the politics of class, with ethnic cooperation occurring at the less important federal level (Rabushka & Shepsle, 1972: 208–12).

Belgian, Spanish, and Swiss representative governments coped with multi-ethnicity in a quite distinctive way, through consociational and confederal forms, but *alongside* class institutions. These distinctive historic forms could be very useful to the much more multiethnic countries of the South of the world today.

Violent cleansing was generally confined to the periphery of Western Europe, where ethnicity and class might reinforce each other. Here exploited classes were also defined as ethnically distinct – indeed, as cultural and civilizational inferiors. This was so in the 1780s of the "Highland clearances" by Anglicized Scottish landlords of their crofters, resulting in much coerced emigration to the New World, many deaths, and the final retreat of Gaelic into the far northwest of the Highlands and islands. The French Revolution had comparable effects on peripheral France. A trace of this survives among Scots, Welsh, and Breton self-conceptions as being proletarian nations exploited by the imperialist English and French. The extreme case was Ireland, in which religion still reinforced ethnicity and class. British discrimination in favor of (Protestant) landlords' rights against (Catholic) tenants and lease-holders worsened the Irish famine of the 1840s. Though this began as a crisis of a mistaken policy of overdependence on a single crop, leading to potato blight, it was worsened by British unwillingness to interfere with market forces blended with callous indifference to primitive Catholic peasants. The result was an ethnocide in which thousands died and thousands more fled to America.

This was the darkest part of early liberal democracy in Europe. Elsewhere. out-groups might be discriminated against, but they were rarely forced out, still less murdered. Their elites voluntarily assimilated or were institutionally coerced into a dominant identity. Later, so were their masses. If contemporary Western Europe contains relatively homogeneous nation-states, this had mostly resulted from cleansing of relatively mild types. The European liberal dark side was found elsewhere, in the colonies.

THE ORGANIC VERSION

The democratizing ideal spread somewhat later in the European center and east, along with the later spread of capitalism and industry. Initially, these regions looked west and north for democratic inspiration. But three differences led toward organic rather than liberal conceptions of the nation-state, giving nationalist movements a chance of trumping class movements.

First, aspirations for democracy appeared later here, when political theory had matured into the notion that the *whole* people must rule, both the people and the populace – though it was still largely limited to adult males. So advocacy of limited propertied franchises of the early Anglo-American type was overwhelmed by more popular demands. Seeking to keep the masses at bay, elites developed another form of partial democracy, limiting not the vote but parliamentary sovereignty. All males might vote, but their deputies must share power with a monarch. The German *Kaiserreich* was the prototype, where a Reichstag, a parliament elected by universal male suffrage, shared powers with the kaiser and his ministers in an essentially dual state. By enhancing executive powers, this first difference enhanced *statist* powers and ideologies beyond liberal levels.

Second, by now states were expected to be more active for their citizens, providing communications infrastructures, economic development, social welfare, and citizen armies. In Perez-Diaz's (1993) words, the state became "the bearer of a moral project." In the 1890s and 1900s statist projects surged on the far right through protofascists, on the center-right through the paternalism of Social Catholicism, and on center-left through movements like the German Socialists of the Chair, British New Liberals, French Radical Republicans, and Russian *zemstvo* intelligentsia. Only the far left lagged. Until after World War I and the Bolshevik Revolution, most socialists remained attached to utopian or communard notions of a minimal postrevolutionary state. In the 20th century the statist surge continued, affecting most of the world.

Third, the region was dominated by multiethnic dynastic empires. The Habsburg (Austrian), Romanov (Russian), and Ottoman (Islamic/Turkish) Empires comprised many historic provinces and kingdoms. The dynasties did not seek to homogenize or legitimate themselves in terms of a nation. In fact, they encouraged further immigration by minorities, like Germans or Jews, with more economic skills than the locals. Any groups willing to act as settler-soldiers in border areas were also welcomed. They were not fully multicultural, however, since the dynasty depended more on the elites of a single, core ethnic or religious group mobilizing patron–client networks among various other ethnic and religious elites and using discriminatory practices against some minorities. So as subordinate classes began to demand political representation, this became entwined with imperial versus proletarian ethnic conflicts.

Disprivileged elites initially claimed representative rights only for themselves, as in the Northwest earlier. But faced with pressures from below, they began to speak in the name of the "whole" people against the imperial ethnicity and its local clients (Mann, 1993: chap. 10). This fostered a leftist version of nationalism. The nation, it was argued, would rise up like a proletariat to overthrow its oppressors. The Italian fascist Corradini invented the label *proletarian nation* in 1911. It aptly describes the ideology of the many nationalisms threatened by a more powerful imperial enemy. Croats, Slovenes, and others might resent past Bosnian/Turkish and present Serb domination, Romanians might resent Hungarians, Slovaks might resent Czechs, and almost everyone might resent the formerly dominant Germans, Russians, and Turks. The three imperial peoples – Germans, Russians, and Turks (and after 1867 the Hungarians as well) – then responded with their own counternationalisms. Their very survival, they claimed, was threatened by these revolts. Later they became particularly worried – as Serbs were later in Yugoslavia – that their own coethnics who had settled abroad might now become exploited minorities in states dominated by other ethnic groups.

But first came the ideal of the organic nation-state. I instance Austria in the 1880s (Schmidt-Hartmann, 1988). In 1882 three young Austrian politicians propounded the Linz Program, which was intended to found a new party, the Deutsche Volkspartei, a German People's Party. The program combined German nationalism, universal suffrage, and progressive social legislation. It denounced equally liberalism, laissez-faire capitalism, and Marxian socialism. The three men declared that whereas liberals advocated a constitution enshrining the conflict of interests, they upheld the "substance" of democracy. Their legitimacy, they said, was grounded in the unity of the people, "the good of all," "the interests of the people." The projected party never materialized. The three split and went off to found their own parties. Adler became a leader of the Social Democrats, Lüger founded the Christian Socialists, and Schönerer founded what became the Pan-German Party. These were the three mass parties of interwar Austria, and two of them generated mass fascist movements.

These young Austrians were endorsing an organic conception of the people and state. The people, they said, was one and indivisible, united, integral. Thus its state need not be grounded upon the institutionalization of diversity or of conflict. One national movement could represent the whole people, ultimately transcending any conflict of interests between social groups within it. Class conflict and sectional interests were not to be compromised but transcended, and displaced onto international conflict. As the 20th century began, the notion emerged that the transcending agent might be the nation-state. These ideas of the trancendent nation and the state helped incubate prewar fascist theory. The fears of dominant and subordinate ethnicities fueled each other, creating a "security dilemma." Austro-German fueled Czech nationalism in the 1890s. In turn, both fueled Slovak nationalism. Tiso, who led the Slovak nationalists in the interwar period, was speaking for all three when he defined the nation as "a community of people who are of a single origin, single physical type, single character, single language, single set of customs and single culture of equal goals, and they constitute an organic whole in a coherent territory" (these Slovak quotes are from Nedelsky, 2001: 221–3). Nationalism, like class conflict, thrives on conflict with like-minded others.

Organic nationalism had two potential vices. First, it might lead from democracy to authoritarian statism. Single parties of the left or right need to maintain internal party democracy, but few can achieve this and they tend to fall to an elite or a dictator. Who is to express the people's supposedly singular essence? Given the real diversity of human communities, a state led by an elite or a dictator claims to speak with a singular voice. Tiso's deputy

Kirschbaum declared, "Because a voluntary inclination toward this single path cannot be expected due to the diversity of opinions and the artificial fostering of many paths, the requirement of authoritative direction logically follows." Second, organicism encouraged the notion that minority communities and political opponents might be excluded from full membership in the nation.

So these nationalists came to believe in (1) an enduring national character, soul, or spirit, distinguishable from that of other nations; (2) their right to a state that would ultimately express this; and (3) their right to exclude out-groups with different characters, who would only weaken the nation. They disliked multiethnic states, and they even sometimes looked askance at assimilation. Thus late-19th-century Eastern minorities were feeling pressures moving from voluntary to coerced assimilation and thence to pressured emigration. Between 1870 and 1910 over 5 million non-Jewish Eastern Europeans emigrated from areas where they constituted minorities – especially Slovaks, Croats, Germans, and Slovenes (Marrus, 1985; Pearson, 1983). But things were worst where new ethnic-racial labels overlaid old religious ones – as they did in Europe for Jews and Muslims. I focus here on Jews, dealing with Muslims in the next chapter.

Jews had been the target of religious and economic resentments for centuries. The "killers of Christ" had been forced into unpopular economic middleman roles by bans against owning land or having public employment. Popular resentment of dominant classes and political elites could also be displaced onto them. A pogrom against Jews allowed peasants to signal their discontent without rebellion. Pogroms involved violence, looting, and rape. If rumors spread about Jews abducting Christian babies or committing ritual murder, then murder might also ensue. But few intended to get rid of the Jews. They were too useful. Forced assimilation through conversion was periodically attempted (as with Moslems), but that was as far as cleansing usually went. Two new escalations were now added: (1) rising democratic sentiments led to Jews being deprived of full citizenship and labeled as aliens to the nation and (2) organic racial theories viewed Jews more as a racial than a religious out-group.

Things were worst where there were most Jews, in Russia. Russian pogroms were escalating to murderous cleansing. During 1881–3 Jews were scapegoated for the assassination of Tsar Alexander II, since a Jewess was one of the assassins. Politicians and the press fanned the flames, and the tsarist authorities seemed unwilling to intervene. Phleve, the minister of the interior, may have helped foment the pogrom, though he publicly claimed to desire only assimilation plus some cultural cleansing. Yet these were mainly outbursts from below. They were proportionately much bigger in industrializing cities; they spread across modern road and rail networks, and the chief perpetrators seem to have been workers in modern industries. In fact, pogroms often resembled contemporary Russian strikes, violent outbursts involving young, single male workers (recent migrants from the country-side) locked into a violent, alcohol-laden, masculine subculture. Over the next decades, modern labor unrest was persistently displaced onto the Jews (Friedgut, 1987; Klier, 1993; Wynn, 1992). But there were still far more beatings, rapes, and lootings than premeditated murders.

The next Russian eruption was more political and so more murderous. It came in 1903–6, fanned by the war with Japan and the 1905 revolution. Jews were believed to be behind other threatening enemies. Pogroms grew as discontent against conscription was displaced onto Jews; they became more deadly when Jews were attacked as supposed socialists by counterrevolutionary mobs egged on by conservative politicians. The tsarist government was alarmed by the scale of the violence (3,000 Jews died), yet recognized that pogroms could be used to whip up popular rightist support. The tsar's private letters reveal alarm at the overrepresentation of Jews among revolutionary leaders. From now on, anti-Semitism featured prominently in the political ideology of Russian rightists. This turned more young Jews leftward or to support of political Zionism, demanding a Jewish homeland in Palestine – an organicist ideal; 2.5 million Eastern European Jews migrated westward in the decades before 1914.

World War I further escalated organic nationalism in this great region. It destroyed most multinational states, weakened traditional conservatism's distrust of the masses, provided an economic model of how statist intervention and planning might achieve development, and through mass citizen armies provided a military and then a paramilitary model of popular collective action in the pursuit of national goals. As I have showed in *Fascists* (2004), many military veterans and political activists embraced paramilitarism. Apart from the Russian and Spanish civil wars, the right specialized more in this than the left. In Italy, Germany, Austria, Hungary, and Romania (even in Spain), civil strife left at least two dead leftists for every dead rightist. Leftist talk of revolution and armed struggle was mostly just that – talk. While Benito Mussolini's *squadristi* organized paramilitary assaults, Italian leftists demonstrated. Class analysis protected most leftists from militarism but doomed them to defeat.

Organic rightists increasingly connected their main political enemy, Bolshevism, with foreign enemies. German and Italian rightists attacked Slavs, though Jews remained the favorite target across Eastern Europe, where the notion of a Judeo-Bolshevik seemed minimally plausible. The Bolsheviks were not anti-Semitic. Lenin denounced this, 6 out of the 21 members of the Central Committee in 1921 were Jewish, and Jews became especially overrepresented in the command structure of the Cheka secret police. Anti-Semitic rightists had a field day identifying Jews with torturers and murderers. Jews were not overrepresented among the rank-and-file Bolsheviks, but exact proportions did not matter; this was the first time Jews had been allowed *any* prominent political role outside their own community.

Immediately after World War I ended, rightists across Russia, the Ukraine, Poland, the Baltic states, Romania, and Hungary led local populations in murders of Jews (Marrus, 1985: 62–4). Though many leftists were also anti-Semitic, their leaders usually recognized that this was in principle wrong, conflicting with socialist or anarchist internationalism. By now Russian industrial workers were also being organized by Marxists and so were less prone to perpetrating ethnic pogroms than in tsarist times.

The Ukraine during the Russian Civil War saw murderous cleansing of Jews in ways that prefigured the far worse slaughter during World War II. Somewhere between 50,000 and 150,000 Jews were killed, between 3 and 10 percent of all Ukrainian Jews. Less than 10 percent of them were killed by the Red Army or the Ukrainian anarchist militia. Perhaps a quarter were killed by Ukrainian nationalists and over half by the White Army. The war also saw much exemplary repression. Villages and towns were treated mercilessly if they were believed to have collaborated with the enemy. Because Jewish communities sometimes collaborated with Red Army units, since they seemed the least bad of the forces ravaging the countryside, they were punished. They were vulnerable to punishment since they were a minority in local populations generally less favorable to the Reds.

Rightist ideology often embraced cleansing. Ukrainian nationalist warlords (Hetmans) rallied their peasant partisans with cries of "Death to the Jews and down with the Communists!", "Death to the Jews! For the Orthodox faith!", and against "our age-old enemies, and their agents, the Jews." Their hostility mixed hatred of outside oppression – a Russian (now a Bolshevik) state aided by cosmopolitan Jews – with Orthodox religious Judeophobia aimed against "the killers of Christ." White leaders mouthed more political anti-Semitism, blaming Russia's misfortunes on the "diseased microbes" of the "Judeo-Bolshevik conspiracy" – anticipating SS language. Even the more liberal Whites, the Kadets, did not condemn the pogroms, since they brought their cause popular support. Shulgin, a politician close to Denikin, the White commander, was shaken by the ferocity, noting that "a dreadful medieval spirit stalked the streets of Kiev." But he nonetheless believed the Jews should "confess and repent . . . before the whole world . . . [for their] active part in the Bolshevik madness." Shulgin hoped that this "torture by fear would . . . show them the right way." After their defeat, fleeing rightists brought west the infamous *Protocols of the Elders of Zion*, a forged manual for a supposed Jewish conquest of the world. The emigres helped incubate ethnic/religious hatreds amid European *völkisch* nationalists. The young Heinrich Himmler read the *Protocols*. He confided to his diary that the book "explains everything and tells us whom we must fight next time" (Altshuler, 1990: 284; Kenez, 1992; Levene, 1993; Mayer, 2000: 377–89, 513–26).

But cleansing by more moderate means also had more respectable supporters. Cleansing by resettlement – partly voluntary but mostly coerced deportations – was officially ratified by the 1918 peace treaties implementing

Woodrow Wilson's doctrine of *national self-determination*. In his speeches President Wilson had consistently confused liberal and organic conceptions of democracy. The Entente Powers, he said, were fighting for "representative democracy" and for "national self-determination" – the combination meaning in practice democracy for each majority nationality. At the time the United States was at its multiethnic high point, having received in the previous decade its greatest ever flow of immigrants. But U.S. immigrants did not challenge the state, and Americans tended (and still tend today) to conceive of minority rights in individual, not collective, terms. Individual rights are protected by the Constitution. American politicians like Wilson – just like British and French politicians of the time – believed that it was sufficient to create unitary nation-states with constitutionally enshrined individual rights.

The Versailles delegates replaced the Austro-Hungarian and European parts of the Russian and Ottoman multinational empires with a dozen new states. Apart from Czechoslovakia and Yugoslavia, each was effectively assigned to a dominant ethnicity comprising at least 65 percent of its population. Anyone dissatisfied had the right to change his or her state within one year. It was expected that minorities might move to a state where they would be part of the ethnic majority. After a year, those staying put had to hope that their state would respect the treaty clauses guaranteeing minority rights. Most did not, and the Entente Powers had no interest in, and the League of Nations no power to, enforce them. The League's secretary, the Habsburg historian Charles Macartney, penetrated to the core of the problem. He noted that for a minority, four things were possible: the revision of frontiers to minimize minorities; emigration and population exchange; "physical slaughter"; or changes in constitutions away from the nation-state form (Hayden, 1996: 735). Macartney preferred the last option, but the nation-state ideal was too strong for him.

The immediate result was discrimination against minorities plus coerced emigration. The war had seen large refugee flows, but the peace settlement increased the flow. By 1926 there were nearly 10 million European refugees, including 1.5 million exchanged between Greece and Turkey, 280,000 exchanged between Greece and Bulgaria, 2 million Poles, over 2 million Russians and Ukrainians, nearly 1 million Germans, nearly 250,000 Hungarians, and 200,000 Estonians, Latvians, and Lithuanians. These numbers are mind-boggling. Over 60 million Europeans had been ruled by a foreign power before 1914 compared to only 25 million afterward. In Eastern Europe subordinate nationalities had been reduced from a half to a quarter of the population. Citizenship was now substantially identified with ethnicity, with minorities in danger of becoming second-class citizens. It was believed that this was better than keeping the ethnicities mixed. Ethnic conflict in the Ottoman Empire had recently brought genocide committed against the Armenians and wild deportations of Greeks. The multiethnic Ottoman Empire had become a Turkish Republic, without Armenians or Greeks, even without most of its Arabs. Population exchanges followed by some discrimination was considered a reasonable solution, encouraged by the Great Powers, both European and American.

So organic nation-statism surged through half of interwar Europe – in Germany, Austria, Italy, Spain, Poland, Lithuania, Latvia, Estonia, Romania, Hungary, Bulgaria, Greece, Czechoslovakia, and Yugoslavia. Organic movements demanding national liberation from foreign rule also grew among Slovakians, Ukrainians, and Croatians. Brubaker (1996: chap. 3) argues that interwar ethnic relations arraigned three main types of actors: *national minorities* (i.e., forming a minority in their present state), *nationalizing states* (where the majority nationality wishes the state to reflect only its identity – i.e., organic nationalism), and foreign *homeland states* (i.e., of national minorities). Jews and gypsies would constitute a fourth *pariah nation* type: minorities without a homeland state. But the most dangerous feature of the early interwar period was that respectable conservatives were moving toward organic nationalism. Instead of justifying their mildly statist rule in the name of an essentially passive people (as in the past), conservatives began to compete with the left by mobilizing the people behind nationalism (Mann, 1995). Conservatives and organic nationalists joined forces in authoritarian movements that seized power in all the states and movements just mentioned, except for the Czech and Bulgarian lands. This was to exacerbate conflict between minorities, nationalizing states, homeland states – and the pariah Jews and gypsies.

Organicists were also denouncing leftists as quasi-ethnic enemies of the nation. Liberals were denounced as foreign internationalists, and socialists as internationalists or *Bolsheviks*, a term conveying both Russian and Asiatic connotations. Religious and ethnic minorities served foreign states. By the 1930s attempts to merely assimilate minorities were fading. Germans and Czechs, Poles and Ukrainians, Croats and Serbs, and other groups claimed to possess different essences, partly biological, partly cultural, but not very malleable. To protect the organic unity of their nation, they discriminated against minorities in education and the civil service and curtailed minorities' freedom of association, hoping to induce their emigration. Yet geopolitics played a moderating role. Almost every national minority was a majority in another state, usually a neighbor. Diplomacy between neighboring states to avoid retaliation could mitigate cleansing nationalism. Only the Jews and the Gypsies had no homeland and no protectors against the organic nation-state. But all minorities might be harmed if the geopolitical balance of Central and Eastern Europe were upset.

CONCLUSION

Modernity generated two different conceptions of democracy. Northwestern European regimes accepted interest group and class conflict within the citizen body. They sought to institutionalize rather than repress it and so developed liberal, not organic, forms of democracy. Class trumped ethnicity, as it had in most of previous history. But in Central and Eastern Europe, democratization struggles increasingly pitted a local ethnicity against a foreign imperial ruler. Here ethnicity began to rival class, though not yet trumping it, since conservative, liberal, and socialist parties dominated until World War I. But in multiethnic circumstances, a majority ethnicity can rule through majoritarian democracy, as elections become ethnic censuses. Bell-Fialkoff (1996: 48) correctly concludes, "The real culprits are the ideals of freedom, self-determination, and representative democracy." Democratization had its dark side. This might potentially be very dark, for unlike classes, ethnic communities are not so interdependent. They can live in their own cleansed communities with their own organic state.

These trends began to encourage ideas of founding the state upon ethnic homogeneity. They encouraged Europeans to consider solving ethnic disputes and a supposed "Jewish question" by population transfers. They produced embittered refugees embracing enhanced nation-statism. And they sat amid broader scientific racism. World War I then saw the defeat of all the major multinational empires; its citizen warfare also boosted paramilitarism. Yet political opposition was generally only banned and imprisoned, while ethnic and religious minorities only suffered discrimination and some coerced emigration. Anti-Semitism remained largely casual, its worst excesses the short-lived pogroms. Organicist movements remained small, and a postwar flurry of paramilitary killings subsided. We can trace Nazi genocide backward to these antecedents, for the Nazis were the most extreme proponents of a tradition of modern science, modern politics, and modern society. Yet no one could have anticipated how these cleansing tendencies would end. Only with hindsight, smoothing over the "twisted path to Auschwitz," can we know that they culminated in the most singlemindedly genocidal regime the world has ever seen.

4

Genocidal Democracies in the New World

"If ever we are constrained to lift the hatchet against any tribe, we shall never lay it down till that tribe is exterminated, or driven beyond the Mississippi. . . . In war, they will kill some of us; we shall destroy all of them." This is the first chapter in which we will meet perpetrators of murderous ethnic cleansing like this man. But he was no colonial desperado. He was Thomas Jefferson, third president of the United States.

The previous two chapters suggested that murderous ethnic cleansing had been uncommon until quite recently. I traced the emergence of dangerous organic conceptions of democracy in 19th-century Eastern and Southern Europe, contrasting them with the more tolerant liberal democracy dominating Northwest Europe. Yet most liberal countries also had colonies. There both organic and liberal conceptions of we, the people coexisted. On the one hand, the settlers recognized themselves as divided into diverse interests and classes, and their political parties represented this diversity amid liberal institutions. On the other hand, this entire people had the singular quality of being "civilized" and did not include "natives," "savages," "orientals," and so on. The difference was later recast as racial. The "lower races" were not a part of we, the people.

Thus some of the states I earlier called liberal were in reality dual, with an extremely dark side many miles away in their colonies. Class compromise, representative rule, and tolerance among Europeans developed above terrible atrocities against very large out-groups. The worst cases, in the United States and Australia, amounted to the most successful cleansing the world may have ever seen. They were committed by settler democracies, at first de facto, then de jure. Such is the doleful story of this chapter.

A GENERAL MODEL OF COLONIAL CLEANSING

Virtually all European colonies were conquered violently, but only some went on to murderous cleansing afterward. I study variations among Spanish Mexico, Australia, the United States, the Russian Caucasus, and German South West Africa. I argue that the more they embodied settler democracy, either de facto or de jure, the more the murderous cleansing. However (unfortunately for such a simple causal analysis), they also differed by other factors that influenced the degree of cleansing – like type of economy or type of rule over natives. So I will pay more attention to variation between authoritarian and democratic periods within each colony than I will to differences between colonies.

Economic Power

Unlike other cases discussed in this book, underlying the ethnic conflict was a direct economic conflict over who should possess and use the land, the natives or the colonists (Smith, 1997: 229, calls it *utilitarian genocide*). But there were five main types of colonial economy bringing ascending levels of violence by settlers against natives.

1. *Trade.* Where Europeans merely traded with natives without settling their land, they were few in number, unable to impose much force. Where trade did lead to conquest, small numbers still usually ensured that they ruled indirectly, through native elites retaining many powers. This was often so in Asia, which was near the rim of the European logistical reach. Trading settlements did not often involve much ethnic cleansing after the initial entry. At the worst, this might degenerate into partial politicide, to eliminate part of the native leadership class. But other local elites were still needed as trading partners and client rulers. I will not discuss trading colonies further.

2. *Plunder and tribute-taking.* This was important in the early stages of colonization. Spanish incursions into America initially involved massive looting of gold and silver. This could result in slaughter in seizing the loot, but not in subsequent ethnic cleansing. For tribute, the conqueror needs live subjects. I will discuss Spanish plunder and tribute-taking in Mexico. These first two types roughly correspond to the first of the four colonial regimes distinguished by Fieldhouse (1965) and Fredrickson (1988) – the *occupation colony*, where the colonial regime seeks military and political control and economic tribute, but does not seek to control land or labor.

3. *Settlement using a dispersed labor force.* Much settler farming was small-scale, using native labor scattered thinly over the colony. Though the initial land seizure might involve violence, severe repression was thereafter impractical and cleansing was not desired – whether free, indentured, or even slave labor was used. This type of economy roughly corresponds to Fieldhouse's and Fredrickson's *mixed* type of colony, which they also see as typically associated with Spanish colonization. It will not figure much in this chapter.

4. *Settlement using a concentrated labor force.* Mining and plantations typically involved large, concentrated labor forces – closely and often brutally supervised. Fieldhouse and Fredrickson saw these *plantation* colonies as pioneered by the Portuguese. Given a labor surplus, the natives might be callously worked to death. If labor was scarce, the colonists might show

more restraint. Despite its brutality, this type of settlement did not usually lead to deliberate murderous cleansing, though it sometimes brought ethnocide, unintended deaths resulting from callous labor practices, requiring further importation of slave labor from elsewhere. I touch upon this type but do not focus upon it.

5. *Settlement not requiring native labor.* The settlers used the land, but with their own or some other labor, not the natives'. This is Fieldhouse's and Fredrickson's *pure settlement* colony, pioneered, they believe, by the English. Max Weber observed that throughout history "conquering peasant communities" have sought to "wipe out" native populations (1958: 165). The Europeans wanted fertile land, which was usually already inhabited. If natives were thinly spread out hunter-gatherers, they needed large spaces for their subsistence. Despite the natural abundance of regions like North America, large settler populations put pressure on the habitat, causing great hardship among natives. Since most colonial economies were much more productive than the natives' one, they generated large economic surpluses capable of provisioning further conquest and cleansings. Such colonies are the main focus of this chapter. They perpetrated mass murder.

Even here, however, two lesser forms of cleansing were still possible. A division of the land might occur, so that the two communities could live segregated from each other. The Europeans would likely take most good land, but survival might remain possible for both. This was what settlers termed *protection* or *reservations*. Alternatively, natives could assimilate, some as small property owners, most as laborers. If native, society was stratified, lateral aristocratic assimilation might result, assimilating elites but not the masses. These were the main economic variations.

Political Power

Political power also brought variations in the treatment of natives. Small settler and trading groups sometimes made no formal political claims on the land. But their desire for monopolies encouraged political claims, and most settlers arrived in the name of states. On landing, Europeans would plant a flag, round up some natives, and make a long speech to them in an utterly unintelligible language, claiming the land and its people for the Crown (or the republic). This political claim to a monopoly over the land and people was nonnegotiable, likely to bring determined resistance. But often Europeans could not enforce the claim. Three types of political enforcement brought ascending levels of violence.

1. *Extraterritoriality.* Europeans could not conquer the most powerful rival states of the world, like the Chinese or Japanese or Ottoman Empires. But they could achieve extraterritorial powers, whereby their merchants would not be subject to local law and would enjoy privileges or monopolies.

Sometimes this brought much violence, as in the Chinese Opium Wars. But it did not bring cleansing, since the locals were regarded as useful trading partners and consumers. I touch upon extraterritoriality when dealing with the Ottoman Empire in Chapter 5.

2. *Indirect rule*. Europeans might conquer – usually with the help of native allies – but not be strong enough to rule on their own. They had to be content with indirect rule or *protectorates*, permitting native rulers to continue while paying obeisance and tribute to the colonial authority. Indirect rule involved compromise and only limited violence and cleansing. Yet further settler waves generally put pressure on the colonial administration to go for more direct rule.

3. *Direct rule*. Where they dominated, the Europeans insisted on direct rule, involving the complete submission of native rulers and masses to their powers and laws. This invariably happened where large numbers of settlers arrived and stayed, claiming their state – "rule by the people" – but not including natives. There now resulted a clash of rival sovereignties over the same territory (my theses 3 and 4).

Whatever the enforcement powers, however, colonial governments almost never wanted to kill the natives beyond what was necessary for conquest. They wanted live natives to tax and conscript. So where settlers wanted to eliminate the native population, governments had a dilemma. They tended to be wavering actors, caught in the middle between more extreme settlers and more moderate churches (see later). But on the ground, the settlers, not themselves, often controlled the territory, especially in newly settled frontier areas. This was often a de facto settler democracy long before it also became de jure. Either might be bad news for the natives.

Europeans could generally wield superior political resources than native polities could. Aztecs and Incas could mobilize, but only through loose and fragile federations of peoples and city-states. Europeans could divide and rule, offering allied elites indirect rule and lateral aristocratic assimilation, culturally assimilating elites but not masses into a civilized identity. Yet in North America natives were usually fragmented into many tribes, clans, or nations, each rather fissiparous. Chiefs had great autonomy but little power, and few could make deals involving lateral aristocratic assimilation since they could not provide stable indirect rule. In the 19th century, U.S. government agencies further exploited this political weakness. They claimed to have made treaties with an Indian nation on the basis of a deal made with a small, unrepresentative group of desperate, starving chiefs prepared to sign away extensive tribal lands in exchange for paltry rewards. Conversely, native survival was helped where Europeans fought against each other, as they did in most early stages of colonization. But when one colonial power was ceded full sovereignty over a territory by its European rivals, this was bad news for the natives, since their powers of maneuver were gone.

Military Power

The clash was solved by war. The Europeans came armed, seeking conquest. The balance of military power varied according to numbers and technical and organizational capacities. Where Europeans were few, they could not easily conquer, but they increasingly made up for numerical weakness by more powerful military organization and technology. Some wars were costly, since natives might long remain dangerous, but the outcome of battles if colonial resources could be focused on them was not generally in doubt, especially in 19th-century colonies after the development of quick-firing guns. If the Europeans wished to cleanse murderously, they could increasingly do so with little risk to themselves – perhaps more easily than any other group of conquerors in history (my thesis 4b). But military power also involves tactical matters. As noted in Chapter 1, certain types of warfare are more likely to tactically lure soldiers into more campaigns aimed against civilians.

Ideological Power

We saw that barbarians invading the Roman Empire had actually been its neighbors. But the Europeans now arrived from afar by means of a navigational revolution, and at first they seemed like aliens. Aztecs debated whether the first *conquistadores* were gods and fatally delayed their initial response; Hawaiians supposedly debated whether Captain Cook might be the god Lono – though if they really did think this, it proved fatal for him, not them. These were examples of native ideological explanations of the great difference and the superiority of European economic, military, political, and biological power – the main thrust of *ideological power*. Little social construction of ethnicity was needed. No European doubted who was native and who was European, though natives had to modify their sense of identity. They had not previously regarded themselves collectively as natives – they were of diverse clans, lineages, nations, and states. They were now forced to construct themselves as collectively distinct from white Europeans. Nonetheless, colonial ethnic conflicts had a degree of facticity to which the constructivist theories discussed in Chapter 1 are less appropriate.

Superiority was not entirely objective, since colonists behaved savagely and treacherously. As Trigger (1994) says, their behavior ensured that they were not regarded as gods for long. But in terms of economic, military, and political resources, colonists were superior. The colonists explained this in terms of models drawn from their own history: "higher" civilizations overcoming "lower" ones and "civilization" overcoming "barbarity" or "savagery." This was the very meaning of history and progress. It was inevitable, what God intended. Being civilized also involved notions of personal hygiene, clothing, and manner that could make repugnant interpersonal contact with "dirty," unclothed, and "unrestrained" natives. Natives were often dying of disease in front of them, seemingly physically unfit to live amid a higher civilization.

Civilizational models of history and progress meant that it was easy for settlers to develop ideologies of superiority to justify whatever treatment they meted out to the natives, insulating themselves from moral risk (as thesis 4b suggested). We should not wonder at their contempt for natives. It seemed self-evident.

Of course, Europeans, like natives, were careful observers and noted differences. If they found complex cities, monuments, irrigation agriculture, or even peoples of proud bearing, they modified their judgment. Pragmatic needs also influenced their ideology. If they needed to rule indirectly through native elites, or if they needed natives as stable sexual partners, they moderated their views.

Christianity complicated their models. It reinforced the savage–civilized dichotomy, since Christians alone had truth. The Christian church also said that Christians had the right to dispossess non-Christians of their land by *right of discovery*. Yet even savages were believed to have souls. Natives were literally in a "state of nature," *naturales*, but they should be led to the true faith – and thence to civilization. Conversion involves assimilation, cleansing culture, not lives. Christianity strengthened dispossession but weakened murderous cleansing. Later, the Enlightenment, liberalism, and socialism brought secular moderating ideologies. So the stronger the power of religious/humanitarian groups, the less the murderous cleansing. This gives us a third colonial actor, professional ideologists – churches, religious orders, missionaries, humanitarian movements. After initial conquest and land seizure, they were usually more restrained in their treatment of natives, though they were not immune to ethnic stereotypes or to their own material interests in dispossessing the natives.

Biology/Ecology

One further form of power lies outside my four-part model. The Europeans had *biological power* superiority in the temperate zones of settlement, where they unwittingly carried lethal disease microbes. Natives in first contact with Europeans (and especially with their animals) succumbed to everyday European diseases, for which they had built up no immunity. Diseases were easily the biggest killers of most native populations, though they worked in conjunction with food shortages and fertility declines that were more deliberately induced by the Europeans (Thornton, 1997). Disease epidemics accompanied European penetration, making conquest much easier. New England colonists found expansion easy amid sick and dying natives unable to work or fight, pleading, arms outstretched for help. This was the main component of ethnocide in the temperate zones – reinforcing Europeans' sense of their power superiority.

Ecology mattered. Cleansing was much greater in the temperate zones of the new continents, which were hospitable to European settlement. This primarily meant the Americas, Australasia, and small zones across Africa.

This is where Europeans imposed what Crosby (1986) calls *ecological imperialism*, domination by European humans, weeds, animals, and disease microbes. The result was cataclysmic, the greatest eliminations of populations ever recorded.

In Australia the aboriginal population before the arrival of the First Fleet in 1788 was probably just above 300,000. By 1901 only about 93,000 remained. The low point was reached in 1921, when about 72,000 survived. Over little more than a century the attrition had been almost 80 percent. Then the aboriginal population stabilized. After 1961 it even began to grow (Smith, 1980: 12, 69–70).

In the Americas, regions with large settler populations lost about 90 percent of their natives. Across the whole continent the total pre-Columbian population may have been 60–100 million. Over half died (Stannard, 1992: 74–5, 81–7, 118, 146, 266–8). In the area now occupied by the United States, estimates of the pre-Columbian Indian population are generally 4–9 million. In the U.S. Census of 1900 there were only 237,000 Indians, a loss of at least 95 percent. Extermination happened last, and so is most visible to us, in California. The Spanish missionaries estimated that there were 310,000 natives on their arrival in 1769. By 1849, when the gold rush began, the population had been halved. Thereafter it fell even faster as settlement expanded. By 1860, after 10 years of statehood, Californian Indians numbered only 31,000 – an 80 percent loss rate over only 12 years! The Third Reich also lasted 12 years and killed 70 percent of European Jews. Finally, things began to ease. By 1880 there were still over 20,000 Californian Indians. In the 20th century their number grew slightly (Almaguer, 1994: 107,000–130,000, but all figures are crude estimates; Thornton, 1997). How did this cataclysm happen, how intentional was it, and who perpetrated it? I explore variations between those wielding political power (colonial and postcolonial political elites), ideological power (mainly churches), and economic power (settlers). Military power might be wielded by either states or settlers. Biological power was wielded, usually unintentionally, by all of them.

MEXICO

The Spanish first entered Caribbean islands where they did not face organized states, usually through privateering ventures. They killed native elites and coerced and overworked natives on their estates and mines. They forced native women into sexual relations so that fewer Indians reproduced Indians. Their pigs and sheep destroyed the vegetation that nourished the natives. But above all, European animals carried diseases that ravaged native populations, including those who never even saw the *conquistadores*. In terrible ethnocides the native populations were wiped out – unintentionally, though with great callousness.

On the mainland, the Spanish confronted an advanced civilization. Cortes noted that these Indians were "of much greater intelligence than those of the other islands. Indeed, they appeared to us to possess such understanding as is sufficient for an ordinary citizen to conduct himself in a civilised country." Though daunted by the size of the armies that the Aztecs could bring into the field, he recognized their divisions, quoting St. Mark: "Every kingdom divided against itself will be brought to destruction" (Thomas, 1993: 576, 245). Cortes recruited as allies city-states that were restive under Aztec rule. His initial Plan A was to impose sovereignty, while allowing allies some political autonomy, and to plunder gold and silver, settle the land, and convert souls. His chronicler, Bernal Diaz del Castillo, cheerfully admitted, "To bring light to those in darkness, and also to get rich, which is what all of us men commonly seek" (quoted by Farris, 1984: 29).

During the conquest the worst Spanish atrocities amounted to exemplary repression. About 20 Mexican towns suspected of betrayal had their men killed, their women and children enslaved, their buildings burned. Dogs were occasionally used to tear victims apart. More commonly, the Spaniards would turn aside while their native allies tore apart their former rulers and ate them. Such were the accusations made by Bartolome de las Casas, bishop of San Cristobal, Chiapas, and the *conquistadores* only denied the details. One defended the destruction of Tepeaca (in retaliation for the murder of 12 Spanish captains): "It was convenient to impose the said punishment for the pacification of the land ... and in order to put fear into the *naturales* so that they did no hurt to the Spaniards." But the Spaniards often lost self-control when they believed someone was concealing gold. Rich Aztecs were tortured to reveal hiding places; a few were ripped apart in search of swallowed jewels. These were emotional outbursts marring what was generally an instrumentally rational campaign. After the fall of the Aztec capital, Tenochtitlan, many of its captains were executed. Yet the other inhabitants were allowed to leave the destroyed city in peace (Thomas, 1995: 243–5, 262, 434–9, 459, 527, 544).

There was a tactical lure away from murderous cleansing toward making distinctions between friendly, neutral, and hostile natives. Allies were desperately needed. This campaign requirement was decisive in luring the *conquistadores* away from undifferentiated murder. In their exemplary repression, the *conquistadores* were traditional imperial conquerors, so their Plan A did not aim at ethnic cleansing. Settlement involved lording it over natives who would do all the work, if necessary by coercion. But they had learned from the Caribbean experience, and in Mexico they developed the *encomienda* system. The Crown granted to Spanish settlers the land and the people on it as virtual serfs. They were not allowed to drive the natives away and they had to protect them, though labor conditions could be very harsh.

Since the settlers were overwhelmingly male, they needed women. Spanish tolerance of ethnic diversity ensured that many native partners became wives, begetting children in stable mixed marriages. Relative numbers – far more natives than Europeans – meant that native marriages and procreation continued alongside mixed marriages. There was no major fertility decline among the natives. The conquest had also been clothed in religious legitimacy by "their Most Catholic Majesties" and always involved clerics saving souls, thus assimilating natives. Priests and religious orders were powerful at the kings' and the viceroys' courts. The Spanish gentry were fighting for command posts in New Spain, and accusations of maltreatment of natives could get rivals barred from office (the charge was raised against Cortes himself). Clerics administered the same rites to mixed and native marriages and helped moderate the regime.

Spanish commanders used natives as client rulers, who complied since they wished to keep their power and wealth. They had to convert, but this was often outward show. In private they practiced whatever rites they chose, and the Spanish learned to avoid idol smashing. Native elites joined in military expeditions, received *encomienda* and Spanish titles, and their daughters were married to Spanish officers. Natives became priests and church musicians; and they used the law courts, often suing Spaniards. Their descendants became in habits and speech indistinguishable from the *conquistadores* (Thomas, 1995: 559–60, 577, 589–90). Regional variations were mainly determined by relative numbers. Spaniards were 50 percent of the population of Mexico City by 1800, and so ruled there directly. But they remained under 4 percent in the central plateau and the Yucatan, and so had to resort to indirect rule through Mayan lords able to retain their local powers. Mayans said they would assimilate the Spaniards, not vice versa (Farris, 1984: chaps. 1, 2). In the Yucatan, they did.

So the Spanish Plan B of long-term settlement involved lateral aristocratic assimilation – assimilation of elites. The southern and central Yucatan was not conquered until the mid-19th century (nor were other *republicas indias* scattered across South America). There were backlash periods of rebellion, repression, and enforcement of a racial sense of caste purity. But the long run saw a *mestizo* (mixed-race) class/caste ruling over the *indios*. Mexico, Guatemala, and Peru saw phases of ethnic cleansing in which peripheral *indios* were brutally displaced, even exterminated by white or *mestizo* elites (Centeno, 2001). But overall a much higher proportion of the native population has survived than in North America. Ethnicity and class entwined, as they still do across Mexico and much of Latin America.

Ferocious initial conquest, pillage, and labor exploitation put the Spaniards among the deadlier of historical conquerors. In the Aztec Valley of Mexico, disease contributed most of the 90 percent population loss in the first century of Spanish rule, an ethnocide. Yet the Spanish remained fewer than the natives, had to rule through native elites, and wanted native laborers. The Spanish government and the Catholic Church added more moderate pressures. Spanish rule moderated. Australia and the United States followed a different trajectory.

AUSTRALIA

Australian colonization began in 1788 and was consolidated through the 19th century. By then, British military and political power was far superior to that of the natives. Aborigines could mobilize only small bands with primitive weapons. There was a rather peculiar Plan A: the establishment of a convict settlement requiring local farming. It was assumed that the natives would trade with the settlers, help them work the land, and be gradually taught civilization. There might have to be a show of force, but no one initially conceived of extermination. This was state-dominated, since British armed force was also needed within the penal colony. The only clerics were subservient to the military authorities. Then the practice of releasing convicts into the colony after they had served their prison term, plus incoming waves of free settlers, meant that the colony needed less native labor. Since the terrain favored the grazing of animals more than arable farming, settlement spread out over very large areas. The aborigines were hunter-gatherers, requiring even more extensive lands for their subsistence. So there was a fundamental conflict over the land, focused on its rivers, water holes, game, and edible grasses. Aborigines did not have the military or political organization to fight wars, but they did raid in search of food, spearing cattle and sheep, stealing sacks of flour, and occasionally killing whites.

To Europeans the hunter-gatherers seemed extraordinarily primitive. They were almost naked and dirty, and they lacked states, one god, and literacy. Many settlers viewed them as intelligent animals; others saw them as children in the bodies of adults; still others were radicalized, seeing them as vermin, the source of pollution and disease. After the distortion of Darwin's theories into social Darwinism after the mid-19th century, most Europeans believed these were two species (Haebich, 1988: 54, 80; Markus, 1994: chap. 1). Since they appeared to have no class differences, none could be regarded as more civilized than the others – there could be no lateral aristocratic assimilation. Though big class differences existed among whites, all whites ranked above all natives. Ethnicity trumped class. The weakness of churches provided little humanitarian opposition to this ideology. Since aborigines bestowed no value on the land through labor, they also had no right to it. Since they were unused to agriculture, most settlers declared that they could not use their labor. Not until the late 19th century did labor shortages force settlers to really try. Before then, aborigines were considered idle and shiftless, without a sense of clock time or a fixed place, unable to accept labor discipline. So aborigines could be not used, only driven off. The settlers responded with Plan B, driving them away by force from the area of settlement, initially termed *dispersal*, that is, policed deportation.

It did not initially seem too callous, for this vast continent seemed big enough for both races. Yet the Industrial Revolution in the mother country fueled expansion of sheep ranches (for wool), followed by cattle ranches (industrialized war meant that cattle reared on even poor-quality grass could produce tallow fat for the greasing of guns). The sheep and cattle ate the edible grasses, drained the water supply, and destroyed the game. Aborigines were driven into the more barren interior to face starvation. They regarded the land as theirs; they felt entitled to its produce. They continued to steal cattle, sheep, and whatever else they could find. Sometimes they just destroyed them, hoping to force the whites into going away. Occasionally they murdered them. Such resistance brought massive retaliation by whites calling for "the extermination of the black fiends." At least 20,000 aborigines, perhaps many more, were killed by the settlers in sporadic frontier skirmishes lasting into the 1920s, some taking the form of killing sprees. The dead whites probably numbered fewer than 200. This became the Plan C of some frontier settlers as deportations became wild and degenerated into local genocide. They felt they had been "driven" to this by aboriginal resistance and encroachment. It was "self-defense" and in frontier areas settlers could act first, without seeking political legitimation from above and with little risk to themselves.

There was also some ethnocide, though disease was not the immediate killer it had been in Spanish America. Aborigines tended to suffer more from prolonged contact. The deadliest diseases were social ones. In frontier areas, white males dominated and settlers forced sex from aboriginal women. There were a few marriages and more stable common-law unions, but even more abductions, rapes, and hunger-induced prostitution. Soon there were far more settlers than natives. All this combined to retard aboriginal reproduction. Young aboriginal women were kept away from their men, ensuring fewer full-blood and more mixed-race infants. Venereal diseases swept through aboriginal camps on the fringes of white settlements, producing physical degeneration and early death in a malnourished population incapable of dealing with alcohol. By 1850 most whites believed the race was dying out.

Settlers' actions were contrary to colonial administrators' intentions. All governors declared benign intentions toward natives, urging settlers to "conciliate their affections" and finance protectorates (reservations) for natives. They offered natives the full protection of the English law. The British allowed only limited settler self-rule until midcentury and persistently tried to restrain cleansing even thereafter. When Britain granted western Australia self-government in 1889, it tried to retain control of native affairs. Yet far across the globe the Westminster Parliament took little interest and provided it with inadequate resources. The settlers had de facto local control, especially in outback regions. A rancher/gold miner who was chief protector of aborigines in western Australia state suggested that "if the government shut their eyes for six months and let the settlers deal with the natives in their own way it would stop the depredations" (Haebich, 1988: 97). The administration lacked funds and local support for benevolent paternalism. In practice it had to abandon it (Markus, 1994: 23–9; Rowley, 1970: Part I).

There was an enormous military difference between local settlers and natives: between guns and spears, between young white men riding horses and running aboriginal families of all ages. The standard settler retaliation for thefts of stock was to surround an aborigine camp at night, attack at dawn, and massacre men, women, and children alike. This was arbitrary justice. After one theft incident, an aboriginal camp was stormed "and men, women and children were shot indiscriminately. Some took to the river and were shot as they swam. Their dead bodies subsequently floated down past the Settlement." The theft was later traced to a white employee (Rowley, 1970: 112–13). When hungry aborigines stole flour, the settlers would leave poisoned sacks of flour for them to find. Settlers rarely had to call in soldiers to help them remove aborigines. A Queensland aborigine gave the native view:

We were hunted from our ground, shot, poisoned and had our daughters, sisters, and wives taken from us...what a number were poisoned at Kilcoy....They stole our ground where we used to get food, and when we got hungry and took a bit of flour or killed a bullock to eat, they shot us or poisoned us. All they give us now for our land is a blanket once a year. (Quoted by Rowley, 1970: 158)

For routine force after the introduction of *responsible statehood*, settlers relied on their own local paramilitaries, Native police forces officered by local whites and manned by detribalized aborigines. This enabled offloading of moral blame onto aborigines, confirming some stereotypes of savagery. Their job was to disperse the natives with gunfire. One officer was asked during an inquiry: "'Do you not think there is any other way of dealing with them, except by shooting them?' Came the response: 'No, I don't think they can understand anything else except by shooting them'" (Rowley, 1970: 158–63). These killing sprees were described euphemistically as "dispersal" or even "having a picnic with the Natives," unlike North American colonists who were usually blunt in admitting "exterminations." The courts were of no practical use to natives. Until the 1840s, they deemed aborigines incapable of understanding the law. Then the colonial administration allowed aboriginal evidence, but settler juries discounted it anyway. Whites were almost never brought to justice for their atrocities (Markus, 1994: 46–8).

There developed what Rowley has termed a *triangle of tension* between settlers, missionaries, and the British government – the settlers being the most hard-line, churchmen favoring conversion and conciliation, and the government favoring compromise. Disputes among settlers were generally decided by "experts" who "knew the aborigine" and concluded that "he needed a firm hand." Social Darwinism helped. There was a world historical inevitability to aborigines' decline: they had no future, so get rid of them now. B. D. Moorehead, later prime minister, declared

What was being done in Queensland was being done in every country.... The colonist had come here as white men and were going to put the black man out.... The lower race must give way before the superior race.... [It was a mistake] ... to try and initiate a course of action by which these poor creatures would be enabled to linger out an existence which was bound to cease on the advance of the Anglo-Saxon.... The blackfellows had to go, and go they must ... the aboriginal race was [not] worth preserving. If there were no aboriginals it would be a very good thing. (Markus, 1994: 36–7)

Hunter-gatherers in the interior and the far north provided most of the full-blooded survivors into the 20th century, though more mixed-blood aborigines lived on the margins of white settlements, somehow eking out livings, despised, coping with poor health, diseases, and alcoholism. Where more intensive agriculture or industry developed after about 1870, surviving aboriginal communities found some opportunities for steady work. After 1900 the "white Australia" immigration policy, devised to "keep the race pure," dried up Asian labor, and some employers ignored union and Labour Party objections and turned to aborigines. By the early 20th century, policy had moderated to protection, that is, segregation – a kind of Plan D. Laws prevented aborigines from entering towns and cities without an official permit. Some states had powers over marriages, preventing aborigines from marrying each other or half-breeds from marrying whites. But some population revival brought recognition that aborigines were not going to die out. Since mass killing was now out of the question, this problem was here to stay.

So coercive assimilation (Plan E) dominated from the 1940s until the 1970s, a product of global decolonization and deracialization. Assimilation was seen as possible, though mixed bloods were viewed as easier cases and aborigines could become citizens only if they renounced their tribal associations and culture. States except for Victoria could remove aboriginal children from their parents, to be brought up as orphans in white institutions or homes. This phase ended only with the election of Gough Whitlam's Labour government in 1972. Full citizenship was proclaimed plus the restoration "to the Aboriginal people of Australia their lost powers of self-determination in economic, social and political affairs." Aborigines now have full citizen rights plus the freedom of their own culture and organizations, though in practice such multiculturalism is combined with discrimination (Haebich, 1988; Hunter, 1993; Markus, 1994; Rowley, 1972). This is far from perfect but a lot better than aboriginal history.

But the southern island of Tasmania took no part in this improvement. Its ecology differed. The island is everywhere hospitable to European small farming, and this occurred early. Here we see what happened when settlers had full powers and no desire to use aboriginal labor. About 4,500 aborigines lived on the island when they arrived in 1804. Every full-blooded aborigine was wiped out inside 80 years. The last man died in 1869, the last woman in 1876. A few of mixed blood survived. Shooting on sight, "hunting parties," and poisoning flour were more common here. The island's colonial administration urged conciliation, but in 1830 Lieutenant-Governor Arthur succumbed to settler pressures on his Legislative Council and declared a massive "drive" launched across the island to round up the remaining 2,000 aborigines and place them on reservations. This was a failure, since the aborigines evaded their pursuers. Reservation policy was now entrusted to George Robinson, known as the "conciliator," who had lived unarmed among the aborigines and believed they presented no threat. His influence among the aborigines enabled him to round them up. Had they stayed on the fringes of farms and sheep stations, the settlers would have killed them all. But Robinson's policed deportations sadly had the same result. The last aborigines were transported to a small island and crowded together with little food. Disease and malnutrition carried them off over the next two decades, to the unconcern of whites (Cocker, 1998: chaps. 7–11; Hughes, 1987: 414–24; Rowley, 1970: 43–53; Smith, 1980: 70). Tasmania was the extreme case of settlers requiring the land but not the labor. This was a rolling genocide that nobody quite planned but to which most contributed their bit. A de facto settler democracy perpetrated it when the colonial government caved in.

This was so right across Australia. From the 1850s on, settler democracy was effectively in control. Rowley says that "no indigenous peoples have been more completely at the mercy of typical settler democracies, where the standards of parliament are those of the settlers" (1972: 23, 72, 132, 137). Elimination came in many short-lived rolling waves of settler penetration, resistance, and deportations – sometimes followed by sudden, mostly unpremeditated genocidal bursts. The language of planning – of Plan A, B, C, and so on – might not be appropriate to the fluid circumstances of the outback before the onset of stabilized political institutions. This combination continued until labor shortages, followed by changing global political and humanitarian climates, forced more assimilatory and eventually more multicultural practices.

THE UNITED STATES

In several respects, North American colonization lay between the Australian and Mexican cases. The natives posed an intermediate level of threat, formidable in battle, persistent in campaigns, but fighting only in smallish groups. Their level of civilization also seemed inferior to that of Europeans. There was more trade with natives than in Australia, but no native empires or many minerals worth the looting, as in Mexico. There was neither the dire initial conquest and enslavement nor the later widespread assimilation of the Spanish Empire. But settler pressure on the land proved as relentless as in Australia.

This happened cumulatively, without long-term premeditation, a mixed ethnocide/genocide of many rolling waves breaking westward over the country. Early on, settlers were few and poorly armed, and nations like the Iroquois and Huron could play off the French against the British. But British victory in 1763 ended this geopolitical space in the East, as later in the West did the American victory in California and Texas over the Spanish. Trade rarely produced terrible consequences. Nash (1992) notes that images of the Indian developed through trading were milder than those of permanent settlement. Trade brought stereotypes of natives as primitive but winsome, perhaps ignorant and sometimes dangerous, but nonetheless viewed as receptive to European ideas and goods. Indians who traded were also useful, not to be removed.

But settler farmers, not traders, eventually predominated. They needed labor, but their early attempts to capture and tie Indians to dependent labor failed. These hunter-gatherers wasted the land; they did not improve it, they were idle. From John Locke to contemporary Israelis dispossessing Palestinians, Europeans have argued that those who work and improve the land are entitled to it. The New World was thus *vacuum domicilium* or *terra nullius*, an "empty" home or land, the bounty of God to civilized peoples. They made lesser attempts to employ the natives, convert them to Christianity, intermarry with them, or culturally assimilate them. The Puritans wished in theory to convert them but felt they had not the resources to do so, and they sometimes described their own frightful atrocities – like the frying of Indian men, women, and children in villages they had torched – as "God laughing at his enemies" (Nash, 1992: 84).

The first genocidal incidents came early, in 1622 in Virginia and in 1637 during the Pequot War in New England. The settlers kept on coming, decade after decade, waves upon waves of them. Some ploughed Indian lands, others grazed cattle, some mined. Merely crossing the land with roads, staging posts, and later railroads scared away the game. But they also hunted the game to extinction, selling meat and hides for the insatiable appetite of the cities. The Indians' environment became degraded and they died, even without wars. Survivors depended on government handouts of essential supplies for which they traded off their lands, sometimes unwittingly. The settlers had the political and military power to achieve these dire ends without much risk to themselves. There were forcible mass deportations of sick and hungry natives, whose chances of survival outside their traditional lands were poor. The Indians were crowded onto smaller and smaller hunting lands and reservations. Many Europeans recognized the relentless ethnocide this involved but did nothing. It provoked some braves to raid settlers' farms out of hunger and anger, and intermittently to rebel. When Indians resisted, Europeans responded with retaliation – actually, fearsome escalation. Some frankly advocated genocide.

Europeans perceived an enormous difference in civilizational level between themselves and natives. The natives were illiterate, "idolatrous," "heathen," "naked," and "dirty." Before their own arrival, this had been a land "full of wild beasts and wild men," "a hideous and desolate wilderness." The settlers could distinguish between the proud bearing and military skills of the Plains Indians and the lightly clad hunter-gatherers of California, described as "beasts," "swine," "dogs," "wolves," "snakes," "pigs," "baboons," and "gorillas." But ultimately, Indians were "savages." Divine Providence was there for all to see in the form of disease. John Winthrop described the smallpox epidemic of 1617 as God's way of "thinning out" the native population "to make room for the Puritans." William Bradford wrote, "It pleased God to visit these Indians with a great sickness and such a mortality that of a thousand, above nine and a half hundred of them died." Followers of the Lord, he said, could only give thanks to "the marvelous goodness and providence of God" (quotes from Nash, 1992: 136; Stannard, 1992: 238). Whatever they did to the natives could be justified ideologically. Some say the English were influenced by experience of the "savage" Irish, but I doubt this. As Chapter 2 showed, the English wished to forcibly assimilate, not eliminate, the Irish. But to even live among the New World natives would pollute – which meant that Indian women and children were also at risk. The ideology had genocidal elements.

But it changed its form during the late 18th and early 19th centuries. Labels for the natives shifted away from "savage" or "heathen" or casual analogies with animals to labels of race, influenced by experience with African slaves. Scientific classification of races as distinct species or as thousands-year-old adaptations to climate, ecology, disease, and so on then added rigidity, linking races hierarchically, conjoining physical, temperamental, and moral qualities, and viewing the whole ensemble of races as natural and God-given (Smedley, 1993: chaps. 4–7). Civilization might be learned, but race was fixed. God plus science reinforced economic, military, and political power to make it difficult for Europeans and Indians to live among each other.

Countertendencies were weaker than in the Spanish colonies. The British colonial state tended to be more moderate than settler communities, partly because of geopolitical calculations in a period of imperial rivalry. Since they wanted Indians as auxiliary soldiers against each other, the British, French, and Spanish authorities were keener to honor Indian treaties than were the settlers. In this period Indian nations could actually increase their power and organization by military alliances with a relatively successful European power, as the Iroquois did in the North and the Creek in the South. But after the warfare died down, the victorious British Crown had less control over settlers than had the Spanish Crown. Nor was the Anglican Church ever in a monopoly position. The various churches were much closer to the white settler communities they served. Though local priests and ministers might be more moderate than their congregations, they had little power over them. As in Australia, they played second humanitarian fiddle to missionary movements, which provided the main early pressure group for assimilating rather than eliminating natives.

There was one great exception: the Quakers of Pennsylvania and New Jersey. Their determined stance of pacifism toward the Indians not only protected local Indians for several generations, it also brought in a great influx of Indians fleeing from cleansing elsewhere. The Quakers could not prevent the spread of disease. Nor in the long run could they retain political control of their region. Eventually, most of its Indians also died. North America was also influenced by the secular Enlightenment. Like the missionaries, this movement wished to civilize the natives through education. Indians might be savages, but they were of the same human race, possessed of reason and often noble, dignified, brave, intelligent, and adaptable to their environment. Through education they could surely be brought to appreciate private property, work, literacy, and religion. This required that Indians abandon the hunter-warrior culture, the tribal order, and the communal ownership of land. Intermarriage was in principle favored, but there was to be no cultural compromise, no multiethnicity (Sheehan, 1973: 10; Wallace, 1999). This would be voluntary assimilation – savages would want to be civilized. Presidents Washington and Jefferson, several secretaries of war, and federal Indian agencies all worked closely with missionaries and schools in this assimilation project. They warned that any resistance would meet with certain defeat, but they did not conceive of assimilation as coercive. This was not popular with most settlers, who opposed all assimilation.

The program attracted a few Indians, but it was blatantly contradicted by the continuous economic, political, and military pressure on them. Since Indian experience of settlers was of greed, exploitation, and betrayal, they came to regard whites with as much contempt as flowed in their direction. Nor could assimilation bring them material gains until after they abandoned the very institutions of tribal collectivism that nourished them. Unlike those of Mexico, most North American Indian societies were egalitarian. Chiefs had few privileges or property that they might be anxious to preserve with lateral aristocratic assimilation. Race trumped class. Neither community was much interested in intermarriage. Prominent colonials and traders fathered children by Indian women, but they rarely legitimized them. Permanent interracial unions were commoner among frontier traders and laborers in southern colonies with a surplus of males. Mixed blood was accepted in Indian communities, but most of the few Indians or half-breeds who tried to join white society were rejected (Nash, 1992: 280–5). Cherokees who had become private propertied planters were rejected in the 1820s, and when Cherokees acquired permanent political institutions, the State of Georgia would not accept them. It lobbied hard for the deportation of the Cherokee and achieved this in 1834 (Champagne, 1992: 133, 143–6).

By the 1820s, the philanthropists were recognizing the failure of assimilation. So they switched to advocate *protection*, the policed deportation of Indians to new tribal lands west of the Mississippi. This, they reasoned, was better than piecemeal elimination through land-grabbing, murder, and degradation, allowing time for assimilation to occur later. But when the deportations occurred during the 1830s, they proved lethal. Many Indians died in the treks, and the survivors only put more pressure on Indians farther west. The reality was that ordinary settlers, supported by their local state governments, refused to have Indians as neighbors, assimilated or not. Nor did many Indians want assimilation on the terms offered.

The late 19th century eventually saw some moderation into a combination of cultural suppression and segregated assimilation, a policy sometimes known as "kill the Indian, spare the man." Indians were now assimilated as a marginalized underclass on peripheral reservations. The irony of this early-20th-century policy of neglect, as Hoxie (1984: 243–4) points out, was that it allowed Indian culture to survive, if in poverty-stricken circumstances. From that base, the current Native American revival could flow.

California contained more Spanish influences, settled for 80 years by the Spanish until conquered by the United States in 1848. But the Spanish state's presence was weak, only a handful of soldiers and administrators protecting a few settlers and missionaries. The central institution dealing with the Indians was the chain of Californian Franciscan missions. They were concerned primarily to save souls, but they also set up entire agricultural communities to sustain those souls. They sought a benevolent goal, using highly coercive means.

Father Fermin Lasuen, a Basque, had taken holy orders at age 15. He was a Franciscan missionary in Mexico at age 24 and then served in the California missions for 30 years, becoming their second head. His intentions were benevolent. He wanted to save the Indians through conversion and assimilation. He knew this was difficult. Indians were "without education, without government, religion, or respect for authority, and they shamelessly pursue without restraint whatever their brutal appetites suggest to them." How could he transform "a savage race... into a society that is human, Christian, civil and industrious"? "This can be accomplished only by denaturalizing them. It is easy to see what an arduous task this is, for it requires them to act against nature. But it is being done successfully by means of patience and by unrelenting effort." Indians were in a "state of nature," different from the Spanish *gente de razon*, people of reason. While in their state of nature, created by God, they were to be treated benignly as free men. Though savages, they could not be exploited, still less driven away or killed.

But once Indians were baptized, everything changed. They were now under the authority of the order, and the order became a prison. Long hours of forced work in the fields were followed by hours of forced prayers in Latin, of which they understood not a word. Indians girls were locked up at night. If Indians showed any independence, or refused to work or pray, they were shackled and whipped and forced to recite more Latin. If they ran away, the soldiers forcibly brought them back, shackled them, and whipped them more. Sometimes they would crop off an ear or brand a lip. The Indians had difficulty escaping, since independent Indian villages would not take them in. Inside the mission, Indians and Spanish were tightly crammed, the Indians forced into heavy labor with inadequate nutrition. The bones of mission Indians were much smaller than those of free Californian Indians, and they were much less likely to survive disease (Stannard, 1992: 138–9). These were what in Table 1.1 are called revolutionary mistakes, attempts to effect wholesale social transformation, driven by overriding commitment to a value, that is, Weber's value-rationality, which instead brought disaster. The Franciscans committed local ethnocide, unintentional but devastating. Half of California's Indians died during the mission period, almost all from diseases introduced there amid a population weakened by too much coerced work and too little food.

European travelers said they appeared apathetic, aimless, without hope. Sir George Simpson had formerly been head of the Hudson's Bay Company, where he had shown benevolence to local Indians and had encouraged intermarriage between them and his employees. But in California in 1841 he noted: "These sons and daughters of bondage – many of them too sadly broken in spirit even to marry – are so rapidly diminishing in numbers that they must soon pass away from the land of their fathers, a result which, as it seems uniformly to spring from all the conflicting varieties of civilized agency, is to be ultimately ascribed to the inscrutable wisdom of mysterious Providence" (La Perousse, 1989: 18–19; Paddison, 1999: 249–50). Even this moderate white man perceived their end as divine Providence. In reality the Franciscans were the Maoists of the 18th century, intending the improvement of the world but achieving its devastation.

The Spanish ranchers in California were more instrumental. Dispossessed Indians could work as free laborers. They intermarried more and murdered much less. Their Plan combined coercive assimilation with limited segregation of the remaining Indian communities. Things seemed set to improve further after Mexico achieved independence from Spain in 1821. The new Mexican government, influenced by Enlightenment ideas, proclaimed in 1826 the emancipation of most mission Indians, and the missions were secularized in 1833, with half of their lands to be distributed to the Indians. Unfortunately, the benevolence of a distant state was undermined by rapacious local settler officials who took most of the land themselves – settler democracy again (Phillips, 1975: chap. 2). By this time, however, incoming settlers were almost all Anglos. In 1848 they seized California from Mexico and made it a U.S. state. This ensured that the rate of deliberate killing rose markedly.

Most native deaths still did not result from murder. Though we lack accurate numbers, the largest killer was disease. In California the interlinked categories of disease, malnutrition, and starvation killed somewhere around 60–80 percent of natives, direct killing about 10 percent, with most of the remainder attributable to reproductive failure. Deliberate killings were usually in cold blood or in situations of such an imbalance of force that the appellation *murder* is applicable. But none of these categories are entirely separable from each other. Malnutrition, starvation, and low fertility often resulted predictably from settler policy, while diseases were not entirely accidental. Diseases spread most rapidly where malnourished natives were herded closely together, as in California missions and the many U.S. Indian reservations located on marginal lands. The settlers were not ignorant of the disease mechanisms involved, yet they rarely took steps against epidemics to which they themselves were immune. Nor were they unhappy with the results. Nash (1992: 300–1) compares the white responses to the spread of disease among Indians and black slaves. Since slaves were valuable, the white community tried to combat epidemics among them. Slaves were inoculated against smallpox. Indians were not. Indeed, some settlers fomented disease. Reports of donations of disease-ridden blankets to Indians have become notorious, though rare.

More important (as in Australia) were gender abuses and diseases. Indian women were raped or reduced by poverty to prostitution. So they transmitted venereal disease, much more deadly to Indians than whites. No controls were attempted. Alcoholism demoralized and killed Indian men. Yet despite attempts at control by government agencies and missionaries, settlers routinely used alcohol as payment for Indian lands and labor. The callousness is clear. They either intended Indian deaths or they welcomed or were indifferent to deaths resulting from their own actions. Disastrous falls in Indian birth rates were also caused by settler's sexual practices. Between 1848 and 1860 the Indian population of California fell from 150,000 to 31,000, while the white population rose from 25,000 to 350,000. Census data for 1860 households reveal that the Indian decline resulted substantially from the forced segregation of the Indian sexes. Young Indian male survivors could work for a bare subsistence living, while the more numerous young women could reproduce – but with whites. Young Indian men and women could not live together so as to reproduce Indians. The final blow to reproduction came in the 1850s and 1860s with a great influx of Anglo miners demanding all the women. Indian males in the mining districts were now more likely to be exterminated than employed (Hurtado, 1994).

Who perpetrated this deadly mixture? Let us first consider political elites. The British colonial government and then the U.S. federal government were initially committed to a Plan A of limited deportations plus partial assimilation, moving some Indians away, converting all to Christianity, and maintaining racial barriers against full assimilation. Faced with further massive waves of settlers, the United States moved toward a Plan B of forcible deportations combined with segregation on reservations that in theory would be adequate for the reproduction of Indian life and culture. But while the federal government and the Supreme Court might often be conciliatory and humane, state/local governments in the frontier areas were more responsive to the interests of the settlers. The Court eventually recognized that properly constituted Indian governments might have sovereign power to enter into treaties over their lands. The differences increased through time, as federal politicians in the East depended on electorates for whom Indians were no longer salient. They could maintain a disinterested enlightenment in relation to natives. The federal government had early set up an Indian Bureau. Its officers had to implement official policy, but they often applied it in relatively humane ways. Some local Indian agents appropriated bureau funds and supplies for their own use, did corrupt deals with settlers and merchants, and generally sold out the Indians in their charge (Nichols, 1978: 10–19). But most higher-level agents lobbied for moderation.

Elected state-level officials in frontier areas tended to be more extreme. The cycle of land encroachment and resistance drove them to develop more coherent policies. In the 1820s and early 1830s southern legislatures pressed successfully for deportations and did not care what happened to the Indians at the end of their journey. Few local politicians supported grants of land or taxes that would make segregation on reservations viable for the Indians after they were deported. They came to believe that deportations, accompanied by exterminist rhetoric, would get them reelected, not pleas for toleration and protection, and especially not taxpayer subsidies to reservations or land grants to Indians. Settler democracy was again bad news.

This was very clear in California. Its constitution of 1850 enshrined full white male suffrage, the most advanced form of democracy of the age. But it also authorized the forcible detention and placing in indentured labor in perpetuity for any Indians who fled the reservations or were found wandering. This included children. The legislature authorized settler militias to enforce the roundup, paying them $1.1 million in 1850 and 1851. Since the reservations, small and on marginal land, could not support the Indian population to be supposedly deported there, in practice the militias killed as many Indians as they deported. The legislature never objected. The California legislature and the California delegation to Congress stymied several presidential and Indian Bureau attempts to offer half-decent treaties to California Indians involving substantial grants of land, plus subsidies and technical assistance for their improvement. The California legislature actually opposed recognizing *any* Indian rights to land in the state. But they then had to face the final consequences of such obduracy, since there was nowhere farther west to which the problem could be sent.

Governor Burnett, having rejected the path of conciliation through adequate reservations, confronted a difficult situation. The settlers were few and poorly armed. Their continual encroachment on Indian land had increased resistance. Indian groups who had been hitherto very loosely organized were ceding more powers to war chiefs (Phillips, 1975: chaps. 3–5). The Indian threat seemed to be growing. Burnett's response was not to conciliate, but to escalate to genocide. He declared "a war of extermination will continue to be waged between the two races until the Indian becomes extinct." His successor, Governor McDougall, agreed: the war "must of necessity be one of extermination to many of the tribes" (Hurtado, 1988: 134–6). It should be noted that Hitler never dared to make such an openly exterminist public statement as these two California governors. He knew most Germans would disapprove; they believed most (white) Californians would approve. So they left "smoking guns"; Hitler did not. Nor was the next governor, Bigler, much better. He wrote to the army expressing his view of Indians:

the acts of these Savages are sometimes signalized by a ferocity worthy of ... cannibals. ... They seem to cherish an instinctive hatred toward the white race, and this is a principle of their nature, which neither time nor vicissitude can impair. This principle of hatred is hereditary. ... The character and conduct of these Indians ... [means] ... that Whites and Indians cannot live in close proximity in peace.

Bigler ended this letter by asking the army to evacuate *all* Indians from four counties. Where to, he didn't say. But he offered the California militia to help (Heizer, 1993: 189–91).

In frontier states many politicians, settlers, and their press agreed with such sentiments. Minnesota Governor Ramsey declared, "The Sioux Indians must be exterminated or driven forever beyond the borders of the state." This became a popular slogan: "Exterminate or Banish." His militia commander was General Sibley, a former fur trader known for swindling Indians and federal government alike. He launched a successful war of extermination against the Santee Sioux. A total of 770 surviving Santee were deported in 1863 by steamship from St. Paul. White Minnesotans lined the river bank, hurling stones and abuse at the Indians (Brown, 1970: 50–65). Colorado's governor was no better, as we will see. He was supported by the Denver press. During 1863, 10 of all of its 27 stories about Indians openly advocated extermination (Churchill, 1997: 172). In response to two 1871 Indian raids stealing horses and cattle and killing four whites, a party led by two leading Tucson citizens attacked an Apache village with no connection to the raids. They massacred 144 Apaches, of whom only 8 were men. Many of the female victims had first been raped. The Denver *News* congratulated the killers, adding, "we only regret that the number was not double." A furore back East caused President Ulysses S. Grant to describe this atrocity as "purely murder" and to apply pressure to bring its ringleaders to trial. Much incriminating evidence was produced in court.

It took the jury 19 minutes of deliberation to acquit them (Brown, 1970: 202–5; Cocker, 1998: 220–1). Juries almost never did find Indian killers guilty, since they consisted of the local settlers and in most states Indian testimony was not accepted against whites (for California, see Heizer, 1993: 11–14).

The federal government and the army often protected Indians, and the missionaries protested loudly, as indeed did some settlers and a few local politicians and newspapers. Yet almost all divisions among the whites could be healed if Indians resisted and killed white men or women. Some Modoc Indians on the Oregon–California border tricked General Canby into a parley and killed him. There followed a national cry for vengeance, to which General William Tecumseh Sherman was able to give expression. He demanded not just the deaths of the small group of offenders but also the killing and scattering of the whole tribe "so that the name of Modoc should cease." After the Lakota Sioux rebelled and killed 80 U.S. soldiers in one skirmish, Sherman was able to do the same. He wrote, "We must act with vindictive earnestness against the Sioux... even to their extermination, men, women, and children." The death of George Armstrong Custer at Little Bighorn in 1876 produced a similar national outcry. There followed a ruthless war, the expropriation of all Sioux lands, and the final surrender of Sitting Bull in 1881 (Uttley, 1994).

The effect of Indian resistance on even enlightened presidents drove them to accept a Plan C, threatening genocide if they did not accept deportation. Consider the five most famous presidents before the 20th century. Washington and Jefferson forgot about the Enlightenment when Indians sided with the British. Washington instructed his generals to attack the Iroquois and "lay waste all the settlements... that the country may not be merely overrun but destroyed," and not to "listen to any overture of peace before the total ruin of their settlements is effected." He likened Indians to wolves, "both being beasts of prey, tho' they differ in shape." He declared that the Indians must be forced west of the Mississippi, and any who remained must be broken by force. Jefferson also changed his tune during Indian wars. He repeatedly recommended either the root-and-branch destruction of hostile tribes or driving them beyond the Mississippi: "nothing is more desirable than total suppression of their savage insolence and cruelties"; "This then is the season for driving them off"; their "ferocious barbarities justified extermination"; "if ever we are constrained to lift the hatchet against any tribe, we shall never lay it down till that tribe is exterminated, or driven beyond the Mississippi.... In war, they will kill some of us; we shall destroy all of them." In 1813 he thought that the defeated Creeks would "submit on the condition of removing them to such settlements beyond the Mississippi as we shall assign them." Neither Washington nor Jefferson ever spoke about the civilized British enemy in exterminist language. Jefferson also supported white land-grabbing. While he was president, 200,000 square miles of Indian territories were acquired by his agents. The method, he told his officials, was to trick the Indians into debt, forcing them to sell their lands. With inadequate land left for hunting, they would have to learn agriculture and then assimilate. If they resisted this, they must be crushed; if they merely languished and starved, that proved the inevitability of their end. His preferred policy was assimilation, then deportations, but extermination might follow if these failed. Jefferson also said he believed in the inherent racial equality of Indians (unlike blacks) with whites (Wallace, 1999: 78), but higher must triumph over lower civilizations. Though many Americans today know that these two presidents were slave owners, their ferocity toward Indians is little known.

Andrew Jackson has left a more ambiguous reputation. During his presidency, the franchise was extended to all white males. Yet he was renowned as an Indian fighter. The revisionist view is that Jackson was merely a pragmatic politician, bending to pressure from southern state legislatures over deportations, prepared to defend Indians against white squatters and other unjust expropriations, but coming to believe that deportations were ultimately the only way to protect Indians from the white man (Prucha, 1994). This is whitewash. When Indians resisted, Jackson was ferocious. When one white woman was taken prisoner by the Creeks, he declared, "I shall penetrate the creek Towns, until the Captive, with her Captors are delivered up, and think myself Justifiable in laying waste their villages, burning their houses, killing their warriors and leading into Captivity their wives and children, untill I do obtain a surrender of the Captive, and the Captors." Prucha (p. 212) sums up such views as follows: "Forthright and hard-hitting, he adopted a no-nonsense policy toward hostile Indians." The terminology reminds me of the euphemisms we find written by superior officers in the files of SS men proficient in a more recent genocide. *Hard-hitting* does not quite convey the sense of the mass murder he was perpetrating. Jackson inveighed on other occasions against "deceitfull" and "unrelenting barbarians" – "the blood of our murdered countrymen must be revenged. The banditti ought to be swept from the face of the earth." He boasted, "I have on all occasions preserved the scalps of my killed." In principle he believed that "fear is better than love with an indian." He urged his soldiers to kill women and children. Not to do so would be like pursuing "a wolf in the hamocks without knowing first where her den and whelps were." Indian wars were the setting for all these remarks, and they helped him become president. Once in office, Jackson broke Indian treaties and launched forcible deportations. He claimed that his Removal Act of 1830 was an act of generosity, yet around 10,000 Creek, 4,000 Cherokee, and 4,000 Choctaw died along the infamous Trail of Tears.

Lincoln was much less involved in Indian affairs (see Nichols, 1978: 3, 76–128, 187, for this para.). As a young politician he used his military experience in the Black Hawk War to cultivate an Indian-fighter image, and he eulogized Zachary Taylor's savage military exploits and Winfield Scott's deportation of the Cherokee. Yet while he was president, Indians were only a peripheral problem. He was confronted by only one major decision. He had sanctioned military expeditions and land-grabbing in Minnesota. This provoked a Sioux rising in 1862 that the army crushed, capturing 309 of the rebels. His decision was whether to approve their execution. The locals and Governor Ramsey clamored for the execution of all 309, for had not whites been killed and raped in the rising? Lincoln was lobbied hard by both exterminists and humanitarians. He seems to have sympathized more with the latter, but (typically) Lincoln compromised, approving the execution of only 39 of the Indians, satisfying no one but defusing the situation. He was glad to turn away from the matter, which he described as a "disagreeable subject." It was still the largest mass execution in American history, and the evidence against any of the individual captives was scant. Almost all the rest of the captives soon died anyway from terrible prison conditions. But Lincoln's actions did make him a relative moderate among presidents, though he shared the general view that the Indians would disappear before a superior white civilization. As he had the impudence to tell a tribal delegation to the White House in 1863:

the pale-faced people are numerous and prosperous because they cultivate the earth, produce bread and depend upon the products of the earth rather than wild game for a subsistence. This is the chief reason of the difference; but there is another ... we are not, as a race, so much disposed to fight and kill one another as our red brethren. (Nichols, 1978: 187)

During 1863 there was a Civil War raging between whites! The truth was that the pale-faced people were more likely to kill each other *and* their red brethren.

At the end of the 19th century, when the rolling genocide was almost over, a fifth great democrat and president, Theodore Roosevelt, no longer needed to contribute to it. The Indians were almost gone. Yet he did declare that extermination "was as ultimately beneficial as it was inevitable," and that the noblest of all wars was one of extermination against savages. "I don't go so far as to think that the only good Indians are dead Indians, but I believe nine out of ten are, and I shouldn't like to inquire too closely into the case of the tenth."[1] Presidents, especially the more democratic ones, responsive to the needs of their constituents, could reveal an arrogant imperial racism that fueled policies beyond an exemplary repression, which remains an ultimately pragmatic policy, toward genocide. For Indian resistance and justification of land-grabbing led them into such temptations. How many of these presidents would be prosecuted today for genocide by an

[1] These presidential quotes are taken from Sheehan (1973: 206, 209, 244), Stannard (1992: 119–22, 245–6), Wallace (1999: 65, 235–8), and Cocker (1998: 206).

international war crimes tribunal? Four, I think – excluding Roosevelt, whose rhetoric was not matched by actions – though Lincoln's sentence would be slight.

What of the ordinary settlers on the frontier, who provided most of the actual killers? Since cleansing came in small, rolling waves in newly settled areas, each settler group only had to dispossess a few natives in order to get the desired land. Then the next wave of local cleansings might be committed by others, and so, on until local cleansing was complete. This whole process might take anywhere between 5 and 50 years, and its violence and murder would vary greatly according to the relative numbers of whites and Indians, the rapidity of the land-grabbing, and the capacity of the Indians to resist. At any one time, only a few Europeans were land-grabbing and even fewer murdered. Subsequent generations experienced only peace, since the Indians had been defeated and removed elsewhere. It is not really appropriate in such contexts to invoke coherent Plans, either A, B, or C, among settlers, since local exigencies, the lack of a highly institutionalized local state, and their own greed and ideology would drive them quickly through varied cleansing means. Afterward they could settle down as peace-loving Americans. Their children bore no taint. Only some of the local founding fathers were genocidal.

Killers usually mounted justifications in terms of self-defense or retaliation for Indian atrocities committed earlier. Yet it was actually escalation. When an Indian retaliated violently for the rape of his wife or when, starving, he stole a cow or horse, self-righteous settler escalation would follow. A Californian farmer testified, "I believe for every beef that has been killed by them ten or fifteen Indians have been killed." The San Francisco *Bulletin*, away from the actual frontier, was a California voice of moderation, advocating protection, that is, humane segregation, not extermination. It editorialized about a man called McElroy who had a deer stolen from him. He retaliated by killing an Indian man and his squaw and wounding a third. Then McElroy was murdered as Indians also retaliated. But the death of a white man brought in the California militia. They found an Indian camp, killed 9 Indian men (the rest fleeing), and then butchered its 40 defenseless women and children. This newspaper reported on another occasion that a 36-strong militia unit looking for the killers of 1 white man found an Indian village and killed all but 2 or 3 of its 150 inhabitants – men, women, and children. The captain of another army unit wrote proudly, "The number killed I confidently report at not less than 75 and have little doubt it extended to nearly double that number." A captain of different sensibilities criticized a Californian rancher who killed two or three Indians, believing that an Indian had stolen some of his cattle. The next day, the cattle were found. Indians then avenged their dead relatives by killing the rancher. The captain was now trying to prevent further escalation (Heizer, 1993: 42–3, 63–79, 84–90, 95–7, 156–7, 245, 249–50).

Retaliation involved blaming all the Indians around. Three Missouri whites said they would shoot the first Indians they came across, since Indians had stolen their horses. Commented a more reflective settler, "this inconsiderate retaliation upon a whole race for the acts of one of its members leads to half the conflicts that occur" (Madsen, 1994: 316). Indians would do the same. Retaliation was mutual, each side denying that it had started the violence. But the whites were more likely to escalate the killing, and their less discriminate killing contradicted their stated goals, since it alienated still more Indians. Either rage had gotten the better of sense or their real goal was complete extermination. The predominance of white escalation did not merely result from their superior weapons and organization. It also resulted from the superior, more "civilized" party being more unpleasantly shocked by violent resistance from the savages below, worsened by an ideologically induced "moral shudder" that settlers often experienced when confronting the "savage," "unclean" Indian. Their world seemed turned upside down, inducing fear, panic, and repression disproportionate to the actual threat – as we saw from the presidents quoted and as we will see in all lopsided cases of murderous cleansing. There can be no doubting the electoral popularity of the removal of the Indians. There was no protest movement comparable to that of those who sought to abolish the slavery of blacks until the formation of an Indian Rights movement in the 1880s – too late to save many.

Military power in cleansings was shared by the army and settler militias. The army could kill far more Indians because of its superior weapons and communications. It contained diverse views. It was mandated to keep the peace, stop Indian raids, repress Indian risings, and enforce their deportation to reservations. A variety of tactics might accomplish these goals. The predominant army Plan A was a combined carrot-and-stick approach: negotiating treaties for policed deportations to segregated reservations, combined with exemplary repression for Indians who would not negotiate. In applying this policy, local army units sometimes sided with Indians against settlers. The California record is full of army officers protesting against murderous settler treatment of local Indians. To protect them, some officers aimed their guns at the settlers, not the Indians; and some gave the Indians army rations or bought them provisions out of their own resources (Heizer, 1993). In the Southwest, General Crook ran pragmatic, sometimes conciliatory campaigns against the Apache and others, preferring negotiations to battles. Other generals had earlier done so elsewhere.

Yet after the Civil War the army developed a Plan B, escalating the callous tactics learned during the war, occasionally sliding further into a Plan C of local genocide committed against the Plains Indians, Apaches, and other, more formidable fighting nations. Sherman was army chief of staff, Sheridan the commander of the Plains army. Sherman explained his tactics to the secretary of war in 1866:

My opinion is, if fifty Indians are allowed to remain between the Arkansas and the Platte we will have to guard every stage station, every train, and all railroad working parties...fifty hostile Indians will checkmate three thousand soldiers, Rather get them out as soon as possible, and it makes little diference whether they be coaxed out by Indian commissioners or killed. (Brown, 1970: 157–8)

To disperse his forces was to play into the hands of the Indians, who were adept at small, mobile operations. So the generals sought to attack the Indians when they were immobilized in their winter quarter villages. The warriors would then be forced to stand and fight to defend their women, children, and possessions. The army believed that its firepower would win fixed-place battles (Uttley, 1994). Yet the firepower would be directed at crowds of men, women, and children attempting to flee from their village. If they succeeded in fleeing, they lost all their possessions, which destroyed their ability to live off the land. If they failed, they would die together. Sherman's subordinate, General Sanborn, was appalled by this genocidal tactic. Writing to the secretary of the interior, he declared:

For a mighty nation like us to be carrying on a war with a few straggling nomads, under such circumstances, is a spectacle most humiliating, an injustice unparalleled, a national crime most revolting, that must, sooner or later, bring down on us or our posterity the judgement of Heaven.

But General Sheridan dismissed critics of these tactics as "good and pious ecclestiastics...aiders and abettors of savages who murdered, without mercy, men, women and children." This was justification in terms of retaliation. Sheridan expressed himself even more clearly in a famous exchange as some Commanches came in to surrender. Their chief introduced himself to Sheridan in the only broken English he knew: "Tosawi, good Indian." Sheridan replied, "The only good Indians I ever saw were dead." Sheridan has been credited with inventing what had already become an old saw in the West. In the retelling, his line became the notorious "The only good Indian is a dead Indian" (Brown, 1970: 157–8, 170–1). Sherman and Sheridan remained in command of the Indian Wars. There was no vengeance of Heaven, their policies were popular with settlers and politicians on the frontiers, and they were successful in achieving their goals.

The degeneration of military tactics is common in murderous cleansing. It may require initial hatred of the enemy, but it also has a tactical logic. It may emerge from the need to deprive the enemy of its supply base contributed by noncombatants or to combat guerrillas who merge into the civilian population. Both figured in the 19th-century Plains Indian Wars. Braves did not wear distinguishing uniforms, so any Indian male might be hostile. To be on the safe side, better kill them all. But it also came from the tactical need to pin the enemy down to fixed-place defense in sites where men, women, and children were intermingled. At the worst, such tactical lures can slide exemplary repression toward genocide – as they did here.

Yet settler militias, financed by state or local government, provided a more routine genocidal thrust. They were part-time volunteer forces receiving a wage, sometimes in the form of a scalp bounty. "My intention is to kill all Indians I come across," said Colonel Chivington, an ex-Methodist minister and leader of the Third Colorado Militia Regiment. He exhorted his men to "kill and scalp all, little and big." "Little" meant children, for as he said, "Nits make lice." An army officer tried to persuade Colorado Governor Evans to negotiate with the Indians. "But what shall I do with the Third Colorado Regiment if I make peace?" the governor responded. "They have been raised to kill Indians, and they must kill Indians." At Sand Creek in 1864 they did. Chivington's force murdered 105 Indian women and children and 28 men, their bodies being afterward mutilated. Militiamen were seen carrying off trophies made of women's vaginas and other body parts. Chivington's action was stupid as well as evil, since he destroyed the power of most Cheyenne and Arapaho chiefs who had been urging peace with the white men (Brown, 1970: 86–93; Stannard, 1992: 171–4). This was more than exemplary repression, since it was so counterproductive to that goal. It was an attempt at local genocide. Some critics tried to bring Chivington and his governor to trial, but they failed. Chivington remained a hero in Denver.

Wallace (1999: 218) comments that the settlers *were* the militia, so woe betide any aspiring politician who went against them. The vigilante posses, militias, and ranger forces described themselves as "a free people in arms," volunteers adapting their skills as herders and hunters. Eastern militia leaders would appeal for "experienced woodsmen," Western ones for "Indian fighters." Some were professional killers. Cocker (1998: 187–8) narrates the biography of "Sugarfoot Jack," a killer on a global scale. He had been transported as a boy from England to Tasmania, where he killed aborigines. Then he turned up in California as a violent militia member and finally became a sadistic killer of Apache babies in Arizona.

It is a terrible story that a few American humanitarians and historians have been seeking to publicize for 100 years. Unlike the descendants of slaves, the descendants of murdered native Americans are few and marginalized. Genocide was a success. As exterminists claimed, out of the elimination of native peoples, a new civilization arose. That is how the more ruthless social Darwinist theorists told the story. Hitler and Himmler both referred to the American genocide as an example to follow when contemplating their own.

MORE RECENT COLONIAL CLEANSINGS: THE CAUCASUS AND SOUTH WEST AFRICA

Colonial cleansing could not go on forever. By the 20th century, native peoples in the worst-affected colonies were disappearing and the land was settled. The first new nations could forget their origins and delude themselves with their unique pacific virtues. But latecomers like Russia, Germany, and

Italy committed their atrocities later. In Chapter 10 I discuss the last case, that of Italy in Ethiopia. Here I discuss Russia in the Caucasus and Germany in South West Africa (present-day Namibia).

As we move into the late 19th century, we encounter colonial countries with much more modern states and armies. Russian colonial expansion was also distinctively overland, as its rule was extended across Asia. Russians moved in their millions to settle newly conquered areas, which brought another land-centered economic conflict between Russians and natives culminating in dispossession of the latter. Russians justified this ideologically in terms of the usual civilized-versus-savage dichotomy. Kazakhs and other nomads were "wasting" the lands and had to give way to superior Russian peasant agriculture. One Russian viceroy in the Caucasus declared, "gentleness, in the eyes of Asiatics, is a sign of weakness, and out of pure humanity I am inexorably severe. One execution saves hundreds of Russians from destruction and thousands of Muslims from treason."

Normal Russian policy amounted to exemplary repression: show ferocity against those who resist in order to persuade others to submit more peacefully. This policy was at its worst against the Chechens, doughty mountain fighters ultimately brought under (uneasy) Russian rule after savage wars in the late 1850s. But the Turkic peoples of the western Caucasus, especially Circassians, were perceived as being a greater problem since they were even less civilized, being splintered into tiny, fractious clans. There was much small-scale guerrilla resistance but no one able to sign a peace treaty. They also inhabited a more strategic part of the Caucasus, next to the Ottoman Empire, they were Muslims, and the Ottomans were supporting them against Christian Russia.

The Russian military hit on the solution (described by Holquist, 2003; Lieven, 2000: 304–15; Shenfield, 1999). Desperately modernizing in order to keep pace with its European rivals, the Russian general staff was influenced by contemporary notions of systematic, "definitive" warfare waged against whole peoples. Collecting statistics on these peoples was a priority, and staff officers began to suggest organized deportations based on supposedly careful calculations of numbers and logistics. When their leading light, Miliutin, became minister of war in 1862, he promptly launched the policy. Over the next three years the army attacked and burned the principal Circassian villages, killed all those who resisted, and forced the population out. The policy was proclaimed as depopulation, not extermination. By 1865 only about 10 percent of the 500,000 or so Circassians in the main areas of attack remained there. Overall, perhaps 1.5 million Circassians were forced out and replaced with Russian, settlers. Perhaps 150,000 Circassians were resettled across Russia and 500,000 were pushed out, forcibly deported, across the border into the Ottoman Empire.

This leaves almost a million unaccounted for. Most of them probably died, perhaps amounting to half of the total Circassian population. Most deaths resulted from malnutrition and disease. Murderous cleansing was certainly intended, but not genocide. Russian troops burned villages and crops, turning out the population onto the roads knowing that many would die. Horrified Russians who protested were told it was too late. "Can anyone really turn back the calamity?" said Count Yevdokimov to one critic. The Russian authorities had committed callous warfare and exemplary repression against other troublesome and "primitive" peoples in Siberia, Kazakhstan, and the Caucasus. But this was worse.

The case combined some of the worst features of imperial exemplary repression, modern militarism, and early modern colonialism. However, it does not fit my first thesis. Though I have no real evidence on Russian settlers, the leading perpetrator seems to have been the tsarist state, taking advice from the army high command – stably authoritarian institutions for many years. This seems a case where a distinctively modern, rigorous, and scientific militarism added its own bite to what was in other respects a typical outburst of colonial murderous cleansing. We will shortly see another example of this. Yet it was a struggle over sovereignty, with an outside ally contributing to the intransigence of the weaker side, so my theses 4 and 5 apply. I also note a consequence, which will prove influential in the next chapter. It left over half a million Circassians, Chechens, and other Muslims as embittered refugees in the Ottoman Empire.

In South West Africa, I am able to again identify three main types of actor. The first was ideological, here principally the Rhineland Missionary Society. By 1904 it was the most moderate actor, welcoming colonization as a chance to Christianize the natives, that is, to partially assimilate them. It did not favor methods beyond those of institutional assimilation. It was opposed to the German atrocities in 1904–5 and pressured Berlin to get them stopped, supported by liberal and socialist deputies in the German parliament, the Reichstag. They were only a minority there, but their humanitarian clamor embarrassed the German government, eventually influencing policy changes.

The second actor, caught in the middle and often factionalized, was the colonial administration in the colony reporting to the Berlin Colonial Department. This came under the dual authority of the chancellor and kaiser. The kaiser retained power over foreign policy and commanded the armed forces independently of the Reichstag. Since this kaiser was not a strong ruler, the army commanders had considerable autonomy, which was to have an escalatory impact on the events of 1904. The local administrators sought to keep the colony pacified and expanding, goals that were difficult to reconcile. Local administrators were prepared to share some power with compliant leaders of tribal groups. This was formally a protectorate, not a direct colony, embodying some indirect rule. The German administration also wanted Africans to work as pliable laborers and had accorded them legal though not political rights. This was an official policy of discrimination, even partial segregation, but coupled with some protection. It was never aimed at murderous cleansing. However, the simultaneous commitment to encouraging more white settlers led to more land expropriations, policed deportations of natives, and resistance.

Major Theodor Leutwein, governor of the protectorate between 1894 and 1904, took care not to provoke the natives. He realized that the underlying conflict, over who should own the land, was especially problematic for the Herero, the second largest tribal group and easily the biggest cattle grazers, who needed very extensive ranges for their herds. As the white settlers expanded, they wanted the best of those lands. They got more of them by combining force, fraudulent treaties, and malevolent use of credit, calling in lands as payment for supposed native debts. Racial strife was perennial. Leutwein sought to reduce it by dividing and ruling among the African tribal groups and by restraining the settlers from excess. He conciliated tribal leaders, increasing their powers over their own people while expropriating the rights of the African masses. He generally pleased his superiors in Berlin with this strategy. Tribal elites often complied on the assumption that they were the status equals of the colonial elite and the status superiors of the uncultured mass of white settlers (Bley, 1971: 88–91). They wanted the policy of lateral aristocratic assimilation. They deluded themselves. Some imagined a future roughly like that of Mexican or Inca aristocrats, sires of a new mestizo ruling class. In Africa this was unlikely. Racism was too strong, and African chiefs were not equal to poor whites, though political pragmatism might temporarily conceal this.

Leutwein understood the contradictions of German policy and knew he was walking a tightrope. Administrators had, on the one hand, "to take land from the natives on the basis of questionable treaties and risk the life...of one's countrymen to this end, and on the other hand to enthuse about humanitarian principles in the Reichstag" (Bley, 1971: 68). The colony's economic adviser, Dr. Paul Rohrbach, expressed a more ruthless logic:

The decision to colonise in South West Africa could mean nothing else but...that the native tribes would have to give up their lands on which they have previously grazed their stock in order that the white man might have the land for the grazing of his stock. When this attitude is questioned from the moral law standpoint, the answer is that for nations of the cultural level of the South African natives, the loss of their free national barbarism and their development into a class of labourers in service of and dependent on the white people is primarily a "law of existence" in the highest degree.... By no argument whatsoever can it be shown that the preservation of any degree of national independence, national prosperity or political organisation by the races of South West Africa, would be of...an equal advantage for the development of mankind. (Cocker, 1998: 301)

Rohrbach countered moral doubts by appealing to the more general benefit for mankind. Progress, he went on to explain, would come from making the "African races" service the "white races" "with the greatest possible working efficiency." In the most elevated world-historical terms he endorsed complete expropriation, forcing officials into near-slave-labor conditions. He was not contemplating eliminating them. Nor was any official.

The third group consisted of settlers, dominated by those living around the capital, Windhoek, a segregated, racist white enclave, and farmers wanting to expand into tribal lands without using Herero workers. Here is a petition sent by settlers to Berlin in response to Reichstag deputies' criticism of their treatment of natives:

From time immemorial our natives have grown to laziness, brutality and stupidity. The dirtier they are, the more they feel at ease. Any white man who has lived among natives finds it impossible to regard them as human beings at all in any European sense. They need centuries of training as human beings, with endless patience, strictness and justice. (Bley, 1971: 97)

The settlers were pressing for further deportations, by all necessary force. One missionary criticized them roundly:

The underlying cause of the resentment which the Hereros bear against the Germans is that the average German looks upon and treats the natives as creatures being more or less on the same level as baboons (their favourite word to describe the natives)....Consequently, the whites value their horses and oxen more highly than they do the natives. Such a mentality breeds harshness, deceit, exploitation, injustice, rape, and, not infrequently, murder as well. (Drechsler, 1980: 167–8, n. 6)

Since many settlers could not distinguish a chief from a landless laborer, their everyday behavior undermined Leutwein's strategy. He was horrified when a German baker flogged a prominent Herero subchief out of his shop "until the blood ran." He reprimanded the baker for so abusing "a proud and respected man and a particularly wealthy cattle-owner" (Bley, 1971: 86; Drechsler, 1980: 136). Such incidents undermined lateral aristocratic assimilation – indeed, this chief was to be one of the main leaders of the 1904 rising. The settlers also felt vulnerable. Any sign of resistance brought terrible fears of being overwhelmed by "dark savages." The merest hint of native resistance led settlers to inflict ferocious punishment. For some this was a pretext for seizing more land and property, deliberately provoking the out-group.

The settlers did not rule. The governor ran the colony, and settlers were perpetually irritated at their inability to dent Leutwein's policies of "false sentimentality." Another petition stated: "It is the function of the government to establish control over the natives, but it can achieve this only when it has sufficient power at its disposal. Moral pressure alone is not enough to impose our laws on the black race" (Bley, 1971: 79–81, 84–5). But settlers did have two important local powers. First, they staffed the lay magistracy and they tried most cases brought by Africans claiming ill treatment by whipping or rape. They almost never found a white man guilty and would not accept evidence based on African testimony alone (Drechsler, 1980: 133–6).

Second, this was capitalism in which settlers had greatly superior resources of capital, knowledge, and access to law. They found it easy to deprive Africans of their lands within the apparent framework of the law, and the colonial administration was usually helpless to restrain them. Outrageous court injustices and settler land-grabbing were the usual sparks of native revolts.

In January 1904 the Herero paramount chief, Samuel Mahareru – hitherto a docile and drunken client of the Germans – was pressured by his subchiefs to make a final stand. He wrote to his headmen that they should avoid killing women, children, missionaries, English, Boers, half-breeds, or Namas (the neighboring tribal group). This injunction was largely adhered to. They killed 120–150 whites, of whom only 3 were women and 7 were Boers. Since Herero attacks failed to take the towns or barracks, their successes fell on more isolated farms (Bridgman, 1981: 74). The revolt was totally unexpected by whites, whose racism had led them to underestimate the Herero. German males could expect little mercy. The Herrero took no prisoners and mutilated corpses. The attacks were launched by enraged warriors believing that this was their last chance to live free. Either they won or they died, exhorted Mahareru. At first they did win, driving the settlers out of their tribal lands and seizing all their cattle.

From previous colonial cases we should expect the killing of over 100 white men, to bring ferocious retaliation. It was also falsely believed that women and children had been slaughtered too. A missionary described settlers' reaction:

The Germans are consumed with unexpiable hatred and a terrible thirst for revenge, one might even say they are thirsting for the blood of the Herero. All you hear these days is words like "make a clean sweep, hang them, shoot them to the last man, give no quarter." I shudder to think what may happen in the months ahead. The Germans will doubtless exact a grim vengeance. (Drechsler, 1980: 145)

Berlin was immediately involved, since the whole colony seemed threatened. But a split developed. Leutwein and his Colonial Department superiors wanted to follow a decisive military action with negotiation. Yet the generals favored a more ruthless military strategy. Hull (2004) says German military thinking had pushed the doctrine of offensive war to its ultimate limit. Victory was defined as complete annihilation (*vernichting*). The meaning of this word was rather vague, but in colonial contexts enemy combatants were more difficult to distinguish from civilians, and they were not likely to fight German troops. How to achieve victory? Annihilation came to indicate the same tactics that General Sherman had used, attacking native village inhabitants and clans on the move in order to suck the warriors into battle. This was accompanied by the tactic recently pioneered by the Spanish and British Empires: to corral the noncombatants in concentration camps in order to isolate the insurgents.

Arguments initially focused on who should head the military expeditionary force sent to the colony. The moderates had better access to Reich Chancellor Bernhard von Bulow, but the radicals, through Chief of Staff von Schlieffen, had much better access to the kaiser (Bridgman, 1981: 63). On von Schlieffen's advice, the kaiser appointed General von Trotha. He had African experience, he had brutally repressed an East African revolt in 1896, and he had helped suppress the Boxer revolt in China in 1900–1. Von Trotha said:

I know enough tribes in Africa. They have all the same mentality insofar as they yield only to force. It was and remains my policy to apply this force by unmitigated terrorism and even cruelty. I shall destroy the rebellious tribes by shedding rivers of blood and money. Only thus will it be possible to sow the seeds of something new that will endure.

He added, "against non-humans one cannot conduct war humanely," and later claimed that "the Emperor only said that he expected me to crush the rebellion by fair means or foul" (Drechsler, 1980: 154). This meant exemplary repression sufficient to crush Herero resistance once and for all to deter all other tribal groups from rebellion. This was bad enough. But egged on by the settlers and fortified by racism, von Trotha and his army escalated to genocide. In October 1904 he issued a proclamation offering blood money to anyone bringing in a Herero. It ended:

Inside German territory every Herero tribesman, armed or unarmed, with or without cattle, will be shot. No women or children will be allowed in the territory: they will be driven back to their people or fired on. These are the last words to Herero nation from me, the great General of the Mighty German Emperor.

He told his troops, "as a result of this order no more male prisoners would be taken." But many women and children were also shot by his soldiers. An eyewitness testified:

After the battle all men, women and children who fell into German hands, wounded or otherwise, were mercilessly put to death. Then the Germans set off in pursuit of the rest, and all those found by the wayside and in the sandveld were shot down or bayoneted to death. The mass of the Herero men were unarmed and thus unable to offer resistance. They were just trying to get away with their cattle.

Von Trotha did not admit ordering the shooting of women and children, but he did admit deliberately driving them into the desert to die. He believed many were diseased, which may have been true since they were half-starved and weakening: "I deem it wiser for the entire nation to perish than to infect our soldiers... over and above this, any gesture of leniency on my part would only be regarded as a sign of weakness by the Herero." Settler militias joined in, their units showing special brutality. A missionary reported, "each member was as wild as hell itself. How many of them had lost everything. Now was the time for revenge."

Firepower enabled the Germans to corral the Herero (men, women, and children) into the desert. Poisoning water holes ensured the death of most of the survivors, watched by the encircling Germans. When the Nama, emboldened by the Herero revolt, joined in, they were treated with brutal repression, though not genocide. Von Trotha wrote to von Schlieffen declaring that he rejected the advice of Leutwein and the "old Africans" to negotiate. They saw the Herero as useful laborers, said von Trotha. "I, however, am of an entirely different opinion. I believe that the Herero must be destroyed as a nation," repeating this sentence three times in his letter. His soldiers obeyed his murderous orders without question, some with enthusiasm (Bley, 1971: 163–4, 179; Drechsler, 1980: 156–61; Hull, 2004).

The German official military report lauded the tactics:

This bold enterprise shows up in the most brilliant light the ruthless energy of the German command in pursuing their beaten enemy. No pains, no sacrifices were spared in eliminating the last remnants of enemy resistance. Like a wounded beast the enemy was tracked down from one water-hole to the next, until finally he became the victim of his own environment. The arid Omaheke [desert] was to complete what the German army had begun: the extermination of the Herero nation. (Bley, 1971: 162)

Not everyone agreed with such exterminism. Chancellor von Bülow told the kaiser that the campaign was "contradictory to all Christian and humane principles." He added that it was also counterproductive, stiffening the African will to resist (Bley, 1971: 163). He, the Colonial Department, missionaries, and some deputies pressured for von Trotha's recall. Even some settlers were horrified. The pressure forced von Schlieffen to order a halt to the shooting of prisoners in December 1904. In November 1905 he recalled von Trotha.

This came too late to save the Herero or the Nama. Those who survived the war were put into concentration camps where malnourishment, overwork, and disease exacted a murderous toll. By 1911 only about 16,000 Herero out of the 60,000 to 80,000 population of 1903 were left. Only about 2,000 of them were men. The Nama loss rate approached "only" 50 percent (Bley, 1971: 150–1; Drechsler, 1980: 244; Hull, 2004). The Herero were wiped out as a people, since the few dispersed survivors were unable to collectively reorganize themselves. The Germans took full advantage. The kaiser approved an Expropriation Order in December 1905 authorizing the seizing of the "entire moveable and fixed property of the tribe" (Bley, 1971: 166). In 1907 all Herero land and almost all the Nama territory were declared government property, and South West Africa was declared a colony. This was a successful genocide. As Rohrbach observed, the peace of the graveyard descended upon South West Africa.

German colonial policy implied ruthless deportation and the violence necessary to achieve it, but mass murder was not envisaged. Many settlers were more radical. Their pressure hastened confrontations and cleansings, their prejudices prevented lateral aristocratic assimilation, and their provocations caused the actual Herero revolt. Some settlers then responded to the killing of 100 of their own kind with savagery. German policy would have probably led to the expropriation and breakup of the Herero nation anyway; many settlers were willing to be on the cutting edge of such policies. The settlers lost no time afterward in reaping the benefits of genocide and continuing their pressure on the remaining African lands in the colony. But they had not intended genocide either.

Genocide resulted after three escalations. First, the Herero unexpectedly revolted, overturning stable settler expectations and unleashing their worst fears and their most ferocious desires for revenge. Second, the revolt produced factional fighting back in Germany, which was won by the military over the civilian half of the state. This faction appointed General von Trotha, considered the man for exemplary repression of natives, though he had not committed genocide before. The third escalation occurred after he arrived in the colony in June 1904, when he discovered how bad the situation was and how dispersed were the colony's military forces. Then he upped the level of response until it became genocidal. His troops were sufficiently disciplined and racist to implement his orders, and von Schlieffen continued to support him during the campaign. He and the kaiser yielded up von Trotha too late, under pressure from the civilian half of the state. Genocide thus resulted suddenly through these unexpected escalations. Had the International Criminal Tribunal existed in 1905, General von Trotha would certainly have been convicted of genocide on the basis of his own testimony. If sufficient evidence could be found, so would some of his officers and men and some of the settler militiamen. Probably not the kaiser or General von Schlieffen, however, or many other civilians.

Only part of this situation conforms to my theses. The German state remained stable and secure, not fitting well into thesis 5, while the main perpetrator was a highly disciplined, professional, and modern army, though its intervention came after bottom-up settler pressures had provoked a genuinely threatening rebellion. Nonetheless, this was a dual state, contested by a traditional military authoritarian monarchy and a newer representative democracy. The Herero revolt brought factional disagreement between them and a shift of power toward the militarist faction's Plan B, exemplary repression. The final escalation was more accidental, however, as the general on the ground independently escalated to Plan C, genocide. Though this alarmed the militarist state faction, it gritted its teeth and let him continue. The civilian state faction, urged on by religious and secular humanitarians, then fought back. The elimination of Herero and Nama power then enabled settlers to resume a more aggressive version of Plan A, deportations. Again in this late colonial power we see escalation coming from modern militarism, though in this case it was abetted by de facto settler democracy.

Finally, might this have been a precursor of Hitler's Final Solution, help-ing develop distinctively German genocidal tendencies? Many see German racism as an independent cause of the Herero genocide (e.g., Cocker, 1998: 293). But was German racism greater than that of others? Bridgman notes (1981: 166–7) that all the colonial powers of this time were harshly repress-ing revolts, buttressed by self-righteous racism. General von Trotha turned such a policy into something much worse. Perhaps his autonomy might be thought distinctively German, since this army was more independent of civil-ian control than most. The link between German militarism and Nazi mil-itarism was real, as we shall see. Some of the German personnel involved later served in Turkey during World War I, being present as military advisers to Turkey during the Armenian genocide. Several members of my sample of Nazi perpetrators had lived in South West Africa or served in Turkey, though I cannot establish any direct influences through such people on the two later cases, except for Paul Rohrbach, who became a prolific defender of German imperial interests and took a close interest in the Armenian deportations. However, he ardently opposed them (Kaiser, 2001b: xxi–xxii).

In 1905 another late colonial power, with a more civilian-controlled mil-itary, was active on Mindanao in the Philippines, suppressing a rebellion among the Moros, a Muslim minority group. Mark Twain was with the American forces. He wrote, "The enemy numbered 600, including women and children, and we abolished them utterly, leaving not even a baby to cry for his mother."

CONCLUSION: PATTERNS OF COLONIAL CLEANSING

My theses have been generally supported in this chapter, though with some qualifications. Thesis 1 has been largely supported: colonial cleansings did represent the first dark side of emerging modern democracy. Where settlers enjoyed de facto self-rule, these were in local reality the most democratic regimes in the world at the time. Their murderous cleansing was usually worse than that committed by imperial authorities like the Spanish, Por-tuguese, and British Crowns, their viceroys and governors, plus Catholic and Protestant churches and orders. In California, deliberate killings escalated as soon as rule passed from the Spanish Crown and missions to American settler statehood. Most Indian nations supported the British colonial state, not the settler revolutionaries in the War of Independence. Wallace (1999: 17–18) notes that the British Empire was hierarchical and authoritarian but ethnically inclusive, whereas the Jeffersonian vision of we, the people was egalitarian and democratic but ethnically exclusive, since the people was cul-turally homogeneous, as civilized. The more the settler democracy, the more the ethnic exclusivity, the worse the treatment. However, the two late colo-nial cases, the Caucasus and South West Africa, differed. Though German settlers were also more extreme than was the colonial administration, in both cases it was a modern army whose ruthlessness seemed distinctly scientific and modern that went over the edge into massive murderous cleansing.

Contrary to the democratic peace theory discussed in Chapter 1, most cases were ethnic wars *between* democracies. Most native political institutions were actually more democratic than the settlers', and philanthropic colonists admired them for it. "The Indians are perfect republicans," said Boudinot, president of the U.S. Congress during the War of Independence. "Every man with them, is perfectly free to follow his own inclinations," said Jefferson (Sheehan, 1973: 111). Democracy was direct rather than representative, ensuring that most males (sometimes also females) enjoyed greater rights than did citizens of representative democracies. They could speak up in tribal assemblies. If they did not agree with their chiefs' final decisions, they could refuse to fight or leave a fight at any time. They could even freely leave the nation. In many councils unanimity was required, which meant that chiefs had to be more skilled at persuasion and compromise than at war. That was also true of aboriginal groups, and to a lesser degree of the Herero and Circassians. None of this applies to the Aztec or other Meso-American states, but their opponents were not democratic either. This is not to endorse a romantic image of the noble savage. Indians fought repeated and often cruel wars against each other and could be more ferocious than settlers. The Fetterman Massacre committed by Plains Indians in 1865 involved disembowelings, hacked limbs, and "private parts severed and indecently placed on the person." Even after we discount the fantastic elements in settler horror stories of Indian atrocities, several Indian nations reveled in torture as a slow, deliberate ritual and artistic process, understandably appalling whites (Brown, 1970: 137; Cocker, 1998: 201, 213–4; Sheehan, 1973: chap. 7).

Democratic peace theory excludes groups like the Indian nations from its calculations because they did not have permanent, differentiated, representative states. Yet some Indian nations did develop such states. The most fully developed was that of the Cherokee, introduced during the 1820s. The Choctaw, Chickasaw, and Creeks followed down the same representative road, though not so far, in the period 1856–67 (Champagne, 1992). It did not save them, since this only further enraged settler state governments. But democratic peace theory does not work well in the colonies. America and Australia were democratic for whites but murdered millions. Murderous ethnic cleansing, amounting at its worst to genocide, was central to the liberal modernity of the New World – committed first by the settler colonies and then by the independent "first new nations." The process continued in North America, some countries of South America, and Australia until there were virtually no more native peoples to exterminate, with reservations preserving the remnants of tribal peoples. And not states, but we, the people (aided by local politicians and popular paramilitaries) perpetrated most of these acts. The central state was called in when its army became necessary, but it was local settler democracy that made it necessary, through settlers taking the law into their own hands in cycles of land-grabbing, raiding/rebellion, and retaliation. Since armed gangs of locals could act on their own, and so polarize the situation, outsiders often had to decide whose side were they on. If even one settler was killed or a family was terrified by natives raiding their stock, outsiders found it difficult not to work up civilized outrage themselves – as we saw U.S. presidents doing.

The explanation of why settler democracies were so murderous differs from most other cases. The two ethnic groups clashed over a monopolistic economic resource, land, and most settlers did not need native labor to work it. Economic power relations were uniquely the prime mover of colonial cleansings. Yet property rights also required settlers to claim exclusive legal sovereignty over the territory at present possessed by natives (thesis 3). This economic-political clash was then exacerbated by the military/ideological imbalance of power described in thesis 4b. The settlers could eliminate the out-group with little military or moral risk to themselves. As military power became even more overwhelming from the 1860s on, a distinct military tactic of overkill, common to Generals Sherman, Miluitin, and von Trotha, began. Ideologically (except for the Caucasus), the clash concerned peoples not previously in contact. Except for Mexico, notions of difference between settlers and natives overwhelmed any ethnic and class differences on each side. Natives were easy to denigrate as savages or inferior races against whom civilizations and higher races should advance by whatever means were necessary. This ideological insulation against moral risk was unlike those found in later cleansings, since it did not mobilize ideologies of modern nationalism or modern statism. Today, colonial cleansing continues in Palestine and in the back lands of Latin America and Asia, chasing indigenous peoples from their lands. Currently, attempts are being made to bring Guatemalan politicians and generals to court for wiping out Mayan highland villages.

Yet, as thesis 6 suggests, even such instrumentally rational settlers did not perpetrate murderous cleansing as a single premeditated plan. Almost all killings came accidentally or from callousness that might not care but did not actually intend to kill. Killings came in rolling waves, involving perpetrators in different localities drawn from different generations. In each wave only a few would actually kill, and they had not intended to do so before they believed themselves provoked by illegitimate and threatening native resistance. Other, more moderate plans had been tried and failed. Now radicalization was finally necessary. Those radicalized were almost all ordinary settlers as a loosely organized social movement urging on the respected politicians and military officers to radical measures – as in thesis 8. Desperados, marginal landless men, and native policemen might be used for nastier work, but even some of their worst atrocities were genuinely popular among the settlers. The most obvious core constituency of murderous cleansing, as searched for by thesis 7 was the rolling frontier itself. That was where the settlers felt most threatened by native resistance.

There was also support for thesis 5. Murderous cleansing succeeded because settlers controlled the frontier zones, but their political institutions had not been securely institutionalized and did not have a monopoly on the military power that most modern states possess. Central states (and churches) sometimes deplored these local rolling waves of killing, but their writ did not run there. Settler democracy was loose and fluid in frontier areas. Radicals could emerge, mobilize crowds and popular local sentiment, and then commit atrocities – while duly constituted authority remained divided or vacillating. Native political institutions had also been disrupted. White aggression, deception, and treaty breaking created factionalism and crisis within tribal assemblies (Champagne, 1992). Younger war chiefs and leaders radicalized and mobilized raiding parties, bringing upon the heads of the nation massive retaliation. Institutionalized settler or Indian democracies were less likely to go over the edge into the perpetration of murderous cleansing than those destabilized and factionalized by local geopolitical crises, leaving a power vacuum in which radicals could mobilize. With these qualifications concerning intentionality and confusion in mind, genocide was the first murderous consequence in modern times of rule by we, the people – the first truly dark side of democracy. The murderous roles of Washington, Jefferson, and Jackson and the moral equivocations of Lincoln reveal how tainted were the greatest democrats of these societies.

5

Armenia, I

Into the Danger Zone

All that I have seen and heard surpasses all imagination. Speaking of 'thousand and one horrors' is very little in this case, I thought I was passing through a part of hell. The few events, which I will relate, taken here and there hastily, give but a weak idea of the lamentable and horrifying tableau. The same scenes repeat in the different localities through which I have passed, everywhere it is the same Governmental barbarism which aims at the systematic annihilation through starvation of the Armenian nation in Turkey, everywhere the same bestial inhumanity on the part of these executioners and the same tortures undergone by these victims all along the Euphrates from Meskene to Der-I-Zor.

So wrote Bernau, an American representative of the Vacuum Oil Company of New York, whose business trip across Anatolia in 1915 proved unexpectedly horrendous (*U.S. Documents*, 1993: III, 131).

This genocide was committed well before the rise of Hitler. It was not the product of "terrible Turks" or "alien Asiatics," as Europeans have often liked to believe. Instead, it was perpetrated by the "Young Turks," secular, European-style modernizing nationalists. The Ottoman Turkish state was also a player in European power politics, being in World War I allied to Germany and Austria-Hungary. This genocide emanated from Europe, even if almost all the killing occurred just over the Bosphorus in Asia. Nor was genocide the culmination of ancient ethnic hatreds, though these tensions were indeed old. The perpetrating state was the multiethnic Ottoman Empire, long tolerant of minorities. Though its tolerance was fraying somewhat in the late 19th century, this was not because of the Young Turks. Until shortly before the genocide, they were allied with the Armenians against the sultan. If the road to Auschwitz was a "twisted path," the path to Deir-el Zor was positively tortuous. I now attempt to navigate its twists and turns.[1]

---

[1] Though the views expressed in these two chapters are my own, I owe a debt of gratitude to Hilmar Kaiser, who has been most generous in assisting my research. Yet there is still a large hole in the literature. We lack frank accounts by Turks. We know more about the victims, which must bias us toward Armenian views of events. As long as Turkish governments

As in other cases in later chapters, I attempt to reconstruct the processes leading into the danger zone of murderous cleansing and then over its brink into actual mass murder. Most accounts of murderous cleansing, especially of genocide, are overorganized and overpremeditated. Early events, early decisions are too often read back from the ghastly known end result. In doing this, we may suppress the complexity and contingency of events. Though prior events may seem like a single chain of escalations, to the actors concerned they may not have been intended as such. Armenian accounts of the genocide often assume too easily that earlier events – like the emergence of Turkish organic nationalism, the 1909 massacres, the formation of the "special forces," and so on – were steps indicating Turkish premeditation of a final solution (Dadrian, 1997a, and Kévorkian, 1999, both make this assumption). They were escalations, but were they planned as such, as part of a ghastly overall sequence? We must prove it, not use hindsight to assume it.

BALKAN BACKGROUND

We must first appreciate the backdrop: a protracted struggle across the Balkans and the Caucasus, ending as the Ottoman Empire was driven by military force out of almost all of Europe and Russia. The victors were Christian states – the old Habsburg and Romanov Empires and the new nation-states of Greece, Serbia, Romania, and Bulgaria (plus one new Muslim state, Albania). It is now forgotten how many European Muslims there were – only a few pockets, like the Kosovo or Bosnian Muslims, remind us – and how they suffered as the Ottoman Empire disintegrated. I suggested in Chapter 3 that in the period of European religious cleansing, things were worse in civilizational frontier zones like Ireland and Lithuania. Now in a period of ethnonationalist cleansing, things were even worse along the frontier zone between Christianity and Islam.

The process differed between the Caucasus and the Balkans. In the Caucasus, Russia was the enemy. As Lieven (2000) points out, the Russian and Ottoman Empires shared characteristics setting them apart from the more westerly empires. They were more autocratic and backward, and their core provinces (Muscovy and Anatolia) were more backward than their most threatened border provinces (European Russia and the Balkans). Attempting to compete in the Great Power game, they were thus forced to increase the tax-extraction rate on their subjects and increase the size of the state relative to the market economy. Taxes were also easiest to extract from those without power. This made both empires more repressive over their own lower classes

continue to deny genocide, as long as Turkish archives remain largely closed, and as long as most Turkish accounts remain implausible, this bias will continue. Only Turkey is harmed by this.

and minorities. Exemplary repression was normal against all ethnic groups. These were not squeamish states.

In the Balkans all statistics of death remain contested. Most of the following figures derive from McCarthy (1995: 1, 91, 162–4, 339), who is often viewed as a scholar on the Turkish side of the debate. Yet even if we reduced his figures by as much as 50 percent, they would still horrify. He estimates that between 1821 and 1922 somewhere around 5 1/2 million Muslims were driven out of Europe and 5 million more were killed or died of disease or starvation while fleeing. Cleansing resulted from Serbian and Greek independence in the 1820s and 1830s, from Bulgarian independence in 1877, and from the Balkan wars culminating in 1912. Though the new states sometimes repressed and murdered Christian ethnic minorities, they also sought to assimilate them. Some Muslims were forcibly converted; others remained as second-class citizens – we will meet them in Chapter 12 in the former Yugoslavia. But most Muslims were killed or chased out. Between 1877 and 1887, says McCarthy, 34 percent of the Muslim population of Bulgaria fled and another 17 percent died. In the final Balkan wars of 1912–13 he estimates that 62 percent of Muslims (27 percent dead, 35 percent refugees) disappeared from the lands conquered by Greece, Serbia, and Bulgaria. This was murderous ethnic cleansing on a stupendous scale not previously seen in Europe, as the report of the Carnegie Endowment (1914) recognized. It left a bitter legacy among Ottoman Turks. Perhaps half a million Christian Ottoman subjects also fled north as refugees from similar pressures in the remaining Ottoman lands. Many Christians were also killed by Muslim perpetrators, and these massacres – like the "Bulgarian atrocities" famously denounced by Gladstone – naturally became the ones known in the Christian West.

Yet, as in most historic empires, the ethnicity of their subjects had been of little concern to Ottoman rulers as long as they were obedient. All was not multicultural sweetness and light. Any signs of rebellion by subject peoples were treated with the severity customary to such historic empires. Lieven believes Ottoman harshness was worsening, for constant defeats tightened the tax screws on the poorest inhabitants. When facing rebellions, the Ottoman Empire, just like its Assyrian predecessor, practiced the policies of what Table 1.1 termed exemplary repression, in which slaughter was a calculated strategy to maintain political compliance. In some cases (as in Assyria) this was reinforced by policed deportations (perhaps degenerating into wild deportations) of rebellious populations and their replacement (in this case) by Muslim settlers. Periodically, such imperial tactics also involved extremely callous warfare on all sides – as it now did in the Balkans. Punitive raids and deportations of the populations of whole villages and towns believed to succor the enemy revealed callous indifference to whether locals lived or died. The combination, which was no longer practiced in the far more pacified European states farther west, is what gave the Ottoman Empire its reputation for being barbarous and backward. But the Balkan Christians were doing the same thing, and in any case the combination did not amount to anything like genocide. The Ottoman Empire – like other historic empires – wanted compliant, not dead, subjects.

Bitterness against Christians and their states was not mere abstract historical memory among Muslims. It was carried in the persons of refugees. By now there were about 400,000 European Muslim refugees, *mohadjis*, in Asia Minor. Many of the refugees were educated and former property owners but were now living in abject poverty, homeless and starving (Bryce Report, 1972: 499). Their numbers were reinforced by more fleeing from Russia. Many of the Russian refugees came as tribal units, capable of furnishing rather wild, irregular soldiers. The European refugees included many intellectuals, soldiers, and former officials capable of articulating their discontent in ideological and political organizations.

By 1914 the Ottoman lands were also less multiethnic, more monoreligious than in the past. In 1820 they had been 60 percent Muslim; by 1914 they were over 80 percent Muslim. If they lost many more territories they might also be a potential nation-state, since Turks were already for the first time a near-majority of the population – and in control of the state and the army. Since the nation-state was now everywhere viewed as the most modern and powerful form of state, Turkish nationalism now emerged, often embittered. Both of these consequences might be turned against Armenians.

Nonetheless, most political leaders retained a stronger sense of an Ottoman than a nationalist identity right down to 1914. The empire's minorities had long enjoyed religious toleration and local autonomy. Each "religion of the book" had its own *millet* (a term signifying both self-rule and nation or community), administered by its church hierarchy. This was supplemented at the local level by the *taifa* system of privileges available to all minorities. Thus there remained a strong sense of distinct communal identities. Armenians, Greeks, Bulgarians, Serbs, Vlachs, Jews, and so on knew they were different from Turks or Albanians or Arabs or Kurds or Circassians (all Muslims). These identities were deep, not newly constructed. Any minority community could control most of its local affairs, including civil legal matters affecting only persons of that community. In return, unconditional political loyalty to the state was required – and any breach of this would be treated with severity. But if minorities kept their noses clean, this status was much more tolerant and closer to genuine multiculturalism than arrangements in Christian states of the period. This was no melting pot but an imperial form of consociationalism. And imperialism had some kind of cultural cement, for all who had more than local horizons also had a sense of being Ottomans.

It was not an egalitarian system. Among Muslims, formal equality was undercut by informal discrimination. Relatively backward Muslim groups like Kurds and Caucasian tribes participated in all political and military institutions, but Turks ultimately controlled them. Arab emirs and sheiks controlled their own regions, but not the center. Turkish elites dominated imperial structures. But though their ethnic identity might be Turkish, their political identity and loyalty was Ottoman. Even when Turkish nationalism surfaced in the late 19th century, it remained primarily cultural, leaving Ottoman political identity unchallenged (Poulton, 1997: chap. 3).

The Christian Greeks and Armenians were neither economically backward nor geopolitically unprotected. The Christian powers had effected a continental encircling movement, bypassing the Middle East and using control of the seas to dominate trade with Asia. Ottoman trading links with the East, hitherto crucial for its economy, decayed, and with it the Muslim merchant class. Trade depended more and more on Europe, and this trade was flourishing. Before World War I about 14 percent of GNP was exported, almost all to Europe and Russia. The two Christian minorities were better adapted to serve as intermediaries, adept at acquiring certificates of protection from foreign diplomatic agents. Thus the Christian powers helped entrench communal controls by the Christian minorities over the economy. As was normal imperial practice the world over, the Great Powers forced the Ottoman rulers to grant them free trade concessions and even extraterritorial privileges – the hated *capitulations*. The apparent upside was the willingness of the French, British, and then Germans, locked in their own interimperial rivalries, to bankroll the Ottoman state (to prevent it from collapsing into Russian or Austrian hands). But even this tactic was double-edged. To prevent the Ottomans from reneging on these loans, the great powers had secured the power to sequester about a third of the fiscal revenues of the Ottoman state at their source. These taxes were paid directly into a Public Debt Administration run by the Christian powers. Peasants' oppressive taxes went conspicuously and directly to foreigners[2]

The more prosperous parts of Constantinople and other port cities were also conspicuously foreign. Only a quarter of the printing houses were in Muslim hands; only a quarter of the newspapers and journals were written in Turkish. All 40 private bankers were non-Muslims, and the vast bulk of Istanbul's international commerce was run by Christians; they were even encroaching on inland trade with Muslim regions. Many Greeks and Armenians were growing wealthier – even buying land in Anatolia – and they seemed to some Turks to be in league with the oppressive Christian powers. Traditional consociational inequality had been disrupted. Economic power no longer buttressed political and military power. There were fewer Turks in privileged positions outside of the state and army, and very few Christians inside them. Muslims complained that when they went away to war, the Christians gained further control of land and commerce (Akcam, 1992: 61).

---

[2] These paragraphs on the economy owe much to Keyder (1987: chaps. 2, 3), Keyder et al. (1993), and Ahmed (1982: 402–5).

As in other countries, nationalism first emerged among highly educated Muslims, which here meant in the state sector. Thus the nationalists were distinctly statist in their aspirations: the state was seen as the way to economic power and development.

Yet this was not a total ethnic niche economy in which Armenians occupied only specialized economic roles. Seventy percent of the 2 million Armenians remained peasants, alongside 80 percent of the Turks. Both differed from the Greeks, most of whom lived in fairly homogeneous coastal commercial and artisanal communities controlled by the Greek Orthodox Church. The patriarch spoke for the whole Greek community. He expressed liberalism on social and economic issues but was constitutionally a conservative. Greeks favored the retention of the *millet* system that protected their privileges (and preserved the power of the patriarch). Wealthy Armenians and the Armenian patriarch often had interests and politics similar to those of their Greek counterparts, but they had less control over their communities since Armenians were very divided by class. The mass of Armenian peasants, and indeed most of the traders and artisans of the Anatolian interior, had less attachment to the *millet* system. They were also involved in a struggle over land ownership with Turks and Kurds in Anatolia, and this was turning more violent. Aspirations to control the land later encouraged them toward nationalism. The struggle over land, more than resentment of an ethnic niche economy, eventually turned conflict over economic power extremely nasty.

Thus ethnicity-religion and class bore complex relations to each other. Before World War I the former did not simply trump the latter (as in my second ethnic thesis). Prosperous Armenians ranked higher on most stratification dimensions than did poor Turks. On the other hand, in crises many Armenians and Turks could be persuaded that their economic interests might divide along ethnic lines. Ottoman politics were structured by both stratification principles. In terms of my second general thesis, the Ottoman position remained ambivalent: religion-ethnicity and class were still fairly equal as stratification axes. And right next door, in the Russian Empire, nationalist resentments were soon to become part of revolutionary class struggles. Why did this not happen also in the Ottoman Empire?

Geopolitically, however, the Christian minorities could also be plausibly linked to foreign oppressors. In their retreat through the Balkans, Ottoman leaders had long and bitter experience of betrayal by Christians. They came to regret that relatively few Turks lived in what were now the two most vulnerable border areas, the European approaches to Constantinople in eastern Thrace and those parts of eastern Anatolia adjacent to Russia. Hence Ottoman polices of resettlement were revived. From 1911 on some Bosnian refugees were resettled in Macedonia, displacing local Christians (Derogy, 1986: 36). From 1913 on, Greeks were replaced as settlers in the Balkan approaches. The settlers were mainly Turkish refugees from the lost territories. Considerable violence was used in these displacements, though it was seen by its perpetrators as retaliation for the worse things that had recently happened to Balkan Muslims.

Again, however, the geopolitical situation of the two Christian communities differed. Greeks had their own neighboring homeland state, Greece, which could intercede diplomatically for them, backed by the European powers – whose statesmen spoke (classical) Greek! Greeks had a choice. If they wanted economic prosperity, they could stay where they were. If they wanted their own state, they could move next door. There was little danger that Greeks within the empire would seek to create their own state. If the *millet* system failed, some might seek irredentist unity of their coastal communities with Greece. But though Greece was nibbling away at Turkish islands, it could not realistically invade the mainland to protect Ottoman Greeks. It needed World War I and Ottoman collapse to produce a Greek invasion and more murderous treatment of Ottoman Greeks in retaliation.

Armenians were not so protected (nor was the smaller Maronite Christian community). Equally spread between the Ottoman and Russian Empires, they had no state anywhere. Any Armenian state would have to be carved out of Turkish or Russian lands. Though Russia had often persecuted its own Armenian minority (and this had generated the first Armenian nationalist movements), Russian governments now began to consider exploiting the discontent of Armenians living within the Ottoman Empire. Russian expansion now constituted the greatest threat to the survival of the Ottoman Empire. One of its tactics might be to foment an Armenian fifth column inside Turkey. Russian leaders began to declare that Armenians were fellow Christians, to be protected. The Treaty of San Stefano in 1878 had ratified Russian seizure of a slice of eastern Anatolia, but it also obliged the Ottomans to effect reforms in the eastern Anatolian provinces, guaranteeing Armenian security there. International treaties now routinely contained clauses guaranteeing human rights for Christians. Was this only for Christians, asked many Turks? One Armenian survivor remembers his uncle predicting the consequences: "the more we persisted in complaining to the Christian nations, the more determined the Turks became to exterminate the Armenian Nations" (Kazanjian, 1989: 351). Thus Armenian–Turkish relations involved geopolitical as well as economic power tensions.

The suspicion that Armenians might not be loyal subjects seemed confirmed when some caught the nationalist virus sweeping across Europe. Armenian nationalists had gone to work in Russia in the usual way, standardizing the language and the literary canon, kindling memories and myths of the medieval Armenian state, hoping to re-create a state out of Russian and Turkish territories. Nationalism was slower to catch on in the Ottoman Empire because of the *millet* system. Most wealthy Armenian community leaders and the Armenian Orthodox patriarch remained committed to communal autonomy within the Ottoman Empire. They were privileged by it. But the *ideal* of most younger and poorer politicized Armenians was now focusing on an independent state. Scattered local risings began in Anatolia in the 1860s. The more conservative nationalists looked to the tsar for support, liberals to Russian reformers, and a few radicals, focusing on the land issue, drew closer to Russian revolutionaries and began to arm themselves.

Ottoman government traditions made them more likely to repress than conciliate such demands. In any case, they had seen it all before (as Dadrian, 1995, emphasizes). They had long and bitter experience of Christian minorities demanding political reforms, supported by the Christian powers. All across the Balkans, Serb, Bulgarian, Greek, and Albanian reformers had at first only demanded regional autonomy, to which the empire had often responded positively. "No region enjoyed a larger measure of administrative autonomy than the island of Crete," says Djemal Pasha in his memoirs. "But did we succeed in compelling the Cretans to abandon their hope of uniting with Greece?" No, he answers bitterly, nor did we in Rumelia, absorbed by Bulgaria, or Egypt, occupied by the British. Abetted by the Christian powers, all such privileged territories had seized their independence or been absorbed by the Christian powers – in the process killing and expelling many Muslims. Djemal sees this as a general modern tendency. Political decentralization had protected the Habsburg Empire no more than it did the Ottomans. Nationalism, he concludes, must be countered with "firmness" and centralization, "Ottoman unity," led by the core imperial people, Turks. Armenia can only be held this way, he concludes (1922: 250–1). Though Turkish leaders knew that almost all Armenians were loyal subjects, they doubted this would last. Indeed, it would need great originality from both Armenian and Turkish politicians to avoid taking the Balkan route. It needed a more egalitarian consociationalism than the old *millet* system provided. Unfortunately, both groups' education in modernity would lead them away from consociationalism toward the ideal of the organic nation-state.

In the 19th century intercommunal conflict intensified in the course of struggles for political democracy. Ottoman rulers adopted divide-and-rule tactics between religious/ethnic communities in order to preserve their personal absolutism. On occasion they asked Christian communities to pay for the costs of repressing Turkish peasant revolts, in return confirming their privileges. In 1839 a liberal grand vizier yielded to class pressure from below by granting formal equality before the law. This was reconfirmed in 1856. But this was a breach of Islamic law and Ottoman tradition, and it alienated many Turks, accustomed to legal privileges. Either policy could stir ethnic resentment, since each could be seen as increasing the privileges of already economically privileged Christians. This further allowed sultans to deflect discontent over class-rooted political issues by scapegoating resented minorities – the same policy that the tsars were practicing vis-à-vis the Jews. The sultans exacerbated ethnic tensions toward pogroms.

The first major pogrom was aimed at the Maronite Christian community of Lebanon and Syria in 1856–60. There 40,000 people were killed, and only French military intervention stopped the pogrom. Abdulhamit II, the "red [i.e., the bloody] sultan," ruling from 1876 to 1909, sought to modernize through greater centralization, legitimated by pan-Islamicism. He extended education, sought to standardize it in Ottoman Turkish (which had considerable Arab and Persian elements), and built up the army. He abolished legal equality and the constitution and created his own "Hamidian" army regiments, largely Kurdish, to specialize in domestic repression. Their activities allowed more land-grabbing by Turks and Kurds. Armenian nationalist groups began to organize their own violence from the 1870s. In 1894 some Armenian communities refused to pay taxes to both the Ottoman authorities and local Kurdish chiefs. Their agitation produced massive exemplary repression in which an enormous number of Armenians died (between 60,000 and 150,000). It was aimed at towns in Cilicia and the East where Armenian nationalist agitation was strongest, and it fed off the land dispute. Class resentment directed against the Armenians was visible in the frenzied looting that accompanied the urban massacres. Then the sultan sent in Hamidian regiments, ostensibly to separate the two sides but actually intensifying the killing. Yet, like the Jews in imperial Russia, the Armenians were something of a safety valve for the regime. Having used massacres to bolster his support, the sultan turned the valve off again, discouraging further murders. Liberal Turks and Armenians were both later to remember this terrible pogrom as decisive in alienating the Armenian community (Izzet Pasa, 1992; Miller & Miller, 1993: 61). This was occurring before Turkish nationalists got anywhere near power. Indeed, they opposed it. As we shall see, the Turkish and Armenian nationalists were allies until very late.

THE RISE OF TURKISH NATIONALISM

An empire in such retreat will encounter internal discontent and demands for reform. There were tax revolts, strikes, and food riots in the big cities, and army mutinies by unpaid and sometimes starving soldiers. Most of the reformers were referred to as "Young Turks," an expression that lives on in our language as indicating youthful, determined, and rather attractive radical reformers. However, in the early stages of the reform movement, the label is not quite appropriate, since most adherents considered themselves more Ottoman than Turkish. "Ottoman liberalism" predominated among them. This demanded Western-style modernization: constitutional monarchy, equality before the law, an extension of education and other public services, and some recognition of local cultural autonomy – and, more problematically, political autonomy for minorities.

But liberalism had three defects. First, there was a tension between individual and communal rights. This tension was never resolved by liberals, and it weakened their cohesion. Second, to the extent that they focused on local communal rights, they saw them as confederal rather than consociational – that is, minority rights were to be entrenched in local communal autonomies more than in the central state. This is the normal bias of liberalism. Yet confederalism was not generally favored amid modernizing states in the 19th or early 20th centuries. Strong centralized states were considered essential to their geopolitical defense. Third, liberals were supporting the same types of reform as those demanded by the foreign powers. Thus they sometimes seemed to be supporting foreign interventions against the sultan and could be labeled as stooges of the imperial oppressors. This was all the easier because liberalism was rather secular, Western, and appeared non-Islamic.

Such abuse was hurled by varied groups – Islamicists, palace loyalists, and another growing Young Turk faction favoring a more centralized and eventually a nationalist state, standing firm against foreigners. Yet faction divisions had not yet hardened. The groups overlapped in membership and recruited among the same core constituency of highly educated Muslims in the bureaucracy, education system, and army. Though at the Young Turk Congress of 1902 (held by exiles abroad) the battle lines were clearly drawn, liberals and radicals continued joint action against the conservative palace.

Both factions were greatly influenced by European political ideas. In Europe liberalism and nationalism were already dominant, alongside two statist currents of thought, French positivist social engineering and German Listian economics. Adapting these ideological currents to the Ottoman experience of peripheral exploitation at the hands of the imperial liberal powers meant that nationalism and statism gradually rose at the expense of liberalism. This was a movement of officials, teachers, and officers, not merchants and manufacturers. The events of 1905 helped redirect this trend down more Asiatic channels. An Asian power, Japan, inflicted the first decisive modern defeat on a European power – the Ottomans' great enemy, Russia. Japan had adapted more nationalist and statist influences than liberal ones. Delighted by the spectacle of Asians humiliating Europeans, many Young Turks resolved to do likewise.

Since the intelligentsia was so influenced by global nationalist thought, the early Turkish nationalist theorists were actually cosmopolitans. Those educated abroad, especially in France, were prominent, and so were ex-Balkan and ex-Russian Muslims who did not at first consider themselves Turks at all. So were Jews, especially those from the cosmopolitan city of Salonika. Socialism and freemasonry also contributed to Turkish nationalism. Some leading nationalist intellectuals were of mixed ethnicity themselves (Turkish/Kurdish, Turkish/Tartar, Bulgarian/Turkish, etc.). Maybe their personal experience with the multiethnic tensions of the empire made them first gravitate toward nationalism (as Zürcher, 1998: 136–7, suggests). But these were no longer isolated peripheries. Kurdish chiefs got the news of the sinking of the Russian fleet the next day, over the telegraph.

The most influential theorist was Gökalp (Astourian, 1995: 28–9; Landau, 1995: 37; Melson, 1992: 166–7). Half-Kurdish, he was born in 1876 in Diyarbakir in eastern Anatolia. He was a veterinary college graduate, a poet, and a professor of sociology, much influenced by Durkheim and Tönnies. He argued that societies had developed through three historical stages. First had come tribal communities, in which language and race generated the normative and ritual solidarity that (like Durkheim) he believed was the core of any society. The tribal stage had been followed by a broader religious solidarity – in this region, Islam. Finally came the third, modern stage, in which normative solidarity rested on the culture of the nation and the institutions of the nation-state. Only national culture and state corporatism could transcend class conflict and the *mutual parasitism* that he perceived an expanding division of labor had brought to a multiethnic society. A Greek/Armenian bourgeoisie and a Turkish bureaucracy were parasitic on each other, and both preyed on the poor Anatolian peasant. Only the nation, he concluded, could provide what Durkheim had termed a *collective conscience*, a moral order capable of holding together a modern society with its sprawling division of labor.[3] Gökalp, drawing from Tönnies, also distinguished between culture (norms, values, and practices within a community) and civilization (a rational, international system of scientific and technological knowledge). Turkish culture was still trapped within the medieval civilization of Islam and Byzantine politics. This needed replacing with European scientific-industrial civilization. But national pride could be reconciled with modernity. Turks could modernize while keeping their distinctive cultural traditions. Gökalp was able to popularize his sociological theory through his poetry, his main source of influence among educated Turks.[4]

His concept of the nation became more Turkish than Ottoman. Given Ottoman traditions, reinforced by the threatening geopolitical context, he saw national norms as decidedly martial and statist, which appealed to younger bureaucrats and officers. But he denounced Ottoman multiethnicity for having stifled the Turkish national spirit. Turks may have won the wars, but they lost the peace by assimilating to the culture of the conquered – a common refrain among imperial revisionists (e.g., Germans and Serbs encountered later in this book).

> We succeeded in conquering many places
> But spiritually we were conquered in all of them.

---

[3] Durkheim himself had suggested that the nation might supplant God as the core of society's moral and ritual order. He had also written at length about countering anomic and disintegrating tendencies within the division of labor with the aid of syndicalist corporations. But he never quite satisfied himself that he had found the answer to his original question: "how do modern societies hold together?" As a liberal, he would have been unhappy with Gökalp's nationalist solution – and with later fascist extensions of his corporatism.

[4] Dadrian (1997b: 239–40) describes the Young Turks as "devoid of any cultivated ideological footing," a "gang" of "bloodthirsty adventurers" – useful in ascribing to them genocidal premeditation but not to understanding their ideals or their appeal.

Assimilation must be rejected. Christian minorities could be allowed Turkish citizenship but not nationality, for they "would remain a foreign body in the national Turkish state." The Turkish nation-state required military discipline:

> What is duty? A voice that comes down from the throne of God,
> Reverberating the consciousness of my nation
> I am a soldier, it is my commander,
> I obey without question all its orders.
> With closed eyes
> I carry out my duties

These sentiments are rather organicist, excluding minorities from full membership in the nation. Militarist tendencies are understandable given the geopolitical position of the country.

Another influential theorist was Agaoglu, born Agayev to a prosperous Muslim family in Russian Azerbaijan in 1869. As a young man he identified himself not as a Turk but as a Persian – as did many educated Muslims proud of the past glories of Persian culture. But he became aware of the exploitation in Russia of local Turks, economically deprived and politically excluded. His early writings demanded political rights for Turks in Russia, though without using nationalist terminology. He then studied in Paris and was influenced by Renan's view of nationalism stressing religion and the Aryan race. This led Agaoglu to identify Shi-ite Islam and Persian ethnic identity as the keys to national modernization (Persians were Aryans; Turks were not). But back in Azerbaijan he was shocked by the atrocities committed by Russians and Armenians against local Turks in the 1905 revolution. He believed Armenians did not want Turks to achieve equality with them. The 1908 coup in Turkey (see later) made him a Young Turk. He became inspector of education, dropping Persian and Islamic in favor of a Turkish identity. His change of name symbolized his embrace of Turkism. His nationalism was now quite similar to Gökalp's. It had been the experience of Russian oppression and divide-and-rule, setting Muslim against Christian minorities, that led such emigres to pioneer Turkish nationalism. Though few in numbers, these writers dominated some of the emerging Turkish nationalist journals (Arai, 1992: 55; Landau, 1995: 35–6; Poulton, 1997: 68–75; Shissler, 2003).

The significance of these intellectuals derived from their ability to give broader meaning and legitimacy to the modernizing aspirations of a highly educated generation of youngish men staffing the middle levels of the civilian and military bureaucracy. The main connection was through the educational institutions in which they taught, especially the Civil Service Academy (the Mülkiye), the War Academy, and the Military Medical College, all located in Constantinople. Their graduates adapted the nationalist ideas learned there to the more worldly domains of the army and provincial administration, especially in the remaining but threatened European provinces of Macedonia and Thrace. Both Gökalp and Agaoglu were honored by the movement and became members of the Central Committee of the Committee of Union and Progress (the CUP), the semisecret ruling body of what gradually became the more radical nationalist wing of the Young Turks, sometimes called Ittihadists (Unionists).

The Ittihadists then moved unevenly toward three main types of policy. First came a theory of ideological power. Reformers said that a modern state required new cultural and educational cement. They were fervent believers in meritocracy based on the acquisition of modern technical and scientific knowledge. This also made them secular. They were hardly strong enough to attack Islam, and in any case they were aware of the fact that it was Islam that gave the empire a powerful ideological cement. But on education and the language issue they revealed their true nationalist colors. They pressed for a simplified Turkish language and literature, purged of Persian and Arabic elements, with poetry rendered in a meter more suitable to mass education because it was better attuned to actual Turkish speech. Gökalp's own popular poetry exemplified this. Language issues dominated the nationalist journals (Arai, 1992). They hoped to make schooling free, compulsory, and in the modernized Turkish language. Turkish was proclaimed as the only language of instruction, a typical forcible assimilation policy of organic nationalists.

The movement was itself meritocratic. Take the three men who later became its "triumvirs." Talaat Pasha was from a family of Bulgarian converts. His mother held the despised occupation of a layer-out of corpses. He began his career as a teacher of Turkish in a Jewish school and then became a government postal and telegraph clerk. He rose to become a senior telegraph official. Enver Pasha was the son of a lower railway official, born in a poor part of Constantinople. He attended military school and was a star pupil. He rapidly rose on his abilities through the officer corps. Djemal Pasha's family was also humble – his grandfather had been the sultan's hangman, his father was a soldier. He also did well at military college and rose rapidly. But though the Ottoman Empire lacked a true aristocracy, its elite had modernized by acquiring a veneer of Western culture, the French language, and diplomatic graces rather than technocratic knowledge. This brought generational status conflict with the Young Turk meritocrats. The German Stuermer wrote snootily, "The Turks of decent birth are disgusted at these parvenus" (1917: 255; cf. Barton, 1998: 190–1; Derogy, 1986: 34–9; Mardin, 1971: 201; Shaw, 1977: chap. 4). Young Turk meritocratic ideals were popular, but their language policy alienated Albanian, Arab, and Christian sympathizers. As these left the movement, it became more committed to Turkification.

Second came a theory of economic power, mostly articulated after about 1910. The Ittihadists turned away from economic liberalism toward the cultivation of a *national economy* led by an *organic national bourgeoisie* coordinated by the state to achieve development. Borrowing from German economists in the tradition of Friedrich List, they emphasized state intervention, protection, abolition of the free trade capitulations, and boy-cotts of "foreign" enterprises, which mostly meant Christians. Though this was popular among many Muslims, it alienated Greeks and Armenians and it encountered resistance from liberals. It only became a prominent policy following successful mass boycotts of Greek and Armenian shops during 1912–13 (Adanir, 1998: 59–60; Kaiser, 1997; Keyder, 1987: 53–4; Zürcher, 1998: 127–31). This, coupled with the land issue, channeled class resent-ments toward ethnonationalism.

Third came a theory of military and political power stressing technoc-racy and centralization, with Germany again the model. Technocracy was embraced by all reformers; centralization appealed more to Turks than to minorities. The Young Turks formally embraced democratic representative ideals but, like the liberals, recognized that the empire was a long way from the ideal. Some also began to argue that only Turks or Muslims would ulti-mately be willing to defend the Ottoman state against its enemies. This led in the organic nationalist direction of allowing only Turks to be full political citizens. But it probably mattered more that in terms of practical action, the movement was being steered away from democracy. Its core lay in the army, Islamic and mostly Turkish. Then the Balkan and North African campaigns converted some Yonng Turk officers to the violent paramilitarism of a peo-ple's war. Enver's Young Turk squads of guerrillas (*fedais*) began waging callous warfare in the Balkan hills. As geopolitical pressure on the empire mounted, radicals also suggested deporting ethnic minorities of doubtful loyalty from strategic regions and resettling Turks in their place.

All these policies were seen, nonetheless, as reformist, and as being aimed against the palace. Yet Armenians, Greeks, Arabs, and Turkish liberals ob-jected to some of them, and they threatened all those with entrenched priv-ileges in the old regime, including Christian elites (Astourian, 1995: 27–31; Shaw, 1977: 301–4). The Turkish nationalists appeared surprised by the strength of the reaction. They seemed fairly free of ethnic prejudice. Their journals talked at length about ethnic diversity but rarely mentioned eth-nic conflict (Arai, 1992). Some articles recommended assimilation into a single Turkish/Ottoman identity, but the only force envisaged was compul-sory teaching of Turkish. As yet there was no confrontation between rival ethnonationalists claiming the same territorial area (as in my third thesis).

YOUNG TURK RADICALIZATION, 1908–13

By 1906 the sultan's regime was unpopular, its fiscal resources stretched, provoking tax revolts, food riots, and demonstrations by unpaid soldiers. The palace could not command enough loyalists to repress these challenges. Reformers demanding the restoration of constitutional rule began to point to the 1905–6 revolutions in Russia and Iran as models. Radical nationalists were involved in many of these disturbances, and CUP branches and *hearths*, Turkish nationalist cultural associations, expanded in Anatolia. They collaborated more with Armenian than with Greek or liberal factions, since they shared their radicalism on constitutional and taxation issues (Ahmad, 1982; Kansu, 1997: 29–72, 78–9). CUP *fedais* and Armenian nationalists fought alongside each other in skirmishes in the eastern Anatolian city of Van against Ottoman troops. Arab sheikhs were more reactionary, since the Islamic/tribal status of the caliph/sultan bolstered their own power. Thus the political lineup at this stage was not between Muslims and Christians. The CUP and Armenian nationalists were allies, if wary ones.

The Ittihadist power base lay in the junior and mid-level officer corps of the European army, quartered in Salonika, Edine (formerly Adrianople), and Monastir (now Bitola in Macedonia). Sixty-three percent of the 505 CUP members in Salonika were officers. These were almost entirely Muslim and predominantly Turkish. Since this was an illegal organization, they organized clandestinely, gathering weapons and soldiers. In 1908 they marched on Constantinople. Aided by some street demonstrations, they pulled off a half-coup against Sultan Abdulhamit, not deposing but sidelining him (Kansu, 1997: 87–113, 221). To describe these events as a revolution would be accurate only in a limited ideological sense. There was little pressure from below, only a little violence and little class content to the Young Turk demands. This was faction fighting among military and political elites, leaving the masses unchanged. Though the Young Turks favored a constitutional and fairly pacific regime, they did not intend the "primitive and superstitious" people to rule. Rather, meritocratic reforms and secularization would gradually civilize the country and make democracy possible (Mardin, 1971). Enver Pasha expressed the new regime's ideals in democratic and rather multicultural terms:

Today arbitrary government has disappeared. We are all brothers. There are no longer in Turkey Bulgarians, Greeks, Servians, Rumanians, Mussulmans, Jews. Under the same blue sky we are all proud to be Ottomans. (Morgenthau, 1918: 18)

Some Greek, Albanian, and Bulgarian nationalist bands voluntarily laid down their arms in the months following the coup (Kansu, 1997: 100–1). The CUP and progressive Christians were allies, since they all favored constitutional rule. There were purges of corrupt civil servants, the constitution was restored, and parties were allowed to organize openly. Semidemocratic elections were held. Male taxpayers over the age of 25 voted for an electoral college whose members were generally local notables. These then voted for the actual deputies. This involved a popular vote, but local notables had preponderant influence upon the result. The parliament then shared power with an executive. This semidemocratic system was still essentially in operation in 1915. Table 5.1 details the election results.

It should be noted, however, that party labels were shallow and fluid. Young Turk candidates were often the same old local notables now jumping on the bandwagon of modernity. Some deputies changed sides once they

TABLE 5.1 *Deputies Elected to the Ottoman Parliament in 1908: Party Grouping by Ethnicity (numbers)*

Ethnicity	CUP Young Turks	Independent Centrists	Monarchist Conservatives	Total
Turks	43	83	27	153
Arabs/Kurds	1	30	22	53
Albanians	2	10	15	27
Bulgarians/Serbs	0	8	0	8
Greeks	0	22		22
Armenians	4	7	0	11
Jews	3	1	0	4
TOTAL	53	c.153	c.72	278

Source: Calculated from Kansu (1997: appendix 1). My calculations of Kansu's data produce slightly different totals of overall party strength than he gives on pages 238–9. There were also at least three deputies whose party affiliation and ethnicity are unknown (though the overall number of deputies is not known with certainty). Turks, Arabs, Kurds, and Albanians were Muslims. Bulgarians, Serbs, Greeks, and Armenians were Christians. The Greek deputies mostly voted as a bloc. They tended to be centrists on social and economic issues but conservative in their support of the monarchy and the *millet* system.

were elected, embracing a conservatism they had eschewed on the popular hustings. Table 5.1 shows that independent centrists dominated, but not as a cohesive group. Most CUP (Young Turk) deputies were Turks, yet the CUP also got many Jewish, Armenian, and Albanian votes and was allied with Bulgarian and Armenian socialists. It received little support from Greeks, who wished to retain their traditional *millet* privileges, or from Arabs or Kurds, whose leaders were more attached to the palace. The CUP did best in Europe and in western Anatolia. In eastern Anatolia, Armenian candidates who might have offered support to the CUP were defeated by conservative Turkish or Kurdish candidates (Ahmad, 1982: 405–21). The CUP appealed to the more modern, less religious, parts of the empire and was the ally of other ethnonationalists. Almost two-thirds of the CUP deputies were officials or teachers compared to less than a third of the other deputies.[5] Non-CUP men were more likely to be lawyers and propertied notables (including Arab sheiks). Islamic muftis and ulemas were found in all parties, including the CUP, though most of the Islamic establishment supported the palace. We see again the Young Turk bureaucratic/educational core.

Parliament lacked a consensus. The CUP could steer some legislation through, since it was the most cohesive group and could pick up support among independents. But everything had to be laboriously negotiated, often in return for corrupt favors. The CUP retained its multiethnic support, while

[5] Regular military officers were banned from standing as candidates, though a few deputies were officers who were also teachers at military colleges.

the powers of the palace were being reduced. But when it came to positive reforms, difficulties arose. The CUP favored more state centralization and Turkish-only education, but Christians and many other Muslims did not. Many Christian, Albanian, and Arab politicians showed their nationalist colors only after the old regime was defeated. Nonetheless, there were repeated attempts at conciliation and compromise right down to 1913, since the Young Turks needed all the allies they could get. They were few, with little influence in many parts of the empire. In most towns they had to continue ruling through local notables and Muslim clerics. In some places even local CUP leaders might have little commitment to Young Turk ideals. Though purges increased the number of reformers in the political and military bureaucracy, even their hold over the European army was shaky. Many of these highly educated officers had never actually served in combat, and their ability to control their men was limited. In the ethnic sphere, therefore, their Plan A remained (in terms of the categories of Table 1.1) an uneasy multiculturalism: alliance with all the sultan's enemies, including the Armenians.

But all hell broke loose next year. Army mutinies were followed in April 1909 by murderous cleansing in Cilicia, around the city of Adana. Over 20,000 Armenians (plus about 1,000 Muslims) were massacred by mobs. It is not entirely clear who organized this. There is no evidence linking the massacres to the sultan or any other higher authority in Constantinople. Some contemporaries believed that a radical Salonika faction of the CUP, led by Dr. Nazim (of whom more later), were implicated in encouraging them (Dadrian, 1997b: 246-7). Dadrian (1992: 274-5) alleges that the massacres were a test of the CUP's already mature plans for genocide but produces no real evidence for this statement. Kévorkian's research (1999) shows that several local Young Turk leaders (including the main Ittihadist newspaper in Adana and the CUP branch heads in Adana and Tarsus) were among the instigators, along with conservative politicians and officials and several clerics. These local notables claimed that Armenians were preparing an armed rebellion, and some of them may have genuinely believed this, though it was probably not true. Since they controlled information sent to the capital, for a time the authorities in Constantinople probably believed this too.

The massacres died down but then restarted when soldiers sent to quell the massacres began joining in after unknown persons fired on them. The local situation had been very tense. Adana was an ethnically divided city experiencing industrial development. Greeks contributed most big capitalists, Armenians most small businessmen, professionals, and skilled workers. Muslims resented Christian economic power. Armenians who had fled abroad during earlier persecutions were now also returning to claim their property, seized by Turks and Kurds. During 1908-9 many Muslim refugees from both Europe and the Caucausus were also being resettled in the area.

So there was a strong economic power component to this ethnic/religious conflict.

The events in Adana resembled some of the deadly riots that have recently broken out across the Indian subcontinent (as documented by Brass, 1997, and Tambiah, 1996, and which I discuss in Chapter 16). There were the same inflamed local tensions, the same fanatics with their own malevolent goals, similar exploitable incidents (in this case, an Armenian youth shot dead two of the Turkish thugs who had attacked him), similar gullible belief in the grossest rumors, and similar complicity by local politicians and police and military authorities. What set the Adana incident apart, and made for such a terrible massacre, was that (unlike the Indian subcontinent) higher state echelons did not intervene decisively to quell the massacres or afterward punish the guilty. Kévorkian suspects (but cannot prove) that the Young Turk regime was involved from the start. I am more inclined to believe that the riots escalated mainly because of the weakness and divisions in the regime. The Young Turks were of various stripes, and they still needed to cooperate with liberals, Islamicists, and palace loyalists. They were warier of alienating them than the Christians. Though the Young Turks were formally allied to the Armenians, they reasoned that unlike Turkish factions, Armenians had nowhere else to go. Thus they were slow to come to the aid of the Armenian community. Their divisions were also revealed in the three separate inquiry commissions set up: a court martial whitewashed the authorities and blamed the Armenians for the troubles, and the members of the two parliamentary inquiries between them produced three rather different reports. The cabinet exonerated Armenians, who it declared were "the victims of the spread of unfounded suspicions and provocations."

After the fact, there was a regime conspiracy. Both Dadrian and Kévorkian imply that this supports the notion that the regime had conspired to perpetrate the massacres. But cover-ups are common, and they do not mean that the regime was itself guilty of the act being covered up. Most Turkish politicians wanted to sweep the atrocity under the carpet. Only a few (egged on by Armenian and Greek politicians) sought to prosecute the leading perpetrators. The compromise was to execute some perpetrators of the second rank while punishing the leading perpetrators with a slap on the wrist. Those military officers who were complicit in the massacres actually seem to have received better subsequent postings than those who tried to stop them.

This sorry aftermath preserved cooperation among Turks but was a disaster for interethnic relations. "Don't trust Turkish governments" was the lesson drawn by most Armenians, badly denting future negotiations with the Young Turks (see also Ahmad, 1982: 421–3; MacFie, 1998: chap. 2). Growing friction with Armenians also made life more difficult for CUP moderates. The party's compromises with palace conservatives and liberals strengthened a Turkish/Islamic identity as the lowest common denominator of the regime, weakening its attachment to democracy. All this strained the alliance between Young Turks and Armenians.

The creaky coalition regime then suffered geopolitical disaster. Austria annexed Bosnia-Herzegovina, Bulgaria proclaimed full independence, and Crete joined Greece. This series of disasters strengthened the hand of central-izers and of Turkish nationalists/Islamicists against liberals and Christians – a stronger, more loyal state was needed, more said. CUP commitment to democracy was now secondary to defense of the state. But their centralizing policies – increasing state powers over conscription and taxation and enforc-ing a Turkish language policy – were not specifically aimed at Christians. Indeed, it was Albanians (some of them Young Turks) who in 1911 launched the first insurrection against centralization, followed by risings by Yemeni tribal chiefs. In response the CUP moderated its centralization policies.

Italy exploited this moment of Ottoman weakness by invading its North African provinces. The coalition government sought appeasement, but some CUP army men broke ranks. They raised volunteer *fedais*, recruited support from Arab chiefs, and thrust back the Italian Army to a narrow coastal strip of territory. This was a tremendous success for the radicals, seem-ing to demonstrate the military power a combined Turkish/Islamicist ide-ology could mobilize in guerrilla warfare against Christian armies. But most Young Turk leaders remained pragmatic politicians, attracted to a variety of Turkish, Ottomanist, and pan-Islamic ideas, blending them flexibly to deal with opposition and stay in power. Moreover, minority issues were not their most pressing problem. They were a by-product of the two main tasks: to secure a constitutional regime against the palace and to secure a stronger state against the Great Powers. Defeats and territorial losses escalated do-mestic conflict to riots and murder in the streets. Defeat tended to discredit whichever group was then fronting the regime. The palace conservatives were overthrown by a half-coup mounted by liberal officers. The Ittihadists feared for their own lives. But with Islamicists also weakened, secular nationalism strengthened. When the liberals were forced by the Great Powers to deliver the city of Edine to Bulgaria in January 1913, they were overthrown by an Ittihadist coup.

The Young Turk coup installed rule by three young triumvirs: Enver (age only 31), Talaat (age 39), and Djemal Pasha (age 41). Ambassador Morgenthau called them a "roughshod crew" (1918: 21), and they had now effectively abandoned democracy. In Constantinople, Djemal was particu-larly ruthless in his repression of opposition. The palace defeated, they had little in common with Christian decentralizers, and they had the military and police powers to repress them. We can see this period from 1908 to 1913 as a period in which the Young Turks grew up and learned the harsh realities of life. From idealism, the exigencies of coups, risings, and wars had lured them tactically into the darker side of traditional Ottoman rule – exemplary repression by military and police authorities, legitimated by reasons of state. The nationalists had been toughened.

So they ruthlessly radicalized the state. Several Ittihadists who were to emerge later as key organizers of genocide now received crucial appointments and promotions within the security apparatuses (Dadrian, 1997b: 259; Kaiser, 2000b). Army purges shed 1,100 unsympathetic officers; others were shunted sideways – including Mustapha Kemal, the officer who under the name Ataturk later ruled his country. This was to remove him from significant participation in the genocide. The Ittihadist youth wing now received military training from the army (Astourian, 1995: 26; Dadrian, 1995: 195–8, 214; Zürcher, 1998: 19–44; 1998: 90–115). The sultan was reduced to a rubber stamp. The cabinet still contained moderates and non-Turks – a Jew converted to Islam, a Circassian, a Christian Arab, and an Armenian. But they occupied "softer" offices – finances, public works, commerce and agriculture, and posts and telegraphs (Morgenthau, 1918: 121). The repressive heart of the state had been seized by nationalists. Some were contemplating extreme measures to achieve their desired goals. This was becoming a radicalized party-state.

In terms of the model laid out in Chapter 1, by 1913 the Ottoman Empire was entering the danger zone of murderous ethnic cleansing. Political leaders amid two ethnic/religious groups were beginning to lay claim to rival states in the same terrain (my third thesis). One possessed the existing state; the other had a historical memory/myth of its own state, buttressed by half-plausible means of attaining it again with help from a neighboring power. The Young Turks were now steering into organic nationalism and radicalizing the repressive heart of the state. Economic resentments were being channeled away from class toward ethnonationalist conflict (my second thesis). The two communities might be on a collision course.

Their progress toward collision had been erratic, and it remained asymmetric. On the Turkish side, radical organic nationalists now controlled the core of the state. A few Armenians sought national independence, some through terrorism. It took only a few of them to bomb, seize banks, and assassinate Turks and conservative Armenians. Sultan Abdulhamit himself had narrowly escaped assassination in 1905. Since this was secretive terrorism, the authorities had difficulty in responding with precise selective repression. Some repressive measures fell on Armenians more generally, alienating more of them. Some Turks reasoned, as they had in the past, that repression would work and bring not love but compliance from Armenians. Others faced with modern nationalist dissidents were less confident, but believed they had seen it all before. Far more Armenians, they believed, would soon embrace revolutionary nationalism – unless they destroyed it now. But the measures had to be more systematic than in the past. Hence a more radical Plan B began to emerge. Some Turks were considering a preemptive strike of forcible "Turkification." Yet even if collision was now likely, it might not be more deadly than traditional tactics of exemplary repression plus Turkification – repress the few hotbeds of radical Armenians to cow the rest into compliance and then Turkify them. But things did get worse, again the result of unexpected geopolitical pressure.

DESCENT TOWARD MURDEROUS CLEANSING

Radical Ittihadists were now discussing variant forms of a Plan B, forcible Turkification. The most incriminating Young Turk statements of the period 1910–14 refer to the desire to achieve Turkification or "Ottomanism," if necessary by force or military means. There is no reason to believe this meant genocide; more likely the radicals were contemplating some combination of coerced assimilation, selective repression, and limited deportations. This policy firmed up and acquired more supporters among the Young Turks through the military power pressures exerted by two wars following in quick succession. In two years the Ottoman Empire was to go right through the danger zone and over the edge into genocide. The Balkan wars ended in humiliating peace terms imposed by the Great Powers in February 1914. Turkish forces, led by Enver Pasha, had been retaking territory in Thrace, but the treaties deprived them of the gains and also demanded more autonomy for the Armenian communities. For the first time this was to be supervised by two inspectors appointed by the Great Powers. Armenian reformers were identified as collaborators with Great Powers imposing national humiliation on Turks. The loss of territories ratified by the peace treaties reduced the ethnic-religious diversity of the Empire. Ottomanism had failed and was less relevant to the rump state anyway. With the sultan sidelined as a constitutional monarch, a more secular Turkish nationalism dominated.

More Young Turks began to embrace ethnic nationalism. Lacking a broad base of support, their theorists had invented one in the Turkish heartland, the neglected and hitherto despised and uncultured peasantry of Anatolia. If the state was to be saved, here were its loyalist masses. This involved displacing notions of class exploitation by a bureaucratic/bourgeois dominant class over an exploited peasantry onto a claim of ethnic-religious exploitation by a foreign and comprador bourgeoisie over a bureaucratic/peasant Turkish proletariat (Keyder, 1987: 61). The leaders of resistance would be the bureaucrats, the followers Anatolian peasants. From this was then spun a broader imperial myth. Theorists like Gökalp, Tekinalp (born Moses Cohen, a Jew from Serres, near Salonika), and Akcura (from a family of Russian Tartar merchants who studied at the War Academy and then in Paris) had been conceiving of their national identity as ultimately less Ottoman, Islamic, or even Turkish than "Turanian" or "pan-Turkic." This entity embraced the Turkic-speaking population living east of Anatolia into the Russian Caucasus, across Central Asia, and up into western Siberia (see the Turanian maps in Baghdjian, 1987: 19 and Landau, 1995: 3 – though both are of later date). Gökalp's 1911 poem "Turan" culminated in

> For the Turks, Fatherland means neither Turkey, nor Turkestan;
> Fatherland is a large and eternal country – Turan!

When faced with World War I, Gökalp advocated conquest to achieve it.

> The land of the enemy shall be devastated,
> Turkey shall be enlarged and become Turan.

For were not Turanians descended from the great conquerors Attila, Genghis, and Timur (Tamburlaine)? Tekinalp described the potential Turanian expansion as "Ghengizism," ruthless conquest followed by forcible Turkification. This was an Asian adaptation of aggressive European organic nationalisms of the period. There was soon even a rival European claimant to this very Turanian mantle – Hungarian fascism (see my companion volume, *Fascists*, chap. 7). Turan would save what had been a half-European empire by reorienting it toward Asia. After the 1908 coup these pan-Turkists became professors in Turkey, influencing young men and women, their ideas resonating amid the turbulent geopolitical climate. Pan-Turkists, Ottomanists, and pan-Islamicists still debated vigorously within the movement. The three triumvirs all differed: Enver was a Turanian enthusiast; Talaat was more statist and opportunist, emphasizing whichever identity would appeal most to his audience; and Djemal compromised, saying that his own identity was primarily Ottoman but that Turks must stage an imperial revival (Arai, 1992: chap. 4; Landau, 1995: 31–52).Yet, emphasizing Turkic rather than Islamic identity created fewer enemies. It did not antagonize Britain or France (which feared that pan-Islamism might undermine their own empires), only Russia. During World War I, Turkey's German ally also encouraged Turkish aggression to focus on the Russian enemy, safely away from possible disputes with allied Austria and neutral Greece. So the war saw a further surge of Turanian sentiments among the Ittihadists.

This was bad news for the main Armenian communities in central and eastern Anatolia, whose own nationalism was intensifying. They lived alongside Turkish and Kurdish peasants, not always amicably. Eastern Anatolia was adjacent to Russia, blocking the lines of communication with the rest of the Turanian people. Armenian nationalists were now relying on Russia for external protection since the Russians were promising a new Armenian statelet. Turanians were identifying a macro-regional conflict between the Turkic peoples and a Christian Russian–Armenian alliance. A leading radical, Dr. Nazim (a graduate of the Military Medical School) argued, "The Ottoman state must be exclusively Turkish. The presence of foreign elements is a pretext for European intervention. They should be forcibly Turkicized." He, and Gökalp at this time, were formally suggesting coercive assimilation,

not deportations or murders. But even this would require considerable repression.

The peace treaties intensified the Turkish sense of being victimized. Per-
versely, said Turks, the Christian powers still saw Turks as the oppressors,
denouncing their militarism and atrocities while ignoring the suffering and
humiliation imposed on them. Akcam (1992: 43–50; cf. Akcam, 1997, and
Dabag, 1994: 104–7) says that Turks became absorbed in the *psychosis of
disappearance*, the fear that this would culminate in the final collapse of the
Turkish state and all aspirations to nationhood, and in *societal paranoia*,
the belief that foreign powers and minorities were destroying them. They
railed justifiably at the biased standards of the West. They saw that during
the wars the loyalty of Christian minorities had been shaky, with some aiding the enemy. Turks alone had to decide on their moral standards and the
measures necessary to achieve them. Such indignation was the moral basis
of the radicalization now under way.

This is a paradox we will repeatedly encounter, of an insecure imperial
nation now claiming it is oppressed. The reasoning is: "We were once a
proud imperial power, but we are now the exploited victim. Since you still
falsely denounce us as an oppressor, we reject all your moral standards. We
will revive our pride and our power within limits imposed only by our own
moral standards, and so by whatever means we deem necessary." Indeed,
this does have a certain terrible logic. I am not for one moment accepting
the common Turkish rationalization that genocide was in effect provoked
by the victim. Yet, *before 1915* both sides could conceive of themselves as
being victimized. The Armenians had suffered terrible pogroms, but the very
survival of Turkey as a state was now threatened, and some Armenians, in
collusion with foreign powers, were helping to try to destroy it. From July
1913 Armenian community leaders – not radical nationalists – began meeting
with foreign diplomats at home and abroad, persuading them to pressure the
Ottoman government to grant more community autonomy to them. They
ignored pleas from Talaat and others to desist. As Dadrian (1997: 254–7)
notes, their contacts with the Russian government were to prove especially
damaging. Now the Young Turk leaders feared collaboration with the foreign
enemy not only from a few radical nationalists but also from respectable,
conservative Armenian community leaders. If all Armenians were enemies,
what then?

The most radical Ittihadists now seem to have resolved on a desperate way
out. We have the testimony of several allied German and Austrian officers (including the most senior Austrian officer, Vice-Marshal Pomiankowski) stationed in Turkey during World War I that some Young Turk leaders decided,
after the Balkan wars, that "next time" they would rectify past mistakes by
eliminating or annihilating disloyal minorities – with the Armenians singled
out for the harshest treatment (Dadrian, 1994a). Though these words may be
a rhetorical flourish not implying actual genocide, they do imply murderous

cleansing, Turkification, and deportations. But a "next time" was still needed. Otherwise, the Young Turks still had two more likely options. They might settle down in power and compromise with varying coalitions of liberals and minority nationalists, issue by issue. Such compromise would help secure effective rule across the whole country. This might also involve compromising with the Great Power demands for Armenian reforms. Alternatively, they might turn to traditional Ottoman policy of exemplary repression to finish off Armenian nationalist activists and scare the rest into submission. The first option was being grudgingly implemented in mid-1914 as two inspectors arranged by the Great Powers, a Norwegian and a Dutchman, were on their way across Turkey to supervise reforms in central and eastern Anatolia. The Ittihadists had been stalling the inspectors, but they were reluctant to alienate all the Great Powers at once. Nor in peacetime did they have the instruments or the cover to accomplish mass murder even if this had been their goal.

But there was a next time, and it promptly sent the two inspectors riding home again before they had inspected anything. It came by way of a much bigger war, which drove an immediate wedge of steel between the supervising Great Powers. World War I began in the first week of August 1914. Turkey signed a secret treaty with Germany on August 2, committing itself to soon join the Central Powers. If Turkey did join in, it was logical to join the German side, for Germany was the only Great Power not trying to grab its territories. Britain had traditionally propped up the Ottoman Empire, but had shifted in the 1880s to a strategy of dividing the spoils of Asia amicably with Russia. The CUP overestimated German strength – they themselves valued statist militarism over liberalism, and ideological bias seems to have contributed to this mistake. The dissident Young Turk Batzaria believed it was all decided rather impulsively by a group of radical leaders who loved action and struggle over caution and peace (Karpat, 1975: 297). But Karsh and Karsh (1999: chap. 7) believe that the radicals, spearheaded by Enver, had a more consistent vision of regeneration through battle and a more calculated strategy for getting what they wanted from Germany. If Germany was going to win, better join its alliance early, for the spoils of victory would be greater. Once neighboring Bulgaria also joined the German alliance, the CUP lost all doubts. For its part, Germany wanted one crucial strategic asset from the Turks: if the Bosphorus and the Black Sea were bottled up, Britain and France could not ship resources to bolster the Russian war effort (Djemal Pasha, 1922: 113–15; MacFie, 1998: chaps. 5, 6). This was indeed achieved by a few German ships, much Turkish artillery, and the bravery of the Turkish infantry in resisting the British landings at Gallipoli.

In the week following the secret treaty, CUP leaders tried for the last time to stick with Plan A. They sought an explicit deal with Armenian nationalists, presenting them a kind of loyalty test. A high-level CUP delegation asked the leaders of the main Armenian party to help organize an insurrection among

Armenians living in the Russian Caucasus. If this was successful, the CUP said it would grant them an autonomous Armenian province under Turkish rule. The Armenian delegates rejected the offer, replying that in the event of war, Armenians on both sides of the frontier should remain loyal to their respective states (Jafarian, 1989: 76). This seemed the most sensible option for them, for to rebel against either state was decidedly risky for a minority lacking military resources. But it was also obvious that if Armenians had to choose loyalty to one of these states, more would choose Russia than the Ottoman Empire – which had been recently murdering them. Armenians' recollections of their youth indicate this. One remembers adults in Sivas talking affectionately of "Uncle Christian," that is, Russia: "the hope of salvation for the Armenians in Anatolia would be the arrival of the Russian army" (Bedoukian, 1978: 7; cf. Jafarian, 1989: 41–4; Kazanjian, 1989: 48).

Of course, a modernized *millet* system embodying entrenched power sharing would have considerably increased Armenian affections for Turkey. But Armenian radicals wanted local freedom *from* centralized rule, whereas since 1908 the Ittihadists had sought to strengthen centralization. As they saw it, decentralization had ended in the loss of province after province. By 1914 they were probably correct. Regional autonomy would have probably led to further Armenian demands for an independent state. That seemed to be the way the whole European world was going. To the radicals, Armenians seemed to be political enemies of the state and ethnic enemies of the Turanian nation. They set the loyalty test too high and the Armenians failed it – and the Ittihadists knew *both* reasons why: the pragmatism and the nationalist sentiments.

The Ottoman Empire formally entered World War I in late October 1914. The declaration of war urged "destruction of our Muscovite enemy" to "unite all branches of our race," that is, of Turanians. Four non-Turkish cabinet members resigned in protest; the grand vizier (an aristocratic Egyptian, a rather marginal Young Turk) dithered but stayed on. The resignations increased Ittihadist control over the state. The poorly organized Turkish forces fought hard, not without success. A British expeditionary force was defeated in Mesopotamia. At Gallipoli a British landing to force open the Straits was thwarted. This state was capable of survival. But in the Caucasus in January 1915 came disaster, the complete defeat of Enver Pasha's Third Army. Enver's attempt to invade Russia seemed foolhardy, in keeping with his reckless ambition and his attraction to the notion of an ethnic Turanian Empire (suggested Stuermer, 1917: 76–7). Less than a quarter of his 90,000 troops made it back to Turkey. Only extreme winter weather held up the Russian counterinvasion.

Over 150,000 Russian Armenians had volunteered for the tsar's army, some through patriotism, some viewing the tsar as the lesser evil, some wanting to get their hands on weapons – which might be used later for Armenian nationalist purposes. A much smaller number of Ottoman Armenians, including some experienced fighters, had crossed the border to join the Russians. Most Armenian sources estimate only 1,000–2,000, though the most detailed account is of 5,000. Turkish army reports suggest 6,000–15,000 (Chalabian, 1988: 218–29; *Documents on Ottoman-Armenians*, 1983: II: 13, 45–6, 63). Derogy's (1986: 44) range of 5,000–8,000 seems the most plausible compromise. Whatever the number, it was dwarfed by the 200,000+ Armenians conscripted into the Turkish forces, few of whom deserted. But though the Armenian volunteers were few, they had value to the Russians. They knew the terrain, the disposition of Turkish forces, and the sympathies of the local populations. For Turkey this was a very threatening front during the first three years of the war, until the 1917 revolution brought the collapse of the Russian armies. Some Armenians were intensifying that threat.

The prior radicalization of parts of the Ottoman state, plus a little Armenian participation in Turkish defeats, explains the next escalation, into murderous reprisals directed only against Armenians. Armenians seemed more threatening, yet were also more vulnerable than Greeks and Jews. Ottoman Greeks knew by now that the *millet* system, which had privileged them, was dead. Their loyalty lay with Athens. But Turkey did not want to provoke neutral Greece. The Jews were neither geographically concentrated (except for Zionists in Palestine) nor plausibly connected to an enemy power. Many Jews were Young Turks, since they remained suspicious of Christians. The German ally also sought to protect Greeks and Jews – but not Armenians (Dadrian, 1996: appendix C). Several Austrian and German officials, American consuls stationed in the European provinces, plus Rafael de Nogales, a Venezuelan mercenary fighting with the Turkish forces, all believed the Young Turk plan was to turn on other minorities later. Less visible Christian minorities did suffer during the war. While riding, de Nogales came upon slaughtered Nestorian Christian villages. Unlike the Armenians, he said, they presented no threat to Turkish rule. The Bryce Report detailed at gruesome length these massacres. But the U.S. consuls reported that few Greeks were slaughtered. Most were forced to leave, their property stolen and some of their young women raped (Bryce, 1972: 99–192; Dadrian, 1994; de Nogales, 1926: 136–7, 206–8; *U.S. Documents*, 1994: 65–70). When Greeks were both more threatening and more vulnerable, during the Greek–Turkish War of 1922, nearly 30,000 Greeks were massacred after the Turks took the city of Smyrna. But for the moment, the main Christian threat seemed to be posed by the Armenian communities in central and eastern Anatolia.

Kurds were much less of a threat, though they were as vulnerable as the Armenians and without foreign protectors. Kurds have been victimized by more recent Turkish (and other) states. But the dominant Turkish policy toward Kurds was coerced assimilation plus some deportations, not mass murder. Kurds are Muslims. Turks viewed them as more primitive and tribal than the Armenians. They could be bribed and modernized through Turkification, and they mounted less of a political threat. They were also so poor as to be not worth looting. During 1916 and 1917 entire Kurdish tribal confederations were deported from eastern border provinces designated as a Turkification region. But they were not murdered. It was expected that they would assimilate into the Turkish population of their new area of residence (Adanir & Kaiser, 2000: 14–15). Only Armenians were the victims of reprisals and deportations, which were to be murderous. The last Balkan war and the first year of the First World War had taken Ottoman Turkey right through the danger zone and over the brink into murderous ethnic cleansing.

CONCLUSION

This chapter has not described an inevitable or premeditated descent into murderous ethnic cleansing. Descent resulted from two persistent and two more contingent pressures.

1. European influence and Christian military and geopolitical power had persistently encouraged nationalist rebellions in the Ottoman Empire. Though the Christian powers had sought to prevent the collapse of the empire, they had negative views of the Turks who dominated it. This empire was the "sick man of Europe," ruled by "terrible Turks," "fanatical Muslims," and "barbarous Asiatics." They had decided that the empire should not survive unless it could somehow become civilized. But their liberal recipes for this civilizing process, though often well intentioned, were not ideally suited to this state or its survival. More significantly, the action was accompanied throughout by land-grabbing and economic exploitation. After all this, it was more or less inevitable that either the Ottoman Empire would collapse or an Ottoman, Muslim, or Turkish attempt at revival would nourish harsh views of Christians.

2. This pressure reinforced long-standing Turkish and Muslim popular economic resentment against Christians within the empire. Populists argued that the Muslim master had become the slave. Since this was not entirely fantasy, a radical organic nationalist movement might mobilize widespread popular Muslim action against Christians. Inland Anatolia nourished a second resentment by local Turks and Kurds of Armenians buying up their land. Turks and Kurds countered with violence conferred by their control of political and military power. In both cases, class resentments were being displaced onto ethnicity. But these two Muslim populist movements arose in different regions and classes. It was not clear that they would ally together. It was even less likely that such an alliance would be under the Young Turks. For most of the prewar period Young Turks were allied with Armenians, not

with those fanning populist violence. No one was intending to trump class with ethnicity.

3. But the Young Turks radicalized as military and political pressures led them to view modernization as requiring more centralization than they had initially believed. Their multiethnic Ottomanism also gave way to greater Turkic nationalism. Turks were nonetheless slow to embrace organic nationalism. The strength of the empire had lain in multiethnicity, and it needed many defeats before they sacrificed this. But Ottoman politics were determined less by mass movements than by quite small groups controlling significant power resources. The economic modernization of the empire was mostly controlled by non-Turks, but Turks controlled political and military modernization, and they were increasingly attracted to statist and nationalist reform. Mobilizing coercive powers within the army and police, and with the ability to call forth popular demonstrations, they seized political power in two stages, in 1908 and 1913. Purges then radicalized the state and the Young Turks themselves. But this did not simply follow the lines indicated in my first ethnic thesis. There was a sense in which this was the darkening of democratic aspirations, the blending of the *demos* and the *ethnos*. But the Young Turks also radicalized and modernized rather dark Ottoman practices, turning repression and divide-and-rule between ethnic communities toward actual cleansing.

4. World War I suddenly intensified militarism and geopolitical destabilization and made this blend much more dangerous. From late 1914, only Germany retained any influence inside the Ottoman Empire, and Germany had no interest in Armenians. Their main protector, "Uncle Russia," was at war with the empire, supported by some Armenians. This raised the specter of a scenario mixing my theses 4a and 4b. Though the Turks possessed overwhelming force within the empire vis-à-vis Armenians, the two sides could be equalized by foreign support that produced a real fear of political extinction among Turks. War also meant that there would now be no external restraints on radical solutions to the ethnic-religious tensions of the empire. This was a contingent and external pressure, since the Ottomans had not contributed to the slide to general war. Their decision to join a war already in motion was also a mistake that might have gone otherwise.

So geopolitical destabilization (thesis 5), linked to Christian economic privileges, made some kind of radical Ottoman Turkish backlash probable. Several times geopolitical crises enabled radicals to win closely contested arguments among the Ottoman reformers. In 1908 the Young Turk and Armenian nationalists had been allies, the Plan A of the Young Turks. It was primarily geopolitical pressures that pushed them apart over the next six years. The final radicalization resulted from World War I. The two coups had provided the potential instrument of radicalism, a state core that could connect the two different populist resentments against Christian privileges, embody a modern organic nationalist solution, and implement radical policies. Only through the second coup, reinforced by the world war, did danger spread to Armenians as a whole. Armenians in eastern Anatolia blocked the organic Turanian nationalist project to save the empire, and both nationalists and conservative Armenian leaders were increasing their contacts with Russia. Tensions between some Armenians and some Turks rose to the boiling point. As this book will show, this was not an atypical combination of the deep-rooted and the contingent as causes of descent into murderous ethnic cleansing. As usual, it was political power – who would control the state – that was ultimately the decisive source of danger.

Note how *late* came the fatal embrace of organic nationalism, statism, and violence. That the Young Turks, rather than palace and Islamic reactionaries, should be the instrument of their doom would have surprised most Armenians in 1912, even perhaps through much of 1913. As late as August 1914 the Young Turks tried a new version of their Plan A, alliance with the Armenians. As we see in the next chapter, their Plan B – mass but strategically confined deportations – emerged quickly and turned even more rapidly into a Plan C of more generalized and much more violent deportations. This was inherently unstable and quickly slid into a genocidal Plan D. This was not as coherent, organized, and premeditated a genocide as is usually argued. It fits clearly my sixth ethnic thesis: murderous cleansing is rarely the initial intent of the perpetrators. Nor was it the only case of the tortuous yet finally rapid perversion of a promising political movement, as we see in later chapters.

6

Armenia, II
Genocide

Genocide requires numbers and intentionality. We don't know the exact number of Armenians killed in the years following 1915 – or even the number living in Turkey.[1] 1.2–1.4 million killed might be a reasonable guess for 1915–16. But sporadic massacres resumed when British and French occupation forces left, accounting for thousands more. Perhaps two-thirds of the Armenians died altogether. Many survived by escaping abroad, so only about 10 percent of the Armenians living in Turkey in 1914 remained in the country in 1922 – the most successful murderous cleansing achieved in the 20th century. Far more men than women and children were killed. Of the 180,000 surviving Armenians in the Deir-Zor camp in May 1916, only 10 percent were men (most being elderly), 30 percent were women, and 60 percent were children (Kévorkian, 1998: 224). But since men, women, and children were all killed in very large numbers, and since many surviving women and children were forcibly assimilated into Muslim identities, this was an attempt to wipe out the Armenian nation. The word *genocide* did not yet exist. But the numbers matched the deed.

But was it intentional? Was it planned by the government in advance? Most writers say it was (e.g., Dadrian, 1995; Melson, 1992). There are a few disseuters (Adanir, 2001; Suny, 1998). I take the latter view: though eventually there was organization and planning, this emerged erratically out of sudden responses to unexpected crises. We have no authenticated smoking gun, no unequivocal order of genocide from the top (nor is there in other cases discussed in this book).[2] Nonetheless, the ruling CUP was radicalizing during

---

[1] Turkish official sources estimate 200,000 to 300,000 dead, which is far too low. McCarthy (1983: 112, 130) goes higher, to 600,000, which he says is 40 percent of the Armenian population. Most others estimate 1.5 million killed, 65–75 percent of a total population of 2.1–2.4 million (Astourian, 1995: 50, fn. 17; Hovannisian, 1986, 1994; Kévorkian, 1998: 14–16, 60–1; Rummel, 1998: 81–5; Yalman, 1970: 326–32).

[2] I do not accept as proved genuine documents in which the Central Committee or the triumvirs seem to order genocide – letters of February 18 and March 15 from the Central Committee to the authorities of Adana or telegrams from Talaat and Enver to underlings in Aleppo in September, November, and December 1915. These were published by Andonian (1920), quoted in several Armenian accounts of the genocide, and are supported by Dadrian (1986a). Turkish scholars suggest that the documents are forgeries. Zürcher (1998: 121) is also

1914, and this later moved toward genocide. Some said the war provided a unique opportunity to remove the Armenians and provide a solution once and for all to the Armenian question. What they meant by this was not clear. They were not yet a majority, nor did they have the clear support of the regime's two powerhouses, Enver and Talaat. Enver seems to have moved toward their viewpoint on his return to Constantinople from his defeat at the hands of the Russians in the Caucasus. On January 22, 1915, he praised the Armenian community and soldiery for their loyalty, but the next month he began to blame them for his own strategic blunders. Some German military advisers urged removing Armenians from strategic areas to prevent them from collaborating with the invading Russians (Dadrian, 1995: 34–42). Talaat later told the American ambassador that deportations had not "been decided upon hastily . . . they were the result of prolonged and careful deliberation" (Morgenthau, 1918: 333).

In early 1915 "deportations" were planned, but what did that mean? Some Turks used the word as a euphemism for something much worse, but probably most did not. Forcible deportations comprised what we might call Plan B, adopted after the final failure of Plan A, compromise with Armenian nationalists against their common enemies. Initially Plan B was designed to move potentially disloyal Armenians away from the theater of war so that they could not interfere with it. But this action contained what I have termed a tactical lure: as a military tactic it could lure the tacticians toward something worse. It could easily escalate to Plan C: deporting Armenians from all vulnerable communications routes and front areas, which might involve the whole of Anatolia and almost all Armenians. They would be forced into "safer" marginal desert areas of the south. This escalation was precipitated by the military disasters of early 1915. The Eastern front was buckling under Russian pressure in late January; the British inflicted defeats at the Suez Canal in February and in Mesopotamia in April. British naval landings were expected imminently on the Syrian coast. Instead, on March 18 an Entente fleet aimed at Constantinople itself, trying to force entry at the Dardelles Straits. When this failed, they landed forces at Gallipoli on April 25 – only a few miles from the capital. This was an attempt to knock Turkey out of the war. There was panic in Constantinople, and plans were laid for a last stand in Anatolia, which had to be secure if there was any chance of survival.

To understand how the Ottoman Empire went over the edge into murderous cleansing of the Armenians, look at Map 6.1. Note the relationship between the fronts and the Armenian deportations. There was also a general

skeptical. Kaiser (1999b: 108), says that more evidence is needed before they can be accepted as authentic. Dadrian's (1993) English version of a document purportedly suggesting that there was an operational blueprint for the genocide is also undated. Unfortunately, forgeries do circulate.

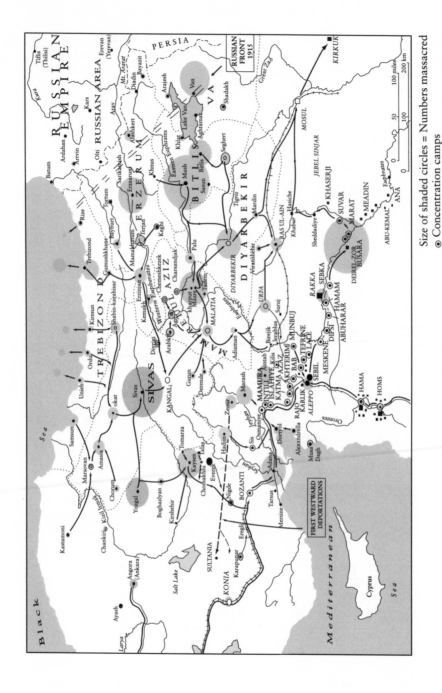

Size of shaded circles = Numbers massacred
◉ Concentration camps

MAP 6.1. The 1915 Armenian genocide in the Turkish Empire. Courtesy of the Armenian National Institute (ANI) (www.armenian-genocide.org).

belief among Turkish leaders that Armenians might collaborate with the enemy and the desire for a "pure" Turkish heartland in Anatolia. Mass deportations were widely seen as the solution to the short-term crisis and by radicals as the way to long-term security for Ottoman Turkey.

Plan B was (and still is) widely seen by Turks as a reasonable policy in the circumstances, given what they saw as Armenian collaboration with the Russians (e.g., Izzet Pasa, 1992: 200–9; Yalman, 1970: 326–32). Plan C is harder to justify, though Halil Berktay (in the leading Turkish newspaper, *Milliyet*, October 20, 2000) explains it in terms of the wartime context:

the Turks had been forced back, and pushed into a corner... with the landings at Gallipoli, Istanbul would also be lost, and that there would be a retreat to Anatolia, and that there would be no place left for the Turks but the Anatolian heartland. And then, just at that point, the activities of Armenian nationalist bands in parallel with the operations of the Russian army on the Eastern Front. The resulting birth of the nightmare that even Anatolia itself was no longer safe.

Plan C was also consistent with the Ottoman practice of forcibly dispersing rebellious peoples. In 1913 Christian villages in eastern Thrace had been destroyed by the Special Organization Forces (of whom more later) to frighten all local Christians into fleeing. In mid-1914 some Greek villages and farms along the Aegean were similarly attacked. In the autumn came police attacks on Zionist communities in Palestine, launched by the radical Jaffa governor (Kaiser, 2000b, 2001a; Karsh & Karsh, 1999: 166–7). This was the type of murderous ethnic cleansing seen in Yugoslavia during the 1990s: massacres, burnings, and rapes to terrorize the rest to leave – but not genocide. Was it the policy of the whole regime or of a faction of CUP radicals controlling repressive resources during a crisis? We don't know, though I veer toward the latter interpretation. It was probably the military disasters of early 1915 that then converted Enver and Talaat to this radical policy.

But in wartime even Plan C was unstable, breaking the orderly bounds of my category policed deportations. This ramshackle empire at war was struggling to provision its own soldiers. A much higher proportion of the total economic surplus went to the war effort than in other major powers, and much of it was extracted by force. Perhaps 240,000 Turks died during the war from disease, alongside the 325,000 who died in battle (Ahmad, 1993; McCarthy, 1983). This is a terrible level of suffering.[3] But given the sufferings of the country, no one could have envisaged deporting hundreds of thousands of Armenians without causing mass deaths. We know of no plans made for their resettlement. They were just dumped into inhospitable

[3] The figures are often adduced by Turkish denialists to claim that as many Turks were killed as Armenians. While not wishing to minimize the extent of the sufferings endured by the Turkish people during this period, the number of Turks actually killed (or led to their deaths) by Armenians must have been a tiny proportion of the total Turkish dead – and a tiny proportion of the number of Armenians killed by Turks.

desert areas. The Armenians were allowed no possessions, had no skills relevant to a desert, and received no government assistance. Most would die. Even if we take the official Turkish views of events, this would involve violent deportations laced with elements of politicide, pervaded by extreme callousness toward the victims, all descending in the direction of ethnocide.

Who initiated such Plans? The unreliable memoirs of Huseyin Cahit (Yalcin) claim that the Central Committee endorsed genocide in mid-February 1915. He says that 3 of the 10 members present (Gökalp, Kara Kemal, and Midhat Sukru) opposed the decision, but they agreed to keep their opposition quiet. He says that the Committee was dominated by radicals, by now comprising Enver Pasha, Talaat Pasha, and the three leaders of the paramilitary Special Organization (the *Teskilat-I Mahsusa*), which had already been involved in Balkan atrocities and which later carried out most of the genocidal murders: Dr. Bahaeddin Sakir, Dr. Nazim, and Atif Reza (Astourian, 1995: 33–41). The third triumvir, Djemal Pasha, was not present, though in these early days observers considered him an advocate of forcible Turkification (Morgenthau, 1918: 172–4).

Yalcin's account may be embroidered, but it seems broadly accurate. The Salonikan upwardly mobile accountant Sukru was a moderate, though we lack evidence of dissent from Gökalp, the intellectual. Enver and Talaat's radicalism is documented from early 1915. From slightly earlier dates, so are Reza's and the two doctors'. Dr. Nazim declared that earlier Ottoman politicians "had not been far-sighted enough to cleanse all the country they ruled of the Christian element" (Bryce, 1972: 8).[4] A German general held Dr. Sakir responsible for massacres in Erzerum in April 1915, and Turkish sources quote him as conceding that deportations "may mean going against national and humanitarian rules. I am willing and ready to pay for the 're-sponsibility' of this with my own life." In the future, he says, it will be recognized "that I have sacrificed myself for service to the country" (quoted by Yalman, 1970). Yet he was known as a humanitarian among Turks. In 1916 he organized a series of public lectures in Constantinople by doctors, social politicians, and politicians on Anatolia, the devastation wrought by syphilis, malaria, and other diseases, and the hopeless poverty, exploitation, and lack of education of the Anatolian peasants. His own lecture managed to pressure Anatolian officials into making new efforts at social and hygienic reform (Stürmer, 1917: 172–3).

All this suggests debates between three positions inside the CUP. A small faction still wanted compromise – Plan A. Centrists favored forcible deportations from the front areas. Yet as the British and Russians attacked, deportations spread to Anatolia as a whole. Plans B and C, deportations, were

---

[4] I am discounting as unreliable the statement of the renegade CUP member, Mevlan Rifat, that on another occasion Nazim had told the Committee that the extermination must be total this time (the supposed speech is quoted in Chalabian, 1988: 226).

both unstable. Plan B was unstable when the fronts moved inward, Plan C because it had to result, even unintentionally, in mass deaths. The third and most radical faction favored Plan D, wholesale extermination. Eventually, they won the debate. The last Balkan war started the debate. World war swung it toward deportations. The official Armenian refusal to foment rebellion against Russia, reinforced by Turkish defeats, led to a radical victory that widened deportations into Plan C and then escalated into Plan D, genocide. These last two escalations were coordinated from the top, in the offices of Talaat, minister of the interior, and Enver, minister of war. Some of the consequences of the policy had not been thought through. Deport people southward from the war zone, even from Anatolia, crushing all resistance – but how severe should be the repression, how could deportation be accomplished, what would happen to the deportees on arrival in the south? Few could have thought it all through in advance. Perhaps only the most radical had, since their Plan D was the simplest and most coherent plan.[5] This seems the most likely scenario. It does not resemble a highly planned genocide, though it did rapidly escalate to that. Yes, this was genocide, though it was very rushed and initially disorganized.

THE GENOCIDAL PROCESS

So genocide was a developing process. Its sequence is discussed by Kaiser (2001a), and it can be traced geographically on Map 6.1. The first incident occurred in late February at Dortyol, a large Armenian village not far from the Syrian coast. Two British-Armenian spies had landed, been given hospitality, and then captured. The place was known as an Armenian nationalist stronghold. The authorities believed that the spies were attempting to organize a diversionary rising while British marines landed on the coast nearby. The British were feeling out what support they could expect from Armenians, and they wanted the Turks to believe they would invade here, since they would not. Many local Armenians had failed to respond to the draft. The government was understandably jittery. It may have believed rumors of a plot of a widespread regional rising and felt it safer to prevent any such possibility with exemplary repression. The Adana governor sent a large military force to Dortyol, and most of the Armenian men were arrested and deported in labor gangs elsewhere.

---

[5] Armenian accounts sometimes "read backward" from the genocide itself to earlier events, which are then seen teleologically as coherent planning for it. For example, the "Armenian Genocide Chronology" circulated on the Internet (www.armenian-genocide.org/chronology) intersperses statements by Turkish radicals, Nazim's boycott of Armenian products, actions against Armenian politicians, and the formation of the Special Organization as if all were the first stages of a planned genocide. This was probably not the case; more likely different strands of anti-Armenian and war preparation came rapidly together.

This incident was then used to justify Enver's order of February 27 to disarm all 200,000+ Armenian draftees in the army. They too were deployed as forced labor battalions. This policy was applied to other non-Muslims too. Aaronsohn (1916) was assigned along with other Zionist soldiers in Palestine to labor battalions, where some were forced to work in terrible conditions. But he does not suggest that Jews were deported or killed. This was obviously an attempt to disarm dangerous Armenian collaborators in a strategic area and all armed Armenians. But was this because they really were considered a threat or merely so that they could not resist the worst that was already being planned? Let us see which scenario is more consistent with later events.

There was now a lull followed by another incident, more suggestive of an ad hoc than a planned response. The first full-scale deportation of a local civilian population occurred a month later, on March 26, in the town of Zeitun in Marash province in Cilicia. Map 6.1 shows that this was nowhere near the front lines, but it was on a major army supply route. It was also renowned as the strongest Armenian town, able to run its own affairs and containing many armed nationalists. There were also Armenian bandit bands enlarged by army deserters active in the nearby hills. When these began to raid army supply caravans in mid-March, pressure was put on local Armenian leaders to cooperate with the army in rounding them up. This worked; most bandits were killed, captured, or dispersed, and the authorities eased their pressure. When bandit activity once again increased, the authorities concluded (with some reason) that the locals were no longer being cooperative. A German officer stationed there wrote to his wife that the local Armenians hated the violent and incompetent gendarmerie commander. This led to fighting in which a dozen gendarmes were shot dead. He commented that the locals were caught in the middle. They "just didn't trust the government any more" and were frightened of the robbers' reprisals should they betray them. They seemed not to realize how dangerous their situation was, he commented, for this was too strategic an area for the authorities to take any risk (Kaiser, 2001b: 13)

So the government decided to end the problem once and for all – and eliminate all future threat from these independent mountaineers. A large military force attacked Zeitun and began to kill Armenian men on April 8, continuing for three days. A few armed Armenians escaped into the hills, where they fought on, to the disapproval of community leaders who feared worse retaliation. But this seems to have already been decided, for deportations began immediately. Most of the local men were sent south to the town of Deir Zor in the Syrian desert. But the women, children, and the elderly were deported in a different direction, northwest to Sultania and Konia – which differed from all later deportations. There were no killings en route, and both groups reached their destinations – again, different from later deportations. Surviving deportees say the authorities did not know what would be done with them. Adding together the actions at Dort Yol and Zeitun, the length of time between them, and the different treatment involved compared to later deportations, this was probably ad hoc exemplary repression – repression so terrible that it set an example for all other Armenians. The disarming of the Armenian soldiers reveals additional fear by the authorities of more general Armenian disloyalty, but these men were still being deployed in construction tasks and there was as yet no mass killing.

There was now another lull, but of only 10 days, followed by two distinct but almost simultaneous escalations. One was another incident, but in a much more important city. Van was a strategic city in eastern Anatolia near the Russian and Persian borders, the biggest city with a substantial Armenian population. A moderate governor, Tahsin Pasha, had been replaced at the end of 1914 by a radical Ittihadist, Djevdet Bey, the brother-in-law of Enver. Returning defeated and angry from the front, he blamed the Armenians for the defeat. On April 16 he tricked five local Armenian leaders into meeting him and had them killed. The alarmed Armenian community erected barricades. Both sides dug in. Sporadic killings began of isolated Armenians in villages around the lake. On the 20th, an attempted rape of an Armenian woman flared up into mass shooting and a bloody siege of the Armenian quarter began. This gradually merged into the war as the Russian advance neared the city, headed by Armenian volunteer detachments. They took the city on June 19, but it was retaken by the Turkish Army and Kurdish irregulars in August. Van was the site of a full-scale ethnic civil war in which the front and rear dissolved into one.

Van deeply alarmed the regime. Its sympathies lay with the local Turks rather than the Armenians, and the radical governor was sending it inflammatory reports. On April 19, as the two sides were digging in, the government informed the German embassy that it could no longer trust the Armenians. Van was constantly used to justify retaliation through mass deportations against Armenian collaborators with the enemy (*Documents on Ottoman-Armenians*, 1983). In the parliament, a few deputies criticized the authorities' exaggerations. Some Turkish officers also alleged that the commander of the Third Army Group, General Kamil, had provoked incidents and then exaggerated them to demonstrate that Armenians were a menace to the war effort, requiring elimination (Dadrian, 1994b: 93). But though the moderate deputy Ahmet Izzet Pasa remained horrified by the Turkish overreaction, he says that when he became commander of the Eastern Front, he realized that Armenian atrocities had been real enough (1992: 200–9). De Nogales, the Venezuelan mercenary commanding a Turkish artillery battery at Van, credibly reported callous warfare on both sides. Neither gave quarter, killing captured combatants and collaborators. Armenians committed atrocities after the city was relieved in June. When Turks and Kurds retook it in August, they escalated to local genocide (for varied accounts of Van, see Bryce, 1972: 32–77; Dadrian, 1996: 31–4; de Nogales, 1926; McCarthy, 1995: 188–92, 223–30; Morgenthau, 1918: 296–300).

At the time that Van was exploding, the capital was also threatened. The government knew of the imminent Entente attack, and indeed the Gallipoli landings came close to breaking through. There was a flurry of political activity in the capital. April 20 produced an order to settle Muslim refugees from Europe in Zeitun: the Armenians were not going to return there. Yet their fate remained unclear. On April 22 or 23 the CUP and military leaders made some big decisions. Preparations began for a guerrilla war in Constantinople itself, including the removal of over 200 Armenian leaders from Constantinople and some other towns, including all revolutionary nationalists who could be found. On April 25 they were sent to prison camps in the interior. A second wave of deportations of Armenian leaders came two days later, after the Entente landings.

On the 24th the Zeitun deportees initially sent northwest to Konia were rerouted south to Deir Zor. This was a decisive change. They might have been expected to survive at Konia, but they would likely die in the Syrian desert. On the 27th, Talaat told the German embassy that the political autonomy of all religious communities was abolished. Between the 25th and the 30th, more towns and villages in Cilicia (Armenian strongholds or on army supply routes) were emptied, the deportees being moved south. As the snows melted on the eastern Armenian plateau in late April, Ottoman troops and Special Organization forces began massacres near Van, Mush, and along the Russian lines. It is unclear when the first killings of the deported political leaders began. Probably revolutionary nationalists were tortured for information and then killed, but most of the leaders may not have been killed until late May or June. It is also unclear when the Armenian army labor battalions began to be killed, though this was under way at the end of May. By July almost 200,000 Armenian soldiers had been killed. Though a few Armenians had been deserting, the vast majority seemed obedient. The Entente now had to confront far fewer Ottoman soldiers and now recruited fleeing Armenians as soldiers. The French Armenian Legion became 4,500 strong. The radicals felt trapped in the security dilemma referred to in Chapter 1. Though the probability of Armenian soldier rebellions was low, the cost of any such rebellion would be extremely high. Better strike first to be on the safe side, they may have reasoned. But few Armenian communities presented much threat to the Turkish war effort. The regime was not striking at an actually threatening movement, but preempting one seen as inevitable in the future. Talaat more or less admitted this.

Thus, before April 23–5, there was probably no coherent Plan, but rather a series of exemplary repression responses to the most threatening situations. A Plan was then formulated during these three days, focused on Armenian leaders, soldiers, strongholds, and strategic towns and villages. It was moving beyond ad hoc exemplary repression and limited forced deportations toward politicide: an attempt to wipe out the entire potential Armenian political and military leadership class to prevent it from collaborating with the enemy. In Armenian communities the police went searching for terrorist arms. They found some. It was legal to possess weapons, and many Armenians had decided that arms were needed for self-protection. If the police didn't find guns, they sometimes planted or sold the householder weapons that they would then "discover." They would then arrest him. It is unclear how many were then killed.

Killings and deportations continued to widen. Much of Cilicia was cleared in May, the Armenian population sent south, as were all later deportees (Bryce, 1972: 465–91, 646–8). Massacres and deportations spread westward from Van. Scattered resistance provoked greater massacres, but most Armenian communities were taken by surprise. Later there was substantial scattered resistance led by bands of nationalists and deserters in the hills. But resistance was rarely successful, suggesting little prior Armenian organization (Bryce, 1972: 84–95; *U.S. Documents*: I, 24–5, 49–50; II, 108; Barton, 1998: 100–3, 108–12; Kaiser, 2001b: 20–8; Kévorkian, 1998: 323; cf. Miller & Miller, 1993: 74–5). By now most Armenians did sympathize with the enemy, since a Turkish defeat was their main hope of survival. Whatever the Plan may have been, in reality, throughout May, escalation was under way toward a Plan D: genocide.

There was a flurry of official activity in the last week of May. The Entente powers warned the Ottoman government on May 24 that those implicated in killings would be held legally liable after the war. We might interpret subsequent administrative orders either as systematizing the murderous deportations or as giving legal cover and an impression of orderliness to them. Either these orders now embodied systematic genocide or the regime was trying to avoid retribution if it lost the war. The orders did not mention killings. On May 26 Talaat ordered that inhabitants of Armenian communities close to the Eastern Front and those in Adana province and Marash district be deported. The next day the government published a more general "Deportation Order" authorizing steps to prevent any collaboration with the enemy, including forced removal and resettlement. There was no mention of regions or particular ethnic or religious groups. But three days later the cabinet authorized Muslim refugees to settle in any vacated homes, while all Armenian property would be expropriated and sold. On June 9–10 there were further deportation and property seizure orders to all provincial authorities (Kaiser, 2001a; texts in Institut für Armenische Fragen, 1988: 12–13).

The pretense continued that this was merely Plan B, war-necessitated deportation. In actuality it was genocide. By early September there were no Armenian communities left, except in the big and visible cities of Constantinople, Smyrna, and Aleppo. Talaat came close to acknowledging genocide in a telegram of July 12, 1915, to the governor of Diyarbekir:

massacres of Amenians and Christians without distinction as to sect have been organized within the province ... in Mardin some seven hundred people from among the Armenians and other Christian inhabitants were recently taken outside of the city at night and, with due authorization, slaughtered like sheep ... the total of those killed to date in these massacres is estimated at two thousand persons...there are fears that, if a speedy and definite end is not put to this, then the Muslim inhabitants of neighboring provinces will rise up and engage in a general slaughter of Christians. As it is not appropriate that the disciplinary and administrative measures adopted with regard to the Armenians be extended to the other Christians...such practices which threaten the lives of Christians indiscriminately [must] be stopped immediately. (Quoted by Berktay in *Milliyet*, October 20, 2000)

He was trying to stop massacres of other Christians but not of Armenians.

The diary of a Protestant missionary teacher, Bertha Morley, enabled Kaiser (1999a) to give a detailed account of the process in one medium-sized town, Marsovan. Her account can be supplemented by a chapter on the area in the Bryce Report (1972: 331–77). It was not a strategic area and the first note of trouble relates to April 29, 1915, when Morley records that 13 leaders of Armenian societies, all men, were arrested; a further 21 were arrested on May 10. During May and early June, she reports police concern about deserters and hidden arms caches. A cache of bombs found in a vineyard was attributed to Armenians. In the Bryce Report (p. 332) the principal of her college says that they seemed rather old arms, but they "aroused the fury of the Turks to white heat." Morley says that those found in possession of arms were arrested and sent off into typhus-infested areas. She does not question whether the arms finds were genuine, but there is no hint in her diary of any Armenian resistance. On June 10 the governor said he did not want "severity," "but much pressure [was] brought on him from without." June 23 saw the way prepared for more general deportations. Those born elsewhere were ordered to return to their birthplaces. All the men were rounded up on June 26 and sent in groups into the countryside.

The first rumor that many Marsovan men were killed en route was heard on July 1. On July 3 the mission's Turkish lawyer let it drop that the deportees "would be disposed of on the way." Morley comments: "It looks as if the crushing or annihilation of the race was aimed at." The next day, she says, the whole Armenian population was being told to leave. She hears of a baker telling an Armenian woman buying several loaves for her journey, "You won't need so much bread, and then he laughed." This indicates that knowledge of the deportees' fate was widespread among local Turks. On July 5, Armenians were desperately trying to sell their property, but some Turks said, "No need to buy these things. Soon they will be ours anyway." "Reliable information" reached them on July 6 that almost all the deported men were killed en route. The next day there was a "real danger" of a massacre in Marsovan itself. But the mayor called together CUP members, and they ensured order. The town saw little serious violence. The principal said that women were deported over the next two weeks, leaving only a few hundred out of an Armenian population of 12,000. By now the people "felt that the Government was determined to exterminate the Armenian race, and they were powerless to resist" (Bryce, 1972: 334).

Miss Morley does not convey images of Turkish ferocity. Killings happened elsewhere, outside her range of vision. Hostile locals seem mainly to have coveted the deportees' property and possessions, while friendly Turks urged Armenians to convert to survive. But such opportunistic conversions rarely worked, since the authorities were not fooled. Morley seems pleased, since apostasy seems to have worried this gatherer of souls as much as the killings! She reports on July 12 that some Turks were mystified by the atrocities, saying "that they and their religion would never do anything so cruel as this, that it must be Germany and Christianity" that were to blame. Bryce (1972: 348) notes that two Turks had been hanged for sheltering or offering to shelter Armenian friends. On July 14 Morley does report killing in the town. A sympathetic soldier tried to hide the Armenian Protestant pastor. But when his comrades threatened to kill him too, he ran away, abandoning the pastor to his fate. The soldiers argued. Some were still reluctant to kill the pastor and repeatedly begged him to accept Islam. He refused, so they killed him and a young acolyte who also refused to convert.

On July 17 the mayor tried to justify the events, saying that they were "only a fraction of what [Armenians] had done to Turks elsewhere...in Van not a Turkish child was left in its cradle." On July 20 Morley says that Armenian women were grateful to escorting Turkish soldiers who had fought off marauding Circassians. The authorities were relentless but disciplined in their pressure. The mission was pressured to yield up more of its Protestant Armenians (who, like Catholics, were often initially spared across the country). On July 18 the local authorities began expropriating Armenian community assets. On August 15 an official said that in his travels he saw executions and many corpses lying along the Euphrates. Morley continues her depressing diary for another month. By then the Armenian community in Marsovan had gone.

From various such reports emerges a common sequence of events indicating the coordinated implementation of a Plan by the beginning of June 1915 (or perhaps a little earlier). First came a sudden roundup of political and intellectual leaders and those supposedly possessing arms. Some of these were imprisoned; most were marched off, and usually not heard of again. Then any remaining Armenian men of military age were assembled, roped together, and marched off, supposedly to be resettled in desert areas in the unthreatened south of the country. Some local massacres were committed in the towns and villages of Cilicia and the Russian frontier regions, but not many elsewhere. In these communities this might initially look like deportations – but why the men first? In reality most of the men were deported only to the nearest desolate area, where they were killed. The remaining Armenians lacked arms, leaders, or even many men. Some weeks later, the women, children, and the elderly were rounded up and marched into the desert. Since they were no threat, they were not immediately killed but marched for several days. Many died as they starved or fell to disease or were butchered in waves of irregular attacks on the straggling columns by tribesmen or brigands. The European provinces differed in this respect. Most European deportees were herded onto trains and arrived at the southern termini relatively unscathed – but not for long. Anatolia and almost all other northern areas were virtually totally cleansed of Armenians – murderously.

American Consul Davies witnessed events in Kharput and what he described as the "slaughterhouse province" of Mamuret-ul-Aziz. His consular travels enabled him to see (and photograph) what he estimated to be 10,000 Armenian corpses strewn around its deserts and valleys. Most of them were naked or half-naked, the result of the final indignity, stripping their bodies by the poorest people of the province (Davies, 1989: esp. 86–7; *United States Official Documents*: 1995, Vol. III). Survivors of all the columns of "deportees" described scenes of terrible cruelty interspersed with a few acts of generosity. Younger women were repeatedly raped, some being taken as prostitutes or slave-mistresses, with an uncertain fate.

The wives of Turkish officials often intervened in the deportations, selecting healthy-looking young women to be their servants. Poor Turks and Kurds seized young women as brides for their sons, which avoided paying ruinous bride prices. Some of these young women presumably lived in rather degraded conditions, but they lived. Most eventually assimilated, losing their sense of being Armenian. Since descent was patrilineal, their children would take the father's identity. We have no idea how many Armenian women survived in this way. It might require revising downward our overall estimate of the death rate. Such practices reveal that racial views of ethnicity were not widespread. Useful, harmless Armenians could be forcibly assimilated. It involved terrible gender and age bias, for while the men and older people were killed, young women survived.

The escalation from the first incidents to genocide occurred within three months, a much more rapid escalation than Hitler's later attack on the Jews. Map 6.1 shows that the massacres and deportations began in the areas of greatest Armenian concentration in Cilicia and the northeastern borders and then spread inward from these borders, west along the Black Sea hinterland, and southeast along the Baghdad Railway. Between 600,000 and 800,000 Armenians, disproportionately male, were killed in this first wave concentrated in Anatolia. A separate rail flow southward began in late 1915 from the European provinces. Those not quickly killed, mostly women, children, and elderly men, were driven south, ending up in the Syrian and Mesopotamian deserts. Very few counterflows were visible, except for the very first deportation from Zeitun.

The second major wave of final exterminations, of perhaps another 630,000, came in the death camps of Syria and Mesopotamia indicated in Map 6.1 with the symbol ⊙. Here most deaths came from starvation and disease (Kévorkian, 1998). Killing resumed from April to September 1916 around these camps, with mopping-up operations elsewhere. The Armenian communities were virtually emptied by then. Only Constantinople, Smyrna, and Aleppo were largely spared, probably because they were too visible. The arrival of British troops in Syria in early 1917 saved most of those still alive in southern areas. But the killings continued in smaller waves right until 1923, intensified by the withdrawal of British and French troops from the region and by the release of some murderous Turkish officials from British custody (Marashlian, 1999).

We have ample documentation of all this. Already by 1916 Lord Bryce had delivered to the British foreign secretary a large volume of eyewitness reports by Armenians and foreigners – missionaries, nurses, travellers, consuls, and others.[6] This remains the best source on the early genocidal process, buttressed by Armenian survivors' memoirs (Kazanjian, 1989; Kévorkian, 1998; Miller & Miller, 1993) and by sources who cannot be accused of bias. The reports of neutral American consuls, businessmen, and missionaries are damning (collected in Barton, 1998; *U.S. Official Documents*, 1993–5). Those located in the north mainly see roundups and deportations, plus a few killings. They hear credible reports of mass murders and death marches but do not witness them. It is different for those in the southern deserts, the destination of the death marches – like Consuls Davies and Jackson or Mr. Bernau, whom I quoted at the beginning of the previous chapter.

Even more damaging are the reports of the allies, high-ranking German and Austrian soldiers, diplomats and railway officials, with access to the regime. They try to believe the best of their allies, initially expressing disbelief, then shock and dismay at what they call the "annihilation," "extermination," "obliteration," or "systematic butchery" of the "Armenian race." Most concede that this was "the deliberate policy of the Young Turk government" or alternatively of "a large segment of the Ittihadist Party."[7] The German employees of the Baghdad Railway had a ringside view. Their trains transported many thousands of deportees; the lines were routes of death marches; and stations became concentration and sometimes death camps. Kaiser (1999b) quotes terrible descriptions by the railwaymen. The higher railway officials also became aware of Talaat's close control of the exterminations. Though he occasionally responded to their protests by publicly denouncing atrocities, it became clear to them that he was then secretly countermanding these statements and covertly urging his officials to move the genocide along.

---

[6] The second (1972) edition of the Bryce Report adds an appendix identifying the places and persons described in the report. Its main defects are a tendency to label the Kurds collectively as perpetrators, a failure to perceive the role of the Special Forces, and the editors' rather negative view of the Ottoman Empire, typical of Europeans of the period.

[7] The Austrian reports are in Institut für Armenische Frage (1988), with mentions of "extermination" on pp. 173, 209, 243, and 265; Austrian and German reports are excerpted in Dadrian (1994a), and German missionary diaries are reprinted in Kévorkian (1998: 263–325; cf. Trumpener, 1968).

During the siege of Van, the Venezuelan soldier of fortune Major Rafael de Nogales was chief of staff of the Turkish gendarmerie troops. But he asked to be relieved of his post:

I was thoroughly disgusted and disheartened by the numerous and utterly unjustified massacres of the Christians, committed, if not at the direct instance, at least through the complaisance of the Commander-in-Chief of our Expeditionary Army, Khalil Bey.

As he rode toward his new posting, his escort urged him to hurry if he was not to miss the action. As he neared the pretty white houses and minarets of Nairt he gasped:

The ghastly slope was crowned by thousands of half-nude and still bleeding corpses, lying in heaps, or interlaced in death's final embrace. Fathers, brothers, sons and grandsons lay there as they had fallen beneath the bullets and yataghans [farming implements] of the assassins. From more than one slashed throat the life gushed forth in mouthfuls of warm blood. Flocks of vultures were perched upon the mound, pecking at the eyes of the dead and dying...while the scavenger dogs struck sharp teeth into the entrails of beings still palpitating with the breath of life. (De Nogales, 1926: 122–4)

In 1919 some Turks also acknowledged the extent of the crime. The new Ottoman government initiated war crimes trials, and the minister of the interior wrote bluntly:

Four or five years ago was committed in this land a crime unique in history, a crime which makes the world shudder. In view of the immense extent of the crime, the authors are not five or ten people but hundreds of thousands. . . . It is already a proven fact that this tragedy was planned by the decisions and orders of the Ittihadist Central Committee. (Andonian, 1920: 167–8; my translation)

Unfortunately, this regime was soon overthrown by a more nationalist one and the trials were discontinued. Ever since, Turkish governments have alternated denials and silence, though the dissident views of a few brave Turkish historians and journalists are being published in national newspapers. Taner Akcam in *Yeni Binyil* (October 8, 2000) states, "it is beyond debate that the events of 1915 qualify as genocide according to the 1948 UN definitions." He adds that Attaturk himself had labeled them as *massacres* – which amounted to saying *genocide* before the word was invented. Halil Berktay in *Radikal* (October 9, 2000) talks just as frankly. He distinguishes between "Armenian gangs," capable of "local violence" and inflicting "one or two thousand" Muslim casualties, and the regime's systematic organization of deportations by murderous Special Forces who killed "at least 600,000."

At the time, the Turkish leaders only acknowledged that they were embarked upon severe deportations, not genocide or even deliberate massacres. Talaat treated American Ambassador Morgenthau to a little speech:

We base our objections to the Armenians on three distinct grounds. In the first place, they have enriched themselves at the expense of the Turks. In the second place, they are determined to domineer over us and to establish a separate state. In the third place, they have openly encouraged our enemies. They have assisted the Russians in the Caucasus and our failure there is largely explained by their actions. We have therefore come to the irrevocable decision that we shall make them powerless before this war is ended.

Morgenthau urged him to consider the disastrous economic consequences of mass deportations. Talaat replied bluntly:

We care nothing about the commercial loss.... We don't worry about that.... We will not have the Armenians anywhere in Anatolia. They can live in the desert but nowhere else.

Of course, these possessionless women and children could not live in the desert. Talaat explained to a German journalist why the policy must involve all Armenians:

We have been reproached for making no distinction between the innocent Armenians and the guilty; but that was utterly impossible, in view of the fact that those who were innocent today might be guilty tomorrow.... Our acts have been dictated by a national and historical necessity. The idea of guaranteeing the existence of Turkey must outweigh every other consideration.

He is admitting that deportations were countering a future as well as a present threat. This was a preemptive strike justified by historical necessity. We later see Himmler using the same reasoning. Enver Pasha opened up similarly to Morgenthau:

The great trouble with the Armenians is that they are separatists.... It is our own experience with revolutions which makes us fear the Armenians. We have therefore adopted the plan of scattering them so that they can do us no harm.... Economic considerations are of no importance at this time. The only important thing is to win. That's the only thing we have in mind. If we win, everything will be all right; if we lose everything will be all wrong any how. Our situation is desperate, I admit it, and we are fighting as desperate men fight.

Morgenthau then offered him a chance to deflect blame to others. The ambassador said he appreciated that subordinates had gone much further than the Committee had ever intended. But Enver was offended by this suggestion, replying:

You are greatly mistaken. We have this country absolutely under control. I have no desire to shift the blame onto our underlings and I am entirely willing to accept the responsibility myself for everything that has taken place. The Cabinet itself has ordered the deportations. (Morgenthau, 1918: 336–8, 347–52; cf. Bryce, 1972: 633, 636)

Only the word deportations is retained as cover. The most extreme measures are necessary for the defense of the country. Until it is saved, both morality and the economy can go to hell.

For the Turk cast as the oppressed, humiliated victim, faced with Allied invasions, forcible deportation from the war zones might have seemed a reasonable response. Relocate the Armenians to a place where they could not collaborate and where Turkish troops would not be needed to watch over them. Deportations were an Ottoman tradition, and forced relocations became standard war policy during the 20th century. We can't be certain whether deportation was ever a genuine policy – or, if it was, at what precise point it was changed to mass murder. But by mid-1915 participants in the deportations knew they were systematically murderous. Many must have known they were an attempt at genocide. The process was not as tightly organized as the later Nazi genocides, and there were more local variations. As we shall see, moderate officials could delay the process as well as save Armenians willing to convert to Islam. In many areas, Armenians who were Protestant or Catholic (rather then belonging to the Armenian Apostolic Church) were exempted, though not by all local officials (Barton, 1998, and Bryce, 1972, detail such variations). Yet the consistent direction of flow of the deportees, the sequencing of phases, and the division into two April-to-September "seasons" suggest an overall plan being consistently implemented (Kévorkian, 1998).

PERPETRATING ELITES

We can identify four main overlapping institutional networks of perpetrators. We know something of who they were, though we have very little evidence of their motivations.

Key Ministerial Elites

This was a decidedly statist genocide, initiated at the highest levels of government and implemented through several civilian state agencies. It did not involve the entire state administration, but it did involve its core. This was an old imperial state operating in a backward economy. It did not have many civilian bureaucracies penetrating the country – education, health, communications, and so on. Its core remained the Interior and War Ministries. The Interior Ministry commanded large armed police and gendarmerie forces, while the War Ministry now commanded a massive army engaged on a four-front war along almost all of its borders. Army units were being constantly moved across the country between the Dardanelles, the Caucasus, Mesopotamia, and Syria and so could make intermittent murderous contributions. The two ministries also dominated the more advanced reaches of the country's communications system, especially the telegraph and the limited railway network.

The two ministries dominated the Young Turk regime, since in them lay the core of their political support. The triumvirs were the interior, war, and navy ministers (Djemal, the navy minister, doubled-up as governor and army commander in Syria). The Interior and War Ministries coordinated the genocide. Orders issued by Talaat and his Interior Ministry assistants were much more important than regulations and laws published by the government as a whole (Kaiser, 2000b). Though the Special Organization described later had some autonomy during the killing process, the telegrams coordinating its movements were sent through the Interior Ministry. The telegraph was a very effective means of coordination. All the mayors and governors involved in the genocide were receiving regular telegraphed orders from Constantinople. They knew quite early what was coming. American missionary Stella Loughridge had conversations during April–May 1915 with officials in Cesarea. They gave her similar warnings: that "not an Armenian was to be left" in the district, that "something terrible was to happen to our school girls and boys," that there "was no hope for the Armenians," and they should all become Muslims to avert their fate (Barton, 1998: 116; cf. Bryce, 1972). This implies official coordination at an early stage.

Two spinoff departments were also involved. A Deportations Department centered in Aleppo supervised the southward flow of deportees. It was within the Ministry of the Interior, but its director general was Shukru, a core member of both the CUP and the Special Forces, so it had both a certain institutional autonomy and a radical fervor. The Interior Ministry's "Directorate for the Settlement of Tribes and Immigrants" was a more subordinate agency that had built up its expertise during the resettlement programs of the previous two years. It made inventories, stored and sold Armenian property, and resettled refugee Muslims in their stead. The Directorate could mobilize popular support since refugee and local Muslims were acquiring property and businesses at knockdown prices. Non-Muslims were barred from acquiring Armenian property (Kaiser, 2000b). The ideological cover provided by a supposedly innocuous "Resettlement" office was also important in legitimizing the process.

The connection between the Young Turks and these institutions endured. After 1918 the initial war crimes trials were hindered by widespread sympathy for the accused in the civil service, and especially in the War Office, Interior Ministry, and police forces. Many were the documents destroyed, the witnesses intimidated, in order to abort the prosecutions. But the relationship had been greatly tightened by the purges of 1913, which constituted an important precondition for genocide – though presumably not an intended one. The state became a party-state, while the army was commanded by many party members. Only a minority of officials or officers can have been Ittihadists, since this was a big state but quite a small party. As we will see, only some officers and officials were perpetrators. Yet almost all the worst perpetrators described by eyewitnesses are identified as hard-line Ittihadists. So we must investigate further within the state to identify these radicalized officials and officers.

Factional Struggles Among Officials

The radical elite did not need the active support of all civilian officials. The CUP could use wartime emergency powers to bypass nonparty administrative channels and replace dissidents. The Deportation Order was railroaded through the full cabinet and Parliament was suspended, cutting short public discussion. There was some dissent at the highest levels, though the sources disagree about the identity of the leading dissenter. Trumpener (1968) suggests that the palace chief minister, the Grand Vizier Said Halim (and his faction), grew unhappy. Halim was too powerful to dismiss, but in October 1915 he was ousted from the Foreign Ministry post he also held. His replacement, says Trumpener, was the more reliable Minister of Justice Halil Bey, from a landowning family, educated in Paris, a Young Turk since at least 1908. Yet Ambassador Morgenthau has it exactly the other way around – suggesting from his conversations that Halim was the radical, while Halil had said to him, "I agree that the government has made serious mistakes in the treatment of the Armenians" (he added that he was not prepared to rock the boat by saying this publicly). The leading cleric in the administration, Shaikh-ul-Islam Khairi, resigned in May 1916 and was replaced as minister of pious foundations by the well-known radical Musa Kiazim (www.armenian-genocide.org/chronology/1916). Yet, in any case, the cabinet was increasingly bypassed as provincial officials took instructions from the CUP rather than it.

By May 1916 there were signs of independence at the very top, from one of the triumvirs, Djemal Pasha. In his memoirs he says he had argued strenuously for resettling the Armenians in the interior of Anatolia, away from all fronts. Deporting them to the south would only obstruct the war effort. He says he was overruled and the deportations implemented through civilian channels in which he played no role. He further claims he saved 150,000 southern deportees by bringing them to Beirut and Aleppo (Djemal Pasha, 1922: 277–9). Others also credit him with saving wealthy Armenians (for money), allowing Armenian artisans to contribute labor to the war effort, and finally offering all Armenians in Syria conversion to Islam. The detailed evidence of the Circassian officer, Hassan Amdja, confirms Djemal's moderation in the summer of 1916. Kévorkian believes this was less humanitarian than geopolitically motivated. Armenians would be useful to an attempted rapprochement with Russia, made through Armenian intermediaries. Djemal exercised considerable autonomy in his own fiefdom as governor and army commander in Syria and Palestine. Now he would make peace if the Russians let him assume the sultancy (Hartunian, 1986: 115, 358–61; Kévorkian, 1998: 53–9, 228–37; MacFie, 1998: 137–9; Morgenthau, 1918: 174; Trumpener, 1968: 124–5, 230–1, 247). Yet all this goes against Djemal's sternness against Arab nationalists and his ferocity when dealing with the Jews of Palestine. After pressure from the German and American ambassadors, the CUP removed the hard-line governor of Jaffa, who was intent on deporting all Jews who were not Ottoman subjects. Yet Djemal subverted this directive from Istanbul, appointing the man to his own staff so that he could continue the policy. He told a Zionist official: "We, the Young Turks, deem the Zionists to be deserving of hanging, but I am tired of hangings. We will disperse you throughout the Turkish state and will not allow you to congregate in any one place." Thus he forced the 9,000 Jews of Jaffa and Tel Aviv northward, and many died en route. He tried to do the same to the Jerusalem Jews before being stopped by Istanbul (again under German pressure). The British advance of 1917 then saved the Jews of Palestine from worse (Karsh & Karsh, 1999: 166–70). It is difficult to see Djemal as a moderate, though he did show considerable independence.

Further down the hierarchy there was more dissent. Morgenthau believed that the authority of the CUP throughout the empire was "exceedingly thin" (1918: 227). Yalman (1972: 326–32) says that "most" of the western regions' officials resisted implementing the deportation. He instances the governor of Smyrna, Rahmi Bey, who prevented the removal of any Armenian from his province, and says that another governor left the order "on paper" and sat passively in office doing nothing to implement it. Berktay says that "governors and commanders" issued "an arrest order for Bahaittin Sakir," the leading perpetrator (in the newspaper *Radikal*, Oct. 9, 2000). Foreign consuls and missionaries, in regular contact with local officials, constantly remark on whether they are moderates or hard-liners. The leading officials in Kharput, Broussa, Urfa, Marash, Zeitun, and Aintab are described as especially ruthless, while there was severe factional fighting among officials in Trebizond, Adana, and Konia (Bryce, 1972).

But dissident administrators were easy to remove. The normal outcome of conflict was that the Interior Ministry dismissed the moderate official (occasionally imprisoning him) and sought to replace him with a hard-liner. This did not always work, whether because the regime misjudged the character of the substitute or because the new man was horrified by the reality of deportations. In this case there was a second replacement, and this seems to have worked (presumably the second time around, the regime selected the new man very carefully). The consequence was postponed rather than canceled genocide. Thus governors or mayors were replaced in Angora (present-day Ankara – together with the police chief), Diyarbekir, Van, Everek, Trebizond, Mersina, Konia, Tarsus, Meskene, Marat, Sebka, Deir El-Zor, and Ras Ul-Ain, and it needed two takes at Aleppo and Yozgad. There were probably more replacements in less well-documented places.

The reshuffling probably involved over one-third of the senior officials in the places where most Armenians were killed. In places where Armenians were merely deported, it was easier for officials to comply with orders and shut their eyes to the consequences occurring elsewhere. In Yozgad, Djemal Bey became the second governor to refuse to allow murder. A Turkish witness described him as declaring with bitter sarcasm, "I will never allow the Gendarmes to kill the deportees, you had better release all the convicts and allow them four days to murder the Armenians, and after allow me to catch, with my Gendarmes, all the convicts and have them killed by my Gendarmes." But the local CUP, aided by a visiting undersecretary from the Ministry of the Interior, managed to oust him and bring in a more compliant replacement. Constantinople selected replacements for their radical views or kin or patronage ties. Only in Marash and isolated Mosul did a moderate governor seem to survive in office during the whole period. But even the powers of moderates were more to stall than to prevent, for these cities were also murderously cleansed of Armenians.[8]

The CUP also had a second arm of control. Consuls, missionaries, and British sources reveal the ubiquitous use of CUP "delegates" brought in to control local officials. Dr. Shakir himself was sent to get things started in Dyakibir and Erzerum, assisted by a second outsider, Djemal Effendi, "a fanatic of the foulest type." In Deir el-Zor, the moderate governor, Ali Suad, ignored one summons to report to the Aleppo Deportations Office and one to report to Constantinople. After three Ittihad delegates visited the town incognito, he was transferred to Baghdad – whose deported Armenians he had been protecting in Deir el-Zor! He was replaced by Salh Zeki, who had already proved his ferocity as vice-governor of Everek. Promotion came that way. In Ras ul-Ain, Kerim Refi, described as a savage refugee Turk from Europe, was the man who as vice-governor actually organized the massacres, utilizing many brigands, especially Circassians. In Hadjin, Court Martial Judge Alai Bey arrived to get things started. To foreigners he was courteous but firm, declaring he would carry out "the necessary actions of the Turkish government against Armenian nationalists." For two weeks he set the deportations in motion; then he left, delegating his organization to reliable local officials (Bryce, 1972: 236, 492–4).

Though the delegates were ideologists, many also benefited materially from looting and career advancement. An enthusiastic Ittihadist delegate was sent to Angora to vet the activities of the moderate governor. He then succeeded him as governor and implicated local councillors and imams (clerics) in the process by ordering them to read out calls to "rid ourselves of all these Armenian parasites" at the streetcorners and mosques. Tahir Jevdet, Enver's brother-in-law, had first expedited atrocities in Van. He was then sent to do the same as governor-general of Adana. Talaat's own undersecretary since 1913 and member of the shadowy "Council on Terrorism," Ali Muenif Bey, was entrusted with enforcing the actual deportations in Adana and Yozgat.

---

[8] These named cities are documented in Barton (1998: 155–6), Bryce (1972: 223, 329, 377, 382–3, 445–6, 474), Hartunian (1986: 62, 84), Kazanjian (1989: 7, 96, 260), Kévorkian (1998: 108–14, 128–9, 181, 191, 223–4), *U.S. Documents* (1993–5, I: 133, 148; II: 38, 78, 87, 96), and Yeghiayan (1991: 196–7, 311, 354).

Yozgat's first two governors balked at their orders, while there was German pressure for moderation in Adana. In Adana, Ali Muenif Bey mollified the Germans by posing as the advocate of "orderly deportations" trying to restrain the more rabid local CUP leader, Ismael Safa (Kaiser, 2000a).

The city of Aleppo was distinctive, with few Armenian residents but the main reception center for deportees and housing the country's Deportations Department. Its director-general, Shukru Bey, and his deputy, Nouri Bey, won a power struggle against two moderate governors by having administrative boundaries redrawn, putting much of the province in safer hands (Bryce, 1972: 469). Then the third governor, Bekir Sami Bey, was doubly reliable, an Ittihadist hard-liner and a kinsman of Talaat. It is said that he was also personally involved in atrocities. Nouri Bey energetically fulfilled his duties, telegraphing to Constantinople on January 10, 1916:

It is established, after a survey, that scarcely 10% of the Armenians submitted to deportation have arrived at their destination. The others died en route through famine, sickness and other similar natural causes. I hope to obtain the same result for the survivors, in treating them with rigour.

These men were aided by Essad Bey, assistant director of the Intelligence Department of the secretive "Directorate for Public Security," which organized the Special Forces. The district's extermination units sent out to finish off Armenian employees of the Baghdad Railway were also under local CUP command (Andonian, 1920: 116–17; Kaiser, 1999b: 91, 102; Kaiser, 2000a). British dossiers on Turkish war criminals detail a dozen instances of local deportations organized by local CUP leaders.[9]

Some officials were zealous because of family or other patronage connections. This overlapped with a second motivation – this was the way to achieve promotion (Bryce, 1972: 23). Others shared a careerist zeal to wipe out past dissent. Hilmi Abdul Kadir was in 1914 a retired army staff colonel. His problem was that earlier he had sided with the sultan and the Ottoman liberals against the CUP. In 1914 he was sidelined as the public engineer in the isolated southeastern city of Mosul. However, he hailed from the town of Kastamoni, an Ittihadist stronghold. Hilmi knew the CUP minister of education, Shukri Bey, who came from there. "Knowing him well," Shuki "took him under his protection" and recommended him to his CUP colleagues. "Having thus made his peace with, but also his show of devotion to the CUP Chiefs, he was ripe for executing all the dishonest or cruel missions, that would be confided to him," said a witness. Along with the Mosul CUP leaders, he bypassed the moderate governor, leading the district brigands

---

[9] The British had taken to Malta 118 Turks whom they suspected of having committed war crimes. Yeghiayan (1991) has listed the charges against 60 of them, together with snatches of evidence. But before the British trial preparations were complete, half of the prisoners were exchanged for British POWs held by the Turks, and then all prosecutions were aborted.

and organizing the killing of thousands of deportees ending up in Mosul. In the process, he enriched himself and raped Armenian boys and girls (Bryce, 1972: 95; Yeghiayan, 1991: 251–7). He was prepared to do just about anything – not a devoted Ittihadist but a devoted careerist. There was a similar man in Adapazar. The mayor and the police chief were moderates, but they were undermined by a man called "the Beast," an outsider, probably a CUP delegate. He had been released from prison for political offenses, "working for his liberty by carrying on this devilish work." He would taunt the Armenians with "What do I care for your Mayor? . . . He says you are good people, but he is no good himself. . . . My orders come from Talaat Bey" (Bryce, 1972: 105). The regime did not need many zealots to replace the recalcitrant governors and mayors. A core of radicals, enlarged by patronage and promotion, provided the men.

Provincial governors were men of stature, not easily intimidated. Few lower officials dared openly resist. They preferred compromises and coping mechanisms. The wife of a village mayor "told our ladies how she had wept over the terrible things she had seen and how she had tried to keep her husband from having anything to do with them." Many disapproved but said they bowed to superior power. Consul Davies says that the governor of Mamouret ul-Aziz allowed many Armenians to escape over the Russian border. But in the end he carried out the government policy, saying "he was obliged to carry out orders" (*U.S. Documents*, 1995: III: 45–6). An official said, "We are living in the twentieth century. Now power is the more essential force, and not morality or principles" (Davidson, 1985: 177). And in the last resort, the capital could undermine official orders by more private ones issued to radicals (Bryce, 1972: 353, 362, 376, 442).

Dissidents held some important offices. But since they had been out of power since the purges of 1913, they had no collective organization that could change the overall policy coming from Talaat. They feared the consequences of individual dissent, and censorship prevented them from knowing much about other dissenters elsewhere. An American missionary believed hundreds of men across Turkey were languishing in prison for dissent (Barton, 1998: 191). Most officials, like most of us, were not that brave.

Moral cowardice and careerism were ordinary motives for compliance. So was wartime patriotism. The missionary Harriet Fisher reports a conversation with a prominent female Ittihadist, Halide Edip, when the two were working together in refugee relief in May 1917:

She was a loyal Turk. At one time she said, "No one can love his country more than I, yet no one can criticize it more severely. . . . Nothing can remove the stain of these massacres from my nation." When I asked her if the leaders had wanted it to go on with such brutality, she said "Some of them did and still do. It is not finished yet. . . . But she added "Some did not. But they were not so practical and did not have executive power. Besides it was put up to us in this way. We are at war. Enemies are

on every side. If we appear divided all will be lost. It is our nation or the Armenians. "
(Barton, 1998: 164)

The ability of the party-state to blend coercion, careerism, and country was
decisive for its officials – as will prove ubiquitous in 20th-century genocide.
Despite all dissent, the radical Ittihadist part of the state was in control.
Orders were transmitted down through party-controlled offices, and the
regime was quickly able to extend the span of this control. This was not
a united state launching genocide. But its radical core could exercise a mixture of ministerial and party powers to enforce its will. Genocide does not
need an entire state as its perpetrator.

Factional Struggles Among Soldiers

Crucial in this army had been the 1913 purges, giving more power to the radicals. Now radical officers were giving the orders on behalf of the legitimate
civilian government of the country. Wartime contributed a second legitimation. The "night and fog" of war – martial law, a front line ranging across
some Armenian settlements and the necessity to kill the enemy – these were
the conditions enabling a radicalized slice of the army to aid mass murder
and for the army as a whole not to obstruct it. Soldiers contributed much of
the early killing against Armenian strongholds in Cilicia and near the Russian
front. They participated more erratically along the Baghdad Railway. They
were the most lethal force, since they were the best armed. But they were
not the main force used. Only a minority of officers or men could have ever
come near atrocities, and only a few thousand could have murdered.

De Nogales focuses the blame more narrowly. He excuses the army as a
whole and regular soldiers in particular. He generally contrasts professional
Turkish officers, for whom he has considerable respect, with officers whose
personal ambitions and political connections, he says, reinforced their defects of character. He is contrasting the "professional soldier" (like himself),
with some respect for the rules of war, and the "political soldier" without
such respect. He adds that the troops used in atrocities by such political soldiers were irregular forces – especially Kurds and some gendarmerie units.
This network of perpetrators was formed (as the Nazis were later to say) of
political soldiers. There were few Ittihadists except at the higher levels, but
not that many were needed. Most soldiers went through the war without
encountering the genocide, as was probably so of General Mustafa Kemal
(later the father of his country, Attaturk). He seems to have had rather cool
relations with the CUP. But like many of his comrades, he focused on fighting the war and said nothing in public about the deportations. Like civilian
officials, the more politically committed soldiers often had connections (the
murderous General Halil was Enver's uncle). Others had had prior careers in
such violence, for example in organizing guerrilla forces and punitive raids

in the Balkans, commanding units containing 4,000 criminals released from prison for the purpose (says Dadrian, 1994b: 97–8). Their experience formed the core of the Special Forces described here.

This was a well-disciplined army. Foreigners routinely praised the bravery and unswerving obedience of the ordinary soldier. We know of no units collectively refusing their assignments. Obedience in the ranks was enforced by brutal discipline and ruthless measures against dissent. Had soldiers refused to follow deportation orders, they would have been shot. When survivors occasionally describe soldiers helping them, the help was covert. Officers would not have been shot, but they had their careers to think of. Some did refuse to implement the orders, including the two highest-ranking Army Group commanders in the East. One of these said he would prefer to see the Armenians merely dispersed and relocated.

Army officers were difficult to remove. Some relinquished their posts and some were sidelined, but others continued to obstruct the genocide. Several officers had murderers court-martialed and shot. One despairing major committed suicide, declaring that he was "ashamed to live as a Turk." The regime tried to assign reliable officers for key missions, and CUP members got rapid promotion and assignment to critical deportation tasks. In the second phase of the genocide, many officers faced a choice between political exterminism and professional protection of Armenian labor. Armenians were useful as artisans making uniforms and other military supplies, working in hospitals, and building roads, railways, and tunnels. Officers from Djemal Pasha and General Ghalib Bey down protected useful Armenians (Bryce, 1972: 242; Dadrian, 1994b: 95–6; Kévorkian, 1998: 151, 191, 228–237; Yalman, 1970: 326–32; Yeghiayan, 1991: 258, 279). The army collectively did little to obstruct genocide, but for routine butchery the regime felt – just as the Nazis did later – that it could not routinely rely on regular officers and men, and so it turned elsewhere.

Paramilitary Killers

The main killers, specializing in massacring bound men and columns of women, children, and the elderly, were the 20,000–30,000 men of the paramilitary forces organized by the Teskilat-I Mahsusa (the Special Organization). These Special Forces were unique among the murdering paramilitaries described in this book. They were not an independent party militia like the Nazi SA or the Rwandan Interahamwe, but nor were they as tightly organized from top to bottom as the Nazi SS. They were organized from within the party-state, but peculiarly. They originated in the CUP *fedais* of the period 1907–11, mentioned in the previous chapter. These were initially Enver Pasha's personal organization within the military, used for covert guerrilla assignments. They were reorganized and renamed the Teskilat-I Mahsusa in 1913 or early 1914, when they were put under the command of the Directorate for Public Security, a secretive organization within the Interior Ministry, but staffed only by CUP members with its own budget. Thus neither the cabinet nor any other collective constitutional body controlled the organization. It appears to have been the core of the radical faction of the CUP from at least 1913 on.

It had acquired two purposes, one a covert but legitimate form of warfare, the other completely hidden and totally illegitimate. The first purpose was guerrilla warfare behind enemy lines. This had begun in 1907 in the Balkans and continued intermittently there for the next seven years. In 1911 they were used very effectively in the North African campaign against the Italians. In 1914 the initial idea was to use the same guerrilla techniques to foment revolt among Muslims in Arabia and Russia. In Arabia its missions were the counterpart to those of Lawrence of Arabia. Both Lawrence and the Turkish Special Forces sought to recruit Arab tribes to their side by bribes, gifts of arms, and spurious promises of freedom. They were not too choosy about the methods used by their clients. This was dirty warfare, but it was not usually mass murder or ethnic cleansing. The Special Forces recruited mainly ex-army officers plus a few civilian adventurers. They were almost all Turks. The higher-ranking officers were Ittihadists, but the organization also recruited many lured by simple patriotism or a desire for adventure and speedy meritocratic advancement – like their counterparts in other countries' special forces. By 1914 the Turks could count on many with experience in previous dirty wars (Stoddart, 1964).

But they did not get the same opportunities against the Russians. The rout of Enver's army prevented Turkish units from crossing the border to foment trouble in Russia. Instead, they began a secret dirty war in Turkey itself, building on their attacks on Macedonian and Greek Christian villages in 1913 and 1914 to eliminate supposedly disloyal ethnic minorities. In 1914 Special Forces officers, in collaboration with Ottoman officials, used murder and deportation to destroy small Zionist communities in Palestine (Aaronsohn, 1917: 47–56). The following year they turned against the far more numerous Armenians, supposedly providing sympathizers and saboteurs for the Russians. Their German liaison officer, Colonel Stange, said flatly that "Military reasons were of secondary importance for the deportation of the Armenians ... an intervention from outside was not expected ... military considerations and insurgent tendencies in certain parts of the country afforded welcome pretexts." Their activities remained somewhat independent of the Committee, and so were deniable by the regime, but they were deliberately given a free hand. The Special Forces may have committed most of the murders of Armenians – with "beastly brutality," said Stange. As their role expanded, care was taken to recruit committed Ittihadists as their officers (Dadrian, 1993: 68; 1994b: 110–11; 1996: 43–9).

The British postwar dossiers reveal several types of local commanders. Halil Bey (later Pasha) had spent his entire career in the Special Forces. He had little education but rose to corporal in a band of brigands in the Balkans. By 1915 he was leading the Special Forces inside Persia, organizing massacres. The Yozgat Special Forces were a family business, its brigands led by four brothers. Two were small leather and shoe merchants and two were rougher types with a reputation for violence – one had served time for murder. The two merchants had been adherents of the CUP since 1908, though they were of too low status for leadership positions in it. They were apparently jealous of the greater wealth of local Armenian merchants – the "national bourgeoisie" in waiting. When CUP pressure ousted the moderate Yozgat governor quoted earlier, the four brothers were deemed suitably motivated to lead the local Special Forces, presumably two for the looting and two for the killing. Instructed by higher-level CUP officials, they organized the killing of 8,000 of the 10,000 local Armenians and helped themselves liberally to their property. A third motivation was revealed by Hodja Ilias, CUP deputy for Marash, but also a religious scholar who wrote venomous pamphlets against Christians. He became "a scandal among the Moslems" for raping Christian girls, but his suitability came from his propaganda supporting the declaration of *Jihad* (holy war). Liaising with local CUP leaders, he led Kurdish chiefs in killing raids in the southeast (Yeghiayan, 1991: 325–7, 342–56, 387–90).

But the rank-and-file were different. Some were uniformed gendarmes, but since most regular gendarmes had been conscripted into the army, the gendarmerie had been forced to draft many raw recruits unsuitable for military service. They were reinforced by two types of irregular unit referred to by all sides as brigands (*cetes*). One was composed of criminals. Edicts, trial transcripts, Stange's reports, and survivors all concur that most of these rank-and-file recruits were conscripted criminals from the prisons, their crimes pardoned for undertaking this atrocious task. The prisons were emptied to find men who would suit. Though they may have been unaware of the full extent of the task ahead, they were not likely to shrink from it, since it entailed their own freedom plus substantial material gains. Looting opportunities were considerable, but in some areas they officially received half of the wealth expropriated from the local Armenians. The second type of brigand unit was tribal, led by Kurdish, Chechen, and Circassian chiefs. Roving Special Forces officers would sometimes offer payment to the chiefs, but again the normal incentive was loot. Kurdish tribes dominated massacres in several eastern regions, Chechens in parts of the south, Circassians in both. These tribal groups rarely helped plan the deportations, but they repeatedly attacked and massacred isolated Armenian villages and refugee columns. In Kharput, said Consul Davies, almost all the killing was done by the gendarmerie and the convicts, not the Kurds. But in Kurdistan proper it was often the reverse (Davies, 1989: 156; Kévorkian, 1998; *U.S. Documents*,

1994: 143–52). I should add that all the killers were male, but they had a fairly normal age structure – without the disproportionate numbers of young males found in many other paramilitary groups discussed in this book. This was because so many young men were at the front. Women were not involved because women almost never bore arms in this society.

Few Kurds and few rankers in any unit can have been ideological killers – though criminals and Kurds probably had little love for the relatively privileged Armenians, nor the Caucasian tribes for Christians (who had expelled them from Russia), nor the Kurds for the Russian forces invading their lands. These motives of retaliation and revenge helped still normal taboos against murdering helpless human beings. Materialist killing probably predominated, though the chiefs had to balance material inducements against geopolitical caution – did the tribe's interest lie in allying with the Turks, with the Entente, or with neutrality? A life of crime or of tribal warfare may also give men pleasure in violence. Survivors often described them killing and raping with relish. These were skilled practitioners of rather wild forms of tribal or criminal violence, and some reveled in their skills. These were willing soldiers of evil.

Ordinary Turks

To what extent were ordinary Turks involved in, or supportive of, genocide, and what were their motivations? It is not easy to be precise, since our main sources, the Armenian survivors and the missionaries active in the Armenian communities, were rarely privy to local Turkish discussions. Their main initial impressions were of mobs and menacing noises coming from inside mosques, followed by villagers silently watching their refugee columns. We cannot get close to many Turks. I reject Dadrian's (1996: 121–7) resort to simplistic nationalist theory. He says that the warrior values of the Turk combined with the intolerance of Islam to generate a cultural predisposition to massacre Christians. But neither Islam nor the army were the main instruments of death. Nor is any whole people or its culture intrinsically murderous.

However, some broad generalizations seem reasonable. Since the regime was actively organizing the whole process of genocide, these events involved less mass involvement than had earlier Ottoman pogroms. Villagers and townspeople were usually required to do little. Mobs might be useful, but a hundred or two rioting in a town of many thousands would suffice to put pressure on the Armenians. An American missionary noted:

In former outbreaks, where the Armenians were attacked by the rabble, the officials had always professed to try to stop the outbreak, and came to the tardy rescue of the sufferers, after a few had been killed; but in this case, the destruction of the Armenians was a plan for which the government itself stood sponsor, and the execution of the plan, in all of its horrid extremes, was pressed on local officials, willing and unwilling alike, by the relentless efficiency of the military staff whose orders could not be resisted... we who had lived all our lives among the Turks and knew something of their ways said again and again at the time, "This is no Turkish outbreak." It was altogether too cold, too calculating and too efficient. The common people liked it not. (Riggs, 1997: 96)

Reverend Riggs is here contradicting a nationalist stereotype of perpetrators that the Turks did it, aided by the Kurds, the Chechens, and others. Like others, Riggs said many Turks initially helped their Armenian neighbors. Missionaries often instance Turks hiding Armenians (Barton, 1998: 45). But the numbers declined drastically once officials declared that their orders were to kill anyone harboring fugitives. Local Turks were intimidated by the proclamation of General Kamil:

Any Muslim who dares to harbor an Armenian will be hanged in front of his house which will also be burned down. If the culprit is an official he will be dismissed and court-martialed. If those protecting the Armenians are military people, they will stripped of their military status and will be handed over to the court-martial. (Dadrian, 1995: 235–8; 1996: 39; 1997: 43–4; Merdjimékian, 1919: 6–10)

We shouldn't underestimate the power of such threats. Since many Turks had rather mixed feelings about Armenians, a little fear would easily deter risk-taking on their behalf.

This Armenian woman's account gives a colder view of "ordinary Turks" in Marsovan:

Fear began to fall on the Armenian population in May; it was felt... the Government was about to take measures against us. There was no question of a popular Turkish rising against us; the whole thing was done by Government order. The Turkish population remained gladly callous throughout. The deportations and massacres that ensued were carried out by the Government only through its officials, though of course very many Turkish men volunteered for the official job of butchering the Christian. In the country the Turkish peasants, men and women, took an active part in massacring and torturing, but always with official sanction. Throughout the massacre period, there was never any excitement among the Turkish populace; all was cold blooded murder by official order or at any rate with official sanction. (Yeghiayan, 1991: 94; cf. Armenian Political Trials, 1985: 6–10, 88–9)

Obviously, Turks behaved variously. Though survivors describe most of their police and gendarme escorts as terrible, they identify a few kindhearted ones (Davidson, 1985: 111–14, 120; Merdjimékian, 1919: 7; Sarafian, 1994: 136, 159). Though most bystanders are described as unhelpful, some neighbors and others helped them. Many Turks urged them to save themselves by converting; many took bribes to help them. "There is not a Turk who does not love to be bribed" is a refrain of survivor stories (Jafarian, 1989: 94, 99; Kazanjian, 1989: 6–8, 106, 128–9, 172, 174–5, 270, 366). Towns generating mobs baying for action, looting, or blood were not common, but more often were found in Anatolian areas where Armenians, Turks, and Kurds had long been struggling over the land. Here Turks and Kurds justified violence as retaliation against past injustices. One survivor describes a crowd yelling, "Be done with the Christians! Long live the nation!" (Davidson, 1985: 76). Another describes shootings "in the presence and to the joy of the local rabble" and another mob jeering at the deportees, "glorifying their prophet for this blessed day" (Hartunian, 1986: 61, 101). Mobs rarely constituted a sizable proportion of a town's population, though the sources allow no precision as to numbers.

One survivor's journey across Turkey conveys a sense of the variety of Turkish reactions. Bedoukian encounters one crowd of villagers viciously assaulting deportee women and children, seeking to kill them. Another crowd "were contemptuous and derided us but did not commit any outright cruelty. I thought they were trying hard to hate the refugees, but not quite succeeding." In a third place, where Turks and Armenians had lived closely among each other, Turks clicked their tongues as a sign of compassion, saying, "It's a pity." Yet they were "embarrassed to approach us, being aware of Armenian–Turk tensions." In the same town, a Turkish youth tried to court Bedoukian's pretty sister by throwing her scented poppy seeds wrapped in a bright handkerchief over the garden wall. Her family did not view this as a suitable match (they had not lost all sense of their superior social status). They threw the handkerchief back – dipped in the contents of the household latrine. The consequence of this contemptuous act? "We were never bothered again by our neighbors" – not the reaction we might expect from Turks now enjoying the upper hand over vulnerable deportees. On the banks of the Euphrates a fifth set of locals unfavorably compared "lazy and obnoxious" Turkish refugees resettled in the homes of deported Armenians with the hardworking, dignified refugee Armenians (Bedoukian, 1978: 21, 27, 30, 59, 73–4, 93–4, 126). Bedoukian had experienced the whole gamut of possible Turkish reactions.

The Bryce Report also reported varying eyewitness accounts. A foreign physician noted ideological support for the genocide growing: "the common people came to believe more and more the grossly exaggerated stories and whole-cloth lies manufactured for the very purpose of exciting the sympathy of the common people towards the scheme" (1972: 412). Regime censorship controlled the flow of information. How would Turks elsewhere know the truth about Van? As the regime consolidated its hold over officials, it closed off alternative sources of knowledge. Only a few Turks killed, more approved, but most remained silent.

Nor were the perpetrators the Kurds – though this collective actor does figure in some accounts. Kurdish tribal bands participated in many massacres. Yet Kurdish villagers helped Armenian refugee columns out of sympathy for suffering human beings (Barton, 1998: 100–4; Davies, 1989: 108; Jafarian, 1989: 108; Marashlian, 1999: 120). In the second phase of the genocide, in

Syria and Mesopotamia, Chechens and Circassians were prominent in the massacres. Some survivors remembered all of them as terrible, attributing this to the fact that they were refugees from Russia. Either they were desperately poor and coveted Armenian riches, or they had suffered in Russia at the hands of Christians. One Syrian Arab village had rushed to massacre Armenian deportees, believing a rumor spread by Ittihadist propagandists that "Zetouni brigands" (Armenians) had just massacred nearby villagers (Kévorkian, 1998: 78–90, 95, 107). Most survivors describe Arabs as being more sympathetic than were Turks or Chechens, with Kurds being somewhere in the middle. Ethnicity did affect attitudes. Yet it is the language of organic nationalism – and not of social science – to attribute action and motives to ethnic groups as wholes. Smaller organized, mobilized groups act. If Turks and Armenians today were to fully realize this, then most would not act so defensively about this genocide, and we could find out more precisely what happened. More importantly, the two communities could begin the process of reconciliation.

Since Armenians tended to be wealthier than their neighbors, class resentment and greed could motivate many. They motivated officials impounding and siphoning off their valuables, local notables acquiring Armenian businesses at knockdown prices, and poor policemen and Kurdish and other militias seizing anything left. Their empty houses were appropriated, often by refugees in government resettlement schemes. Baghdjian (1987: 75) estimates that even a partial valuation of Armenian property seized would be $1 billion. Local villagers almost all joined in looting around Harput, reported American consuls and missionaries (Davies, 1989: 146–7, 170, 179; Sarafian, 1994: 144, 148). Some joined in the butchery, killing with knives and axes, raping, stripping, and cutting up bodies in the search for hidden or swallowed coins or jewels. If the Armenians were not actually killed, they might be left naked, as the poorest locals stripped off their clothing. This happened twice to an Armenian Catholic priest during his flight (Merdjimékian, 1919: 8, 14). If a government legitimizes looting and the victim is resented as a foreign-cum-class exploiter, then murder may result – in many places besides Turkey.

Young Turk leaders claimed this was a shortcut to the creation of the missing national bourgeoisie, a Muslim economic elite that would be duly grateful to the CUP for its elevation (Adanir & Kaiser, 2000: 14; Kaiser, 2000b; Keyder, 1987: 66). De Nogales said, "the Young Turks, to give them their due, had been honest until the beginning of the war. That pouring torrent of gold, however, blinded and corrupted them" (1926: 169). Looters justified their seizures ideologically in terms of proletarian economic redistribution. Human beings are capable of righteousness even in justifying greed and loot.

This is very mundane human evil. It was coupled with more ferocious, but again recognizably human evil. If the regime declares that the victim is the enemy of the nation and of Islam, is threatening the Turkish state itself, is burning babies in Van, then murder can be committed in a spirit of righteous rage. The disguised Armenian Shiragian (1976: 24) listened to off-duty brigands in Constantinople coffee houses boasting appallingly of cutting off and collecting Armenian women's nipples and of the wealth they had stripped from the infidels:

Not one of these men displayed the slightest vestige of regret, disgust or guilt. They acted as if the Ittihad government were performing a great service for the country. And the same could be said for their listeners.... Other Turks almost cried with jealousy. They kept repeating that the [brigands] were lucky and that not everyone was so fortunate.

Such incidents are common in all the case studies of this book, as well as in other contexts. As Katz (1988) notes in his study of recent American murderers (of their close kin), a sense of righteousness and murder are not opposite but causally linked human qualities.

Economic rationality might be important at the level of the individual perpetrator, but overall this was not an economically rational policy – as Talaat Pasha admitted earlier. German General Liman von Sanders reported that over the winter of 1916–17 the Turkish Army on the Caucasian front lost 60,000 men to disease and starvation, the result, he said, of the destruction of local agriculture because of Armenian deportations. The effects were obvious to many Turks. The American consuls in Aleppo, Mersina, and Mamuret ul-Aziz all noted that local Turks thought it would result in economic disaster. In Mamuret, Davies remarked, "it was killing the goose that laid the golden egg." In Aleppo, Jackson said that with 90 percent of the commerce of the interior in Armenian hands, their elimination was a disaster.

Though few Young Turks were very religious, they found the notion of *Jihad* (declared by the government in November 1914) a useful mobilizer. During World War I the regime was encouraging pan-Islamism to stir up Muslims in areas ruled by Russia, Britain, and France – though without much success. They advocated deporting all Christians, Armenians, Greeks, Nestorians, Jacobites, and Maronites. Some policemen and villagers legitimated killing in terms of *Jihad* (Bishop Balakian's testimony in Armenian Political Trials, 1985: 88–9; Stoddart, 1963: 51–75). Where local massacres began in similar fashion to earlier pogroms, they mobilized mobs shouting Islamic slogans. But in Ras ul-Ain an observer noted that it was the least religious Chechens who first took up the cry of *Jihad*. For them it was a ritual learned ago – and also a cover for material looting (Kévorkian, 1998: 197).

Indeed, some Muslims objected to the massacres because they saw them contradicting the Koran. The Marsovan Turks mentioned by Miss Morley had believed that Christians, not Muslims, must be behind such terrible things. Bryce's reports give varied accounts of Muslim clerics (1972: 250, 497–8). A *hodja* (learned teacher) in Erzindjan justified the local massacre: "The Armenians have committed atrocities at Van. That happened because their religion is inferior. The Moslems should not have followed their example, but should have carried out the massacre with more humanity." I wonder what a humane massacre would look like! Yet the mufti of Hadjin refused to sanction the actions of the CUP delegate brought in to start the city's deportations – "he could see no good in it" (nor did many of the locals in this city or its surrounding villages). This was not primarily an Islamic but a secular nationalist genocide, though the long European struggle between Christian and Muslim had left deep marks on community enmities.

There were many guilty consciences in Turkey. Turks were not the fanatics whom Armenians often described them as being. But genocide does not need to be backed by a whole people. Thirty thousand murderers set amid the silent millions will suffice.

THE BACKGROUNDS OF PERPETRATORS

I know little of the backgrounds of individual perpetrators. Among those initially charged by the British, middle-aged men predominated, and there were no women. This was probably because most were higher-ranking perpetrators. Among CUP militants of lower rank, lower officials, teachers, and professors predominated. As we saw in the previous chapter, this was the core area of recruitment for the radical Young Turks. At the higher levels, people with army officer backgrounds, especially army medical doctors, dominated the inner circles. There were several doctors on the Central Committee, and of about 100 leading perpetrators at least 23 were doctors. A few were apparently performing grisly experiments on Armenian prisoners (injecting them with diseased microbes), and there were reports (not yet authenticated) that gassing occurred. Dr. Resid declared:

though I am a physician, I cannot ignore my nationhood. I came into this world a Turk. My national identification takes precedence over everything else.... Armenian traitors had found a niche for themselves in the bosom of the fatherland; they were dangerous microbes. Isn't it the duty of a doctor to destroy these microbes? (Dadrian, 1986b: 175)

Overrepresented were refugees from the Turkish lost territories, mainly in the European Balkans, though also including Caucasians. The Deportation Edict permitted refugees to occupy deportees' homes. Stürmer sees Muslim refugees (*mohadjis*) as constituting the main thrust of the atrocities (1917: 53, 166–8). Davidson (1985: 77–8) remarks that the police chief of Adana "was someone from the Balkans and when he saw an Armenian he would behave like a mad dog." Another survivor says that the numbers of Ittihadists had been swollen greatly by "a crowd of officials made available at the end of the Balkan War" (Merdjimekian, 1920: 5). The Turkish writer Taner Akcam (1992: 77) stresses the revenge desired by refugees who came to Anatolia from the Balkan wars: they were "beyond being the surviving victims of atrocities, to become the voluntary executioners of the other minorities who were to be destroyed in mass in Anatolia, most especially the Armenians." Refugee nationalists will be overrepresented in almost all the ethnic and political cleansing movements discussed in this book. There were also many Turks from the threatened borders – which will also be a familiar pattern. In trials begun by the postwar Turkish government, one of the main defendants said he was avenging his father-in-law, who had suffered at the hands of the invading Russians aided by local Armenians (Bedrossyan, 1983: 161; Dadrian, 1996: 229; 1997b; Yeghiayan, 1990, 1991).

These are sparse data. They may indicate that the leading perpetrators – except for the Special Forces' rank-and-file – came from the core constituencies of Turkish organic nationalism. But more research is necessary.

THE COMPLICITY OF FOREIGNERS AND THE GERMAN CONNECTION

The Entente powers bore a little indirect responsibility. They had supported Armenian demands for freedom and were trying to force this on Turkey when war broke out. The ferocious Turkish backlash was to some degree a reaction against the link between Armenians and the Christian Entente. Thereafter, the Entente was powerless to intervene. This was a secondary theater of war for the allies, and the Russian and British advances were insufficiently resolute to rescue many Armenians from their fate. Armenians eagerly followed news of the war hoping for Entente breakthroughs, praying that the British landings at Gallipoli would succeed (for that might end the war). The Entente powers had encouraged them but then left them to their fate. We will see that this has been a common failing of the Great Powers when confronted by murderous cleansing. But it is only relatively minor culpability, given the overwhelming salience for the Entente of other fronts more crucial to their war effort.

There was more direct German and Austrian responsibility. Germany, the dominant ally, was the only foreign power that could have conceivably restrained Turkey. Most members of the German and Austrian community in Turkey knew what deportations meant by late 1915. Many of their missionaries, officers, and consuls deplored them. The German embassy did make a belated formal protest, declaring that deportations were acceptable only if they were a military necessity. Of course, the Turkish government replied that they were, and this initially satisfied the embassy. But protests by Germans in Turkey then began to go directly to Berlin and they greatly disturbed the Wilhemstrasse, the German Foreign Ministry. Chancellor Bethmann Hollweg himself overruled a Wilhelmstrasse plan to censure their ally. He observed with lack of humanity yet irrefutable geopolitical logic, "The suggested public condemnation of an ally during the present war would be a measure unlike any in history. Our sole object is to keep Turkey on our side until the end of the war, no matter if Armenians perish over that or not" (Kaiser, 1996: 43–4). The German journalist Stürmer characterized the German attitude as "boundless *cowardice*" (1917: 65; his emphasis). Yet most German diplomats and officers condemned the massacres once their scale and scant military rationale became apparent (Dadrian, 1994a; Trumpener, 1968). A few continued to remain loyal to their ally. Among those involved in the Baghdad Railway, there was no overall unity of viewpoint, concludes Kaiser (1999b). This would seem to hold for the German official community as a whole.

Can we also reverse the causality and hold the Young Turks partially responsible for Nazi genocide? There were similarities between the two genocides (say Astourian, 1995, and Melson, 1992). Armenians viewed as threatening political-ethnic enemies of the nation, their geopolitical wartime vulnerability, and their relative wealth all resemble the Jews in relation to Nazi Germany. Dadrian (1993: 80) also remarks the murderous fusion of "political militarism and militaristic politics" among the Young Turks – so evident also in the SS and in the German Wehrmacht operating on the Eastern Front. Melson also recognizes differences between the two genocides. The Turks were not nearly as racist as the Nazis. Nor did they declare that they wished to wipe out the world's Armenians – as the Nazis declared they would wipe out all Jews. Melson says they only murdered Armenians supposedly blocking national purification, not the smaller Armenian populations in "unthreatened" Turkish Lebanon and Palestine. Armenian women and children were much more likely to survive than were Jewish women and children under the Nazis, which is really the decisive indicator that this was not biological racism. The perpetrators were confident in the strength of patriarchal Turkish society to absorb and assimilate Armenian women and children. The survival rate of rich big-city Armenians was also quite high, since many could bribe their way out of trouble. Nonetheless, some racism had penetrated into Young Turkish ideology, as we saw in the case of the doctors, while Turkish nationalists did later turn on other Armenian communities and on the Greeks as well. More Armenians and Greeks were able to flee abroad than were killed in these final massacres, but the result was the near-total cleansing of the country (Graber, 1996: 140–50; Rummel, 1994: 233–5). But even if the Young Turks might be thought to resemble the Nazi Party, and the Special Forces officer corps the SS, there were far fewer ideological perpetrators among the Turks. Only a few of the rank-and-file perpetrators could have shared much of the Young Turk ideology, beyond a proletarian sense of resentment of Armenian/foreign exploitation. The SS would have also deplored the Turks' methods as wild – not like their own orderly genocide.

Nor in this case were the techniques of genocide very modern. True, the telegraph enabled the ordering and coordinating of the deportations, but modern small arms figured alongside axes, knives, and drownings. The few rail lines were used, but virtually no motorized transport (there was little in the country). The vast majority of deportees walked, as did most accompanying gendarmes. The Turkish government was reserving its modern resources for the war effort, unlike the Nazis. There was also as much bribery as bureaucracy in the organization of the deportations. Obviously, the Nazis were to use more modern methods than these, since theirs was a more advanced country perpetrating murder a generation later. Yet the Turkish genocide was modern in one important sense – I will later argue that this was also the true modernity of the Nazis. The Young Turks initiated genocide because they were committed to the modern ideology of organic nationalism in its mixed proletarian-cum-imperial-revisionist form carried to its genocidal extreme. They carried this through as a modern party-state. The Final Solution to the Jewish question was not unique. But neither, as we shall see, was this pair of attempted genocides. They were part of broader organic nationalist movements, which when placed in certain dangerous macro-situations with certain micro-relations between collective actors could lead to murderous ethnic cleansing, and even to genocide.

Was there a causal influence of the Turkish on the Nazi genocide? This seems unlikely. Peace with the Soviet Union in 1922 and with Greece in 1923, followed by Attaturk's stable rule, eased tensions in the region and led Turks to deny rather than complete genocide. Though Europe had influenced the Young Turks and now influenced Attaturk, there was little reverse influence. Insofar as most Europeans were aware of the Armenian tragedy, they viewed it in "Orientalist" terms as Asiatic barbarous backwardness, not as political modernity. There was a large German military mission to Turkey, its World War I ally, and this did include a few men who later became committed Nazis – including a boy-soldier, later the Auschwitz commandant, Rudolf Höss (these men are listed in Dadrian, 1996: 199–204; see Höss's biography presented later, in Chapter 8). But it is doubtful that the proportion graduating to murderous Nazism was greater than from other theaters of war. Nor is there evidence that Nazism was much influenced by observing the Armenian genocide. We know of one direct connection, which should make us pause. In a speech to his commanders before invading Poland, Hitler justified the killing of Polish civilians (not, let it be noted, Jews) in these terms:

I have placed my death-head formations in readiness – for the present only in the East – with orders to them to send to death mercilessly and without compassion men, women and children of Polish derivation and language. Only thus shall we gain the living space which we need. Who, after all, speaks today of the annihilation of the Armenians? (Marrus, 1987: 20)

But for most Europeans, Armenia seemed tragic in a quite opposite sense – it was *not* seen as a warning against others embarking on organic nation-statism. Just as the Nazi genocide has been predominantly interpreted as indicating that the Germans had some distinctive character or *Sonderweg* (special path) that led them into genocide, so has the Armenian genocide been interpreted as resulting from a peculiar Turkish character, conjuring up Orientalist images of the terrible Turk. This was not so. I have explained this genocide in terms of more general social processes – rival claims for political sovereignty, Great Power rivalry, political factionalism and radicalization, the unequal distribution of political and military power within societies, and mundane motives of greed, careerism, fear – and hatred.

CONCLUSION: AN EXPLANATION OF THE GENOCIDE

Was this the dark side of democracy? Not in the direct form found in the settler democracies, nor even in the sense of perverted democratization we will see in the Yugoslav case. There was, indeed, a perversion of a movement originally seeking government by the people as it moved toward authoritarianism and militarism. There was also the emergence of an organic and ultimately exclusionary nation-statism. But this state remained throughout World War I the Ottoman Empire, and the Young Turks radicalized some of its dark side as well – its divide-and-rule between Muslims and other *millets*, its exemplary repression of dissent, its resort to deportations of troublesome minorities. The Young Turks came to embody at the beginning of World War I a unique conjoining of the dark side of the modern nation-state and the older multiethnic empire. Not until after the genocide and after World War I did another cohort of Young Turks convert fully to organic nationalism. Then the rule of Attaturk could be a light and progressive one, for Turkey had lost most of its minorities.

My other ethnic theses apply more directly in explaining this genocide. This was an asymmetric clash between two rival and predominantly ethnonationalist movements claiming ideologically plausible and practically achievable sovereignty over the same territory. The Ottoman Turks had long possessed legitimate sovereignty over the territories where Armenians lived, and they had the political and military power monopoly to enforce their claim. Armenian nationalists were beginning to claim their own state, asserting historical legitimacy rooted in past Armenian states. Though with few political or military resources of their own, they were aided by an invading Great Power in whose territories millions of Armenians lived. Russia was a quasi-homeland state stiffening the will of the weaker side to fight. Though they were weak now, they believed political nationalism was ultimately unstoppable in the modern world. Turks had reason to fear these last two resources. Any Ottoman government feared Russian aid for the Armenians, since this threatened core Anatolian territories of the empire. Turkish nationalists also feared Armenian nationalism since they too now believed that the nation-state was an unstoppable ideal.

Thus there was a clash between leadership factions of two ethnic groups claiming sovereignty over the same territory, one aided by a quasi-homeland Great Power neighbor. It then unfolded as the mixed scenario of my fourth thesis, a preemptive genocide, launched by a still-dominant group believing that the tide of history might be turning against it, requiring radical action now. This level of cause might suggest deep-rooted structural forces leading toward genocide.

But there were also more contingent causes. The destabilization of political and geopolitical institutions transformed the goals of powerful social actors, as in my fifth thesis. This was not a stable confrontation between two well-defined and entrenched enemies. As the previous chapter emphasized, Ottoman power was collapsing in the face of Christian nationalists and Christian Great Powers. A series of catastrophes resulted in successive political crises as different factions clashed, their identities, powers, and goals being transformed by crisis. The drift, as in most of Europe, was toward organic nationalism, but it was an unsteady drift. In two coups, in 1908 and 1913, the Young Turks came into power. Within their ranks, state-strengthening centralizers grew in influence. It was as a by-product of their commitment to centralization that the Ittihadists began to embrace a more organic nationalism intolerant of decentralized diversity. This threatened the alliance that these advocates of constitutional rule had made with other ethnonationalists, including Armenians. Two final crises resulted from Young Turk blunders – overconfident entry into World War I and the reckless despatch of Enver Pasha's army into Russia. Defeats worsened the crisis, radicalized more Young Turks, and gave radicals control of key political and military institutions.

Ethnicity was a basic organizing principle of Ottoman society, structuring conflict relations, displacing class resentments, and generally reinforced by religion. Yet the trumping of class by ethnicity occurred only during the war. The war made some Armenians into traitors. Outbreaks of violence in Van and Cilicia turned into an ethnic civil war, dissolving the difference between the front and the rear. Now class differences among Armenians mattered only for purposes of bribing to achieve survival. Age and gender differences remained to give greater or lesser chances of survival. But in general, Ottoman subjects were forced by both conventional and ethnic war mobilizations into a singular identity, as Armenians versus Turks (and Kurds, Circassians, etc.). Ethnicity trumped class and all other divisions, as in my second thesis.

As both this chapter and the preceding one have emphasized, genocide arrived as a policy choice late and suddenly – as my sixth thesis suggested. The Young Turk Plan A, dominant over two decades, given a last try in early August 1914, was for alliance with the Armenian nationalist parties against their common opponents. Sometime between August 1914 and February 1915, Plan A was replaced by its main competitor over the previous two years, Plan B – forcible deportations. This was unstable, first because military pressures threatened retreat and a last stand in the Turkish heartland, where there also lived a disloyal minority. In this sense, in 1915 there also occurred a struggle over the particular territory that was most crucial to both groups. The situation, believed those possessing overwhelming military force, required ethnic cleansing by whatever means worked. They used their formal and covert military superiority to accomplish this, and it predictably produced mass deaths. From an unknown point between April 23 and late May 1915, the Ottoman Turkish government began to organize genocide. This was committed by a state possessing overwhelming military superiority, recently destabilized, factionalized, and radicalized, mostly by unexpected geopolitical crises. It would not have happened without such contingent pressures, and it was not long premeditated.

The accomplishment of genocide is murkier. But once under way, it was predominantly top-down. This was only half a party-state, being less of a mass popular movement from below than the product of a small nationalist elite. Its core constituencies lay among the military and political middle classes of the empire, especially those who were refugees and emigres. These radicalizing nationalists controlled enough key state apparatuses to dismiss a third of the provincial administrators who dissented from genocide, and they possessed enough competent officials from their own ranks to replace them. They then commanded the state's repressive powers – police, specially formed paramilitaries, and parts of the army. As in my seventh ethnic thesis, these core militants consisted mainly of ideological killers, recently radicalized – though careerism also kicked into their motivations. The officers of the Special Forces had also been socialized over the previous two or more years into violent perpetrator motives.

Thus armed, the radicals could exploit mundane instrumental motives among more ordinary Turks and others. The criminals recruited into the Special Forces were lured by freedom and loot. Kurdish and Circassian chieftains acquired more local political autonomy and land, and their followers acquired loot. They and the thousands of ordinary Turks involved seem very materialist killers. Yet both also shared a degree of casual envy-driven bigotry directed against Armenians, as well as a wartime patriotism making them more disciplined killers, obeying the orders they were given. In the end, ordinary Turks, Kurds, Circassians, and others participated in genocide, as in my eighth thesis, but with material motives of greed unusually prominent.

The combination produced a messy, nonrational outcome. The perpetrators were not "the Turks" (as nationalist theories would have it). Rather, some Turks (and others) were embroiled in a decidedly top-down process of murderous cleansing (as statist theories suggest). Yet statism was the end product of factionalism and radicalization induced by repeated crises emanating from the unstable geopolitics of war. It was not the product of ancient hatreds (as primitive or even perennial theories would have it), yet two degrees of ethnic age were involved. There were quite old (at least a century old) religious-ethnic tensions between Christians and Muslims. But these were exacerbated and given direction by a modern organic nationalism, generating massive ethnic hatred only in the previous two years. It was committed by actors struggling to rationally attain their goals (as in rational choice theory), but amid a situation that they could neither control nor make rational decisions. They resorted to genocide when other solutions seemed not to work. They believed the final decision was one of last-ditch desperation.

They erred, not only morally but also factually. Armenians did not constitute such a threat, and their elimination weakened the Ottoman war effort. Genocide contributed to defeat. The leaders then fled into exile, where they fell to the bullets of Armenian assassins. They might claim that the genocide was a long-term success, since the disappearance of Armenians made it easier after the war to unite and centralize Turkey. Yet the country remains bedeviled by two Young Turk legacies: military authoritarianism and an organic nationalism that now represses Kurds rather than Armenians. The Young Turks fatally weakened their country by pursuing organic nationalism; their successors struggle in their shadow.

7

Nazis, I

Radicalization

We approach the most notorious and best-evidenced case of genocide. My book *Fascists* shows that fascism was essentially a movement committed to extreme organic nationalism and statism, claiming to transcend social conflict, especially class conflict, by using paramilitary and state violence to "knock both their heads together." But there were two additionally dangerous features of Nazism compared to other fascist movements: its conception of the nation was more racial than cultural, and it advocated an aggressive *imperial revisionism* to restore German's former power. I will argue that when both were turned into eastward expansion in Europe, they brought about Nazi genocide, though only after a series of radicalizations of leaders and militants. This chapter deals with the radicalizations, the following two with genocide.

Why did Germany nourish racial sentiments that the Nazis then took to extremes? This is the German Question. But perhaps it is slightly misplaced, for Germany was not alone. Northern Europe nourished racialism. As we saw in Chapter 4, Spaniards and Portuguese abroad were much readier to assimilate (and intermarry with) natives than were Northern European colonists. The late 19th and early 20th centuries also nourished racism. Social Darwinism now blended with biology, medicine, sociology, and psychology to generate racial-genetic notions of human progress. Many believed that the Germans or the British were genetically distinct from Slavs and Jews, that one race might be superior to another, and that social problems like crime or mental illness might be combated by eugenic, "race-purifying" policies. The Nazi policy of murdering mentally retarded persons only took further the compulsory sterilization practiced by other Northern Europeans at the time. Third came the general rise of organic nationalism throughout much of Europe in the late 19th century, discussed earlier.

But between these three broad encouragements and the commission of genocide lay a great gulf. Why did some Germans bridge it? Some seek answers mainly within German nationalism. It is conventional to identify two main types of nationalism, *ethnic* and *civic*, and to identify German nationalism as being decidedly ethnic and so more dangerous (e.g., Brubaker,

1992). Any long-term resident of French or Italian territory is considered a member of the French or Italian nation. This is a civic definition of citizenship allowing for assimilation of people of various ethnic origins. But in Germany, only ethnic Germans, wherever they live, have been securely considered full members of the German nation. This is held to be the root of the German problem because it is more exclusionary than is civic nationalism.

There is some truth in this. Yet, as I noted in Chapter 1, ethnicity cannot be objectively measured. Germans still have to decide who is ethnically German. German states have used two criteria: the ability to speak German as one's native tongue and blood descent. Language can be learned, but blood descent is given by heredity. So the precise mix of these two criteria would influence how exclusionary German nationalism would be. In the late 19th century, Jews and Poles living in the *Kaiserreich* were partially assimilating into the German nation by speaking and culturally becoming German, though Poles were discriminated against and often regarded as second-class citizens. Jews and Slavs were being "cleansed" by the peaceful means of voluntary assimilation and institutional coercion. But German anti-Semitism was no greater than French anti-Semitism before World War I. Indeed, to explain why things got much worse, we must also look for causes lying outside of German nationalism itself.

But where exactly was Germany? It was more than the mere "geographical expression" of earlier centuries. But before 1914 two major German states remained, and millions of Germans lived in neither of them. Germany was incomplete. Thus any analysis of German nationalism must involve geopolitical relations (between states) and transnational relations (among Germans, and between Germans and others) that ran across state borders. This will be true at all stages of German radicalization. The transnational and geopolitical embroilment of Germans in Eastern questions was to radicalize German nationalism and anti-Semitism.

German nationalists aimed to unite all ethnically defined Germans into one state. This was now tantalizingly close, for many German states had been consolidated into two great ones – Prussian Germany and Habsburg Austria. But to include almost all Germans in any single state would require imperial expansion in regions dominated by other ethnic groups. The distinguishing feature of German nationalism in the late 19th century was less that it was ethnic than that it implied imperialism – Germans conquering and ruling over others. Though imperial expansion was not unusual in Europe, German imperialism came late, and so would be more ethnic than had been the earlier English or French imperialism. By now the whole people should rule, not just the upper classes, so imperialism could mobilize the people into a more ethnonational imperialism. Under the influence of social Darwinism, wars might decide which nation was the fittest to survive. In Germany, race theorists said that the Danish and French minorities were of similar Aryan stock, but not Slavs and Jews, who lived across the eastern borders of the two Germanies. Such eastern ethnicities might be considered alien to the German race.

Both German states were ruled by dynastic monarchs opposing rule by the people. Yet the two differed. Prussian expansion had been mainly among Germans, so this was an ethnic German state, a *kleindeutsch* (small German) nation-state, but with only partial popular sovereignty and potential second-class citizenship and/or assimilation for non-Germans. By contrast, Austrian expansion was in the east and south, mainly over non-Germans, a *grossdeutsch* (great German) imperium but not an ethnic one. It was an empire of diverse ethnicities ruled by a German dynasty. The Habsburgs could not be nationalists. They had to rule by combining assimilation (getting others to speak German and adopt German culture) and multicultural confederalism (allowing other ethnic elites to share in rule). The Austrian version of Germany was *grossdeutsch* imperialism, but it was not organicist. As Chapter 3 showed, the struggle for rule by the people across Habsburg lands spread organic nationalism among subordinate ethnicities, and Germans and Magyars reacted to this by demanding more ethnic, not merely cultural, rule. Thus by 1900 Austrian Germans were mobilizing the largest organic German nationalist movement in reaction to attacks by subordinate nationalists on them.

Two ethnic groups seemed especially threatening. Most Germanic expansion was eastward, which meant that Russia was seen as the most threatening rival power – massive, primitive, and Slav. Germans began to see alien, primitive Slav hordes as threatening "higher" Germanic civilization. The second threat was posed by Jews, seen as old religious enemies and "pariah exploiters" throughout Europe. Yet Western European states were now secularizing, and Jews seemed embarked on assimilation there – as in Prussian Germany itself. This was less so in countries farther east. But Jews were in a peculiar position in the Habsburg Empire. The dynasty disliked nationalists – including German nationalists – and encouraged religious toleration and cosmopolitan groups like the Jews as counterweights. The state was assimilating Jews, but German nationalists and Jews were more on a collision course in the Habsburg than in the Prussian Empire. This conflict was reinforced by the flight into Habsburg lands of Orthodox Jews from the pogroms of the Russian Empire. Their strange language, garb, and ringlets seemed alien and primitive. German fear of eastern Slavs and Jews increased at the end of the 19th century.

Jointly, these tendencies increased aggressive elements in German nationalism, though more in Austria than in Germany. But then World War I brought two decisive changes. Austria and Germany suffered disastrous defeat. This finished off both dynasties and dashed both German imperial projects. The Habsburg Empire ceased to exist as Austria was reduced to the small republic it is today. Its other domains were granted to states with a single dominant ethnicity, mostly Slav, in which Germans now suffered discrimination as second-class citizens. Prussian Germany also became a republic but remained a Great Power, if reduced in territories and population and shorn of dynastic restraints on nationalism. The two republics were politically polarized into a Marxian left and a nationalist right. German rightist discontent about the Versailles peace treaties now emerged as ethnic imperial revisionism – revise the borders to incorporate the "lost territories" and create an ethnic German Empire. With Austria dismembered, only the Prussian German state, now simply known as Germany, could do this. The Habsburg cultural *grossdeutsch* ideal was dead, the Prussian ethnic ideal transformed into a new *grossdeutsch* expansionism. But, as Burleigh (2000) emphasizes, the aggression of the Third Reich derived from an acute sense of victimhood.

The second consequence of the war period was that the Bolshevik Revolution created a specter across Europe of class revolution and chaos, viewed as distinctively Russian and also as Jewish, since so many prominent Bolsheviks were Jews. In 1918–19 Germany, Austria, and Hungary all had to repress Communist uprisings in which Jews were prominent. This seemed to further entwine the two eastern racial enemies, Slavs and Jews. Jews were also seen as capitalist and linked to enemy powers in the West, but the Soviet Union was the main enemy of German expansion, and a Judeo-Bolshevik enemy might threaten inside Germany. Ethnic and class enemies were seen as jointly conspiring to found their own state over Germans. Of course, Jews were not actually seeking their own rival state (at least not in Europe), but they were seen as inspiring Slavs and Communists who were.

The Great Depression added economic discontents, and the Nazis swept into power not mainly because of anti-Semitism, but because they presented a plausible program of restoring economic growth by transcending class conflict, wrapped in organic nationalist rhetoric. The elections of the period 1928–32 first saw a decline of the centrist liberal and special interest parties, with most of their votes going to conservative nationalists. The Nazis at first picked up lesser numbers. Then the conservatives began to lose ground, and the Nazis were the main beneficiaries. Unlike conservative nationalism, the Nazi variety seemed classless, popular, and so genuinely organic. Hitler promised strong leadership to knock the heads of all the classes and interest groups together, unify the nation, and make Germany great again. Though the Nazis played down anti-Semitism at election times, few doubted they would put pressure on the Jews, and many approved. Though the Nazis did not urge war, since this would have been very unpopular, most Germans expected and wanted them to reassert German power and recover the lost territories. So the Nazis rose up in free elections to acquire over a third of the votes, with only the socialists and Communists remaining as a substantial opposition. Since the remaining conservative parties had also radicalized to compete with Hitler, the Nazis effectively had a Reichstag majority, which they used to engineer a more or less legal coup. The Nazis came to power through a democracy turning organic (see Mann, 2004: chap. 4). Then they immediately terminated democracy. But only a minority of Germans had expected this beforehand, and most of them had voted socialist or Communist. And even they did not expect a world war or genocide.

In some ways these elections resembled those of Serbia in 1990–1. People voted for Hitler or Milosevic to a similar extent and for similarly varied reasons. Both appeared to have strong economic policies, and both expressed popular organic nationalism. Imperial revisionism and the rechanneling of class sentiments amid destabilized geopolitics and an economic crisis had made German nationalism thoroughly organic. Liberal and socialist notions of rule by a diverse people were initially defeated by democratic means by notions of organic rule. Then the winners destroyed democracy by force, ensuring that ethnonationalism would be expressed by racial fascism. Germany and Austria had thoroughly entwined the two senses of rule by the people – *demos* and *ethnos*. Then the party of the *ethnos* murdered the *demos*. It was a party dictatorship that was to perpetrate genocide.

Enhanced anti-Slav and anti-Semitic sentiments were not original to German nationalism, but were unintended by-products of its encounter with eastern geopolitical and transnational realities. In the Final Solution, Jews were not exterminated merely as Jews, but also because they become entangled in German struggles against others. Only in this indirect sense did Nazi genocide embody my third thesis: murderous cleansing threatens where two rival ethnic movements claim states over the same territory, each believing in the legitimacy and practicality of its claim. This only applies from the perspective of the Nazis themselves, since Jews were not in reality conspiring to found their own state in German lands. But the Nazis believed Jews were behind Slav/Communist expansion. For this reason also, the Nazi case fits (indirectly again) into the mixed version of my fourth ethnic thesis. Threatened by the thought of a Jewish-fomented conspiracy of powers, the Nazis launched what they believed to be a preemptive strike against a weak group, Jews, to prevent Judeo-Bolshevism growing stronger in the future.

THE SCALE OF NAZI GENOCIDE

In the last 4 years of its 12-year life, the Nazi regime caused the murders of approximately 20 million unarmed persons.[1] Though Jews became the main victims, they comprised under a third of the total and their genocide occurred only well into the killing sequence. First came the escalating street, police, and concentration camp violence of Germany in the 1930s – killing only a few thousand, but important in inuring and training perpetrators

---

[1] No one can give an exact tally of the dead, either in total or for any of the groups of victims. Rummel (1992) reviews many estimates and suggests that we use the midpoint of the more plausible ones. This calculation yields 21 million.

and the general population. This first phase was focused less on Jews than on German political opponents, especially on the left. This was essential in removing moderates from politics – as also occurred in the other cases of murderous cleansing. Though this was a politically aimed selective repression, the political enemies were also castigated with organic, ethnic epithets, as "alien," "un-German," and so on. In 1938 *Kristallnacht* and the Austrian *Anschluss* briefly focused Nazi fury on Jews, but in the following year this was overshadowed by the start of the first systematic killing in the so-called euthanasia project, code-named T4 (after the Berlin address of its headquarters, 4 Tiergartenstrasse).

T4 killed mentally retarded and disturbed Germans so that they would not have children. In all, perhaps 250,000 of these particularly helpless victims may have been murdered, a large percentage of all the mentally disabled persons within reach (Burleigh, 1994; de Mildt, 1996; Klee, 1983). This was genocide under the UN definition, though it was not ethnic genocide. Biological-racial reasoning also led the Nazis to order the killings of "asocials" (including repeat criminals), homosexuals, and those with grievous birth defects or unusual physiques, like dwarves, supposedly introducing biological impurities into the Aryan breeding stock. Their killing was erratic, leaving too many alive to be genocidal, but small non-Aryan ethnic minorities like Kashubians and Sorbians in Germany and Krimtchaks in the Crimea did suffer genocide.

Gypsies were also murdered after a delay. They confronted Nazis with an ideological dilemma. By 1939 some leading Nazis viewed them as subhuman, as they did Jews and Poles. Their roaming and supposed petty thievery got them alternatively classified as antisocials. Yet Nazi theorists recognized gypsies as of Aryan descent. Himmler suggested preserving the "ancient purity" of their "stock" by segregating the "purer tribes" in reservations – until Martin Bormann (speaking for Hitler) silenced him. From late 1942, gypsies at Auschwitz were shot, starved, worked to death, or perished in Josef Mengele's ghastly experiments. Their systemic gassing began in 1944. Gypsies in Belgium, Croatia, Estonia, the Netherlands, and Lithuania were mostly wiped out, as were three-quarters of Austrian and German gypsies. But others were adept at evasion. Estimates of their dead are generally around 200,000–260,000, about a quarter of Europe's gypsies, though defining who is a gypsy is difficult (Crowe, 1996; Hancock, 1996; Höss et al., 1978: 62–8; Kenrick & Puxon, 1972: 183–4; Pearson, 1983: 200). There is much dispute about how genocidal this was. The intent was there but thwarted by an elusive quarry, so this was attempted genocide. It would have been accomplished had the Nazis won the war.

More Slavs were killed than anyone else (Hunczak, 1990: 122–4; Kumanev, 1990: 140). In the 1939 conquest of Poland, the Nazis went beyond the bounds of even the most *callous warfare* of European history, discussed in Chapter 2. Major General Lahousen testified after the war that the fuhrer had decreed dual military/civil control of occupied Poland to accomplish "the extermination of the people" and "political field-clearing" (Nuremberg Tribunal, 1946: VIII: 588). The Nazis did kill almost all the highly educated Poles they could lay their hands on. SS General Berger urged: "Better shoot two Poles too many than two too few. A savage country cannot be governed in a decent manner." Just under 3 million non-Jewish Poles were killed, perhaps the most thorough 20th-century case of politicide, the wiping out of an enemy elite. As Poles watched the extermination of the Jews, many believed that after the war they would be next for genocide (Gordon, 1984: 101; Gutman, 1990). Actually, the Nazis planned a more mixed fate for them – *politicide* for up to a third, *segregation* for another third, and *wild deportations* into Russia of the rest. The intended outcome was not quite genocide.

With the invasion of the Soviet Union in mid-1941, killing centered on Soviet civilians and Jews, at first mainly by *Einsatzgruppen* ("special forces") shooting squads, then by combined SS, police, and Wehrmacht forces and in death camps. The Nazis killed 6–7 million non-Jewish Soviet civilians (nearly 4 million Ukrainians, nearly 2 million Belarussians, and 1.5 million in the Russian Republic) plus 3.3 million Soviet POWs, 57 percent of all their Soviet POWs – compared to less than 4 percent of British and American POWs who died in German captivity (they were viewed by the Nazis as Aryans). About one-third of these Soviet civilians and POWs were shot or gassed; the rest were wastage, worked to death or simply not fed enough to avoid disease and starvation (Streit, 1978: 10). "Only" about 15 percent of Ukrainian non-Jews died in these ways, about 10 percent of Poles, and about 10 percent of Belarussians – whereas 90 percent of Polish Jews died. But the absolute numbers are horrific. This was not quite genocide since there were too many Soviet Slavs to contemplate killing them all. Instead, the Nazi aim was to eliminate those who might conceivably oppose them (politicide), push vast numbers of the rest into central Asia in wild deportations, and then rule over the 30 percent remaining as helots in slavelike segregation. Russians were intended to suffer the same fate as Poles, but they were better equipped to resist.

The Italian writer Malaparte, traveling with the German forces, provides a graphic eyewitness account of the policy. In a ruined Ukrainian village, 118 captured Russian soldiers were asked to read aloud from *Pravda*. Those who read best, they were told, would be given clerical jobs in the POW administration, an easier job than the quarrying awaiting those who failed. Thirty-one passed this literacy test and stood in a group, "laughing contentedly" at their good fortune. They were then lined up against the nearest wall and shot. The sergeant in charge told Malaparte:

Russia must be cleared of all this learned rabble. The peasants and workers who can read and write too well are dangerous. They are all communists. (Malaparte, 1946: 213–15).

The political victims were described in racial terms as *Untermenschen*, sub-humanity, just as Jews, sometimes described as not human at all, were also given political labels. Heydrich said, "Judaism...was the source of Bolshevism and must therefore be wiped out." Killing orders routinely en-twined political and racial targets – "Jews, gypsies, racial inferiors, asocials and Soviet political commissars" or "all racially and politically undesirable elements among the prisoners" or "second-class Asiatics." Headland (1992: 54) lists 44 overlapping "target groups" identified in the SS *Einsatzgruppen* reports, some ethnic, some political, some vague (like hostiles, saboteurs, and agitators). The notorious "Commissar Order" stated that all Soviet com-missars must be killed since they had "initiated barbaric, Asiatic methods of warfare." Many Soviet citizens with Asian "facial features" were also killed (Gordon, 1984: 143; Jacobsen, 1968: 530; Krausnick, 1993: 62–3, 532). Compared to Jews, mental patients, and gypsies, a lower proportion of Slav women and children were killed, revealing that the intent was not strictly genocidal. But almost all victims were harmless civilians, neither armed nor even Communist. Hence the startlingly unbalanced statistics of SS and Wehrmacht reports: in a typical action, 1,500 killed partisans turned out to have only 100 rifles among them. Against Slavs, the Nazis undertook mixed political-ethnic cleansing with genocidal tendencies. Against Jews the same combat became genocide.

From 1939 to 1941, killing of Slavs outweighed that of Jews. In September 1941 the first trials of Zyklon B gas were conducted on Russian POWs at Auschwitz. The next month, 40 Russians were used to test the first gas van at Sachsenhausen. Naked, they were forced into the truck, which was driven to the local cemetery, the engine left running. After 20 minutes the banging and groaning from inside had finished. The van was opened, the bodies pushed out. To the satisfaction of the SS men, the bodies were pink – which indicated that they were poisoned, not asphyxiated (Browning, 1985: 62–5). The gas vans then ranged across Eastern Europe from Poland to Serbia, though the new technique was brought to its killing peak in death camp gas chambers against Jews.

But from early 1942 the Jewish Final Solution, also known as the Shoah or Holocaust, became the centerpiece of Nazi genocide. Gassing was largely reserved for Jews, while most Slavs were shot or starved. Nor were Slavs murdered so pitilessly. The ghettoes were liquidated, the five death camps were set in motion, the attrition rate of Jews in the thousands of other camps accelerated, and then pressure from advancing Red armies turned camp evacuations into death marches for the survivors. Even final liberation left many prisoners too enfeebled to survive. The oft-repeated total of 6 million Jews murdered may be slightly too high. Hilberg (1978) carefully calculates 5.1 million, and Maksudov (1993) adds 300,000 more Russian Jews. Per-haps 5.5 million might be the best overall estimate of murdered Jews. Almost three-quarters of European Jews died, most survivors being in countries not fully under Nazi control. Most of the victims were in the East, but extermination was just as ruthless in the West. This was clearly genocide, the only really large genocide attempted by the Nazis.

The Final Solution was the most single-minded attempt at genocide the world has ever seen. The Nazi leaders aimed to kill *all* European Jews. When dreaming of world empire, they envisaged killing all Jews everywhere – single-minded pursuit of extermination whatever the cost. It made no sense in terms of instrumental rationality. It made no sense in economic or military power terms. It diverted enormous resources of manpower, transport, supplies, and so on from the war effort. It lasted into the last days of the war. This was not instrumental rationality but value rationality in Weber's sense, to a degree that was unique to this case. For some Nazis it *was* the goal of their endeavors, it *was* the war effort, the single greatest achievement for which they would be remembered. This proved to be true in entirely the opposite sense to the one they had intended. For remembrance of the evil they inflicted dominates our view of the entire Nazi regime, and for many it dominates the image they have of Germany itself.

A sense of encounter with evil inspired the unparalleled proliferation of survivor memoirs and war crimes trials. Since so many have felt compelled to bear witness, we can read about it until our brains reel and our stomachs churn. In its overall scope, its consistent intent, and its relentless cruelty, the extermination of the Jews represents unparalleled human evil on a scale almost unimaginable to us – as it was to uncomprehending victims who went incredulously, and so comparatively meekly, to their deaths. But the trials and the memoirs also give us the evidence to penetrate close to the heart of human evil. Why was genocide done? How could people kill and continue killing so relentlessly? Though no one can fully answer these questions, I can provide essential clues. By focusing on processes and perpetrators, I trace how the genocide developed and what its perpetrators thought they were doing. As in other cases, we may view each phase in the process as a step in a single escalatory sequence, either planned from the beginning or related to each other in an orderly progression. Or we may regard them as unplanned, escalating in a more contingent way. I again adopt the methodology of formally isolating a Plan in each phase, identifying a Plan A, Plan B, Plan C, and so on. I identify planners and perpetrators, attempting to discern their intentions at each stage of the process.

PERPETRATOR MOTIVES

Two broad contrasting initial conclusions might seem to stand out. First, victim groups were killed in pursuit of a ferocious ideology: to complete the cleansing of the German *Volk* and *Reich*. This certainly permeated the thinking of the Nazi elite. In *Fascists* I emphasize that from the beginning, Nazism had pursued a project of extreme nation-statism (extreme nationalism plus extreme statism). In this chapter we shall see how this project radicalized between 1933 and 1941 into an ideology of murderous cleansing to "purify the race."

But this necessarily involved masses of perpetrators across many institutions – euthanasia hospitals, *Einsatzgruppen*, Waffen-SS and Wehrmacht units, hundreds of liquidated ghettos, five death camps plus over 1,000 other camps and industrial slave labor factories, the final death marches, and all the offices and transports necessary for all their functioning. Most, though not all, of the perpetrators were Germans. Their total number is unknowable. Goldhagen (1996: 168) hazards a guess that about 330,000 persons killed, so that the average perpetrator would have killed about 65 people. This was mass, repetitive killing involving many thousands whose prior attachment to Nazism must have been slight. Many ordinary persons must also have been mass murderers, as my eighth ethnic thesis suggests.

Chapter 1 identified a number of ordinary motives. Bigoted killers were imbued with the normal prejudices of Germany. Ordinary Germans were murderous anti-Semites, says Goldhagen (1996), without much urging from Nazis. So were ordinary Ukrainians, suggests Sabrin (1991: 242). Others were ordinary people trapped into the coercive yet also comradely organizations described earlier. Noncompliance might bring punishment by superiors or withdrawal of comradeship by peers. People can murder under social pressures, says Browning (1993) of the *Einsatzgruppen* support troops of Police Battalion 101. For this reason, Birn (in Finkelstein & Birn, 1998: 98–100) says that so many perpetrators were "perfectly normal men who knew the difference between right and wrong" – "ordinary men and women" with "personalities found in any country" who could "commit history's greatest crimes." She concludes, "that is the really sensational truth about the perpetrators of the final solution." These would be fearful, disciplined, or comradely killers. Others were functionaries in the bureaucracies of modernity, in which compliance is neither ideological nor socially pressured but the product of institutionalized routines, caught up in Hannah Arendt's (1965) banality of evil as bureaucratic killers. Finally, ordinary people might be cultivating a career or just a secure job amid difficult wartime conditions – careerist killers – or their materialism might be crasser, killing to loot and pillage the victims – materialist killers. Since these are all ideal types, most perpetrators had mixed motives, combining several of them, and they changed through time.

NAZI RADICALIZATION

Thus we must place perpetrators amid changing historical and social contexts and amid their own life careers. I identify the core constituencies of Nazism and the varying motivations they might yield. Perpetrators were affected by their lifetime experiences – in World War I, the Weimar period, during Nazi rule and World War II. Nazi conceptions of the enemy as variously political, racial, and Jewish changed through time. Mommsen (1991, 1997), Broszat (1981), and others have established a sequence of cumulative radicalization of the Nazi movement between 1933 and 1941. Let us see how this affected the perpetrators.

Remember that mass murder was only a late addition to the Nazi repertoire. Killings intensified throughout the period, from individuals to batches of tens, to the hundreds, to the thousands. In the 1930s most deaths resulted either as wild street violence escalated or in institutions accustomed to death, where it is not always considered entirely outrageous, like prisons or hospitals. In 1940 and 1941 most killing moved into theaters of war, committed with the weapons and legitimacy of war. Only from 1942 was most killing institutionalized well away from these more legitimate sites of death. Later killings might need more toughness than earlier ones, yet earlier ones might help inure perpetrators as demands on them escalated. Nor should we commit the democratic fallacy of believing that macro-outcomes are the product of the sum of the motivations or ideologies of individuals. That would be naive sociology. Mass movements involve power institutions in which some people, and their ideologies, are more important than others. Leaders, militants, and rank-and-file bystanders caught up more casually in their projects have different degrees of power and different motives for action.

Goldhagen (1996) is quite wrong to suggest that many Germans had previously espoused murderous anti-Semitism (see the criticisms of Finkelstein & Birn, 1998, and Pohl, 1997). There had been no pogroms in Germany since the 1880s, and pre–World War I German anti-Semitism had peaked at the end of the 19th century. Even the Nazis downplayed anti-Semitism at election time, since a group that constitutes 0.7 percent of the population is not easy to blame for the major problems of the country. Anti-Semitic *völkisch* parties had only a little success before World War I, mainly in Austria. Germans were casual anti-Semites, but this ideology had not been central in their lives or their politics. Between casual anti-Semitism and mass murder is an *enormous* distance. Even after three years in power, Nazism did not seem particularly dangerous. Only a few Jews were leaving Germany. Most expected things to soon settle down. The eventual scourge of Nazism was withholding judgment. Winston Churchill wrote:

We cannot tell whether Hitler will be the man who will once again let loose upon the world another war in which civilization will irretrievably succumb, or whether he will go down in history as the man who restored honour and peace of mind to the great Germanic Nation. (Churchill, 1937: 165)

Churchill still did not fully comprehend Hitler or his movement. Nor did Stalin. Nor did most Jews. This was because Nazism had not then completed its radicalization.

There were several radicalizing surges. German racism and anti-Semitism surged in the 1920s among a few political aficionados on the far right, then among a larger number of Nazi militants through the mid-1930s, then among more ordinary Nazis and Germans from 1939, and then again more radically from 1941. We cannot understand these surges without considering that they emerged within a *fascist* movement with a distinct power structure and distinct constituencies of support. The Nazi movement embodied two main organizational characteristics: hierarchy and paramilitary comradeship. I will trace their impact beginning with the Nazi leadership, then move to the mass movement of militants, and finally turn to the radicalization of ordinary Germans.

RADICALIZATION OF THE HIERARCHY

Despite avoiding written orders, despite never witnessing a single murder, despite never committing violence himself, Hitler was the prime mover of genocide. Participants described extermination orders as *"Führer* orders" (Gordon, 1984: 141). Hitler had two near-absolute values: anti-Semitism and commitment to imperial ethnic revisionism, both focused eastward. He said Jews had caused World War I and the Bolshevik Revolution. From 1919 to 1945 he advocated "the removal of the Jews from our people." His revisionism went beyond restoration of pre-1914 borders to demand *Lebensraum* (living room) in the East. But a Judeo-Bolshevik regime stood in the way. From 1919 a call to eliminate *both* Jews and Bolsheviks from an expanded German Reich pervaded Hitler's speeches, the two volumes of *Mein Kampf*, and his recorded "table talk."

Only the timing of eastward expansion and the method of elimination remained to be determined. Hitler and other elite Nazis used several terms interchangeably – *Vernictung* ("destruction"), *Entfernung* ("removal"), and *Verbannung* ("banishment"). *Ausrottung* ("extermination") was little used before 1940, but even it did not necessarily mean killing. Hitler sometimes endorsed aggression that would force the Jews to flee Germany "voluntarily" (Naimark, 2001: 62–4). But his tendency to label Jews subhuman or vermin, Bolsheviks as irreconcilable enemies, and Slavs as an inferior race indicates that he would lack moral qualms whatever the means involved. He wrote in *Mein Kampf* that "the sacrifice of millions at the front" in World War I would not have been necessary if "twelve or fifteen thousand of these Hebrew corrupters of the people had been held under poison gas." The number might suggest murdering thousands to terrorize the rest to flee (Kershaw, 1998: 151–2, 249–50; 2000: 41–2, 146, 151).

Thus Hitler's Jewish Plan A was probably total ethnic cleansing through pressured emigration, then escalating to the Plan B of wild deportation. He was vaguer on Slavs and Bolsheviks, though callous warfare was implied by creating "living room" for Germans. But his commitment to ethnic cleansing and imperialism became pure value rationality: policy was subordinated to them, whatever the cost, whatever the means. Any rational choice theory of Hitler's strategy would come up short against his increasing willingness to risk all – eventually, devastation for Germany and death for himself – for these values.

Since Hitler became chancellor of Germany, he could act on his values to start a major war whose central aim was *Lebensraum* and ethnic cleansing in the East. Unexpectedly, the supposedly degenerate democracies forced him to also fight a war in the West. He explained this in terms of an international Jewish conspiracy, and his rage at this frustration of his goal led him closer to his final radicalization. In January 1939 he uttered a terrible threat:

if international finance Jewry inside and outside Europe should succeed in plunging the nations once more into a world war, the result will not be the bolshevization of the earth and thereby the victory of Jewry, but the annihilation [*Vernichtung*] of the Jewish race in Europe. (Kershaw, 2000: 127)

Without Hitler, there might have been Nazi-inspired pogroms of Jews and a degree of callous warfare, but probably no genocide. Without Hitler, the disabled would have been abused and neglected, the Jews and gypsies would have been kicked around, with scattered pogroms across the East, leftists would have been attacked until they gave in, perhaps Germany's borders would have been taken back. The subjugation or expulsion, not the death, of minorities was considered necessary for the achievement of a cleansed society by most organic nation-statists elsewhere in Europe. Thus genocide first belonged to Hitler, an extraordinary example less of the role of the individual in history than of the individual placed in such a powerful role by a state-worshipping movement – the most extreme form of fascism's Leadership Principle.

Yet genocide did not belong to Hitler alone. Extreme statism, anti-Semitism, and anti-Bolshevism were common among far right activists in Germany and Austria. The core influences on Hitler and the early Nazis came mainly from ex-Catholic writers and journalists from Bavaria, Austria, and parts of Bohemia and Moravia offering a new *Grossdeutschland*, union of all Germans in a single eastward-tilting *Reich*. They saw Jews as particularly dangerous because of their cosmopolitan and rootless way of life. They linked Jews to the Bolshevik risings in 1918–19 in Budapest, Vienna, Berlin, and Munich. Semites and Bolsheviks jointly threatened Western and Aryan civilization from the East. Friedländer (1997: 87) calls this *redemptive anti-semitism*. Jews had penetrated the German racial bloodstream. Redemption would come if they could be expelled.

After World War I these southeastern ideologists linked up with revisionist German and Austrian military veterans refusing to accept war defeat, launching irregular warfare around German borders. In the middle to late

1920s this altered the composition of the leadership and produced the first electoral surge across broader swathes of the country. Anti-Semitism seems to have been downplayed. Only a few leading Nazis said they joined the movement because of anti-Semitism. The best sample of Nazi militants is those who wrote autobiographies in response to an essay competition on "Why I became a Nazi" (see Mann, 2004: 144). Twice as many of them chose Bolsheviks as their main enemy as chose Jews.

Until the Nazis neared power, theirs was largely rhetorical aggression. Few gave much thought to actual cleansing policy. For two years after seizing power, violence was directed mainly against Bolsheviks. But by 1935 Communists, socialists, and liberals were defeated, and the concentration camps now stagnated. This left Jews as the main remaining potential target of violence. Since the Nazis viewed Jews as a racial, not a religious or cultural enemy, Jews (unlike Communists) could not simply give in and assimilate. The seizure of power in 1933 had already begun national and local anti-Semitic legislation. Jews were expelled from the civil service, the armed forces, teaching, and the arts, then from the professions. The year 1935 saw a flood of local bans against Jews in public halls, arenas, swimming pools. The Nuremberg Laws defined who was Jewish and proscribed intermarriage between Jews and Germans (Friedländer, 1997: 141–51).

The regime was now committed to severe discrimination amounting to segregation designed to force Jews out of the country in pressured emigration. This combination was the leadership's Plan A. Yet more conservative Nazis, including some high-ranking ones, believed the policy amounted only to partial segregation with Jews as second-class subjects, not citizens – as the new Citizenship Law stated. Thus a split developed within the Nazi movement, described by contemporaries as between legal or orderly means and wild violence. Conservative Nazis (and almost all Germans outside the movement) preferred the former, the few Nazi radicals the latter. Over an eight-year period the radicals won, for four main reasons.

1. Between 1933 and 1938 Hitler destroyed the power of non-Nazi elites. The political parties, the civil service, big capital, the churches, and finally the high command were subordinated. Since they had been Western-oriented, this strengthened the Eastern orientation of the regime. It also shifted the balance of power among Nazis. Since no more institutional compromises with conservative elites were required, the influence waned of Nazi conservatives like Schacht, hitherto useful in brokering such deals. Herman Göring, another conservative, radicalized in order to retain his power. Emboldened, the radicals introduced new laws in 1938. Jews were excluded from all welfare benefits, Jewish children were expelled from German schools, most Jewish business activity was proscribed, and many Jewish businesses were expropriated. Nazi conservatives still sometimes greeted these laws with relief, since they appeared to limit disorderly violence against Jews. Though it was now difficult for Jews to make a living in Germany, most still hung on. They

considered themselves Germans and could not quite believe that the Nazis did not.

2. Hitler's recovery of lost territories between 1936 and 1938 were radical successes opposed by conservatives. With the Rhineland recovered, attention shifted east, first to Austria, then to the Sudetenland and Poland, which were supposedly subjugating millions of ethnic Germans. This strengthened *Lebensraum*, the influence of transnational ethnic Germans, and the supposed threat of the Judeo-Bolsheviks. The *Anschluss* (union with Austria) of March 1938 brought in the more virulent Austrian strain of political anti-Semitism, sparking a veritable pogrom, more violent than anything seen in Germany for over a century. Thousands of Jews fled abroad, others were dumped over the border, and some were ransomed for emigration. Plan B of wild deportations had arrived. In November the leadership tried to spread it to Germany, Hitler privately saying, "The Jews should for once get to feel the anger of the people." The wilder SA, not the orderly SS, were to lead it (Kershaw, 2000: 138–9). In *Kristallnacht* over 100 Jews were killed and 80,000 fled the country. But the violence went too far, shocking Nazis and non-Nazis alike. Some *Gauleiter* refused to transmit the pogrom orders. Michael Müller-Claudius wrote a book in 1947 detailing conversations with 41 fairly elite Nazis in 1938 that 28 (63 percent) expressed strong disapproval and only 2 (5 percent) clearly approved (quoted by Gordon, 1984: 263–5). Göring was upset about the potential damage to the economy, and even Hitler worried about looting getting out of hand. The regime pulled back.

3. Radicals were aided by the diffusion of the Leadership Principle. More and more Nazis and careerists practiced what Kershaw (1997, 1998: chap. 13) calls "working towards the Fuhrer," that is, acting to anticipate what they perceived to be his intent, which they correctly saw as radical. Few Nazis were contemplating mass murder, but when pushed to its edge, few opposed it since this would also oppose the fuhrer – ensuring career's end. This encouraged disciplined and careerist more than ideological killers. The deeds of Nazis who could get things done became known in Nazi networks, putting pressure on their more cautious colleagues and superiors. Radicalization was a nonbureaucratic, diffuse process. It involved little open dissent, though a few drifted off to the sidelines.

4. War with Poland and the Western powers in 1939, and then with the Soviet Union in mid-1941, strengthened the radicals with ordinary wartime patriotism. War made opposition to Hitler impossible. By 1942 Müller-Claudius recorded that in conversations with 61 elite Nazis, 15 (26 percent) endorsed the racial policies, 42 (69 percent) were noncommittal or indifferent, and only 3 (5 percent) expressed disapproval (Gordon, 1984: 263–6). When war began in 1939, and especially when it spread to Russia in 1941, *Reichsleiter*, *Gauleiter*, SS leaders, civilian governors, and generals came to endorse elimination.

All of Hitler's inner circle conspired to effect this drift. Himmler told his top SS men in 1938 that the next decade would see an "ideological struggle of the entire Jewry, freemasonry, Marxism, and churches of the world. These forces – of which I presume the Jews to be the driving spirit, the origin of all the negatives – are clear that if Germany and Italy are not annihilated, they will be annihilated ... we will drive them out with an unprecedented ruthlessness" (Kershaw, 2000: 130). Once mass murder started, Himmler confided to his doctor the burden he shared with the earlier North American colonists: "It is the curse of greatness that it must step over dead bodies to create new life. Yet we must create new life, we must cleanse the soil or it will never bear fruit. It will be a great burden for me to bear." In 1941 Göring, Himmler, and Heydrich together formulated the Final Solution. Göring declared, "This is not the Second World War, this is the Great Racial War." Goebbels's diary describes "a life and death struggle between the Aryan race and the Jewish bacillus." Germans must rule "brutally" over Eastern nations – though Goebbels's instrumental reason made him later suggest gentler treatment until the war was over, when subjugation could resume (Goebbels, 1948: 126, 148, 185, 225, 246; Gordon, 1984: 100; Kersten, 1956: 120). These leaders were aware of how present-day humanity would judge them, yet believed their actions were historically necessary and morally desirable. In the future, they said, they would be thanked for their tough capacity as an elite to overcome conventional morality. These were ideological killers.

RADICALIZATION THROUGH COMRADELY PARAMILITARISM

To understand the increasing violence of the Nazi movement, we must move lower down the movement to examine a number of organizations that encouraged radicalization through violence. I view these as "cages" trapping their inmates into escalating violence. They were interlinked, and many moved between them as their Nazi and work careers developed. The first two cages predated the growth of the Nazi movement itself.

1. *Postwar paramilitaries.* Irregular volunteer fighters sprang up in 1918, refusing to accept defeat. The Freikorps fought across the eastern borders, attempting to drive out Slavs from formerly German lands. The Wehrverbände trained, stockpiled weapons, and skirmished more cautiously against the French and Belgian occupiers of the western borders and against German and Austrian Reds. They were disproportionately drawn from Germans fled from the lost territories. Their main targets were not Jews, though they were permeated by *völkisch* anti-Semitism. They introduced over 100,000 young German men to the notion that political problems could be solved through military power. Elias (1996: 182–97) sees them as crucial to "the decay of German civilization," since they blurred the moral line between legal and illegal force, as all these cages did, and as is normal among volunteer paramilitaries. Most Germans and Austrians wanted the lost territories back, and

many blamed Reds for the supposed "stab in the back" that had lost them. They admired the bravery of the paramilitaries and sometimes viewed their killings as justified acts of war, not illegal murder. The paramilitaries were also relatively egalitarian and classless. Officers led through example, not rank, and strong comradeship caged together these young men drawn from all social classes. For them, nationalism did trump class.

The paramilitaries produced many Nazis (as I show in *Fascists*, chap. 4). Campbell (1998) says the Wehrverbände provided many SA leaders, while almost 30 percent of the 265 highest-ranking Waffen-SS officers during World War II had Freikorps experience. As we shall see, these paramilitary veterans also contributed disproportionately to genocide. Yet much subsequent experience was also needed to produce such escalation. Equivalent World War I veterans in Italy rapidly became fascist *squadristi*, killing some socialists. But after the fascist seizure of power they seem to have settled down into the comfortable enjoyment of power. The U.S. equivalent (the radical wing of the American Legion) contented itself with murdering a few Communists. What contributed to continuing radicalization in Germany? I turn to subsequent cages.

2. *Refugee camps/associations.* Millions of refugees flocked into Germany at war's end. Their camps and associations bred embittered nationalism and kept them apart from normal society. Most of these ethnic Germans were from the lost territories of Poland, Denmark, and Alsace-Lorraine, though some were from the Soviet Union and the Baltic states. There were also half-refugees from western parts of Germany occupied by Allied troops. These were self-selected ethnic Germans: those indifferent to foreign rule had stayed at home. But the refugees wanted their homelands back, inside the German Reich. The Easterners also tended to identify Jews as Soviet collaborators, bringing westward notions of the Judeo-Bolshevik enemy. Then in 1934 came an influx of radicalized Nazis, 4,000 Austrians driven out by the Dollfuss regime after the failure of their attempted coup. But Germans remaining in the ccupied territories also proved generally quite receptive to Hitler. His march into the Rhineland brought cheering crowds. In the Saar plebiscite of 1935, 91 percent voted for union with Hitler's Germany. Many refugees became full-time activists in the SA, the SS, the Austrian Legion, or the Nazi Party, engaging in illegal violence that filled and caged their lives, preventing normal civilian life. These "old fighters" (members before 1929) or "old Nazis" (members before 1933) began early and then graduated through escalating stages of violence. As we see in the next chapter, genocidal institutions were staffed disproportionately by these transnational ethnic Germans. Most were men, though a few were women, and they were drawn from all social classes.

Let me illustrate these men with the first short biographies from my sample of genocide perpetrators. The family of Gustav Sorge (the anonymous case "S2" in Dick, 1972) were forced out of their Silesian hometown in 1919 when they refused Polish citizenship. But 8-year-old Gustav was left behind with an aunt so that one day he could claim back the title to their house and smallholding. Since the Poles "stopped us learning in German," Gustav and his friends became more anti-Polish. He venerated an extremist ex-Freikorps veteran who taught him sailing. In 1930 he was forced out of Poland and lived in German Silesia with an uncle, a Nazi militant. He joined the party and the SS in 1931: "All of us lads joined instinctively against the Poles and Czechs." Unemployed, he was prominent in Nazi street battles against the Reds and was soon a full-time SS fighter. He liked fighting. By now he had lost touch with his family and the SS was his home. He was a bodyguard for prominent Nazis and participated in the "Night of the Long Knives" in 1934, when Hitler had the SA murderously purged. He was then trained as a camp guard. Later an NCO in a death camp, he was known as "Iron George," a Nazi fanatic and a brutal killer. Here we see how an embittered German refugee found his home in a violent paramilitary movement.

3. *The SA*. This was by far the biggest Nazi paramilitary organization until the late 1930s, organized all over Germany, with no obvious regional bias. After 1930 rapid expansion made it predominantly working class, especially recruiting young unemployed males. It specialized in rowdyism and, unlike the SS, was more interested in action than ideology. It satisfied the needs of young males directly, giving food, lodging, excitement, and comradeship to the unemployed. For them it was a working-class peer group, a home, a comradely cage of proletarian paramilitary comradeship. For its leader, Ernst Röhm, and some of the officer corps, it was initially also a safe haven for homosexual activity. There is evidence that Hitler considered homosexuals malleable instruments of violence. Before 1933 the SA lived uneasily with the police authorities, which variably abetted, tolerated, or opposed it. In 1933 the state became Nazi and the SA was deployed as an auxiliary police force specializing in wild violence, mostly against the left, though other parties and Jews also felt its blows. The SA roamed the streets, intimidating, beating up, and rounding up political enemies into hastily organized SA camps, where at least 500 were killed and many more tortured. Such state-licensed thuggery might attract many young men in modern societies. Yet the army began to see the SA as a potential rival, and Hitler wanted to buy time by placating the generals. He arranged the Night of the Long Knives, murdering Röhm and his leadership cronies. SA manpower was now reduced by about 40 percent and its powers reined in.

The SA survived, more subordinated to the Leadership Principle. But by now it had socialized many Nazis into the normalcy of collective, comradely violence, often unpremeditated but sometimes culminating in killing. But by 1935, with the leftists destroyed, a movement geared to paramilitary thuggery was running out of enemies. I have written elsewhere (Mann, 1997) of "the contradictions of continuous revolution" faced by both fascist and communist movements once they seize state power: on the one hand, the movements embody an ideology of radical transformation; on the other hand, the regime seeks to institutionalize and bureaucratize its rule through compromise with elites – in this case German capitalists, the army, and the churches – whose entrenched powers can otherwise frustrate its designs. Many Germans and many Nazis perceived this contradiction, and most preferred compromise and order to wildness. To *displace* revolutionary wildness onto enemies who are not viewed favorably may sidestep the contradiction and allow both radicalization and compromise to go forward. The solution was to displace wildness onto an unpopular out-group, Jews (Kershaw, 1984: 275–6). This was also the displacement of proletarian resentments onto ethnicity.

Being a Nazi militant had always meant street brawling. Now it involved smashing Jewish shop windows and intimidating Jews. This is what ordinary SA and (to a lesser extent) SS and Hitler Youth members were actually *doing* from the mid-1930s and how they established successful careers. Young working-class males dominated, reveling in their "manhood" and "toughness" – like street gangs and football hooligans of today, but state-licensed. *Kristallnacht* escalated this licensed thuggery. It could not be defined as self-defense, since unlike Communists the Jews mounted no collective resistance. The targets were respectable property-owning shopkeepers and professionals – exactly the kind of people normally well protected by law from working-class violence. As the brawling proceeded in lockstep with anti-Jewish legislation, the bounds of legality and morality blurred – with consequences for public opinion generally. In 1938 rank-and-file Nazis escalated violence into murder committed in public. Nationalist commitment, careerism, and paramilitary skills all reinforced one another in a gradual process of caging. After *Kristallnacht* the SA was again sidelined, but many of its hard-core members were transferred to other killing institutions. The SA provided the main initial bands of violent, bigoted, and comradely killers, able also to find careers in violence.

4. *The SS*. The SS later became the main killing organization. It began small, as Hitler's personal bodyguard, but its size, functions, and influence increased throughout the 1930s. From 1934 the SS ran the concentration camps. From 1936 it controlled most of the Reich security police forces. In 1941 it gave the orders to the *Einsatzgruppen*. In most occupied countries the SS controlled the killings behind the front lines. If the SA represented early wild violence, the SS represented the orderly, ideological violence that actually captured much of the state apparatus and accomplished genocide. It was not easy to remain in the SS and not be implicated. The SS produced much more literate ideology than did the SA, and its order and apparent sophistication appealed to a more middle-class and educated core constituency. The SS also had a regional core constituency. Most of the SS elite were not from Protestant, Prussian parts of Germany. Himmler and Heydrich were Catholics from Munich and Halle. Rosenberg was a Baltic ethnic German,

and Berger was a Catholic Swabian with family in Eastern Europe. SS organization was strongest in the East and Southeast, and was clearly rather eastern-tilting.

SS ideology rested on biological racism, the Leadership Principle, and paramilitarism. Its training manuals taught that "Teutonic Aryans" possessed a "racial purity" embodying "idealism" and "virtue." Lesser Aryans, like the British or the French, had degenerated through decadent democratic practices but could be set right under German tutelage. Non-Aryans formed "anti-races," biologically inferior and polluting, "subhuman," "leeches," "lice," against whom a life-or-death struggle must be waged. By 1940 a distinction was being made. Inferior races with states could be conquered and cleansed of hostile elements. Where they could not found a state, cleansing had to go further, to elimination. For the SS this meant mostly Jews, then gypsies, but also blacks – which proved a death sentence for many French colonial troops captured by SS troops in 1940. SS leaders later defended mass murder in moral terms. Himmler declared: "We had the moral right vis-a-vis our people to annihilate this people which wanted to annihilate us."[2] Most ordinary SS men were uninterested in the arcane racialism of the elite. Even Eichmann scorned "Teutonic-Germanic Party bigwigs who behaved as if they were clad in horns and pelt." But the SS constantly parroted a simple racist slogan: Slavs were subhuman, Jews not human at all. SS General Bach-Zalewski later sought to explain genocide at his Nuremburg trial: "If for years, for decades, one preaches that the Slavic race is an inferior race, that the Jews are not human beings at all, then the inevitable end result must be such an explosion."

Second, the SS intensified the Leadership Principle. Himmler identified two SS mottoes: "the one which the *Führer* has bestowed upon us, 'Loyalty Is Mine Honor,' and the motto of ancient German Law, 'All Honor Comes from Loyalty.'" SS members were taught that Hitler embodied the German *Volk* – his will was law. Disobedience was treason to the *Volk*. No God existed above the fuhrer, nor any law of conduct above SS rules. The Leadership Principle was extended down through the SS, but since Hitler despised bureaucracy and the SS grew so rapidly, the authority of any lesser fuhrer was dwarfed by the Hitler cult (Buchheim et al., 1968: 320, 366). And unthinking obedience was a postwar defense strategy tapping into Allied notions that Germans had been brainwashed. Few perpetrators were passive internalizers of ideology. Rather, the Leadership Principle gave them a sense of absolution from guilt. Responsibility was shifted away from them, more toward the leader. Idealization of Hitler was psychologically useful.

---

[2] The Nazis and the SS were sometimes more opportunistic. When Germany allied with Japan, the racial status of the Japanese was upgraded. In Europe, however, they scorned opportunism. A less racist view of Ukrainians and Russians would have given them useful allies against communism. They never trusted or used effectively Ukrainian and White Russian troops.

But third, the SS plugged the gap between self and leader with elitist paramilitary comradeship. Its "political soldiers" were the true "bearers of the national-socialist revolution." Responsibility shifted to the comradely peer group. Wegner says that rescuing and purifying the Reich required "a comprehensive elite of 'political soldiery', freed from outdated legal barriers and transcending the limits of the 'normal' state apparatus" (1990: 126–7). The elitism of the SS caged its comrades, protecting them from the reach of conventional morality and legality. Guilt for murder could be countered by shame for not murdering, for flinching meant your comrades would reproach you with the cowardice and weakness of the ordinary (i.e., nonelite) man. These pressures would produce comradely and especially disciplined killers.

The three principles underlay SS recruitment and training. In the 1930s less attention was paid to the skills of recruits than to their racial purity. They had to produce genealogies stretching back to 1800, to be fine physical specimens, and to "look Aryan." All this encouraged a view of themselves as an elite, entitled to rule. Ideological instruction took up to a fifth of training time so that "every man should be trained to be a fanatical hater," as an SS general declared. The ideology also resonated amid commonplace virtues like loyalty, obedience, comradeship, dutifulness, honor, and patriotism, which were especially strong among the SS core recruitment constituency of ex-soldiers, policemen, civil servants, and educated professionals. It is generally believed that the SS also recruited more among Austrians and Bavarians (Wegner, 1990: 15, 206–7). By about 1937 the 20,000-strong SS was a cohesive all-male volunteer elite. And though the war saw a massive increase in recruitment that weakened SS cohesion, by then two important subcages had emerged within it that specifically encouraged violence unto murder.

5. *Concentration camps.* The prewar camps reveal an eastern regional bias. Six of the seven German concentration camps existing in mid-1939 were arranged in an arc around the east and south of the country. Dachau and Flossenburg were in Bavaria, Mathausen was near Linz in Austria, Sachsenhausen and Ravensbrück were in Prussia north of Berlin, and Buchenwald was a little more centrally located, in Weimar. The exception was the small camp of Neuengamme, located near Hamburg. None were in the west of the country. Since six of these seven camps catered to Germans (and not at first to Jews), it is not clear why they tilted geographically to the east and south – except that this was also the SS recruitment bias.

These were not initially supposed to be killing camps, but they were tough. As the first SS camp opened, at Dachau in 1933, the guard commander gave his pep talk:

Comrades of the SS! You all know what the Fuhrer has called upon us to do. We haven't come here to treat those swine inside like human beings. . . . Any man in our ranks who can't stand the sight of blood doesn't belong here, he should get out. The more of these bastards we shoot, the fewer we'll have to feed. (Sofsky, 1996: 4)

When this led to a spate of wild murders, SS leaders became alarmed and appointed a new commandant in 1934 to install a more orderly regime. Theodor Eicke was a refugee from Alsace, the son of a village station master. He was a patriotic and restless 17-year-old World War I volunteer. He left Alsace in 1919 at age 20 without a proper home in the Weimar Republic, hating it for the loss of his homeland to France. He fought with the Freikorps. As a veteran he could get hired as a policeman anywhere in Germany, but he was repeatedly fired by police forces for his nationalist activism. A Nazi by 1928, he feuded violently with the local Nazi *Gauleiter*, who almost managed to get him incarcerated in a mental hospital (we meet Heyde, the psychiatrist who prevented this, in Chapter 9). Sentenced for possessing explosives, he fled abroad. In 1933 Himmler invited him back to help in the Night of the Long Knives. He shot Röhm and was rewarded with command at Dachau, where he pioneered the terrible Nazi camp system. He recruited experienced SS men, preferring Freikorps veterans. Later, as the camps expanded and the supply of experienced Nazis dried up, he recruited young party members, whom he said were more malleable. He rejected ex-Wehrmacht NCOs, who had internalized softer standards of discipline. He believed men so picked could be socialized into a segregated camp world that would become their home. Thus the camps caged the guards as well as the prisoners. His career pinnacle was to become the commanding general of Waffen-SS front divisions. He was killed at the Eastern Front in early 1943.

Eicke's regime became the model for all prewar German camps and later for the death camps. Dachau trained the core officers and NCOs of the other major camps, apart from the *Aktion Reinhard* camps (as we see in Chapter 9). Eicke instructed guards not to arbitrarily beat or maltreat prisoners according to their mood, but to do so routinely as systematic intimidation. He lectured his men that prisoners were "subhuman enemies of the state." Höss (the Auschwitz commandant) got his training there and remembered that prisoners would plaintively ask, "Why do the SS hate us so? After all, we are men like them." The Eicke regime was not one of rules. Staff were told to enforce compliance through violence and were left alone to get on with it. They became like-minded, talked the same camp slang, imbibing a camp culture. They knew what to do without thinking too much about it (Orth, 2000).

Franz Hoffman was a typical camp guard, a Bavarian semiskilled worker who joined the Nazi Party and the SS in 1932 at age 26. A Dachau guard in 1933, he was toughened by Eicke and proved himself fit to join this toughened elite. First, he shot an elderly Jew he found in the toilet after curfew; then he joined in the sport of driving prisoners to the camp wire and then shooting them "while trying to escape." He spent the next 12 years in camps, rising to captain, the commandant of several small camps. He showed special hatred of gypsies. After the war he claimed that he was a "little man" oppressed by Jewish and SS big shots. In 1965 he was sentenced to life for complicity in over 2,000 murders and the actual commission of at least 30 murders.

The guards were given absolute power, to use repeatedly, violently, so as to liberate "a perpetrator from all inhibitions." Excessive violence was routinized, producing "habitual perpetrators who do without reasons for their actions," blurring the line between torture to extract information and torture as "pure, purposeless torment." Terror became a binding group norm that diffused the guard's sense of personal responsibility onto the camp as a whole (rather like the fuhrer principle). One could never be disciplined for it unless it was uncontrolled. As the camps expanded, conditions worsened, exaggerating the social distance between well-fed, smartly uniformed perpetrators and emaciated, filthy, shivering, lice-infested victims incapable of self-defense. They became deindividualized, dehumanized in the sight of the guards. Then in the death camps murder became required behavior (Sofsky, 1997: 16–24, 223–40).

But there were also close to 1,000 forced labor camps, and they were more varied. In some camps even Jews could strike a modus vivendi with the guards and managers – and survive (Straede, 1999). But all camps tended to be occupational communities, segregated from society, offering secure careers to not very qualified persons, exerting social control over them. Until 1941 their practices were terroristic. Thereafter only the death camps were genocidal. But each progressive shift from violence through more ubiquitous individual killing to genocide might take no great moral effort from guards. From 1941 for ordinary Germans in uniform, the concentration camp was a safe, secure, and well-paid place to be, infinitely preferable to the Eastern Front. Under the camp regime we might therefore expect a mixture of bigoted, careerist, comradely, and disciplined killers – and disturbed violent guards would be allowed to flourish in the core camps.

6. *The SD*. From 1935 the SS acquired control over the Kripo (criminal police) and Gestapo (political police). They were brought into the SD, the SS security police branch. Himmler declared that its prime purpose was "the internal defense of the people" in "one of the greatest struggles of human history" against "the universally destructive force of Bolshevism." Werner Best, the Gestapo head, described it as "a fighting formation" defending "the political health of the nation" (Kershaw, 1998: 541). Few Kripo or Gestapo officials had been Nazi or SS members before the coup (this would have been often illegal), though 20–40 percent had been members of Nazi vocational organizations. In 1933 a few policemen were purged, replaced by Old Nazis. But most policemen bent with the wind as police functions were Nazified (Browder, 1996; Gellately, 1990: 50ff.). In any case, Nazi concern with enemies undermining the state suited most policemen, who reveled in their new freedom to smash the enemies of the state. Himmler and his deputy Heydrich (the SD head) also wished their own empire to be independent

of party bosses and so often preferred efficient, tough policemen to more political and potentially wilder Nazis.

Heinrich Müller was ideal for them. From Munich, a much-decorated aviator in World War I, he followed his father into the Munich police force, acquiring the reputation of a fervent anti-Communist willing to exceed legal norms to get a conviction. Though specializing in harassing the left, he was not a member of any political organization and claimed to be uninterested in politics. This is because he conceived of rightist values as providing an objective justice above mere legal norms. He was also exceedingly blunt. Schellenberg, an SD officer who considered himself an intellectual, says in his memoirs that he was shocked when Müller, in his "crude Bavarian accent," confided to him, "One really ought to drive all the intellectuals into a coalmine and then blow it up" (1956: 8). Müller was loyal, delighted to see his talents used to the full by the SS. He rose to head the Gestapo, with the rank of SS major-general. He disappeared in 1945, probably dead. Rumors abound of his survival – first in U.S. military custody, then in South America, though his fate remains unknown. He must be dead by now.

Wilhelm Harster was more political, yet still exemplifies the resonance Nazism had for people from military-police backgrounds. Also the son of a policeman, from near Munich, he was a model student in high school, where he also joined a Freikorps youth movement. He graduated from university with a law degree and joined the police in 1929. He was described as a "conscientious, obedient civil servant" and an authoritarian conservative nationalist. He joined the Nazi Party and the SA in 1932 and greeted the coup with delight: it would mean the end of "streetfighting, unemployment and Versailles." He was immediately transferred to the Gestapo, where he served in ascending spheres of violence – Berlin and Württemburg in the 1930s, Austria during and after the *Anschluss*, Poland in 1939, and then in occupied Belgium and Holland, where he supervised deportations – he was later found guilty of complicity in the deaths of 82,956 people (including Anne Frank). No evidence of personal cruelty, or indeed of much hatred, was revealed. He claimed he had Jewish friends but believed "in separating Jews from the nation."

The state judicial apparatus also became infected. Senior police officers interacted closely with the state prosecutors, with whom they shared a background of university law degrees. Together they produced "idealistic," "ethical" Nazis. One was Walter Schellenberg, from the Saar, the son of a piano manufacturer who went bankrupt because of the French occupation. Yet the family adapted and provided a happy home. He was close to his cultured, religious mother. He was educationally successful, fluent in French, with cosmopolitan poise and ambitions. He graduated with a law degree in 1933 and says that a judge advised him to further his career by joining the Nazis (he may have been more Nazi than this implies). He promptly joined both the party and the SS at age 23, being also attracted, he admits, by the glamour of the SS uniform and the prospects of joining an elite of "the better type of people." He gave ideological lectures to the SS, and his strongly anti-Catholic views attracted Heydrich's attention and got him into the local SD, which was worried by Catholic opposition. He rose to the top of the internal intelligence wing of the SD, where he was known for his mainstream Nazi views and his attempts to build up more professional and objective state intelligence reporting. He was somewhat segregated both from dirtier police work and from Himmler's rather quirky racialism. He also claimed in postwar testimony that he had avoided several attempts to get him into the *Einsatzgruppen*. Though he embraced Nazism with some enthusiasm, he does not seem to have been a murderous Nazi. But he was also lucky in that his headquarters SD roles kept him away from the killing fields. Most SD men were not so fortunate.

The SD expanded the tough side of police work as legal restraints diminished. By 1939 many policemen had experience of methods of extracting information and "neutralizing" enemies of the state that in most countries would have transgressed legal due process. From 1939 the term *enemy* acquired an extra wartime intensity. Thus, when the SS bosses came to form the murderous *Einsatzgruppen*, the core came from the SD – an environment in which professionalism might fuse together ideological, careerist, and bureaucratic motives for killing.

7. *The Euthanasia project – T4*. The only prewar mass killing occurred in the Euthanasia project. Neither anti-Semitic nor anti-Slav, it rested on reputable biomedical models embraced by geneticists, anthropologists, and clinical practitioners in many countries. Psychiatrists and doctors believed that some patients were incurable and so accepted that there was "life unworthy of life." Hitler had initiated T4, which further enhanced its status, and bonuses were paid for its "difficult" work. T4 found it easy to attract administrators, doctors, nurses, administrative staff, orderlies, and soldiers committed to a Germany that valued their own professional expertise and careers. Hospitals, regional medical authorities, and universities were all implicated, and the project involved many women as doctors, nurses, and clerical staff. Again, there was a regional bias since its institutions were located around the eastern and southern edge of Germany. T4 also introduced the Nazi movement and the German public to cleansing the German *Volk* through legitimate killing. It pioneered the techniques of administrative secrecy, with few written orders, sanitized records, and insulated institutions, and quiet, methodical, "scientific" killing without much bloodshed. It trained and inured death camp personnel. One hundred staff were to transfer their methods to the death camps of Poland, refining their techniques on Jews and Slavs.

Dr. Hans-Bodo Gorgass, the son of a Leipzig railway inspector, came from a family of depressives, though he seems to have come through unscathed. He was in the SA in 1933 at age 24, a committed Nazi. He worked from

1937 in state hospitals under Bernotat, a euthanasia pioneer, who recommended him to T4 in 1939. He was told baldly by Brack, its head, that a "particularly trusted doctor" was needed to kill mental patients. He says his qualms were stilled by the prestigious doctors associated with the project. Later, in Buchenwald, he behaved "more like a butcher than a doctor."

Dr. Georg Renno was an emigre from Alsace, the son of a clerk. He had been a Nazi student, and joined the party in 1930, at age 23, and the SS in 1931. He played the flute in an SS band but was not otherwise prominent. During the 1930s patients called him a "friendly, humane doctor." He caught the eye of the Nazi hospital head, Nitsche, who picked him for the first experiments there. He was briefly a Waffen-SS regimental doctor and then joined T4 formally in 1940. At his trial he said, "At the time I viewed euthanasia as a blessing for the patients" and "The notion that a state could pass a law that was illegal was beyond my comprehension." In a less guarded moment he said, "Turning on the [gas] taps was no big deal."

T4 contained many low-level employees. Paul Reuter (Burleigh's Paul R.) was a farm servant and then a gardener from Hessen-Nassau. He became a Nazi in 1930 to improve his employment prospects, he claims. He regularly attended Nuremberg rallies. In 1936, unemployed, his Nazi record got him trained as a male nurse. After serving in Poland he was transferred to a T4 hospital. He joined the transport section, assuring patients that "they were going for a bath," then administered lethal injections and dug graves. He says he was told, "This is a fuhrer order and we must carry out the orders of the fuhrer."

Pauline Kneissler (Burleigh's Pauline K.) fled with her family from Odessa as the Bolsheviks seized it in 1918. They acquired a small farm in Westphalia, but the Depression forced its sale. Her father found work on the railways and Pauline was a seamstress, then a nurse. Though joining the Nazi Party only in 1937 at age 37, she was in the Nazi Evangelical Church organization in 1934 and had minor leadership roles in Nazi women's organizations. She came to believe that religion conflicted with "the laws of nature." All this got her recruited for T4. She did not like the deception involved in euthanasia and claimed that the relentless killing got on her nerves, but she killed more patients than any other nurse.

The next chapters reveal that all these interlinked cages of violence, located at the fringes of illegality, trained and toughened Nazis who would murder. Together they spanned all the classes of German society. Most were all-male, and most tilted the social geography of Nazism southward and eastward. The enemies they perceived were varied, though Bolsheviks dominated until the mid-1930s and Jews later. By the time they were asked to commit mass murder routinely, many had long experience of violence. Not all of them were real Nazis, but their work environments tended to produce bigoted, comradely, disciplined, and careerist killers. For these were Nazi and work careers in ascending violence.

THE RADICALIZATION OF ORDINARY GERMANS

Obviously Germans differed greatly. If they voted for the Nazis, this could have been for reasons trivial as well as ideological. In *Fascists* I identified the core constituencies of Nazi support. There was no significant class or gender bias. The main constituencies lay in military, police, and public sector backgrounds; economic sectors lying outside the key class conflict zones between capital and labor (i.e., not from large-scale, urban manufacturing or mining sectors); the more educated middle classes; lost and threatened territories around the frontiers of Germany (and Austria); and Protestants rather than Catholics. Persons from such backgrounds tended to find extreme nationalist or statist solutions to Germany's problems more plausible, and this led them toward Nazism. Before 1933 little suggested that this might culminate in mass murder. But perhaps such backgrounds might also push *some* ordinary Germans down that path. With the exception of the Protestant religion, this was indeed the case.

The German opposition had been smashed by the mid-1930s. Half of the 300,000 German Communists spent time in concentration camps. Since no one could safely express public dissent, racism was the only ideology heard in public by ordinary Germans. Our closest guides to the mood of the population are Gestapo and clandestine Socialist Party reports, supplemented by eyewitness memoirs (see Bankier, 1996; Gellately, 1990; Gordon, 1984; Kershaw, 1984; Kirk, 1996). Kershaw (1984) summarizes them: "The road to Auschwitz was built by hate, but paved with indifference." Few Germans went beyond privatization or withdrawal from victims and regime alike. They focused their energies on family, career, or church, daring at most to make private jokes about prominent Nazis. Laws removing Jews from the civil service, from higher education, and from their shops and businesses met more approval than disapproval – as across Europe – partly out of greed but partly because Germans believed the Nuremberg Laws defined what was legal and so would put a stop to wild Nazi violence. Most Germans reacted negatively to the 1941 edict forcing Jews to wear the yellow star, and they often showed public kindness to Jews. Wild violence like *Kristallnacht* caused outrage. Germans wanted Jewish influence lessened through discriminatory laws. When the time came, they did not oppose their physical removal, but – like most Nazis – they preferred legal means.

Yet the new regime was popular and Hitler seemed surefooted. A third had freely voted Nazi; another fifth supported authoritarian nationalist parties. Hitler surged to power on a wave of hope for a new order. A Gestapo officer later involved in assassination plots against Hitler remembered: "Seldom had a nation so readily surrendered all its rights and liberties as did ours in those first hopeful, intoxicated months of the new millennium" (Gisevius, 1947: 102). Hitler's *military Keynsianism* brought jobs, created order, and cleaned up streets. An overheated economy spread some discontent at the end of the 1930s, scurrilous jokes spread about Hitler, and many resented attacks on their church. But Gestapo informers made dissent dangerous. On the positive side, Hitler's foreign adventures brought success at virtually no cost between 1936 and 1941, restoring German national pride and the legitimacy of *grossdeutsch* ethnic nationalism. From 1933 the reasons given by persons joining the Nazi Party or the SS reveal a generalized national pride into which legitimate personal careerism could be inserted. "I wanted to help build the new Germany" – this simple equation of self and country overwhelmed whatever qualms many ordinary Germans felt about the Nazis.

From 1939 the regime appropriated wartime mobilization and patriotism. Jews were declared enemy collaborators, to be rounded up and imprisoned. Most Germans had more pressing concerns – bombing, war shortages, and the fate of kin at the front. The Jew had been depersonalized, made abstract by propaganda and then made absent by imprisonment and deportation. Bankier (1996) says indifference was a psychological defense mechanism. To worry about the Jews would increase unease, even guilt – therefore, repress all knowledge. This, he believes, intensified once extermination began. The mass shootings were widely reported by returning soldiers, the death camps by the BBC and Allied leaflet drops. Germans knew but tried to keep the knowledge at the back of their minds. It occasionally popped out. When Goebbels publicized the Soviet massacre of Polish officers at Katyn, the SD reported mutterings like "Germans have no right to get worked up about this action... from the German side Poles and Jews have been done away with in much greater numbers." Yet many agreed that the Eastern Front was "a fight to the death" against Judeo-Bolshevism, while "Jewish capitalism" was often blamed for the British bombing of German cities. This was no ethnic civil war, but bombing did blur the distinction between the front and the rear. To be a German, almost regardless of class, determined one's fate. To be a Jew was death. Ethnicity transcended class and other axes of stratification.

From 1941 the presence of foreign workers became normal across much of Germany. Their pitiable condition brought many expressions of sympathy. The first defeats in 1942 brought forebodings. If Germany was defeated, Allied retribution would be terrible. Bombing raids were thought to be direct retaliation for the concentration camps. Thus anti-Slav and anti-Semitic sentiments were now rarely voiced: Germans kept their heads down and their thoughts private, taking the least risky option of silence. That silence makes it difficult to be certain whether they viewed the Jews as an enemy serious enough to merit death. But since the regime constantly stressed their enmity, since the war brought death and destruction to Germans, and since the Jews were now an absent abstraction, many Germans probably believed so.

All this is necessary to understanding the ordinary German perpetrators encountered in the next chapters. Until 1942 Germany became more hospitable to Nazi ideology. Hitler's domestic successes were followed by remarkable geopolitical gains. Wartime patriotism then enveloped him, and wartime mobilization enveloped the Germans. Though there were core constituencies of radical Nazism, there were no antidote constituencies. Class had been trumped by racial ethnonationalism, a version of my second general ethnic thesis. At the end of the war came more varied behavior: perpetrators seeking to curry favor with prisoners or wiping out the remaining witnesses, desperately retreating soldiers and an angry but cowed civilian population. But before this finale, many ordinary Germans may also have been radicalized. They were almost all mobilized into compliance by the world war.

FINAL RADICALIZATION: INTO GENOCIDE

The final surges into genocide came within the Nazi movement. There were no broader popular pressures at this stage. Though ordinary Germans participated later in the genocide, they were not much involved in its initiation. Since radicalization of the Nazi movement was continuous, we cannot attach precise dates to it. Historians have spent great energy searching for a decision authorizing the Final Solution, yet it remains elusive. Hitler wished to eliminate the Jews, but pressured emigration escalating into violent deportation remained the preferred solutions until 1941. In 1939 and 1940 Eichmann worked on plans to deport the Jews to Palestine or Madagascar. It was assumed that most would not survive the inhospitable conditions at the receiving end. Yet Britain ruled the waves and would not permit any such scheme. Eichmann went back to the drawing board.

But decisions about Jews were not taken in a vacuum. In 1939 their fate was linked to that of Poles. This was not a conventional war of conquest, since the defeated Poles were not absorbed into the Reich. Hitler declared:

The *volkisch* state must on the contrary take the decision either to seal off these racially alien elements in order not again to allow the blood of our own people to be debased, or it must remove them forthwith and transfer the land made available to our people's comrades. (Kershaw, 2000: 237)

Goebbels noted, "The Fuehrer's judgement on the Poles is annihilatory. More animals than human beings.... The filth of the Poles is unimaginable." Hitler said he would not make the mistake of former German conquerors. By assimilating Poles, they had produced a "slavified" German mongrel race. "Now at least we know the laws of race and act accordingly." The western third of the country was to be incorporated into the Reich – but cleansed of Poles and Jews. The middle third was to be a protectorate, containing Poles, but only as seasonal labor living in segregated slave quarters. Its Jews would be herded into ghettos, joined there by the Reich Jews, pending a final solution of the Jewish question. The eastern third was ceded to the Soviet Union and so, for the moment, was not a German problem. All this was accomplished with extremely violent deportations plus the mass murders of the Polish intelligentsia amounting to a Plan C of politicide. The justification given (as usual in such atrocities) was retaliation, though the elite knew this was phony. Ethnic Germans were now organized by the SS into militias. Their commander exhorted them: "You are now the master race here.... Don't be soft, be merciless, and clear out everything that is not German." Army Chief of Staff Halder, a noted Nazi, declared, "it was the intention of the Fuehrer and Goering to annihilate and exterminate the Polish people." He added, "the rest could not even be hinted at in writing" (all quotes from Kershaw, 2000: 237–52).

But this brought logistical problems. Over a million Jews and several hundred thousand Poles were to be moved eastward into the Polish protectorate, but the Nazi leadership there lacked the facilities to accommodate them. They objected to their fiefdoms becoming dumping grounds for *Untermenschen*. It would undermine all their attempts to impose order over the protectorate. Fierce intraparty wrangling commenced over the fate of Jews and Poles.

Once the invasion of Russia came, the fate of Jews was entwined with that of Russians. This was planned as a war of extermination. It included the elimination of the Jewish-Bolshevik intelligentsia and all captured Communists. All this was openly stated in the master plan for Operation Barbarossa, the invasion of Russia. Gerlach says that the army planned to feed itself from occupied Belarus This would produce mass local starvation, indicating a "genocidal intent." Since Belarussian Jews were mainly urban, they would suffer disporportionately. This, he says, was "the final, decisive impulse for the complete liquidation of the Jews" (1999: 44–81). But a speedy victory might have solved the Jewish Question short of genocide, since the plan was for all Jews and millions of Poles to be driven east into former Soviet territories by whatever means were necessary. Heydrich, through Göring or Himmler, had been asked to plan for a "final solution project" in January 1941, but this still seems to have been a territorial deportation, not genocide. Eichmann was laying plans to move 5.8 million people. Yet even Göring's letter to Heydrich of July 31 is cagey as to means:

Complementing the task that was assigned to you on 24 January 1939, which dealt with arriving at – through furtherance of emigration and evacuation – a solution of the Jewish problem, ... I hereby charge you with making all necessary preparations ... for bringing about a complete solution of the Jewish question in the German sphere of influence in Europe. (Nuremberg War Crimes Tribunal, 1946: Einsatzgruppen Case, Part IV, 133)

No means are specified. But high Nazi and SS functionaries stated that they expected deportees to starve, freeze, or be worked to death as slave laborers. The Plan was becoming genocidal before there was any formal decision on genocide. The Nazis running Reich Poland wanted Jews and potentially troublesome Slavs deported from their fiefdoms, but those running eastern Poland did not want them there. The agreed-upon solution was to drive them farther east into the vast expanse of Russia. Himmler had asked his planners two days after the launch of Barbarossa to organize eastward deportation of the almost unbelievable number of 31 million persons, mostly Slavs. But for Jews and any potential troublemakers, many planners assumed – but did not openly state – that the goal was to "kill them all, but outside of Europe." Brack, the head of T4, said after the war that now "the destruction of the Jews ... was an open secret in high party circles."

The *Einsatzgruppen* officers received orders in the early summer of 1941 to kill Bolsheviks and partisans. Based on SS experience in Poland in 1939, parts of the army were expected to oppose civilian killings. And the invasion plan was so optimistic that the 3,000 *Einsatzgruppen* could not possibly have killed all the Jews in the vast territories assigned to them. But the army cooperated because its purged officer corps, panicked by partisan activity, accepted the Nazi view that the Judeo-Bolshevik was the enemy. Some killed with enthusiasm (Streit, 1978). So did many local collaborators. So Heydrich received more help than anticipated. In July 1941 he increased the number of *Einsatzgruppen* and extended the scope of the killing. Some commanders now received orders to kill all adult male Jews, and some women and children too. The numbers killed jumped (sometimes 10-fold) in mid-August. By the end of 1942 *Einsatzgruppen* numbers had increased 11-fold and the killing had escalated way beyond even the wildest of deportations. Yet there still seems to have been no master plan. Some were killing young males; others were killing those unable to do labor. Militants in numerous agencies – the SS, the Wehrmacht, and the civilian administration – all had some local autonomy, but they tended to share similar anti-Semitic, Nazi, and careerist values, and they were all frustrated by Soviet and partisan resistance and by having too many mouths to feed. They were now rivaling each other to provide technical solutions for mass murder – shooting, gassing, starving (Gerlach, 1999; Lower, 2002; Musial, 1999; Pohl, 1996; Sankühler, 1996).

Yet stiffening Soviet resistance and hardening front lines at the end of 1941 meant that all versions of Plan A, deportation from the Reich, be-came impossible for the foreseeable future. There was again a contradiction between eastward deportations and the lack of any place to deport popu-lations to. In this context Plan D, genocide, became the only solution that could actually eliminate the Jews from the German sphere of influence and that did not backtrack on the radical momentum of Nazi rule. It may have been decided by the top Nazis at the end of the year and steered through the German state hierarchy at the Wannsee Conference in January 1942. But there is no "smoking gun" document, and there was probably no sin-gle order. In practice, large numbers of Germans in the East were already embarked upon genocide, believing this was what the fuhrer wanted.[3] This

---

[3] The decisional process remains controversial. I have drawn on those already cited, plus Breitman (1991), Browning (1985, 1992), Friedländer (1995), Gordon (1984), Mayer (1990), and Naimark (2001: chap. 2).

was less an orderly series of decisions than a general process of escalation among like-minded elites whose initial plans were frustrated.

CONCLUSION

Of all my cases, this one fits least well into my theses. It was the most statist and the most premeditated, with the most coherent, least destabilized state. Its unchallenged dictator traveled the least distance between his Plans. Already by 1919 Hitler intended to eliminate Jews and Bolsheviks from a Greater German Reich. To accomplish these two unwavering "absolute values," he was always prepared to use whatever violence was necessary. Though he never seems to have had a master plan, his successive Plans – pressured emigration, deportations, politicide, genocide – flowed easily into each other as each met obstacles. He never considered pulling back, except tactically, when encountering opposition during the 1930s. But he did not seem to contemplate genocide until after the war began. It is sobering to realize that had the other Great Powers combined to deter German expansion during the period 1936–9, then genocide would not have occurred. Then escalation was justified as self-defense, as it was by Goebbels, Himmler, Heydrich, and others. German historians have recently emphasized that the younger generation of university-trained Nazis shared exactly the same values and recognized equally that desperate times required desperate remedies. Plan D, genocide, was the logical outcome of the frustration of their earlier Plans on the Eastern Front. War fighting and exterminist strategies were now combined against the Judeo-Bolshevik enemy.

Thus the Jews were not exterminated merely because of strong anti-Semitism. Extermination required entangling the Jews with the broader ethnonationalist and political enemies of Germany, as these were perceived by Nazi radicals. For most Nazis and Germans, however, the distance traveled was much greater, since they were unaware of Plan A in the first place – and nor were most German Jews. In order for Nazis and Germans to begin to form the required army of perpetrators, far more was needed. The stages by which this occurred will become clearer by tracing actual careers in genocide in the next two chapters.

8

Nazis, II

Fifteen Hundred Perpetrators

Our knowledge of individual perpetrators must necessarily rely quite heavily upon testimony drawn from postwar trials. But this has certain difficulties. It is biased toward three of the motives distinguished in the previous chapter: perpetrators said they complied because they were fearful, disciplined, or bureaucratic. Persons accused of war crimes desperately denied having Nazi, racist, anti-Semitic, or murderous intent, claiming, "I was only following orders," "I was frightened," "I was only a small cog in a giant machine," "I was in the motor pool/personnel records/cookhouse all the time." No one admitted having enjoyed killing; few liked to talk about their SS career achievements. Few incriminated each other or even admitted having had conversations with their colleagues about the genocide cascading around them. From their testimony, this would seem to be an ideology-free environment in which ordinary people were trapped inside coercive and bureaucratic institutions. Yet to accept the self-serving testimony of mass murderers would be unwise.

When motives are so occluded, it is doubtful that we can fully test whether killers might have been of the psychologically disturbed violent type. Court-appointed psychologists did carefully assess a few defendants, usually concluding that they were sane. A court psychologist reported that the Nuremberg defendants' personalities "are not unique or insane . . . they could be duplicated in any country of the world today." Most camp survivors report that only a handful of guards were sadists in the sense of being noticeably disturbed individuals. Rather, the environment produced a collective sadism, they say – which needs a sociological explanation. Yet it should be frankly admitted that we cannot penetrate far into the characters of most perpetrators, since we lack reliable psychological data.

Consider, for example, one of the more seemingly honest perpetrators, the commandant of Auschwitz. It is easy to feel that we know Major Rudolf Höss, since he composed a frank *Memoir* in 1945 (Höss et al., 1978). Already sentenced to death, with nothing more to lose, Höss did not try to conceal the enormity of the killing machine he had supervised. The *Memoir* is a calm, measured account of the organization and personnel of the death camp by an obviously sane senior manager. Some have stressed his ordinary qualities. Katz (1993: 61–79) calls him "a Nazi bureaucrat," "an administrative functionary," attached to order, cleanliness, tidiness, and obedience to authority – the epitome, he concludes, of "the ordinary modern bureaucrat."

Yet this seems an extravagant extension of ordinariness. Consider Höss's career. He began as a teenage volunteer soldier in World War I. After the war, at age 19, he joined a Freikorps, killing Latvians, Poles, and German Communists. His unit was dissolved after it killed one of its own members, a suspected traitor. The leading killer, Höss, was convicted of murder. Released in 1928, he went straight into the Artamen League, a Nazi agrarian organization; he was a full-time party militant until 1934, when he became one of the first concentration camp guards, at Dachau. He served in the camps until 1945. Höss may have been an efficient manager, but he certainly was a highly ideological Nazi, his adult life caged entirely within proto-Nazi and Nazi organizations, steeped in violence. It is difficult to picture him as an ordinary manager or as representing modernity. Such is the justification for my method here: I throw light on the perpetrators by analyzing simple, objective features of their backgrounds and careers. What kinds of biography preceded their terrible actions? What motivations might they support?

Previous studies do not permit authoritative answers. No study treats the entire corps of perpetrators, only particular subgroups. But most stress three rather ordinary features of perpetrators' lives. They maintained fairly normal private lives amid their ghastly work, living with their families or writing loving letters home, celebrating life's rituals, having affairs. Seventy-two percent of West German war crimes trial defendants remained married at the time of their trial (Oppitz, 1976: 170). Second, they were ordinary in the sense of having unexceptional talents. Arad (1987: 198) speaks for many authors when he describes the *Aktion Reinhard* death camp staff as people without exceptional qualities or characteristics. Third, their prior occupations seem typical of Germany. Hilberg says, "the machinery of destruction was a remarkable cross-section of the German population. Every profession, every skill, and every social status was represented" (1978: 649). Lasik (1994a: 279) says that pre-Auschwitz occupations reveal a "camp staff very much like the society from which it was drawn" (cf. Browning, 1993; Goldhagen, 1996; von Hentig, 1977). Recent research on Nazis in general has also tended to argue that they were drawn from all the social classes (see my *Fascists*: chaps. 4, 5; Fischer, 1995). Shorn of their uniforms, swagger, and cause, the aging, sober-suited defendants in postwar trials looked remarkably like the German man and woman in the street outside. It might comfort us if the evil of mass murderers was visible in their bearing: then they might have nothing in common with us. But this is not so.

But we really know rather little about perpetrators' biographies. We have no precise data on economic sectors, though the public sector must have been overrepresented. We know little about their regional origins. Researchers on Nazis in general have concluded that they were drawn from all areas of Germany, yet this statement has usually been based on rather formal categorizations of region (north versus south, east versus west, Prussia versus other states, etc.), uninformed by any theoretical hypothesis. Merkl's reexamination of the sample of 1930s Nazi militants that Abel originally studied is the exception (1975: 133–8). He found men from the lost territories and threatened borders overrepresented – because these areas were likely to produce extreme nationalists. These were examples of what I call core Nazi constituencies. Perhaps they also provided many perpetrators. Most scholars also see Austrians and ethnic Germans from abroad as overrepresented. Koehl (1983) believes the SS was especially successful at recruiting Austrians and Sudetens, though he produces no actual figures. Banach's (1998: 50) figures for security policemen do not suggest Austrian or Sudeten overrepresentation or much skewed representation among the German states – except that the more Catholic states (Baden and Bavaria) are somewhat underrepresented. He also found Catholics underrepresented among security policemen (1998: 142). Lasik (1994a) intriguingly found the reverse among Auschwitz staff, which is at odds with our knowledge of Nazis in general, who were disproportionately from Protestant backgrounds. Yet Lasik could not distinguish between Germans and Austrians in his sample and accepts that Catholic Austria might be biasing his result.

Did perpetrators already have careers in Nazism and violence? We know most about T4 personnel. Since they killed non-Jewish Germans, they were the group most likely to be brought to postwar trial in Germany. Most scholars emphasize how varied they were, some being highly selected through party or personal networks for their known reliability, others being ordinary party members, totally unaware of the tasks awaiting them (e.g., Horwitz, 1990: 64–8). Yet de Mildt (1996: 311) believes that careerism shines through this variety:

> they were not killers by conviction but by circumstance and opportunity. Instead of matching the image of the paranoiac ideological warriors . . . their background profile far more closely matches that of rather ordinary citizens with a well-developed calculating instinct for their private interests. . . . The key word which springs to mind . . . is not "idealism" but "opportunism."

Banach (1998), Browder (1996), and Gellately (1990) emphasize variety among the Gestapo and other security policemen. Yet though they tend to identify more ordinary men than ideological Nazis, their work helps us break down the dichotomy with which I began my analysis of motivations. For they stress a congruence between the ordinary values and practices of police work at this time and the general ethos of Nazism. Though only a minority had been Nazis before 1933, almost all appreciated the special powers the Nazis conferred on them to hunt and interrogate suspects. Browder argues that the institutional identity conferred by security police work had a kind of elective affinity with Nazism. Policemen were further seduced into more radical Nazism by the escalating routine violence of their profession during the 1930s. Rather tough conceptions of public order were thus compatible with the Nazi stress on statism – as two leading but initially non-Nazi policemen in my sample, Müller and Nebe, discovered on their way to becoming major perpetrators.

Proctor (1988) interprets medical practice under the Third Reich similarly. Since race was a natural object of German medical science even before the Nazis came to power, there was already a strong scientific affinity between medical science and Nazi championing of racial biomedical science. Nazism appealed professionally to them. Allen (2002) likewise notes that the administrators and engineers of the WVHA (the SS camps' headquarters) found an affinity between their commitment to scientific management and the seeming Nazi commitment to an ordered, rational society. Thus professional institutions and subcultures might draw innocent people toward Nazism – and then perhaps into murder. This sociological view of ideology sees it less as an abstract, fixed doctrine than as the drawing of conclusions from one's own cumulative experience – blurring the simple distinction between the ordinary person and the real Nazi. I will build on these insights. Ordinary policemen, doctors, and engineers, not ordinary men, might have been predisposed toward radical Nazism.

Among the *Einsatzgruppen,* the mobile killing units, the two studies of Auxiliary Police Battalion 101 agree that most of the policemen had little background in Nazism. Browning says they were ordinary men, trapped into committing genocide by the pressures of hierarchy and comradeship. Goldhagen says they were ordinary Germans, murdering because (like all Germans) they were bursting with "eliminationist anti-Semitism," though he is silent on their motives when killing Russians. Both stress that the policemen were draftees and not individually selected, few were Nazis before the war, and their prior occupations were representative of Hamburg, whence most came. I will cast some doubt on these conclusions in the next chapter.

Obviously, the perpetrators had rather varied biographies, as Browning's studies indicate (1978, 1985, 1993). But some variations were predictable. The higher the rank, the greater the Nazism; and there were more committed Nazis in core SS and party organizations than in auxiliary police forces (Browning, 1993: 45–48; Jansen & Weckbecker, 1992: 79–81; Lichtenstein, 1990; Pohl, 1996: 81–96; Sandkühler, 1996). The higher *Einsatzgruppen* officers were ideological Nazis (and highly educated; Headland, 1992: 208). Thus the higher ranks in core institutions were brimming with long-term Nazis. Birn finds imposing histories of Nazism, and usually of political violence, in the careers of the 45 highest-ranked SS police officers. Himmler himself selected them, and he "compared himself to a plant breeder – selecting, weeding out and nurturing" (1986, 1991: 351). Segev (1987) reveals long-term Nazi careers, if more hit-and-miss selection procedures, among 30 concentration camp commanders. So does Safrian (1993) in his work on Eichmann's staff.

Scholars have also noted how genocidal institutions changed over time. Set up with tough tasks in mind, their founders recruited people up to such tasks – Old Fighters or others deemed reliable, ice-cold, tough, or sound. Later institutions were initially staffed from earlier ones already involved in the encouragement of violent practices. Austrians picked for tough tasks after the *Anschluss* were often those who had fled Austria after the unsuccessful Nazi rising of 1934 and then trained in Germany as full-time revolutionaries in the Austrian Legion. The first actual death camps (Sobibor, Belzec, and Treblinka) were opened with 97 staff drawn from T4. Auschwitz was started with personnel trained under the tough prewar camp regime pioneered by Eicke at Dachau. Applicants to the SS were screened up to the mid-1930s, but then came great expansion, escalating during wartime, when the camps had to compete against the needs of the front: the luxury of selecting known individuals declined and recruits were found any which way – including drafting older police reservists and wounded soldiers unable to serve in combat. And thus perpetrators became more ordinary as their numbers expanded. Obviously we must investigate the social relationships involved in this expansion – between officers and men, between experienced killers and increasingly raw recruits. Sofsky (1997) argues that these relations helped the death camps accomplish genocide. Was this more generally so?

SAMPLES OF PERPETRATORS

To cope with the variety revealed in previous studies, we need to sample the whole perpetrator corps. Otherwise, scholars can forever generalize on the basis of subgroups, using a few biographies to support their own pet theory. Yet there is no known population of perpetrators from which a sample might be selected. The obvious strategy is to rely on convicted war criminals, but some undoubted perpetrators died in the war, others disappeared, some were never tried, and some were bizarrely acquitted – because they had killed almost all the potential witnesses or because the court showed unusual leniency (as in acquitting T4 killer doctors because "they did not realize this was wrong"). Some countries' courts were more lenient than those of others, and all were operating under their particular national laws. Thus West German courts can press murder charges only where they can show "base motives" (anti-Semitism would count) or "cruelty" (requiring direct contact with the victim).[1] Such particularities mean that some perpetrators were more likely to be tried and convicted than others. Most at risk were those directing notorious killing sites, persons from killing sites where witnesses survived (especially camp doctors, whose prisoner assistants often survived), and those whose personal brutality made them memorable. Most rank-and-file perpetrators who just kept their heads down and killed

---

[1] I am grateful to Christopher Browning for this point.

remained anonymous and free. Thus, among convicted war criminals there are far more officers than rankers, and more men, since women were not officers.

Two imperfect sampling strategies remain. We can avoid selection biases by using the limited data available from the files of all the staff of a particular murderous setting, as Lasik (1994a) did for Auschwitz or Browning (1993) did for Police Battalion 101. This was a minor part of my research. I have limited biographical data on two groups collectively involved in genocidal activities but by no means all committing war crimes.

1a. *KL officers in 1945*. This includes all concentration camp officers listed on a 1945 roster of SS officers.[2] Since women could not become SS officers, this yielded an all-male population of 357 officers. Of these, incomplete details were given for 80. Almost all of these 80 had entered the camp system in 1944, had only reached the rank of lieutenant or captain, and were born before or just after 1900. These were probably middle-aged draftees into the Wehrmacht or Waffen-SS front-line formations who were wounded and then invalided out into SS rearguard activities like those in the camps. They were the more fleeting members of the KL staff. Though some may have had time to commit atrocities, most were probably relatively minor accessories to genocide. Thus I concentrate on the remaining 257 men for whom I have rank, date of entry to the Nazi Party, date present rank was attained, birthplace, and birth date. I could check data accuracy in the case of the 39 men who were also in my main sample. Only their Nazi Party membership was unreliably recorded. Of the 12 who were not listed as party members in this roster, 6 were in reality members. So I have not used this information.

These KL officers range downward in rank and notoriety from Major-General Richard Glücks (head of the inspectorate for all the camps) to men who have left no personal mark on the historical record. Most were never brought to trial. They form the overwhelming majority of the officers present in the hard core of genocide, the major concentration camps, though they may have personally committed no serious crimes.

1b. *SD officers in 1945*. From the same SS source, I drew a sample of officers recruited from the much larger state security police, the SD. I chose all men with family names beginning with *H* and *I* (selected as having no obvious regional or religious bias). This yields the same biographical details for 406 men as sample 1a.[3] These men were probably more varied in their activities than the KL officers. Some would have been routinely involved in the ferreting out of Jews, Bolsheviks, and other enemies and in interrogating suspects. Some were drawn into shooting sprees, torturing, beating, and so on. Yet most studies of the SD argue that many were career policemen, often

---

[2] I consulted a microfiche copy of this roster in the Museum of Tolerance, Los Angeles.
[3] I wish to thank Gareth Mann for collecting these data.

drawn reluctantly and partially into SS codes of violence, retaining some attachment to the more correct code of conduct of the security policeman. Only 15 were also in my main sample of actual perpetrators. Unfortunately, the roster list gives no clue as to where these officers were serving. This must have made a significant difference. SD men serving in Germany itself were less likely to be drawn into war crimes than those drafted to Poland or Yugoslavia.

A NEW SAMPLE OF 1,581 WAR CRIMINALS

We can draw a sample from war crimes trials, despite their biases, and so use the richer detail provided to the court. Then we can add data on the most likely criminals among the disappeared, the dead, and the dead lucky. These would be actual or highly likely war criminals and are my main subject here. I collected biographical data on 1,581 presumed German war criminals derived from published court accounts, newspaper clipping files, and scholarly studies of perpetrators.[4] *Justiz und NS-Verbrechen*, the 22-volume digest of West German trials occurring between 1947 and 1965 (Bauer, 1968–81), provided over one-third of my sample. The rest came from a large number of sources, almost all published, marked with an asterisk in the bibliography attached to Mann (2000). My analysis is based overwhelmingly on secondary research, a first attempt at quantitative analysis of perpetrators. It could and should in the future be strengthened by further primary research in the archives. I included persons found guilty of murder or of directly organizing or assisting in murder in postwar trials in various countries (993 persons), plus persons whose guilt of the same crimes seems probable but who either died in the war (101), committed suicide at its end (62), escaped conviction (339), or whose fate is unknown to me (87). In these last four categories, much depends on my judgment of likely guilt. I could have avoided this by studying only those found guilty by the courts, but this would increase sample reliability at the cost of decreasing its validity.

Included are the top Nazis: the SS High Command (the RuSHA), higher SS and police leaders, Nazi Party *Gauleiter*, and senior *Einsatzgruppen* officers. As we descend through the ranks, representation of the total number of perpetrators becomes thinner. The most notorious mid-level officers are men like Eichmann and Klaus Barbie. Josef Mengele leads the infamous company of doctors. Many of the lower ranks tend to be remembered not by their real names but by terrible nicknames – a second "Angel of Death" (i.e., besides Mengele), the "Beast of Belsen," the "Bitch of Buchenwald," and so on. They come from all over the killing fields, men and women who ordered

---

[4] I thank the library staff at UCLA, the Wiener Library, London, and the Simon Wiesenthal Center, Los Angeles, for placing their collections at my disposal. Fuller details of the sample, including a complete list of sources from which it was drawn, can be found in Mann (2000).

or committed repeated killing of Jews, Slavs, gypsies, mental patients, and others. Nor is this sample without bias. It has far more leaders than led, more of those who had left paper trails and more of those who were memorable to the victim group. I do not claim that my sample is representative of all perpetrators, but rather that it does represent the hard core and can be used to reveal something of their relations with the larger mass of perpetrators. It is also the largest sample of mass murderers yet collected.

I collected data on place and date of birth, religion, normal or disturbed family backgrounds, prior occupations of self and father, prior history in the Nazi movement, prior involvement in violence, wartime activities, and postwar fate. The bane of such research is variable data – complete for some individuals, sparse for others. The sample could be enlarged and missing data could be found by archival work amid SS and Nazi Party files of Berlin, the prosecutors' files of Ludwigsburg and Vienna, and the postwar files of the former Communist states. I have consulted none of these, though someone clearly should.

In this study I sought answers to four main biographical questions: (1) Were the perpetrators drawn from core Nazi constituencies? Pre-1933 Nazis had been disproportionately drawn from military, police, and public sector backgrounds; economic sectors lying outside the key class conflict zones between capital and labor (i.e., not from urban large-scale manufacturing and mining, where class conflict trumped nationalism); the highly educated middle classes; lost and threatened territories; and, amid all these environments, from Protestants rather than from Catholics. Such backgrounds had tended to favor extreme nationalism or extreme statism and so generated Nazis before 1933.[5] Of course, before 1933 little suggested that such views might lead to mass murder. But would such backgrounds be even more characteristic of the perpetrators, suggesting that their involvement in mass murder might have partially flowed from such broader ideological commitments? (2) Were they involved early and/or youthfully in Nazism? Had they been full-time and/or highly committed Nazis? (3) Were they involved early and/or youthfully in illegal, violent, or murderous activities before the main phase of exterminations? This might indicate careers in and inurement to violence. (4) Did they experience social marginality, downward mobility, unemployment, or family trauma? What Staub (1992: chap. 3) has termed the *psychology of hard times* might push people to aggression or scapegoating of others. Without real psychological data, this is as close as I can get to evidence for disturbed personalities leading to violent motivations. Note that the combination of (1) through (3) might also indicate a process of career caging inside violent Nazism, led by socialization and initial ideological preference toward becoming real Nazis. Conversely, in all four respects the perpetrators might not be unusual but broadly representative of ordinary Germans.

---

[5] I have compiled and analyzed all this evidence in my book, *Fascists* (2004).

FINDINGS

Table 8.1 summarizes the sample's characteristics, divided into the main genocidal institutions.[6] Ninety-five percent of my sample were men. Women formed more than 5 percent only in T4 (as nurses and secretaries) and in the camps (as warders of female prisoners). This reflects the real level of female participation in Nazi genocide. Women formed about 10 percent of death camp staff, as they did among all camp staff (Schwarz, 1994: 35). Given women's subordinate roles at the time and their exclusion from full SS membership, other participation was usually limited to indirect administrative assistance. The women in my sample were much less educated and middle-class than the men, and only the six female doctors had a rank equivalent to that of officer. Few had a Nazi track record. Only 16 percent are recorded as having joined an adult Nazi organization before 1939. None were known to have participated in prior violence, and few chose their positions. Most female warders said they were conscripted into their positions and then spent two to four weeks training at one of the main camps (Schwarz, 1994). The postwar prosecutors usually failed to show that accused women were real Nazis. Some had male family members who were active Nazis (my sample contains one married couple, the infamous Kochs of Buchenwald), and surviving prisoners said that only a few of the women had strong Nazi sympathies. Unfortunately, I lack systematic data on either, since the courts recorded this only sporadically. The women illustrate most acutely a methodological difficulty of this kind of research. Does lack of information mean actual absence? Not necessarily. Some must have had strong Nazi views, though few had previously acted upon them and few seem caged within Nazism or prewar violence. But German patriarchy and its gender biases protected women from much participation in genocide, whatever their inclinations might have been.

The second row of Table 8.1 reveals that most of my sample were officers (or higher-status civilians to whom I accorded equivalent rank). Though they did not form a majority in my camp subsample, they were still overrepresented there compared to Lasik's (1994a: 282) more complete data on Auschwitz staff. Since my coverage of the major camps is good, the bias was probably in the prosecution process, not in my sample selection. This also explains my skewed distribution of occupational class (compared to Lasik's). Other than for the camps and T4, the working class figures little in my sample, while elite occupations are almost 10 times overrepresented. Approximately 41 percent of the sample had a university education. Obviously, this is a sample composed substantially of fairly prominent perpetrators.

---

[6] The category "Other" groups together a motley collection of civil servants, businessmen, propagandists, and Wehrmacht and Waffen-SS personnel.

TABLE 8.1 *Nazi Perpetrators: Characteristics of Sample by War Crimes Sector*

	T4	Doctors	Camp	Einsatzgruppen	Security Police	Nazi Party	Other	All	Total N
% women	22	5	9	0	1	0	4	5	1,581
% NCOs or below	67	0	71	28	16	3	18	36	1,562
% working class	63	0	64	35	29	14	22	37	1,216
% university graduates	25	99	5	34	43	54	49	41	912
% state employees	24	6+[a]	21	58	53	51	57	40	1,152
% with absent parent(s)	20	11	19	20	19	2	13	16	650
% with disrupted careers	21	11	47	16	30	9	13	24	765
% full-time/violent Nazis	53	51	62	72	95	100	60	72	784
Average age when joined Nazis	27	29	28	27	28	29	33	28	1,159
Average age in 1939	34	35	32	33	35	41	41	35	1,562
% birthplace rural	30	25	38	32	25	36	28	32	1,471
% birthplace 80%+ Catholic	46	37	32	31	30	40	30	33	1,556
% foreign ethnic Germans	33	23	31	28	28	31	16	28	1,581
% sentenced to life/death[b]	28	46	35	35	44	41	32	37	1,580
Number in sample	141[c]	109	458[d]	291	305	121	200[e]	1,581	1,581

[a] This figure is much too low. Whether doctors had previously worked in the public or private sector was rarely made clear in the sources. Where it was unclear, I coded as private.

[b] This figure includes estimates of likely sentences of persons dead or evading arrest.

[c] Excludes doctors and dentists, who appear in a separate column.

[d] Excludes doctors and dentists, who appear in a separate column.

[e] Composed of 72 civil servants, 58 military persons (mostly Waffen-SS), and 70 diverse civilians (journalists, businessmen, etc.).

TABLE 8.2 *Nazi Perpetrators: Intergenerational Social Mobility Among Men: Percentage of All Men in Each Category*

Father's Occupational Class	Own Occupational Class			
	Elite	Lower Middle	Workers	Total %
Elite occupations	19.6	12.0	1.2	32.9
Lower middle class	5.7	20.7	12.0	38.4
Workers	2.4	6.0	20.3	28.7
Total %	27.7	38.7	33.6	100.0
% in German labor force	2.8	42.7	54.6	100.0
Ratio of representation	9.89	0.91	0.62	

Notes:

Total $N = 581$ male perpetrators for whom both occupations are known.

The occupation coded was the principal occupation stated for (1) father and (2) self during the pre-Nazi career. Occupations and classes categorized as in the 1933 German census:

　Elite occupations: substantial landowners, entrepreneurs, higher managers, higher civil servants, academically trained professionals.

　Lower middle class: independent craftsmen. nonacademic professionals, white-collar workers, lower civil servants, small merchants, and farmers.

　Workers: unskilled, semiskilled, and skilled.

LIFE TRAUMAS

Tables 8.1 and 8.2 contain the rather limited data that are relevant to life traumas and hypothesis 1b – that these might be violent killers. Only 16 percent of the sample suffered the loss or incapacitation of a parent (through death, severe injury, divorce, or desertion) while under 19 years of age. This figure seems low in a period when average life expectancy was around 50 and that included World War I. Only 30 persons (4.6 percent) among the 650 with adequate family histories had lost a parent or seen a parent psychologically shattered in the war (22 fathers, 5 mothers, 3 both). The disturbed biography of the Gestapo torturer Klaus Barbie is well known (Linklater et al., 1984). His father returned home shattered by his experiences in World War I. He drank heavily and beat his family. Klaus was not a happy boy, and his schoolboy worship of Hitler may have been displaced father worship. Yet such traumas seem few in my sample, running against the grain of Loewenberg's (1983: 259–80) theory that loss of a father figure led to authoritarianism and fuhrer worship – if this was assumed to lead to the commission of war crimes at Hitler's behest. In any case, the decisive point about Barbie's biography is that he was informing for the Gestapo while still at school, joined it full-time on graduation, and never subsequently left its embrace. It was his home, his cage.

Disrupted employment affected 24 percent (Table 8.1, row 7). Again, this figure seems low. Unemployment was over 30 percent in 1933 alone. Browder (1996) found that at least 32 percent of his SD officers had been unemployed.

My measure includes, as well as unemployment, business failure and charges of embezzlement at work. But for a third of these, Nazi or SA or SS membership had come first; for them disruption could have been a consequence of spending too much time with the movement (some said this). For half, Nazism had come after career disruption and could therefore have been a consequence of it; for the remaining one-sixth, Nazism and disruption appeared too closely together to separate cause and effect. Thus, at most, 16 percent of the sample might have had career disruption that could conceivably have led through the psychology of hard times to extremist reactions. These people were not usually failures. Unemployment preceding Nazism mostly occurred among workers in my sample. Some said they had joined the Nazis hoping to get work from them. Though this was a self-serving claim in a war crimes trial (i.e., "I wasn't a real Nazi, just an ordinary German joining to get work"), it was probably often true for the "Bandwagon Nazis," joining after 1933, who joined for careerist reasons.

Evidence of prewar criminal marginality was rare. Only 10 had been convicted or even formally accused of prewar crimes other than political ones. The true figure was presumably higher, since this was not information to be revealed freely. But had I included Kapos (prisoner foremen) in my sample, this would have been different. Many of their records reveal a lifetime of drifting, petty crime, family disruption, and unemployment – indeed, most were in the camps because they were criminals. They had not been prewar Nazis. Table 8.2 provides a rather crude overall assessment of social mobility. Most perpetrators (60.6 percent) were neither upwardly nor downwardly mobile compared with their fathers. Rather more were mobile in a downward (25.2 percent) than an upward (14.1 percent) direction. However, at least half of the difference among the best-documented persons seemed the result rather than the cause of their political commitment: militant Nazis rarely cultivated their careers. Unlike the prewar Nazi leadership (especially the *Gauleiter;* Rogowski, 1977), the perpetrators had not previously experienced much upward mobility. They resembled Jamin's (1984) prewar SA sample: mostly rather static, though with a little more downward mobility (which she tends to overplay). Thus few perpetrators seem to have had very disrupted lives of the kind that might produce severe frustrations, aggression, or scapegoating for personal unhappiness. This was the most highly organized case in this book, probably not typical of the others. But it did not depend on marginal or criminal types.

CORE CONSTITUENCIES: THREATENED BORDER REGIONS AND REFUGEES

For many variables we want to know if the sample differed from the German population as a whole. Thus I calculate a *ratio of representation*, the percentage of perpetrators with a given characteristic divided by the percentage contribution of people with this characteristic in the German population or labor force as a whole. A ratio of more than 1.0 means overrepresentation of perpetrators with this characteristic, a ratio of less than 1.0 underrepresentation.

Were perpetrators drawn from particular regions? I coded birthplaces into the provinces and subprovinces distinguished in the Reich census of 1933 (as reported in Statistisches Reichsamt, 1935), plus areas abroad containing ethnic Germans potentially available for recruitment to genocidal institutions: 6.4 million Austrians (the German 94 percent of the Austrian population of 6.8 million); 1.5 million Germans in the lands lost to Poland and Czechoslovakia after World War I, 600,000 more in the rest of Poland; 3.2 million Sudeten Germans; 2 million Germans in the rest of Czechoslovakia, Hungary, Yugoslavia, the Baltic states, and Italy combined; and 350,000 in the western lost territories of Schleswig-Holstein, Alsace-Lorraine, and the Malmedy area of Belgium. There can be no exact population of available ethnic Germans, but my estimate of 14 million cannot be far off. Map 8.1 shows birthplaces, with each region given a ratio of representation. The Reich German provinces have two further ratios: the ratio of perpetrators among Reich Germans alone and the Nazi voting ratio in the Reichstag election of July 1932.

I hypothesized that some regions might nurture extreme nation-statists, favoring an aggressive state capable of attacking the enemies of the German nation. Possible candidates would be Germans living abroad amid supposedly threatening non-Germans, Germans living in the lost territories, and Germans living in regions adjacent to threatened borders. Germany had lost territories around most of its borders: in the northwest (northern Schleswig, population 166,000); the northeast (Danzig, the Polish corridor, and the east Prussian border with Lithuania, population 3 million); the east-center (parts of Silesia, population almost 1 million); and the southwest (Alsace-Lorraine and small areas handed over to Belgium, population 1.9 million). In the center-west, the Saar was controlled by the victorious powers and the Rhineland was occupied from 1923; along the entire central-western and southwestern borders, the Allies claimed the right of military intervention along a further 50-kilometer strip. Map 8.1 shows these territories. Had the supposed exploitation of Germany by foreign powers stimulated the emergence of more future Nazi perpetrators there?

The most striking finding of Map 8.1 is that all ethnic German regions abroad, except for the Sudetenland, are overrepresented. The most overrepresented are the westerners, almost all from Alsace-Lorraine and areas lost to Denmark and Belgium. They are followed by ethnic Germans from Poland and other Eastern countries. Most of those from Poland and a handful of those from Eastern Europe also came from lost territories. These groups are more overrepresented than those born in any region of Germany itself. Austrians are also somewhat overrepresented, though my sample probably

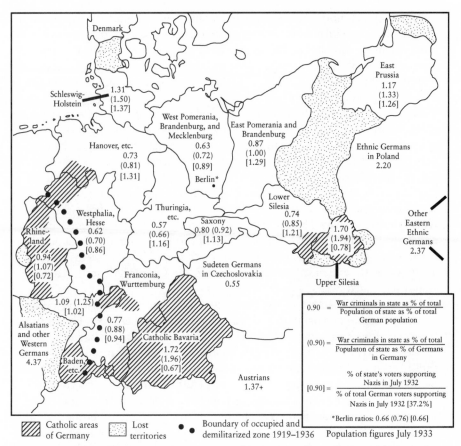

MAP 8.1. Regional ratios of over- and underrepresentation of German war criminals and Nazi electoral support.

understates things, for there were fewer Austrian postwar trials than German trials and more Austrian perpetrators probably disappeared into anonymity.

But we must also distinguish ethnic Germans who had returned to Germany before or after their country was "liberated" by the German armies (1938 for Austria and the Sudetenland, later elsewhere). The earlier refugees had fled under pressure, often to refugee camps whose atmosphere fueled aggressive revisionism. In the previous chapter I noted that this was one of the distinctive cages of violence of the Nazi movement. Most of these refugees had come early, shortly after World War I, though Austrian refugees tended to be Nazis fleeing their country after their coup of 1934 failed. Many of the Austrians then attained high positions in the German Nazi Party or SS. Excluding the Austrians, there were 100 refugees, and most had shown some commitment to Nazism well before World War II. They were older than the sample average, more likely to have been early and/or young Nazis, to have engaged in prior violence, to have attained higher rank, and to have received larger postwar sentences.[7] Of the Austrians, 45 percent received death or life sentences; of the refugees, 42 percent; and of both the Sudetens and the liberated ethnic Germans, only 31 percent. The Reich Germans lay in the middle, at 36 percent.

Map 8.1 shows that these refugees proved to be the most overrepresented group among the perpetrators. In the 1933 census, those born abroad who spoke German as a mother tongue comprised less than 1 percent of the population. Yet they formed over 6 percent of the perpetrators (and just under 6 percent of those arriving after 1933). This group contained almost all the ethnic Germans from Alsace-Lorraine, Schleswig-Holstein, most of those from the Baltic states, about half of those from Poland and few from elsewhere. It is obviously a highly self-selected group of ethnic Germans, highly and early committed to Nazism as a militant form of nationalist revisionism, prepared to go to extreme lengths in support of it. This also seems true, to a slightly lesser extent, of most Austrians in my sample. All seem real and somewhat caged Nazis.

This alters our picture of the remaining 108 ethnic Germans (excluding Austrians and Sudetens) who had waited abroad for liberation. Their ratio was much lower, though still high, at 1.5. They were younger, had less Nazi or violent experience, and were predominantly workers with low wartime rank. Seventy of them worked in concentration camps, almost all as ordinary guards (some were sergeants by war's end). Their sentences were lower than the sample average. They also seemed to have been recruited more accidentally into genocide. Few were eligible for the Wehrmacht but they could serve in the SS, rendering them more likely to be sucked into murder. The SS attempted to screen them in terms of racial purity (often measured by fluency in German), by skills, and by political reliability. Yet few were Nazis, since most of the liberated ethnic German communities had been locally oriented, relatively uninterested in which state they belonged to. The main choices they faced on liberation were conscription into the Reich labor force (not much better than corvée labor), selection as colonists on farmsteads seized from Slavs (alluring but dangerous), or volunteering for the SS – dangerous if assigned to the Waffen-SS front line but comfortable if assigned to the camps. Health and strength usually determined which of these two assignments occurred; being wounded at the front might result in transfer to the camps. These selection processes seem to have produced a fairly representative collection of the less healthy workers and peasants of these regions now available to assist genocide (Komjathy & Stockwell, 1980; Lumans, 1993).

---

[7] These findings disposed of one potential sample bias I had feared – that the ethnic Germans might be more vulnerable to postwar prosecution and severe penalties, being less protected by social support networks in postwar Germany.

Most were initially assigned to the bottom jobs distant from killings, though some became block commanders. From this group came many war criminals. In the smaller camps, ethnic Germans performed various "dirty" tasks, including murders. Surviving prisoners recall tensions between the ethnic German guards and their Reich German NCOs, who despised them for their crude German and rough peasant ways. Thus, in Polish war crimes trials, witnesses described the ethnic Germans in varied terms: some were said to have been decent, turning a blind eye to prisoners' practices or abusing them only in the presence of their superiors. A few even helped the Polish underground. Others behaved very cruelly, but their atrocities seem rooted less in prior Nazism than in the license granted them by the SS to reverse local class hierarchies and turn murderously against the Polish officials and Jewish traders and professionals who had previously bossed them about. All of this produced motivations distinctive to the Eastern European Germans.

Among the Reich Germans, ethnic revisionism was also important. Regions adjacent to the lost territories or that were occupied and/or demilitarized by the Allies after 1918 provided most perpetrators. This is so of Schleswig-Holstein, East Prussia, Upper Silesia, and (marginally) Baden/Saar/Rhine-Palatinate. By removing the ethnic Germans from the calculation, we can compare them to the other Reich Germans. The second set of ratios in the map show whether each region is overrepresented among Reich Germans only. This pushes up the ratio of the Rhineland to over 1.0 and that of Eastern Pomerania and eastern Brandenburg to exactly 1.0. Note that for all border regions, the region lying farther inside Germany has a distinctly lower ratio. Inner Germany provided fewer perpetrators: only two inner German cities are overrepresented, Bremen and Osnabruck. By contrast, the East Prussians and the Upper Silesians, virtually surrounded by foreign states, were greatly overrepresented. Eastern Pomerania and Brandenburg are at parity, while Lower Silesians and Saxons are underrepresented (confirming that the Sudetenland border seems not to have produced a sense of threat).

The most striking feature of this map is that virtually all lost territories and threatened borders disproportionately provided perpetrators. Western ethnic Germans were the most overrepresented, and refugees were more overrepresented than liberated Germans. Was the main factor contributing to murderous Nazism the degree of local outrage over the perceived treatment of Germans after World War I rather than the local intensity of anti-Semitism? The findings support the suggestion made in the previous chapter: the origins of mass murder lay substantially in embittered ethnic imperial revisionism, whatever specific bite local anti-Semitic sentiments may have added.

But the other surprise was the Sudetenland. Was the explanation that interwar Czechoslovakia treated its Sudeten German minority quite well? It was more democratic than other Eastern European countries, and Germans were granted more local autonomies and collective rights than elsewhere. Though two-thirds of ethnic German voters supported the nationalist Sudeten German Party in 1935, this only then sought more rights within the framework of the Czech and Slovak state. When Hitler marched in, fewer than 2 percent of Sudetens were in the Nazi Party (Komjathy & Stockwell, 1980). Czech guards at Theresienstadt have been singled out as the mildest of the camp staffs. The few Sudetens in my sample were mainly workers conscripted into the SS and serving as camp guards. Their sentences were lower than the sample average. Perhaps higher-level Sudetens and Sudeten Nazis were still getting used to ruling their region and so could less easily be tempted into genocidal institutions.

When I analyzed the birthplaces of my KL and SD comparison samples, neither revealed such striking findings. There was a big reduction in the proportion of ethnic Germans from abroad. Only the fairly small group of western refugees (dominated by those from Alsace-Lorraine) remained overrepresented. Austrians and ethnic Germans from Poland were in the SD in about their right proportions; the rest of the ethnic Germans were substantially underrepresented, as were the most exposed border Germans, those in East Prussia. Among the Reich Germans, the two types of officers differed a little. Camp officers came disproportionately from the south of the country, especially from Catholic Bavaria. Men from Schleswig-Holstein were the only significantly overrepresented northerners. Among the SD, Catholic Bavaria and Protestant Schleswig-Holstein are substantially overrepresented, while a central (Protestant) belt of the country was a little less so – but there are no other striking deviations. It seems that the camp officers were disproportionately southern, especially Bavarian, while the SD (though showing some small biases) was more representative of Reich Germans.

Remember that these two comparison groups were composed overwhelmingly of persons never brought to trial. Many of the SD officers – and even some of the KL officers – may never have committed indictable crimes. Though these SS officers can hardly be considered ordinary Germans in terms of their wartime occupations, as groups they were far less steeped in murder than were my main sample. They were perhaps not atypical of the Germans who joined the SS: committed Nazis but not necessarily murderous. Thus the SS as a whole was a little southern, somewhat Bavarian, but otherwise fairly representative of the German Reich. It probably lacked the ferocity toward murder provided by experience of lost territories and threatened borders. But we must now turn back to address the special problem raised by Bavaria: religion.

CORE CONSTITUENCIES: RENEGADE CATHOLICS

Bavarians were overrepresented among my perpetrators and among the SS as a whole – especially those from Upper Bavaria (including Munich). They were the neighbors of the unthreatening Swiss, Sudetens, and Austrians and

TABLE 8.3 *Nazi Perpetrators: Religion of Family of Origin and Birthplace Census District*

	Religion of Family			Religion of Birthplace			
	Protestant	Catholic	N	Protestant	Mixed	Catholic	N
% in whole sample	54	46	338	39	30	31	1519
% among sample ethnic Germans	37	63	95	38	10	52	394
% among sample Reich Germans[a]	61	39	243	39	37	24	1125
% in entire population of German Reich	66	34		51	29	21	
Ratio of each religion among sample Reich Germans to entire population of German Reich[b]	0.95	1.21	243	0.78	1.29	1.15	1125

[a] This and urban–rural birthplace calculated from the 1933 Reich census (Statistisches Reichsamt, 1935). Faiths other than Protestantism and Catholicism among Germans excluded from the calculation.

[b] That is, the ratio of the percentage of this religion among the perpetrators compared to the percentage of this religion among all Reich Germans (1933 census). Ratios higher than 1.0 signify overrepresentation of this religion among the perpetrators. A ratio of more than 1.0 signifies overrepresentation of perpetrators in that occupational sector; less than 1.0 signifies underrepresentation. Data for the sectoral distribution of the whole labor force are from the German census for 1925.

surely cannot have feared them. But these were predominantly Catholic regions. Did Catholicism generate SS men and perpetrators? Map 8.1 also indicated the German subprovinces that were over 80 percent Catholic. These provided more perpetrators than neighboring Protestant areas, though this tendency becomes somewhat confused with the effects exerted by threatened borders. Thus Upper Silesia seems more threatened than Lower Silesia but it is also solidly Catholic, unlike Lower Silesia. South Baden and parts of the Rhineland may also confuse threat with Catholicism.

Table 8.3 divides the census district of birth into 80 percent-plus Protestant, 80 percent-plus Catholic, and religiously mixed. Protestant districts were underrepresented, Catholic and mixed areas overrepresented. Yet the results may elide provincial and religious effects. In the main sample most predominantly Protestant provinces are underrepresented, while in all the samples Bavaria alone provided two-thirds of the predominantly Catholic districts. There were only four provinces providing many Catholic as well as

TABLE 8.4 *Nazi Perpetrators: Urban–Rural Birthplace*

	City: 100,000+	Town: 2,000–100,000	Rural: Less Than 2,000	Total
% among whole sample	35	33	32	
% among sample ethnic Germans	31	31	39	100
% among sample Reich Germans	37	34	29	100
% among entire population of German Reich	31	37	33	100
Ratio of sample Reich Germans to entire population of German Reich	1.20	0.093	0.88	
Sample N	517	490	465	1,472

mixed or Protestant districts. In three (Bavaria, Silesia, and the Rhineland – but not Westphalia) the Protestant districts provided proportionately fewer perpetrators, though the numbers were sometimes small (preventing further analysis of my two comparison samples). In any case, maybe the perpetrators from Catholic regions were actually drawn from local minority Protestant populations embittered by local Catholic dominance.

So the second measure in Table 8.3 is more direct, the religion of the perpetrator's own family. This datum was available only for the main sample – and indeed for only 22 percent of it. But, among this group, Catholics are indeed overrepresented. They also got more severe sentences: 56 percent got life imprisonment or death sentences compared to 42 percent of Protestants (half of this difference is due to the foreign ethnic Germans). These findings offer tentative support for Lasik's conclusions based on Auschwitz. Catholics – actually, probably lapsed Catholics – seemed more likely to become perpetrators, reversing the pattern found among the mainly Protestant pre-coup Nazis. Yet this conclusion would be on firmer ground if data had been available for more of the sample. Further primary research might overcome this problem.

Such findings could be the product of intervening variables. Therefore, in Table 8.4, I consider urbanization, the presence of ethnic-religious minorities, and institutional accident. We see that Catholic, Bavarian, and threatened border regions of Germany did not provide more perpetrators because of urban–rural differences. Though perpetrators came slightly more often from big cities than did Germans as a whole, the threatened and Catholic regions actually supplied the same proportion of big-city perpetrators and more rural perpetrators (32 percent to 25 percent) than did unthreatened regions. The camp officers (sample 1a) were a little more rural, while again the SD officers (sample 1b) were closer to the German norm as a whole. This differs from Browder's (1996: 135–6) finding that prewar SD officers were distinctly more big-city in their origins. It seems, however, that the wartime SD tended to be officered by men who were not dissimilar to most Germans, while the camps (containing worse atrocities) were halfway to the background biases found among the actual war criminals.

Nor is the explanation that perpetrators came from areas with more Jews. In the 1933 census, Jews were only 0.7 percent of the German population, so it is unlikely that many perpetrators had much personal experience with Jews. A third of German Jews lived in Berlin, underrepresented among the perpetrators. Most of the rest were scattered in tiny numbers across all the bigger cities. Though many Jews lived in Silesia (7 percent of all Jews), most were in Lower, not Upper, Silesia – the reverse of the distribution of the perpetrators. Except for eastern ethnic Germans, many in my sample had never encountered Jews until they began killing them. Slavs were obviously present in the lives of eastern ethnic Germans and those of East Prussia. But in the rest of the northeast of the Reich, perpetrators were underrepresented. I do not know the distribution of gypsies, but it is unlikely that such a small group affected the Nazi sympathies of many Germans.

Was the pattern a mere accident of location, perhaps from bureaucratic siting of genocidal institutions in Catholic regions and then hiring local labor to staff them? In the previous chapter I noted that T4 hospitals were located in southern Catholic regions. Yet most killing institutions transported their staff much farther. The major extermination camps were mostly outside of Germany, in northeastern Europe, far from Bavaria and the Southwest. Some were partly staffed by local ethnic Germans. Yet Auschwitz was in Poland, where the local ethnic German population was mostly Protestant, while the staff were mainly Catholic. Indeed, a second locational accident would suggest that my results actually understate the number of ex-Catholic perpetrators. Bavarian and Austrian courts have been notoriously reluctant to prosecute Nazis, while Protestant cities like Hamburg, Frankfurt, and Dortmund have been the most zealous. Had trials been spread evenly across Germany and Austria, they would have yielded a sample containing more ex-Catholics.[8]

Looking at Europe as a whole, Catholicism was associated with conservative politics and specifically with anti-Semitism. The Catholic Church did on occasion stand up to the Nazis, but as its critics point out, this was usually to preserve its own interests, not the lives of the victims. Perhaps ex-Catholics had been initially socialized into some Catholic reactionary anti-Semitism and then rejected the church as an institution. But this is speculation. I prefer the less direct explanation begun in Chapter 7. A Vienna–Munich axis had provided most of the early leaders and intellectuals of Nazism, furnishing a

---

[8] I am grateful to Christopher Browning for this point.

distinctly Austrian anti-Semitism. This retained the territorial ambition of the old Habsburg ideal of *grossdeutsch* nationalism (an eastward-tilting union of all Germans in a single Reich), while changing this from a cultural-political union to an ethnic-racial one. These Nazis attacked Habsburg multiethnicity and Jewish cosmopolitanism.

During the later 1920s and early 1930s German and Austrian Nazism then grew apart. German rightism, including Nazism, became dominated by Protestants, more *kleindeutsch* in territorial scope, being preoccupied with Weimar Germany's internal enemies, especially Communists. By 1936, however, the Rhineland was reoccupied, the Reich's internal enemies had been defeated, and a flood of refugee Austrian Nazis had entered Germany. Hitler now sought to exploit the Sudeten issue, linking it to *Lebensraum* in the East. The Nazi regime also feared the disruptive effects of SA radicalism – now without an obvious enemy on which to vent its violence. Thus Nazism made a second shift, back toward the southeast. This emphasized *grossdeutsch* and racial aspirations. Expansion was justified in terms of German racial superiority in which anti-Semitism, anti-Slavism, and anti-Bolshevism played vitriolic roles. Nazi genocide resonated amid the more *grossdeutsch* eastern-tilting sentiments of former Catholics.

Thus refugee ethnic Germans and those from threatened border, Catholic, and Austro-Bavarian areas were all more likely to become perpetrators because genocide flowed from their ethnic *grossdeutsch* imperialism. It was racist because it was eastern-oriented, anti-Slav, and anti-Semitic. Jews and Slavs were murdered for reasons of imperial ethnic revisionism. They allegedly stood in the way of the unity and power of the German nation. This explains the perpetrators' regional biases in terms of the resonance in their regions of Nazi ideology as a whole, not merely of its anti-Semitic component.

CORE CONSTITUENCIES: SECTORS OF LOW CLASS CONFLICT

Table 8.5 contains data on economic sectors for men only. The few women were mostly in light industry (usually textiles), health services, and shops, hotels, or cafes.

The ratios here are extremely skewed. Those previously working in agriculture or industry are strongly underrepresented. That there are few manual workers in the sample cannot explain this, since workers constitute over half of those serving construction, service trades (such as transport, shops, hotels, and restaurants), and the military/police/prisons – in all of which perpetrators were overrepresented. During the war, workers and managers in key industrial and agricultural sectors were exempted from conscription, but by then most of these perpetrators were embarked on their ghastly careers anyway. And although the sample is disproportionately middle class, commerce (merchants, banks, insurance, etc.) is not overrepresented. These results

TABLE 8.5 *Nazi Perpetrators: Ratios of Over- and Underrepresentation of Occupational Sectors in Sample*

Occupational Sector	Ratio – Whole Sample	Ratio – Men Only	% in Whole Sample
Agriculture, forestry	0.20	0.21	6.24
Heavy industry	0.49	0.51	7.46
Light industry	0.46	0.43	7.89
Construction	1.25	1.31	6.68
Transport, shops, hotels, cafes	1.66	1.54	6.16
Commerce	0.96	0.98	7.20
Education	5.52	5.51	6.24
Health	10.74	9.38	13.53
Civilian state	5.54	5.74	12.92
Military, police, prisons	5.57	5.80	22.29
Law	9.94	10.50	3.38
Total N or %	1,153	1,091	100.00

Note: A ratio of more than 1.0 signifies overrepresentation of perpetrators in that occupational sector; less than 1.0 signifies underrepresentation. Data for sectoral distribution of the whole labor force are from the German census for 1925.

support my more general evidence (see my *Fascists*, chap. 5) that the Nazi appeal lay partly in the claim to transcend class conflict by nation-statism: the Nazis received support from all those classes lying outside the main zone of struggle between capital and labor, who endorsed the notion that a strong state should knock both their heads together to restore the integral unity of the nation.

Professionals and the public sector were extraordinarily overrepresented. Those in education and the media were almost all teachers, those in the law were lawyers, and those in health included many doctors. These were professions with many Nazis (Jarausch, 1990; Proctor, 1988: 66–7), and they were closely entwined with the German state. Most of the lawyers had spent some time in prosecutors' offices, in close contact with the police. Conversely, 62 percent of Nazi security policemen who were university graduates had studied law (Banach, 1998: 79). Most of the doctors had worked in public hospitals. These institutions were heavily Nazi, and they were entrusted with crucial roles in genocide.

Both the civilian and military/police parts of the state are strongly overrepresented among perpetrators. Perhaps we might expect employees of the Nazi state to appear among the perpetrators. Yet there had not been major purges of the public sector. None was needed since the state had long been a breeding ground for authoritarian ideas, including Nazism. Over a quarter of Abel's sample of Nazi militants (Merkl, 1975: 50–61), over a third of Nazi security policemen (Banach, 1998: 42), and over half of high-ranking SS officers (Wegner, 1990: 240–1) came from military and civil service backgrounds. Authoritarian-leaning civil servants easily (if at first covertly) embraced Nazism (Caplan, 1988; Mommsen, 1991). Nazism mostly seems to have proved quite a congenial extension of these people's own statism (as Browning, 1978, shows in the case of the Foreign Office). The importance of the professions and of the civil service also explains why the perpetrators were so well educated.

All these ratios indicate that perpetrators were overwhelmingly drawn from core Nazi constituencies. Few came from agriculture and industry, the main homes of organized class conflict and the orthodox parties of the left and right. Far more workers were drawn from construction, the service sector, and the state; far more middle-class persons came from professions active in the state sector. Were some parts of these sectors less liable for war service, more recruitable into the SS? This is possible. But they had all been core Nazi constituencies even before coming to power in 1933. These people came from sectors most likely to be attracted by the Nazi ideology of extreme nation-statism: advocacy of a strong state to enhance the organic unity of the nation by suppressing class, political, and ethnic conflict. These were the core constituencies wishing the nation to trump class.

Genocide sucked in some occupations for obvious reasons. Most of the SD perpetrators had been career policemen; so had many of the *Einsatzgruppen* and some camp personnel. By virtue of their training in capturing, interrogating, and intimidating criminals and extremists, policemen were relatively toughened, with skills useful to the project of genocide. If we exclude policemen from the "military state" category, the ratio for the remainder (mostly military men) declines to 1.65. Doctors, too, were caught up in T4 and experiments and selections in the camps; and networks of prosecuting lawyers, policemen, and civil servants together supplied most *Einsatzgruppen* officers. Again, however, these are not artifacts, but real features of Nazi genocide. Perpetrators were embedded in institutional and professional subcultures already favorable to tough physical, legal, and biological remedies for social ills before genocide was initiated. The Nazis could more easily accomplish genocide by using such a willing core.

CAREERS IN NAZI VIOLENCE

I have five measures of prior Nazism or violence.[9] I first divided the sample into three age cohorts. Those born before 1901 could have fought in World War I (measure 1) and in the Freikorps militias (measure 2). Measure 3 distinguishes Nazis according to the age and year they joined the Party, the SA, or the SS. All but 16 of the Reich German, Austrian, and refugee men

---

[9] Since women, Sudetens, and ethnic Germans liberated by the German armies scored minimally on these measures, I have confined analysis in this section to Reich German, Austrian, and refugee ethnic German men.

were members of at least one of these – indicating at least a basic commitment to Nazism. The second age cohort, men born between 1901 and 1912, were almost all too young to fight in the war or the postwar Freikorps militias but could join the Nazi movement before it seized power. Persons joining before January 1933 were styled *Old Nazis*. The third age cohort was born after 1912. Among them, those joining after 1933 under the age of 25 were termed *Young Nazis*. Older persons joining during 1933–8 (i.e., when the Nazis were already in power) I call *Bandwagon Nazis*. Wartime Nazis joined from 1939 on, perhaps from simple patriotic motives or from immaturity (e.g., joining the SS for the powerful, if sinister, aura the uniform conveyed or joining the party because one's comrades were members). The few youngsters joining during the war are termed *Raw Nazis*. I assume that Old and Young Nazis were closer to being real Nazis than the others – though obviously, all five types will have included Nazis of varying hues.

Measure 4 identifies those who worked full-time in the movement for at least three prewar years – a measure of Nazi caging. Measure 5 identifies those committing serious prewar physical violence or who were described in prewar records as especially fanatic Nazis. I had information on this measure for only half of the sample. Of these 784 persons, 101 had been involved in prewar violence, and 81 were singled out in the sources as being ideological fanatics. Violence means distinguishing oneself (i.e., within the movement) in street brawling or the prewar camps, being deployed in murderous violence like the Röhm purge or *Kristallnacht*, or being described as tough or by some others euphemism in prewar Nazi records – men like Hermann Florstedt (whose drunken street brawling brought him into continuous trouble with the police) or Heinz-Karl Fanslau (who killed at least one SA man during the Röhm purge). Fanatics were either described as such or are recorded as making very extreme declarations, like the doctor Kurt Heissmeyer, experimenting on camp children, declaring that there was no difference "between Jews and guinea pigs," or Ernst Weinman, described in the 1930s as an "uncompromising National Socialist."

These measures provide the sequence and escalation of Nazi radicalization. But though membership of organizations was almost always recorded, evidence concerning any violence or fanaticism was available for only half of the sample. Maybe perpetrators were more likely to be prosecuted and end up in my sample if they were party or SS members. Nazi membership and activism were relevant evidence in postwar trials, while the Allies considered the SS a criminal organization. SS men were also more vulnerable to arrest in 1945 since they bore the incriminating SS body tattoo. Yet I found no trials where memberships were decisive to the verdict, though they did sometimes affect the severity of the sentence. Thus this sample bias may not be severe.

Table 8.6 presents the results sequentially, indicating the percentages of men sharing an earlier experience who also shared a later one. Earlier

TABLE 8.6 *Careers in Nazism and Violence, by Cohort (Reich German, Austrian, and Ethnic German Refugee Men only)*

	World War I Veteran?	Participated in Freikorps?	Type of Nazi?	Full-Time Nazi?	Prewar Violence or Extremism?	N
Cohort born 1900 or before	No 11% Yes 39%	No 70% → Yes 30% →	*Old Nazi?* No 43% → Yes 52% ↗ All yes 57% → Yes 68% ↖	No 45% → Yes 34% ↗ All yes 55% → Yes 71% ↖	Yes 43% → All yes 40% → Yes 37% ↖	282
Cohort born 1901–12	No 98% Yes 2%	No 91% → Yes 9% →	*Either Old or Young Nazi?* No 29% → Yes 69% ↗ All yes 71% → Yes 81% ↖	No 41% → Yes 43% ↗ All yes 59 → Yes 69% ↖	Yes 39% → All yes 37% → Yes 35% ↖	332
Cohort born 1913 on	No 100% Yes 0%	No 100% → Yes 0%	*Young Nazi?* No 36% → Yes 64% →	No 51% → Yes 4% ↗ All yes 49% → Yes 74% ↖	Yes 25% → All yes 29% → Yes 31% ↖	78
Whole sample			Yes 65%	Yes 55%	Yes 37%	692

Note: An arrow indicates the movement of a group of perpetrators with one experience to a later experience. Thus, Yes 50% to Yes 20% indicates that 20% of those to whom the first measure applies also fall into the second category. "All yes" is therefore the total of those to whom a measure applies. *N* signifies the number of individuals in each cohort for whom information is available on all men.

experiences appear on the left-hand side of the table, later ones on the right. The starting point is World War I service. Of the men in my sample who were born in the German Empire in the period 1875–1900, 89 percent served in World War I. This is the same percentage as in Browder's (1996: 138) sample of SD officers but is distinctly higher than the national average of 81 percent (Winter, 1988: 27, 30). In itself this may only indicate a somewhat heightened patriotism. Yet for some, military values quickly became radicalized. Of the Germans born before 1901, 30 percent fought after the war in the Freikorps (so did 30 percent of the Austrians and 24 percent of those born between 1901 and 1904, too young to fight in the war). Only about 3.5 percent of all the surviving 11.1 million German veterans can have served in the Freikorps. Thus many of my older perpetrators had been engaged in political killings long before they became Nazis.

Over two-thirds of my Freikorps veterans then went into the Nazi movement before 1933. In the three age cohorts, 57, 71, and 64 percent – and 65 percent overall – were Old or Young Nazis. Seventy-one percent of these and 55 percent of the whole group then went on to become full-time Nazis. Thus most had shown considerable commitment to Nazism, and a disproportionate contribution at each stage was made by persons already experienced in an earlier violent or Nazi activity. These are all signs of radicalizing careers in Nazism. This pattern changes somewhat when we arrive at the measure of violence or fanaticism. Only 37 percent scored positively here, and in two of the three cohorts the violent fanatics were slightly less likely to have been full-time Nazis. Perhaps there were two distinct routes to genocide – full-time commitment and commitment of violence or fanaticism.

So on these measures, about two-thirds of the Reich, Austrian, and refugee German men might loosely qualify as real Nazis before the war, with just over one-third adding a track record of violence or marked fanaticism. These men received higher postwar sentences. T4 staff and all doctors tended to have had less of a track record as Nazis, but they started earlier and served longer in genocidal institutions. Thus caged careers were common.

Table 8.7 shows a clear, expected relationship with rank. Almost all of those with the highest ranks were Old Nazis. Over half of the rankers and NCOs joined only during the war. Most of the NCOs were Old or Young Nazis, most of the rankers wartime or Raw Nazis. Hierarchy is again important: those giving orders were longer-term Nazis. Table 8.8 contains information on twice as many perpetrators as Table 8.1 and reveals 6–11 percent fewer Old or Young Nazis across the three age cohorts. Perhaps those for whom I have the fullest data were the worst Nazis. If so, my estimate of those who loosely qualify as real Nazis might be reduced slightly, to between 55 and 60 percent, with a third adding prior violence or fanaticism. Table 8.8 also shows that Old Nazis alone formed 44 percent of the sample. Mature wartime Nazis comprised 29 percent, and there were very

TABLE 8.7 *Type of Nazi by Rank (Reich German, Austrian, and Ethnic German Refugee Men Only)*

	Rank or Equivalent Office					
Type of Nazi	NCO and Below	Lieut., Captain	Major to Brig. Gen.	Major Gen. Up	All Ranks	N
Old Nazi: joined before 1933	21	43	54	70	44	584
Young Nazi: joined 1933–7, age 25 or less	15	17	10	−1	12	161
Bandwagon Nazi: joined 1933–7, age 26 or more	11	16	17	9	14	181
Raw Nazi: joined 1938–, age 25 or less	4	1	0	0	2	20
Wartime Nazi: joined 1938–, age 26 or more	49	23	16	21	29	387
Total %	100	100	100	100	100	
N	378	410	326	219	1,333	1,333

Note: Type of Nazi measured by date and age joined first adult Nazi organization (Nazi Party, SA, SS, or Nazi front organization in another country).

TABLE 8.8 *Type of Nazi by Age Cohort (Reich German, Austrian, and Ethnic German Refugee Men Only)*

	Born 1900	Born 1901–12	Born 1913–	All Cohorts	N
Old Nazis	48	47	18	44	589
Young Nazis	0	14	40	12	164
Bandwagon Nazis	21	12	0	14	182
Raw Nazis	0	0	13	1	20
Wartime Nazis	31	27	30	29	386
Total %	100	100	100	100	
N	450	732	159	1,341	1,341

few Raw Nazis (most liberated ethnic Germans and women). We still see a sample dominated by real Nazis, mostly fairly caged into careers of ascending violence. Indeed, only about 10 perpetrators had any kind of track record as members or supporters of leftist, liberal, or centrist parties. Doubtless, more had voted for these parties and some (though still few) implied that their parental homes had such sympathies. Of the main Weimar parties, only the rightist German National People's Party (DNVP) had supplied many perpetrators. This means that whole areas of German political life were relatively untouched by war crimes. Fascists and their rightist sympathizers committed serious war crimes.

CONCLUSION

These findings point in the same direction: these hard-core perpetrators were overwhelmingly drawn from core Nazi constituencies. Few came from agriculture and industry, the main place where class conflict trumped nationalism, organized by orthodox parties of the left and right. Far more workers were drawn from construction, the service sector, and the state; far more middle-class persons were from the professions and the state. The actual perpetrators – not the whole body of camp officers or security policemen – were disproportionately drawn from lost territories or threatened borders. The perpetrators came from sectors and regions most likely to be attracted by radicalized Nazism. This suggests that most of these perpetrators were probably ideological killers – though such a motivation was reinforced by others, to be explored in the next chapter. Many perpetrators were also embedded in institutional and professional subcultures already favorable to tough physical, legal, and biological remedies for social ills before genocide was requested. Approximately two-thirds of the sample had also had full-fledged careers in ascending violence and Nazism. The Nazis could presumably more easily accomplish genocide by using such a willing core of ideological and violent careerists. I examine more closely their careers in violence and Nazism in the next chapter.

9

Nazis, III
Genocidal Careers

The previous chapter treated my perpetrators as a statistical sample of individuals, abstracting them from their institutional environments. Yet to understand the process of Nazi genocide, we must investigate its institutions that constrained their members and the careers that they allowed them. Some see Nazi genocide as highly institutionalized, even bureaucratic. Baumann's famous linking of modernity and the Holocaust is in terms of technology and technical reason:

the choice of physical extermination as the right means to the task of *Entfernung* [removal] was a product of routine bureaucratic procedures: means–ends calculus, budget balancing, universal rule application. (1989: 17)

Feingold elaborates the argument:

The Final Solution marked the juncture where the European industrial system went awry.... Auschwitz [was] a mundane extension of the modern factory system. Rather than producing goods, the raw material was human beings and the end-product was death, so many units per day marked carefully on the manager's production charts. The chimneys, the very symbol of the modern factory system, poured forth acrid smoke produced by burning human flesh. The brilliantly organized railroad grid of modern Europe carried a new kind of raw material to the factories. It did so in the same manner as with other cargo. In the gas chambers, the victims inhaled noxious gas generated by prussic acid pellets, which were produced by the advanced chemical industry of Germany. Engineers designed the crematoria; managers designed the system of bureaucracy that worked with a zest and efficiency more backward nations would envy. Even the overall plan itself was a reflection of the modern scientific spirit gone awry. (1983: 399–400)

This is the Holocaust as bureaucratic modernity, the banality of genocide. Indeed, memos, inventories, transport schedules, and so on rarely mention death – sometimes "final solution," more commonly "evacuation," "special treatment," "special actions," "resettlement," or "labor in the East." Memos refer to the movement of Jews, their property, their clothes, their hair, their teeth, but the prim language seems to denote a large distribution company moving products around Europe – with no need for ideological justification. Do warehouse workers and transport managers need ideologies? Do they need to explain their behavior? No – it is their normal work routine.

The memos thus appear to be written by ordinary bureaucratic clerks and managers, without motives, without ideologies.

But the banality was illusion, not reality. The paperwork was *deliberately* denuded of murderous language in order to conceal mass murder. Most extermination institutions were neither bureaucratic nor dispassionate. True, Germany was an advanced society under fairly efficient rule, with a very efficient army. Obviously it used the railways, the paperwork, and the weapons of modernity. IBM Hollerith machines and punch cards, the very latest office technology, stored camp records. Yet foreign collaborators, Romanian and Croatian fascists, used primitive techniques to almost as devastating effect. Croatian Ustasha bludgeoned thousands to death with hammers and crowbars; they pushed many thousands over the edge of ravines, throwing (modern) sticks of dynamite on the writhing bodies below to finish them off. As we saw in the previous chapter, Turks had earlier used knives, axes, and bolt-action rifles to achieve comparable results. We see in Chapter 15 in Rwanda that the quickest genocide – over half a million in 12 weeks – came mainly with machetes and hoes. Each group of perpetrators used the highest level of modernity and technology available to it. That is the sole, and rather banal, truth of Baumann's and Feingold's argument.

Dispassionate methods did not dominate even among Germans. Prewar SA and SS men were better trained in beating people to death than in shooting them. The euthanasia project did begin with fairly calm, rational, scientific organization of killing, consonant with the modernist nightmare. Yet as it developed into cynical, brutal murder of all patients, regardless of any real diagnosis, all that remained bureaucratic was the continuous stream of lies told to the outside world – a repertoire of fake diagnoses of incurable mental illness, fake causes of death, delivery to relatives of a pot of random ashes. As patients realized the dreadful truth, screaming, struggling, incontinent victims disturbed all calm. Then began the shooting of Jews and Slavs by the *Einsatzgruppen* – point-blank, blood-spattered butchery by soldiers of over a million defenseless victims. The handguns, trucks, trains, and radios were indeed modern, but this was not dispassionate, scientific, banal, or bureaucratic killing.

The five death camps, especially their gas chambers, have formed the core of the modernist nightmare. Yet they were not very high-tech. Zyklon B gas was routinely used in Germany for the extermination of insects and rodents. The gas engine was produced by skilled motor mechanics aided by graduate chemists, competent technicians, not high flyers. True, the Europewide collection and distribution system of the victims embodied a formidably efficient bureaucracy. Its core lay ironically in the bureaucracy of the welfare state. Records of welfare entitlements in Germany, Belgium, the Netherlands, and other countries provided names, addresses, and religions, thus identifying Jews.

Yet the actual killings were not bureaucratic. In the death camps, screaming, naked, bloodied, defecating prisoners were beaten toward the gas chambers by drunken guards with whips and rifle butts under a pall of nauseous smoke. The perpetrators were not insulated from the horror, except by the alcohol that they (and all killing units) consumed in enormous quantities. Railway personnel witnessed beatings to death, while the property-disposal staff saw blood, hair, and teeth. Headquarters staff were insulated – the traditional privilege of the leaders of massacres throughout history. Nor in the 1,000 nondeath camps were most of the casual murders, ruthless beatings, workings to death, neglect, and starvation distinctively modern (though lethal injections might finish people off). The accused in war crimes trials often compared their roles to those of Allied bomber pilots. Aerial bombing is indeed an insulated and modernist form of mass killing, usually without sight of the victim, banal and easy to do. But most Nazi killing was different, and they knew it. Heydrich's 1941 directive to the Wehrmacht to murder captured Bolsheviks and Jews read: "the special situation of the campaign in the East ... demands special measures which have to be carried out in a spirit free from bureaucratic and administrative influences and with an eagerness to assume responsibility" (*Trials of the War Criminals Before the Nuremberg Military Tribunals*, 1946, The Einsatzgruppen case, Part IV, 127). All case studies of Nazi killings in the East emphasize local administrations free from bureaucratic restrictions, able to use their own initiative (Herbert, 2000, summarizes them). This was no bureaucracy.

Even desk-killers knew what they were doing and believed they had good reasons for doing it. Their motives were diverse – careerism, fear of authority, comradely conformity, enjoyment of arbitrary power, bigoted views of Jews or Slavs, broader Nazi ideology. Much of this involved the ideology rather than the technology of modernity. Baumann's theory is based on Weber's notion of instrumental or technical reason. This is wrong. Weber's action of value rationality – commitment to absolute values – would be more appropriate. Nazis believed they were exterminating their enemies for good ideological reasons. Modernity's evil has been more ideological and blood-spattered than bureaucratic and dispassionate. Bureaucratic states do not commit murderous cleansing; radicalized ones do. But they also gave perpetrators genocidal careers.

CAREER ROUTE ONE: ELITE DESK-KILLERS

The top Nazis and the non-Nazi elites who abetted them enjoyed distinctive careers, privileged as desk-killers from having to personally kill. By the time serious killing began, the Nazi leaders had been in power six or more years, alongside initially non-Nazi elites. Their mutual complicity had had time to mature. But overall genocidal policy was decided by Hitler's inner circle and implemented by a few hundred higher party and SS functionaries, virtually all Old Nazis, party members before 1933. Most became ideological desk-killers, though they had not become Nazis because they wanted to be mass murderers. They got there by stages.

The SS supervised the camps through an administrative agency, the Office of Economic Policy (WVHA). It was headed by Oswald Pohl, who reported directly to Himmler. From the occupied Ruhr, the son of a Thyssen steel plant foreman, he worked for the navy, known as a modernizing administrator, frustrated by the navy's conservatism, early attracted by the Nazi progressive brand of nationalism. He joined the party in 1922 at age 30. Though a fierce Nazi, his talents were organizational. He introduced effective budgetary controls into the SS, organizing the camp industries, which made them financially independent of the state. The forced labor camps produced goods and profits. So Pohl favored well-fed slave laborers, not corpses – though he never questioned Himmler's exterminist orders. Navy-cultivated loyalty and strong SS comradeship helped him solve his dilemmas. Though the slave-versus-corpse debate could be quite intense, the SS elite all accepted collective responsibility for decisions finally taken.

Beneath Pohl were three camp overseers. I described Gestapo boss Heinrich Müller in Chapter 7. Richard Glücks was also from the occupied Ruhr. He served in the Freikorps, was a Nazi member in 1926, and worked for Eicke in camp administration during the 1930s. He became an extermination fanatic, and decided the numbers to be killed at each site, but didn't want to know much about the killings. Gerhard Maurer was a Saxon businessman, a Nazi by 1928. As boss of the slave labor camps, he favored laborers over corpses – though he never carried his views into a public debate. Except for Müller, these leaders were early Nazis. Their commitment was ideological, but rather abstract and cold. These Nazi organization men were implementing an ideal conception of a cleansed Reich from their desks. Shielded from the stench of death, they found ideological rigor easy to maintain.

The other main genocidal arm of the SS was its security apparatus, the Reich Security Main Office (RSHA). Ernst Kaltenbrunner succeeded Heydrich as its boss. He was selected because of his Austrian connection to Hitler, his reputation for toughness, and his lack of political guile. He was no threat to his superiors. His extremism and anti-Semitism were learned from his father. A very big man, the young Kaltenbrunner physically bullied Reds, Catholics, and Jews. He seemed quite normal, became a good family man, and began a promising career as a lawyer. He joined the Austro-fascist Heimwehr in 1929, at age 26, and the Nazi Party the next year. Declaring that he wished to "be 100% National Socialist," he joined the SS in 1931 and made speeches laying out in "gripping, convincing words" the "essence and goals of National Socialism." Arrested several times and imprisoned once, he became a full-time revolutionary. His SD work involved supervision of steadily more violence, though it is unclear if he ever himself murdered. He was very anti-Semitic and anti-Slav. For him Nazism was "a *Weltanschauung* encompassing life in its entirety." Race was "the divinely-inspired building-block of mankind." At his trial, he conceded only that Nazism had been sullied by "deviations" and that Hitler had made geopolitical mistakes. Kaltenbrunner saw himself as the ideal SS "Political Soldier" (Black, 1984). He had graduated through violence to genocide believing in the justice of his cause.

Most of the RSHA were not so used to violence. They were of a single generation, born in the first decade of the 20th century, too young to fight in World War I. They were successful and highly educated, two-thirds with university degrees, a third with doctorates. Most had been Nazis or radical rightists while at university, joining the Nazis before 1933. By the mid-1930s they were ready to remake the world according to Nazi racial-national doctrine. They knew that action was required, and few flinched from it when the time came (Herbert, 2000: 26–7; Wildt, 2002).

Adolf Eichmann was a man known for getting things done. He supervised the deportation machinery linking Nazi, military, and civilian administrative agencies to the death camps. At his trial in Jerusalem psychiatrists said he was a good family man – "more normal than I am after having examined him," one exclaimed. He had been born in the Rhineland, though when he was eight his mother died and the family moved to Austria. His performance at secondary school and then as a salesman was mediocre. He joined the Austrian Nazi Party in 1932, at age 26, and the SS in 1934, during the illegal period, on the advice of his friend Kaltenbrunner. The reasons he then gave for joining were the unjust Treaty of Versailles and mass unemployment, but career frustration also contributed. He was trained as a sergeant at the Dachau camp in 1934 and was in the SD Jewish Section the next year, where he became an expert on Zionism. He described himself as "unemotional" and "objective." For Arendt (1965) he epitomized the banality of evil (a phrase she later came to regret). She thought that morally he "never realized what he was doing." This was not true. Eichmann was very anti-Semitic, and his expertise on the Jewish Question and its various solutions had made him ready for anything. Höss (1978: 105), the commandant of Auschwitz, recalled their wartime conversations:

even when we were quite alone together and the drink [flowed] freely, so that he was in his most expansive mood, he showed that he was obsessed with the idea of destroying every single Jew that he could lay his hands on. Without pity and in cold blood we must complete this extermination as rapidly as possible. Any compromise, even the slightest, would have to be paid for bitterly at a later date. (Höss et al., 1987: 105)

He repeatedly told friends that Jews were of no value except as laborers – and only 20–25 percent were capable of hard work. Dieter Wisliceny (see later) said:

he was not immoral, he was amoral and completely ice-cold in his attitudes. He said to me... in February 1945, at which time we were discussing our fates upon losing the war: "I laugh when I jump into the grave because of the feeling that I have killed 5,000,000 Jews. That gives me great satisfaction and gratification." (*Trials of the War Criminals*, 1946: VIII).

"Ice-cold" meant ruthless, not detached. Only his technique in court was banal, trying to hide behind duty and orders. But he himself often took initiatives. He opposed deporting Serbian Jews, a colleague minuting, "Eichmann proposes shooting." He opposed deporting foreign Jews from Hungary in 1942. Better, he said, to wait until all 700,000 Jews in Hungary could be dealt with at once. His advice was taken in both cases. This was not a rule-governed bureaucracy: it was fluid, allowing officials to innovate in radical directions. Eichmann's evil was neither unthinking nor banal, but innovative, ruthless, and ideological (Losowick, 2000, agrees).

I follow the deportations into a single country. Working closely with Eichmann in deporting Hungary's Jews were two Nazis from privileged backgrounds. The senior Foreign Office man was Edmund Veesenmayer, a Catholic from Lower Franconia (Bavaria). He had been a lecturer in economics and a successful businessman. An extreme nationalist, he turned to the Nazi Party in 1932. From 1933 the SS sponsored his diplomatic career. He rose to brigadier-general in the SS and was crucial in persuading the Hungarian government to back mass deportations. He wrote, "the Jews are enemy No. 1 and the 1.1 million Jews amount to as many saboteurs...as Bolshevik vanguards." The ranking SD man was Lieutenant-General Otto Winkelman, born in Schleswig-Holstein, the son of a city official. While a student, he fought the French in the Ruhr in 1923 and was imprisoned. A conservative nationalist, he turned to the Nazi Party in 1932 at age 28. Dieter Wisliceny had the Hungarian desk in the "Jewish Emigration" Office. Born in 1911, he was in the Nazi Party at age 22 and in the SS and SD at age 23.

Their staffs – men like Burger, Grell, Hunsche, Krumey, Novak, and Sprinz – were Old or Young Nazis with Freikorps and/or street fighting experience in Germany or Austria (Krumey was the exception, a Sudeten active only in the mid-1930s in nationalist, then Nazi front organizations). The Hungarian deportations were deliberately placed in safe hands – as they were in all occupied countries. These were ideological Nazis, rewarded with careers. As with the camp elite, their purpose and efficiency flowed more easily from a systematic, rigorous ideology: the pursuit of "moral" cleansing. This eventually meant not sparing a single Jew or Bolshevik. As Losowick (2000: 8) says, this was an elite group carrying out a world-historical mission, ideological efficiency experts, not banal bureaucrats. They knew exactly what they were doing, to the last drop of blood.

The governors and police chiefs of the occupied territories oversaw killings in the field. They were tough Nazis, often experienced in street fighting before the coup. Unlike the desk killers, they saw and participated in the carnage. They declaimed a blunt racist ideology: "We are a master race of which the lowliest German is racially and biologically one thousand times more valuable than the local population," said Ernst Koch, from the Ruhr, a railway clerk fired for early political activities. After being *Gauleiter* of East Prussia from the late 1920s, he was *Reichskommissar* for the Ukraine. "I ask nothing of the Jews except that they should disappear," said Hans Frank from Baden, a Freikorps veteran, a Nazi Party lawyer, then Reich minister of justice and governor of Poland. Josef Bürckel was more hesitant. He was from the Rhine Palatinate, the son of an artisan, a Freikorps veteran then a teacher, then in the late 1920s a party functionary. He was a conservative, order-loving Nazi. In 1938 he was *Gauleiter* of Vienna, where he tried to restrain wild looting and violence against the Jews. But when told Hitler supported this, he changed his views. He was working toward the fuhrer.

The doyen of Eastern police commanders was Erich von dem Bach-Zalewski, born in Pomerania to a Junker military family. He served in World War I, then in the Freikorps and then in the Weimar army. Impressed by Hitler, he resigned his commission and joined the Nazi Party in 1930, at age 31, and the SS the following year. A Nazi Reichstag deputy for 12 years, and a commander of the Röhm purge and SS and Gestapo units, he was Hitler's favorite general, commended by Hitler for "beating Communist opposition to a pulp." He boasted after one *Einsatzgruppe* operation: "There is not a Jew left in Estonia." Later he liquidated the Warsaw ghetto.

But he had qualms. In 1941 Himmler went to see an *Einsatzgruppe* liquidation. Visibly nervy, he flinched and averted his gaze as each volley crashed out. As the firing finished, Bach-Zalewski revealed his own discomfort, saying:

Reichsführer, those were only a hundred [killings]. . . . Look at the eyes of the men in this *Kommando*, how deeply shaken they are! These are finished for the rest of their lives. What kinds of followers are we training here? Either neurotics or savages!

Thereupon Himmler made an emotional speech to the men. He acknowledged that the soldiers had a repulsive duty. He would not like it if Germans did such a thing gladly. But it should not impair their conscience. Soldiers had to carry out every order unconditionally. He alone had responsibility before God and Hitler. They had undoubtedly noticed that he hated this bloody business and that he had been aroused to the depths of his soul. But he too was obeying a higher law by doing his duty. Look at nature. There was combat everywhere, not only among men but also in the world of animals and plants. Whoever was too tired to fight must go under. Didn't bedbugs and rats have a purpose also? But man must defend himself against vermin. (Hilberg, 1978: 218–19).

In 1942 Bach-Zalewski suffered psychic exhaustion involving hallucinations of the shootings of Jews. He suggested to Himmler that they stop. Himmler was now safely away from the killing, and his retort was sharp: "That is a Führer order. The Jews are the disseminators of Bolshevism. . . . If you don't keep your nose out of the Jewish business, you'll see what'll happen to you" (Lifton, 1986: 15, 159, 437). Bach-Zalewski recovered and resumed killing. Yet at Nuremberg he confessed and repented. Usually, toughness faltered only into self-pity. One officer declared: "The people really worthy of pity were we, the liquidators, because our men were in worse nervous condition than those who had to be shot" (Dicks, 1972: 61).

A very different police commander was Friedrich Katzmann, the son of a Ruhr miner, trained as a carpenter. He was in the Nazi Party and the SA in 1927 at age 21. His activism made him unemployable. The leader of a brawling gang of SA miners, he was promoted beyond his abilities because he was a political soldier with fanaticism, favoring radical solutions, able to get things done. Odilo Globocnik was more middle class, born in Trieste, the son of an Austrian army captain concealing a part-Slovenian descent. Educated in cadet school, after the war he moved to Austria and worked as a construction manager. He joined the Austrian Nazis early, in 1922, at age 18, and the SS in 1932. In 1933 his activism cost him his job and he became a full-time revolutionary. A fanatic Nazi and anti-Semite, he was also corrupt, dismissed as *Gauleiter* of Vienna for currency speculation. His friend Himmler cushioned his fall and asked him to set up the first death camps of *Aktion Reinhard*. Globocnik probably remained corrupt. He boasted openly of murders and opposed the policy of concealing genocide by burning the corpses:

> if after us such a cowardly and rotten generation should arise that it does not understand our work, which is so good and so necessary, then, gentlemen, all National Socialism will have been for nothing. On the contrary, bronze plaques should be put up with the inscription that it was we, we who had the courage to achieve this gigantic task. (*Trials of the War Criminals*, Nuremberg, "The Medical Case," Vol. I, 866–7)

Yet even he reported pangs of conscience, saying he could not look at his little niece without thinking of the children he had killed (Hilberg, 1978: 332, 628; Höffkes, 1986: 92–4).

Few higher Nazis experienced killing without moral qualms. Most tried to subordinate them to a supposedly higher moral purpose. Birn (1986) attributes this to rigid, militaristic upbringing, experience in the war, an emotional conversion to National Socialism, and extreme obedience to Hitler. But obedience also gave them a sense of idealism, subordinating personal feelings to the common cause. Such perverted idealism was prevalent among higher-educated perpetrators. Ideological rigor assisted perpetrators to stick to their task when other motives were failing.

Non-Nazi institutions were also complicit. Without the civil service, little could have been accomplished. Few civil servants had any history of violence or fanaticism. In the Foreign Office, Browning (1978) identifies two groups of complicit officials. The first were rather intellectual Nazi members before 1933 and before joining the Foreign Office. Luther was born in Berlin, the son of a senior civil servant. After war service, he ran a furniture import-export business. He was in the Nazi Party and the SS by March 1932 at age 37, but he already knew many Nazis and was a friend of Ribbentrop. He quickly became a Nazi Berlin city councillor. Browning calls him "an amoral technician of power," but that isn't quite right. He was a career Nazi before he was a career diplomat, only entering the Foreign Office in 1936 and then being rapidly promoted.

Browning's second group were mere careerists, joining the Nazi Party (and not the SS) as Bandwagon Nazis after the coup. They included aristocratic conservative diplomats like Otto von Neurath and upwardly mobile men like Franz Rademacher, the son of a railway engineer from Mecklenburg, who joined the Nazis only in 1933, working his way up to the Jewish desk. Browning considers these men better exemplars of the banality of evil than Eichmann. Yet most were from military and civil servant backgrounds, while the whole service was permeated by anti-Semitic conservative nationalism. Rademacher believed strongly in scientific racism, his main qualification for helping to draw up the Madagascar Plan and then the Final Solution. In my sample, almost all the civil servants – compared to few of the businessmen – were drawn into Nazi membership. But their Nazi ideology was rarely expressed in rabid speech, still less in violence. Instead it resonated in their professional experience in a fairly authoritarian civil service.

The infamous Conference of the Undersecretaries at Wannsee in 1942 laid down the collaboration required between the SS and the civil service to implement the Final Solution. The Nazi leaders expected civil service dissent, yet all went smoothly – probably because all the participants except Kritzinger (an ethnic German from Poland)) were Old Nazis. Most discussion concerned technical issues arising from mixed marriages between Jews and Christians. After only an hour and a half the conference ended, followed by drinks and lunch. News of the Final Solution then diffused through the ministries without causing much fuss (Hilberg, 1978: 264–5). Careerism now chipped in. Seniors, concerned that they might lose influence, got their ministries to devise killing schemes, while mid-level officials could advance their careers by staffing the Jewish desks springing up everywhere. The Finance Office made property inventories of the deportees and turned them over to the Tax Office, the Labor Office collected work books, the Housing Office disposed of vacant housing, and the state railway built lines to the camps and transported the prisoners.

Virtually none of these men killed, and few had a history of violence. Browning (1978) says they mixed a "depersonalized bureaucratic mode of operation," "the organizational achievement of a bureaucratic society," and "ideological indoctrination." But their prior rightist ideologies moved relatively easily into a statist Nazism, giving a principled cast to their careerism. Bureaucracy was the *means* of genocide in civil service areas removed from the killing, yet the resonance of Nazi ideology gave the ends. Farther east, the combination was more desperate. Civil servants knew there what their ideology actually meant, but their careerism was also more naked. Postings to Poland and Russia were not desirable and often resulted from career lapses, even criminal activities. Musial (1999) sees these officials as venal and overtly racist, trying to redeem themselves and restore their careers through murderous zeal.

Things were different in industry. I stressed in *Fascists* that neither capital nor labor was in the core Nazi constituency. Few businessmen were ideological Nazis, though many jumped on the bandwagon after 1933. They ran slave labor factories, but for profit. Almost all became complicit, since labor shortages became desperate as the war progressed. Industrialists with Nazi connections, like Porsche, lobbied to use prisoners as laborers – first Western Europeans, then Slavs, finally Jews. By the end of 1942 a third of the German labor force were slaves. Their treatment varied considerably. A few Jews were well treated, better than French or Dutch laborers in other factories. Yet IG Farben directors asked that laborers who fell ill be replaced, knowing they would then be killed, and managers routinely entered the camps to select their labor, says Straede (1999).

Even the few industrialists and managers charged with war crimes had rarely joined the Nazi Party before 1933. Gustav Krupp "used up" many thousands of Russian and Jewish slave laborers and so was exempted from inheritance tax, but he never joined the party. Kurt Schroeder and Friedrich Flick had helped finance the party from 1932, though Flick had given more to other rightist parties and joined only in 1937. Schroeder joined in 1933. Even the "shameless and brutal" Erich Dittrich, from the Polish lost territories, who recruited workers for his business from the local ghetto and handed over enfeebled ones to the Gestapo to be shot, joined the party only around 1935. Industrialists and financiers also took lucrative government economic positions, often working closely with the SS. Bank director Hans Fischböck was in the post-*Anchluss* Austrian cabinet and then helped run the Dutch economy. He was a rightist, though not formally a Nazi until 1940, when he received the honorary rank of SS colonel. Among German capitalists we come closest to genuine banality – mass killings as the by-product of something routinized and legitimate in modern society: the extraction of maximum profit from minimum costs. Since free labor was in short and costly supply, capitalists gladly used slaves. Of course, capitalists, managers, and even foremen did not have to kill. They handed the slaves over to the SS and then tried to forget about them. They were mainly materialist accomplices to killing.

There were some moderates among elites. They ridiculed reports revealing that 6,000 dead partisans had only had 480 rifles among them; civil servants wrote "yes, but" memos back to delay terrible orders (Buchheim et al., 1968: 346, 377–9). Generals, economic planners, and industrialists preferred healthy slave laborers to corpses. Many warned against alienating subject peoples; some wanted to spare Jewish war veterans. But whenever they realized that the radical line came down from on high, probably from Hitler himself, they desisted. The fuhrer principle legitimated careerists' moral evasions. To obey was apparently sacred, but it also brought career or profit. Some asked for transfers but did not resign. A few leading Nazis were sidelined. But Eichmann said that general acceptance of the great task deterred individual deviance. For Nazis, the movement had long been their home. They could hardly conceive of life outside it. Middle-aged men had privileged families. Compliance was reinforced by mundane motives of which we are all capable.

Courageous opposition generally required an alternative ideology. The socialist physician in charge of Warsaw, Dr. Wilhelm Hagen, kept up a running battle with the SS administration to improve ghetto conditions (though as a German doctor of his time, he still believed Jews spread typhus). A few traditionalist officers disobeyed, like Lieutenant-General Moser. Drafted to eastern Poland, he smelled a death camp and went in to investigate. Horrified, he declared, "every decent German must disavow a government that has ordered such an organised mass murder" and walked over the Russian lines to surrender (Boehnert, 1981: 211–12). The Stauffenberg family, plotters against Hitler, were also old-school militarists. SS officer Kurt Gerstein remains enigmatic, though the deep evangelical faith of his Prussian family clearly sustained him. He risked all to give church leaders and a Swedish diplomat details of the Final Solution. Lieutenant Colonel Grosscurth, a professional officer, the son of an evangelical minister, tried to block the shooting of women and children by the *Einsatzgruppen* – until overruled by his superiors. Catholicism helped Albert Hartl, a former priest, resign his SS position in disgust. Most conspirators were longtime leftists, religious activists or old-school militarists (Hoffmann, 1988). But even most people with track records opposing Nazism kept their mouths shut, since they had most to fear from nonconformity.

A very few top Nazis sought to block policy from within. Karl-Siegmund Litzmann was the son of a general and became an officer himself. After World War I he was in the Freikorps, then the Stahlhelm. He joined the Nazis in 1929. He became an SA leader but was sidelined over policy differences. In World War II, as general commissioner for Estonia, he opposed murderous policies that he said turned Germany's potential friends into enemies. But he ultimately shrugged his shoulders, allowing his objections to be bypassed (Kersten, 1956: 223–5). Wilhelm Kube, governor of Belarus, provided more determined opposition. His fascism was more cultural than racial, and he opposed exterminating "cultured" Western Jews:

I am certainly hard and I am ready to help solve the Jewish question, but people who come from our cultural milieu are certainly something else than the native animalized hordes [from the East]. . . . I ask you, consider the honour of our Reich and our party . . . to take care of what is necessary in a form which is humane.

When SS Colonel Strauch shot 70 "cultured" Jews, Strauch says Kube blew his top:

my men and I were reproached for barbarism and sadism, whereas I did nothing but fulfil my duty. Kube asserted that [removing Jewish gold fillings]... was unworthy of a German man and of the Germany of Kant and Goethe. It was our fault that the reputation of Germany was being ruined in the whole world. It was also true, he said, that my men liberally satisfied their sexual lust during these executions. I protested energetically against that statement and emphasized that it was regrettable that we, in addition to having to perform this nasty job, were also made the target of mudslinging.

Kube died soon after these exchanges, but he might have ended badly anyway. Himmler said his conduct "bordered on treason." He was considerably older, and denounced young Nazis for having lost the early ideals of the movement. Born in Polish Silesia, the son of an infantry sergeant, with a university degree in history, he had joined prewar nationalist movements. After serving in World War I, he joined the conservative DNVP Party. He joined the Nazis in 1927, though at the unusually advanced age of 40. Perhaps he was too old to be fully socialized (Black, 1984: 175; Hilberg, 1978: 233, 253–4; Höffkes, 1986: 195–8). But such men were uncommon.

Nazism had always preached hatred of enemies, the movement and its Leadership Principle was their life, and they were steeped in violence before this escalated to mass killing. This is why they were assigned to their genocidal positions. Their ideology also had a systemic quality, from which the efficient organization of genocide might easily flow. Then the war entwined real enemies with their ideological ones. Koehl says that fewer than 2,000 SS officers were directly involved in extermination; fewer than 200 above the rank of major ran it. But "that fraction was damned by its training, its selection, and the conditions of unrelenting warfare to be devils incarnate ... decisive in warping and constraining hundreds of thousands more who passed through the ... system" (1983: 167, 177–86). But most elites had it easy. They were desk-killers.

CAREER ROUTE TWO: THE MAIN CAMPS

This was not so in the camps, in which victims were killed by men and women of only moderate rank, lower-middle and working-class people in secure and quite well-paid jobs that also involved killing. Not many articulated principled Nazi ideology. Their racist and anti-Semitic statements tend more toward simple bigotry. But the camps were also occupational communities. Some lived there with their families. Parties, drinking bouts, and affairs were part of quite intensive socialization, generating conformity to group norms. Since the *Aktion Reinhard* death camps had their own recruiting methods, I treat them separately. There were stronger threads connecting together the prewar German camps, Auschwitz and Majdenek death camps, and the many other camps.

Violence first escalated to routinized murder in the prewar German camps. Eight percent (115) of my male sample had served there. None had experienced mass murder, but they were vetted. All but three were prior Nazi Party, SS, or SA members. In my sample, 286 men served in the Auschwitz or Majdanek camp complexes. Only 14 percent were raw recruits. These were all rankers, and almost all were liberated ethnic Germans recruited after 1942. The rest were already party or SS members. Forty-one had also served in the prewar camps, 35 in other nondeath camps, 14 in the *Einsatzgruppen*, 12 in the *Aktion Reinhard* death camps, and one in T4. They were very experienced.

A total of 295 men served in nondeath camps during the war. Only 5 percent were raw recruits, again mostly liberated ethnic Germans. Twenty-two percent had previously served only with Waffen-SS divisions, mostly transfered to the camps when wounded on the Eastern Front. Another 22 percent had only been party or SS members. Forty-four percent were more experienced, having served with T4 (5 persons), the *Einsatzgruppen* (14), the prewar camps (66), or a death camp (40) – and all but 9 of these were also party or SS members. This is similar to the Auschwitz pattern, except for the wounded Waffen-SS men. Again, we glimpse systematic selection and transfer procedures making use of experience and deeds.

We saw that Eicke's regime at Dachau became the model for all camps. So persons with promotions went from Dachau and other prewar camps to the death camps. At least nine commandants and eight deputy commandants of major camps had begun their career at Dachau. Special care was taken over the filling of senior Auschwitz officer positions, the routinized core of the genocide. The three commandants Höss (already encountered), Arthur Liebenhenschel (an Old Nazi from Polish Silesia who had followed his father into the lower reaches of the civil service), and Richard Baer (a pastry cook from Bavaria, who joined the Nazi Party in 1930 at age 20 and the SS the next year) had become NCOs at Dachau. So did Deputy commandant Hans Aumeier (a Bavarian lathe operator, an Old Nazi, and a career SS man, who later went on to be a camp commandant), Baer's adjutant Karl Höcker (from Westphalia, the son of a building contractor, himself a bank clerk, a Young Nazi joining the party at age 22 in 1933), Franz Hoffman (already discussed), in charge of the actual killing area, and Karl Fritzsche, a Sudeten riverboat hand who joined the party and the SS in 1930. Fritzsche valued the intense brotherhood of the SS and served seven years at Dachau, supervised protective custody at Auschwitz, and finally headed the Flossenburg camp, where he "exceeded his authority," that is, led wild atrocities.

Josef Jarolin, an Alsatian, at Dachau for nine years before being given command of the Allach camp, had joined the Nazi Party only in 1933, at age 29, yet Allach prisoners described him as a fanatic. Karl Koch, from the Ruhr, an anti-Red street fighter of the 1920s and an Old Nazi, later the wild and corrupt commandant of Buchenwald, learned his trade at prewar Sachsenhausen (so did his terrible Old Nazi wife, Ilse, who made lampshades out of tattooed prisoners' skins). Hermine Braunsteiner, a Viennese housemaid, then a munitions worker, had been only 20 in 1939 when she volunteered for the SS. She was assigned to Ravensbrück and later supervised the female warders of the Majdanek death camp.

Some had only violence to recommend them. Promotion came more slowly for the Bavarian Josef Kramer, the son of a lower civil servant, a Nazi by 1931. Trained at Dachau in 1934, he became a clerk, though moving toward the killing zone. He became deputy commandant at Matthausen, an officer at Auschwitz, commandant at Natzweiler, and supervised the death camp area at Auschwitz-Birkenau before finally becoming the "Beast of Belsen." His wife said, "the movement gave him great hope...Nazism was a deep emotional experience. The movement...allowed him to believe in himself once again. He would tell me that what drew him to the SS more than anything else was the desire to be in the company of other young men of his age, in the same situation, found close friends in the organization" (Segev, 1987: 50-1, 218).

A minority were transferred to camps from other SS activities. Amon Goeth was the commandant at Plaszow depicted in the film *Schindler's List* (by a much shorter actor – in reality Amon was 6 feet 4 inches tall). He was from Vienna, the only son of a publisher of military books. He was good at high school but got hijacked by Nazism. He probably joined the party in 1925, at age 17, and was definitely in the SS in 1930. In 1933 he had to flee after police connected him to a Nazi arms cache. He was active in illegal activities, including the Dollfuss murder, after which he fled to Germany. He reveled in brawling, and the party valued him for it. He was profoundly racist. He commanded a detachment of ethnic Germans, liquidated ghettos, and was then moved to command Plaszow. Hanged by the Poles for causing the deaths of 8,000 prisoners, he died "at peace, a political soldier," said his widow.

It was essentially violence that united the camp officers and drew them in upon themselves as a unique, elite body of toughened men. Orth (2000) shows that they were quite well educated, certainly not declassé. On average they had joined the Nazi Party by September 1931, but they saw themselves as men of action, not words, and Orth emphasizes that they shared almost without reflection an ethos of violence.

Josef Klehr stayed an NCO. He was from Upper Silesia, the son of a reform school teacher, trained as a cabinet maker but then an orderly. He was active in the SS from 1932 and a camp guard from 1938. He went from Buchenwald to Dachau to Auschwitz, becoming a sergeant. He may have the record number of personal murders (475), a man of "enormous psychopathic potential." Herbert Scherpe, from Upper Silesia, trained as a butcher but worked for his saddler father and then as a policeman and customs official. After spells of unemployment he joined the Nazi Party in 1932, at age 24, and was given full-time SS employment the next year. He was a camp guard in 1936 and in Dachau in 1939. Wounded on the Eastern Front, he volunteered for Auschwitz in 1943. There he murdered many children until one day he shouted, "I can't do any more." He was transferred to a less murderous part of the camp. Bernhard Walter, a Bavarian plasterer, a Nazi in 1933 at age 22, began at Dachau and became prominent in selecting who would die in Auschwitz. These were more limited men whose commitment to Nazi ideology is unclear but who held NCO rank by fulfilling ascending requirements of violence.

Some were very young. Johannes Stark was from Darmstadt, his policeman father a strict disciplinarian whose motto was "He who cannot obey cannot give orders." At 17 he was a guard at Buchenwald, then Dachau, then most murderously at Auschwitz. A court psychiatrist commented that his only training had been as a Nazi camp guard, where he had learned to brush aside conscience "by calling compassion a weakness." Corporal Perry Broad wrote an Auschwitz *Memoir* (Höss et al., 1978). He was in the Hitler Youth, then the SS, was assigned to Auschwitz, and at age 21 was required to torture and execute. Auschwitz was his only adult experience, his conception of normality. Survivors attested to his brutality, though he preferred to label his colleagues "bloodthirsty butchers," "cruel sadists," and "fanatics." He says executioners would whistle and exchange small talk between shots, feigning indifference while "finishing off that rabble" "to boast how tough" they were. "Toughness" conveyed social status.

Josef Schwammberger was a refugee from the Austrian South Tyrol ceded to Italy in 1918. His father was a postal clerk, and he was a chemist's clerk until unemployment struck in 1931. He became an active Nazi – though he may have joined the party earlier. He was a street fighter and had to flee to Germany in 1933. He received SS military training, but health problems forced transfer to SS clerking. But when posted to a killing office in occupied Poland, he was promoted to sergeant by asserting his skills as an old fighter with military training. He was assigned a small forced labor camp of Jews. Within months all were dead. He proceeded through ghetto clearances including wild shooting sprees by his Ukrainians. A survivor said, "I couldn't call him a beast because I wouldn't want to embarrass the beast. He just killed because he wanted to kill." It would be almost impossible to disentangle the Nazism, violence, and careerism in this man, since his skills were in Nazi violence.

Some of the younger men, the liberated ethnic Germans, and the women were marginal Nazis or not Nazis at all – though we cannot be certain, since rankers' records were skimpy. Günther Hinze served briefly on the Eastern Front at age 20. He received a severe head wound, joined the Nazi Party at age 21, and was posted as a guard to the Fürstengrube subcamp at age 22. There he was bent on simple revenge, asking, "You know why the Jews are punished? Because they are the cause of the war" (Jacobs, 1995: 144–5). Emil Hantl was the son of a Sudeten factory worker. A weaver until unemployment forced him to be a farm laborer, he was not very political but his nationalist gymnastics club was absorbed into the SS in 1938. He was drafted into the Waffen-SS in 1940 and then moved to Auschwitz as a guard, then an orderly. At Auschwitz he assisted 350 murders, though survivors called him "one of the decent medics.... He looked as if he was carrying out his duties with great reluctance." After the killing of 120 Polish children, he emerged "in a state of total collapse" and "completely went to pieces, cursing the war."

The women tended to be single and young or with career moves dependent on Nazi partners. Irma Grese's father was a Pomeranian agricultural worker who thrashed her in 1942 when at age 19 she volunteered for the SS. She was trained at Ravensbrück, then moved to Auschwitz, then Bergen-Belsen. She spouted Nazi beliefs and was extremely violent, confessing to "making sport with the prisoners." Hildegard Lächert, from Berlin, was the daughter of a metal worker. She was in Nazi youth organizations and then in a women's organization in 1938 at age 18. She worked in various factories, then lived at the front with a Luftwaffe officer and then with an SS man. They were both posted to Madjanek, Auschwitz, and then Ravensbrück. Her two children were brought up by her mother. She was known as "Bloody Brygida." We lack the data to penetrate far into these women's motives.

In the main camps, doctors selected prisoners for life or death and might conduct gruesome racial experiments on them. They were the best-educated men and women in the camps and seem more varied than regular camp officers. In Auschwitz, Enno Lolling was from the Rhineland, joining the Nazi Party and the SS in 1931. He was a fanatic Nazi, considered by some an incompetent drunk. He began in Dachau but rose to head the WVHA medical inspections of the camps. Friedrich Entress first served at prewar Gross-Rosen. He was a refugee from Poland, a Nazi at age 21 in 1935, in the SS next year, a man of "ideological intensity" who favored killing because Slavs were *Untermenschen* and Jews were not human at all. He seemed psychologically harried by his own "Polish half," pretending not to understand Polish prisoners and treating them cruelly. These were real Nazi doctors.

Others seem more careerist. Johann Paul Kremer kept a startlingly un-eventful Auschwitz diary. We learn of dinner menus and career concerns, anger at his university's slowness to promote him, outrage at his brother-in-law's lack of patriotism. But we learn little of the death camp. He was from the Rhineland, the son of a farmer, perhaps the oldest doctor at Auschwitz. A rightist nationalist, in 1927 he headed a university anatomical institute. At-tracted by Nazi bioracial theory, he joined the Nazi Party in 1932 and the SS in 1934. He was in the medical service at the front and then briefly assigned to experiments at Auschwitz. He comes across as a frustrated careerist, not very political but blending nationalism into biomedical racism. Friedrich

Mennecke was the Westphalian son of a socialist bricklayer. He struggled to get through medical school and joined the Nazis in 1932 to advance his career. He advanced, to his own considerable satisfaction, through T4 to wild euthanasia to Buchenwald. His scribbled notes on patients reveal anti-Semitism allied to conventional Nazi views, but he was at heart a careerist.

Some were idealistic Nazis. The notorious Josef Mengele was the son of a Bavarian self-made machinery manufacturer. He was a star pupil, a nationalist and a devoted racial biomedic. He joined the Nazi Party in 1937 at age 26. He served as a doctor on the Eastern Front, and was decorated and wounded. He was transferred to Auschwitz to experiment on prisoners. After grisly procedures, he personally killed many of his subjects, demonstrating "absolute ideological firmness." Yet he was considered by colleagues as "open, honest, firm," lacking in cruelty, affectionate to camp children, a rare nondrinker. As Lifton (1986: 377) says, Mengele "exemplified the Nazi biological revolutionary," improving humanity by killing. Eduard Wirths was the son of a successful (and pacifist) stonemason. He imbibed *völkisch* ideals as a student and became an ardent, idealistic Nazi in 1933 at age 25. He joined the SS the next year and wrote of his "love for the biological tasks set by the SS." He was a principled anti-Semite, declaring that "the Jews were a danger to Germany" – while continuing to treat Jewish patients even after this became illegal. He served as a doctor on the Eastern Front, then was Dachau camp physician and chief garrison physician at Auschwitz from 1942. The doctors said he was "the best physician in all the concentration camps" (Höss agreed). He cared for his prisoner-patients, tried to improve camp health facilities, and once forcefully intervened against the terrible Irme Grese, shouting, "Do not beat my women." Yet he never disobeyed killing orders and made a point of implementing them himself, experimenting on prisoners, joining in selections, and reprimanding squeamish colleagues. Lifton (1986: chap. 18) believes he was split between his Nazi and his humane doctor self, and that he exemplified the "Nazi-German principle of killing as a difficult but necessary form of personal ordeal." A prisoner-doctor remembered him as a "Nazi ideologist who did not like the methods of the gas chamber . . . a Nazi in spirit but not a cruel one." He was a victim of Nazi idealism, which enabled highly educated Nazis to implement "principled genocide" over moral revulsion at its concrete practices.

CAREER ROUTE THREE: FROM T4 TO THE *AKTION*
REINHARD CAMPS

In T4[1] the status relations distinct to medical practice affected the practice of genocide. The main sites were occupational communities – hospitals and

---

[1] My main sources for T4 perpetrators were Burleigh (1994), de Mildt (1996), Friedländer (1995), Horwitz (1990: chap. 3), Klee (1983), Lifton (1986), and Müller-Hill (1988).

homes in isolated rural areas, with the staff living as well as working together. This solidified two distinct groups of comrades, doctors/administrators and SS NCOs/rankers. Most T4 people were chosen carefully. Over 90 percent of the 118 men in my sample who served there were prior Nazi or SS members. Nine were additionally policemen, and 13 had been in the camps or the *Einsatzgruppen*. Forty-one percent had relatives or friends already working there when they arrived, and a further 47 percent were known by the recruiter to be reliable. These were people with track records, though rarely yet of actual murder. Of 17 administrators at T4 headquarters, all but one (Becker) were Old Nazis. For at least 10, family or friendship connections had helped recruit them. They had respectable administrative, usually civil service careers, but they were also Nazis with good Nazi connections. Allers said "most people got in through connections. They would hear of the job as being 'attached to the Führer Chancellery' and that sounded good. Then of course these jobs carried extra pay; and it meant not having to go to the front." Material and ideal considerations were entwined.

Medical science was essential to T4's cover, authority, and procedures. University genetic, psychiatric, and anthropological research had converged upon a belief in the hereditary transmission of physical and mental characteristics (Müller-Hill, 1988). In German universities no great distance lay between heredity and race, and the regime gave researchers the funds to bridge it. Their commitment was primarily ideological in a professional sense: they believed in *racial science*. About five among this entire scientific community are known to have refused to comply. But one professor's daughter said, "What should he have done? He would have sold himself to the devil, in order to obtain money for his institute and his research." The temptations are still there. Colleagues at the University of California get large research grants to work on battlefield nuclear weapons. The German researchers were chosen by four top Nazi doctors for their standing in the profession and sympathy for Nazism and euthanasia. Of my 27 doctors who passed through T4, 18 had been Old Nazis, 4 others had joined before their 24th birthday, and 2 (Nitsche and Mauthe) were well known before 1933 as proponents of biomedical racism. This leaves only three probable Bandwagon Nazis. At least five had been in the Freikorps, though probably no others had been involved in violence before entering T4. But all were now in the SS.

The head doctor was Karl Brandt, born in 1904, the son of a policeman. He left Alsace in 1918 when it became French, and was later prevented by the French from joining Albert Schweitzer in French Africa. A fervent nationalist, he became a Nazi in 1932. He saw Nazism as "the avenger, the party of hope." His two heroes were Schweitzer and Hitler! Introduced to Hitler by his fiancee, a German swimming champion, he became a medical adviser in Hitler's entourage and was then offered the T4 position. He accepted because of ambition, veneration for Hitler, and a desire to join in the "collective revitalization" of Germany. Noted neither for cruelty nor for anti-Semitism, he was regarded as an idealist, an ethical Nazi, countering the influence of cruder Nazis in the project. Werner Heyde was one such. The son of a textile manufacturer in Polish Silesia, he enlisted in World War I at age 16 and then fought in the Freikorps. He was involved in the Kapp Putsch and other agitation. Asked by the Nazis to make a psychological assessment of Eicke in 1933, he pronounced him sane, no psychopath. He was an SS captain by 1936. He did part-time work in the camps, acquiring "wonderful research material," and was a Gestapo advisor, probably on torture methods. He was the doctor who killed most people at T4. His SD file also details his sexuality. He was traumatized as a 15-year-old when seduced by an older female relative and became homosexual. Perhaps this vulnerability helped him obey orders. Yet it was mainly commitment to extreme nationalism and biomedical racism that led him to kill.

Exercising mid-level authority were SS captains and lieutenants supervising T4 killing centers. Of 12, 10 had been career policemen and 10 had been Old Nazis or covert sympathizers (we can't always tell when policemen joined). They led the social environment of lower ranks, who mostly lived on site. The NCOs were also committed Nazis. They issued the essential drinks ration and organized the frequent parties. As we descend the hierarchy, information becomes less detailed. The lower nonmedical male staff (orderlies, cooks, chauffeurs, stokers, building tradesmen, and clerks) were working-class men with minimal education. All were already Nazi Party members and most were in the SS. A third (and over half of the NCOs) had previous violent activism. They had experienced more unemployment than any other group of perpetrators, and some had joined the party to get work. The female typists and nurses were the least likely to have Nazi records, though they were vetted, usually recruited by local Nazi bosses from their own networks. Some nurses were already working at the hospitals or homes before killing commenced and were selected by their superiors to stay on. So the women may have had more Nazi sympathies than the sparse files reveal.

Very few had prior knowledge of what T4 might involve. When told, they were often threatened that noncompliance would mean trouble, but their compliance seems to have been overdetermined by legimate authority. These were men and women of low status to whom Nazism had been kind. War crimes defendants in this sector were most likely to justify their actions in terms of their legality. This rationale was buttressed by their acceptance of medical authority, especially among nurses and orderlies. The state had declared these medical practices legitimate, and prestigious doctors were implementing them. These were general principles to hide behind, relieving psychological pressure.

I instance some of the men later, when discussing *Aktion Reinhard* camps. But Irmgard Huber was an Austrian domestic servant and then a nurse. She arrived at Hadamar Hospital in 1932, long before it was a killing center. She was active in Nazi women's organizations and had a long-term liaison with a

Nazi doctor. She was promoted over better-qualified nurses to the euthanasia project. She was troubled by having to kill Germans, though not Russians or Poles. Anna Katschenka came from a Viennese socialist background and never joined a Nazi organization. But she was divorced from a Jewish man and had a liaison with a Nazi doctor. Her postwar trial concluded that she was weak and easily led. Nurses' trained respect for doctors assisted their compliance. T4 most resembled Milgram's experiments (referred to in Chapter 1). The ideological authority of medical science and the personal authority of the white-coated doctor induced persons of low social status to murder.

This was not initially viewed as murder. T4 selected "hopeless" cases for whom "mercy killing" might be a "release." Their families often approved. Then the perpetrators became inured – and dependent on the bonuses this work paid. De Mildt (1996) emphasizes their careerism. Friedländer (1995: 187) concludes that they were "dull and unimaginative men and women" leading "conventional lives," though Burleigh (1994: 125) notes that those "at the sharp end were carefully selected for their proven brutality and ideological dedication." All these contrasting conclusions have merit. There were individuals of all these types, but they were bound together by hierarchy and comradeship. Hierarchy was entwined with Nazi medical authority, comradeship with an occupational community whose esprit de corps and social life were led by Old Nazis.

As T4 degenerated into killing of all patients, with no pretense of diagnosis, the veneer of science became stripped away. The doctors, nurses, orderlies, drivers, stokers, and clerks were now involved in continuous killing and faking of medical records. The older doctors are usually described as developing more qualms than ones trained only in a Nazi society. But qualms were overcome by a blend of inurement to routine, institutional loyalty, privileged careerism, and commitment to the regime. Many claimed at their trials that they had merely obeyed legal orders even if they were unpleasant and sometimes wrong: "I did my duty as a German official. God is my witness." For them to escape the pit of evil into which they were descending would have needed some countervailing social source of identity or ideology. This they lacked: profession and community were both Nazi-defined.

When T4 was formally wound up in 1941, some remained in the shadowy, wilder gassing program of mentally retarded persons, POWs, and political prisoners that continued throughout the war. But 97 T4 personnel went to staff the first *Aktion Reinhard* death camps – Belzec, Sobibor, and Treblinka. They were chosen for their commitment and skill; they were old hands, able to teach the ropes to new recruits into their occupational community. The death camps were in safe hands.

In my sample, 67 men served in the *Aktion Reinhard* camps. Two-thirds had been at T4. Thirty-one were prior Nazis who had also served at T4, and 11 more were prior Nazis who had served both at T4 and at other camps or the *Einsatzgruppen*. Only three were raw recruits. Burleigh (1994: 232) bluntly characterizes the transferees as "hardened psychopaths." The senior administrator was Dietrich Allers, from Schleswig-Holstein, the son of a prosecutor killed in the war. He joined the Nazis in 1932 at age 22, used family connections to get into T4, and remained an unrepentant Nazi after 1945. He says that the transferred staff could have backed out of what they knew would be mass killing of Jews: "they *were* asked. There *was* an element of choice." Allers later revealed a casual anti-Semitism during an interview: "the press, the banks, business; in Berlin all of it was in the hands of Jews. That wasn't right. There should have been *some* Germans" (Sereny, 1974: 60–90, 225–6). They kept at it throughout the war. After serving at the Polish death camps they were moved to other killing activities, ending the war staffing camps in Italy and Trieste.

Christian Wirth, the "savage Christian," was unusually brutal and vulgar for an SS colonel. He was the roving superviser of the euthanasia project, then of the *Action Reinhard* death camps. Most colleagues were appalled by him. Stangl, the commandant of Treblinka, disliked Wirth's contempt for "sentimental slobber" about euthanasia – it made him puke, Wirth would say. In fact, it was "doing away with useless mouths." Once Wirth arrived to investigate delays in preparing the Sobibor gas ovens. He shouted at Stangl and others for lax discipline. They must kill all Jews who didn't work properly: "If any of you don't like that, you can leave. But under the earth, not over it." Told that the gas chamber still didn't work, he said, "Right, we'll try it out now with those twenty-five work-Jews; get them in here." They were pushed in and gassed. Wirth lost his temper when the doors didn't shut properly. Eichmann shuddered at Wirth's "vulgar uneducated harsh" talk of "poisoning" Jews. Prisoners said that the SS men were terrified of him. Allers's wife, also in T4, described him as "a vulgar horrible man," "awful with his men." But Allers thought Wirth was just a Württemberger, "a rough lot who use coarse language and gestures," a "good soldier" chosen because "he was a tough sort of man." Indeed he was – a much-decorated NCO from World War I, an early Nazi, and a Gestapo officer who had been arraigned before the Stuttgart Landtag for atrocities. But, curiously, when later supervising camps supplying slave labor, he increased food rations and improved conditions. Was he any worse in his actions, as opposed to his language, than the prim Eichmann or the cautious Stangl? Wirth has attracted much horrified interest (e.g., Arad, 1987: 182–4; Goldhagen, 1996: 305–6; Sereny, 1974: 54, 80, 97, 110; Wistrich, 1982: 341–2).

Irmfried Eberl was the first Treblinka commandant. In the Nazi Party by 1931 at age 20, a full-time revolutionary during the illegal period in Austria, with a fiercely Nazi wife, he had been a doctor at T4. But he left dead bodies lying around Treblinka and was fired. Franz Stangl had moved from T4 to command Sobibor and now replaced him at Treblinka. Franz Reichleitner, a career police officer and an Old Nazi, replaced him at Sobibor. These three Austrians were selected by Wirth from among reliable Nazis known to him personally. Stangl was an efficient administrator. His soldier father beat his children but died when Stangl was 8. He qualified as a master weaver in a local factory but joined the Austrian police. "They drilled the feeling into us that everyone was against us: that all men were rotten." He volunteered for special political duties and received medals. In 1936 he probably secretly joined the Austrian Nazi Party and was assigned to special police duties in the absorption of Czechoslovakia and in the first steps against the Jews. He was absorbed into the Gestapo and the SS in 1939, renouncing the Catholic Church. His widow is unsure to what extent this reflected careerism or ideology (Sereny, 1974: 232–3). Stangl was too plain a man to be much of an ideologist. But for a policeman enjoying special assignments, Nazism seems to have resonated in his professional life.

Among the *Aktion Reinhard* NCOs was Kurt Franz, from the occupied Ruhr, the stepson of an extreme nationalist. He was a cook, in the Nazi Party in 1932 at age 18. He was trained at Buchenwald, then at T4, Belzec, and Treblinka, where he would command his huge dog to bite off prisoners' genitalia with the supposedly humorous words "Human, bite the dog." His photo album of Treblinka was captioned "the best years of my life." Willi Mentz was an ethnic German refugee from Poland. He worked as a laborer in the sawmill where his father was foreman. He joined the party in 1932 at age 28, though with little Nazi track record until assigned to T4 as a hospital estate worker. He did not kill but got used to seeing it. Transferred to Treblinka in 1941 he became one of the worst guards, called "Frankenstein," "an animal and a sadist." Gustav Münzberger, a Sudeten carpenter, joined a German nationalist front organization later absorbed into the SS. At T4 he was an assistant cook, marginal to the killings, but at Treblinka he drove prisoners to the gas chambers day in, day out, for over a year. Another guard said:

One of his jobs was to stand at the door to the gas chambers and drive them in. He had a whip of course. He did that, day after day. He was drunk most of the time. What else could he do? Could he have got out of that job? I don't know. I think finally he no longer cared – he drank.

Münzberger's son said, "My father? – I can quite imagine that he would have approached Treblinka with the same thoroughness with which he approached his carpentry at home; it was his principal quality as a craftsman" (Sereny, 1974: 221–5).

Gustav Wagner, from Vienna, joined the Nazi Party in 1931 at age 20. An activist, he was arrested but fled to Germany in 1934. He joined the SS, was posted to T4, and transferred to Sobibor, where he got the Iron Cross for his proficiency. Known as the "Human Beast," he killed even babies on a whim. "For him, torturing and killing was a pleasure. When he killed, he smiled." "Wagner didn't eat his lunch if he didn't kill daily. With an axe, shovel or even his hands. He had to have blood." He himself said, "I had no feelings.... It just became another job. In the evening we never discussed our work, but just drank and played cards." Karl Frenzel, "one of the most brutal" guards, with a "very loose" whip, had joined the Nazi Party and the SA in 1930 at age 19. At his trial he declared, "under the prevailing war conditions... I unfortunately believed that what was going on... was lawful. To my regret, I was then convinced of its necessity."

Survivors often distinguished between a few "decent" SS men, relaxing when no colleagues were around, a few "monsters," and most who just killed without much obvious feeling. One said Franz Suchomel (a Sudeten from T4) was "relatively decent. That doesn't mean Suchomel didn't beat us; all of them beat us." They had a "deep fundamental indifference" deriving from "their incredible power" and from their "inner demoralization" at the evil they did. Some could falter. Stangl's wife says Ludwig blurted out to her: "The Jews are being done away with... with gas... fantastic numbers of them." She remembered: "He went on about how awful it was and then he said, in the same maudlin way he had, 'But we are doing it for our Fuhrer. For him we sacrifice ourselves to do this – we obey his orders.... Can you imagine what would happen if the Jews ever got hold of us?'" When Stangl arrived home, his wife questioned him. Stangl offered a typical officer's rationalization: "My work is purely administrative.... Oh yes, I see it. But I don't *do* anything to anybody" (Sereny, 1974: 136, 178–82).

In the death camps the killing process was permeated with sadism – rape when desire swelled, beatings for the slightest dissent or on whim, tearing out gold fillings, stripping prisoners naked, bludgeoning them toward the killing zone with rifle butts, battering noisy babies against walls. The SS officially distinguished between killing for "historical necessity" or "political motives" and motives that were "selfish, sadistic or sexual." If a guard killed Jews because he actually *wanted* to kill them, this was officially considered abnormal, characteristic not of Aryans but of an inferior race (Buchheim et al., 1968: 349–63; Hilberg, 1978: 214; Littman, 1983: 44). On the fringes some kept their eyes shut. The gas van involved mechanics from SS motor pools. Their memos reveal an attempt to maintain technical composure amid descent into genocide, developing euphemistic language: dying people attempting to beat down the back door became a "cargo" problem; excrement, urine, vomit, and menstrual blood became "thicker filth" and "thin fluid" that unfortunately produced rusting and cleaning problems (Browning, 1985: chap. 3). But in the camps, violence was overwhelming. A Sobibor guard said, "I cannot exclude any member of the Sobibor camp staff of taking part in the extermination operation. We were a 'blood brotherhood gang' in a foreign land" (Arad, 1987: 198).

CAREER ROUTE FOUR: LAW ENFORCEMENT
TO THE *EINSATZGRUPPEN*

Genocide escalated in 1941. About 6,000 men rotated through the core units of the *Einsatzgruppen*, supported by 15,000 strong police auxiliary battalions, flanked by 25,000 Waffen-SS troops. Combined, they killed over a million Jews. Not all the troops killed – probably not the radio operators, the motorcycle riders, the desk officers, or the female clerks. But most men were rotated through the execution squads. In some units, all were required to be present at shootings – bound together as comrades by *Bluttkit*, blood cement (Arendt, 1965: 105, 141; Hilberg, 1978: 189–96, 214–18).

Virtually none of them had volunteered in order to kill Slavs or Jews. They were suddenly informed of the task waiting them. Reitlinger (1968) believes even Himmler's own staff – men like Berger, Wolff, Lorenz, and Schellenberg – were largely unprepared for genocide, being "amateurish, muddled men, not without repulsion for their tasks... slightly cranks and slightly misfits, ambitious, idealist." Hilberg (1978: 649) sees the officers drawn to the SS by mixed nationalism and careerism. They then got assignments leading them gradually into the murder zone. He says every lawyer in the SS was presumed suitable for the *Einsatzgruppen*, every finance expert for death camp administration. But they were also committed Nazis. Of my 311 *Einsatzgruppen* men, only 35 were raw recruits (including 21 career policemen), 76 had merely been Nazi or SS members, 6 had been only in the Waffen-SS, 144 had been Nazis and policemen, and 48 were Nazis and had served in a camp or at T4. Police experience figured importantly among all ranks, while experience as government prosecutors was also common among officers.

Senior officers were selected by Himmler and Heydrich. Almost all the senior *Einsatzgruppen* officers had entered the Nazi Party, the SA, or the SS at the earliest moment they could, usually at university. Most then worked in the professions, especially law, or in the Ministry of the Interior. They were marked out as an elite destined for higher things. Their violence had previously been largely rhetorical, but they did not want to sit on the sidelines. They wanted Nazi careers, and that required action. They proved themselves in the *Einsatzgruppen* and then moved up. Virtually all the top 400 leaders of the RSHA toward the end of the war had served there (Wildt, 2002).

Otto von Ohlendorf was born in 1907 near Hanover to a secure bourgeois family. He joined the SA in 1925, while still at school, and the SS the next year. After obtaining a law doctorate, he became an academic sociologist, and in 1936 economics adviser to the SD. His conversations with Himmler's Finnish doctor (Kersten, 1956: 206–17) indicate an intellectual rather than a man of action, favoring a "third way" economic policy between "the big business outlook" of Goering and Ley's "Bolshevik collectivism." He believed societies should be based on races as "natural communities" but denounced German brutality against Ukrainians and boasted of having Crimean Tartars as friends. Himmler mocked him as the self-righteous "Galahad of National Socialism." He had no experience in violence before 1941. Like Biberstein (a former Protestant minister), he was felt to need toughening up. He delayed obeying orders to join an *Einsatzgruppe* but was stung by peers reproaching him for cowardice into accepting a command. He ordered the deaths of thousands of Judeo-Bolsheviks but objected if his men enjoyed the executions. He repented when on trial at Nuremberg, though the effect was spoiled by a letter to his wife in which he asked: "What else could we have done when confronted with demons at work, engaged in a struggle against us?"

The Weinman brothers, Ernst and Erwin, were born in Tübingen in the Catholic south; their father was killed in World War I. They became Nazis while students. Ernst became a dentist, Erwin a doctor. Ernst closed his practice to become the Nazi mayor of Tübingen. Erwin closed his practice to join the SS security police. Both were later promoted to become higher SS and police officers. Dr. Alfred Filbert (Dicks, 1972: 204–27, "case-study PF") was born in the occupied Ruhr, the son of an army officer turned postal employee, a Nazi himself. He joined the party and the SS in 1932 while a law student. After obtaining his doctorate, he became a prosecutor, then an SD intelligence officer from 1935. He was rapidly promoted to lieutenant colonel and was at the Wannsee Conference. He set an example by leading the shooting and ensured that all his men killed, threatening "hard consequences" if anyone showed mercy. He would not allow his men to use the same eating utensils as any Jew. An officer on his staff later sobbed, "I have allowed myself to be abused as a hangman's serf"; another said "If anyone *now* tells me he was no anti-semite, he is in my eyes just a bastard." These commanders all had to report daily to headquarters. Their reports were permeated by racial slurs against Jews, Slavs, "asocials," and "inferiors."

Walter Blume is a contrast, a weak and then a wild commander, causing concern to the hierarchy. He was the son of a Dortmund schoolteacher, a Nazi by 1933, probably earlier. After obtaining a doctorate in law he was posted to the Dortmund Gestapo and rose to a senior position at the RSHA. But he proved poor at making decisions and was squeamish about shooting women and children. His fellow officers described him as "weak and bureaucratic." He was recalled to Berlin and then sent as chief of police to Athens, a peripheral posting. He was known there for his adoration of Hitler and his unimaginative, bureaucratic habits and was called "a dogged bloodhound." When defeat loomed in mid-1944, Blume grew wilder, urging a scorched earth policy, his "Chaos Thesis." But by now the Foreign Office Nazis and Greek collaborators had more influence up the hierarchy and got him recalled (Mazower, 1993: 231–4). There were limits. Killing was supposed to be rigorous and systematic, not an indiscriminate suicidal *Götterdammerung*.

Lower officers, NCOs, and rankers were initially drawn from prewar SS volunteers. Most also seemed committed to their task. Sergeant Helmut Rauca was a career policeman and an Old Nazi. He impressed his superiors with his bearing and respect for order. He had written to them, "It is my aspiration to be active in the National Socialist spirit in a responsible position within the Security Police." He served with murderous distinction in ghetto liquidations. At his trial, witnesses called him "ruthlessly dedicated, a true believer in Hitler's dogma, a convinced member of the master race" (Littman, 1983: 15–16, 161). Max Krahner was a Rhinelander who worked in his father's tanning workshop, an Old Nazi who was in the Gestapo from 1937. He had volunteered for the *Einsatzgruppe* and shot 50 Russian civilians near Minsk, saying, "I was always a nationalist and wanted to fight communism." The Austrian Sergeant-Major Felix Landau had a Jewish stepfather. He was expelled from his Catholic school for Nazi agitation and trained as a cabinet maker but became a career soldier. An Old Nazi, he participated in the Austrian Nazi coup of 1934 and was imprisoned. On his release in 1937 he joined the German Gestapo, with which he served in the Polish campaign of 1939. His *Einsatzgruppe* diary agonizes mainly about his girlfriend's failure to write. He justifies shooting Jews in terms of their prior crimes, though he does say, "I have little inclination to shoot defenceless people – even if they are only Jews. I would far rather good honest open combat." But he was "completely unmoved. No pity, nothing." He calls a Wehrmacht officer seeking to protect Jews "the worst kind of state enemy." "Who could have thought such a thing possible? That's no National Socialist." Lieutenant Karl Kretschmer told his children that since the Jews had started the war, they deserved what they got – "it is a weakness not to be able to stand the sight of dead people; the best way of overcoming it is to do it more often. Then it becomes a habit.... Our faith in the Führer fulfils us and gives us the strength to carry out our difficult and thankless task." The two Maurer brothers, Wilhelm and Johann, were ethnic Germans from Poland, conscripted in 1939 into the Polish army against Germany. They were picked out of a POW camp to help the German cause. Their language skills in Polish and Ukrainian got them assigned to the SD. Though they were not apparently Nazi Party members, their diligence got them promoted to sergeant, one training and leading Ukrainian auxiliaries. Both participated willingly in mass shootings. Careerism plus acceptance of the doctrine of German racial superiority seems to have motivated them.

But expansion then brought middle-aged reservists and wounded soldiers from the front, given only a month's training (including ideological instruction in the Judeo-Bolshevik-partisan). Some managed. Sergeant Magill was a cavalryman, favored by the SS for his horsemanship. He was eventually assigned to the *Einsatzgruppe*. Like other sportsmen favored by this would-be muscular regime he was sucked in, seemingly too grateful for the attention to protest. Lieutenant Hans Ritz, from East Prussia, was the son of a liberal schoolteacher. He was a Hitler Youth officeholder and joined the Nazi Party in 1937 at age 18. He was drafted in 1939 but discharged due to sickness. He was drafted again in 1943 into the Kharkhov SD. On arrival, his superior officer urged him to "Show us what you can do." "Not wanting to create a bad impression, I took a machine pistol from an SS man and shot the prisoners." Thereafter he killed as required.

Others baulked. Teleprinter engineer Kiebach was not a Nazi and had no training for murder. He could fire only five times before feeling sick. He stood down and was laughed at for weakness by his comrades. Major Franz Lechthaler was a career policeman, age 51, from the Rhineland, not a Nazi. Promotion had come slowly, since he was believed to have leftist sympathies and made anti-Hitler jokes. Ordered to kill Minsk Jews, he protested. Overruled by his superiors, he took evasive action, assigning the shooting to Lithuanian support troops and removing himself from the scene. The ranker Hans-Ulrich Werner killed but said, "It's almost impossible to imagine what nerves of steel it took to carry out that dirty work down there. It was horrible." Gas van drivers refused to finish off gasping victims, so the officer swore and did it himself. A war correspondent confirms the varied responses: "I saw SD personnel weeping because they could not cope mentally with what was going on. Then again I encountered others who kept a score-sheet of how many people they had sent to their death...some had already committed suicide....Who today can determine which were those who wept as they carried out their duties and which were the ones who kept a score-sheet?" (Klee, 1991: 62, 67, 72, 129, 169–71). These had become a more varied group of murderers than in the camps.

ORDINARY KILLERS? AUXILIARY POLICE BATTALION 101

We know most about Reserve Police Battalion 101. In Poland between July 1942 and November 1943, its 550 men shot and killed 38,000 Jews, plus many Poles and Russians. They forcibly deported another 50,000 Jews to certain death at Treblinka. The average policeman killed 100 victims, mostly in shooting volleys by groups of 10 to 20 policemen. Since they were not skilled marksmen, the policemen were sometimes up to their knees in writhing bodies, covered in blood and excrement. This churned their stomachs and loosened their bowels, inducing nightmares and shattering nerves. They "consumed amazing quantities of alcohol" to dull the senses (Hilberg, 1978: 218, 249; Höss et al., 1978: 95).

Police battalions were initially formed for local duties in Germany. Prewar recruits were volunteers, but wartime recruits were conscripts, older than army recruits. Their training was minimal, and they were not trained at all for mass murder. The battalion has been analyzed by Browning (1993) and Goldhagen (1996). They say that most of the rank-and-file were Hamburg conscripts, with an average age of 36. Of the 100 whose marital status is known, 99 were married and 72 had children. The most common previous occupation had been policeman, and most of the others had been workers. Browning believes these ordinary men murdered, primarily because they were fearful and conformist killers, Goldhagen believes these ordinary Germans killed because they were anti-Semitic bigots.

This was not in battle. They were safely behind the front line, and only one policeman was killed by partisans. Battlefield anger did not motivate them. Why did they *continue* killing routinely? The question could be asked of all the 15,000 men of the 30 police battalions. This was mass murder – mass victims, mass perpetrators. When ordered to begin the first shooting, the commander, Major Trapp, had palpable qualms and unexpectedly offered his men the chance to be excused. Only 12 stepped forward and were assigned elsewhere, receiving no punishment. On later atrocity occasions, with more time for thought, Browning (1993) says 10–20 percent of the battalion would absent themselves, sometimes officially, sometimes unofficially. They would lag behind, disappear, or shoot to miss. A few hinted at ethical reasons or cited Communist or socialist sympathies or said they had no career aspirations in the police. More referred to physical revulsion or weakness and squeamishness. But few put in for transfers. A man might occasionally recognize a victim, a former neighbor, work colleague, or comrade from World War I. They had to shoot Jews who had spent weeks as their servants. So they would ask someone else to do the killing, or they would do it suddenly, in the back, to "spare" the victim. This is low-level pity indeed.

At the other extreme, Goldhagen (1996) cites policemen murdering with obvious relish. Photographs of "Jew hunts" resemble carefree country picnics. He claims that most perpetrators were driven by "eliminationist anti-semitism," though this seems overly simple. Browning says most had only imbibed a casual anti-Semitism that in wartime could strengthen into an "image of the enemy." Haberer (2001) says of German policemen in Belarus that only a few were ferocious anti-Semites, balanced by the few who refused orders, helped Jews, or shot wide. Most complied with authority after initial hesitancy (cf. Birn, 1998: 122–8). Browning's policemen needed to avoid postwar prosecution and so claimed that "I only obeyed orders," offloading all Nazi or anti-Semitic zeal onto a handful of officers and NCOs described as "brutal," "ruthless," "a hundred and ten percent Nazi," given nicknames like "the poisoned dwarf" and "Slugger." Asked why they had killed, most had difficulty replying. Some said they had not thought much about it, others that their own shooting did not matter since the Jews were going "to meet their fate anyway." Some admitted they had shown weakness or cowardice: they should have stood up and refused. They only occasionally admitted racism or anti-Semitism. One recalled: "The Jew was not acknowledged by us to be a human being." Yet genuine expressions of sympathy for Jews (or Poles) are lacking.

Battalion 101 appeared in a state of shock after the first massacre. Unusually, it had been of men, women, and children together. There had been no inurement through the initial killing of young men only – who might plausibly be partisans. It was traumatic, and no one would talk about it afterward. They tried to pretend it hadn't happened and drank heavily that night. Yet, like other perpetrators, the policemen became somewhat inured, learning to make their killing methods swifter and cleaner, and delegating more of the killing to foreign auxiliary troops. There were limits. An officer described as a "fanatical Nazi" brought his pregnant wife along to watch the men shooting Jews. She seemed to enjoy it, but the men were appalled. They felt outraged that a pregnant woman was viewing the terrible things they were doing.

We must also situate the men institutionally, within their isolated, cohesive, and disciplined military formations. Could they have refused an order to murder? Were they simply fearful killers? The postwar West German war crimes prosecution service attempted to answer the question definitively. After a search of their extensive records, they said they found no case "in which refusal to carry out an order would have entailed an objective danger for the life and limb of the recipient of that order." This might have constituted an acceptable legal defense against war crimes charges (Rueckert, 1979: 80–1). Thus some say that Germans asked to commit murder could refuse without serious consequences (Buchheim et al., 1968: 390–5; Goldhagen, 1996: 278–9). Bach-Zalewski himself said that refusal might involve "a certain disciplinary punishment. A danger to one's life, however, was not at all involved."

At least three *Kommandoführer* did refuse. Ernst-Boje Ehlers refused at the outset and was transferred to an office job. Erwin Schulz, from Berlin, was a conservative Nazi, spying within the police from 1931, declaring himself openly as a Nazi in 1933. He was assigned to the SD in 1935 but spoke up against *Kristallnacht*. He helped establish the first shadowy *Einsatzgruppen* in Austria and Czechoslovakia in 1938. In 1941 he was head of training at RSHA and criticized students returning from shootings in Russia. His reward was to be posted there himself. He obeyed and supervised killings between July and August 1941. Then he refused and was transferred back to his old position at the Berlin Police Academy, where he stayed (Klee, 1991: 82, 86; *Trials of the War Criminals*, 1946: Einsatzgruppen case Part IV: "Affidavit of Schulz"). Otto Rasch, the son of an East Prussian bricklayer, was an Old Nazi, in the Gestapo since 1936. He was initially a conscientious *Einsatzgruppe* commander, but drew the line at the massive Kiev shootings and refused to participate. None of the three was punished, nor was any known officer. Most probably knew of Paragraph 47 of the German Army Code, allowing them to resist illegal or immoral orders. Of course, refusal would destroy their careers. But noncompliance may be more serious for rankers. The mere "possibility of injury" is not an acceptable legal defense, but it might nonetheless deter most of us. As rational choice theorists remind us, we may be terrified by only an outside chance of being killed. We do have cases of credible threats. Hartheim hospital staff were given a welcoming speech by Christian Wirth. He explained the work and then concluded, "Above all, this means silence on pain of the death penalty. Whoever does not keep silent will go to a concentration camp or will be shot." Nurses, orderlies, and secretaries say that Wirth repeatedly threatened them with the alternatives "concentration camp or shooting" (Horwitz, 1990: 70–9). *Einsatzgruppen* commanders Filbert and Stahlecker also threatened their men. SS Lieutenant Hartl, who refused to command a firing squad, said:

very many men of the lower rank under the then authoritarian regime and under such strict and tough commanders as Stahlecker never even entertained the thought of giving expression to their inner conflict, fearing privately that a refusal to take part in a shooting would have had very serious consequences. In my opinion, amongst the lower ranks there was not so much an objective necessity to obey orders, more of a subjective one. (Klee et al., 1991: 84–6)

This is surely correct. Ordinary soldiers in most armies are unaware or skeptical of their constitutional rights. Reluctant rankers rarely asked for transfers; rather, they asked to stand down. One *Kommandoführer*, Dr. Martin Sandberger, was himself ambivalent. He was a convinced Old Nazi, yet a career policeman with some moral rectitude. He had been attracted to the SD by its "idealistic intellectual image," but *Kristallnacht* made him regret this. But he answered the *Einsatzgruppe* call and dutifully did the dirty work. His offer to his men was double-edged: "if a man does not do his duty here, I will transfer him home," but then he added, "this would not exactly help us in our future careers." One man said he complied so that "my chances of promotion would not be spoilt." Others testified that those standing down would risk being shamed in front of all the others for "cowardice," "uselessness for "tough action" or for being "not as hard as an *SS-Mann* ought to have been." Fear merged into careerist, disciplined, and comradely motives.

Corporal Lüdke (DL in Dicks, 1972) exemplifies this, though in a camp setting. Born in Danzig, the son of a master joiner, a salesman for a Jewish firm, he joined the Nazi Party and the SS in 1934 for conventional patriotic reasons but was soon involved in secretive Nazi police work. After Danzig was liberated in 1939, he was assigned to a concentration camp. He repeatedly asked for transfer to active duty but was refused. He was an orderly giving lethal injections and gas "disinfections." At his postwar trial he turned prosecution witness and said that he had hated his terrible duties. Fearing retaliation, he would not openly refuse orders. "I had tried to be a hard and loyal SS man," ferocious "when others were around." But his nerve broke during a shooting session and he collapsed. There were no bad consequences. He was transferred to a quiet back room job, since all could see that he had reached his breaking point. His lack of moral courage had sucked him in for a year; he was afraid of his superiors and of his colleagues calling him a "sissy." Fear merged into conformism.

We return to Battalion 101. Two men testified that "one could keep away from the executions . . . if one did not feel up to the task." But to do more was risky. Since few did opt out, they could be accommodated quietly by their officers, who wished to appear effective commanders. Had the objectors been numerous enough to threaten the mission, the SS hierarchy would have surely begun reprisals, as in other military mutinies. The policemen had reason to be afraid – if they believed their comrades would also refuse. This was a difficult call for them to make – and for us to make about them. They certainly lacked moral courage, but so might we.

Goldhagen (1996) writes as if the wishes of ordinary policemen sum up to the behavior of a police battalion. This is too individualist and "democratic" an assumption. As Hartl noted, these units were coercive military formations, under SS orders "from the Fuhrer himself." Browning has more sociological awareness, stressing hierarchical and especially comradely pressures. Shirkers were shamed with weakness, and if a man shot to miss, his comrades had to kill more (1993: 185). Buchheim et al. (1968: 343, 386) agrees: "Considerable courage is required to make oneself 'unacceptable' to one's social environment and sever one's links with it." SS comradeship mitigated harsh discipline, bringing warmth and "a minimum moral subsistence level." Shame at not killing countered guilt at killing. Officers recognized this. Ohlendorf forbade individual shootings by his *Einsatzgruppe*, "so that the men who were to perform the executions were not faced with the task of making individual decisions" (*Trials of the War Criminals*, 1946: VIII, "affidavit of Ohlendorf").

Moreover, Police Battalion 101 was not entirely ordinary. Thirty-eight percent of the policemen were Nazi Party members, double the membership level among all German men at this time. The higher the rank, the more the Nazis. Though Major Trapp was a career policeman and not a Nazi, his two captains were zealous party and SS members. At least five of the seven lieutenants were party members, though none belonged to the SS. The 32 NCOs were all career policemen. Twenty-two of them were party members, and seven were also in the SS. The main officers, NCOs, and the more experienced rankers were career policemen: 20 percent had several years' career experience of policing in a fascist state where police work was becoming more violent, unrestrained by the law (Burleigh, 2000: 158–86). And the worse the complicity in genocide, the more these tendencies appeared. Ten of the 13 persons from the battalion who were actually convicted of war crimes were Nazi members (two Old Nazis, four Young Nazis, and three Bandwagon Nazis). Seven of the 13 were career policemen (only one had served before the Nazi seizure of power), 2 had been conscripted into the police in 1939, and only 4 had been conscripted in 1941. Only six were actually from the Hamburg region; three were from Saxony, one was an

Austrian, and three were from threatened borders. The Austrian had been in the Nazi rising of 1934 and at least four had served in the Polish campaign of 1939, when German police battalions had already killed many civilians. Even here – where recruitment into genocide had been somewhat haphazard – the hierarchy and the experienced core were mostly Nazis or initiates in violence, ordering and socializing the rawer recruits into genocide.

Indeed, says Birn (1998: 117–20), Battalion 101 was probably less Nazi, less steeped in violence than other police battalions. The "300 Level" battalions were formed only from career policemen and volunteers, and several had served as whole units in Poland in 1939. In Battalion 309, of 14 men charged with war crimes, 13 were career policemen and 8 were Nazi members. Dean (2000: 64) says that of the German policemen in Belarus and the Ukraine, about half had been vetted by Himmler, while half were more ordinary, older policemen. Remember also that the police battalions comprised less than half of the *Einsatzgruppen*. The core were specially selected units, though the largest numbers came from the Waffen-SS, inflicting and sustaining very high losses at the front. On occasion these soldiers also perpetrated massacres of prisoners. Those on the Western Front (of British troops and French colonial troops in 1940, and of Canadians and Americans in 1944) are the best documented. There were also regular transfers between the Waffen-SS, the *Einsatzgruppen*, and the camp staff, which increased their brutality (Stein, 1966: 76–8, 258–64; Sydnor, 1977: 106–17, 313–42). Many of these troops were not virgins in violence.

In late summer 1941 the Nazi leadership suddenly needed many more perpetrators who could shoot, too many to be individually selected. It sought reliable men through collective selection. It chose Waffen-SS units plus reserve police battalions, since both were already bent to the will of the Nazi state, had already killed civilians in Poland, and were likely to contain a disproportionate number of Nazis. This was not an ordinary bunch of Germans. Then they were given a more singular purpose by hierarchical and comradely pressures. Casual anti-Semitism was transformed into hatred and dehumanization of a wartime enemy to help remove moral inhibitions against killing unarmed human beings. Though some killed enthusiastically or grimly, propelled by ideology, few could kill without physical or moral qualms. Then alcohol kicked in.

These mixed motives helped 50,000 Germans shoot a million victims. But the Nazi elite came to doubt they could finish the job. A psychiatrist with the *Einsatzgruppen* estimated that 20 percent of the troops suffered from psychological "decomposition," half from the "unpleasantness" of their task, half from moral qualms. An officer testified:

After the first wave of shootings it emerged that the men, particularly the officers, could not cope with the demands made on them. Many abandoned themselves to alcohol, many suffered nervous breakdowns and psychological illnesses; for example, we had suicides and there were cases where some men cracked up and shot wildly around them and completely lost control. When this happened Himmler issued an order stating that any man who no longer felt able to take the psychological stresses should report to his superior officer. These men were to be released from their current duties and would be detailed for other work back home. As I recall Himmler even had a convalescent home set up close to Berlin for such cases. . . . In my view this . . . was a trick . . . for after all which officer or SS-Mann would have shown himself up in such a way? Any officer who had declared that he was too weak to do such things would have been considered unfit to be an officer. (Klee et al., 1991: 81–2, 111)

But Himmler did take note. He searched for a killing method that would not demoralize German troops. The mass shootings were abandoned in favor of gas and death camps manned mainly by non-Germans. This is the clearest indication that Goldhagen exaggerates his case that ordinary German *Einsatzgruppen* murdered enthusiastically because they were bigots. They murdered for more varied motives and under social pressures, resulting in damaged psyches. Of course, Jews and bandits died, just the same.

CAREER ROUTE SIX: THE WEHRMACHT

The Wehrmacht probably perpetrated the most killing of civilians by ordinary Germans – perhaps a million all told. Since these killings were not routinized, very few perpetrators have been identified. German scholarship now emphasizes the army's role in genocide, stressing an elective affinity between the armed forces and the Nazis (Gerlach, 1999; Heer, 1997). As my book *Fascists* shows, Nazism resonated strongly among those with military-bureaucratic backgrounds. As in many modern wars, soldiers were also quick to pick up racist stereotypes of the enemy. In 1939 German soldiers' letters home demonstrate this in relation to Poles and Jews. Both were described as *Untermenschen*. "Polish dogs" behaved in an "un-European," even "inhuman" way. Jews were termed "enemies." This did not routinely lead to murder, since the soldiers did not expect to act upon their prejudices and the army punished atrocities (Rossino, 1997). This was similar to the attitudes and behavior of U.S. troops in the Pacific campaign (as Dower, 1986, notes). Many officers, schooled by older rules of war, were unhappy at *Einsatzgruppen* activities in the Polish campaign, though this was partly because they considered them militarily superfluous, since the Polish army was collapsing anyway.

By 1941 Hitler had purged the High Command and declared that martial law overrode the military courts. Nazis were now in charge. In the early days of the Russian campaign army resistance persisted. A counterintelligence colonel wrote in December 1941, "In all cases of extended conversations with officers, they asked me about the shootings of Jews without my having brought it up. I have had the impression that the shooting of Jews, of prisoners and also of the commissars was rejected by the officer corps nearly unanimously" (Hoffman, 1988: 132). Yet most squeamish officers chose a middle way out of their dilemma, handing prisoners over to the SS rather than either protecting or killing them themselves. A few did refuse to hand them over, but further High Command orders "improved" the situation and ensured a more "pleasant relationship," said *Einsatzgruppen* reports (Arad, 1989: 211–12, 218–20). The Nazi General Reichenau reminded officers that the war was against the "Jewish-Bolshevist system" threatening Germany. The soldier must understand "the necessity for harsh but just counter-measures against Jewish subhumanity." Partisan "uprisings were always instigated by Jews." General von Manstein proclaimed that the Jew was the liaison between the Red Army and partisans. When some generals still refused to execute orders to kill Russian POWs, a debate was arranged. General Reinecke argued that this was not a war between states and armies, but between the ideologies of National Socialism and Bolshevism "to the death." Soviet prisoners could not expect the same treatment as those on the Western front: "Bolshevist subhumanity" was to be "annihilated." Colonel Lahousen (not a Nazi) dissented, arguing that executions carried out in front of the troops impaired their morale and deterred Russians from surrendering, thus costing German lives. Admiral Canaris had warned him not to try humanitarian arguments. Lahousen lost the debate (*Trials of the War Criminals*, 1946: VIII, "Affidavit of Lahousen").

Hitler continued to dismiss generals who dissented, while German soldiers soon agreed that this was a war of annihilation against a very ruthless and formidable enemy. Bartov (1985, 1991) says Nazification of officers and men intensified throughout the war as casualties grew and the age of recruits lessened. In 1944 29 percent of officers were Nazi Party members compared to only 16 percent of the German middle classes as a whole. Nazi officers were also more educated. Racism permeated routine orders: "in the political commissar we encounter the Asiatic depravity of the entire Red system" or "Bolshevism has raised Russian youth not to carry on an idea, but rather to criminality. Its means of battle are aberrations of the Asiatic brain" (Heer, 1997: 88). Bartov (1991) says that only strongly socialist or Communist backgrounds provided an antidote to racism and fuhrer worship among younger soldiers. Unlike 1939, license was given to kill, rape, and loot Slav and Jewish civilians without punishment, though all other breaches of discipline were treated ruthlessly. The high casualty rate also weakened the primary group as an independent force for socialization.

Faith in the fuhrer remained undiminished to the end. The officers plotting against Hitler in 1944 knew they could not rely on support from a single army unit. Soldiers' letters home became more racist. Russians were termed "cannibalized heaps of soldiers" and "uncultivated multi-raced men." The Wehrmacht was fighting to dam the "Asiatic-Bolshevik" flood, defending humanity against a demonic enemy. When they saw starving captives killing each other to grab the inadequate scraps of food tossed to them, this seemed to confirm their "subhumanity." Sergeant Fuchs wrote home to his wife, "Hardly ever do you see the face of a person who seems rational and intelligent... the wild, half-crazy look in their eyes makes them look like imbeciles" (Bartov, 1994: 128).

Not all of this was directly due to Nazi racism. I accept Hull's (forthcoming) argument that modern German militarism had come to embrace a more ruthless "total" warfare "to the death." This was an extremely callous war. The Wehrmacht High Command increasingly enjoined brutal means against any signs of dissent from any civilian population, whether Aryans or not. Here is Field Marshal Wilhelm Keitel instructing an Italian general on how to deal with Greek defiance: "issue urgent instructions to crush this emerging banditry most brutally. In German experience, for instance in Norway, it helped to adopt such a ruthless approach from the start. And should a village be burned down without justification, that does no harm either – the word of a fast and tough strike is passed around, and helps too." In Nazi eyes, Norwegians were fellow Nordics and Greeks had founded European civilization, yet both should be treated brutally. Keitel was a Nazi, but he was also acting like the more ruthless and callous generals throughout history. In 1944 the Wehrmacht in Greece even turned most brutally against their former Axis allies after Italy left the war. On Cefalonia almost 5,000 Italian soldiers were killed by firing squads after they had surrendered (Mazower, 1993: 146–7, 150).

Most Balkan atrocities were committed by order of the High Command (Browning, 1985: chap. 2; Hilberg, 1978: 433–42; Mazower, 1993: 155–218; Steinberg, 1990). Surprised by fierce partisan resistance, the army launched reprisals against civilians with troops often brutalized by experience on the Eastern Front. Field Marshal Wilhelm List, not a Nazi and an early moderate on the Eastern Front, was by now ferocioius. The Serbs were "hotblooded and... cruel." "The individual in Serbia is obviously like every other peasant, under normal conditions, but as soon as differences arise, then caused by the hot blood in their veins, the cruelty caused by hundreds of years of Turkish domination erupts." His Austrian subordinate, General Franz Böhme, said this was "the country in which German blood flowed in 1914 through the treachery of Serbs, men and women. You are avengers of these dead. An intimidating example must be set for the whole of Serbia." Most of these Wehrmacht regiments were Austrians, whom Hitler believed were best suited to pacify the Balkans (Bukey, 1992: 221–2). A general explained that they had inherited the Habsburg contempt for the "nonhistoric" peoples of the empire, including Serbs (Steinberg, 1990: 37). It was an Austrian quartermaster who first suggested that 100 Serbs be shot for every German soldier killed, 50 for each wounded. If possible, the unit suffering the losses should do the shootings, encouraging the motive of revenge. As usual in guerrilla warfare, they could rarely identify the actual partisans. Böhme's staff selected "all communists, all those suspected as such, all Jews, and a certain number of nationalist and democratically-inclined inhabitants." Gypsies were routinely added, "criminals and so forth" occasionally. SS Colonel Turner, trying to get local authorities to deport them, was delighted that the army was shooting them instead. He reported, "Serbia only country in which Jewish question and Gypsy question solved." A few officers warned that if the wrong Serbs or Greeks were executed, more locals would become partisans. But on Crete, General Student ordered "Revenge Operations" against the local population who had resisted the German invasion. He ordered "1) Shootings; 2) Forced Levies; 3) Burning down villages; 4) Extermination of the male population of the entire region." The High Command offered the troops judicial immunity while they "exterminated this plague." Use "any means, even against women and children, provided they are conducive to success." Over 1,000 Greek villages were destroyed (Mazower, 1993: 173, 176, 183).

Fairly ordinary officers were caught up in such brutality. Kurt Waldheim's postwar prominence as UN Secretary General and Austrian president gives a unique glimpse of one army lieutenant. The exposure of his past does not reveal anything comparable to the atrocities of most SS men detailed here. Nonetheless (despite his denials), Waldheim must have been present during revenge beatings and murders during 1942–4. The son of an Austrian school administrator, he was a student in Vienna, where he joined the Nazi student union and the SA (during the illegal period). He volunteered for the Wehrmacht in 1936 at age 18 but was drafted only in 1939, becoming an intelligence officer. The Yugoslav government's file compiled on Waldheim in 1947 (before he became prominent) cited eyewitness testimony that he helped organize "murder" and "hostage executions," though not pulling the trigger himself. Army records list him as assigned to "special tasks," which his division's reports explained were "final liquidation" of "subhumans" carried out "without pity or mercy" because "only a cold heart can command what needs to be commanded." Most victims were not Jews but Serb and Greek villagers. His own reports mention cleansings and the familiar killing of many partisans with suspiciously few weapons (739 dead, 63 weapons). He was decorated by the Croatian fascists (so were many others). He went on brief leave in 1942 to finish his doctoral dissertation on a 19th-century pan-German nationalist. In it he wrote, "In consequence of the current great conflict of the Reich with the non-European world, in magnificent collaboration of all the peoples of Europe under the leadership of the Reich, the way is being prepared against...the danger from the east. The realization of the [Reich] is the rational calling of Germany....Europe has fallen through Germany, but it is through Germany that it must be resurrected" (Ashman & Wagman, 1988: chap. 4). Waldheim was probably an idealist Nazi without previous entrapment in violence. A combination of such Nazism and inurement to army tactics of exemplary repression must have dispelled the moral qualms of many of his generation of young army officers.

Many were unhappy. In Yugoslavia, Austrian soldiers developed "psychological blocks" after reflecting alone at night after a mass killing. In Greece, soldiers who had killed all the villagers of Komeno went very quiet afterward. "Most of the comrades were very depressed. Almost none agreed with the action." Some protested afterward. An NCO shouted at his fervently Nazi officer, "Herr Oberleutnant, just remember, that's the last time I take part in something like that. That was a Schweinerei [(disgrace)] which had nothing to do fighting a war." A lieutenant said he "felt sick...such an operation was unworthy of a German soldier." But they stopped their protests when an officer screamed at them to obey, threatening reprisals if they did not act with "necessary severity." The Corfu Wehrmacht commander, Emil Jaeger, tried determinedly to stop the deportation of the island's Jews. But he was outflanked when the navy arranged the deportation instead. There was one other alternative for soldiers, but "in the end we lacked the courage to desert. Not a single man deserted." Rarely was anyone punished who went over the top into wildness (Mazower, 1993: 195–200, 211–15, 253–4). This was the best-trained army in the world, cohesive up to the end. But such splendid militarism could be subverted into efficient murdering of civilians.

CONCLUSION TO CHAPTERS 8 AND 9

Most of my sample of hard-core perpetrators were real Nazis. A third had experience of serious prewar violence, and most were inducted through careers in ascending violence into full-scale genocide. Raw recruits constituted only 10 percent of the perpetrators in groups containing many foreign ethnic Germans liberated by the advancing German armies. The median man in my sample served for four years in three different murderous types of genocidal institutions. Though they had almost all begun in these institutions by being unexpectedly asked to kill, by about 1942 they were embarked on careers in murder.

They were overwhelmingly men, but from all social classes. They were drawn disproportionately from core nation-statist Nazi constituencies – from threatened or lost border regions; from sectors of the economy already favorable to the Nazis; and from particular occupations (medicine, education, law, the military, and the police) where Nazi ideology resonated amid professional proto-Nazi predispositions. But the usual correlation of Nazism with Protestantism had been reversed. Now perpetrators were disproportionately Catholic, probably the result of a shift from a more defensive *kleindeutsch* to a more racial-expansionist *grossdeutsch* nationalism within Nazism. Thus the majority of Nazi genocide, as represented by my sample, was accomplished by ideological, experienced Nazis.

Escalating violence brought inurement. Nazi ideology demonized and dehumanized the enemy, appropriated normal wartime patriotism, and helped acceptance of militarism and the Leadership Principle. It provided defense mechanisms against revulsion or guilt. The perpetrator was subordinating himself or herself to principle, the *Volk*, the fuhrer, science, and the future. This attitude helped desk-murderers design efficient genocidal systems and withstand the occasional pricks of conscience that their indirect connection to killing might bring. Educated killers elaborated this in ethical or idealistic terms. For those actually killing, revulsion could be diffused by accepting a higher, more scientific, or elitist level of morality. The less educated voiced ideology in more personal terms by blaming the victim: Jews and Slavs were the enemy, responsible for the war, provoking justified self-defense. Ideology also legitimated aggressive impulses, found especially among young males, refugees, and perhaps those of distinct somatic makeup. However perverted they may seem, many sincerely believed murder was justified. Individual responsibility was diffused onto collectivities – onto a movement enforcing the Leadership Principle, onto the camp "order of terror," onto a medical profession embodying scientific truth and status, onto police institutions enforcing order. These were normative and usually occupational communities entailing both hierarchical and peer pressure.

Of course, neither prior experience nor committed ideology can have characterized the perpetrators as a whole. My sample cannot be representative of all perpetrators. Despite its size, it must represent well under 10 percent of all perpetrators. It overrepresents repetitive murder away from the front lines, and hard-core rather than casual perpetrators. These real Nazis operated among many more ordinary people. Among Wehrmacht killers we might find little more than the overreacting retaliation against civilian enemy populations ubiquitous among desperate, frightened troops embroiled in a savage war. Nonetheless, they were also given license to kill by a Nazi High Command, increasing the role of both fearful and disciplined killers. Among lower administrators in transport and other agencies smoothing the flow of victims, we would doubtless find many Germans with virtually no prior history of Nazism or violence, exhibiting the whole range of prejudices, equivocations, and moral evasions that studies have suggested characterized the German population as a whole. Germans facilitated the transport of the victims, turned a blind eye, thought about matters of more personal concern, cared nothing for disliked Jews or Slavs – with practiced and entirely normal human moral weakness. Perhaps research simply cannot penetrate deeply enough into the full range of Nazi genocide to permit a decisive resolution of such issues. Yet obviously, considered as individuals, the corps of perpetrators *must* have included many ordinary Germans.

Yet genocide was not perpetrated by atomized individuals. Real Nazis, ordinary Nazis, ordinary policemen, ordinary Germans, and so on were engaged in a collective project. In this fascist movement, hierarchy and violent comradeship were central. In this fascist regime, well-rewarded careers involved violence. The higher up the hierarchy, the more fervent the Nazi. Nazis ordered their subordinates to murder, and orders are not easy to disobey. Comradeship heightened the influence of more experienced, inured personnel, men who knew that police forces must combat enemies by tough means. They taught their experience to novices who knew less of police work. In occupational communities, comradely pressures flow from veterans to raw recruits. Killing institutions also had many Nazis at all ranks selected for genocide. The dominant ethos of some selected professions – especially medicine, the police, and the military – offered a conducive subculture in which Nazi ideology resonated. There were also material motives. Higher-level personnel got career advancement, lower-level ones steady jobs. Bonuses and relative safety were also material lures. But careerism was often expressed in principled terms. Nazi lawyers and policemen wanted to advance by contributing to the new Germany. Propagandists wanted to advance by half-consciously bending the truth and then being forced to bend more by fearsome censorship. Many became cynical of the propaganda. Broad tells us that his fellow Auschwitz guards did. Most had difficulty justifying killing to their own minds and bodies. When the psychological protection offered by ideology, discipline, comradeship, and career collapsed, alcohol lowered sensitivity and induced oblivion. These are mixed motives indeed.

But there were few banal, bureaucratic killers. Capitalists pursued profit as a routine, and killed people incidentally and indirectly; so presumably did many lower-level desk killers – though higher-level desk-killers had ideological motives. But the vast majority of those involved in actual killing knew what they were doing. Most thought there was good reason for it. Of modernity I see rather more. But what made this and other modern killings so genocidal was less bureaucracy than the modern mass movement. Discipline, comradeship, and careerism have presumably assisted many historical massacres. But for them to be so tightly interwoven, across the classes and across the diverse sectors of society, reinforced by a shared ideology, seems to be specific to modern movements of perverted democratic sentiments, whereby the unitary sacred collectivity (in this case a nation) is "organically represented" by an authoritarian state.

My position is closer to those that stress real Nazis rather than ordinary Germans. But I add sociology. Exterminist ideology emerged as a process and through institutions and subcultures. Radicalized Nazism was implemented through the careful selection of appropriate institutions and personnel that could employ hierarchy, comradeship, and career to accomplish genocide. Of course, I have not yet attempted to answer *the* questions in this perverted area of human activity – what would you or I have done had we been caged into genocide? Before attempting to answer that question, examine the non-German perpetrators of genocide.

10

Germany's Allies and Auxiliaries

Germans did not stand alone in the genocidal mire. There were many foreign perpetrators too. A million men from 15 countries joined the Waffen-SS and fought as soldiers at the front.[1] Probably only a few of them were war criminals. I will discuss not them but those complicit in cold-blooded killing of unarmed people: collaborating regimes, auxiliary police forces, and concentration camp guards. I confine myself to East and Southeast Europe, areas ruled fairly directly by the Germans – Poland, Estonia, Latvia, Lithuania, Belarus, and the Ukraine – and those ruled by their Axis allies – Italy, Hungary, Romania, Bulgaria, Croatia, and Slovakia. Unfortunately, there is much less evidence on them than on Germans. Among the few comparative studies, Helen Fein's *Accounting for Genocide* (1979) stands out. She explains the proportion of Jews killed in each country in terms of two variables: degrees of prior anti-Semitism and direct SS rule. She suggests that these two variables were often inversely related. In the Netherlands and Greece, at least 75 percent of the Jews were killed, whereas in Romania only about half were – although Romanian anti-Semitism was much stronger than that of the Dutch or Greeks. This was due, she says, to direct SS control in the latter countries but not in Romania. Since the Nazis were the keenest to kill Jews, and the SS was their leading killing machine, occupied countries saw more mass murder than allied ones.

But administrations were more complex than this. The SS, the Nazi Party, German Ministry officials, and the Wehrmacht all ran large slices of occupied countries, and their powers varied. All tended to work toward the fuhrer, and the fuhrer generally wanted people dead. But Germans had two major goals – exterminating enemies and winning the war – and different occupation authorities had different strategies and resources to achieve them. If

---

[1] The 125,000 Western Europeans blended adventurers, ne'er-do-wells, and fascist true believers. Among the 22,000 Dutch volunteers, about 30 percent were from far right parties; more were working-class adventurers (in't Veld, 1976: II, 1513–23). Far more came from Eastern Europe – half a million from the Ukraine, Belarus, and the small Baltic states, 70,000 Cossacks, 110,000 Turkomen, 35,000 Tartars, 20,000 Bosnian Muslims. See Reitlinger (1968: 155–60, 196–206), Stein (1966: 137–96), and Sydnor (1977).

they identified Jews as aiding the enemy, they would be given greater military resources to destroy them. But others might be more cautious or have more limited resources. The specter of the Judeo-Bolshevik tended to link the two goals, but this was more plausible in some contexts than others. The Axis allies also had to balance the desire to please the Germans against their own strategic considerations – adjusted by their own anti-Semitism and fear of other local enemies. If the Germans would assist them against these enemies, they would be more willing to collaborate. Yet some German authorities might worry about whether forcing the locals to hand over Jews might harm the alliance and the war effort. If they did not always ask this question as carefully as they might, this was because Nazi racism persistently prevented them from giving sufficient respect to their non-Aryan allies. So I broaden Fein's two measures, identifying more perpetrator motives and more complex power relations among Germans and locals. I discuss the countries in order of the autonomy they enjoyed from the Germans, starting with the least autonomous.

EASTERN AUXILIARIES

Poland

Across the European East and Southeast, only Poland and Greece fought against the Germans and so were conquered.[2] Poland had the least autonomous regime I discuss. One-third of it was even incorporated into the Reich, and all of it was ruled by Germans. Thus it had the highest killing rate of all: 2–3 million non-Jews and 90 percent of the Jewish population of over 3 million. Yet it still seems that not many were killed by Poles.

This was despite the fact that Poland had been very anti-Semitic. Jews formed 10 percent of the population, more than in any other European country. They were 30 percent of the population in the cities and over 60 percent of those in commerce. Though most Jews were actually quite poor, many Poles felt exploited by them. Polish nationalism was organicist, intolerant of minorities: Poland was for the Poles. Most political parties said that Ukrainian, German, and Lithuanian minorities could be assimilated, but not the more "alien" Jews. They should be forced to emigrate. Murderous pogroms erupted in 1920 and 1935, instigated by nationalists. The Catholic Church was also anti-Semitic. In the 1930s Jews were deprived of economic rights, and by 1939 some government spokesmen were advocating their

---

[2] Greece's Jews also suffered near-total elimination, despite the low level of anti-Semitism in the country. I excluded Greece and Serbia from this chapter, since both were fighting guerrilla wars against the Germans, complicating any analysis. Neither provided many collaborators, though Serb Chetnik nationalists were trapped into complicity in genocide like other nationalist movements discussed here.

policed deportation. The Left parties (receiving 30 percent of the vote in elections) favored only assimilation, while fear of neighboring Germany restricted the appeal of fascism. Nonetheless, Polish anti-Semitism seemed as intense as any in Europe (Hagen, 1996; Mendelsohn, 1983: chap. 1). Indeed, the last European pogrom occurred in Poland as soon as the Nazi yoke lifted. In 1946 in Kielce, 100 miles from Warsaw, 46 Jews were murdered to avenge the fictitious kidnapping of a child by Jewish survivors of the Final Solution.

But in 1939 Poland fought against Nazi Germany and lost. This made all the difference. Few Poles were permitted to bear arms or hold positions of authority. Rightist nationalists became not fascist collaborators but resistance fighters, their anti-Semitism largely irrelevant. Amid their own sufferings, few Poles spared sympathy for the Jews. Poles had a grandstand view of the Holocaust, and some liked what they saw. They turned over Jews more often than they assisted them, and profited from the black market in Jewish possessions. But not many Poles participated in genocide (Karay, 1996; Piotrowski, 1998: 82–127).

The ghastly events in the village of Jedwabne in 1941 (unearthed by Gross, 2001) was one of the exceptions. The villagers, newly liberated from Soviet control, may have killed the local Jews before the Germans arrived. They certainly did most of the killing on their own. Half of the local adult males participated with some enthusiasm, partly in search of loot but justifying their actions as destroying Judeo-Bolsheviks. Poland's Institute of National Remembrance (2002) then dug further, uncovering one other substantial massacre and about 20 other small ones. They were all in ethnically Polish areas occupied by the Soviets since 1939, and in all of them rightist nationalists, including priests, had been strong and Jews relatively few. Looting was significant, but more important was the belief that Jews had collaborated with the Soviet occupation. Indeed, some had. The Judeo-Bolshevik specter dominated genocide across the whole of Eastern Europe. But luckily for Poles, the Germans rarely permitted them arms or authority to accomplish such deeds as occurred at Jedwabne.

The Baltic States

The three new post-1918 states of Lithuania, Latvia, and Estonia were "liberated" by the Germans from a brief Soviet occupation and "restored" as fairly puppet states. This provided many willing perpetrators. All three states had experienced coups in the 1930s by authoritarian nationalists. Their Plan A had been to preserve national independence, squeezed between two superpowers, Germany and the Soviet Union. The regimes had also been somewhat anti-Semitic and organicist, discriminating against minorities. Language and religion were the badges of national identity, and both excluded Jews, who spoke Yiddish, Polish, or Russian. They also wished to nationalize their economies away from "Jewish control." Yet there was little violence, and few Jews felt threatened (Mendelsohn, 1983: chaps. 5, 6). Goldhagen (1996: 409) is wrong to attribute Baltic complicity in the Final Solution to "cultures that were profoundly anti-semitic" encouraging "vehement hatred of Jews." The major cause of radicalization toward murderous cleansing in 1941 was geopolitical. Nationalists were forced by the puny size of their countries to become clients of either the Nazis or the Soviets. The rightist governments were pushed toward a Plan B, a German alliance. The small Baltic left chose as its Plan B a Soviet alliance. Most Jews preferred the Soviets as the lesser of two evils – life imprisonment was better than a death sentence, remarked one. The few Jewish political activists were also leftists. Baltic nationalists claimed that Jews were enthusiastic Communists. Jews were overrepresented among the Communist rank-and-file, though not among the leaders. Jews were 7 percent of the general Lithuanian population. They were 15–16 percent of Communist Party and Komsomol members but less than 5 percent of party leaders and People's Commissariat of Internal Affairs (NKVD) security police (McQueen, 1998: 33). So a Judeo-Bolshevik threat seemed minimally plausible, and that proved decisive.

The Red Army occupied all three countries in 1940 (under the amended terms of the Nazi–Soviet Non-Aggression Pact). Soviet rule was very oppressive, for this was the height of Stalinism. Property was expropriated, political freedoms were abrogated. The poor were aided by positive discrimination in favor of the propertyless, though the economic slump harmed almost everyone. The Soviets also implemented mass policed deportations to Siberia. Between 1.5 percent and 4 percent of the three populations – disproportionately nationalists and property owners – were deported, few to return. But Soviet rule was brief. The Germans invaded and conquered in June 1941, welcomed as liberators by most locals (Kangeris, 1998). They restored the nationalist regimes and slaughtered those they perceived as aiding the Communist regime, especially Judeo-Bolsheviks. By 1945 only 5 percent of the 160,000 Lithuanian Jews survived. In Latvia 9 percent of the 66,000 Jews survived. Estonian Jews almost all perished, though there were only 4,500 of them. The directors of these terrible events were Germans, and they dominated these tiny puppet states. But they found enough willing Baltic clients, whose participation in genocide was a kind of Plan C, an initially unintended consequence of their choosing a German alliance against a Judeo-Bolshevik enemy.

The key collaborating organizations came from the far right. In Estonia the fascist Vaps movement led the German puppet regime. In Latvia the core collaborators were the 5,000–6,000 members of the fascist Thunder Cross, modeled on Italian fascism and the Romanian Iron Guard. It demanded "Latvia to the Latvians, bread and work to the Latvians," since "the sovereign power in Latvia belongs to the Latvians and not to the people of Latvia." It was very anti-Semitic, virulently denouncing Judeo-Bolsheviks.

But since it was also somewhat anti-German, the Nazis soon banned it, though many of its members collaborated as individuals, some becoming the worst war criminals. Initially, the Lithuanian Activist Front led collaboration there. It was much bigger, better organized, and initially more integrated into the Nazi war machine. Its militants had fled to Germany in 1940 and were there organized into a Police Auxiliary Unit to be used in the coming invasion. The Front was not fascist. It favored liberal democracy for Lithuanians but not for others, and it hated Judeo-Bolsheviks. As the Germans marched eastward in 1941, the Front proclaimed:

Lithuanian brothers and sisters, the fateful and final hour has come to settle accounts with the Jews.... Every Jew without exception is hereby warned to leave Lithuania without delay.

There was also a smaller fascist, pro-German Iron Wolf movement, and after the invasion the Germans allowed it to take over the main leadership positions.

When the Germans arrived in Estonia, the main burden of executions was thrust on a collaborating Self-Defense Force that murdered as many gypsies as Jews. Since there weren't many of either, they were quickly disposed of (Weiss-Wendt, 1998). I have found no details of the actual perpetrators.

In Latvia the Germans initially failed to get pogroms going. Latvian militias had been hastily formed to attack the retreating Soviet forces, but these did not turn against the Jews. New paramilitary forces were formed from volunteers. The notorious unit of 300 men led by Major Viktor Arajs murdered about 26,000 of the 85,000 Latvian civilian victims, the remainder being killed by German *Einsatzgruppen* and SD units (in which Latvian-born ethnic Germans were prominent). Of these 26,000 victims, 22,000 were labeled as Jews, 2,000 as Communists, and 2,000 as gypsies or insane. The average Arajs man thus murdered 87 persons. Latvian Auxiliary Police battalions, 3,000–5,000 strong in 1941, rising to 12,000 in mid-1944, helped drive Jews out of the ghettos, in the process seizing Jewish property, and a few participated in shootings. Perhaps 150 mayors and other officials and propagandists assisted in all this. Fewer than 1,000 men actually killed, though a much larger number benefited from the looting. The perpetrators came from overlapping rightist and militarist backgrounds. There were Latvian fascists plus rightist officers and NCOs from the former army, police, and civil defense guards. They were spoiling to fight Bolshevism, frustrated by their government's tame surrender in 1940. The nationalist student fraternities provided supportive elite networks permeating many Latvian institutions, especially the civil service. Former members dominated the leadership of the SD units. Relatives of the deported also participated. Nationalists evading arrest by the Soviets had not anticipated that their families would be deported. This understandably hardened their anticommunism. Stahlecker, the leader of *Einsatzgruppe A*, said he had paid "particular attention" to recruiting people seeking revenge. The auxiliaries' rank-and-file were less ideological and younger. Since the universities were closed and the economy was in tatters, most young men were unoccupied. They appreciated a job, pay, and the chance for adventurous activity. They were not marginal types. They included many athletes. As in other countries, physical prowess could be turned toward violence. There was male bonding between young men who liked the company of other men (without any suggestion of homosexuality) – soldiers, athletes, fraternity members – fostering SS-type toughness; and comradeship.

When later put on trial, they admitted only to patriotism and anticommunism, and denied being anti-Semitic bigots, looters, or careerist killers. They rarely expressed remorse, and few refused the initial shooting order, though some refused to go back a second time. An officer said of one man, "Ten horses will not bring him back again." Alcohol was as important as among the Germans described in the previous chapter. Perpetrators were liberally supplied with vodka before, during, and after the killings. Ezergailis (1996) says it was "the lubricant of commando life... it... broke down the inhibitions of the young men and enabled them to kill for the first time, and it was alcohol that brought them back to the killing pits. After the killings the men drank themselves into a stupor." Arajs voiced remorse of a somewhat self-pitying kind. He advised a friend against collaborating with the Germans with these words:

With Germans it is thus, if they get hold of your finger, then the whole of you is lost, because soon enough one is forced to do things that one would never do if one could get out of it.

The Latvian "finger," freely offered to the Germans as their Plan B, was anticommunist nationalist ideology fueled by anti-Semitic bigotry. This was routinized and coarsened by more material motives of wages and looting. SS leadership brought them to the edge of the killing pits. Were they then held fast to Plan C of genocide by fear, as Arajs suggests? The German SS commander Stahlecker did report to Berlin that compared to Lithuania, "It was significantly more difficult to start clean-up operations and pogroms in Latvia" (details from Vestermanis, 1992, and Ezergailis, 1996; quotes from 105, 194, 255–6).

Having already penetrated the country's police forces, the Lithuanian Front could seize some cities from Soviet forces and set up a provisional government before the Germans even arrived. We view events through the reports of the German *Einsatzgruppen* commanders (excerpted in Arad et al., 1989, and Klee et al., 1989, 1991; I often quote them in this chapter). Most commanders reported a friendly, positive, and pro-German reception in Lithuania. Front bands had already launched wild pogroms focused on adult male Jews. Though the Germans reported that in Kaunas it was "initially surprisingly difficult to set a fairly large-scale pogrom in motion," elsewhere they wrote, "Lithuanians are voluntarily and untiringly at our disposal for all measures against Jews; sometimes they even execute such measures on their own." There are eyewitness accounts from German soldiers (some appalled) of murders committed by young Lithuanian men in front of cheering crowds of men, women, and children, cleaving their victims with knives and axes. These were more than just a "handful of local rabble" (as Misiunas & Taagepera, 1993: 62, claim).

After the Iron Wolf activists took control, only fascists, radical rightists, and anti-Semites remained as officers (Budreckis, 1968: 121–2; MacQueen, 1998: 37–9). They moved to accomplish genocide. SS men led Lithuanian police bands, killing all the Jews they could find, including women and children. Thirty thousand-strong police auxiliary battalions were formed from reliable anti-Semitic and anticommunist locals. The notorious 2nd Battalion murdered 500 Jews per day. Looting accompanied most killings. Senior officials supervised property redistribution after ghetto liquidations. Over half of the Lithuanian Jews died at the hands of fellow Lithuanians, the highest proportion of any Nazi-occupied country. The 2nd Battalion was later transferred to Belarus, where its wildness alienated locals. Forty thousand Lithuanians fought for the Germans, including perhaps 10,000 actual perpetrators. More shared in the spoils, but most Lithuanians just watched. Up to 1,000 may have sheltered Jews, risking their own lives. A tiny underground lamented, "Do we have to be the arch-hangmen of Europe?" Again, relatives of the deported were overrepresented (Arad, 1989; Budreckis, 1968; Littman, 1983; Neshamit, 1977; Piotrowski, 1998: 163–76; Porat, 1994; Sochat, 1974).

Among 18 Lithuanian war criminals (data from German trials plus Hutchinson, 1994, and McKenzie, 1995), 17 were under the age of 25; the exception was an older emigre who had fought against the Bolsheviks in 1918. Five of the six officers had been Front or Iron Wolf members. Antanas Gecas came from a family of devout Catholic farmers. A conscientious but unremarkable student, he joined the air force, training under another of the perpetrators. He there joined the Front. His brother had fled to Germany and worked with the Nazis. When the Germans invaded, Gecas volunteered for the auxiliary police and became an officer. He participated in killings in Kaunas and Belarus. Motiejus Migonis was a young policeman in the 2nd/12th Battalion. He later recalled that his first four years of adulthood "had consisted entirely of executing civilians." Aleksynas was a trade union official who fled when the Germans invaded. But "since I was a nationalist," he returned and volunteered for the police, believing the country should be "scourged" and brought to "order." These seem key code words of organic nationalist and police/military values. He was the only 1 of the 18 who later backed off. He deserted to the Soviets in May 1942 in disgust at the constant executions. The Soviets gave him a light sentence: 10 years in Siberia.

In all three countries the ideological and revenge-seeking leaders and militants mobilized broader support from materialist opportunists keen to seize Jewish spoils. The common ideology for them all was a cleansing of the nation of Judeo-Bolshevism (Gordon, 1990; Hilberg, 1980: 96–102; Misiunas and Taagepera, 1993). But everywhere collaboration then flagged. By January 1942 the SS police chief in Latvia reported, "Regret about the fate of the Jews is constantly expressed; there are few voices to be heard which are in favour of the elimination of the Jews." It was now being rumored that the Nazis favored harsh treatment for the Balts. The plan was to deport two-thirds of them east, replacing them with ethnic German settlers. Some of the remaining third could be incorporated into the master race, though most would be helots. And the Nazis continued to transfer local property to Germans. Young men had to join the forced labor brigades going to Germany or "volunteer" for army or police battalions. So, over 100,000 Balts chose to don the German uniform. They fought against the Soviets as long as possible in the vain hope that the Western allies would be the ones to liberate them and restore their national independence. But as the Red Army neared, the Germans attempted to evacuate the main collaborators and their families. These totaled 100,000 Estonians, 180,000 Latvians, and perhaps 300,000 Lithuanians, indicating the scale of collaboration (Kangeris, 1998: 141). They had done their murderous damage early, some with enthusiasm, more of them trapped when, in support of their organic nationalism, they had subordinated themselves to the Nazis. The Nazis were very satisfied. The Jews had been destroyed, the front protected from the supposed Judeo-Bolshevik enemy lurking in the rear, and all with the deployment of few German troops.

Belarus

The Germans could find only a few collaborators here, led by anti-Soviet nationalists who had fled to Germany in the 1920s as Belarus fell under Soviet control. Their Plans A and B were similar to those of the Baltic nationalists. By 1941 Belarussian nationalism was close to Nazism, especially its hatred of Judeo-Bolshevism. They returned home with the German forces. But they had few followers. Most of the city population was Russian, Polish, or Jewish. Ninety percent of Belarussians were peasants, few of whom glamorized an ethnicity that guaranteed them low status. The nationalists lacked much of either an urban or a peasant base, though the anticommunist Orthodox Church welcomed the Germans, ensuring that many peasants did too.

The *Einsatzgruppen* said that especially in the East, "There is practically no Byelorussian national consciousness... pronounced anti-semitism is missing." It was "almost impossible to stage pogroms against the Jews because of the passivity and the political disinterest of the Byelorussians." If nationalism was weak, the SS reasoned, so was anti-Semitism – right across Eastern Europe. The SS coped by declaring that only those helping the *Einsatzgruppen* could join the new Belarus administration. This brought careerist volunteers. The nationalists selected men known as anticommunists or anti-Semites to lead the auxiliary police battalions, the "Ravens," numbering somewhere between 10,000 and 40,000. Some were formed from local Soviet POWs. The leaders could not have had personal knowledge of many of these men, though a "snowball sample" helped: each group of initiates gave the names of further supposed reliables.

As always, career policemen were favored recruits. Szymon Serafinowicz was an intelligent but poorly educated man brought up in Polish Belarus. He became a soldier, then a policeman. His prospects under Polish rule were limited. He was rebuffed as an unsuitable match by the parents of a Polish girl with whom he had fallen in love. The Soviet occupation improved the status of Belarussians and lowered that of Poles, so Szymon was then able to marry the younger sister of his beloved (the rest of the Polish family had been deported east by the Soviets). But he seized his real opportunity when the Germans arrived, volunteering assistance. Rising to sergeant, he headed the auxiliary police of the small town of Mir, reveling in the power conferred by a uniform, a gun, and a horse – and by his friendship with the all-conquering Germans. Like the other local Belarus policemen, Szymon killed whoever the Germans ordered. But whereas the rankers were content with a guaranteed income and easy work, Szymon showed "excessive killing zeal." He was ambitious, hoping for promotion from the Germans, and strongly anticommunist (they had deported his first love). Though not a rabid anti-Semite, he was "very cold" toward Jews and saw the cosmopolitan Jews as a threat to "national order." He dulled the tensions of his dire work with wild drinking bouts during which he became violent. We know all this because his German interpreter, living in his household, was a covert Jew who lived to tell his tale (Tec, 1990). Szymon's own story ended in Britain in 1996. His death at age 85 aborted Britain's only Nazi war crimes trial as it was beginning.

The auxiliary units ranged from routine police work to brutal murders of Soviet POWs and Jews. The wildness of their alcohol-assisted atrocities – infants smashed against walls, children thrown down wells with grenades tossed down to finish them off, savage rapes followed by bayoneting – supposedly shocked the SS (who habitually reported that wild atrocities were the work of non-Aryans). Many were later drafted into frontline Waffen-SS divisions, but they were less effective as soldiers, and at the end were keen to surrender to the anticommunist Americans. Many are ending their days as U.S. citizens, emphasizing the anticommunism rather than the anti-Semitism of their past careers (Loftus, 1982; Piotrowski, 1998: 148–57).

The few thousand Belarus perpetrators were greatly outnumbered by partisans and victims. The *Einsatzgruppen* repored that the murders of Jews had led to a "feeling of insecurity and even anxiety in the population." Even educated circles "were not used to such a procedure during the Soviet regime and it was impossible to estimate the consequence of such measures." There has been a "deterioration of the popular mood"; "Generally speaking, it may be said that the civilian population will side with those who wield the power in the area." In areas beset by partisans, the peasant "will obey the orders of his former rulers." Most Belarussians, caught in the middle, developed a shell-shocked detachment (concludes Headland, 1992, 118–19). The Germans had to do much of the killing here. Since this remained a front area, they were willing to commit German forces to the task.

The Ukraine

The Ukraine provided more collaborators. There had been murderous anti-Semitism here during the Russian Civil War. But Ukrainians had been subsequently split between Soviet and Polish rule, and the two regions differed. Jews were quite well integrated in the Soviet part. During the 1930s they were 5 percent of the population but constituted over 10 percent of the Communist Party and of the delegates to the Ukrainian Soviet (Altshuler, 1990: 290–4). Thus they were tarnished with blame for Stalin's murderous policies in the Ukraine, discussed in the next chapter. Though very few Jews could have been Communists, the Judeo-Bolshevik enemy thesis might again attain minimal plausibility.

But since Stalin eliminated most of the Ukrainian nationalists in the Soviet area, it was Ukrainians living under the milder Polish rule who were better organized. Their Plan A was again national independence. During the 1920s they became influenced by Italian fascism, especially its paramilitarism, necessary to achieve national liberation. The main nationalist organization, the (ONU), affirmed principles of freedom and democracy – for ethnic Ukrainians. "Ukraine is for the Ukrainians," it repeatedly proclaimed. "The nation is the highest form of organic human community." It veered in the 1930s toward Nazi racism, hopeful that the Nazis might liberate them from Polish and Soviet rule: to achieve a "pure," "organic," and "biological" Ukrainian nation, Poles, Russians, and Jews should be "removed." So Plan B was ethnic cleansing, though not by murder. As across most of Eastern Europe, religion also mattered. The Ukrainian Orthodox Churches emphasized the purity of the Ukrainian national soul. As in Romania, a distinctively Christian and anti-Semitic nationalism emerged (Armstrong, 1963; Kosyk, 1986: Appendix, Documents 6, 44, 61, 68, 75; Motyl, 1980: 143; Piotrowski, 1998: 189–95; Weiner, 2001: 240–8).

The Soviets occupied the Polish Ukraine in 1939, as per the Nazi–Soviet Pact. Many Polish Ukrainian nationalists fled to the German Reich, perceived as Stalin's main enemy. His rule was immediately oppressive, pushing more Ukrainians toward Nazi sympathies. Jews were slightly overrepresented in the new regime, but as Gross (2000: 98) notes, locals were struck by "how unseeemly, how jarring, how offensive it was to see a Jew in *any* position of authority – as an engineer, a foreman, an accountant, a civil servant, a teacher or a militiaman" – not *over*-represented, but shockingly represented!

Thus began the love–hate relationship between Ukrainian nationalists and the Nazis. Their alliance radicalized during the initial invasion into Plan C, genocide. The two ONU factions were organized into two SS-trained Ukrainian *Einsatzgruppen* battalions to purge occupied areas of undesirable elements, that is, Communists and Jews. It is unclear how much they were used in the invasion. As the Soviets retreated, the NKVD police killed most of their Ukrainian political prisoners. Ukrainian nationalists understandably sought vengeance. Many Jews – forced again to choose between Nazi Germany and Soviet Russia – were fleeing east with the Red Army, though few Jews were Communists, and Jewish organizations and property owners' businesses had also been suppressed by the Soviets. It is unclear whether the nationalists believed the bizarre claims of the *Einsatzgruppen* that "the Jews without exception served Bolshevism" and the graves of the NKVD's victims "do not contain Jewish corpses, not even in one single instance." But Ukrainian collaborators showed little reluctance to join in genocide. It did not just reflect entrapment by the Nazis. Twenty-four thousand Jews were killed immediately, some even before the Germans arrived. In some towns new ONU administrations and militias embarked on killing sprees. In the Volhynia region, looting was much bigger than murder, though nationalists defended this as helping the normal development of a modern Ukrainian nation in which industry and commerce were liberated from foreign control. The ONU proclaimed: "The Ukrainian city is now a clean page. Come, take over and develop it" (Spector, 1990: 64–79, 238–9; Zbikowski, 1993).

Einsatzgruppen reports say that the retreating Soviets, helped by Jews, killed hundreds of Ukrainians, especially the intelligentsia; then local Ukrainians wreaked righteous vengeance on the Jews. In Kremenets 100–50 Ukrainians had been killed by the Reds. When it was reported that some of their corpses lacked skins, the rumor spread that they had been boiled alive – evoking old Christian fantasies of Jewish ritual murder. The retaliation, often by relatives of the dead, was to batter 130 Jews to death with clubs. Vengeance was wreaked on an available and alien group plausibly connected to the perpetrators. Pohl (1996: 175–9) believes the NKVD murders radicalized ONU militants into genocide, making anti-Semitism central to their nationalism. ONU strongholds saw the worst pogroms, while regions with more Poles and fewer Ukainians saw the fewest. Jews now had only two choices – flee or help the Reds. But the Germans reported varied local reactions. Some Ukrainians "actively co-operated," "visibly relieved" by the severe measures that "are accepted with understanding." Other reports stressed "indifference to the total liquidation of the Jews," noting that "racial and ideological antisemitism is absent in the population." Again, the Germans attributed indifference to weak nationalism. Nationalists would murder, the SS believed, while peasants were reluctant. Though ambivalent about Jews and Poles, they did hate Russians (Weiner, 2001: 248–56).

Almost all the 35,000-strong Ukrainian auxiliary police battalions were Soviet deserters or POWs. The SS reported that "well-screened politically reliables" were selected with the help of local mayors and police chiefs. Most POWs did not volunteer, despite the lure of being released from captivity. Many volunteers had material reasons, feigning whatever political views were required. But Bohdan Kosiy, later tried as a war criminal, was a 19-year-old tailor's assistant, already a member of the ONU – an obviously desirable recruit. Field intelligence was mostly provided by ethnic Germans. The policemen assisted in ghetto liquidations that killed 150,00 Jews, mostly in 1942. But one report casually states, "All Asiatics found on the highways are also liquidated." Germans gave the orders and provided the organization, though Ukrainian auxiliaries outnumbered German SD and order police battalions by about 10 to 1 and so possessed autonomy in day-to-day operations About half of the survivors refer to the rank-and-file killers as simply "Ukrainians," but half call them "Ukrainian nationalists" or even "Nationalist Committees" (Arad et al., 1989: 128, 140; Dean, 1996, 2000; Kosyk, 1986: 155; Sabrin, 1991; Sandkühler 1996: 409, 417). Survivors were making the same equation between nationalism and genocide as the SS.

As usual, perpetrators had mixed motives: greed, alcohol, ideological nationalism, vengeful anticommunism, casual anti-Semitic bigotry – combining after Soviet occupation into hatred of Judeo-Bolshevism (Arad et al., 1989: 210; Armstrong, 1963: 158–9; Dean, 2000; Piotrowski, 1998: 209–37; Weiss, 1990a: 414; 1990b: 110). Nationalists grimly recognized that genocide was a condition of German support for a national independence of which they never despaired. Some hoped to eventually use their German training and weapons against both the Soviets and the Germans. The SS Galician Division was inundated with more volunteers than it needed, and it was blessed by the Orthodox Church. By war's end 200,000 Ukrainians were in German uniform, 20,000 had fled to ONU partisan bands fighting against both sides, and perhaps about the same number were in Red partisan bands – who said later that they had enjoyed little support from the local population (Weiner, 2001: 156–7). Nationalists were still fighting Soviet forces in the forests into the 1950s.

Sabrin (1991: 242) believes "hundreds of thousands of Ukrainian nationalists were partners in crime with German Nazism, committing warcrimes, crimes against humanity, crimes of collaboration, leading to . . . genocide." Israel's War Crimes Investigations Office more cautiously estimates that 11,000 Ukrainians committed murder or participated in brutal deportations that caused deaths. Though this is a larger number than in neighboring countries, there were also more Ukrainians. As elsewhere, far more participated in looting. Perhaps even a majority quietly approved of the removal of the Jews as long as they did not think too closely about the methods. Much of the

Ukrainian Orthodox Church sided with the Nazis against the Communist foe. Yet about 1,000 priests risked their lives to protect Jews. Baptists were overrepresented among these brave people, though the Orthodox Church's own primate was the most prominent protector. Vivitsky (1990: 107) notes that the primate needed a network of 550 monks and nuns to provide shelter for only 200 Jewish children, yet one Ukrainian informer could easily turn in 200 Jews. Most Ukrainians were probably in the middle – hating Germans, Communists, and Jews equally (Bilinsky, 1990: 381–2; Hilberg, 1993: 94–6, 289; Spector, 1990: 172–87, 243–56; Vivitsky, 1990; Weiner, 2001). Most Ukrainian peasants had little love for either side or for the Jews. But their main concern was to stay alive. This required keeping one's head down until it became clear who was winning.

"Ukrainians"

Many camp guards were described as "Ukrainians" and are often assumed to be Ukrainians (e.g., Piotrowski, 1998: 218–20). Yet Nazis and Jews tended to describe all Eastern European camp auxiliaries as Ukrainians. Genuine Ukrainians may have been the largest single group, yet the term was a generic one. Just as the Bolshevik stooge was supposedly Judeo, the Nazi one was Ukrainian – two pariah peoples, unequal in their power to kill.

Most camp guards in the East were recruited from among Red Army POWs. Three thousand five hundred screened volunteers were sent for 3– 6 weeks to the Trawnicki training camp, staffed by ethnic Germans, Then they were sent in units of 90–120 men to the camps and ghettos. The *Aktion Reinhard* death camps were staffed by 100 Germans and 500 "Ukrainians." Yet Bilinsky (1990: 378–9) says that out of a list of 12 men who died during training at Trawnicki, only 6 had Ukrainian names, the others being probably Russian or German. A Ukrainian prisoner in Auschwitz said that the "Ukrainian SS unit" there included mainly Russians, Belarussians, and Caucasians. They were all looked down on by the German SS guards. Karay (1996) describes a dire Polish labor camp stratified into Germans at the top, then ethnic Germans, then Poles, then Ukrainians, then the mostly Jewish *kapos*, then Jews with resources, and finally, at the bottom, Jews without resources. In this context, demonstrating anti-Semitism was a useful strategy to endear ethnic Germans, Poles, and Ukrainians to their German bosses.

This stratified regime brutalized and corrupted all the guards into complicity in beatings, rapes, and murders. Some atrocities were spontaneous; others were routine policy – especially where prisoners were now too feeble to work. Ukrainian guards were those most often placed in roles where cruelty was required. One said, "When I was handed a truncheon, I became a different person." Prisoners remembered some as appalling, others as quite humane. One said, "When I looked at them and heard them singing 'Dumka' with such longing, it was hard for me to believe that these cheerful lads were the same ones who carried out the terrible executions in the forest." But, like policemen, guards also had mundane motives. They were not in danger of starving, unlike their compatriots. They had avoided hard labor service in Germany. These mainly working-class men were privileged, stealing and extorting what they needed from Jews, including sex. Alcohol insulated. They all drank heavily. Unlike Germans, fear loomed large once they were trapped as guards. When a German SS sergeant failed to start the first diesel gassing engine at the Belzec death camp, the terrible Wirth turned savagely not on him but on his "Ukrainian" assistant, lashing him 11 or 12 times across the face (Trials of the War Criminals, Nuremberg, "The Medical Case," Vol. I, 866). The SS did not much value "Ukrainian" lives. They were commonly called *Askari* by the Germans, the Swahili term for African troops serving their colonial masters, indicating racial disdain. The Jew posing as a German interpreter with the Belarus police unit says that policemen had no choice but to play their murderous role (Tec, 1990: 102; cf. Matthäus, 1996). When "Ukrainian" laxness allowed prisoners to escape, the guards were shot. The Auschwitz guard Broad (Höss et al., 1978: 181–2) said they believed "they would be liquidated one day because they were foreigners." One day 20 fled, fighting a pitched battle with SS troops. They killed two SS men, taking seven dead themselves. Six then escaped, six committed suicide, and one was captured and executed. The costs of noncompliance were high.

Survivors describe them variously as exhibiting sadism, decency, and glazed indifference. There were varying national stereotypes. A Polish railwayman at Sobibor remarked:

the Lithuanians who mostly guarded the trains were much worse than the Ukrainians; they really were sadists; they used to shoot at people, blind, through the windows of the cars, when they begged for doctors, water and to be allowed to relieve themselves. They did it as a sport – they laughed and joked and bet while they did it.

Yet a soldier at Treblinka stressed the drunken brutality of Ukrainian guards, while an Auschwitz survivor said the Ukrainians "were worse than the Nazis. They were there because of their politics" (Ashman & Wagman, 1988: 172; Browning, 1992: 52, 83–5; Sereny, 1974: 157–9).

Anti-Semitic, anticommunist organic nationalism, reinforced by greed and careerism, first trapped these young Eastern European men. Anticommunism had more personal bite than among Germans since they had experience of Stalin's works. Jews were also a more active presence here. Economic resentment more directly legitimated violence. But the main difference emerged as the trap closed. As Arajs knew, once the Germans held them fast, they were damned in a collective hell, becoming the Devil's drunken, grinning, yet fearful disciples. Some were more ideological, coming to accept that an organic nation-state required murderous cleansing. They embraced genocide as ideological Nazis did, with a sense that historical necessity overruled normal moral norms. Others, aware they had passed well beyond the bounds of moral human behavior, decided to enjoy and abuse their devilish powers. They embraced genocide with ghastly enthusiasm.

CLIENT STATES: SLOVAKIA AND CROATIA

The two Nazi-created client states were in an intermediary position. They were grateful to and dependent on the Nazis for granting them their own state, and knew that an Allied victory might deliver them back to their former Czech and Serb rulers. Both states had only limited autonomy, but neither tested these limits by resisting the main Nazi pressure to kill the Jews. The Jews could be sacrificed in order to revenge themselves on their real local enemy. Slovaks had been liberated from the Czechs, who were now firmly subordinated to Germany. Thus Slovaks did not need to pursue Czechs further. In contrast, Croats were still fighting alongside Germans against the Serbs. So Croats also turned murderously against Serbs – and this was their initiative, not a German one.

Slovakia

Interwar Czechoslovakia contained three main ethnic groups. Among Czechs fascism had been fairly insignificant (Kelly, 1995), and even their nationalism was relatively mild. Thus few Czechs liked the Nazis, who ruled the Czech lands directly. Czech Theresienstadt concentration camp guards were described by survivors as being unenthusiastic accomplices of their SS officers. Sudeten Germans had first looked askance at Hitler but came to embrace him in 1938 (Smelser, 1975). Yet Sudetens were underrepresented among the war criminals, as we saw in Chapter 8.

Slovaks provided the most collaborators. Most had lived under Habsburg rule until 1918, and they became restive under Czech dominance. The backward Slovak economy now had to compete with the more advanced Czech lands, with its natural trade routes and subsidies from Hungary cut (Pryor, 1973). As across most of Eastern Europe, education and literacy rates were the main interwar success story. The disjunction between Czech economic exploitation and an increase in Slovak literary and linguistic identity fueled nationalism – as in other countries. The Hlinka Slovak Populist Party capitalized on this to acquire 40 percent of Slovak votes in local elections in 1938, becoming the largest Slovak party. Catholic clerics provided most party leaders, followed by schoolteachers, with students dominating the younger militants. The church was ambivalent toward democracy and somewhat anti-Semitic, yet it was also suspicious of fascism. As the Czechoslovak Republic weakened, more Hlinkas called for an independent state. Younger radicals dominated the paramilitary Hlinka Guard, admiring Hitler and causing a party split. As Hitler's aggressive diplomacy weakened the moderates, party leaders declared they would "cleanse the Slovak land of foreign elements."

The 1938 manifesto declared, "We shall persevere at the side of all nations fighting against Jewish Marxism, its ideology, revolution and violence." After he annexed Czechoslovakia, Hitler rewarded the Hlinkas with a one-party constitution for the new Slovak Republic (El Mallakh, 1979; Felak, 1994; Havranek, 1971; Jelinek, 1976; Leff, 1988; Nardini, 1983; Nedelsky, 2001; Schmidt, 1983; Vago, 1987: 294–5; Zacek, 1971). Since Slovaks had suffered only mild discrimination in Czechoslovakia, they would not have come this far unaided. But now they were clients of Hitler.

The Hlinkas cooperated in the Final Solution up to mid-1942. Though without great ideological zeal, and lacking Nazi racial conceptions of Jews, they yielded up the Jews without much pressure, as a necessary by-product of their Plan A, national independence. Material motives were important. The Nazis taxed them for every local Jew, and they received a cut from redistributed Jewish property. The Hungarian border police noted that Hlinka guards would take bribes to delay deporting richer Jews. They also spared gypsy musicians. Where skilled and business Jews could not be easily replaced, the Hlinka regime also often protected them.

In any case, Slovak cooperation then declined. By mid-1942 a German diplomat reported that "the deportations became unpopular in large circles of the population." Slovak desertions from the front increased as the soldiers became disgusted by the Germans' treatment of Russians and Jews. Since the Nazis did not want to divert German troops from the front, they depended increasingly upon the Hlinka Guards, especially after they jointly put down an attempted Slovak uprising in October 1944. Yet Hlinka zeal weakened as German defeat loomed (Hilberg, 1978: 458–73; Jelinek, 1989; Rothkirchen, 1989; Schmidt, 1983: 165). The hard-core perpetrators appear to have been younger, educated radicals and near-fascists of the Hlinka Guard.

Croatia

Croats had lived within an interwar Yugoslavia ruled by King Alexander's rightist authoritarian and Serb-dominated regime. There was only a small Serb fascist party, mainly led by students, seminarists, and priests from the Serb Orthodox Church. They gave it a somewhat religious tone and an ability to mobilize some of the rural poor, as in Romania. The Serb Chetnik movement was more important. Though not fascist, it combined organic nationalism and paramilitarism. As Croat discontent grew, Alexander became more dependent on them for help in repressing it, which further fueled Croat opposition (Avakumovic, 1971: 138; Djordjevic, 1971: 130; Kuljic, 1998: 828; Vago, 1987: 294–5).

The most extreme Croat nationalists were the Ustasha ("insurgents"). Initially patterned on Italian fascism, this small movement grew to over 30,000 members as Chetnik repression increased. Though formally fascist, its core was a simpler organic nationalism. The Ustasha proclaimed that Croatians were "Europeans and Gothic, not Eastern and Slavic" like Serbs. Foreigners could be assimilated into the Croatian nation if they converted to Catholicism. They were mostly young, led by intellectuals and students, with support from younger Catholic clerics and young workers in nonunionized sectors. Their paramilitaries drew from the upland border regions with Serbia and Bosnia, where households kept guns and where there was a sense of Serb threat. Fascism thrived off the local national antagonisms in Yugoslavia, the enemies seen not as Jews or Communists but as each other. During the war Jews were killed to please the Germans, but Jews also fought in the resistance movements.

In 1941 the Wehrmacht occupied Croatia, receiving a friendly welcome. Ustasha leaders returned from exile and set up the client "Independent State of Croatia," supported by the nationalist Catholic Church and by enough deputies of the Peasant Party to form a parliamentary majority. This fascist regime maintained a parliament, though a servile one lacking control over the Ustasha paramilitaries. Over the next four years, many Yugoslavs were murdered. Rival statistics are still brandished as weapons in the region's nationalist struggles – recently, for example, by Tudjman, the former president of Croatia. Mirkovic (1993; cf. Hayden, 1996: 746–8) has estimated the dead at 487,000 Serbs (7 percent of the Serb population), 207,000 Croats (5 percent), 86,000 Muslims (7 percent), 60,000 Jews (78 percent), and 27,000 gypsies (31 percent). In a dirty war, many atrocities were committed by all sides. The lineup of forces was actually complex. There were two occupying powers, Germany and Italy, each with its distinct goals and enemies. The two main Serb-led forces, Tito's Partisans and the rightist Chetniks, fought against each other as well as against the Germans, Italians, and Ustasha. The Chetniks identified with Serbian nationalist goals, while the Communist Partisans appealed to nonnationalists in all communities. Thus some Croats from Dalmatia fought with the Partisans against the Germans and Italians, while the Italians financed some Chetnik bands. Bosnian Muslims were caught in the middle and fought on all sides. But since Muslims feared Serbs more than Croats, many collaborated with the Germans. They supplied the SS Sandzak Division. One way or another, about 140,000 Yugoslavs fought on the German side during the war, recruited from all the major ethnic groups except Jews (Völkl, 1998).

We need to appreciate these complexities not only to understand World War II events, but also to distance ourselves from postwar nationalist simplifications of the war, which were to play an important myth-making role in the atrocities of the 1990s. However, despite the complications, most of the terrible wartime atrocities *were* committed by Croatian Ustasha. Serbs in Croatia were, after Jews, the group most at risk. They did get their revenge. At least one-third of the dead Croats were Ustasha forces massacred as they surrendered in 1945.

Ustasha strategy was genocidal only vis-à-vis Jews and gypsies. Serbs were treated to murderous cleansing through wild deportation and forced conversion. From 200,000 to 300,000 Serbs were expelled into German-controlled territories, many dying on the way, and 240,000–350,000 Orthodox Serbs were forcibly converted to Catholicism. Catholic priests and Franciscans combed the area, giving Serb peasants the alternative to "convert or go to concentration camps." Since it became clear that most persons going to the camps died, it was not much of a choice. As in German killings in Poland, class distinctions were important, indicating politicidal tendencies. Business-people, Orthodox priests and intellectuals, and richer peasants were most likely to be killed. Out of 577 Orthodox priests living in Croatian territory in April 1941, 38 percent were killed by the end of the year and 58 percent were forcibly deported, with 4 percent in prison or in hiding (Ramet, 1992: 150–1). In some areas whole Serb populations were killed. This might seem a throwback to the religious conflict of earlier centuries. Yet the Ustasha justified it in ethnic terms. The foreign minister explained: "In Croatia we can find few real Serbs. The majority of Pravoslavs [i.e., Serbs] are as a matter of fact Croats who were forced by foreign invaders to accept the infidel faith. Now it's our duty to bring them back into the Roman Catholic fold" (Shelah, 1990: 77). The Ustasha goal, openly stated, was one-third expelled, one-third converted, one-third slaughtered. The goal was two-thirds achieved. In the census of 1921 the Serb population of the territories of Independent Croatia had been 1.6 million. By 1944 it was down to 600,000 – a cleansing of 63 percent. The Chetniks also sought a "homogeneous Serbia," cleansing the territories of alien elements. But they had less power, since Tito's Partisans dominated most of the area, ruthless but not pursuing ethnic goals.

The most notorious concentration camp was Jasenovac. We know most about it from the belated trial in Croatia in 1999 of one of its commandants, Dinko Savic (see various reports by HINA, the Croatian News Agency, March–October 1999). A Croatian historian testified that about 60 percent of what he estimated to be 85,000 murdered prisoners (an underestimate) were Serbs, 15 percent were Jews, 14 percent were Croats and 12 percent were gypsies. Virtually all the Jews and gypsies had been killed, but the killing of Serbs and Croats was more erratic. Croat victims were political dissidents, while the Serbs were mostly described as "intellectuals." Other witnesses testified that death was by axes, mallets, and knives, more than by guns, and the methods were extremely brutal. They said they had feared teenage Ustasha guards most. A few guards and officers had treated them sympathetically, and some even attempted to thwart the killing. However, they were executed when the authorities got wind of their actions, and this stifled criticism and made guards more zealous.

Sakic himself was 23 at the time he became commandant in 1944. He had become a Croatian nationalist while still only 11 years old, and was excluded from his school and then banned from all schools in Croatia at age 17. He left for Germany and joined the Ustasha in Berlin in 1938. He was first posted to Jasenovac as a guard in 1942. Witnesses charged him with personally shooting some prisoners. He was sentenced to 20 years' imprisonment. His predecessor as commandant had been a defrocked Franciscan friar. A survivor said that he had "favored a mystical approach to the killings." After personally shooting prisoners, he would proclaim "justice has been done" and then hold a Holy Mass that all Croats were compelled to attend. "He then used to preach about love for one's neighbor, and on Monday he would continue with the executions."

Recruitment to the Ustasha was disproportionately from the poor mountainous border regions of Bosnia most threatened by Serbia. Ethnic Germans from the Banat northern border region also assisted. Chetniks came disproportionately from Serb villages in the same Bosnian areas. Mirkovic (1993) and Paris (1961) both paint conventional class portraits of the perpetrators. Paris says most were not peasants but petty bourgeois – "artisans, shopkeepers, functionaries or officers of low rank." Mirkovic says the killers were generally recruited from the "socially declassed segments of society, from pariahs with little education or prestige in society." Neither presents evidence supporting these comforting judgments – which we have seen disproved in better-documented countries. They are on firmer ground describing leaders. Mirkovic presents lists of lawyers and Catholic clerics and suggests that doctors were numerous. Paris emphasizes students, seminarists, and priests, especially Franciscans and Jesuits. The archbishop of Zagreb and the Franciscan order were supportive, and almost half of the 21 concentration camps were commanded by clerics. Church newspapers proclaimed Hitler as the "Crusader of the Lord" and declared, "the Serbs are the greatest enemies of the Croats, while the Jews and Masons are the greatest enemies of all Europe." Jews were declared to be cosmopolitans and aliens who could not become true Croats. The church emphasized the eternal hostility of Jews to Christ but said that Serbs and Muslims could be converted.

One Ustasha camp commandant described his inurement to the daily killing of 3,000–4,000 arrivals: "after a time the destruction made no impression. I became used to it." This low-tech genocide used knives, hammers, and axes. Victims were driven over ravines, with grenades thrown down on them to finish them off. The Ustasha did not conceal their murders. The minister of justice proclaimed:

This state, our country, is only for Croats and for no one else. There are no ways and means which we Croats will not use to make our country truly ours, and to cleanse it of all Orthodox Serbs. All those who came into our country 300 years ago must disappear. We make no attempt to conceal our intention.

A priest declared:

In this country nobody can live except Croats. We know very well how to deal with those that oppose conversion. I personally have put an end to whole provinces, killing everyone – chicks and men alike. It gives me no remorse to kill a small child when he stands in the path of the Ustasha. (Alexander, 1987; Avakumovic, 1971: 139–40; Hilberg, 1978: 453–8; Laurière, 1951; Mirkovic, 1993; Paris, 1961; Steinberg, 1994; Tomasic, 1946)

Though Jews and gypsies were also ruthlessly eliminated, this was mainly a trade-off with the Germans, the price exacted for being allowed to run their own state. The Wehrmacht was present to enforce the contract, if necessary. But the murderous cleansing of the Serbs was substantially autonomous of the Nazis.

ALLIED PERPETRATORS

The Axis allies were independent states, not mere puppets but with real though varying freedom of action – Hungary least, then Romania, then Bulgaria, and finally Italy, the most autonomous.

Hungary

Fein uses Hungary as evidence for her thesis that the Jewish dead piled higher where interwar anti-Semitism had been stronger – as in Hungary, she says. But Hungarian anti-Semitism had actually been very erratic. It had peaked briefly between 1887 and 1892 and then again after World War I, when revolution raised a brief Judeo-Bolshevik specter. There was violence and anti-Semitic legislation. But things were quiet for a decade after 1926. The Soviet Union seemed quite far away, and Jews were resented more as capitalist than as Communists. But in the late 1930s Hitler's successes shifted Hungarian politics rightward, factionalizing the government. A reactionary authoritarian group clustered around Admiral Horthy, the regent (i.e., a president); there was a more radical, pro-German corporatist faction, and there was a large fascist movement, the Arrow Cross, sniping around the fringes of the regime. From 1938 the Hungarian government began intensifying anti-Semitic legislation before German pressure mounted. But as the state radicalized, all three factions got control of different state institutions, frustrating any coherent Plan. Until 1944 the Germans did not want to risk harming the alliance by imposing one.

Regent Horthy's Plan A was the familiar one of preserving national autonomy. Though geopolitics forced him into a German alliance, he strove to assert Hungarian autonomy. His desire was only strengthened by Nazi racial arrogance, so destructive of Germany's relations with its allies. Horthy bent to German *force majeure* while seeking not to alienate the Allies (just in case Germany lost the war). Yet his hatred of Bolshevism limited his flexibility – for it was the Soviets who counted in this theater of war. So Horthy deployed his army against Russia but dragged his feet on Jews. His faction made two distinctions. One was between their own legal anti-Semitism of discrimination (restricting Jewish education, job, property, and residence rights) and physical policed or wild deportations as urged by radicals, fascists, and the Germans. His prime minister, Kallay, said that the Jewish problem was not racial but economic. "Social justice" required discrimination. Jewish economic power must be removed (Don, 1989). Second, the Horthy faction distinguished "Magyar Jews" from "foreign Jews," recent refugees who merely resided in Hungary. They also denied citizenship to Jews from territories restored to Hungary during 1938–41. These foreign Jews were expendable. A German SS officer reported, "Horthy considered the assimilated Jews of Budapest as Hungarians but the poorer ones of the provinces only as rabble." This was a more cultural than racial view of the nation. Assimilation of the civilized, cleansing of the rest through deportations was Horthy's Plan B. This plus his geopolitical pragmatism kept him away from genocide.

Yet all over Axis Europe, German pressure accelerated discriminatory legislation into residential segregation, ghettoization, and, finally, deportation to death camps. Germans and their Hungarian radical and fascist supporters applied presssure, and in August 1941 Horthy yielded up 18,000 non-Magyar Jews from northern regions, who were driven by the Hungarian authorities across the old Polish border. They were supposedly Judeo-Bolsheviks collaborating with the Soviets. The operation was run by the Interior Ministry, regional prefectures, and rural gendarmeries staffed by radicals and fascists who called for "a territory free of all Jews." The economy could now "be rid of its Jewish parasites and the economic advantages of the border area may be secured for Christians" (Fejes, 1997). Perhaps two-thirds of the deportees were actually Hungarian citizens (Horthy may not have known this).

The regime was not of one mind. Its radicals favored a final solution, cleansing all Jews by policed or wild deportations. Their motives were mixed: casual anti-Semitic bigotry, ideological organic nationalism seeing Jews as the main enemy, and material greed. They assumed the Germans would finish off the Jews they had driven over the border, but the Wehrmacht was unwilling and drove them back again. A compromise was reached. Hungary took 5,000 of the Jews into its army labor battalions, alongside leftist political prisoners. As war defeat loomed, the treatment of these work Jews deteriorated and most died. The 12,000 Jews remaining along the border were then slaughtered by German *Einsatzgruppen* helped by Ukrainian auxiliaries and some Hungarian troops.

The army was also split. It did not run the 1941 deportations, though some units became involved, especially ethnic German Swabians (among whom Nazi sympathies were strong). Other units tried to save Jews (Zbikowski, 1993: 178). It was different along the contested Yugoslav border, where national interests seemed at stake. In January 1942, 3,300 civilians were murdered by Hungarian soldiers and gendarmes in a Yugoslav district annexed by Hungary in 1941. Seventy-seven percent of the victims were Serbs; only 21 percent were Jews (there were also a few gypsies). The need to come to terms with the Serb minority then brought the High Command to try some of the perpetrators, radical rightists, with Swabians again overrepresented (Braham, 1989a). But the army become more Germanophile as the war developed. Many middle and lower officers supported the Arrow Cross and demanded that Hungary be cleansed of the Judeo-Bolshevik conspiracy. An officer later testified:

The Jewish question had a catastrophic effect upon the armed forces. It had a terrible corrupting effect. Every value underwent a revaluation. Cruelty becomes love for the fatherland, atrocities became acts of heroism, corruption was transformed into virtue...against [the Jews] any action was permissible.... (Braham, 1981: 317)

Horthy held out until early 1944. Then he yielded up 100,000 more "alien" Jews, telling a confidant:

The Germans have cheated me. Now they wish to deport the Jews. I don't mind. I hate the Galician Jews and the Communists. Out with them, out of the country! But...there are some Jews who are as good Hungarians as you and I...here are little Chorin and Vida [Jewish industrialists and members of the Senate, Chorin also a Christian convert] – aren't they good Hungarians? I can't allow these to be taken away. But they can take the rest.

But Horthy's fierce anti-Bolshevism prevented him from changing sides as early as Antonescu did in Romania. The fortunes of war were shifting, and Hitler desperately needed Hungarian troops. Horthy probably could have stalled and done nothing about the Jews. But the Germans worked through Hungarian radicals, assisting them into office, and they pressured Horthy from within. Cabinet ministers called for cleansing of the Judeo-Bolshevik menace by physical means. Younger government deputies called for a "hard, militant, right-wing policy, based on the Szeged Idea [i.e., fascism] at home, with stern measures against subversive elements and new and effective measures against the Jews" (Braham, 1989a: 587; 1989b: 602).

Eichmann expected difficulties in 1944 when he asked for the remaining Hungarian Jews. Yet he got all the cooperation he needed from radicals in the key state agencies. He said that Endre, the fascist secretary of the interior responsible for Jewish affairs, "wanted to eat Jews with paprika." His deputy, the fascist Baky, provided the link with the gendarmerie. The Germans offered two trains a day for the deportations; the Hungarian planners asked for six. They compromised on four, since there was a war on. In two months almost 450,000 Jews were deported, mostly to their death. Over the autumn and winter at least 60,000 more died in shootings and forced marches. There had been 825,000 Jews in Hungary in 1941. Four years later, 68 percent were gone. Braham concludes, "the Germans would have been quite helpless...without the wholehearted and effective co-operation of the Hungarian authorities." That is also what SS officials Veesenmeyer and Winckelmann reported to Berlin. A few prefects, mayors, policemen, and civil servants dragged their heels and a handful resigned. Most prefects had been replaced by radical rightists, and some were moved to areas where they knew no one and so could not organize resistance. But most of their deputies and town mayors had remained in place and carried out orders. Teachers and civil servants predominated among the radical leaders. Most Hungarians seemed pleased to see the Jews leave, not thinking much about their destination. Around 1 million profited from the prompt redistribution of Jewish assets. About 1,000 men of the state security police, 3,000–5,000 of the 20,000 gendarmerie, and 3,000–5,000 fascist Arrow Cross militiamen perpetrated murders or severe beatings. The army was not heavily involved – it had its hands full elsewhere. SS officers again expressed distaste for local wildness. Some deportees said they had feared the Hungarians more than the Germans (Arendt, 1965: 140; Braham, 1981: 374, 403, 841–2; Braham, 1995; Herczl, 1993: 186–8; Höss, 1978: 135–6; Levai, 1948: 335–421; Molnar, 1997; Nagy-Talavera, 1997; Sagvari, 1997; Szinai, 1997; Szita, 1990).

In 1946 a Hungarian court in Cluj (now Kolosvar) found 185 persons guilty of war crimes during the deportations. They were mostly organizers rather than rank-and-file personnel, so most were middle-aged. Their occupations reveal the complicity of the authorities. Of the 179 whose occupations are clear, 143 worked in the public sector. Thirty-six were prefects, deputy prefects, or mayors, 17 were lower-level officials, 22 were police chiefs, 18 were policemen, 38 were gendarmerie officers, 6 were gendarme NCOs or men, 5 were army officers, and 1 was a soldier. The rest were scattered throughout the class structure: 6 businessmen, 6 professionals, 6 artisans/traders, 3 white-collar workers, 6 workers, and 9 women – including 3 midwives specializing in brutal vaginal searches. Many were Arrow Cross activists, and deportations were often organized from local party headquarters. One mayor grotesquely inverted reality, evoking a specter of Soviet deportations:

Blood and tears, the old and children, men and women, with their corpses will mark the trek of these new exiles toward Asia. And who would it be, with whip in hand, that would beat those staggering on bloody feet? The Jews...Bolshevism and Jewry are the same thing. A society that wants to fight against them must extirpate this species because the Jew does not want to, and cannot assimilate. (Braham, 1983: 84, 201–14)

The rural gendarmerie quickly cleansed the countryside, its commanding general having drafted the deportation plan. Most peasants seemed indifferent and were little involved. But Budapest was only cleansed in two bursts in 1944. The main street perpetrators were Arrow Cross paramilitaries abetted by gangs of young thugs. Horthy, the army, and church hierarchies had supported anti-Semitic legislation in 1938 and 1939 but were unhappy at the violence. The churches began to protest to the Germans and aid some Jews, but many lower clerics radicalized. One brutal Arrow Cross gang leader was a Catholic priest, while banners were dipped in honor when religious parades passed Arrow Cross buildings (Herczl, 1993). Newspapers also inflamed anti-Semitic feelings. But Horthy's faction dug in when foreign protests ensued, protecting Budapest Jews, helped by loyal police and army units who deterred radical gendarmerie units from entering the city (Karsai, 1998: 104–5). In July, Horthy was negotiating with the Soviets, trying belatedly to change sides – bizarrely using the bloodstained gendarmerie commander as his emissary (Erez, 1989: 624, 639). When the Germans got wind of this (through radicals within the regime), they arrested and replaced Horthy with the Arrow Cross leader Szalasi. He brought back the worst perpetrators for another burst of murderous deportations. Luckily the Red Army soon swept into Budapest, saving most of the capital's Jews.

Once again, the perpetrators cannot have numbered more than a few thousand. Once again, their core comprised fascists and paramilitary police units. My book *Fascists* shows that fascists were drawn from extreme nation-statist constituencies. There was some Nazi pressure. Without Hitler's war and German power, genocide would not have been attempted in Hungary. But almost all the perpetrators were Hungarian. The regime as a whole wanted ethnic cleansing of Jews, being divided over the means. Genocide was attempted by some radicalized state agencies as the state began to fragment under divisions exacerbated by war. Unfortunately, radicals came to control those state agencies possessing the weapons, training, and communications technology best suited to genocide. The core perpetrators seem to have been ideologically motivated by organic nationalism. However, once cleansing took the form of violent deportation, it created massive opportunities for profit. Many more Hungarians were sucked in by materialist motives, legitimated by those state agencies that normally maintain law and order against such motives.

Romania

Chapter 9 of *Fascists* stressed how central violent anti-Semitism had been to Romanian nationalism and to the country's large fascist movement, the Legion of the Archangel Michael. Wartime governments, the Romanian Orthodox Church, the military, fascists, and many others were complicit in what followed, if in varying degrees. Most Romanian atrocities were their own. Ioanid (2000: 108–9) says that anti-Semitic riots became genuinely popular during the 1930s and then became a "government enterprise" as

Romania entered the war on Germany's side. Hilberg says that Romania had the only government outside of Germany to itself implement all the stages of the killing process – from bureaucratic definition of who is a Jew, through discrimination, ghettoization, and deportation, to mass murder (1978: 485–509). But even all this did not bring up the killing rate to the level of countries ruled directly or through puppets by the Germans.

In 1937–8 the Romanian government had withdrawn citizenship from one-quarter of Jews – without Nazi influence. A pause lasted until August 1940, just before Romania's entry into the war, when the head of state, Marshal Antonescu, declared the country's Jews stateless, except for the few whose families had possessed citizenship before 1914. Antonescu was an ambiguous character in a weak position, but Romania was close to the Soviet threat, and like many nationalists he believed in the Judeo-Bolshevik enemy. He said Jews were "the most dangerous internal enemy" and favored deporting them even before the rise of Hitler – this was his Plan A, policed deportations (Ancel, 1993: 225). The government office of "Romanianization," originally seeking cultural suppression and economic discrimination against minorities, became more focused on heavier coercion of Jews. Trying to impress the Germans (so that they would stop supporting the fascist Legion that he had suppressed), through 1941 he repeatedly called for cleansing or purification:

we are living at the historical moment most propitious for a total ethnic emancipation, for a national revision, and for the purification of our Nation from all those elements foreign to its heart, which have grown like mistletoe, darkening its future. We must be implacable so as not to miss this unique opportunity.

The deputy prime minister told a Council of Ministers meeting in June 1941:

the Romanian nation ... must use this hour to cleanse the population.... As to the ethnic populations, let me assure you that it is not just the Jews but all the ethnic minorities – we shall apply a policy of full and violent removal of the foreign population. (Ioanid, 1990: 214; 1994: 158–9)

Church leaders urged that Christian Romania be purified of Bolshevik, Jewish, and "Satanic" blood. They described Hitler and Antonescu as God's "Archangels on Earth" "with the sign of the cross on their chests" fighting against "the Synagogue of Satan" (Ancel, 1989). The first murders, in 1939–40, came from the less respectable quasi-fascist LANC and the fascist Legion. Then during the Legion's botched coup of January 1941, 120 Bucharest Jews were killed and about 1,400 were beaten or robbed. In one terrifying incident, Jews were put through the machinery of an animal slaughterhouse. Ioanid (1991; cf. 2000: 57–60) calls this "the last Tsarist pogrom," but this was not a mere political diversion. It was a populist fascist coup involving murderous cleansing to eliminate Jews from Romania. Valerian Trifan headed the Fascist Union of Christian Romanian Students, the student wing of the Iron Guard. He was a theology student and a fascist and anti-Semitic propagandist. Just before the rising he broadcast radio calls for action: "The Jews, even if they were hidden in the nest of the serpent, we will find them there and we will kill them there." During the rising he led attacks on the Bucharest Jewish quarter. When the coup failed, he was smuggled out to Germany in an SS uniform. He ended up a respected American citizen.

Antonescu was now sucked in by a combination of domestic and German pressure similar to the one that had ensnared Horthy. But given his own views and the violence of Romanian anti-Semitism, he had less far to go. Hitler liked the marshal and let him into the secret of the Final Solution early. Antonescu was keen to prove himself. The Romanian Army was to invade the Russian-ruled provinces of Bessarabia and Bukovina. Antonescu took an active interest in the ensuing atrocities (Ancel, 1993, 1994; Butnaru, 1992: 89–133; Ioanid 1990, 1994, 2000). His gendarmerie commander called for "the cleansing of the land." "Echelon" elite units were formed, imitating the *Einsatzgruppen*. Romanian methods were neither rigorous nor orderly, and the Germans said they were both too sporadic and excessive, with too many rapes, lootings, and wild murders. Romanians had not entirely abandoned the pogrom, but the regime aimed at more systematic murderous cleansing.

The first massacre of between 3,000 and 13,000 Jews occurred in July 1941 in the Romanian border town of Jassy before the troops had even crossed the frontier. Antonescu was disturbed by this massacre since its wildness blew all secrecy from the operation. Fascist Legionaries were among those inciting the crowds to murder, armed by Echelon units acting on orders from the High Command. Whereas at this stage of the war the Hungarian Army sometimes obstructed the work of the *Einsatzgruppen*, the Romanian Army jumped right in. The Italian war correspondent Malaparte described the scene:

Hordes of Jews pursued by soldiers and maddened civilians armed with knives and crowbars fled along the streets; groups of policemen smashed in house doors with their rifle butts.... Squads of soldiers hurled hand grenades...into the cellars where many people had vainly sought safety; some soldiers...turned laughing faces to their companions. Where the slaughter had been heaviest, the feet slipped in blood; everywhere the hysterical and ferocious toll of the pogrom filled the houses and streets with shots, with weeping, with terrible screams and cruel laughter. (1946: 138)

Slaughter spread across the two provinces as the Romanian Army secured them. The remaining Jews were driven into neighboring Ukraine, where the SS was expected to finish them off. Many died, looting was ubiquitous, and a few Jews rich enough to pay ransoms were spared – a Romanian, not a German practice, indicating that greed might triumph over ideology. Not all Romanians were complicit: Ioanid (1990) names dissenting officers and cites cases of sympathy shown by soldiers, railwaymen, and local peasants. Yet the scale required mass perpetrators – half of the 330,000 Jews of the two provinces were dead by September. Then the Germans complained that they couldn't cope. The deportees were driven back, this time into the "Transnistrian reservation," the Ukraine around Odessa occupied by Romanian troops, joined by the first batches of Jews deported from the core Romanian territories, the Regat. Over the next three years 200,000 Jews confined there suffered waves of killings, deliberate starvation, and cruel maltreatment. It is unclear whether Antonescu was involved in these or if he now had a coherent Plan. But he did nothing even after official commissions of inquiry detailed the horrors. The regime was radicalizing toward mass murder. Only 50,000 of these Jews survived to the end of 1943 (Ioanid, 2000: 174; Schechtman, 1989).

Wild deportation began of the 200,000 Transylvanian Jews, more than 20,000 gypsies, and smaller groups of enemies like Orthodox minority sects (the Innocentists) and Ukrainian intelligentsia. The Germans reported with alarm, "The Rumanians are inclined to exterminate the stratum of Ukrainian leadership in order to settle the Ukrainian problem in the North Bukovina once and for all." The Germans struck a deal: if the Romanians handed over Ukrainians, the Germans would hand back Romanian Communists. Yet German reports continued to complain that murders of "absolutely unprotected and helpless" Ukrainian ONU members threatened "constant unrest." Antonescu declared: "It's all the same to me that in the eyes of History we should look like barbarians.... Fire with the machine guns if need be." The worst atrocity followed the bombing of Romanian army headquarters in Odessa (probably with delayed-action bombs planted by the departing Russians). Antonescu ordered reprisals, killing 200 "Communists" (i.e., civilians) for every dead Romanian officer, 100 for each soldier. The quotas were exceeded as 60,000 Jews were killed over three days, the biggest massacre in the entire Final Solution, outstripping anything the SS could do. Its scale and speed required modern weapons like the machine gun and the grenade, but the killing was not bureaucratic. It involved scenes of utter carnage in which groups of soldiers strove to outdo each other in bestiality. Judeo-Bolshevism was once again the pretext (Hilberg, 1978: 199–201; Ioanid, 1990: 199–234; 2000: 177–82; Mayer, 1990: 261–3). This was now genocidal. The diary of the Jew Dorian (1982: 163–4) reveals hatred of the Judeo-Bolshevik at its most bizarre. Here Russian POWs are considered Kikes – Jews:

I was horrified by the pervasive hatred toward Jews, whom everybody considers traitors, commandos, Communists, vipers – an uncontrollable hatred spreading like a contagious disease: people dont know when the epidemic has touched them – suddenly the sickness is in their blood. Any slanderous remark about Jews...no matter how nonsensical, is immediately believed. A third-class car, full of Russian sailors, prisoners of war, was attached to my train.... In a second, civilians emptied the platforms and soldiers left their cars, rushing to see the prisoners. An understandable curiosity – except that the majority clamored for knives, axes, picks, anything to gouge the eyes and chop off the noses of the "kikes."

The number of perpetrators was large but unknown. Very few Romanians helped the Jews; most remained passive. Fascist Legionaries were prominent in the killings. Chapter 9 of *Fascists* showed that the Legion was predominantly proletarian, though led by civil servants, professionals, students, and priests, and that it appealed especially to border counties where Romanians lived amid Jews and other threatening nationalities. It is unclear whether extermination had the same core constituency. The leaders were a wider spectrum of rightist nationalists, including members of the government, for whom Jews, especially those of border regions threatened by Bolshevism, Magyars, or the newest threat, Ukrainian nationalists, seemed essentially anti-Romanian.

But in 1942 Antonescu drew back from genocide. Like the Bulgarian and Hungarian regimes, he distinguished between types of Jew. Jews from Bessarabia and Bukovina (Romanian only between 1918 and 1940 and newly reconquered from the Soviets) were generally considered alien Judeo-Bolsheviks. Faced with a choice, most politically active Bessarabian Jews understandably preferred Soviet rule – though once again, few Jews were actually Communists. In Transylvania (held only since 1918) Jews were accused of collaborating with the Magyars. Indeed, many local Jews had been economic middlemen between Romanian peasants and a Magyar upper class. Had they been given a plebiscite in 1918, most Transylvanian Jews would have chosen Hungarian, not Romanian, rule. But Hungarians were allies, much less threatening, and these Jews were more Westernized. So they were considered only mildly alien. Third, Antonescu viewed the Jews of the old Romanian core lands, the Regat, as civilized and Romanian; they were also the wealthiest and most useful.

In making these cultural distinctions, Antonescu was separating himself from Romanian fascists, committed to racial cleansing of all Jews. Liberals, royalist circles, and the Vatican were pestering him to draw back, and the United States was trying to get him to change sides. He correctly thought the Allies might restore Transylvania to Romania. As the fortunes of war swung, so did Antonescu. The first German reverses on the Eastern Front in late September 1942 made him decide not to implement an agreement to begin deportations from Bucharest. He publicly rejected this plan the day the German surrender at Stalingrad became known in Romania. He was buying credit with the Allies. "The Jews became for Antonescu a possible form of exchangeable currency" (says Ioanid, 2000: 238–58, 271–83; cf. Ancel, 1993, 1994). He had more autonomy from the Germans than did Horthy, who was closer to the Reich, but he was also more flexible. Without Stalingrad, Antonescu would have willingly gone further; he later reportedly regretted his inability to cleanse all Jews. But most Jews from the Regat survived, thanks to his geopolitical sense. Finally, in August 1944, Antonescu allied with the Russians, though too late to save himself. They executed him the next year. He had led a local genocide, seeking to have cleansed by murder all Jews outside the Regat.

Bulgaria

Bulgaria was the only Axis power to largely resist the Final Solution. Tsar Boris, the leading politicians, and the church hierarchy have often received the credit, yet the survival of most Bulgarian Jews derived from much broader sources (Hilberg, 1978: 474–84; Oren, 1989). Jews were less than 1 percent of the population, did not dominate any branch of this overwhelmingly rural economy, and had little impact on politics. The main historic enemy of Bulgarian nationalism was not the Jew but the Turk, the enemy of "civilized Europeans" like the Bulgars, Greeks, Russians, Armenians, and even Jews. "Orientals" like the local Turkish population, Pomaks (Slav-speaking Muslims), gypsies, and Gagauz (Turkish-speaking Christians) were more marginal out-groups. Muslims were 14 percent of the population, the only substantial alien group. Organic nationalism grew after 1934, directed not at Jews but at coercive institutional assimilation of Muslims, mainly through compulsory schooling measures. In other wartime circumstances Turks might have been more likely enemies and victims. They had been 30 years earlier in the Balkan wars, and they were again after 1945. But Turkey was now neutral.

Nor was there much Bulgarian anti-Bolshevism. The struggle against the Turks had allied Bulgaria with Russia, so nationalists were often Slavophile – and few wished to alienate the massive Soviet neighbor. Bulgaria declared war on the Greeks, Serbs, and British but was careful not to declare war on the Soviets. Hitler understood, and he was mainly interested in Bulgaria's trade and in the assisted passage of his troops through the Balkans. The Judeo-Bolshevik enemy was nowhere to be seen, as even Hitler realized. Most Bulgarians, not just elites, were relatively immune to the hatreds sweeping much of Eastern and Southeastern Europe, and the Germans did not greatly pressure them.

Hitler did demand discriminatory and ghettoizing anti-Semitic legislation, and more was demanded by local nationalists influenced by Russian White emigres, then by Italian fascism and Nazism (some had been students in Germany). The regime became a little factionalized as these radical rightists infiltrated the Department of Jewish Affairs established under German pressure. A compromise was found. Hitler had rewarded his Bulgarian ally with Thrace and Macedonia, won from Greece. The 11,000 Jews of these provinces were more marginal members of the Bulgarian nation, unfortunate pawns, delivered up to the Nazis to preserve Bulgarian autonomy – and the rest of Bulgaria's Jews. When the Nazis and local rightists pushed for more, the government agreed to deport 9,000 additional Jews, but local politicians backed by large demonstrations halted this plan. The Germans did not want to divert troops to repress them. The remaining Bulgarian Jews suffered discrimination, but they lived. As in Poland, war-fighting strategy thwarted any local cleansing nationalism directed against Jews. But here it also affected the Germans. Thus were Bulgarians saved from perpetrating much evil.

The rulers of these three southeastern Axis states had all drawn distinctions between categories of Jew. Yet they were also drawn further into the genocidal project than they had initially intended. Hedging their geopolitical bets on the war outcome, they compromised over which Jews they would kill. But their motives were also political. Whatever the level of racial and religious anti-Semitism, Jews were believed to pose variable political threats to the organic nation-state. Those long settled in core territories were not considered fully alien, antinational, or Bolshevik, in contrast to those in threatened border territories. Except in Bulgaria, most politicians wished to cleanse their nation of Jews. But they drew the line at murdering them all. We have seen some signs that the usual core nation-statist constituency, including threatened border nationalists, were the most likely to cross this line. But the evidence is thin.

Italy

Italy was the only fully independent Axis ally, able to resist all German pressures – certainly until November 1943, when Mussolini was deposed and then reinstated, this time as a German puppet ruler. Until then, any atrocities were Italian initiatives; thereafter they might be more pressured. As Chapter 4 of *Fascists* showed, early Italian fascist atrocities had mostly fallen short of murder. Nor had racism or anti-Semitism figured much. Race was considered more cultural than biological. The Italian nation was formed by an act of willed unity by diverse groups, said Mussolini. All nations, he said, were biologically diverse. The Jewish question did not much interest him. Count Ciano, the Italian foreign minister, confided to his diary: "There are not many Jews and, with some exceptions, there is no harm in them." There was no Judeo-Bolshevik specter. Ten percent of Jews were supposedly party members. Yet from 1934 Mussolini occasionally, opportunistically stirred up anti-Semitism, and from 1936 joint Italian–German intervention in the Spanish Civil War brought more Nazi influence (Michaelis, 1995).

But it was in Africa that fascists discovered murderous ethnic cleansing in a way that returns us to the colonial themes of Chapter 4. Italy acquired North African colonies late, near the end of the 19th century, and developed conventional European racist views toward conquered natives: only whites were colonial citizens. Fascist writers like Corradini had a eugenicist vision of expanding the Italian population through colonies. Since settling large numbers of Italians in Africa required clearing the land of natives, Mussolini's Libyan and Ethiopian ventures led to mass killings. During 1928–32 the pacification of Libya killed almost a quarter of the 225,000 people of Cyrenica. Yet even this paled beside Ethiopia. Far more Ethiopians were killed during 1936–8 than there were Jews in Italy, though racism has prevented them from receiving comparable scholarly attention.

Del Boca (1969) details three types of brutality in Ethiopia, which I will convert into the categories of Table 1.1. First came callous warfare: the use of mustard and other gases, banned under the Geneva Convention, since they killed or maimed all life caught beneath the spraying planes. An American journalist estimated that 250,000 Ethiopians were killed or seriously affected. Observers said they saw "countless bodies of men and beasts" on plains and in rivers, and "thousands of corpses in an advanced state of putrefaction." The effects were long-lasting. An Italian Jewish doctor serving with the invading British forces in 1941 has told me that he saw many Ethiopians whose feet had been reduced to bones after walking through infected areas. The effects of mustard gas were soon dwarfed by those of the fire bombing and atom bombing of callous warfare in World War II. Yet this was massive overkill against a backward, numerically inferior enemy. Indeed, it had a second and deliberately cleansing purpose: to create space for the million Italian settlers envisaged. This was the equivalent not of the Final Solution, but (on a smaller scale) of the Nazi mass murders of Poles.

Second, the Italian occupation authorities committed exemplary repression escalating to politicide after the conquest. Mussolini had tersely wired to General Graziani, "All rebels captured are to be shot." Renowned for his ferocity in Libya, Graziani was reported as replying, "The Duce shall have Ethiopia, with the Ethiopians or without them, just as he pleases." To his fellow generals Graziani wired, "We must continue with the work of total destruction." Surrendering Ethiopian soldiers were executed by the thousands. Many civilians in resisting areas were murdered. In Addis Ababa squads of fascist Blackshirts went on a "Hunt the Moor" rampage, dousing streets with petrol and finishing off fleeing inhabitants with hand grenades. The small Ethiopian intelligentsia was liquidated: perhaps 3,000 were killed in Addis, followed by about 1,000 Coptic clerics elsewhere. Rome wired a caution to be secretive. But politicide in such a large, thinly settled country was counterproductive, since fearful Ethiopians could flee and intensify resistance. By the time the milder duke of Aosta took over from Graziani, it was too late. Italy could now rule only with a large apparatus of repression. Again, this paralleled Nazi rule over Poland or other occupied Eastern peoples. It was not genocide. It stopped short of mass murder sufficient to clear the necessary space and at politicide to wipe out all potential Ethiopian resistance. How far it might have eventually gone would have depended on how many colonists were introduced.

Third, racist segregation underlay fascist colonial policy after the repression was over. Racial intermingling was banned. A journalist noted that the policy was "to preserve the purity of the white race in East Africa ... racism can be considered ... as the crown of Fascist colonial policy" (Del Boca, 1969). Yet a contradiction emerged between fascists and Italians. Official policy was often thwarted by ordinary Italian soldiers and settlers, who were not racist. The Italian character, they said, favored conviviality, generosity, and consenting or purchased (but not raped) sex with Ethiopian women.

None of this was on the scale of Nazi genocide. In Libya, Mussolini even for a time struck a pose as the protector of Islamic civilization. This was normal colonialism. But by the mid-1930s only Italy and Japan were bent on establishing settler colonies. At worst Japan's policy rivaled the callous warfare of the Italians, though after conquest the Japanese imposed the most coercive form of assimilation, cultural suppression, not exclusion through mass murder. Of the Western colonists only those of South Africa were heading toward complete racial segregation, and this was never so murderous. That Italian mid-20th-century colonial cleansing through mass murder was so bad seems attributable to fascism.

In turn, Italian colonialism also made its fascism more racist. Combined with Mussolini's commitment to march with Hitler to the end, this generated anti-Semitic legislation in 1938. This did not result from German pressure (Preti, 1974). Mussolini was increasingly denouncing Jews, spurring on fascist students and journalists to anti-Jewish campaigns. Only Germany had supported the Ethiopian venture, pushing Mussolini further into the Nazi ideological embrace. Jews had called the loudest for League of Nations sanctions against Italy, since they feared all racism. Mussolini had long believed that "internationalist world Jewry" opposed his regime, but he had preferred not to provoke it. Now that it was publicly attacking him, he declared that Jews were not part of the Italian nation. All these strands entwined as his view of the enemy radicalized. He became concerned that fascism might stagnate (it had done so after his seizure of power), and so he demanded "progressive totalitarianization" from the movement. This radicalization was much less than the Nazi one discussed in Chapter 7, but it was in a similar direction.

The anti-Jewish laws were not popular, except in the Trieste region (Szajder, 1995). There were more Jews there (though still only 4 percent of the population), and anti-Semitism was (as usual) inserted into broader national conflicts, in this case between Italians, Germans, and Slovenes. The cosmopolitan Jews of Trieste were viewed as allies of foreign enemies. Elsewhere fascist street brawling only occasionally turned against Jews. SS reports said most Italians and most officials opposed the deportations. Some Italians tried to thwart genocide in occupied France, Croatia, and Greece.

Fierce resistance by Dalmatian Croatian guerrillas to Italian occupation did lead to mass execution of hostages and terror bombing of villages (Tomasic, 1946: 113). But, says Steinberg, the Italian Army "inhabited a different moral universe" than the German Army. Its fascists were traditional monarchists and nationalists. Nor was there an Italian fascist equivalent to the SS undermining the traditions of the German army. Jews, Serbs, and Greeks certainly suffered much less at the hands of Italians (Mazower, 1993: 150–5; Steinberg, 1990: 206–27).

Yet in November 1943 the final rump fascist state in northern Italy, the Salo or Italian Social Republic, was installed. Organized by the new Revolutionary Fascist Party, the Republic considered itself leftist and anticapitalist. Since the Germans opposed such leftism, fearing it would disrupt wartime production, the radicalism of these fascists was redirected toward anti-Semitism – rather like the radical redirection of the German SA during the 1930s (discussed in Chapter 7). Salo paramilitaries committed mayhem against Jews and locals suspected of partisan sympathies. Most of the *carabinieri* and draftees seemed to lack enthusiasm. But the more radical bands, totaling somewhere over 2,000 men, relieved the SS of most of the burden of the final deportations. Some were independent freebooters; others came from fascist formations like the African Blackshirts or the MSVN, a fascist paramilitary police force. These fascist veterans had turned toward a more ethnic conception of the enemy influenced by the African wars and Nazi power. Some denounced the Judeo-Bolshevik enemy. Zucotti calls them "fanatic fascists ... vicious, dedicated men with nothing left to lose and nowhere else to go ... idealists, opportunists, sadists, ex-convicts, adventurers and adolescents" (1987: 148–54; cf. Bernardini, 1989; Fargion, 1989; Hilberg, 1978: 421–32; Ledeen, 1989). This jumble of identities is not entirely convincing, and the perpetrators remain murky. Many were tried after the war, so more data must surely be available. Yet it is clear that in both Africa and Italy, real fascists were guiltier than ordinary Italians.

CONCLUSION: THE SOCIAL STRUCTURE OF ALLIED AND AUXILIARY GENOCIDE

In the interwar period, almost all of Eastern Europe moved further toward the organic conceptions of democracy described in Chapter 3. The new governments set up after 1918 were designed as representative governments heading toward liberal democracies, but all privileged the dominant (and usually titular) ethnic group. Poland was essentially for the Poles, Romania for the Romanians, and so on. Political parties of majorities and minorities alike styled themselves as nationalist, claiming to speak for the single, integral nation. Their leaders, alongside generals and monarchs, claimed to be its mouthpiece, and so democracy degraded into authoritarianism. Yet their nationalism and their discriminatory policies against other ethnic groups were also popular. Several minority parties abandoned multiculturalism (their first line of defense) and reacted with their own organicism, claiming their own states. Ukrainian and Croatian nationalists eventually embraced their own authoritarianism. The region's regimes thus embodied my ethnic theses 1a and 1c, supposedly seeking democratization but in reality moving toward ethnic cleansing. Of course, the most serious cleansing occurred in World War II under collaborating regimes that were not at all democratic. But by that time, Nazi Germany had intervened.

I have discussed murderous cleansing committed by somewhat more than 50,000 non-Germans. Including Western Europeans would raise the total above 60,000. This was mass murder but obviously nowhere near majority collaboration in genocide. Almost everywhere, organic nationalists led the killers, as earlier they had led milder discrimination and cleansing. These leaders were led toward ideological killing by their anticommunism and organic nationalism. They wielded ethnonationalist, not class, models of interest. They were then trapped in the Nazi embrace by German mobilization of military and political power. Their compliance became double-edged: though most local allies and auxiliaries seem to have killed rather willingly, they were also disciplined under German orders. The allies were more autonomous than the puppets, the clients, and the auxiliaries, and though Italian and Croatian fascists took their opportunity to murder their own enemies, greater autonomy almost always meant less systematic killing. Their more autonomous killings also usually had the ambiguous quality of wildness. Though wild killings seem more horrific (including to Germans), their momentum could not be easily maintained over time. Wild killings were in a sense escalated pogroms, and so included much materialist looting. Looting perpetrators were often too busy to kill very efficiently. This is why even the most violent anti-Semitism, in Romania perhaps, though much greater than any earlier found in Germany, could not lead on its own to genocide. It needed Nazi reinforcement to get anywhere near that end.

These perpetrators were stratified. German Nazis constituted a genocidal "upper class" whose career radicalization (described in previous chapters) was almost complete by the time these collaborators were asked to join in. Thousands of fascists and organic nationalists dominated the collaborating administrations of routinized genocide then set in place. They were the genocidal "middle class," probably drawn from core constituencies similar to those I identified in the case of the Nazis. Yet very few were driven by the near-absolute value rationality dominating Hitler and his inner circle. They got into murderous cleansing and then into genocide indirectly, as milder Plans for national independence and rule by the majority ethnicity were frustrated by political and geopolitical crises. State boundaries had been transformed by the post-1918 peace treaties. New states were created, while older states nourished ethnic revisionism. Nationalist movements were seeking their own states, bringing competing demands for the same territorial area (as in my third ethnic thesis). The growth in power of Soviet Russia, Nazi Germany, and fascist Italy brought further destabilization. All this brought distinct channeling of class toward ethnicity (my second ethnic thesis) – the supposed Judeo-Bolshevik exploiter, or Serb or Czech exploitation of Croats, Muslims, and Slovaks. Geopolitical destabilization then exploded into a second world war in which these nationalists had to choose their side. Those who were to become middle-class perpetrators predictably chose Nazi ethnonationalism over Soviet class revolution. War mobilization kept them firmly to their choice, ensuring that for several years ethnic trumped class conflict.

Amid this crisis, all the nationalist movements discussed in this chapter radicalized as their states' autonomy weakened or collapsed. Thus their behavior fits well into my fifth general thesis: state factionalism and radicalization amid geopolitical crisis. These nationalist collaborators moved quickly, though often ambivalently, to secure Nazi support to attain their two primary goals: the achievement or preservation of state autonomy and the organic ethnic unity of their nation. Down this path lay genocide, though the local "middle class" had intended only a rather lesser evil.

More ordinary people in the tens of thousands volunteered to be the rank-and-file, the genocidal working class. The collaborators came from all classes, from social constituencies among which ideological violence resonated. They were disproportionately young men with military or police backgrounds, anticommunist and rightist. Sometimes they were from threatened borders. There were very few women among the perpetrators. Many women approved of the killings (Gross, 2001, says this was so in the Polish village of Jedwabne), but they were rarely allowed to join in. On the side of the victims there was little gender bias. Women (and children) were generally killed alongside men, though often after being raped.

Initial entry to this genocidal "class structure" was voluntary, unlike entry to real classes. The perpetrators were not random Lithuanians, Ukrainians, Croatians, and so on but self-selected volunteers for tasks that most knew would involve some killing. The full extent of German goals must have eluded their initial understanding. But nationalist leaders, police auxiliaries, and camp guards must have known the job would be tough and dirty. Some performed their tasks with enthusiasm; others conceived of toughness as enforcing order, which their rightist or police/military backgrounds valued. Some committed nationalists grimly believed that the end, an organic nation-state, justified dirty means. The initial ideological motives of both the middle class and the working class seem to have mixed anti-Semitic bigotry, vengeful anticommunism, organic nationalism, and a more general admiration for the all-conquering Germans. Yet many were lured over the brink by materialism, and were then additionally trapped by careerism, enjoyment of their own power (including sadism), and hierarchical pressures of conformity and discipline. Motives were mixed, especially at the lower levels.

Some merely followed their friends, their elders, or respected local elites; some had admired the Germans or Hitler from afar, with little knowledge of their methods; some just wanted a steady job and food, or to loot the possessions of Jews and others. Auxiliary and Axis perpetrators seems to have had even more mixed motivations than their German masters.

This class structure also contained an unusually severe penalty for exit. Changing one's mind was hazardous. It was easier for the allied Axis powers once the fortunes of war had turned. Only the real fascists among them conspicuously spurned this opportunity to withdraw selectively from murders that had become geopolitically disadvantageous (since the Allies did not like them). But exit was difficult for the puppet leaders and for the auxiliary formations under German officers, operating in the midst of vastly superior German forces. Germans had enormous military and political power to secure compliance – which is what actually made the Solution in the occupied territories Final. Arajs was correct. After volunteering, he and thousands like him were held fast in the Nazi embrace. Coercion (aided by inurement and alcohol) was an important bond. It would have required unusual bravery to seek escape. Only a few attempted it until the final months of the war. There was a much higher proportion of disciplined killers here than among Germans.

Broad factors underlay their initial compliance. There was the strength of casual anti-Semitism across Central and Eastern Europe. This rested on twin ancient traditions: Christian and economic hostility to Jews as pariah exploiters. The Final Solution was built on a very old base, and it contained important traditional religious and material motivations. Many perpetrators believed wild rumors about Jews similar to those existing in their fathers' and grandfathers' time – Judeo-Bolsheviks were in the same mythic tradition as Judaic baby stealers. Perpetrators cloaked their greed in Christian legitimacy and rhetoric about ending exploitation. In the early 20th century both traditions had been modernized. Christian churches had harnessed themselves to local organic nationalisms that could supposedly transcend class and other social conflicts. Protestant, Catholic, or Orthodox churches now reinforced almost every nation's sense of its essential difference from aliens abroad and within. Anti-Semitic avarice was wrapped up in more modern ideology: a populist nationalism that was exploited by foreign capitalists and Bolsheviks alike. Religion and populism jointly reinforced the turn of nationalism rightward to organicism and toward fascism.

This reinforced the plausibility of the notion that Jews threatened the desired modern nation-state. The cosmopolitan Jews were almost everywhere regarded as alien to the nation. Only Bulgarians had other, more important enemies that effectively sidelined their own casual anti-Semitism. Only Croats had the autonomy plus another, more important enemy to subordinate Jewish genocide to murderous cleansing of Serbs. There were echoes of this in other cases – Romanian murders of Ukrainians, for example – but the Jew was usually in Central and Eastern Europe the national enemy. Unexpectedly, the ideologically driven fate of the Jews also sealed the fate of another, smaller group of cosmopolitans: gypsies. Yet, as I have emphasized in these chapters, anti-Semitism was not a stand-alone phenomenon. Jews got worse treatment when plausibly linked to other enemies of the organic nation-state. Fein (1979: 44–58, 88) found that only 1 out of the 9 ethnically homogeneous states in Europe (where 75 percent of the population shared the same language and church) had successful anti-Semitic movements compared to 6 out of 10 ethnically mixed states. Jews were more likely to be the victims where organic nationalists also felt some other threat besides Jews. I have provided the most sustained analysis of this link in the case of Romania in Chapter 9 of *Fascists*. There the level of fascist voting was systematically higher in Romanian counties where both Jews and either Germans or Magyars lived in large numbers. As usual, Jews were at risk when they seemed connected to other enemies of the organic nation-state

What would have transpired without the Nazi upper class and its stunning military successes and domination over its auxiliaries? Though "counterfactual history" is hazardous, we have seen an aggressive organic nationalism surging throughout this region between the world wars. The rise of Nazi Germany fueled the surge but did not cause it. As early as 1925, most governments were subverting the multicultural promises of their constitutions. Poland was in practice for the Poles, Estonia for the Estonians, Romania for the Romanians, and so on. Three countries had relatively mild nationalisms. Italian fascism began with a more flexible and cultural than a fixed and ethnic sense of the nation, though it drew the line at Africans. And though its treatment of conquered Slavs was fairly mild, it was reluctant to admit them to full citizenship. Hostility toward Slavs (and therefore Jews) in the Trieste region provided one of its main thrusts from the beginning (see *Fascists*, chap. 4). Luckily for Bulgaria, organic strains in its nationalism (aimed against Turks and other Muslims) were not exacerbated by the geopolitics of this period. Czechoslovakia was perhaps the most liberal society, though even its multiculturalism had limits and these spurred some Sudetens and Slovaks toward fascist fellow-traveling and murderous cleansing.

Nationalism was stronger than statism across most of the region – though these movements have attracted scholarly attention mostly because they murdered large numbers of Jews, justifying this in terms of organic nationalism. This was also wartime, when constitutional debates about state forms were less appropriate than killing enemies. But they had turned against liberal democracy, endorsing authoritarian organization, whose model was militarism and paramilitarism. Statism was more real than rhetorical. Thus unless some major countertrend had emerged, organic nationalist and statist pressures upon ethnic and political minorities would have likely increased anyway – without the Nazis.

The pressures would have probably been of very different strengths in the three cases of gypsies (and other small minorities), Jews, and other larger minorities. For gypsies, unanticipated victims of SS ideology, the likely counterfactual scenario seems the clearest. Without the Nazis, they would have lived, suffering discrimination (as they do today), but breathing and flourishing. Perhaps the same can be said of mentally disabled persons, Jehova's Witnesses, Innocentists, homosexuals, and other groups. For larger Gentile minorities, the likely counterfactual scenario would also have been discrimination, living as second-class citizens, plus some pressured emigration. In the relations between Croats and Serbs, worse might have transpired, and later did so. But without the power of Nazi Germany, other large minorities – like the Germans or Ukrainians of Poland – would have had two options: either stay, facing discrimination in economic and educational opportunities and community rights, or emigrate. Emigration might be more attractive for Germans than Ukrainians, since Germans had their own homeland state. Either eventuality might have been accompanied by violence and perhaps the death of hundreds. Political minorities would also have suffered persecution, arrest, and a few deaths. It is difficult to imagine an Eastern and Central Europe in this period that would not have tended toward ethnic cleansing, if by mostly nonmurderous means. Indeed, this was the trend throughout 20th-century Europe. The drift of this half of Europe was also against political toleration. Liberals and social democrats were being repressed – which was doubly unfortunate since they provided the main bulwark against organic nationalism and anti-Semitism.

But what counterfactual scenario awaited the Jews? Even without the Nazis, there was a secular trend toward seeing Jews as inimical to the modern nation-state. Jews were responding with Zionism, seeking their own nation-state in Palestine – which has also become a decidedly organic and repressive one. It was not a steady trend, since economic or political crises tended to suddenly escalate anti-Jewish sentiments and lurch toward organic nationalism. Liberals seemed fairly helpless against such surges. They would have been rather stronger across the continent if the Nazis had not conquered Germany. Conservatives had more power to deflect the direst consequences for Jews by compromising with populist nationalism on economic and civil discrimination without murder.

One thing seems clear: without Hitler's Judeo-Bolshevik ideology, without the power structure of the Nazi movement, and without the military power of Germany, no genocide. It is difficult to imagine any of the groups discussed in this chapter, even the Romanian Legionaries or the Ustasha, as pursuing genocide on their own. They responded mainly in terms of the local plausibility of the specter. Violence, terror, killings they contemplated, but the main aim was pressured emigration, to drive Jews and other aliens out. Many minorities would have buckled and fled under such pressure, as Jews in the Russian Empire and Muslims in the Balkans had been doing since the 1880s. Conservatives might have maintained distinctions between national and alien Jews. Pragmatic politicians did not want the massive economic disruption that followed large-scale emigration of hard-working Jews. Unpleasant scenes would have become widespread – poorer Jews being driven across borders, being driven back again, stinking refugee camps, and unseaworthy ships. These, the familiar scenes of other refugee groups, may have been the most characteristic conditions of European Jews as well. This is not a pleasant scenario, but it is far short of the Final Solution. Thus genocide was everywhere linked to organic nationalism, usually to a pronounced degree of statism – the leading edge of both being Nazi fascism. Germans and Slavs, Serbs and Croats, could have murdered each other so freely only in the 20th century. The ultimate tragedy of the Jews was also essentially modern: to be the main target of this cleansing organic nation-statism. In this way, I have indirectly incorporated the Final Solution into my first ethnic thesis: it was the dark side of the democratizing nation-state.

11

Communist Cleansing

Stalin, Mao, Pol Pot

INTRODUCTION: MARXIST REVOLUTIONARIES

All accounts of 20th-century mass murder include the Communist regimes. Some call their deeds genocide, though I shall not. I discuss the three that caused the most terrible human losses: Stalin's USSR, Mao's China, and Pol Pot's Cambodia. These saw themselves as belonging to a single socialist family, and all referred to a Marxist tradition of development theory. They murderously cleansed in similar ways, though to different degrees. Later regimes consciously adapted their practices to the perceived successes and failures of earlier ones. The Khmer Rouge used China and the Soviet Union (and Vietnam and North Korea) as reference societies, while China used the Soviet Union. All addressed the same basic problem – how to apply a revolutionary vision of a future industrial society to a presently agrarian one. Cambodia was more agrarian than China, which was more agrarian than the Soviet Union. These two dimensions, of time and agrarian backwardness, help account for many of their differences.

These cases differ from those discussed so far. They were not mainly targeted against ethnic groups, and so key terms used so far do not quite fit. Not genocide, since the intent was almost never to eliminate whole peoples, and ethnic targeting was uncommon. Communists perceived their main enemies in terms of class, not ethnicity. For them, the notion of *rule by the people* became confused with *rule by the proletariat* or, rather, *rule by the vanguard party of the proletariat*, not rule by an ethnic group. Yet their revolutions succeeded only when old regimes had been undermined by war, and so Communists also acquired nationalist credentials by resisting foreign enemies. As the party of the proletariat became the party of the nation, domestic enemies became seen as traitors to the nation, puppets of exploiting imperialist powers. Thus class movements captured and channeled ethnonationalism, rather than the reverse suggested by my second thesis.

These revolutionary parties mobilized ideological power. Marxian theory gave them (they believed) scientific knowledge of historical dynamics and schemes of wholesale social transformation. This centered on economic and political transformation, the creation of a society of genuine abundance for all, and a more genuine democracy than that provided by mere liberal democracy. The two came together in the notion that the workers themselves would control the means of production and so make a genuine democracy possible. This was very future-oriented, since the present hardly conformed at all to it: the economy was backward and agrarian, while they had overthrown one dictatorship and were ruling through another one. But the notion of a hopefully temporary dictatorship of the proletariat, through a vanguard party, was an organic adaptation of genuinely democratic aspirations to their present reality. At first, organicism was restrained by commitment to democracy within the party. But this was rapidly perverted into dictatorship by and over the party.

The driving force of such values created (in Weber's terms) value rational actors, committed to certain goals over all others, willing to subordinate instrumental rationality for the future and for the party that would achieve it. The vision required purifying the movement itself to transform party members into *new socialist men and women* and to overcome class enemies by force. Earlier Marxists had assumed that after a short burst of revolutionary violence, opposed classes would submit and assimilate into socialist society. But the Bolsheviks learned otherwise. From their experiences, Chinese and Khmer Rouge Communists started with grimmer expectations. They also wielded increasing military powers. In Russia state power was quickly seized but a bloody Civil War followed. In the Chinese and Cambodian cases, state power was seized only after long and extremely bloody civil wars entwined with international wars. Armed struggles brought militarism into Marxism. These were now party-states embodying a highly ideological and militarized socialism.

Between victory and revolutionary transformation lay a great distance. The vanguard party was faced with an obdurate society and enemies at home and abroad. Capitalists, landlords, petty bourgeoisies, monarchs, and churches were marked out for elimination. But they resisted, aided from abroad. Some revolutionaries suggested pragmatic compromise to move more gradually toward social transformation, "settling down" into power and bureaucratizing the party-state. Radicals refused such unprincipled compromise, resolving to overcome resistance by any means necessary, whatever the costs. Civil wars encouraged this resolve, leading to a radicalism buttressed by military violence never implied in the revolutionary ideals of Marxism, but that had become necessary to accomplish or consolidate revolution.

Most deaths inflicted under Communist regimes were not intentional murders. They originated from Marxian schemes of revolutionary transformation through mobilized, coerced labor. This sometimes resulted in malnutrition, disease, and death, as it had in the Franciscan missions of 18th-century California, discussed in Chapter 4. The missionaries sought fundamental improvement of the world, but they actually brought death. Table 1.1 classifies this as mistaken revolutionary projects. Yet some Communists escalated beyond this. When their transformational policies failed, they blamed failure on the victims, whom they accused of sabotaging the transformation. They did not care about their fate, which I termed callous revolutionary projects in Table 1.1. Landlords suffered thus in China, kulaks in the Soviet Union. But if Communists deliberately increased the death rate as legitimate retaliation for sabotage, this escalated into politicide, killing off all conceivable opposition. Yet, further, Marxists generated an organic view of the people, defined not by ethnicity but by class. The people was the proletariat, and classes opposed to the proletariat were enemies of the people. Communists might be tempted to eliminate classes through murder. I term this *classicide*,[1] committed by all three regimes, though dominant only in Cambodia.

There was also dissent between radical and pragmatic Communists. Unlike fascists, who had the Leadership Principle, Communists had difficulty handling dissent. Despite being ideologically committed to democracy within the party, they had originated as a band of conspirators, came under military discipline during their civil wars, and emerged into power with no routinized institutions for handling conflict. So when their programs went wrong, factionalism could not be easily handled. Violence ensued, which I term *fratricide*, carrying off hundreds of thousands of Soviet, Chinese, and Cambodian comrades in purges. These greatly weakened the Soviet and Chinese movements and destroyed the Khmer Rouge.

Politicide, classicide, and fratricide are thus the main forms of murderous cleansing discussed in this chapter; while mistaken revolutionary projects contributed most of the deaths. Even bouts of apparently ethnic cleansing (in Chechnya, Tibet, and Cambodia) derived mainly from them. Leftist cleansing was distinctive, since the people was defined by the ideology, the economics, the military force, and the politics of class, not ethnic struggle. Yet leftist mass murders resembled those of rightist nationalists in one important respect – capturing and channeling ethnonationalism (as in my second thesis), they too developed a version of organic nation-statism, if distinctively based on class analysis. Such is the main argument of this chapter.

Like scholars of ethnic cleansing, most observers of leftist atrocities have adhered to a statist view of the perpetrators: mass killings were the top-down work of a dictator or political elite or of totalitarian regimes (e.g., Conquest, 1990; Courtois et al., 1999; Locard, 1996: 131; Rummel, 1992). They emphasize the coherence, premeditation, and planning of the killing. Indeed, these were highly statist regimes, not remotely democratic. They had abandoned their original minimalist view of the state to embrace a decidedly statist (and militarist) view of social transformation, dictatorial top-down planning backed by military-police repression. Most deaths came from a plan perpetrated by the military and police apparatuses of the state. Yet

---

[1] Margolin (2000: 177) comes closest to this concept, suggesting the term *class genocide* for the Cambodian case.

the process by which this eventuated was complex, for these were party-states. Ordinary party members were also ideologically driven, believing that in order to create a new socialist society, they must lead in socialist zeal. Killings were often popular, the rank-and-file as keen to exceed killing quotas as production quotas. The pervasive role of the party inside the state also meant that authority structures were not fully institutionalized but faction-alized, even chaotic, as revisionists studying the Soviet Union have argued. *Both* centralized control and mass party factionalism were involved in the killings.

STALINISM

The Bolsheviks seized power and quickly repressed their enemies and dissenting erstwhile allies. By September 1918 the independence of the worker soviets, the unions, and the law was almost gone, the Cheka secret police was into its first murders, concentration camps were built, and the Red Terror had started. Perhaps 10,000–15,000 were quickly killed, some in armed conflict, most in executions (Harding, 1984; Pipes, 1991: chaps. 15–18; Werth, 1999a: 71–80). The Civil War then increased the military power of the state and the paramilitary power of the party. The war was fought viciously. Both sides executed political opponents, the Reds sometimes extending killings to enemy classes and the Whites to Jews. Both killed well over 100,000 prisoners or civilians. Militarism began to color party rhetoric. This was *war Communism*. Economic problems, declared Leon Trotsky, had to be "stormed" with "disciplined armies" of workers. Like the fascists, the Bolsheviks praised discipline and comradeship. Both movements privileged old fighters; leaders wore military tunics and used metaphors of war for politics and economics – "storm troopers," "fortress storming," "shock troops," "light cavalry," "campaigns," "brigades," and so on. Violence wielded by the vanguard party would encourage "socialist morality" and create the "Soviet man," declared leading Bolsheviks, rather like the Nazi faith in a "consciously German" elite developing the "new man."

But the Bolsheviks had little conception of ethnic enemies. They fought in the Civil War against Ukrainian nationalists and Cossacks, and subjected Cossacks to policed deportations. But they viewed them through a class prism, as military allies of tsarism and the old ruling classes. Their own state would embody not a nation but a transnational proletariat. Since the USSR contained many nationalities, they built ethnic confederalism (see Table 1.1) into the Soviet constitution. This was a federation of sovereign national republics, each with republican autonomy. There was officially no place for ethnic cleansing. Instead, the enemies of the revolution were viewed as targets for cleansing. Whites, kadets, socialist revolutionaries, Mensheviks, then Trotskyites and Left and Right oppositions were seen as being fronts for opposed classes – the bourgeoisie, the petty bourgeoisie, feudal classes, and the kulaks. Since the Soviet Union was encircled by hostile powers aiding some of these enemies, quasi-nationalist denunciations were added. They were aliens, traitors, spies, and saboteurs. These accusations blended political, class, and national hatreds. But from 1920 Lenin described enemies in terms eerily anticipating the SS: "bloodsuckers," "spiders," "leeches," "parasites," "insects," "bedbugs," "fleas," the language suggesting threatening and dehumanized enemies infecting the people, requiring cleansing.

Relaxation came after the Civil War. Many ex-tsarist officials, Whites and socialist revolutionaries were accepted into the party in the early to mid-1920s. Up to 1928, during the the New Economic Policy (NEP), economic controls were also relaxed as independent proprietors were allowed to produce goods for the markets. National minorities were allowed greater autonomy. But from about 1928, Stalin and other radicals demanded more central controls and more force. The role of ideological power was critical here, for Marxism provided a model of a better classless society. The future was known, and it required massive industrial development. Radicals argued that structural transformation must be imposed, whatever the opposition. The regime could have conciliated – and did so later. But in the late 1920s and the 1930s, the radicals won and sought to eliminate enemies by whatever means worked. Mass purges, deportations, famine, and killing escalated through four phases: the cultural revolution and forced collectivization of 1928–32, the Great Famine of 1932–3, the Great Purge of 1935–8, and the ethnic cleansings of World War II. These all occurred under Stalin's leadership. Millions were still suffering in the forced labor camps of the gulag at his death in 1953. Then the regime moderated and stagnated.

The first cultural revolution launched class war by a younger, more proletarian generation of radical Communists against the bourgeois intelligentsia and bureaucrats who had infiltrated the party-state. This was mainly a bottom-up party movement. In response, Stalin zigzagged, initiating some actions, reining others in (Fitzpatrick, 1978). But this was soon dwarfed by the forced industrialization of the 1928 Five Year Plan, their Plan A. The Plan was not intended to kill, but it brought very callous treatment of enemy classes. Bourgeois and petty bourgeois entrepreneurs were expropriated and declared "nonlaboring," "alien," "declasse," "people of the past." A few were executed, more were deported eastward, but most were subjected only to *discrimination*, deprived of citizen rights. At the extreme this involved deprivation of food rations and lodging, threatening malnutrition and starvation. But the greater problem lay in the countryside, where there were few Bolsheviks and less stable state institutions. Agricultural surpluses had to pay for forced industrialization – as in all Marxist economic planning of the 20th century. Peasants had to deliver their grain at low prices to feed urban workers and to pay for the import of manufactured goods. Not unexpectedly, the peasants, the mass of the population, resisted. At first they merely withheld grain, hoping to push up prices.

The Bolsheviks responded with their perennial callousness when dealing with the rural population. They blamed the victim by proclaiming this a class war against a *kulak class*, a term used by Lenin to describe middling-to-rich peasant proprietors. The term had little resonance in the Russian countryside. Few peasants matched the definition. In any case, most peasants, not just richer ones, were now antiregime. Since the party lacked rural mobilizing power, it could not respond to opposition through institutionalized controls. After hesitating, it resorted to force imposed from outside by security police aided by militias consisting of party members and urban workers, its power base. This intensified waves of peasant resistance, leading to thousands of terrorist acts and assassinations of local Communist officials. Peasant men dominated terrorism, women the more openly organized protests. Since the resistance only had local organization and did not dare take openly military forms, it was doomed to failure unless the regime compromised (Viola, 1996).

But the regime deployed greatly superior political and military power and so felt it did not need to compromise. A class version of thesis 4b developed. In early 1930 it radicalized to Plan B, the collectivization of agriculture (Fitzpatrick, 1994: chap. 2). The surplus could be taken if peasants were moved away from their own household economy into state-controlled collective farms, *kolkhozes*. Class analysis was broadened to cope with the opposition. Rich peasants remained the true kulak enemy, "avaricious, bloated and bestial," "the most brutal, callous, and savage exploiters." They were "leeches" and "vampires" sucking the blood from the Russian people. Middle peasants were labeled as a "wavering" class, to be brought with firmness to the correct class line. Even the poor peasants were said to be "under the kulaks," an indication of how Bolsheviks "infantilized" the peasants (says Viola, 1996: 29–36). Thus *all* peasants would be moved into collective farms. Private ownership of land was abolished, and village institutions were destroyed. With so few rural militants, even the *kolkhozes* were not under effective control. In came security police and paramilitary "worker brigades" for enforcement. Plan A, forced industrialization, had escalated to Plan B, selective policed repression, initially aimed only at limiting kulak powers. But continuing resistance led Stalin to declare in December 1929 that kulaks were to be liquidated or eliminated as a class (killing the economic category, not the person). Plan B then broadened into Plan C, policed deportations. Middle and poor peasants were moved to nearby collective farms; kulaks were sent farther off. The most dangerous, 60,000 estimated male heads of household, were to be executed or put in internment camps. Their families were to be deported to the farthest reaches of the country. A further 150,000 families constituted a middling level of danger and were to be deported not quite so far, but into barren parts of the country. The remaining 600,000 kulak families were to be expropriated and then resettled in their own region, though not necessarily in their own locality. So far this had been an orderly sequence of escalation, resulting from the clash between top-down revolutionary projects and determined resistance from below.

But there was such an enthusiastic response from party activists that the pace and violence of collectivization escalated into the more disorderly categories in Table 1.1, pogroms and wild deportations. This alternately pleased and alarmed the leadership, which sometimes felt it was losing control. I call this combination Plan D, though it was much less orderly than a Plan implies, reflecting complex power relations between different party levels and regions. Stalin then tried to slow things down in March 1930, accusing the party of losing its reason through being "dizzy with success." Collectivization slackened and some peasants now attacked local Communists for opposing Comrade Stalin.

But underneath these policy waverings, radicalization was leading to the second phase of atrocities, driven by the rhythms of grain expropriations. The Bolsheviks remained committed to Plan A, removing farm produce to feed the cities and pay for manufactured imports. Each year the regime set regional procurement levels. When the harvest of 1931 proved poor, high quotas inflicted great hardship on the peasants. Worker brigades extracted the grain by force, killing those who resisted. Peasants starved; others hoarded their grain, ate their animals, or stole collective farm produce. The harvest for 1932 was thus even worse, and the procurements worsened suffering. Each year resistance strengthened into terrorism according to the monthly cycle of produce expropriation (Viola, 1996: 102–10). The regime stepped up coercion using hastily assembled worker militias, the 25,000ers, named after their number. Mikhail Sholokhov, honored author of *And Quiet Flows the Don*, wrote to Stalin to protest this treatment of "the respected tillers of the soil." Stalin riposted:

the respected tillers of the soil . . . have conducted a sabotage and would not have any qualms about leaving the working class and the Red Army without bread . . . that the sabotage was quiet and overtly innocent (without blood) . . . does not change the position that the respected tillers of the soil in essence conducted a "quiet" war against Soviet power. A war to starve us out, comrade Sholokhov. (Fitzpatrick, 1994: 75)

This was now in effect a Plan E, callous class war, the main killer during Stalin's rule. Peasant deaths mounted to an incredible 6–8 million during the Great Famine through malnutrition, disease, and starvation. This had never been intended by Stalin or by other radicals, except against the supposed kulak core. It was the unintended consequence of revolutionary transformation projects, worsened by callousness, sometimes hatred, toward the victim, shown by both party elites and rank-and-file.

During this phase the identity of enemies broadened uncontrollably. Class is not as self-evident as ethnicity. Since no one knew exactly who the kulak was, official definitions kept changing (Lewin, 1985). Officials strove to produce definitions that would target richer peasants, not alienate most of the middling peasants, and appeal to the poorer rural families who supplied Red Army soldiers and industrial workers. And were the pettiest of traders selling cigarettes or potatoes in the street really petty bourgeois class enemies? If landlords or capitalists are deprived of their property, do they remain class enemies? Is class an ascribed, permanent characteristic of the person that no reeducation can change? Is class a characteristic of the individual or the family? Are spouses and children also kulaks or petty bourgeois? Were classes hereditary: were children, cousins, grandchildren class enemies in perpetuity? If the class enemy is defined by bloodline, milder forms of cleansing, like assimilation or cultural suppression, become impossible. The class enemy must be removed violently from the body of the proletariat as people.

Local officials and roving paramilitaries had to fill in forms titled "Purging of Class-Alien and Anti-Kolkhoz Elements from the Collective Farms." Required to be lay sociologists, they struggled. *Kulak* became an adjective, not a noun, referring to the kulak-like character of anyone resisting – people connected to the old regime of landowners, clergy, church elders, members of non-Orthodox sects like Baptists and Evangelicals, wealthy peasants, "separating" peasants who had joined the Stolypin reforms of the late tsarist period, entrepreneurs, merchants, traders, tsarist officers, and policemen, Cossack headmen, estate stewards, and village elders – or anyone who had supported the Whites, socialist revolutionaries, or Ukrainian nationalists during the Civil War period. Middle-class outsiders like imported rural schoolteachers, doctors, veterinarians, and agronomists were attacked. Local officials sometimes targeted nonconformists unrelated to class, such as single women violating sexual convention – like witch hunts of earlier centuries. Central and regional party officials complained that locals were taking out local resentments on the second and third generations. The party elite (unlike their Maoist counterparts) formally condemned such bloodlines, but wavered over whether a class enemy could be reformed. Some were persecuted, then rehabilitated, then persecuted again. This was "a compound of political warfare unleashed from on high and traditional antagonisms" unleashed from below, from a "countryside closed in on itself in the midst of profound crisis" (says Viola, 1993; 1996: 113).

From the mid-1930s this led to the third phase, in which cleansing turned inward, to the party itself. Forced industrialization, collectivization, and famine all produced major policy disputes. But there were no genuine elections during the 1920s and 1930s. Dissent and factions were tolerated, provided that all toed the party line once taken. But dissent was not regulated by clear norms or institutions. The party had developed procedures for screening clearly unsuitable members through the *chistka*, a sweeping or cleansing, though "purge" is now the universal translation. The party undertook regular purges to weed out those considered criminal, corrupt, drunken, or merely careerist, though "ideological deviation" and "alien" connections (with enemy classes) each provided about 10 percent of those purged. In the purge of 1929–30 most rural victims were judged incompetent or opportunist, though 20 percent were classified as having ties to the old regime. These early purges shed 10–25 percent of the total party membership at all levels except the very top. Few received any further punishment, and expulsion resulted from collective decision making involving questions of fact, though sometimes affected by chicanery, corruption, and nepotism. The purge of 1933 saw a slight escalation, as more were imprisoned and a few were murdered. Smolensk data for 1935 reveal an increase to 30 percent of those expelled as class or political enemies (Getty, 1985: chaps. 2, 3). But the prison population did not grow until 1937.

During the Great Terror of 1937–8 fratricide exploded. It was never quite planned, but rolled on in a series of expanding attacks. Collectivization may have decreased central control, as local party elites were told to fulfil their quotas by whatever means worked. The Terror could have been a way of reestablishing central control by using party members' resentments against their bosses. Geopolitical fears also fed domestic ones. War was looming, and the Spanish Civil War revealed Soviet isolation. Whatever the causes, the Great Terror saw 1.5 million accused of crimes against the state, of whom 1.3 million were given a penal sentence and 680,000 were executed (Werth, 1999a: 190; 1990b: 100). The higher the position, the more the punishment. Nikita Khrushchev said that almost 70 percent of the Central Committe members of the period were killed. In the factories workers were safest, managers and technical specialists most at risk, and prisoners' education levels rose sharply (Hoffman, 1993; Thurston, 1993; Werth, 1999a: 191). Former political opponents from the early 1920s who had later joined the party and early opposition groups within the party suffered more than did Old Bolsheviks (Getty & Chase, 1993: 230). But targeting was rarely precise, and accusations grew wilder. Many were fantastically accused of working for foreign powers, international capitalism, or fascism.

As the terror intensified, it engulfed many with lesser or no party connections. Industrial managers, engineers, and planners were charged with sabotage if they did not meet production quotas. Arrest quotas were set and rose. Millions were incarcerated in the gulag, whose camps were now contributing forced labor for forced industrialization. Railways, canals, and roads were built, and coal was mined, by slave labor worked to its limits. Most of these prisoners came from the low end of the social scale. The collapse of legality meant that the police dealt with all social problems in the same way. Criminals, juvenile delinquents, those living without papers at the margins of society, erratic workers, drunks, prostitutes, suspect social or ethnic groups, local opponents, and so on could all be rounded up, condemned as saboteurs or enemies of the people, and deported to the gulag with minimal legal process.

Stalin initiated the Terror, his hand in virtually every new initiative, aided by two leadership groups, one involving the political/military security apparatus, the other more ideological, urging radical renewal of the party from below to cleanse it of bureaucracy and corruption (Getty, 1985: chaps. 4–7). There was no alternative leader. As one official said, "any change of leadership would be extremely dangerous . . . [and] to stop now or attempt a retreat would mean the loss of everything" (Conquest, 1990: 29, 34–5, 80–3). Slacken the rural repression, and forced industrialization could not be achieved. No one could come up with an alternative way of achieving that goal. Waverers and opponents could be picked off one by one in the purges, abandoning each other with confessions induced by torture or to protect families or close associates, always realizing they had no alternative but to bow to Stalin's control of the party.

Yet Stalin was aided by rank-and-file party radicals railing against local party bosses, "little tsars," accused of "bad connections," mismanagement, nepotism, and corruption. Rural attacks demanded "kolkhoz democracy." The locals tended to exceed quotas for arrests and executions. By 1938 the Central Committee was trying to rein in the repression (Fitzpatrick, 1994: 194–8; Manning 1993: 193). Lupher (1996: 110–23) says the Great Purge was an alliance between the top (Stalin and his circle) and the bottom (new men, ex-workers achieving technical qualifications and mobility through the party) against the middle stratum of party elites, the *nomenklatura*, which had achieved its power during forced industrialization. Many of the radicals of the first cultural revolution phase had now become the bureaucratized enemies of the revolution, as defined by newer radicals. So not even this third phase reflected true totalitarianism. There was a strong top-down line, enforceable through the security police, enthusiastically amplified at lower party levels. The result was increasing factionalism within the party-state.

Killings also contained ethnic undercurrents. Famine and deportations were unevenly distributed by region. Minorities who could be associated with a foreign power – especially Poles and Germans – were targeted almost regardless of their class position (Weiner, 2001: 140). Famines and deportations also fell more heavily on the Ukraine than elsewhere. It had generated the biggest anti-Soviet nationalist movement during the Civil War, and Ukrainian nationalism was thriving just over the Polish border (as we saw in the previous chapter). Stalin ordered the deaths of about 80 percent of the Ukrainian intelligentsia by 1935. Some see his goal as "re-Russifying" Ukrainian cities and "pastoralizing" the Ukrainians, directly comparable to Hitler's policy in Poland in 1939. The Ukrainian mortality rate was over twice the national rate in the period 1932–3, and one official newspaper declared in 1930 that the policy was "to destroy the social basis of Ukrainian nationalism – individual peasant agriculture" (cf. Mace, 1984, 1997). Yet broader mortality figures cast doubt on this conclusion. Not just the Ukraine, but all "black earth" grain-producing regions (north Caucasus, Moldavia, and the lower Volga) had the highest mortality rates, while the main consumer regions had the lowest rates (Wheatcroft, 1993: 282–4). The party-state was probably focusing limited coercive resources on areas where the largest grain surplus could be seized – and where there was faster forced collectivization. There was also more resistance there, better peasant organization, and more help from sympathizers abroad, which redoubled repression (Fitzpatrick, 1994: 71–4; Viola, 1996: 158–60). Indirectly, Russian nationalism might have contributed, since the main consumer regions were in Russia and the main producer regions were not. The language of a (Russian) "center" versus an "enemy periphery" was now also penetrating the Bolshevik party and state (says Tucker, 1990: 109). Yet despite these nationalist undercurrents, the main driving force was Marxist ideology of class struggle and development.

Yet more nationalism emerged in killings after the Great Famine. Many interwar Marxists realized that to take and retain power, they needed a broader base of support than just the industrial proletariat, so they enlarged the proletariat into a broader constituency, variously called the people, "working people," "the toiling masses," or "workers and peasants." By the mid-1930s the main class enemies had been defeated. Now Stalin began to use the old term *narodny* to denote peasants as well as workers. Fascism also grew into a menacing, virulently anti-Bolshevik presence in Europe, and the Soviet Union seemed isolated. Some border nationalities were defined as ethnic enemies – Germans, Poles, Latvians, Koreans. Proletariat and people were fusing into a singular organic whole beset by alien out-groups. Then the "Great Patriotic War" (World War II) intensified nationalism. Those accused of cowardice or incompetence in the war, and Russians taken prisoner by the Nazis, were called traitors, spies, saboteurs. Thousands of Soviet citizens, including POWs who had survived terrible German treatment, were incarcerated in the gulag when they returned home in 1945. Many died there.

There were also ethnic victims. A few ethnic deportations from strategic border regions had begun before the war. In 1937–8, 180,000 Koreans around Vladivostock were deported into Central Asia in fear of a war with Japan. But during World War II eight entire Soviet nationalities were identified by the regime as potential German collaborators. Over 80 percent of the 1.5 million ethnic German Soviet citizens were forcibly deported eastward during 1941 and 1942. Men were separated from their families, and they were scattered to the far reaches of the USSR, with virtually no provision made for their livelihood. They were to live in varying but often dreadful conditions for about 14 years, a far more callous version of U.S. relocation camps for Japanese Americans. The other seven nationalities were Balkars, Chechens, Crimean Tartars, Ingushi, Karachi, Kalmyks, and Meskhetians. Some did ask the Germans to support their autonomy aspirations. Several hundred Chechen fighters fought with the Germans. These were all border nationalities who might change their allegiance.

But cleansing of these seven nationalities intensified only toward the end of 1943, when the Wehrmacht was being driven out of the Soviet Union. Since collaboration was no longer a serious threat, the opportunity was

being seized to dispose of smaller warlike border peoples who had long resisted Russian imperialism. As Lieven (2000: 314–16) notes, Stalin's deportations seem more explicable as a far more ruthless "final solution" to the
traditional problem of Turkey and the Turkic peoples than as part of the war
with Germany. From 1943, 3–5 million persons of these nationalities were
deported. Escorts were provided by 119,000 NKVD troops – a significant
subtraction from the forces available against the Germans. The deportees
were dispersed on arrival so as to destroy them as collectivities, going through
numerous improvised gulag camps and labor brigades. Killing was rare, and
since this was better organized than earlier deportations fewer died through
callous neglect or overwork, though many thousands still died. The small
Ingushi nation probably lost the highest proportion, then Crimean Tartars.
All their ethnic homelands were resettled with Russians, and cultural residues
were erased. Only from 1956 did the Soviet Union acknowledge these great
crimes and begin the return of these peoples to their homelands (Legters,
1997; Naimark, 2001: chap. 3; Rummel, 1998; Werth, 1999a: 216–25).
This murderous ethnic cleansing was genocide under the UN definition,
which includes attempts to erase a group's collective cultural identity. Yet
it was not deliberate mass murder.

It was highly statist, planned by Stalin through the Supreme Soviet, implemented by state agencies, with state security police being the actual murderers. It was a preventive security measure during wartime initiated by a
paranoid yet strategically minded leader against troublesome groups whom
the war had rendered vulnerable. Though the policies were popular among
the Russian settlers, ethnic cleansing was not a response to, nor was it radicalized by, popular forces from below. But it was more an imperial than a
Communist policy, and it was not repeated. After the war, the USSR returned
to socialist transnationalism and domestic federation of nations. Some say
that by recognizing nationality and granting political autonomy even to ethnic groups who lacked national aspirations, the Soviet regime may have
unintentionally fomented ethnic nationalism (Brubaker, 1996: 26–40). The
contemporary phase of ethnic cleansing in Chechnya is being perpetrated by
a democratically elected regime.

Most of the victims of Stalinism were peasants. A total of 1.8 million
were officially deported during dekulakization, and total deportation deaths
may have been around 600,000 (Fitzpatrick, 1994: 80–8; Werth, 1999a:
155, 207). During the Great Famine perhaps 6–8 million died in all. Werth
estimates that in the Great Terror 685,000 were executed. In the ethnic deportations about 100,000 Chechens, upward of 50,000 Tartars, and perhaps
50,000 others died. Recent estimates of the number of gulag prisoners have
varied between 5 and 10 million, and many of these died (Nove, 1993;
Werth, 1999a: 206; Wheatcroft, 1993). The total dead in all phases combined is unknowable. The most careful estimates place it at 8–10 million,
though some are much higher (Conquest, 1986: 306; 1990: 484–90; Mace,

1984; Rummel, 1994: 83). Of these, perhaps just under 1 million were exe-cuted or otherwise directly murdered. As a proportion of the whole Soviet population the dead amount to only 4–6 percent, nowhere near genocide. But they are still horrific atrocities.

They were not simply totalitarian, since they were both top-down and bottom-up. Getty (1985: 36–7) sees Stalinism as fairly chaotic, since the party was small, divided, and undisciplined, with little planning capacity or record keeping. Werth (1999b: 103–6) prefers the term *variable geometry*, induced by the different rhythms and motivations of its several phases. Cleansing was set in motion at the top and implemented through chains of command, some of which were hierarchical (like the army and security police) and others were very loose (like the worker militias). Werth instances the deportations of 1930–3. The decisions were taken on high, so police, worker militias, and party radicals hastily despatched half a million families, assuming they would be resettled on collective farms or in labor camps, but those at the receiving end did not have the resources. In practice, says Werth, the policy became "deportation-abandonment," unintentionally resulting in the kinds of deaths that occur when people are herded into camps without adequate food or sanitation. Nonetheless, he also sees elements of uniformity among the various agencies. All believed in enemies, were obsessed by statistics and quotas, and were merging farms, factories, deportations, and prisons into a single terrorized industrialization (1999a: 266–7). I would add that coherence came as pragmatists and bureaucrats were defeated by radicals committed to a revolutionary transformation in which cleansing of enemies was ultimately seen as moral. At its worst this amounted to deliberate classicide/politicide. But this terrible outcome had not been originally in-tended. It was the unintended consequence of transformational goals with-out the stabilized political institutions to accomplish them peacefully.

CHINA

The Communists gradually seized power across China during a 20-year Civil War entwined with a war against Japanese invading armies. Sometimes local circumstances dictated compromise with political and class enemies, some-times massive repression and transformation was attempted. Kicked out of the towns, the Communists had led a predominantly peasant army, and dur-ing World War II they became the main leaders of Chinese national resistance against the Japanese. Being militarized, the party/army had exceptional disci-pline and unity, and Mao's leadership was unchallenged, since he had proved a remarkable strategist of victory.

In victory after the war the Chinese Communist Party (CCP) Plan was to immediately execute Kuomintang (KMT) and Japanese cadres and collab-orators, and the land was to be forcibly redistributed. It divided the rural population into landlords, three peasant categories – rich, middling, and poor – and landless laborers. In each locality, landlords and rich peasants were to be leveled down to somewhere around the status of middle peasants, their surplus lands, animals, and property being redistributed to the poorer peasants and laborers. Party and village organizations were to be controlled by the poorer categories. All this was to be accomplished by armed force.

The CCP had ample militants in areas it already controlled. There redistribution was often already half-completed and could be finalized in an orderly fashion. But most of China had only just fallen into its lap. Student militias and other outside militants came in to hastily recruit local members. Less than a dozen of them might have to control several villages, confronted by a functioning, hostile local social order controlled by landlords and their bully boys, with patronage ties stretching through every peasant stratum. Even if peasants were in debt to the landlord, they were cautious. They had already witnessed the ebbs and flows of the Civil War. What if the KMT, the Japanese, or local warlords returned? As one landless man told the two young students effecting land reform in Longxiang village (one was a playwright, the other a comic actor): "What if I stick my neck out and things don't go as you say they will? I'll be left out on a limb." He pulled his jacket collar down to show them where landlord Chi's cudgel had left a great weal on his back. An old peasant told them he had seen outsiders before: "They talked like you do.... They seemed to be nice people. But the landlords came back with their militia ... and an army ... with shiny new arms.... The landlords settled accounts and killed us like flies" (Chen, 1980: 97–8). In Fanshen militiamen led a landlord's donkey all over the village, begging household after household to take it. No one would, fearing reprisals (Hinton, 1966: 124).

So the party militants sought to translate official class categories into tactics. Attack landlords, declare that rich peasants must give up only some of their land, state that middle peasants need fear nothing, and poorer peasants and laborers would receive land and could join a village militia to do the attacking. Then demonstrate their powers first on relatively easy targets. A lesser landlord might be forced to pay back the "exploitive rents" of recent years. Even haggling weakened the inviolability of traditional landlord–tenant relations. Or a crowd might be assembled to take an inventory of the nearest landlord's house. The militants could push aside his household retainers, break down his imposing door, or open his food store. The crowd might then start looting, declaring that this was only payment for what the landlord had stolen from them over many years. The landlord and his family suffered ritual humiliation as they cowered in fear in the courtyard. Or locals could be egged on in an "anti–local bully campaign" to attack landlords' thugs or corrupt or cruel collaborators with the KMT or the Japanese. The leading villain might be executed, his minions cowed or expelled. A landlord relying more on violence than patronage might be next; he might have reduced debtors to slaves or concubines or even arbitrarily killed them. These hated figures were tried in the village square, with villagers denouncing and sentencing them, for to "speak bitterness...must heighten the class-consciousness of the masses and strengthen the thoroughness of our work" (Kuo-Chun, 1960: 121).

Those who helped more got more benefits than those who did not. Where militants attacked religion, or where they expropriated ordinary peasants, or where they were really just young toughs seizing power and property for themselves, they lost popularity. But over the months more and more peasants joined in, settling their own scores, widening the scope of redistribution, widening vengeance, seizing and beating the relatives of landlords. By September 1951 land redistribution had been completed for an incredible 400 million people, 80 percent of the entire rural population. It reached over 90 percent a year later. The new local leaders were overwhelmingly from the middle and poor peasants.

This was the most massive class revolution in history and naturally involved many killings. The elimination of the landlord class was initiated top-down. But that it involved mass killings, elements of classicide, was due more to the bitterness and rage of the poorer peasantry now dominating the party base. Landlordism had been unpopular, kept in place by routine, patronage, and coercion.[2] Once all three props were removed, there was widespread and enthusiastic support for the Communists. The tables turned, peasants could get revenge on their oppressors with impunity and license. They were not bound to the party by ideology, but the party's ideology made immediate practical sense of their experience and interests. Landlords, rich peasants, and their poorer clients were killed as soon as the peasants felt safe. Some were killed as they resisted, others as "speak bitterness," "settle account," or "struggle" meetings turned into beatings and then executions. Landlords were tortured to reveal where they had hidden their riches. The CCP repeatedly denounced "illegal" violence, but seemed truly unhappy only if killing seemed driven by corruption rather than class or if it increased local disorder. But in most localities the process was actually increasing order, cementing the party-state among core constituencies of class support among the lower and middling peasants. Classicide was accomplishing class transformation and state-building. This reverses the causality of statist theory of murderous cleansing: cleansing generated the powerful state, not vice versa.

Most estimates of the dead vary between 1 and 2 million, including 200,000 to 800,000 executions – large numbers but tiny proportions of a population of 580 million. Between 4 and 6 million more were sent to penal labor camps, and many of these died there through overwork and disease. Repression of urban political and class enemies was also ferocious. Restoring social order across China also involved killing and incarcerating many bandits, criminals, prostitutes, and opium dealers. Many other local

---

[2] This account of land reform depends on Chen (1980), Crook and Crook (1979), Hinton (1966), Kuo-Chun (1960), Friedman et al. (1991), Teiwes (1987), and Yang (1959).

scores must have been settled. Perhaps 1 million were killed in the cities and 2 million were sent to the camps. Altogether, Plan A may have caused the death of between 1 percent and 2 percent of the population, either directly or in penal camps. Its scale was not premeditated, though it was received with indifference by the planners – for these were enemies of the people as proletariat in a callous civil war.

The CCP retained a stronger pragmatic streak (and was also more united) than the Bolsheviks. It eased political repression and even recruited nonparty and ex-KMT officials. The political side of the regime's Plan B moderated, mixing bursts of policed repression of potential dissidents, followed by imprisonment rather than executions, plus discrimination that had hereditary tinges. The class position of the family head in 1946–9 continued to define a person's own class position into the 1990s. The children and later the grandchildren of that person remained privileged by an originally "good" (worker, peasant, or revolutionary militant) class position and disprivileged by a "bad" one (landlord, rich peasant, counterrevolutionary). It was assumed that in a couple of generations the effects of bad class backgrounds would disappear.

The former ruling class had been eliminated, but the economy was not yet socialist. Land redistribution had left the peasant household intact. Mao argued that peasant households working on their own were essentially capitalist, and so could not significantly raise production levels. Mutual aid and cooperation must be promoted, since "If socialism does not occupy the rural positions, capitalism inevitably will" (Yang, 1966: 26). The CCP theory of economic development remained broadly orthodox and followed Soviet precedents: it could only be achieved by agrarian collectivization subordinated to industrialization. Since China was even more agrarian than the Soviet Union, industrialization would require exporting even more of the agricultural surplus to pay for the import of machinery. The CCP recognized that Stalin had gone down this road with appalling results. Mao said Stalin had "fished by emptying the water of the pond." They must avoid extreme militarism and instead follow a "unity-criticism-unity" political sequence. Liu Shaoqi argued that "the socialist economy must be planned but at the same time multi-faceted and flexible" (MacFarquhar, 1974: I, 185, 313; 1983: II, 151). Lupher (1996) suggests that the CCP followed a dual "authority–social mobilization" approach, balancing top-down rule with mobilizing the energies of the masses through local party militants.

Thus the CCP began the economic side of its Plan B, step-by-step moves toward collectivization during the early 1950s, culminating in the "little leap forward" of 1955–6. Peasant villages were grouped into smallish collectives or labor brigades. Participation in some brigade activities was voluntary. This partial collectivization seemed quite successful, achieved with little opposition. With the land redistribution already complete, the CCP was well entrenched in the villages – much more so than the Bolsheviks had been

(Lupher, 1996: 175). But Mao began his economic Plan C, the Great Leap Forward, in 1958. He promised "Three years of hard work and suffering and a thousand years of prosperity." Everything was to be communalized, including eating. Investment was to be diverted from agriculture to industry, including the much-touted backyard steel furnaces; "human wave" tactics diverted labor to massive Soviet-style irrigation works. Massive labor mobilization would secure agricultural growth, whose surplus would be used to promote industrial growth. As the Great Leap began, Mao and Liu were in agreement. Liu, the pragmatic bureaucrat, described this as "organizational mobilization"; Mao, the radical voluntarist, proclaimed, "let the initiative and creativity of the laboring people explode." There was still unity among the leadership (MacFarquhar, 1983: II, 51–5; Teiwes, 1987: 51–63; Yang, 1996: 33–6). So far the Plans had come in a very orderly sequence, through party unity more than any totalitarianism.

The Plan was Soviet-derived, though with Soviet militarism modified by Maoist ideological voluntarism. The Plan combined central planning with local initiative through a complicated set of production quotas. The central planners laid down two quotas: one that must be accomplished and was publicized, and a higher one that was expected to be reached but that remained private. But local planners were privately told that this higher level was the one they must attain. The local planners were also told to set a third, still higher quota that they were expected to accomplish. This elaborate system was intended to balance central directives with encouragement of local party initiatives to achieve higher goals.

But the multiple quota system had terrible inflationary consequences on forecasting. Inflation first happened as quotas came down the hierarchy and each level tried to impress the party by choosing a more optimistic quota. Then inflation happened again as the central planners received the most optimistic forecasts back and responded by again raising their quotas (MacFarquhar, 1983: II, 31). There was also inflation between the provinces. Provincial radicals who shared Mao's voluntarism were drawn from the ranks of poor peasants, their power dependent on collectivization. When they reported back inflated goals, the central planners put pressure on more pragmatic provincial officials whose lower targets seemed to indicate that they were performing less efficiently, with lesser commitment to CCP goals. This produced regional factionalism, and the CCP lost some of its cohesion Yet cautious local officials then felt constrained to falsely inflate their actual production rates.

These two sets of inflation led the central planners to continue wrongly believing that the Great Leap Forward was working. There were labor shortages in agriculture as peasants were siphoned off to irrigation and industrial projects. The backyard furnaces were a disaster, and they lured local radicals into depriving agriculture of labor. Agricultural yields dropped. But the planners, misled by statistics showing the reverse, felt they could extract even more of the agricultural surplus for export (to pay for manufactured imports), which then left insufficient food for local peasant subsistence. The peasants, engaged in endless, backbreaking labor, needed more calories than in the past. But they actually got less. They tried to defend themselves by hoarding, but much of the grain was now stored in commune granaries. Radical officials could remove it without using much police or military force. When peasants faced starvation, some did resist by rioting, while others communicated their distress to their kinsmen in the army, generating disaffection there. As in the Soviet Union, some radicals responded by blaming the victims as saboteurs and traitors. As Friedman et al. (1991: 240) note, local zealots had been rewarded for exposing class traitors ever since 1947. They could do so again *and* increase the quotas they sent to the state – at least in the short term.

Senior officials became aware of the problem after a year. Few shared Stalin's hatred of the peasants. Unlike him, they had led a peasant army to victory. Yet they were also attached to an orthodox Marxist economic Plan that placed industry first. They were split, as were local officials. Some saw moving back to more household-oriented incentives as the solution but knew this would increase inequality, which was undesirable. Others wanted further radicalization, yet were aware that it would cause more pain in the short run. Thus the initiatives from both the top and the bottom were diverse, producing serious factional conflict for the first time (Yang, 1996: 48–50). Economic Plan C was losing its coherence. Top officials wrestled with the statistical contradiction between a supposed bumper harvest in 1958 and an apparent grain shortage and hunger. Most recognized the failure of the backyard furnaces, which were abandoned. Mao knew there was false reporting but underestimated its extent. He rejected requests by regional radicals to use more police and military powers to stop hoarding. That would be the Stalinist path to disaster – the peasants were right to hoard what they could, Mao said. That was the only rational thing to do when collectivization had deprived them of control over the surplus. He advocated slowing down the pace of change but would not abandon the whole program, especially since the figures showed progress in industrialization. Decision making stalled and the famine spread. More top officials became aware of the inflated figures and the famine, but were reluctant to risk Mao's wrath by producing statistics that exposed its true size. He had worked miracles in the past, against the counsel of pragmatists. They delayed. The famine worsened.

Defense Minister Peng Dehuai was outside of the economic policy-making loop and so was not implicated in the Plan. He was from a poor peasant background and spoke his mind. In his military tours in late 1958, Peng Dehuai saw crops uncollected because the peasants had been diverted to industrial tasks. He also saw soldiers ordered to abandon their training to make steel in backyard furnaces. He listened to their accounts of their families' sufferings. In July 1959 he protested publicly to Mao, backed by a handful of top officials. He unwisely attributed the radicals' mistakes to "petty bourgeois fanaticism" (a phrase drawn from the only work of Lenin he had probably read). Mao, incensed by this terrible Marxist insult against his own policy, replied that Peng was a rightist trying to "sabotage the dictatorship of the proletariat, split the Communist Party, organize factions within the Party and spread their influence, to demoralize the vanguard of the proletariat and to build another opposition party." Peng responded that he would not shut up. He intended to continue "screwing your mother" (MacFarquhar, 1983: II, 193–223). He was promptly disgraced and dismissed. In 1966 he was imprisoned, and he died in 1974. This fortuitous confrontation prolonged the famine. It made Mao less likely to change course and others less likely to pressure him. Procrastination obviously involved callousness toward peasant suffering, which was less significant than one's own career. The famine was not intended, but more officials were unintentionally becoming careerist killers.

The truth seeped upward nonetheless. Liu Shaoqi and Deng Xiaoping were quietly urging policy reversal. This began in some provinces and produced increases in yields. The Great Leap Forward was quietly abandoned at the end of 1960, and incentives were restored for a local family farming system. The CCP investigated some of the most radical, worst-affected counties. About a quarter of the party cadres were judged to have made mistakes, but only 5 percent were purged. A few were publicly executed, but they were mainly lower officials. Throughout this period of disaster, the CCP protected its own, tolerant even of flagrant abuses of power at a time when it knew all officials were massively unpopular (Becker, 1996: 146–7; Friedman et al., 1991: 243–51). Only in 1981, with Mao dead, did the CCP openly admit its collective mistake: "Comrade Mao Tse-tung and many leading comrades, both at the centre and in the localities, had become smug about their successes, were impatient for quick results and overestimated the role of man's subjective will and efforts" (MacFarquhar, 1983: II, 331).

This was a correct verdict, though it neglected to mention that somewhere between 20 and 30 million people of the then total Chinese population of 650 million had died. Provinces dominated by radicals had death rates over twice those of the others. This may have been the largest number of deaths in any famine in human history (Becker, 1996: 270–4), though others have killed larger proportions of the population. The Irish famine of 1845 killed 11–12 percent of the population, where the opposite state policy contributed heavily. The British government persistently refused to intervene against the "natural workings of the market." Laissez faire can assist famines as well as Communist statism.

The main contributor in China was a mistaken revolutionary project. This was unlike the situation in the Soviet Union, where collectivization had been deliberately pushed through whatever the human cost. The Chinese plan was also top-down, but its most disastrous results were the unintended consequences of interactions between central planning and local initiatives, which reduced the coherence of Plan and party. But it was also laced with callousness toward the victims once famine became visible – though less than in Stalinism. There were even faint tinges of classicide and politicide. Those with "bad," "black" class identities and those in penal labor camps were given lower food rationing priority and were more likely to die. Yet overall this was a terrible mistake, much less a consequence of vindictive dictatorship and class hatred than Stalin's famine had been. The terrible irony was that it killed far more people than either the Stalinist or Maoist (or Khmer Rouge) phases of deliberate killing.

Through the famine the CCP and Mao lost much of their earlier legitimacy. Villagers retreated to clan, lineage, and village institutions to survive against what they perceived as a distant, hostile regime. At the top the CCP remained badly split, causing the fratricide of the third phase of killings, the Cultural Revolution, beginning in 1966. It began among elite party youth members in high schools and universities, encouraged by Mao to attack and purge the pragmatists and reradicalize the movement by mobilizing its base. Mao believed the Soviet Union had allowed a new bureaucratic class within the party leadership to "take the capitalist road." He would use the Red Guards to squash them and keep the revolution on track. It was in a sense a political Plan C. The young Red Guards brought the ideology of class enemies within the party for the first time. Their theory of "natural redness" revived the importance of "good, red classes" and "bad, black classes." The "five red categories," the children of workers, peasants, soldiers, revolutionary cadres, and martyrs, persecuted the "five black categories," the children of landlords, rich peasants, counterrevolutionaries, bad criminal elements, and rightists (Lee, 1978: 68–75). As persecution and counterattack escalated, both radicals and conservatives seized weapons. This brought a minor bloodbath, the disruption of communications and production, and even threatened the collapse of public order and the fragmentation of the army, some of whose units joined the radicals. A frightened Mao now turned to a political Plan D, betraying the Red Guards. He ordered the army to repress the radicals. Somewhere between 400,000 and 1 million people were killed, almost all CCP members, overwhelmingly young radicals killed by army firepower. No one had initially intended this to happen. It resulted as factionalism produced a temporary disintegration of the party-state.

Through the Cultural Revolution the CCP lost most of its original collective leadership (purged) and also a younger generation of members (killed) who might have reenergized it. Thereafter the regime was in no shape to pursue radicalization or, indeed, much mobilization of any kind. It was now terrified of radical action and factionalism. By default, it moderated. The penal work camps remain, but the number of killings has declined. The regime has deployed only selective policed repression for the past 30 years – like many of the world's more authoritarian regimes.

Things had gotten distinctively worse in Tibet, where the targets were also ethnic.[3] Though they were long subordinated to the Chinese Empire, a period of relative autonomy ended in 1950 with the arrival of the Chinese Army. This set off cycles of repression, and resistance culminating in 1959 with a full-scale rising, massive repression, and the flight of 100,000 Tibetans and the young Dalai Lama to India. The famine was also bad there, and the reaction of the CCP was especially callous. Becker (1996: 181) suggests that 500,000 Tibetans died, one in six of the population. Though famine losses must have claimed most of them, the rate of direct killing was higher than in the rest of China, since resistance was much stronger. *Cultural genocide* (the UN's slightly odd term) was practiced there in the destruction of most of Tibet's temples.

Chinese policy toward other minorities living around its fringes has been milder. There has been intermittent repression of resistance in Xinyiang (Chinese Turkestan), which still simmers today. However, killing has never reached anywhere near Tibetan levels. The Mongol population actually increased by 25 percent between the censuses of 1953 and 1964, when the Tibetan population fell by 10 percent. In no other case was there an attempt to wipe out the whole leadership class of an ethnic group. Thus strategic border considerations are unlikely to have been the primary factor in Tibet. Since the Han Chinese are over 90 percent of the population and consider themselves the bearers of modernity, they do not feel threatened by such small and backward minorities. Indeed, they hope to civilize them through partial assimilation.

But in Tibet the CCP uniquely faced a minority with its own quasi-state, perhaps the last theocracy in the world, ruled by a hierarchy of supposedly reincarnated lamas with their seats in great monasteries. Each of these had its own soldiers and estates, dominating the region's economic life. One in four adult men were lamas. Almost all Tibetans who were not pastoral nomads worked on the estates. Not only Marxists defined this system as feudalism, exploiting unfree labor, legitimated by superstition. The CCP believed it was liberating the Tibetans and bringing them into the modern world. It expropriated monastic lands and redistributed land to the poorer peasants. It brought secular schools and hospitals to a land that lacked any. But 1 out of 7 Tibetans were defined as enemy classes compared to 1 out of 20 elsewhere in China. Most killing was launched against the lamas and their monastery and pastoral nomad soldiers.

So the core of the Tibetan killing was not genocide (as some exiles claim) but politicide, dictated by the regime's need to overthrow a rival state, as interpreted by an ideology of class struggle. In fact, it was not directly ethnically motivated. The CCP might have accomplished its goals in Tibet with

---

[3] I have taken most of my factual material on Tibet from Becker (1996) and Margolin (1999a: 542–6), though my explanation of Chinese atrocities differs from theirs.

more limited policed repression coupled with modernizing reforms. This was probably its Plan A. Some of its reforms were popular; the theocracy was oppressive. But reform came entwined with disastrous economic policies – China's economic Plan C, the Great Leap Forward. Tibetan nomads were forcibly settled and collectivized, partly because they constituted a military threat; nomads and former monastery peasants were forced to grow foreign "great crops" of which they were ignorant. This collectivized economy failed worse than almost anywhere in China. Unusually, Tibetans possessed the collective organization to rebel. They rallied around their lamas. Chinese repression deepened, and the CCP became more callous to famine and labor camp deaths. The conflict was eventually defused by the failure of the Cultural Revolution and the subsequent moderating of Chinese regimes. The last serious bout of repression came in 1989.

CAMBODIA

In the early 1970s Cambodia endured a bloody civil war between the military regime of General Lon Nol and an insurgent Communist guerrilla movement, the Khmer Rouge (Red Cambodians). This became entwined with the Vietnam War, since the Lon Nol regime was a client of the United States and the Khmer Rouge were allied to the Vietnamese Communists. In this combined war, half a million Cambodians died, 8 percent of the population. Many were killed by indiscriminate American bombing aimed at the supply routes through Cambodia of the Vietnamese Communists. The bombing of civilian areas of a neutral country was a major American war crime.

But its death toll was soon dwarfed. In 1975 the Khmer Rouge swept to victory in the civil war. Over the next four years they caused the deaths of 1–3 million of the 7.5 million Cambodians. I follow Sliwinsky's estimate of 1.8 million, 24 percent of the population, though higher estimates are currently being aired. He calibrates direct estimates of the dead with demographic data on the overall population loss rate during the period. From 400,000 to 600,000 were executed or so abused as to die. Almost 30 percent of the murders were by shooting, the rest by more primitive means, especially battering in the skull – not high-tech murder. But most deaths resulted from famine, the unintended consequence of callous policies of revolutionary transformation (for figures see Chandler, 1991: 261; Chandler, 1992: 168; Etcheson, 2000; Heuveline, 2001; Kiernan, 1996: 456–60; Kiernan, 2003; Locard, 1996: 140, 157; Rummel, 1998: Table 4.1; Sliwinsky, 1995; Vickery, 1984). Release came only when a Communist Vietnamese army invaded and overthrew the Khmer Rouge. Ironically, the biggest and most successful case of what was later called *humanitarian interventionism* was launched by a Communist state, ending the most horrendous case of Communist cleansing, the only one where a quarter of the population died and at least a third of the deaths were intended.

Since the vast majority of the dead were also Khmer, this was not *centrally* genocide or even ethnic cleansing, though there was genocide attempted against some ethnic and religious minorities. There was politicide (Harff & Gurr, 1988, and Locard, 1996, concur), directed against those believed to be supporters of the civil war enemy. But this term does not capture the extent of the killing, which went far beyond any potential rival leadership group (as Margolin, 2000, observes). Some call it *autogenocide* (self-genocide), but since most of the victims were defined as enemy classes, this was essentially classicide, though the Khmer Rouge view of class was very broad, entwining regional and even ethnic identities with class. As killing turned inward in terrible party purges, we can also identify fratricide.

The Khmer Rouge was formed by leftist nationalists struggling against French colonialism and then conservative Khmer regimes. A few of them went to France for a college education and were warmly received by the French Communist Party. Neighboring Vietnam offered inspiration as its Communists defeated first the French and then the Americans. This initially drew them toward toward Soviet-style communism. But Vietnamese regional dominance was resented, and the Khmer Rouge wanted out of their war. In the 1960s, Pol Pot's cohort of French-educated cadres took over the party, killing many Hanoi-trained members. They shifted toward a Maoist line, emphasizing rapid collectivization of agriculture that could transcend normal trajectories of development. Though they also broke with the Chinese, they continued to believe that revolutionary will could overcome material obstacles (Locard, 1996: 155; 2000a: 51–3).

They retained their nationalism, seeing Cambodia as a formerly great imperial nation now fallen into a proletarian position, exploited by its neighbors and Great Powers, violated by their wars. The restoration of the stupendous ruins of Angkor Vat had made a big impact on educated Cambodians. The Khmer Rouge gave them a Maoist interpretation: national greatness could overcome backwardness through massive labor mobilization – no need of transition phases that made other Communist movements more cautious. Their ideology combined Maoist emphasis on collective will and two distinct Khmer contributions, peasant antiurbanism, and proletarian nationalism Unlike their Russian, Chinese, or Vietnamese comrades, they had no contact with an urban proletariat. The rubber plantation workers were mostly ethnic Vietnamese. Khmer Rouge experience was of a long guerrilla war in the backward mountainous northeast. The leaders were almost all ex-teachers with a marginal relationship to the urban economy. The ordinary soldiers were poor peasants from these marginal areas. The party had no base in the cities or the more advanced rural areas. They belonged to the enemy (Thion, 1993; 86–90). A secret party document of 1977 explained that there were no workers, only peasants: "Therefore we did not copy anyone." As Pol Pot remarked in his 1975 victory speech, "We have won total, definitive and *clean* victory, meaning that we have won it without any foreign connection or involvement" (Kiernan, 1997: 56–7).

The Khmer Rouge immediately made clear their contempt for the urban middle classes. On April 17, 1975, they took the capital, Phnom Penh. The soldiers immediately began deporting the inhabitants of the cities (a third of the national population) into the countryside. Two days later, the cities were deserted and largely remained so until the Vietnamese arrived. This dramatic act may have been decided only a few days in advance by the Party Central Committee, along with the abolition of money and markets, the replacement of private property by cooperatives, the defrocking of Buddhist priests, the expulsion of ethnic Vietnamese, and the execution of leading Lon Nol personnel (Kiernan, 1983: 178). So their Plan A, was class cleansing by policed deportations combined with selective policed repression of former enemies. They then cut off mail, telephone, telegraph, and cable connections abroad. They traded only with selected Communist countries. It seems that not all leaders agreed with these policies, but they accepted party discipline. But no Plan was formally communicated to the cadres or soldiers below, who appeared surprised by the deportations (Chandler, 1992: 107; Vickery, 1983: 108–9).

Deportations soon also involved minority populations situated along the borders, especially along the Vietnamese border. This is easy to understand as a military lure, reminiscent of Stalin's World War II deportations or those of the tsars and the Ottoman Empire. Vietnam was a potential enemy, so possible collaboration along the border had to be eliminated. Yet the urban deportations were stunning. We can begin to understand them if we recall that the Khmer Rouge was a marginal peasant movement led by intellectuals marginal to the economy of the cities they came from. A Khmer Rouge officer told the prisoner Yathay (1987: 67), "we evacuated the city to destroy any resistance, to destroy the cradles of reactionary and mercantile capitalism. To expel the city meant eliminating the germs of anti-Khmer Rouge resistance." Plan A thus matured as the dispersal of the urban population to the countryside, where it could be politically and militarily controlled and forced to contribute to rural development. Along the way, Lon Nol loyalists would be killed.

Thus the deportations were at first mostly orderly, with few deaths except for Lon Nol officers and officials. But soon some units proved much more murderous than others, probably reflecting different orders from above (Vickery, 1983: 109). In Battambang province this spiraled into what was in effect a Plan B, politicide. The retribution in some localities was escalating beyond Chinese and Vietnamese levels. Their victorious Communists had killed only a few surrendering opponents, sending most to reeducation camps from which they might eventually emerge battered but alive (Locard, 1996: 135; Margolin, 1999: 628). Thion (1993: 166) estimates the killing of supposed Lon Nol personnel, including relatives, as eventually reaching to 100,000–200,000 people. This Plan B, combining forced deportations and politicide, was horrendous, but explicable as the severe end of retribution at the end of a bloody civil war. The definition of the enemy then expanded again, as class, and then ethnicity and region, also became indicators of potential opposition. This was Plan C, classicide.

From Sliwinski (1995), we gather that men were more than twice as likely as women to die (34 to 16 percent). By 1985 64 percent of the adult population were women, clear evidence of homicide. Targeting men is a feature of politicide, since men are more likely to organize resistance. Young adults suffered the greatest losses: men age 20–30 and women age 15–20. Young men were the most likely to bear arms, while young women were at the age of maximum fecundity, killed to ensure that enemies did not reproduce themselves. Military officers suffered the highest death rate of all (83 percent), followed by policemen (67 percent), also suggesting politicide. But those in middle-class occupations all had fairly high rates, led by health professionals (49 percent) and teachers (47 percent). Fifty-two percent of those with higher education died, 38 percent of those with secondary education, and only 29 percent of those with primary education or less. Ordinary soldiers suffered the worst among lower occupations (47 percent), industrial workers suffered at about the national average (33 percent), and peasants had the lowest rate (20 percent). The Cambodian middle class soon learned to conceal their class origins, doctors claiming to be farmers or taxi drivers and spectacles rapidly disappearing. This suggests classicide directed against the upper and middle classes.

But some class enemies were also ethnic. *Imperialist* could mean anyone foreign, since proletarian Cambodia was exploited by all foreign countries. Minorities or anyone plausibly associated with foreign powers might be identified as imperialists. *Comprador capitalists* often referred to the Chinese minority, who ran most big business (Becker, 1998: 228). Sliwinsky estimates that the small Catholic population – potential collaborators with Western powers – had a death rate of 49 percent. The Muslim Chams, differing in religion and ethnicity, and with their own paramilitary formations, declined by 41 percent. The Chinese and the Vietnamese (agents of threatening powers) declined by at least 40 percent – and Kiernan (2001) believes that *all* the Vietnamese were either killed or deported. But not all minorities were targeted. Hill peoples' death rate was only 5–8 percent, since they were civil war allies (Locard, 2000b: 301). All religious leaders were targeted, regardless of ethnicity: Muslim and Buddhist leaders suffered loss rates of over 90 percent (Kiernan, 1996: chap. 7; Margolin, 1999a: 591–5).

Ethnicity even acquired racial tinges. The Vietnamese were described as the "hereditary enemy" of the Khmer people (Kiernan, 1997: 59). Since the Khmer were the darkest-skinned people in the region, dark was declared beautiful. Survivors recount that anyone with a light skin was vulnerable. The Khmer Rouge also saw classes as hereditary. Whole families, including wives and children, were identified as enemies, and many young women of childbearing age were killed if they belonged to enemy classes. Only the Khmer Rouge took bloodlines into mass murder. Unlike Stalinists and Maoists, they often talked of blood in contexts of both race and violence. Newspapers and

Pol Pot called for "national and class indignation and blood rancor" and "flaming national hatred, class hatred and seething blood debts." Some biological metaphors seem rather Nazi. Killings were to "clean," "purify" the people of the "buried microbes," "germs," and "worms" deep within the party that would "rot society, rot the Party, and rot the army" (Chandler, 1992: 136–7; Chandler, 1999: 44; Kiernan, 1996: 336, 388). The national anthem used the word *blood* in both senses in four of its first five lines. Cadres were trained to chant in unison "BLOOD AVENGES BLOOD! BLOOD AVENGES BLOOD!" (Ngor, 1988: 139–40, 203).

Kiernan (1996: 26) says that "Khmer Rouge conceptions of race overshadowed those of class." Ethnic differences in killing rates certainly paralleled class ones, and Pol Pot declared, "counterrevolutionary elements which betray and sabotage the revolution are not to be regarded as our people" (Chandler, 1999: 118) – an organic conception of the nation as proletariat. Race and class were uniquely entwined in Cambodia.

Between September and November 1975 most deportees were herded into the Khmer Rouge "base" areas conquered earlier in the civil war. Their populations, named the *old* or *base* people, were considered reliable and placed in control of the unreliable deportees, called the *new* people, from areas only just conquered. The base areas were mostly backward, containing large tracts of virgin land, so the Khmer Rouge nurtured plans for their rapid development through penal labor camps, a more militaristic version of Stalin's and Mao's forced collectivization. This was given its final form in the Four Year Plan of August 1976. The Plan would intensify agriculture, coercing labor to double the cultivated area of the country and triple the yield per hectare. As in other Communist development plans, this agricultural surplus, essentially rice, could be exported to pay for the import of machinery, first for agriculture and light industry, later for heavy industry (Chandler, 1992: 120–8).

Since the new people were mostly middle-class people from former Lon Nol areas, region also indicated political and class enemies. Their death rates approached 40 percent, while those of the base or old people were only around 10 percent. Old/base people remained in their villages, their children recruited into the movement. One boy had been six years old when Khmer Rouge soldiers entered his village:

I was very lucky to be from the village. Villagers were thought of as the old people. We were treated differently by the Khmer Rouge because we were peasants. The Khmer Rouge hated and were suspicious of the educated, savvy city people.... Since they [the soldiers] had guns, we listened to them and took care of them. We fed, clothed and sheltered them. The land became communal. We stopped eating meals with our families. Instead, all the children had to eat together, and all the adults ate together.

The boys were taken to a school that taught Khmer Rouge values. They were well fed but had to work hard in the fields. This lad was proud to be selected for leadership school, but

the school was tough. . . . We had to wear student uniforms and had very long indoctrination sessions. The soldiers taught us about Angka and the wrongs of capitalism.
Angka was great. The revolution was great. We were going to be Angka's helpers in
the war against evil. (Pran, 1997: 123–5)

The "Angka" he refers to was the "Center" of the Khmer Rouge movement.
It remained secretive, mysterious. Only in 1977 did Pol Pot reveal himself as
the head of the Communist Party of Kampuchea (Cambodia). Even then its
institutions remained unclear.

The "evil" the boy mentioned was personified by the "new people," "royalists," "capitalists," or "petit bourgeois," to be used as slave labor. Yet this
simple distinction was later refined. Among the new people, "bad biographies" of politics and class might bring death or slave labor. The base people
were subdivided into "full rights people" with "good politics" or "good [or
"clean"] biographies," persons with "bad [or "complicated"] biographies"
who were labeled "depositees," and an intermediate category of "candidate
members." Only the worst statuses were considered fixed, even hereditary.
But base people could be raised or lowered according to whether their work
was "vigorous, medium or weak," even for some with fairly "bad biographies." Pol Pot told his subordinates, "life stories must be good and must
conform to our requirements," implying that biographies could be massaged.
In 1975 the Khmer Rouge enjoyed widespread peasant support in the base
areas, but they tended to lose this as the severity of their rule increased. They
responded by repressing all those deemed recalcitrant, regardless of formal
status (Chandler, 1999: 90–1; Kiernan, 1996: chap. 5).

Penal collectivization proved disastrous. Crop yields could not be raised
by intensive labor from inexperienced urbanites. The plan disrupted the most
productive parts of the economy and diverted resources to the most marginal
land, requiring large-scale irrigation projects in a land of abundant rainfall.
Yet the party (like other Communist parties) was proud of these gigantic
waterworks, the most visible product of mass mobilized labor. The Plan also
involved working the fittest the hardest, often to death. It sacrificed variety
of produce to an obsession with the rice yield. But the leaders knew nothing
of agriculture or industry. Overall production fell precipitously (Margolin,
1999: 598–602). Deaths increased as soon as the deportees were herded into
the penal camps to work on such futile projects. They were worked harder
as production and food fell. They fell to diseases and starved. More than
in other Communist societies the victims were blamed for the failure and
executed for the least sign of dissent or slacking. The higher their social
class, the more vulnerable they were.

But there was also trouble within the party. Many were surprised by
the abandonment of the cities and money, and they expected killings to
soon ease. In the eastern region, many had stronger links with the more
moderate Vietnamese Communists. Refugees give many accounts of policy

disagreements among cadres. Former prisoners have testified to great variations in the humanity of party officials, food supplies, the labor regime, and the number of executions (Kiernan, 1983; Vickery, 1983). Center policy wavered in response to disagreements. Political killings eased at the end of 1975, and killings in the penal camps eased in July 1977. There were mysterious explosions and small arms fire in Pnom Penh. One of these incidents may have been an attempt to assassinate Pol Pot.

But he remained in control. The party journal declared: "There are enemies everywhere within our ranks, in the center, at headquarters, in the zones, and out in the villages" (Chandler, 1991: 298). Declining harvest yields, malnutrition, and Vietnamese border pressure were called sabotage from within. Purges began in May 1976 of senior party dissidents, especially those trained in Vietnam rather than France or China. The Agriculture Ministry was the radical bastion. One group of "traitors" was rumored to be "democratic activists"; a leader was said to favor the return of money or dislike communal eating or advocate machinery rather than labor. Yathay (1987: 64) says that in August 1975 his camp chief publicly announced that use of money would be restored at the end of the year. Yathay saw splits between moderates and Maoists. An officer said his regional commander thought "that Pol Pot was on the wrong road, although he didn't often say so" (Kiernan, 1983: 179). One dissident declared, "How can we [succeed] if there is no solution to the problem of machinery? We cannot. This is not my fault, it's the fault of the Standing Committee." The purges escalated into murderous fratricide, leading to greater confusion, mistrust, lower production, murder – and collapse.

Border tensions with Vietnam were heightened by Khmer Rouge killings of local ethnic Vietnamese, followed by armed incursions into Vietnam. This was folly since Vietnam had a battle-hardened army that had just defeated the Americans. In late 1978 Vietnam launched a full-scale invasion. The Center was forced to reduce its killings and announced the end of distinctions between the old and new people. As the war went badly, it was blamed on party leaders in the frontier districts with "Cambodian bodies and Vietnamese heads." This provoked a virtual civil war in the eastern zone in which perhaps 10,000 people died, fatally destroying the war effort. Purges eliminated all but one of the zone party secretaries, most of their replacements, and most factory and hospital administrators, plus at least 20,000 party members. Controlling the Security Police, Angka was torturing its cadres to make false confessions to incriminate other "conspirators," who were then rounded up. After "confessing," they were murdered by having their skulls bashed in with ox-cart axles. Their wives and children were often killed too. About 14,000, including 1,200 children, were killed in the main prison alone, including 418 killed on one day. Pol Pot declared, "there is a sickness in the Party.... We search for germs within the Party" and "we all carry vestiges of our old class character, deep-rooted for generations." This was described as "sweeping clean." The main prison commandant described enemies as "worms" or "germs" infiltrating Cambodia "the way that weevils bore into wood." Victims confessed, "I am a termite boring from within." The purges revealed a truly paranoid party (Chandler, 1999: 36–76). The movement fell apart in a welter of fratricide. Three thousand Khmer Rouge dissidents fled to the Vietnamese forces, providing the public face for the new Vietnamese puppet regime.

The Khmer Rouge soldiers had numbered 68,000 in 1975, and there were 14,000 party members. Since many were stationed in areas that saw little killing, the actual murderers must have engaged in truly serial killing. Almost all the leaders came from middling families who had secured education scholarships for their children. Pol Pot's family had a small farm, but his sister's and cousin's positions as court dancers and concubines ensured that Pol Pot left the farm at age six to spend his formative years in royal boarding schools (Chandler, 1992: 7–25; Kiernan, 1997: 53–4). Of the 20 national and local leaders for whom Kiernan (1996) gives details, 12 had been schoolteachers (4 more were their relatives). A businessman, a peasant, a railway worker, and an electrical mechanic were the only ones with experience of the productive economy. There were three women. Chandler (1999: 18–36, 61–2, 69) has analyzed the autobiographies of staff at the terrible main prison, Tuol Sleng, code-named S-21. Its top officials were long-time party members. Most were ex-schoolteachers (especially of math and biology), as were most high party prisoners there. Kiernan suggests that high school graduates drifted into political dissidence because they were unable to find work, a materialist explanation of student dissidence. Yet this was not true of the top leaders, who became dissidents while still students. Nor did S-21 officials or prisoners mention unemployment in their autobiographies. These teachers probably combined nationalism with communism because these were the modernizing ideals of the country circulating in schools and colleges at the time.

One hundred sixty-six of the S-21 staff's records survive. The staff were drawn from pre-1975 Khmer Rouge soldiers from nearby provinces. They were almost all unmarried. Sixty-five percent were aged 18–22 and 12 percent were younger still. Most had joined the movement as teenagers, some as young as age 10. Photographs of these self-satisfied teenagers decorate the walls of the prison camp (now a museum). Angka, Chandler says, "had replaced their fathers and mothers" (1999: 33). At least two staff and 7 percent of the party victims were women. Many wives of party members were also killed there. The army also contained women's battalions, and soldiers were young and got younger each year as war and purges began to kill the veterans. Ly Heng remembers that the last recruiting campaign of 1978 aimed at boys and girls aged 13–18 (Heng & Demeure, 1994: 189–90). Camp survivors estimated the local soldiers as being between 12 and 14, with some as young as 9. They feared the youngest most, for they were easily disciplined and the most callous. For them, killing a person was like swatting a fly. Nine- to 13-year-old child doctors could barely read but were wielding syringes (Picq, 1989: 114; Yathay, 1987: 116). Relying on child-soldiers indicates deliberate use of quasi-parental socialization of the impressionable young into the more murderous tasks.

Almost all the Khmer Rouge rank-and-file were illiterate peasants from the base areas. Almost all the 166 S-21 staff were poor or lower middle peasants. Chandler says these were the "poor and blank," the least corrupted by capitalism or schooling. They were attracted to the Khmer Rouge by a promise of land redistribution, antiurban rhetoric, and anger at the American bombing. The Khmer Rouge said the Americans were imperialist devils, and the bombing did seem capriciously malevolent, devilish – what had Cambodian peasants ever done to harm the Americans? The Khmer Rouge said the Lon Nol regime were the lackies of those devils, and this too was half-correct. The Khmer Rouge provided peasants with the most plausible explanation of their own predicament. Vickery (1984: 66) goes too far in calling this a "victorious peasant revolution," since vast numbers of peasants were killed and the victorious peasants were under the thumb of the vanguard intelligentsia, which mobilized them with simple but plausible Maoist/nationalist doctrines.

Unlike their Soviet and Chinese counterparts, few rank-and-file Khmer Rouge had any experience of a world beyond peasant farms and rural autarchy. The leaders lacked experience of industry and agriculture. So the movement had no appreciation of the division of labor or the market. Yet they saw themselves as ultramodernists, believing they could adapt socialism to accomplish in only a few years what Western societies had labored on for over a century (Becker, 1998: 184, 188). Of course, the notion of penal work camps policed by a mass party was a 20th-century notion. Like the leaders in Moscow, Beijing, and Hanoi, they had an ideal of modern industry (detailed in the Four Year Plan). But this was for the future. It did not exist even in embryo form in the present. Marx's first ideal of the communist society, in *The German Ideology*, was a transfigured past – that man might be a hunter in the morning, a fisherman in the afternoon, and a critic in the evening. This image of rural freedom had been turned upside-down by the Khmer Rouge into penal camps worked by slave laborers.

Survivors describe guards and officials as "villagers, the farmers and the uneducated...the most violent and ignorant people," "ferocious animals, illiterate and brainwashed." Ngor (1988: 158) says they never said "communism." He himself calls them "revenge-people": "All they know is that city people like us used to lord it over them and this is their chance to get back. That's what they are: communist at the top and...[revenge-people]...at the bottom." A guard declared:

We are free at last...from tycoons and feudalism. We have liberty and justice, liberty and justice. All people are equal. No one will be rich and no one will be poor. We have destroyed a fictitious belief. It is nonsense, such as God! God!

They spat out class hatred for their educated victims:

How do you bourgeoisie feel now? Where were you when we were suffering, living in the jungle, fighting the Americans and the puppet regime? You were home sleeping with wives on comfortable beds and making a mockery of us who were trying to liberate our country from French, Japanese, and American imperialism. We didn't then, and we certainly don't need you now. To keep you is no benefit and to destroy you is no loss. (Pran, 1997: 13, 59, 130–1)

This last sentence became a movement catch phrase – a perversion of the Marxist labor theory of value. Only peasants produced value; all special-ized occupations were unproductive and could be eliminated. Doctors were slaughtered as parasites; only peasant folk medicine was needed:

We don't need the technology of the capitalists. We don't need any of it at all. Under our new system, we don't need to send our young people to school. Our school is the farm. The land is our paper. The plow is our pen.... Knowing how to farm and knowing how to dig canals – those are our certificates.... We dont need any of the capitalist professions!

Guards parroted Angka's slogan that it had gone back to "ground zero" to rebuild Kampuchea. The principles of the "Three Mountains" were "independence-sovereignty, rely on our own strengths and take destiny in hand" (Ngor, 1988: 139, 161).

Collectivization would be unsullied by individualism, divisions, and for-eign influence. "The Khmer Rouge soldiers told us not to love our parents or to depend on them." A disciplined organicism dominated the movement's ideals. Everyone would dress the same, eat the same, repeat the same slogans, think the same. "No one can question Angka," said one cadre. "If you have courage to question Angka, you will be taken to the reeducation learning institute," that is, to execution (Pran, 1997: 156, 30; cf. Margolin, 1999: 603–5). Its guerrilla history influenced a rhetoric of perpetual struggle. Ngor (1988: 197) says, " 'Struggle' was military talk, like 'front lines' " – the ex-pression used for critical agricultural tasks like building irrigation systems. "On the frontlines we didn't just work, we 'struggled' or else 'launched of-fensives,' " as for example in "launch an offensive to plant strategic crops" to achieve "mastery" or "victory over the elements." There were obvious Maoist influences here.

The S-21 prison elite were predominantly ideological killers, believing in their orders and carrying them out efficiently, mostly without sadism. The guards, interrogators, and executioners seemed to internalize the regime's definition of prisoners as irredeemable enemies, but any hesitation in front of their colleagues was also perceived as dangerous. They often became fear-ful killers. Chandler admits that he cannot decipher their motives. He won-ders whether Cambodians might be unusually prone to follow orders, but concludes that most ordinary men placed under such pressures would also have been compliant perpetrators (1999: 141). Most killing environments were not as bureaucratized as S-21. Soldiers did almost all of the killing in far more erratic, casual, and brutal ways. They had served for years in a half-guerrilla party-army, lightly armed, somewhat decentralized, accustomed to tactics of terror. They were probably gradually lured by military tactics toward becoming bigoted and violent killers.

Scholars disagree on how statist the killings were. Barnett (1983) sees "a highly centralized dictatorship," since all of its main radical policies were implemented across almost all of the country by terror directed from the top. Kiernan (1996: 27) says, "the power accumulated by the CPK Center was unprecedented in history." In contrast, Thion (1983: 91) says:

at no time... were the central authorities close to having complete control over the national economy, the state power system, the army, the Party, and possibly even the State security office, S-21. All of these were riddled with political factions, military brotherhoods, regional powers, personal networks, all contending for influence, and the purging of rival forces. The state never stood on its feet.

There were marked variations between regions and levels of authority. Becker (1998: 173–7, 209) says that only the Center initiated formal policy, and it controlled half of the army divisions. But, she says, the Center could only rule through the six or seven regional zone party secretaries. These had their own army division and were effectively autonomous warlords, but they had little power over the penal camps, which were ruled by triumvirates from the local party (cf. Vickery, 1983: 104). They were also local dictators, operating without routine written instructions (Yathay, 1987: 168). Becker (1998) says that the purges of the zone secretaries was a desperate, failed attempt to bring them into compliance. This state was not effectively centralized.

Vickery (1983) emphasizes regional variations. The southwest was staffed by Pol Pot's faction, the east by moderates following a more Vietnamese line. In the southwest new people were ruthlessly killed for minor rule infractions, but there was no initial politicide, laborers were rarely worked to death, and food was usually adequate – yielding a quite low death rate. Had Cambodia been totalitarian (or even as centralized as Barnett suggests) under Pol Pot's control, it might have seen fewer deaths. The eastern region initially saw few killings and even some attempts to improve living standards. But eventually Security Police troops were despatched to the east to purge and replace them with Pol Potists from the southwest. What had been the safest region of Cambodia suddenly became the most dangerous (says Kiernan, 1983: 138). But these were the two most efficiently administered regions, and the highest death rates came elsewhere. Areas with more new people faced greater difficulties: no prior institutionalization of power, a population inexperienced in agriculture, poorer-quality soils. Quotas were rarely reached amid shocking death tolls from hunger and illness resulting from incompetence of leaders and workers and a barren environment. Some local regimes responded with more violence, trying desperately to fulfill quotas set on high. Others were purged by the Center for being too soft or corrupt. The worst conditions occurred after they were replaced by Pol Potists from the southwest. Their radicalism escalated into mass executions, overwork, and undernourishment of the new (and sometimes the old) people. So the most killing occurred where there was less established statism and most radicalization.

Centralized authoritarianism, provincial warlordism, and guerrilla paramilitarism were competing organizational principles within the Khmer Rouge. The combinations of the centralized and the factionalized, the intended and the unintended, escalated killings beyond what any other Communists had perpetrated. So my previous identification of Plans C and D is not ultimately helpful. Classicide was never quite planned; purges were planned but degenerated unexpectedly into fratricide and defeat. Yet descent into the abyss had a certain coherence. Angka had hit upon very simple control techniques. It had limited human resources, but it deported a third of the population to penal camps and guarded villages and monopolized the food supply. Whatever the people produced was handed over to officials. They handed some of it back to the locals, in driblets and communally, so few could subsist outside of Angka (Picq, 1989: 114; Yathay, 1987: 149; cf. Thion, 1993: 93). Regime tasks were simple: coerce labor in the fields, eliminate alternative bases for organization, and kill dissenters. This was totalitarianism in the sense that most Cambodians could not live outside Angka. Yet it comprised a very narrow set of goals, and when it failed to achieve even these goals, killing increased, leading to its collapse. The regime survived as a coherent entity for little more than two years. Yet its simplified nature enabled a horrendous scale of killing and social regress within this short period.

CONCLUSION

Despite their differences, radical ethnonationalism and revolutionary Communism nourished *organic* conceptions of we, the people, the people as a singular ethnic nation or a single proletarian class, as in my thesis 1a. They saw states as the bearers of a moral project to cleanse the nation/proletariat of its enemies to further social and economic development. They were the dark side of a state supposedly representing the people, where the people was viewed as a singular organic whole, not as stratified into plural interest groups, as in liberal or social democracy. This took them away from true democracy. Stalinist, Maoist, or Khmer Rouge atrocities were socialist versions of modern organicism, perverting socialist and class theories of democracy just as ethnically aimed atrocities perverted nationalist theories of democracy. The geopolitical notion of a proletarian nation oppressed by foreign imperialist powers also gave class theory nationalist and (for the

Khmer Rouge) ethnonationalist coloring. In the Communist cases, nation did not transcend class, but nor did class simply transcend nation. Nation and ethnicity were channeled toward a class vision of the organic people – the inverse of my second thesis.

Though my third and fourth theses proved specific to ethnic cleansing, civil wars linked to international wars did intensify class hatreds and add militarism to Communist movements. These regimes were more likely to attempt to reach their ideological goals by military force. This brought Communist movements into the danger zone where the policed repression normal to postrevolutionary conditions might escalate to politicide and classicide. This escalation began (analogously to my fifth thesis) as a result of geopolitical and civil war instability. But the first wave of atrocities occurring after victory differed from ethnic ones. They cemented party-states and brought together elites, militants, and class resentments from below to dispose of their enemies. But factionalism then surfaced. It proved difficult to institutionalize party rule. Passions and hatreds aroused at the bottom – often first nurtured from the top – spiraled out of control, making pragmatic, selective repression more difficult to maintain. Then factionalism appeared within the party, creating radicals determined to achieve utopian goals by any means necessary. The death rate now escalated, not with pressures toward totalitarianism but as factionalization and radicalization intensified – just as we saw in ethnic cleansing. These cycles of state building and state factionalizing were distinctive to class cleansing. Indeed, another phase of rising factionalism in the 1980s was to utterly destroy the Soviet Union from the top down. So far China has avoided that fate by encouraging pluralism within the party and, more recently, by removing the party from economic planning.

This also made for Plans nurtured by these regimes that differed from those envisaged in my sixth thesis. Much of the Communist organization of killing was more orderly than that of ethnonationalists. Communists were more statist. But only the Plans that killed fewest people were fully intended and occurred at early stages of the process. There is no equivalent of the final solution, the last desperate attempt to achieve goals by mass murder after all other Plans have failed. The greatest Communist death rates were not intended but resulted from gigantic policy mistakes worsened by factionalism, and also somewhat by callous or revengeful views of the victims. But – with the Khmer Rouge as a borderline case – no Communist regime contemplated genocide. This is the biggest difference between Communist and ethnic killers: Communists caused mass deaths mainly through disastrous policy mistakes; ethnonationalists killed more deliberately.

The gigantic famines of the 20th-century Soviet Union and China resulted mainly from disastrous statism. But the inverse had occurred in the late 19th century, when disastrous market-led famines, late Victorian holocausts, killed well over 30 million people. "Natural" *El Nino* effects did generate severe droughts. But the emergence of world capitalist markets meant that grain storage in case of need largely ceased, prices rose as supplies diminished, and grain was actually exported from famine areas in search of higher profits. Governments also refused to intervene because of their ideological belief that markets were the best way to supply human needs (Davis, 2001). Perhaps in the 21st century, with statism in decline, our gigantic policy mistakes will once again result from ideological overcommitment to markets rather than states.

12

Yugoslavia, I

Into the Danger Zone

The defeat of Nazi Germany did not end ethnic cleansing in Europe. It redirected it against the losing master race. In 1945, 18 million ethnic Germans lived abroad in the East. Germans in the Soviet Union mostly stayed put, but most of the rest were now forcibly deported westward. Almost 12 million reached Germany, but over 2 million died en route, the targets of murderous vengeance by the locals. Only a few thousand of them can have been Nazi perpetrators. Oskar Schindler, declared a Righteous Person by both the state of Israel and Hollywood, was one of 3 million German Sudetens expelled, losing his property but staying alive. All leading Polish and Czech politicians supported the expulsions, and so did the Allies. Churchill told the British House of Commons in 1944 that deportations would provide the "most satisfactory and lasting" solution to ethnic problems. "There will be no mixture of populations to cause endless trouble as in Alsace-Lorraine. A clean sweep will be made." Czech President Benes said the Sudeten Germans were a "nonviable population" and a Czech general declared, "a good German is a dead one." A Lieutenant Smrcina "cleaned up" a German village by killing 25 men and two women without provocation. Another officer removed from a train and had shot 265 Germans, men, women, and children. Germans said the Red Army treated them better than did ordinary Czechs or Poles – except for rape, since the Red Army raped countless thousands of German women (Hayden, 1996: 727–8; Naimark, 2001: chap. 4; Seifert, 1994: 54, 67). Germans were suddenly victims, and the new perpetrators saw this as righteous retaliation. Less than 3 million Germans now remained in the East – an 85 percent cleansing rate and a major way station on the road to an ethnically cleansed Europe.

In Czechoslovakia the Germans were replaced by Czech and Slovak settlers. In Poland, borders as well as people were moved. An agreement with the Soviet Union to move the Polish borders about 150 miles west was coupled with the resettlement of 4.3 million Poles and 520,000 Ukrainians, White Russians, and Lithuanians into the USSR. Poland moved from 67 percent to over 90 percent Polish. In Yugoslavia vengeance was also wreaked on Croatian, Bosnian Muslim, and Serb collaborators. Nearly 100,000 men, mainly Croats, were put to the sword by the mostly Serb partisans as they surrendered. Germans were cleansed from Vojvodina in Serbia, replaced by Serb settlers.

Population transfers were justified as the lesser of two evils: rather policed deportations and exchanges than the mayhem of ethnonationalist democracy. Schechtman (1962: 369ff.) suggested that more negotiated transfers of minority populations was the best way to avoid ethnic wars. Hindsight must also make us respect Croat sociology Professor Tomasic's scheme for the UN to transfer Serb and Croatian minorities to their respective homeland republics. This, he believed, would create two stable federations, one an Eastern Orthodox union of Serbia, Macedonia, and Montenegro, the other a Catholic union of Croatia and Slovenia – though, like most experts then, he did not consider that Bosnian or Albanian Muslims deserved their own state.

The oldest European cleansing tradition was renewed with the forcible expulsion of 150,000 Turks from Bulgaria. The half million Greek community in Turkey declined to 100,000 after riots in 1955. In the 1970s Cyprus was cleansed as 200,000 Greeks and Turks fled to "their" two statelets on the island. Minorities now total fewer than 1,000 people on the island. In 1993 four-fifths of the last 15,000 Greeks were evacuated from the Russian Republic of Abkhazia on the north shore of the Black Sea. Greeks and Turks had been cosmopolitan peoples living in multicultural environments. Now they live within their own nation-states. The Turkish Republic and neighboring states still discriminate against Kurdish minorities, though this appears to have ended for the moment in Iraq.

Communist Soviet and Yugoslav regimes succeeded in damping down ethnic conflict for 40 years, probably the greatest achievement of Communism, unmatched by later democratizing countries. True, the Soviet Union privileged Russians, and in both regimes individual republics implicitly "belonged" to particular nationalities, though Communist parties generally sought ethnic compromise under the banner of transnational class solidarity. The late Communist period saw some faltering. From the mid-1970s, millions of Russians, feeling under pressure, left the Central Asian republics for their ethnic homeland. Only the small Baltic states were still attracting Russians in this period (Bell-Fialkoff, 1996: 178–9). Communist Bulgaria mounted pressure on Turks, and 350,000 left in 1989. The remaining Turks (along with gypsies and others) were forced to take Bulgarian names, a form of cultural suppression. Nonetheless, the Communist version of rule by the people, however flawed in other ways, was transnational. For Marxists, class trumped ethnicity.

When the Soviet Empire collapsed between 1985 and 1991, the first secessions brought little violence. Most successor states remained semi-authoritarian and conservative, fearful of social mobilization and conflict.

The future was seen as resting with pluralist democracy and social market capitalism. Most Eastern political leaders internalized the Western view that organic nationalism was a regression. It was also an obstacle to cutting a deal with the European Union. Nationalist parties have generally played third fiddle to liberal/capitalist and ex-Communist/social democratic parties. Where states inherited clear-cut boundaries, nationalists failed to mobilize revisionist sentiments to change them. Romania remains careful not to provoke its Magyar minority. Twenty-five million Russians now live in states dominated by other ethnicities, easily the biggest ethnic minority remaining in Greater Europe, bearing the opprobrium of former imperial oppressors. Except in Chechnya, they have not been the targets of much violence. As long as these Russians make no major political demands, discrimination rather than cleansing is their lot. They are unlikely to make such claims, since they lack a historically plausible title to their own state. My third ethnic thesis can explain their docility. Most Western commentators seem optimistic (Brubaker, 1996; Laitin, 1999).

Chechnya apart, the violence has tended to pit non-Russian ethnic groups against each other, not against Russians, especially in those parts of the Caucasus and Central Asia where new states had borders cutting through ethnically mixed populations. Border disputes between Armenians and Azeris, Georgians and Ossetians, Georgians and Abkhazis, and the more complex ethnic and religious border wars of Tajikhistan and Uzbekhistan provided almost all the serious violence of the post-Soviet period. In these cases, both contending groups do have plausible and achievable claims to their own state over the same territory. Beissinger (2002) says that rising ethnic violence became a "tidal wave" where republican borders were disputed as the Soviet Union collapsed. The implicit ethnofederalist constitution of the Soviet Union had not played a significant role in causing the Soviet collapse (despite Bunce, 1999). But it did structure the form of the breakup and the subsequent violence. Communist politicians found themselves de facto leaders of the ethnonationalists, police and security forces often sided with them, and embittered refugees supplied the ethnonationalist hard core. All of them, plus criminals, could loot weapons from nonfunctioning Soviet armories and so escalate the level of violence. Some states lie devastated, others are reviving, but all are now far more mono-ethnic.

The Eastern European successor states are substantially mono-ethnic and peaceful. Almost a million more Germans flocked peacefully home from the East to a reunited Germany. There remained only two exceptional multiethnic states. But Czechoslovakia broke up peacefully in 1992–3 into two mono-ethnic states. Prague began the century as a cosmopolitan Czech-German-Slovak-Jewish city and ended it as Czech. But the fall of the other multiethnic state was to prove much more violent.

YUGOSLAVIA: THE PROBLEM

The ethnic wars of Yugoslavia imprinted the term ethnic cleansing on global consciousness.[1] The total casualties may amount to 300,000 dead, two-thirds of them civilians or POWs, numerous thousands raped, and over 4 million made refugees. The area affected by the violence is quite small, with a population of only about 10 million (the total Yugoslav population was 23 million). Here over a third of the local population has been murderously cleansed. The vast majority were casualties of the three-way struggle among Serbs, Croats, and Bosnian Muslims, though the Serb–Albanian conflict escalated during 1999 to produce in Kosovo the most fully cleansed province of the former Yugoslavia. Tensions continued to simmer in 2003 across the Muslim–Croat federation of Bosnia, in the tiny Republika Srpska, in Kosovo, and in Macedonia, though the situation in Serbia improved after the overthrow of Slobodan Milosevic. The states and statelets of the former Yugoslavia – except for Macedonia – are over 70 percent mono-ethnic. Bosnia-Herzegovina has been split into six distinct territorial statelets/political enclaves in which the dominant single ethnicity comprised between 82 and 99 percent of the total population. This massive cleansing is what we must explain.

Persons of all ethnicities have committed murderous cleansing. Serbs probably committed most murders, but most refugees were also Serbs. During early 1999 even more Kosovan Albanians (perhaps 800,000) were forced out of their homes, but then they turned the tables on their Serb oppressors, pressuring almost 200,000 (two-thirds of them) to leave. Even after we correct for the anti-Serb bias in Western reporting, most of the worst atrocities were committed by Serbs (Helsinki Watch, 1992, 1993; UN Security Council, 1994). This resulted more from greater opportunity and incentive for a "first strike" than from any greater ferocity of character or nationalism. I will not allocate blame among ethnicities, since whole ethnicities do not commit ethnic cleansing.

Atrocities have been of four main types. The worst was mass murder, normally reserved for men. On over 20 occasions local men of fighting age were rounded up and massacred. Over 3,000 Croatian men were taken and presumed killed after the town of Vukovar was seized by Serb forces in November 1991. In July 1995, 7,000–8,000 Bosnian Muslims, almost all men, were killed after Serb forces took Srebrenica – some executed in large batches, others hunted down in the woods around the city. These were highly organized atrocities, involving coordination of troops, transports, and body disposal (Honig & Both, 1996: 175–9; ICTY, Krstic Case, Judgment, 2.8.01). The largest non-Serb single atrocity that has so far come to light was

---

[1] I would like to thank Aleksandra Milicevic for assistance both linguistic and intellectual in the two chapters on Yugoslavia.

the 119 Bosniaks killed by Croats in Ahmici in 1994 (see the next chapter), though perhaps 600 Serbs were killed over several weeks as they tried to flee from the Krajina in 1995. Such incidents amount to ethnically aimed politicide, with the intent to murder every local man who might in the future fight back. Second, much more often, people were rounded up, driven off, beaten, and sometimes killed in exemplary repression, to terrorize entire ethnic communities to flee, in pressured emigration, or in wild deportations. In parts of western Slavonia, the Baranja and Krajina Croats so terrorized Serbs into flight. It was also the main Serb tactic in Kosovo, where perhaps 3,000–6,000 Albanians were killed (just over 2,000 corpses have been found so far). Then the terror was reversed as perhaps 1,000 Serbs became victims after the Albanians took control of the province (all these estimates are highly provisional, and they remain political footballs between the sides). Third, *cultural cleansing* has sought to erase the out-group's culture in these territories. Mosques, libraries, and other Muslim monuments were systematically razed to the ground in Serb-occupied areas, while a few Catholic and Orthodox churches were also destroyed.

Fourth, there have been many rapes.[2] Most known rapes were committed by Serb men against Bosnian Muslim women. Feminists have helped make these rapes the best-documented ones in the annals of war. Some suggest that rape expresses less a fundamental male desire for sexual gratification than one to do violence to women. But the overwhelming mass of male violence in all my cases was directed against other men. Is this also an expression of a fundamental desire to do violence to men? Such psychologizing seems banal. Though evidence of male motivations is hard to find, their social aspect seems rather striking. Most were gang rapes, committed by groups of men, in which there are collective male pressures on potentially reluctant men, constrained by the machismo ideology that reluctance indicates lack of masculinity. Wartime also introduces its own causes. Violence is increased by the conqueror's desire to humiliate the conquered men, who are exposed as unable to protect their women. It also attacks the entire culture of the conquered in its most intimate and reproductive sphere.

But do *ethnic* wars add more? Some say that nationalism is especially patriarchal and sexist. Wars of ethnic cleansing do add a collective intent to terrify women so that they flee their homeland. In accounts by female survivors of Yugoslav rapes, images of brutal violation, cruelty, and humiliation seem to dominate those of sexual desire, though it remains possible that the perpetrators began with absurd fantasies of sexual consent that then had to give way to violence. Many women were then killed or disappeared. Some survivors became pregnant and were imprisoned until too late in their term to allow abortion. Their captors often taunted them that they would bear

---

[2] These have been documented and analyzed by Allen (1996), Gutman (1993: 64–73, 144–9, 157–67), Stiglmayer (1994), and Vulliamy (1994: 195–201).

Chetnik babies. This seems like a bizarrely misconceived ethnic cleansing, since when released the Bosnian women fled back to their communities, where the babies were brought up as Muslims (though not always by the shamed mother). Perhaps the explanation is that this reasoning is "founded on the negation of all cultural identities of its victims, reducing those victims to mere sexual containers" of Serb men (suggests Allen, 1996: 100). But many perpetrators did believe that the woman's sense of shame, community blame heaped on her, and actual bodily damage would prevent her from marrying or having further babies. All these hypotheses would be testable if we had quantitative data on rapes in both conventional and ethnic wars. But we do not, and so they remain speculative.

Some consider this combination of atrocities genocide. Western leaders, like U.S. President Bill Clinton, compared it to the Holocaust. International Criminal Tribunal for Yugoslavia (ICTY) prosecutors have brought several charges of genocide against individuals, and one has stuck. General Krstic has been convicted of aiding and abetting genocide in the case of Srebrenica. This massacre does seem a genocidal outburst, though set amid a broader ensemble of murderous cleansing – mass murder and rape were intended to terrorize most of the ethnic group into flight. I would not term Yugoslav cleansings in general as genocide. They were also wild – with perpetrators sometimes out of control (not in Srebrenica), and with great local variations in their practices. It was not like the Nazi Final Solution. Nor was it like the Rwandan cleansing, which though wild was also efficiently genocidal. Yugoslav erratic wildness needs specific explanation.

These horrors were unexpected. *Why*, asked the bewildered survivors? Why did they hate us so? Why had God and humanity so deserted us? These are frightening questions posed by Europeans in the 1990s, accustomed to regard atrocities as belonging to the distant past or to primitive peoples. Simple explanations have been the most popular. Nationalist theories see perpetrators as the Serbs, the Croats, the Muslims, the Albanians. These groups are seen as having collective histories of cleansing. Some Serbs offer a half-justification of Serb retaliation against Croats today in terms of the crimes that Croats (Ustasha) committed during World War II. Some Croats respond in kind: Serbs are Chetniks reincarnated. The sins of the father and the grandfather are blamed on their offspring today. Yet ethnic groups are not collective actors; atrocities are not committed by the Serbs or the Croats or the Bosniaks or the Albanians, but by some Serbs, some Croats, some Bosniaks, some Albanians, and so on – with particular social characteristics, motivations and powers I attempt to identify.

Many others stress the ideological power of ancient hatreds. They tell us of the traumatic defeat of the Serbs at Kosovo Field in 1389, of the medieval religious divisions between Catholicism, Eastern Orthodoxy, and Islam. They stress the divisions between the Ottoman and Habsburg Empires, whose military frontier created a human shield dividing Croats, Serbs, and Bosnians along what proved to be the main fault line of conflict in the 1990s. They note the terrible atrocities of World War II (Chapter 10), plus the violence punctuating 20th-century Kosovan history. They see historic nationalism as having ideological power today because Serbs and Croats imbibe it with their mothers' milk. This is the account essentially given by the journalists Glenny (1992) and Vulliamy (1994).

True, the political and religious aspects of Balkan conflict are old and have occasionally mobilized whole communities. Chapter 2 argued that religious conflict was most violent, popular, and ethnically tinged in Europe's frontier areas. Udovicki (1997: 35) overstates in declaring that "until World War II no ethnically-motivated armed conflicts ever erupted." In the 19th and 20th centuries religious conflicts gradually turned more ethnic, especially in Kosovo, which was seeing intermittently murderous ethnic conflict even before World War I (Judah, 2000: chap. 1). Serb dominance of interwar Yugoslavia was also widely resented. These tensions led some Croats, Serbs, Muslims, and Albanians to choose different sides in World War II. Under pressure from the Nazis, they then committed ethnically targeted atrocities (as we saw in Chapter 10). Yet these had come unexpectedly and were fewest in Kosovo, which had up to then been the biggest flashpoint. It also required an ideological shift among Serb nationalists. Up until then, most had assumed that since Bosniaks and most Croats were "really" Serbs who had acquired a surface veneer of another culture, a Greater Serbia could be achieved by forced assimilation. Only the Albanians of Kosovo were considered so alien that deportations might be necessary. But under the pressure of World War II, some Serb Chetniks radicalized to advocate cleansing through wild deportations and Nazi-policed population exchanges involving Bosniaks and Croats (Grmek et al., 1993). But Communist victory in 1945 suppressed ethnic conflict between these groups. Thereafter, Kosovo, not Bosnia or Croatia, remained the hot spot. Yet Kosovo only exploded late in the 1990s, well after the other provinces. So ethnic conflict in Yugoslavia was old, but neither ancient nor continuous; and though it intensified in the 20th century, it did so unevenly.

So most observers also reject interpretations based on ancient hatreds. A historian of Bosnia says, "Having travelled widely over fifteen years, and having stayed in Muslim, Croat and Serb villages, I cannot believe...that the country was forever seething with ethnic hatreds" (Malcolm, 1994: 252). Many Yugoslavs testified before the International Criminal Tribunal that these groups had long lived peacefully amid each other. A Croatian Catholic priest, witness to atrocities in his ethnically mixed parish, was bewildered: "There had been no tensions or confrontations before. Even the Orthodox people would greet me in the street; some Orthodox grandmas would also attend the mass, and some Orthodox children would attend the Sunday School...[yet]...when the war started raging in this area, the local Serbs became the main killers" (Botica et al., 1992: 253; cf. Scharf, 1997: 150).

Croat and Serb sociologists agree. Letica (1996: 99–100) and Kuzmanovic (1995: 242–7; cf. Gordy, 1999: 4–5) say that surveys in the 1980s revealed levels of prejudice and hostility among Croats, Serbs, and others that were actually less than those characteristically found in studies of ethnic attitudes in the United States. These peoples did not seem to hate each other until the troubles actually started – a seeming paradox.

Most of those rejecting ideological ancient hatreds instead blame the political power of elites. Richard Holbrooke, the leading American peace negotiator in Yugoslavia, says, Yugoslavia's tragedy was not foreordained. It was the product of bad, even criminal, political leaders who encouraged ethnic confrontation for personal, political and financial gain" (1998: 23–4). Cigar says of Serbia: "Genocide...was a national policy, the direct and planned consequence of conscious policy decisions taken by the Serb establishment in Serbia and Bosnia-Herzegovina" (1995: 4–6; cf. Silber & Little, 1995). Mueller (2000) offers a paramilitary slant on "the few bad guys" thesis: "the violence that erupted in Yugoslavia principally derived from...the actions of recently empowered and unpoliced thugs," and then he gives a detailed account of the ethnic wars in which the leading actors are tiny bands of paramilitary thugs.

None of these accounts convinces. If a few bad guys were responsible, how did they acquire such magical powers of coercion and manipulation? And were they quite so coherent in their planning, so in charge of events? After all, atrocities were committed by thousands of persons, and many more thousands stood around, either egging them on or doing nothing to stop them. Many of their bad guys were politicians trying to win elections, currying popular favor. Does the leading American diplomat in the region understand so little about how societies or politics work? It is more likely Holbrooke finds it politically expedient to blame a few bad guys.

Serious analysis must recognize that elites, militants, and ordinary people were all involved. Cohen (1995) offers us a two-phase theory, blaming "quarrelsome leaders" of the republics for the collapse of the federation, which then unleashed more popular nationalist hatreds below. Brubaker says popular ethnic identities *became* "nationalized" and seemingly "essentialized," but this resulted from a "contingent, eventful" process: while cynical and opportunistic misrepresentation by elites promoted this escalation, this alone cannot explain the resonance of local ethnonationalism (1996: 20–1, 71–2). Though Milosevic and Franjo Tudjman, the president of Croatia, did worsen the outcomes, more fundamental processes were also involved. Between the ancient and the contingent or manipulative lay macro forces and micro power relations within and between groups. Numerous social groups became involved – not just leaders and masses, but also radical and moderate movements and core constituencies. Much of the macro derived from the growing power of the nation-state ideal in the 20th century (here built on top of older fault lines), while the micro involved particular economic, ideological, military, and political power relations on the ground. All were involved in a descent from a multinational Yugoslav Federation to murderous ethnic cleansing by organic nationalists. This comprised five main steps:

1. The breakup of the Yugoslav Federation;
2. Its replacement by organic-leaning nation-states;
3. The outbreak of violent incidents between these states and their ethnic minorities;
4. The escalation of such incidents into war between ethnically based states and statelets;
5. The escalation of war into murderous ethnic cleansing.

In this process, steps 2 and 3 overlapped, while steps 4 and 5 happened almost simultaneously. Each thrust different actors into prominence and radicalized them to overcome opposition to their desired goal by all means necessary, cleansing an organic nation-state of out-groups – finally, if necessary, by murder. This chapter deals with steps 1 and 2 of the escalation and the following one with steps 3 to 5.

The progression was neither inevitable nor preplanned. Yugoslavia might have found a peaceful solution either through a single republic with a confederal/consociational constitution or through compromise between separate republics. Even without a lasting solution, conflict may have remained at a niggling but not disastrous level. At worst, cleansed nation-states might have resulted from peaceful population exchanges. Why was each of these solutions rejected, and by whom? Luckily, the processes of radicalization and escalation are better documented than those in any of my other cases. They happened recently in Europe in the glare of global publicity, followed by International Criminal Tribunal trials in which many locals, UN soldiers and officials, social scientists, and journalists described what they saw.

TOWARD THE DANGER ZONE

The ancient matters only when ideologically reinterpreted into the modern ideal of the nation-state. Three historic religions inhabit this frontier area of Europe, and Orthodox, Catholic, and Muslim identities are also powerfully transmitted through intimate rituals of birth, marriage, death, and the seasons of the year. Such identities were only erratically relevant to politics before the 20th century. But though earlier battles and banners are vividly recalled by today's religious/ethnic communities, they are misremembered. Wars had actually mobilized regional and dynastic, not ethnic, armies. At the Battle of Kosovo Field in 1389, the Balkan Army defeated by the Turks was led by the Serb Prince Lazar but comprised Serbs, Croats, Hungarians, Vlachs, Albanians, and others. The records of the time reveal no trace of a Serb ethnopolitical identity. Over the next centuries the myth of Kosovo became more religious, centered on the Christian martyr-king sacrificing life for faith. In some versions, Prince Lazar chose martyrdom and eternal life over worldly victory and state survival. These "memories" were part of a rich panoply of myths, some religious, some ethnic, some more local. But late-19th-century nationalists produced an ethnonationalist version of a brave Serb defeat at the hand of the Turks, and in 20th-century school systems this was taught to all children. Now it became real for most Serbs. The French and English learn similar doctored history about their struggles of earlier epochs – of St. Joan and the field of Crecy and Agincourt. It encourages national rivalry, but not usually murder.

But mid-20th-century Yugoslavia could add on the atrocities of the Ustasha, the Chetniks, and the Muslim Sandzak SS regiment. Some Croats, some Serbs, and some Muslims did indeed do terrible things to the parents and grandparents of those active in the events of the 1990s. Some leading actors had experienced these atrocities as small children. If, in the telling, the actions of *some* persons were then attributed to all Croats, all Serbs, and all Muslims, then organic nationalism added the notion that whole nations share ethnic character attributes. This collective memory, based on a real recent historical core, then amplified by organic nationalism, boosted ethnic cleansing in Yugoslavia – but only after serious political tensions had emerged.

Yugoslavia did have problems. These ethnic groups lived somewhat segregated from each other, so that nation-states could be achieved by the secession of territories in which a single ethnicity constituted over 70 percent of the population. This had happened for short periods in the 20th century, and Yugoslavia's Federal Constitution gave them the right to do so again. This was technically a federation of *nations* (*narodi*) and these, not republics, had the right to secede and form their own majoritarian democracies (Hayden, 1996: 786–7). This might move them into the danger zone specified by my third ethnic thesis. The Serb nation had been hitherto privileged, but Serbs saw this position as now threatened. If they responded with imperial revisionism, things might get nasty. In the Republic of Bosnia-Herzegovina, both Serb and Croat nationalists might develop imperial revisionism, seeking to annex territories inhabited by Bosnian Muslims, whom they regarded as Serbs or Croats. Finally, swathes of mixed population lay in the borders between them, containing minorities, locally dominant, potentially at odds with the republic in which they lived. These might plausibly aspire to union with their homeland republic next door. In this context, rival ethnonationalists might claim sovereignty over the same territory, the weaker side being aided by a neighboring homeland state – as in my ethnic thesis 4a. However, this is to jump the gun. We need to know how escalation began, who carried such nationalist sentiments, and how they became so forceful or persuasive.

ETHNICITY AND POLITICS IN THE YUGOSLAV REPUBLICS

Postwar Yugoslav censuses had allowed people to define their own ethnic identity. Ninety percent chose only one of them. Ethnicity was real enough, not merely constructed out of the contingent events of the 1980s or 1990s or invented by nationalist leaders. The Yugoslav Communist federation consisted of six republics. One of them, Serbia, also contained Vojvodina and Kosovo, two regions enjoying less autonomy. The census of 1991 (taken just before cleansing began) revealed that five of the six republics were substantially mono-ethnic, Bosnia-Herzegovina being the exception. In Slovenia, 88 percent of adults identified themselves as Slovenes, Croatia was 78 percent Croat, Serbia was 66 percent Serb, Macedonia was 65 percent Macedonian, and Montenegro was 62 percent Montenegrin (Bogosavljevic, 1995; Woodward, 1995: Table 2.2). Since most Kosovo Albanians boycotted the 1991 census, we have to estimate their population, at around 85 percent of the province. Within Serbia, Vojvodina was more mixed, Serbs constituting 44 percent and Hungarians 25 percent of the population. It saw little trouble, since Hungarians and other minorities had little alternative to remaining part of Serbia. Thus all the republics except Bosnia, plus the province of Kosovo, *could* have their own predominantly mono-ethnic nation-state, just as we have seen had become the 20th-century European ideal. But for this to happen, two problems involving Serbs and Bosnia would have to be surmounted.

Serbs were the local imperial nation, having formed the first independent state and leading both interwar and Titoist Yugoslavia. Like other imperial nations like Germany and Russia, their past dominance ensured that many Serbs now lived outside Serbia. Those living in other republics, the *precani* Serbs, totaled 2.1 million, 25 percent of all Serbs in Yugoslavia. Most lived just over Serbia's borders. In Croatia and Bosnia they formed only 12 percent and 32 percent of the population, respectively, but they dominated some border areas. They also ran the province of Kosovo, though forming only 10 percent of its population. Their imperial past also meant that Serbs were politically and militarily the best-organized ethnic group, overrepresented in the police, interior ministries, and armed forces. In the 1981 Yugoslav Army, 60 percent of the NCO and officer corps was Serb, overrepresented by a ratio of 1.51 (Bebler, 1993: 117; Gow's evidence to the ICTY, Nikolic Case; Grmek et al., 1993: 240; Vujacic, 1995: 116–17).

But Serbian domination had been twice threatened. During World War II, Croat nationalists and some Bosnian Muslims had allied with Hitler, while Serb partisans had led the resistance. Almost half of the Serb young men had died in the war, so we can understand the moral claims that Serb nationalists made due to their wartime sacrifices, and perhaps even their hysteria at any sign of a Ustasha revival (for we understand Jewish outrage at swastikas daubed on synagogues). Serb nationalists also identified a more recent "demographic threat." Between the censuses of 1961 and 1991, Serbs in Bosnia-Herzegovina declined from 43 to 31 percent of the population, while Muslims rose from 26 to 44 percent. In Kosovo, Serbs had declined from 24 to 13 percent between 1961 and 1981 and to probably below 10 percent in 1991. Kosovo's Albanians had risen to about 85 percent by 1991. The Muslim birth rate was higher, and Albanians had begun pressuring Serbs after Tito granted some regional autonomy in 1974. In 30 years Serbs had lost their position in Bosnia as the largest single group, and in Kosovo they were now so few that they needed to rule by repression. Any breakup of Yugoslavia obviously threatened these imperial remnants.

There was also economic conflict in this failing state socialist economy disrupted by global recession and Soviet collapse. Exports declined and foreign debts mounted. Unemployment was high, but the northern republics of Slovenia and Croatia suffered least, being more developed and closer to European Union markets. In Serbia, Vojvodina and Belgrade were doing quite well, but most Serbs were rural and poor, dependent on the public sector, while recession was shrinking the tax base. Most industry and commerce was publicly owned, while privatization gave assets to those with political connections. Who controlled the state, at both the republican and local levels, controlled economic resources. Whether economic conflict in Yugoslavia would be between classes, sectors, republics or ethnicities, it would be politicized and rather zero-sum: for one group to gain, another would lose, for the economy was shrinking. Economic difficulties worsened tensions, especially since many Serbs felt threatened by a more decentralized division of the cake.

The most famous expression of Serb anxiety was the Serb Academy of Sciences and Arts *Memorandum* of 1986 (English edition, 1999). Outside of Serbia this document is much reviled. Thompson (1994: 54) calls it "self-pitying, morbid and vengeful." This is not how I read it. It was drawn up by 16 prominent intellectuals, mainly historians and literary figures with moderate and covertly anticommunist views. The *Memorandum* was leaked while still in draft form and so is uneven, revealing an uncertain grasp of economics. It begins by pointing out, incontrovertibly, that the Yugoslav economy is now a basket case. Market reforms have decentralized economic decision making only to the republican level. Thus each republic's economy, it says, is rather autarchic, run by a "top-heavy [Communist] bureaucracy, whose costs represent an intolerable burden for the economy." Economic cronyism now appropriates for private gain what had previously been socially owned property. This, declares the *Memorandum*, is not just an economic but "a moral crisis." It then laments Tito's constitutional changes of 1974. Serbia's two provinces of Kosovo and Vojvodina had been given autonomy plus independent representation at both the federal and Serbian republican levels. Constitutional change now requires unanimity among the republican/provincial delegates, which makes central decision making cumbersome and constitutional change almost impossible.

The non-Serb representatives of the two provinces can ally with others to outvote Serbs at the federal level, and they can even stymie change within the

Serbian republican assembly. These Serb complaints were substantially true. As Walker Connor observes, Tito had "gerrymandered" the constitution "as a means of weakening the state's largest ethnic element," the Serbs (1994: 333; cf. Udovicki & Torov, 1997: 80–4; Vujacic, 1995: 108–112). Only Serbia is being frustrated in the quest for a nation-state, says the *Memorandum*: "A worse historical defeat in peacetime cannot be imagined" (pp. 117, 125–6). It neglects to mention Serb strengths – control of the military, the security agencies, and the capital city and overrepresentation of *precani* Serbs in the party and security apparatuses of all the republics. It alludes to this obliquely when complaining that the other republics and provinces portray Serbs as "oppressors," "centralists," and "policemen" (pp. 119–22). It also blames the lagging Serbian economy on lack of federal investment and unfair terms of trade with the other republics. In reality the main cause of the lag was the rural and southern location of most Serbs, far from European markets.

The consequence, the *Memorandum* argues, is that the *precani* Serbs are being forced to emigrate. Then comes the notorious phrase, quoted by all critics: Kosovo is experiencing a "physical, political, legal and cultural genocide" of the Serb people (p. 127). The word genocide is repeated three times. Serbs were leaving Kosovo because of discrimination and intimidation (Vujacic, 1995: 218–25). This was ethnic cleansing, but nowhere near genocide. The *Memorandum* concludes with moderation, inviting dialogue about constitutional changes toward "a democratic, integrating federalism" (p. 105). This must guarantee the rights of all ethnicities, regions, and classes and must strengthen both federal institutions and popular sovereignty (an implicit attack on the Communist Party). It demands equality for all groups, and an end to Serbia's "flawed nationhood." It does not demand more "Serbian power" or an enlarged Serbia. Despite its many critics, it was simply a Serb view, biased here and there, of the federation's defects (cf. Grmek et al., 1993: 235). It was an early version of the "strong federal" option: the federation should be kept but its center strengthened.

Yet some Serbs were demanding more. Serb rule should be extended over all areas where Serb minorities lived in Kosovo and border areas of Croatia and Bosnia; the morbid version of this was that Serbs should rule wherever there were Serb cemeteries. This was the option of "Greater Serbia." Though not massively expansionist (not remotely comparable to Nazi plans for *Lebensraum*), it would infringe on the rights of other ethnic groups there. This ideal had core constituencies among rural Serbs (suffering from recession and decentralization), privileged but vulnerable public sector workers, threatened *precani* Serb communities, and returning Serb refugees. Kosovo Serbs felt the most threatened and were the most extreme. So for Croatia and Bosnia to have their own states, their Serb minorities would have to be handled sensitively; otherwise, they might throw in their lot with Greater Serb nationalists. Solving the Serb problem would not be easy.

The second problem concerns the only republic that could not become a mono-ethnic nation-state. In the 1991 census, 44 percent of the population of Bosnia-Herzegovina identified themselves as Muslims, 32 percent as Serbs, 17 percent as Croats, and 5 percent as Yugoslavs. Sixteen percent of the population were also the children of mixed marriages, much more than in the other republics. Intermarriage was mainly recent and urban, and rural dwellers often described it as risky. The ethnic map of Bosnia was also a patchwork, containing small pockets of each main ethnic group. Even if several statelets emerged, each would contain substantial minorities. An independent state of Bosnia-Herzegovina would need consociational power sharing between the communities. Solving ethnic tensions in Bosnia would not be easy.

By 1990 Federal Yugoslavia was unpopular. Most Yugoslavs wanted to move from Communism to democracy, yet they associated federation with Communism and Serb domination. Outside of Serbia almost all wanted decentralizing reforms, but most Serbs disliked the decentralization that had already occurred. As the political regime teetered, international capitalism wielded neo-liberal butchery, granting credits only in return for reduced state planning and budgets. GDP began to decline from the 1986 level. The official unemployment rate was 17 percent in 1988, but the rate for those under 25 was above 30 percent. Rural areas were hit worse. Jobs and consumer goods depended increasingly on family, patronage, and barter networks in the public sphere and in the market sphere created out of public resources. As the Serb *Memorandum* had noted, markets were structured by the individual republics, increasing the relevance of ethnicity for subsistence. More Yugoslavs were linking their personal and familial interests to those of their ethnic group. Nation was ascending over class, and this was ominous for federalism.

Yugoslavia had been formed in the settlement of World War I, accepted by Croat, Serb, and Slovenian leaders for geopolitical reasons. They had been constrained to fight against each other in that war – Slovenes and Croats had been in the Habsburg Empire, fighting against Serbia – and they now sought Balkan peace through union. United, they also formed a second-rank power able to defend its territory against any regional rival. Interwar Yugoslavia was shaken by nationalist rivalries but geopolitical reasoning had held it together, and the same geopolitical logic reemerged after 1945. When Tito broke away from Stalin in 1948, Yugoslavia was able to exploit its neutrality between the superpowers. So Yugoslavia had always been a geopolitical entity. It still had one of the largest armies in Europe. But the Soviet collapse made the geopolitical logic redundant. In 1990 Yugoslavs no longer needed federation for their defense, and they disliked the form of federation they actually had – Communist, militarist and somewhat Serb-dominated.

THE REJECTION OF YUGOSLAV FEDERALISM:
THE ELECTIONS OF 1990

Democracy killed off Yugoslav federalism (Snyder, 2000). Yugoslavs wanted rule by we, the people, but fairly free elections in the six republics between April and December 1990 brought rule by organic nationalists committed to majoritarian ethnic democracy. In accordance with the Constitution, the elections were organized by each republic separately, and so were almost all the parties. The elections proved an ethnic census. Among the bigger parties, only ex-Communist ones attracted many votes across ethnic boundaries, and even they mostly appealed to ethnic minorities, except in Serbia. The other successful parties were mostly mono-ethnic in leadership and support. Nationalist parties did best, dominating the symbolic and sentimental realm, milking their sufferings under Communism. Leaders like Tudjman and the near-fascist Paraga in Croatia, Izetbegovic in Bosnia, and Seselj and Draskovic in Serbia had acquired moral authority under Communism, suffering imprisonment and beatings. Like the liberals, many of them also stood for market reforms that would supposedly bring prosperity. But only the nationalists defined material interests as belonging collectively to the ethnic group, and this brought increasing plausibility in the Yugoslav economy (Cohen, 1995; Crnobrnja, 1994, Part II), especially since Marxist conceptions of class interest were unpopular. Ethnicity had not yet trumped class, but most Yugoslavs were turning toward it.

The results varied among the republics. In Croatia a nationalist coalition centered on Tudjman's (HDZ) won an absolute majority of seats (though not of votes). Tudjman now remained president of Croatia until his death in 1999. The ex-Communist Party and a centrist alliance did respectably, and some of them preached multiethnicity. They did best among minorities. There were no significant differences between male and female voters. Croat nationalist party voters were attracted less by any actual party program than by feelings of threat from other ethnic groups. Siber (1993: 197) says that in Croatia "the stereotype of a non-ethnic voter or a non-nationalist party does not exist." But the winners wanted rule by the Croat people.

Since Slovenia had many parties, none won an absolute majority. But though they labeled themselves as socialist, Christian democrat, liberal, conservative, and so on, most were primarily nationalist, prepared to suspend their arguments until they had jointly established national autonomy inside or outside of the federation. Slovenia felt as close culturally to Europe as to the rest of Yugoslavia, and it had some support in Europe for independence. In both Slovenia and Croatia there was tension between a principled desire for a nation-state and a pragmatic desire for peace and continuity. A peaceful secession was desired by most of the main political actors in both republics. But they would be cautious in pushing for it.

The two smallest republics were to see less trouble. Montenegrins have an ambivalent sense of ethnicity. The majority parties said that Montenegrins were essentially Serb; the minority said they were ethnically distinct. The majority supported the Serb conception of a strong federation, with minor reservations. Montenegrins remained in the Serb rump federation. Milosevic's failures were to increase Montenegrins' reservations. In 2003 a looser federation was established between the two republics with an agreement to hold a referendum in each republic in 2006 on full independence. In Macedonia moderate nationalists won the election, with more radical nationalists coming in second. The new government supported a federation but mainly for geopolitical reasons, since it felt threatened by its Greek and Bulgarian neighbors. It favored a compromise of "asymmetric federation" where different republics would be granted different degrees of autonomy according to their needs. When that failed, they declared independence while Serb attention was distracted elsewhere. Macedonia's discrimination against its 25–30 percent Albanian minority eventually produced armed skirmishes in 2001, though these have now lessened. This ethnic conflict seems capable of compromise.

The other initial compromiser was Bosnia. Since Bosnia could not become a nation-state, this restrained its nationalists. Yet even here, the three victorious parties were all ethnically based, one in each main community. Together they got nearly 90 percent of the votes, with no significant class or gender differences. The biggest social organizations not tainted by Communism were ethnic ones, and these translated into the most effective political parties. Even in this multiethnic republic, compromise would have to be brokered by ethnic parties. Initially they agreed to preserve the federation, but this was just geopolitical pragmatism. Serb and Croat leaders in Bosnia expected that the influence of their homeland republic inside federal institutions would protect their interests. The Muslim leader (later president) Izetbegovic argued in 1989:

We are not on the road to a national state.... Some people may want that ... but this is not a realistic wish. Even though the Muslims are the most numerous nation in the republic, there are not enough of them ... they would have to comprise about seventy percent of the population. (Silber & Little, 1995: 230)

He apparently agreed that 70 percent is the requisite level for establishing a nation-state.

Communist Party leaders in each of the three main communities had previously each possessed effective veto power over policy, which had necessitated constant consultations among them. But as Communism disintegrated, Bosnian politics began to fragment along ethnic lines. Though Muslim parties at first favored federation, some became attracted by a majoritarian democracy that would favor them, the largest group. Bosnian collective identity had lagged behind other ethnic identities in Yugoslavia, helping Croats and Serbs persist in believing that Muslims really belonged to them. But the autonomy conferred by the 1974 Constitution and market reforms had disseminated (first in Sarajevo) a common *Bosniak* identity. Some included local Serbs and Croats within its rubric; others restricted it to Muslims. The latter usage began to predominate during the 1990 election (Bringa, 1995: chap. 1). I shall use the term Bosniak in this sense in these chapters. Bosnian Croats were also tempted by an alliance with the Muslims over the Serbs. So the largest Bosnian Serb party, Milosevic's SDS, having originally favored federation, began to favor stronger links with its own homeland nation-state just across the border, resulting perhaps in a Greater Serbia. Trinational parity began to falter amid these maneuvers.

Thus *all* of these victorious party leaders outside of Serbia began to think of the nation-state as their ideal, even in Bosnia. Pragmatism might make them settle for less, but ideally they preferred sovereignty for their nation. The new republican constitutions they proposed, except Bosnia, explicitly guaranteed the majority nation its own state through self-determination (so later did the Serb and Croat statelets formed amid other republics). The Bosnia-Herzegovina proposed constitution declared a sovereign state of the plural "nations of Bosnia and Herzegovina – Muslims, Serbs and Croats, and members of other nations and nationalities living within it." The decision was made that the right of self-determination belonged to each republic and its majority nation (Hayden, 1996: 790–2; Woodward, 1995: 108).

This was majoritarian democracy, degrading the rights of minorities. With ethnic groups living amid each other, this might induce a downward reciprocal spiral of border disputes. People asked, "Why should I be a minority in your state when you can be a minority in mine?" Nonetheless, pragmatic compromise might still prevail. I now turn to the biggest and most important republic.

THE RISE OF SLOBODAN MILOSEVIC

Most of the evils of Yugoslavia have been attributed to one rather dumpy gray man. Milosevic was only opportunistically a nationalist. He began as a Communist apparatchik favoring reform, sharing the antibureaucratic sentiments common among young Communists. Ambitious, he hoped this would propel him into power. He seemed to stumble almost by accident on the nationalist card in April 1987, in the small town of Kosovo Field, next to the famous battlefield. Tito's grant of local autonomy to Kosovo in 1974 had enabled Albanians to take over the province's administrative and police powers. Under this pressure, many Serbs left. Others moved within Kosovo, clustering especially around Kosovo Field, which became a hotbed of Serb nationalism (Vujacic, 1995: 220–1). In 1987 Milosevic was sent there as deputy leader of the Serbian Communist Party to help cool the locals with the usual public talk of brotherhood and back-room deals. Their public meeting and subsequent events were filmed and then broadcast across the world in the BBC documentary *Death of a Nation* (1998).

The film reveals Milosevic in the meeting hall, expecting the deference due to a senior Communist. Instead he was drowned out by an angry crowd of Serbs in the street outside demanding entrance, shouting that they had been beaten up by the Albanian police. As elsewhere in Yugoslavia, police powers were often wielded brutally. But the organizers of this demonstration subsequently acknowledged that they had staged a provocation, throwing two truckloads of stones at Albanian policemen to get the desired police retaliation. Milosevic then went outside, apparently hoping to calm the crowd down. He failed. Visibly shaken, he blurted out, "never again will you be beaten" and "never again will Serbs be beaten." He then returned to the meeting inside, spending all night patiently listening to Serb complaints before rising at dawn to promise them "speed and efficiency" in addressing all their grievances. He appeared sympathetic. "Sloba's ours," Kosovo Serbs began to say (Judah, 2000: 53, and Udovicki & Torov, 1997: 87–8, suspect Milosevic had prearranged much of this).

Later in 1987 at a televised party Central Committee meeting, Milosevic denounced the party leadership for having failed to defend Kosovo Serbs. Over the next two years he used Serb nationalism as part of an "antibureaucratic revolution," taking over the Serbian Party leadership, stripping Kosovo and Vojvodina of their provincial autonomy, purging both of their Communist Party leaderships, and acquiring substantial influence in the Macedonian Party. He then revamped the party as an apparently social democratic party, the SPS. He was on the brink of acquiring a majority vote in the supreme body of Yugoslavia, the Federal Council – a very worrying prospect for Croatian and Slovenian political elites. The culmination came in 1989, when he addressed several hundred thousand Serbs gathered at the great battlefield to celebrate its 600th anniversary. His final words became famous: "Six centuries later we are once again in battles, and facing battles. They are not armed battles, though the possibility of those cannot be excluded" (translation of Vujacic, 1995: 394).

Milosevic spoke much more directly to his audience than had his Communist predecessors. His image was of a plain-spoken man who was also a skilled politician, able to first listen and then deliver the goods. He rarely spouted inflammatory nationalism, though his supporters did. At this time he favored a "compact federation" with more powers at the center, which was his Plan A. He mobilized the core constituencies of Greater Serb nationalism – Serb refugees, Serbs in threatened areas, especially Kosovo, and some rural Serbs who expected more economic development from a stronger federation. They could turn out 80,000 demonstrators, claiming to be the people, demanding the dismissal of "uncaring bureaucrats" among the Serbian, Kosovan, and Vojvodina party leaders. Milosevic encouraged them, saying,

"No force on earth can stop the people of Serbia," while claiming he could not control their popular anger.

He wanted an antibureaucratic revolution with himself as party leader. Though he was supported by many army officers, the High Command was divided and could not yet be collectively mobilized. More useful were the police and the murky Serbian State Security Service, the SDB. Since 1972, when 19 supposed Ustasha terrorists had penetrated into Yugoslavia, the SDB had used the criminal underworld to murder and intimidate dissidents at home and abroad. This is how the notorious "Arkan" first moved from criminal to political violence. So did "Beli" and "Giska," close to the nationalist leader Vuc Draskovic. As Giska himself noted, "All over the world in liberation and resistance movements, patriotic 'criminals' have taken to the frontlines and made a great contribution such as only they, in such circumstances, could make" (Knezevic, 1995).

Yet in 1990 elections mattered most. Milosevic's Socialist Party, the SPS, stood for moderate reforming nationalism, protecting Serbs though a compact federation. Only if the federation collapsed would Milosevic seek a revision of republican borders to protect Serb minorities. This would be his Plan B. The SPS enjoyed unfair electoral advantages, for it had inherited Communist state apparatuses, especially radio and TV, plus the police and security police. The opposition parties were also unprepared for a hastily declared election. Unlike elections in the other republics, Serb elections were only half-democratic.

But the biggest opposition parties were even more nationalist than Milosevic. This is the main obstacle to blaming Serb aggression on Milosevic (as do Cigar, 1996, and Gagnon, 1997, though Snyder, 2000, differs). The main opposition leader, Vuk Draskovic, was demanding "unity of all Serb lands" and making territorial claims against other republics. He declared, "all those who like Turkey [i.e., Muslims] should go to Turkey," and said he would personally cut off any arm raising the green (i.e., Muslim) flag. The nationalist parties emerged from Orthodox cultural-educational societies like St. Sava (named after a Serb martyr), which called for the elimination of godless Communism and the restoration of a Greater Serbia. Nationalists claimed that Muslims were really Serbs, just as Tudjman claimed that they were really Croats – allowing each to claim half of Bosnia. The liberal democratic parties, unlike the SPS and the nationalists, started with no already existing mass organizations. They were formed out of associations of intellectuals and professionals capable of some mobilization in Belgrade, other urban middle-class areas, and among ethnic minorities, but much less elsewhere. They denounced Milosevic as a manipulating dictator and favored federation and autonomy for minorities. Yet even they agreed that if federation were to collapse, the existing borders should be expanded to provide Serbs with more protection (Goati, 1995: 76). Almost all Serb parties shared ethnonationalism. They agreed on a Plan A, demanding a reformed, asymmetric federation that would better protect Serb interests – as elaborated by the Serb Academy. A common Plan B existed if this failed – a Greater Serbia. This was not a conspiracy of elites. They were expressing anxieties widespread among Serbs, and like normal democratic politicians they wanted reelection.

But Serb voters were not obsessed by ethnonationalism. Preelection surveys revealed that the most salient negative issue was removing the Communist legacy, and the most salient positive issues were the economy and the standard of living, followed by building good international relations while at the same time defending the nation. Aggressive nationalism came nowhere. Warmongering rarely wins elections. Draskovic thrived on his anticommunist and nationalist rhetoric and his charismatic presence, but his economic policy seemed naive and he seemed inconsistent on the ethnic issue. Milosevic had to downplay his Communist past, but he scored well on his firm yet supposedly moderate defense of the nation and his economic competence (*Vreme*, January 6, 1992). Voters evaluated the parties on various criteria, as in most elections.

Milosevic's votes came disproportionately from older Serbs, from the less educated, from workers and peasants (though the unemployed spread their votes around the parties), from the large public sector, and from rural areas, especially in backward south Serbia. Milosevic's control over state TV was especially important in rural areas and among less educated groups with less access to other media. They were the people most worried about living standards and security. In attitude surveys, SPS voters were more statist and more likely to approve of authoritarian rule. The liberal democrats were the mirror image of this, recruiting heavily from ethnic minorities, the middle class and the educated, northerners, and residents of Belgrade and other cities. The SPS taunted them as "cosmopolitans who can't see Serbia from the center of Belgrade." In turn, they derided the SPS as "Belgrade mountain nationalists." The SPS and the liberal democrats both drew equally from men and women. The nationalist parties' voters were slightly more male, but were spread evenly across the classes and both towns and countryside. The highest nationalist vote came from Serb *precanis* and refugees, especially those in and from Kosovo. And the nationalist party voters had more nationalist views than did SPS voters.

Milosevic seemed the centrist, steering between the old and the new politics and between rabid nationalism and cosmopolitan liberalism. The SPS declared itself as "the right choice for those who want to live in peace and not in national hatred and national conflicts; who want a brighter tomorrow for their children instead of uncertainty and a fratricidal war; who want to live well on the fruits of their labor; who in the freedom of others find the condition for their own freedom." Milosevic's drew most support from those apprehensive of change and disorder, depending on state patronage for economic survival, drawing them toward nationalism. The SPS slogan

"With us, there is no uncertainty" was especially popular.[3] At this stage, Milosevic was semiauthoritarian but not an extremist. But his policy and his core constituency favored a union of statism and nationalism that elevated nation above class and drew them toward violence. Most of these core constituencies of support endured. Opinion polls reported in *Vreme* in 1992 showed a slide in SPS popularity, especially in the cities, in the north, and among the educated. Only 15 percent of Belgraders supported the SPS compared to 51 percent of those in south Serbia. Milosevic came to depend more on the core constituencies of Serb nationalism.

A first-past-the-post electoral system and an Albanian election boycott meant that a vote of 46 percent for the SPS garnered 77 percent of the parliamentary seats. Milosevic now had parliamentary as well as executive power. Yet over 90 percent of Serbs who voted had supported parties favoring a similar Plan A: a compact federation incompatible with the aspirations of almost all the other republics' major parties. They continued to advocate Plan B, redrawing boundaries in favor of Serbia if federation did not work. Throughout the stormy 1991 negotiations between the republics, all major Serb parties supported Milosevic's position. They rejected not only Slovene and Croat arguments for a weaker confederation, but also the compromise suggestions of Bosnians and Macedonians for an asymmetric federation attuned to the peculiarities of each republic (Goati, 1995: 76). When negotiations failed, the opposition parties could not easily oppose Milosevic's Plan B of a Greater Serbia, since this had been their Plan too. Most Serbs were pessimistic about the prospects for multiculturalism. Only 11 percent of those in one poll thought that the different nations could live in accord with each other, and the majority believed it was best for each state to be mono-ethnic (*Vreme*, November 30, 1992).

The disastrous ethnic wars were to reduce Milosevic's popularity. Faced by public opposition, in 1991 and 1993 he resorted to coercion. His formidable police powers ultimately swept demonstrators off the streets and closed down independent media on trumped-up charges. War also enhanced his powers. The president of the dissident Social Democratic Party of Vojvodina was labeled an "ally of the fascist bandits in Croatia" and then arrested and conscripted into the army. Milosevic also wielded covert economic power. About one-half of Serbian industry was still state-owned, and it covertly financed the SPS and some of its paramilitary allies. Workers who refused to go to war might be laid off (*Vreme*, November 11, December 9, and December 12, 1991). Milosevic also benefited from an opposition divided into a smaller liberal antiwar bloc and a larger nationalist prowar bloc – with Draskovic now wavering between the two. Needing more support,

[3] Electoral data are drawn from Cohen (1995: 152), Gordy (1999: 34 and chap. 2), Mihajlovic et al. (1991), Vujacic (1995: 421–38), Vukomanovic (1995: 82–8), and from the Serb opposition journal *Vreme* over the period.

Milosevic entered into a coalition with Seselj's nationalists. By mid-1992, 200,000 Yugoslavs had emigrated, including a disproportionate number of liberal university graduates (*Vreme*, April 6, 1992). A Milosevic/nationalist coalition now ruled Serbia – lessening his freedom to maneuver.

Gordy (1999; cf. Snyder, 2000) overstates Milosevic's role in what he calls "the destruction of political alternatives." Though Milosevic did use police and media powers and was buttressed by wartime patriotism, the fundamental problem derived from the initial national consensus on greater defense for Serbs. Then, when opposition strengthened, it was divided, some of it being more extreme than Milosevic himself. Unfortunately, Serb politicians and voters began to relinquish views that were inflammatory to other ethnic groups only *after* cleansing had commenced. For Draskovic the terrible sack of Vukovar in November 1991 produced a personal moral crisis (Grmek et al., 1993: 316–17). He had not realized that his own rhetorical slogan of "extending Serb rule to wherever there are Serb cemeteries" would produce even larger cemeteries. Before this, most Serbs supported a firm national stance against threats from outside. As yet, this involved neither personal costs nor a commitment to violence.

In none of the republics did a majority support murderous ethnic cleansing. Yet two radicalizing political forces had been set in motion in Serbia. Milosevic was beginning to trap himself. He had to deliver "more defense" of the Serbs in the form of a compact federalism or a redrawing of boundaries. If he backtracked, he might be overwhelmed by popular nationalist forces unless he allied with liberal parties, which opposed his authoritarian leanings. His own support straddled nationalist and statist constituencies that were vulnerable to further nationalist seduction. He was part controller, but also part prisoner of his core constituency and of the coalition he was building with the nationalists. Second, a Serb nationalist hard core was beginning to use paramilitary violence against opponents, with support from the Serb security police, the SDB. From the 1970s the SDB had been using criminals to assassinate opponents abroad. Now its agents began to arm and organize paramilitaries in the Serb *precani* communities in Croatia and Bosnia and to assist paramilitaries being organized by the Serb nationalist parties (Knezevic & Tufegdzic, 1995; Milicevic, forthcoming). The growth of more radical and violent populism connected to murky regions of the state were now destabilizing politics.

Negotiations over a reformed confederation made little progress, and Slovenia and Milosevic turned to other options. Slovenia saw the chance of an unopposed secession; Milosevic had an army to enforce his demands. Tension worsened. When they all sent representatives to the Federal Parliament in Belgrade to haggle over the new constitution, they failed to form socialist, liberal, or conservative caucuses – as, for example, do their national counterparts in the federal European Parliament. Instead they caucused as nationalists – as Croats, Slovenians, Serbs, and so on. Ethnicity was trumping class (my second thesis). The Serb and Croat delegations from Bosnia remained ambivalent, caucusing in two ways, one with the whole Bosnian delegation, the other with their ethnic comrades elsewhere. The federal budget collapsed when only Serbia and Montenegro made their republics' contributions. The economic crisis and the burden of foreign debt led to trade and currency wars as each republic tried to unload its burdens on the others. Milosevic escalated this process at the end of 1990 by robbing the National Bank to pay for Serbia's debt. The other republics responded in kind.

By now the federation was collapsing. Step one had occurred more or less inevitably, given the nationalist forces emerging in the republics. They opposed an initially Communist federation that now lacked either geopolitical rationale or economic success, supported mainly by Serb nationalists. Federalism was now deviant within a Europe of nation-states. The individual republics now had centralized, unitary parliamentary institutions reinforced by winner-take-all rather than proportional representation elections, and nationalists had won them. We cannot tell what Yugoslavs really wanted. We know only what they chose at the ballot box when confronted with a given range of parties in a given electoral process. But we can assume that very few of them wanted what they were soon to get – murderous ethnic cleansing.

Defensive ethnic nationalism was growing. Croatian survey data show that nationalist parties especially attracted people feeling ethnically victimized, resenting out-group privileges (Siber, 1993: 152–3). The most insistent nationalist slogan across the Yugoslav elections of 1990 was the primacy of the hearth and the need to defend it. Democracy rewarded this moral nationalism with electoral victory led by politicians who had proved their principles through bravery. Two preexisting social organizations had mobilized best. The largest were the Communist youth leagues, trade unions, and professional and cultural associations. But since most people wanted a break with Communism, these multiethnic organizations began to fade. So the most mobilizing organizations were ethnic ones. Under Communism they had kept out of politics but organized music, dance, football, parades, and picnics, formidable everyday mobilization. At the end of the 1980s republicwide cultural organizations joined them. These became the civil society mobilizers of the nationalist parties. A distant third were multicultural groups supported by the educated professional classes of the cities. They wrote the most informed pamphlets and gave the most sophisticated speeches. They talked about feminism and human rights. But they lacked mass mobilization. For all their talk of civil society, this was being mobilized by nationalist organizations and identities; again, civil society was to turn out more evil than civil.

Liberal democracy and its social science often has a rather atomized model of individual opinion and electoral choice. Through the opinion poll and the social survey, it continually asks what the people think and so is baffled (as were Holbrooke, the Croatian priest, and the sociologists measuring social distance) when the result seems quite different from the sum of the individual preferences. Yet since most people have complex and often contradictory political thoughts, it is organization that brings some of these thoughts, and not others, into the voting booth. Manipulation helped bring Milosevic rather than other Serb nationalists into power – and this made a difference. But most elite manipulations in 1990 were those of cleverer versus more naive democratic politicians – the normal stuff of democracy. Democratization had brought Yugoslavia into the danger zone. For the election of nationalists to power in most republics strengthened their mutual fears, creating a security dilemma.

THE EMERGENCE OF ORGANIC NATIONALISM

Organicist nation-states emerged over the next nine months. In late June 1991 both Slovenia and Croatia declared independence from Yugoslavia. These two regimes, plus Serbia, refused all compromise during this period. Between Serbian compact federation and Croatian/Slovenian weak confederation there seemed no compromise. All three regimes were ready to risk further escalation rather than compromise. The Slovenian government had a relatively easy choice. Slovenia was the richest and most European-oriented republic, with the fewest ties to Serbia and little interest in federation. Slovenia also ran the lowest risk from a declaration of independence. It had uncontested frontiers, no border with Serbia, and virtually no Serbs. Slovenian politicians doubted that Serbia would contest a declaration of independence if they acted firmly and with unity.

Slovenia declared independence with little internal dissent. After Slovenian police forces showed that they would resist a token thrust from the JNA, the Serbian-led Yugoslav army, Milosevic let Slovenia go. Army morale was low, the High Command divided. The fiasco did radicalize some generals, appalled that federation was being abandoned without a fight. But as State Council President Jovic (a close Serb ally of Milosevic) later said on camera, "It was an ethnically pure state. No Serbs. We couldn't care less if Slovenia left Yugoslavia" (BBC, 1998). Slovenia, with few minorities, has been spared ethnic war. I will not discuss it further. Yet Slovenes had now done their bit to help destroy Yugoslav federalism. It is sometimes argued that by promptly recognizing Slovenia as an independent state, the European powers also did their bit. But not much can be blamed on outsiders. Perhaps all shared collective responsibility for the dominance of the nation-state ideal. But it was Yugoslavs who tore apart their own country.

The Croatian declaration of independence then finished off confederal Yugoslavia and risked much worse. Croatia had a long border with Serbia and a large Serb minority. Unlike Slovenia, Serbia had strong interests there, so the risks of secession were much higher. Negotiations were now between half-sovereign republics, and conflict was potentially warlike. Serbia controlled most of the Yugoslav army, the JNA, a massive resource in such an eventuality. Thus the Serb regime felt it had the military power to pressure Croatia to remain in the federation. Would Croatia take a big risk and try to break away? The outcome would probably determine other republics' moves toward independence. Its politicians and parties were the crucial initial actors in stage two.

Tudjman, now in power, did not initially favor Croatian independence for pragmatic reasons: a former army general, he feared a JNA invasion. So while bargaining, he was covertly seeking arms and military advisers abroad (as Izetbegovic in Bosnia was not). The longer the delay, the more he could arm. Croat emigres were important in funneling money from the United States, Canada, and elsewhere. In the emigre communities, more than in Croatia itself, Ustasha ideology lived on – especially the belief that defending Croatian independence required armed struggle. Many emigres returned to Croatia and became prominent in the HDZ as hard-liners controlling access to guns. Much of the administration in the "softer" realms of this new state was inherited from the federal republic's. But for its "hard" functions, it lacked an army, and its police forces in Serb-populated areas were mostly Serb. The army was forming secretively, in the hands of hard-liners; the police forces were fragmenting. Croatia had a distinctive form of the destabilized state that my fifth thesis suggests is important in going over the brink into ethnic war.

Tudjman's true desire was for a Croat nation-state, and he was prepared to fight to achieve it. He had become a historian of sorts. One of his books minimized the casualties at the terrible Ustasha death camp, Jasenovac. In *Nationalism and Contemporary Europe* he said that a separate Bosnia-Herzegovina would make "the economic and geographical position of Croatia extremely unnatural in the economic sense and therefore in the broadest political sense very unfavourable for life and development." Bosnian Muslims were really Croats, and so he calculated ethnic populations by counting Croats and Muslims as one, justifying a Croatian state sprawling over most of Bosnia (English edition, 1981: 112–15). To implement this vision would be dynamite for both Muslims and Serbs living there.

During the election campaign Tudjman's HDZ repeatedly demanded "Croatian sovereignty" and a "state for the Croats," without reference to minorities. Even antiabortionists got in on the act, their campaign posters declaring, "Even a fetus is a little Croat." The HDZ was substantially financed by the emigres (Pusic, 1997: 98). Tudjman repeatedly declared, "We alone will decide the fate of our Croatia." This state would culminate "one thousand years of uninterrupted Croatian aspirations for sovereign statehood." Tudjman sometimes defended the Ustasha:

Our opponents see nothing in our programme but the claim for the restoration of the independent Croatian Ustase state. These people fail to see that the state was not the creation of fascist criminals; it also stood for the historic aspirations of the Croatian people for an independent state. They knew that Hitler planned to build a new European order. (Silber & Little, 1995: 91)

Unlike Milosevic, Tudjman was not mealy-mouthed. He publicly thanked God that his wife was neither a Jew nor a Serb. He declared that while Croats were Eastern Europeans, "the Serbs belong to the East. They are Eastern peoples, like the Turks.... Despite similarities in language, we cannot be together" (Cohen, 1995: 211). This of a Serb people whose own nationalist myth saw themselves as defenders of the whole of Christian Europe against the Turks! Since Tudjman's party sometimes linked anti-Serb with anti-Semitic vitriol, Serbs could be forgiven thoughts that the Ustasha might be returning.

The new state's draft constitution tried to reassure them, embodying more pluralism than might have been expected from the campaign rhetoric. It proclaimed:

the Republic of Croatia is comprised as the national state of the Croatian people and all minorities who are citizens of Croatia, including Serbs, Muslims, Slovaks, Czechs, Jews [etc etc]... for whom equality with those citizens of Croatian nationality is guaranteed.[4]

This guaranteed equal rights for non-Croats, but for Serbs and Muslims in Croatia it seemed to reduce their political rights. They had been defined as an "equal nation" within Yugoslavia, and federal institutions had collectively entrenched their national rights. Now they were promised the lesser status of a minority like Czechs or Jews, who had enjoyed only individual civil rights under Yugslav law. Individual rights were insufficient; collective confederal or consociational rights were necessary, argued many Serbs. Croat nationalists argued identically when they were in a minority. The Bosnian Croat leader Mate Boban told a journalist that he could not accept the constitution of Bosnia-Herzegovina, since "although it defended individual rights, it did not defend the rights of the ... narod" (evidence in the Blaskic trial, April 24, 1998). Unfortunately, the major powers, especially the United States, had liberal constitutions, and so believed that a guarantee of individual rights was sufficient protection for minorities. This was incorrect. Serbs argued that areas with non-Croat majorities should have political autonomy (federalism) or that ethnic minorities should have entrenched rights within the central state (consociationalism). But the powers failed to understand arguments

---

[4] Other republics had comparable clauses appearing to confer second-class rights on minorities. The Macedonian Constitution declares that Macedonia is "a national state of the Macedonian people," adding that other ethnic groups should have "full civic equality." Albanians are currently agitating for its revision.

couched in terms of collective rather than individual rights. They applied no outside pressure on Croatia – nor had they on Slovenia. That was a mistake.

Tudjman's tactics lessened the chances for compromise. Most Serbs in Croatia had voted not for Serb nationalist parties but for the ex-Communist Party or centrist parties. Tudjman saw these parties as his main electoral rivals and did not wish to negotiate with them. Since he was a democratically elected leader with a majority (a 42 percent vote had translated into 68 percent of the parliamentary seats), he did not have to. Tudjman said he expressed the view of the true Croats through a legitimate parliamentary majority. It was left to the small Serb nationalist party, best represented in the Krajina (literally "border") district, to lead Serb negotiations. It did not initially have a clear position, since the leadership was being challenged by a more radical faction. But it tended to think in terms of confederal protections – autonomy for the border region. Croats feared that another purpose lay behind this demand. If the border Serbs were granted some autonomy, they could exploit it to attain union with Serbia. Tudjman's own strategy was reinforcing this possibility, since he was shifting the conflict to one that could be expressed territorially – between Zagreb and the Krajina. The conflict, as Brubaker (1996) observes, was no longer merely one between two ethnic states. It was three-way, involving what he calls a *nationalizing state* (Croatia) and a *national minority* (Serbs), aided by a *homeland state* (Serbia). The second and third might fuse into a single Greater Serbia.

Many Serbs also feared the Law on Croatian Citizenship of 1991. This said that a citizen must "adhere to the laws and customs prevailing in the Republic of Croatia and that he accepts Croatian culture." The last phrase might exclude Serbs altogether. The language and symbols of state might also alienate them. Though the two ethnic groups speak basically the same language, they write it in different scripts. Most Serbs can use Latin script; few Croats use or read Cyrillic script. The official state script was to be Latin, though local government and schools in majority Serb areas could also use Cyrillic. This was a concession, though not a two-language policy. Language and symbols also played more emotional roles. The new flag and coat of arms, everywhere displayed, were of ancient provenance but they were known to most Yugoslavs only as Ustasha symbols, especially the hated checkerboard symbol, which seemed to evoke fascism (as it did to me when I first saw Croat football supporters flourishing it). Latin script and checkerboards were an in-your-face demonstration typical of organic nationalism: "This is our state." The regime tried to ban the worst excesses, like best-selling reproductions of Ustasha photographs and maps.

All these disputes were capable of settlement, but Croat radicals did not want compromise. The members of the smallish fascist party, the Croatian Party of Rights, and extremists in Tudjman's own HDZ were flourishing Croat symbols in mixed-population areas as a deliberate provocation, so as to get a violent reaction from radical Serbs, which in turn would strengthen the plausibility of their own arguments among Croats. HDZ radicals were routinely called fascists by their Serb counterparts, a very resonant label within the threatened Serb community. Seselj, a Serb nationalist leader, proclaimed on television, "We Serbs are in danger. Croat fascist hordes attack Serb women and children in our villages. The Croat fascist hordes are planning genocide for the Serbs." One Serb in the Krajina town of Knin told the journalist Glenny, "Most of the Croats in Knin are fine people.... They're not like those dreadful Ustashas in Split" (1993: 19). Thompson provides a vivid glimpse of HDZ radicals. He had arrived in the town of Zadar just after the first Croat policeman had been killed. By the bus station he came across a gang of teenage boys wielding table legs and iron bars, smashing and looting Serb shops, with Croat policemen looking indulgently on. One young man, asking him questions about rock music, took him to Croat road blocks and to the local HDZ party headquarters, manned by "sullen, boorish" men with guns and knives. These were sending off alarm bells around local Serb communities, encouraged by radical Serbs. The next day, Thompson was told by a local Serb, "What happened in Zadar yesterday was total genocide" (1992: 261–4, 276). Both sides were claiming to act in retaliation for actions committed earlier by the members of the other group.

Some of Tudjman's advisers urged conciliation. They knew they could not retain all their territory if the JNA attacked. Tudjman should have dissociated himself from the Ustasha regime, though this would have broken the "thousand-year" rhetoric of his own election campaign. Had Tudjman or Milosevic been a genuine statesman, capable of vision and magnanimity, then perhaps – with the aid of moderates in all the communities – he could have averted catastrophe. But such statesmen are rare anywhere, especially if they have won an election using nationalist rhetoric. Tudjman, unlike Milosevic, was an unwavering nationalist, and he had been electorally rewarded for this. The problem was not yet Tudjman as a semiauthoritarian manipulator (which he was soon to become), but Tudjman the democratic politician, responsive to those who had voted for him, repeating slogans that had worked electorally, inattentive to those unlikely to vote for him. Serb deputies called for a less ethnic definition of citizenship, but Tudjman's majority was large; he had no need of their support. He refused.

The initial Serb SDP leader in Croatia was Jovan Raskovic. He had mouthed Greater Serb rhetoric in the election campaign, but he was aware of the local Serbs' weak position and wanted compromise. Yet Tudjman's intransigence led the SDP to force Raskovic to reject the vice-presidency of the parliament. He began to speak more favorably of Milosevic, and his deputies walked out of parliament. The party radicalized. Raskovic's problem – and that of other such politicians – was that he could not actually deliver a compromise, since the other side thought it had the political power to refuse him. As tensions increased, Tudjman's support grew. He was unchallenged until after the war ended. His core support came from men more than women;

from conservatives, especially religious conservatives; from rural areas; from those most negatively affected by the war (i.e., Croats in border regions); and (like any normal party) from those doing better out of his economic reforms. But the war silenced even most of the discontented, for they did not want to be unpatriotic. Authoritarian controls, half-legitimated by the war, finished off the opposition. This had become a party-state, though a fairly popular one (Pusic, 1997; Sekulic & Sporer, 1997). It was not disposed to compromise.

Rival referenda were held in Croatia in May 1991. Ninety-three percent of Croat voters favored creating a sovereign and independent country, with individual rights guaranteed to minorities. Krajina Serbs boycotted this referendum, since a week earlier they had organized their own referendum and voted overwhelmingly for union of their region with Serbia. People were asked to vote for or against the nation, so who would dare stand up and organize a "No" vote? But the consequences were to confer legitimacy on the nationalists. It was now their state.

Tudjman and Milosevic met secretly to head off disaster. They discussed dividing Bosnia between them, at the expense of Muslims, but reached no agreement. Milosevic, Jovic, the Serb generals, the Security Police, and the SPS controlled a state and an army, confident that they could roll over the opposition. If it came to war, it would be over in weeks. Greater Serbia could be achieved quickly, with few costs. But Tudjman and much of the HDZ had fought long and hard, as underdogs, against what they saw as a Communist/Serb dictatorship. They saw a future battle with Serbia as a long haul, but they were used to this. This gave Serbia an incentive to strike quickly, before the Croats could build up their military power. The gains for either side were to be far outweighed by the destruction of war, a mistake often made by state elites launching war. Descent into the danger zone had been dominated by democratic processes. But voters were now replaced by armed men.

13

Yugoslavia, II
Murderous Cleansing

The previous chapter discussed the descent into the danger zone of murderous cleansing as democratic processes degenerated across Yugoslavia. But to explain descent over the brink into violence we must turn to the armed men who first committed violence in the mixed Croat/Serb areas of the Krajina within Croatia. Later came those from the mixed Muslim/Serb/Croat areas of Bosnia, while Kosovans in 1998 and Macedonians in 2001 lagged far behind. All these conflicts fit into my third thesis: danger threatened because representatives of two rival ethnic communities made sovereign claims on the same territory, their claims being both morally plausible and achievable. One constituted the majority population in the existing state; the other constituted a local majority in particular border districts, the weaker side supported by its homeland state next door. But further descent involved not democratic but authoritarian processes.

Sovereignty claims are not easy to settle. They appear as a zero-sum game: "Either you or I have sovereignty over this plot of land." Conflict can be defused by the minority's enjoying federal autonomy within the majority's state or by consociational power-sharing arrangements at the center. Yet sovereignty immediately also involved concrete issues of military and economic power: who should have the guns and jobs? The initial flash points were in Serb-majority parts of the Krajina, where Serbs had previously provided most policemen and held most of the guns. When Croatia claimed sovereignty, it tried to bring in its own policemen. In some localities Serb radicals reacted by proclaiming local self-rule, throwing up road blocks, organizing ad hoc militias of ex-policemen (Cohen, 1995: 132–3). Jobs were also involved. The new Croat government began antidiscriminatory firing of hitherto privileged Serbs. Most industries were still state-owned. The Domovnica, a document proving Croatian citizenship, was also used. This had to be presented to open a private business or obtain medical coverage, retirement pay, a passport, or a driving license. Serbs found it insulting and harder to get, since an applicant had to know "the Croatian language and the Latin script" and show "acceptance of Croatian culture" (Udovicki & Torov, 1997: 95; *Vreme*, March 8, 1993). Class conceptions of interest were being displaced onto ethnicity. Offices and factories saw confrontations over jobs. The Croat border areas were fragmenting into rival administrations lacking routinized procedures for settling disputes. They were destabilized, factionalized, and radicalizing – as in my fifth thesis.

In May and especially June came the first clashes between rival police forces. Most of the first killings were committed in the heat of skirmishes and were not premeditated. Yet beatings and shootings became more deliberate as nationalists aimed at well-known moderates in their own community and at the other community. All violence was justified as self-defense or retaliation. Someone else had started it. It was rarely directed against the actual perpetrators of previous violence. Thus violence spread as innocent victims retaliated against innocent victims. The attacks silenced moderates and made exposed communities feel insecure. They fled to the shelter of their ethnic group, from which trust and defense might come. Mutual flight produced more mono-ethnic villages and towns, each with its own emerging police forces. Class privileges counted for almost nothing in such violence, except that the rich might seek to bribe their assailants to desist. One's fate was determined by one's ethnicity – the most potent way in which ethnicity trumps class.

Segregation also heightened ideological power barriers. Telephone lines from Serbia to Croatia and Bosnia were cut. Radicals took over local radio and TV stations. It became harder to learn of political alternatives. Refugees were also placing themselves under the protection of armed radicals This might initially happen in only one local village, but the demonstration effect and the mutual fears it engendered might lead to the same sequence in nearby villages. The locals were tempted to loot abandoned houses or move in their own refugee relatives from elsewhere. This implicated more ordinary and victimized people in the cleansing policies of radicals. Small groups of radicals on both sides, playing a double act of mutual provocation, could set local ethnic cleansing in motion. Though they included some thugs, most were genuine nationalists feeling under threat, affected by the sequence of emotions identified by Katz (1988) among other murderers: threat, humiliation, righteous rage.

Some local conditions favored escalation. These rural areas had youth unemployment of over 30 percent. Young men were hanging around squares and bars, with plenty of time but little income or prospects. Ethnonationalists offered them the out-group's jobs, or they craved excitement or status that did not depend on educational or occupational attainments. Antidiscriminatory firings brought angry unemployed men, receiving a sympathetic hearing from radical nationalists. Class interest was rechanneled toward ethnicity. These areas also had guns, part of the patriarchal household culture. Men cherished them and debated their virtues in local bars. Young men brawled to show their fitness to enter adult society. Here was the potential raw material for paramilitary nationalism. These areas also had low ethnic intermarriage rates. People were less ambiguous about ethnic identity and could identify with the righteous defense of their own ethnic group. These areas had seen more World War II atrocities. More parents or grandparents had suffered, and the labels "Ustasha" and "Chetnik" resonated. The connection between then and now was weaved into the myth of ancient enmity. Krajina Serbs said they were "the remnants of a slaughtered people." In 1945 avenging Partisans had swept through the area, to become the local ruling group, buttressed by incoming Serb settlers. The insecurities of these colonists – alternatively viewed as stealing the land or taking it from fascists – fueled tension (Glenny, 1993: 107–8, Silber & Little, 1995: 98–112).

Other conditions favored compromise. There had not been serious ethnic conflict here for 40 years, and witnesses at the Hague Tribunal testified that before 1990 the communities had lived peacefully together, aware of their cultural differences but assuming they had little political relevance. Though the 1990 elections made ethnic identity more salient, few advocated solving political problems by violence. Most people knew they had much to lose by violence – as the events of the 1990s were to prove. It is not easy to overcome the norm of stably functioning societies that violence is irrational and immoral, and Yugoslavia had long been such a society. The nationalist parties had also emerged out of cultural associations and were led by ideologists, not men of violence – novelists, poets, scientists, dentists, psychiatrists, whose "violence" was largely rhetorical. Babic the dentist or Raskovic or Karadzic the psychiatrists or Plavsic the biology professor did not want to kill people. Rather, they hoped their rhetoric would rally their own community and scare the other into concessions.

Throughout the first half of 1991 these contradictory pressures intensified factionalism *within* each ethnic community. This happened quickly in Croatia, more slowly in Bosnia, and according to a different rhythm altogether in Kosovo. The Krajina saw conflict between Serb factions led by the more moderate Raskovic versus Babic and Martic. Among the Croats of central Bosnia the moderate Klujic opposed the radical Boban. Only in Serb areas of central and eastern Bosnia did a radicalizing leader, Radovan Karadzic, seem to control his party, though his deputy was the more ambiguous Koljevic, and Karadzic had not yet passed the point of no return. In these settings moderates had two initial advantages – they were in power and they stood for order. Yet power was fragmenting.

Osijek was a mainly Croat town in eastern Slavonia surrounded by Serb villages. A local civil war could break out, and some on both sides were urging armed consolidation of territory. So the beginning of the troubles found the moderate Croat police chief, Reichl-Kir, patrolling the area unarmed, arranging truces between rival ad hoc barricades, defusing tensions. He had support from both sides since most locals were terrified by the specter of civil war. The villages that had been colonized by displaced Serbs were 10 times more likely to cause trouble, said Reichl-Kir, taking special trouble to placate them (Stitkovac, 1997: 160, 170). The Croat leaders of Osijek did not want trouble. Nor did the Serb SDS leader Vucevic. But they were both confronted by radical opposition.

In such settings, three alternative scenarios might play out. First, the existing forces of law and order and moderate politicians might be reinforced from above by the emerging Croat, Serb, and Bosnian states, suppressing local radicals. This is the usual outcome of ethnic conflict across the world. As we see in Chapter 16, communal rioting in India and Indonesia ends if the police intervene against all armed locals. Repression of those rioting or flourishing arms virtually always works in the limited sense of restoring communal order, at least until the next spasm of violence occurs. Unfortunately, this scenario was becoming unlikely, since neither the Croat nor the Serb state seemed capable of acting impartially or with only a little bias. They declared proudly that they represented their own ethnic group. That is how they had just won elections.

Second, local politicians and policemen might be left on their own to settle their own dispute. In the brief period in which locals did operate on their own, we can observe one tipping factor. Extremists could counter the moderates' advantage of appearing as the party of order if they could plausibly claim an overwhelming monopoly of military or police force. Then any violence would likely be short-lived and victory assured through a low-risk first-strike option (as in my thesis 4b). This repeatedly occurred in the early days of conflict. Towns and groups of villages in which one ethnicity possessed military superiority were more likely to see local radical coups. These had additive effects. The victors carried their recipe for defense elsewhere, to less troubled communities, over which they might possess military superiority. Radicals from the Krajinan Serb stronghold of Knin organized a paramilitary unit known as the Marticevci and took over the town. Then they attacked and overcame the police station at Glina, a small town in which the multiethnic Croatian Democratic Party had enjoyed much Serb support. The Glina Serbs were forcibly liberated (Stitkovac, 1997: 161). Such coups generated refugees who fled to a safer ethnic enclave, embittered, demanding action to get their homes back, or determined to keep possession of a home they had now seized. This lured them tactically toward a first-strike option against a small minority in their new area of residence. The vulnerable in each community were easily picked off.

Yet the opposite might prevail in more ethnically balanced towns and villages. Here radical arguments seemed risky, since a first strike might fail and lead to spiraling violence. Balanced areas like Osijek, Vitez (Croat/Muslim), Sarajevo, and Bratunac (Muslim majorities but better-organized Serbs) established joint emergency authorities. Ethnically balanced villages set up joint patrols to enforce order, like Visnjica, detailed later. Local peculiarities might aggravate or reduce trouble. Mostar's great ravine divided two majority communities of Croats and Muslims. There was a quick Croat takeover of one side and a Muslim takeover of the other. The sides became armed camps dug in on either side of the ravine. A few shots turned into artillery cannonades, in the course of which Croat militiamen destroyed the world-famous bridge. This resembled conventional warfare.

In World War II the Bosnian Croat village of Medjugorje had been a Ustasha stronghold. Its Croats remembered not Ustasha atrocities but Serb postwar revenge during which "barely a family in this part of the plateau survived the atrocities unscathed. Incarceration, torture, rapes: these were only a few of the horrors of the Partizan reign" (Bax, 1995: 74). The Ustasha bands fled into the mountains, resisting for 12 years until the last remnants fled abroad – handing over their guns to local Croats. Tito forced local Croats to erect a giant war memorial to the "Victims of Fascist Oppression." It remained a potent symbol of Serb domination. But locals adjusted.

During the 1980s the village become a major site of Catholic pilgrimage after local women and children reported visions of the Virgin Mary. One village clan, the Ostojici, originally Serb but now mixed by considerable intermarriage, reaped the profits of the pilgrim trade by virtue of its political influence. Resentments built up, influenced by rising Croat nationalism. The site was run by the Franciscans, whose dubious wartime activities I detailed in Chapter 11. The local Franciscans (though not the order as a whole) were now implicated again in Croat nationalism. Their souvenir shop sold Ustasha and Nazi trinkets alongside Catholic ones, and the Virgin of Medjugorje was absorbed into the new nationalist iconography. Croatian independence was declared on the anniversary of the Virgin's appearance in the village. The leading hard-liner in Tudjman's entourage, Susak, had been born in the village and retained influence there. As the crisis erupted in this region in September 1991, the Ostociji were denounced as being in contact with Serb "Chetniks." As a warning, their graves were blown up – a common act across the contested areas of Yugoslavia during 1991, a gesture of denial of a group's claim to historic local roots. The Ostociji defended themselves with the help of refugees from cleansed villages elsewhere. The final solution came in May 1992, when villagers elicited the aid of a passing Croat HVO army detachment. Almost 100 of the Ostociji, mostly men, were captured, taken to a ravine, and killed (Bax, 1995; Sells, 1996: chap. 5).

Yet the entire province of Kosovo went the other way, toward damping down violence. This was the only region of Yugoslavia in which severe conflicts had erupted throughout the 1970s and 1980s. Kosovo had been a police state after Milosevic's 1989 crackdown. As Judah (2000: 84) notes, this was "a fundamental struggle between two people for control over the same piece of land," as in my third ethnic thesis. Yet it remained relatively quiet until the late 1990s. Since the province was 85 percent Albanian, the Albanian community could not be controlled by the Serb authorities. Nor could the neighboring homeland state of Albania intervene. The hard-line Communist regime of Albania had been distasteful to most Kosovo Albanians, but its postcommunist successor was disintegrating. Kosovo Albanian politicians were free to determine their own tactics of resistance. Ibrahim Rugova's nonviolent strategy won out. His Democratic League of Kosovo boycotted Serb-run elections, schools, and hospitals and set up its own instead (Maliqui, 1995). The Serb authorities were prepared to let things ride. Their control over Kosovo was internationally recognized, and they did not want trouble while preoccupied elsewhere. But the Dayton Agreement of 1995 legitimized Serb control of Kosovo. This undermined Rugova's nonviolent strategy as many Albanians switched to the armed struggle advocated by the Kosovo Liberation Army (KLA). When neighboring Albania imploded in 1997, Kosovo became awash with arms. The final drama began in February 1998 as Serb police and soldiers attempted to wipe out the KLA.

Given such local variations, it is not easy to answer the historical counterfactual question – what if locals had been left to settle their own differences? But they were not left on their own. The third scenario dominated. The balance was tipped by ethnonationalist armed intervention from outside. Among the Krajina Serbs, Raskovic, the SDS leader, relied for his core constituency on urban areas, where many Serbs favored negotiations with the Croat government. He was conscious of representing Serbs where they were both majorities and minorities, and of the exposed position of the Krajina. He said he didn't want a Serbian state in Croatia or even an autonomous province in Croatia, only local power sharing. But his power was challenged by radical SDS members, mainly from rural areas in Lika and Dalmatia, with the town of Knin their stronghold. In Knin they formed a "Serbian National Council" led by the dentist-mayor Babic and the police inspector Martic. In August 1990 their "Declaration on the Sovereignty and Autonomy of the Serbian People" claimed that Serbs in Croatia "on the basis of their geographical, historical, social, and cultural specificities, are a sovereign people with all the rights that constitute the sovereignty of peoples." Should Croatia secede from the Yugoslav Federation, they declared they would seek sovereignty. This they did, and founded the Serb Republic of Krajina, the RSK.

They were emboldened by contacts with Milosevic, the JNA, and the SDB security police, which supplied them with arms and volunteers. The contacts were admitted by Babic himself (Witness C-061) and two intelligence officials in the Milosevic trial. In Knin, they said, Milosevic was known as "the boss," and he personally arranged finances and arms for the supposedly independent RSK. They knew they could win a local show of force. When the Croat interior minister arrived to conciliate, they assembled a hostile crowd of armed Serbs to force him out. The Knin deputy mayor, Macura, an English teacher and director of the local radio, was presenting a map on the day of the local referendum. It showed large parts of Croatia under Serb rule. Boasted Macura, "I don't expect war because the Croats would have no chance of winning. . . . You must have bloodshed to make a country" (quoted by Judah, 1997: 181). Unless Croatia caved in, these radical Serbs rejoicing in their little stronghold would find it difficult in the long run to hold on to the Krajina, but they were insulated by their local domination and the promises of Milosevic.

Raskovic felt trapped by what he described as Tudjman's "outmoded claims for national and ethnic sovereignty." Tudjman declared, "Territorial autonomy for the Serbs is out of the question. We will not allow it." But in October, serious negotiations began between his HDZ and a SDS delegation led by the moderate Serb doctor Vukcevic. It was rumored that the Croat delegation was making concessions. The phrase that Croatia was the "national state of Croats" would be cut out of the Constitution, and economic grievances would be addressed. But while negotiations were proceeding, Raskovic and Vukcevic were undermined from within. The Knin radicals leaked a recording of a conversation with Tudjman in which Raskovic could be heard describing his fellow Serbs as "crazy people" – an obvious bargaining ploy ("You must give me some concessions so I can outmaneuver my crazy extremists"). Yet it enabled Babic and Martic to depose him as the SDS leader. Since there were no routinized party debate and voting procedures, coercion played a large role. Moderate Serbs who had joined the rival Serbian Renewal Party were also cowed into silence (Judah, 1997: 168–9; *Vreme*, October 28, 1991). HDZ promises of concessions were never tested, for they now faced no one who would negotiate. Croatia prepared secretly for war, just in case, and the influence of the emigres and hard-liners increased.

Osijek quickly felt more deadly pressures. Reichl-Kir's conciliation attempts ended when armed Croats arrived from Dalmatia, sent by Susak on July 1, 1991. They were briefed by Glavas, a local radical HDZ policeman, who feared the dossier that Reichl-Kir had built up on his own provocations. These Croats fired 22 bullets into Reichl-Kir's car, killing him and his Serbian and Croatian helpers (one of them vice president of the Osijek municipality). Control of the Croat police now passed to Glavas and his paramilitary unit (Stitkovac, 1997: 160). In response. Vukcevic, the SDS moderate, was pushed aside by members of the Serbian National Council. Pressured emigration of Croats now began in outlying villages, and JNA army and paramilitary units began to mass over the Drina River. On September 3 mortar duels began. Osijek Serbs "found themselves between the Army hammer and the Croatian anvil" (remarked *Vreme*, December 2, 1991). However, Serb military pressure now switched to Vukovar, and Osijek remained quiet for a while.

The Bosnian Serb leader Radovan Karadzic wavered. Before the elections he had declared, "Our Moslems are much closer to us than many Christian European nations." The election campaign had involved a mutual understanding between the three Bosnian ethnic parties that each could lead its own community. Karadzic and his deputy, Biljana Plavsic, then supported Izetbegovic, the leader of the largest community, as Bosnian president. But, affected by rising tensions, they began to shift. Plavsic declared, "six million Serbs can die so that the remaining six million can live in freedom." With the authority of a biology professor, she declared that ethnic cleansing was "a natural phenomenon." Karadzic said, "Serbs here are ready for war. If someone forces them to live as a national minority, they are ready for war. This nation remembers well the genocide" (i.e., World War II). In July 1991 he let slip "I hear the people are arming, but . . . Serbs have no need to arm. If they are attacked, it will mean that Yugoslavia has been attacked, and all Serbs will voluntarily join the Yugoslav People's Army [JNA] in defending the country." Believing the JNA was behind him, he threatened Muslim deputies: "If you decide on war, you will be wiped off the face of the earth." Once hostilities started, he repeatedly said that Serbs and Muslims could never live together, for Bosnian Serbs had lived for 70 years under the threat of "genocidal annihilation" (Sudetic, 1998: 84; *Vreme*, May 3, 1993). Proximity to Serbia emboldened and radicalized him. He believed the JNA army could achieve Greater Serbia. He was embracing my thesis 4b: overwhelming military power could achieve Serb nationalist goals at little risk.

Milosevic's SPS and Serb nationalist parties were staging meetings and demonstrations in the region for months before the Croat declaration of independence. These outsiders had no special powers. Locals could still discuss the options with out-group neighbors. They received newspapers and radio and TV messages with varied perspectives. Big peace rallies were held in Sarajevo, Mostar, and Banja Luka. But radicals were now distributing arms. Local Serbs accepted them for varied reasons – nationalism, the delight of owning a modern weapon, the feeling of power it conferred, fear of not being a good Serb or a real man if one refused. But having accepted a gun, one might find it difficult to refuse to use it. This was to trap many ordinary Serbs like this Sarajevo man:

I'm a pacifist basically. I knew there was going to be a war but I don't want to admit it to myself. Coming home from a cafe I was stopped by SDS people I knew. . . . They said "We've all got to take up arms or we'll all disappear from here, it's 80% Muslim." . . . The 6 January was the Orthodox Christmas. There was a lot of shooting – testing – a signal to show how strong we were. On all religious days people were shooting. It was an important thing. We were much more afraid than they were. (Quoted by Judah, 1997: 195)

Stage three had been reached: an armed standoff flaring into violence between ethnonationalist militants. But the Croatian government contained moderates, and it feared the JNA. Most communities hesitated. Had there been no further outside influences on the area, and had the two groups been of roughly equal strength, mutual interest and deterrence might have defused the violence and persuaded the two sides to compromise. Unfortunately, neither condition was met – and these were the decisive escalations into civil war and murderous cleansing.

SERBIA INITIATES CIVIL WAR AND MURDEROUS CLEANSING

Tudjman hoped Milosevic would back off but would not do so himself, prepared to take the consequence of war if it broke out. He was smuggling in arms and would settle in for the long haul if necessary. But Milosevic gambled on possessing military power sufficient for an easy first-strike victory. This turned local violence into ethnic civil war and murderous cleansing. Once things started, in the few areas where Croats could get gains, they too escalated. But for a time, the government of Serbia was the main perpetrator.

By March 1991 Milosevic had abandoned compact federalism (Plan A), instead seeking to enlarge the Serbian-controlled territory (Plan B). He repeatedly called for "All Serbs in one state." The code for Plan B was "the military line," which meant covertly arming the Serb *precani* communities. In May 1991 the top leaders of the SDB, close associates of Milosevic, reorganized its agents in Croatia into a paramilitary force known as the Red Berets to arm radical *precani* Serbs – and later to kill moderate Serbs (Milicevic, forthcoming). Thus armed and assisted, the *precani* Serbs might control their territorial pockets and then turn to him to negotiate a division of spoils. He was also willing to threaten a JNA invasion to back them up: this would force Croatia and Bosnia to negotiate on his terms. Probably in the late summer he drew up an actual JNA invasion plan just in case. This was his Plan C, code-named "RAM," meaning "frame" or "framework" (Judah, 1997: 170). Overwhelming military force would quickly redraw Serbia's boundaries and force many Croats and Muslims to flee, for only this would make the new Serb lands secure. Milosevic assumed this would only involve exemplary repression plus pressured emigration, since he expected to then strike a deal with Tudjman to carve up Bosnia between them. At the Hague Tribunal, Babic quoted Milicevic as saying that Croatia could leave the federation "after they establish new borders with us."

Milosevic must have anticipated some killing, though probably nothing on the scale of the ensuing atrocities. Plan C involved miscalculations. First, he overestimated Serb support. In August 1991 a survey showed that 78 percent of Serbs favored keeping the peace at all costs, yet 55 percent declared, "I do not want to go to war, but if one has to go, one has to go" (*Vreme*, November 18, 1991). But few expected war, and the government had not prepared them for it. War patriotism needs time and a crisis to cultivate it. The Slovenian and Croatian declarations of independence came suddenly. Milosevic immediately ordered the reservists mobilized, but within days it was clear that most Serbs were not responding. Estimates put the level of response at below 50 percent, perhaps only just above 30 percent. Only 15–20 percent are said to have responded in Belgrade and Vojvodina. In the cities, mothers demonstrated against their sons' conscription. (Gordy, 1999: 126; *Vreme*, September 30, 1991; Zabka, 1994: 41). Whatever threat Serbs might feel, over half did not want to risk their lives to counter it.

Since he could not rely on Serbs as a whole, Milosevic had to fall back on his two core constituencies. The first was the party-state. This one had two parties (details from Williams & Cigar, 1996). The bigger party was Milosevic's SPS, its 50,000 members strategically placed within the state agencies and nationalized industries involved in the war effort. It was allied with the only other party to which officials were permitted to belong, the SK-PJ, a supposedly Communist Party conveniently headed by his wife, Mirjana Markovic. This was important inside the JNA officer corps and among nationalized industry bosses channeling money into the venture. A decade later, Milosevic effectively confessed to this part of Plan D. In denying charges that he had embezzled government funds for his private use, he said the funds had been actually used to finance Serb armies in Bosnia and Croatia. His lawyer added, "To this very day, the army of Republika Srpska is being paid . . . by that money" (*Los Angeles Times*, April 3, 2001). Milosevic's direct role in these financial operations was confirmed by the expert witness Torkildsen at his trial.

He kept things secret, believing most Serbs and some state officials would disapprove. Most federal officials were kept out of the action. The key agency was the Serbian Interior Ministry, deploying the Red Berets. But selected JNA generals were also brought into dinners discussing the operation. War then enabled Milosevic to extend his control of the state. Two-thirds of the rival Federal Ministry of the Interior's staff were forced into early retirement. In October 1992 armed Serbian security police seized its buildings. The two ministries were now merged and enlarged so that the Interior Ministry commanded three divisions, about 35,000 security policemen, a virtual private army (*Vreme*, October 26, 1992). This force was to be key in the cleansings, especially in Kosovo.

But Milosevic did not head a totalitarian or even a very bureaucratic state. Parliament remained rumbunctious, the opposition media difficult, the civil service and army factionalized. *Vreme* was full of reports of factionalism, especially within the army High Command, though resignations, retirements, and reassignments gradually increased the army's coherence. Milosevic's parliamentary base was a shifting coalition of parties. The 1992 elections gave him only 29 percent of the vote and 40 percent of the seats. He now had to ally with Seselj's ultranationalist SRS for his majority. In the elections of 1993, under U.S. pressure, Milosevic supported the Vance–Owen Plan and ditched the Bosnian Serbs. He lost Seselj's support, but with no major centrist rival left, he posed as the peacemaker. His vote rose to 37 percent, which gave him 49 percent of the seats in Parliament. Using state patronage, he bribed a few opposition deputies into supporting him (Gordy, 1999: 43–51). By exploiting the divisions and ambiguities of his opponents, he withstood all the disasters to remain in power until the year 2000.

He could also rely on a second core constituency, the nationalist parties and paramilitaries. Though most Serbs dodged the draft, a substantial minority volunteered for the war. Some of these volunteers went directly to the front to join JNA units and others went into the local territorial forces, but many joined nationalist paramilitaries with names such as "Chetniks," "Knights of Serbia," the "Serbian Guard," "Dusan the Mighty" (a medieval Serb prince), "White Eagles," and the "Serbian Volunteer Guard" (more commonly known as "Arkan's Tigers"). It is said that most volunteers were rural Serbs, often *precanis*. Some say criminals were in their ranks, released so that they could kill (Vasic, 1996). Some stress their poverty (Mueller, 2000). Sikavica says that the officers were petty bourgeois, "former bar owners, self-employed truck drivers and warehouse clerks," while the rank-and-file came from the "underclass" (1997: 140). I doubt all this, but we lack real data on their backgrounds. Universal male conscription and an active reserve system meant that a large, experienced paramilitary force could be assembled from only a minority of reservists. Military power did not depend on majorities. It needed only a few thousand Serbs to provide a popular army with varied motives – fired-up patriotism, adventure-seeking, employment, or loot.

Unlike Milosevic, paramilitary leaders openly called for cleansing. White Eagle leader Mirko Jovic said, "We are not only interested in Serbia but in a Christian, Orthodox Serbia, with no mosques or unbelievers"; "I'm all for the 'clearing operations.' I've seen handsome guys amongst them (although they are Croatians) who are laughing. They have never experienced a genocide and thus should be given the opportunity to see what it's like. I applaud the genocide of the Croatians! For this reason they should be given arms, the more the better. Their resistance would last longer and here we have the chance to get rid of them once and for all." Chetnik boss Seselj, leader of the Serb Radical Party, declared, "we must cut the Croats' throats, not with a knife, but with a rusty spoon." In Parliament he threatened non-Serb deputies: "You can be sure that when Serbia's government changes, we will expel all of you.... We won't kill you, we'll just put you in trucks." "Croats should move outside the frontiers of this state." SPS deputies shouted in agreement, "So they should!" Another declared, "My goal is not only to defend Serbianness but to cleanse territory, to have an ethnically clean state" (Grmek, 1993: 302–9; *Vreme*, December 9, 1991, April 6, 1992; Williams & Cigar, 1996: 17).

These two core constituencies shared a culture born amid authoritarian Communism and then organic nationalism. They were also linked materially. Arkan's Tigers were armed and trained by the Serb Ministry of the Interior, Seselj's Chetniks by the JNA. Arkan's secretary (Witness B-129) said at the Milosevic trial that when she needed government assistance, she lifted the telephone and said *Pauk* ("spider"). This code word connected her directly to the head of the Red Berets. She said he gave Arkan his missions and delivered to her sacks containing millions of German marks. Seselj was frank about Milosevic's help, telling the BBC, "Milosevic organized everything. We gathered volunteers and he gave us special barracks...all our uniforms, arms, military technology and buses. All our units were always under the command of the Krajina, or the Republika Srbska or the JA" (BBC, 1998; Silber & Little, 1995: 230). Ron (2000) sees the paramilitaries as "state sub-contractors," doing Milosevic's bidding but allowing him to deny responsibility for their actions. Ron also shows that in the Serbian statelets, parallel networks connected local paramilitaries and local politicians. Milicevic (forthcoming) also stresses SDB control over the party paramilitaries. Troublesome leaders were mysteriously killed – as were the former criminals Beli and Giska in 1991. A paramilitary formed by an uncooperative party was dissolved.

Nevertheless, control remained imperfect. In the field, most paramilitaries were formally integrated into the JNA command structure, but in practice they operated on their own, while Milosevic was part initiator, part beholden to these extremists. Increasingly, refugees added their embittered rage. By late 1992 there were over 550,000 refugees in Serbia, cleansed from elsewhere, the visible sign of the abject failure of this regime. Milosevic desperately wanted to disperse them. Their numbers surged again in 1995, when Croatia recaptured the Krajina. This may have crystallized Milosevic's plan to cleanse Kosovo, for this was the solution to his refugee problem. But Croatian, Bosniak, and Kosovan resistance forced him into more radical Plans than he had intended.

Babic said there were two chains of command, both reporting to Milosevic. One involved the JNA, the other the security forces and the paramiliatries. But they also had to connect on the ground. Without the JNA, the nationalist paramilitaries would have had no artillery or tank support. Stalemate would have resulted. During a tapped telephone conversation in July 1991, Karadzic asked Milosevic for more help.

> MILOSEVIC: Speak to Uzelac [chief of staff, Sarajevo Army Corps]. If you have any problems, contact me.
>
> KARADZIC: I am having problems with Kupres [in central Bosnia]. A sizeable portion of the Serbian population there is rebellious.
>
> MILOSEVIC: Don't worry, we'll take care of it. Just call Uzelac.... Don't worry, you'll have everything. We have the power.
>
> KARADZIC: Yes, yes.
>
> MILOSEVIC: Don't worry. As long as the Army is there, no one can touch us....
>
> KARADZIC: That is OK. But what about the bombing of...
>
> MILOSEVIC: Today it is not convenient for the aviation to act, since the European Community is holding a session.... (Quoted in *Vreme*, September 30, 1991).

Milosevic here seems confident in the power of the JNA to override the "sizeable proportion" of "rebellious" Serbs opposing the war. After the JNA formally withdrew from Croatia in November 1991, the new Serb statelet armies were formed from JNA units. But the performance of the army, however it was formally named, was disappointing, with low morale. Thousands of soldiers had deserted from the front as early as December 1991 (*Vreme*, December 9, 1991, April 6, 1992). Despite its numbers and equipment, it could not sustain offensive infantry warfare against small-scale but determined resistance. The JNA was no Waffen-SS or even a Wehrmacht.

But, unfortunately, that only made things worse. Morale was too low for the JNA to capture villages and towns by means of rapid infantry advances. So it used its massive artillery superiority to rain down shells indiscriminately upon them, killing many civilians. It sat in front of Vukovar for four months raining destruction on the city. Such callous warfare is common in modern war, as the U.S. bombing of Vietnam and of neutral Cambodia reveals. NATO high-altitude bombing of Serbia in 1999 is another Yugoslav example of using superior resources at minimal cost to oneself. From 1991 to 1994 only Serb leaders could plausibly believe they had the option of using such a low-risk overkill strategy. We do not need ethnic stereotypes of murderous Serbs; there were tactical lures toward atrocities. When resistance eventually crumbled before the bombardment, the paramilitaries were sent in to finish them off, given license to kill, rape, or loot. Asked why the JNA did not dispense with such thugs, a general replied, "Because they were the only ones prepared to charge" (*Vreme*, March 8, 1993). By 1993, 70,000 paramilitaries were operating west of the Drina River (the boundary of Serbia), half the size of the JNA itself (Zabka, 1994: 59–60). Milosevic's Plan C had degenerated into a wilder Plan D.

The JNA officer corps was divided. Some officers protested atrocities. Lieutenant Colonel Eremija reported to headquarters that the main goal of "paramilitary formations from Serbia" was "not to fight the enemy, but to pillage public property and harass the innocent Croatian population." He detailed tortures and killing of civilians, which he complained "negatively affect the morale of the division units." His report produced a stir but no action. At the Milosevic trial, General Vasiljevic, head of the JNA security services, said he and other officers complained repeatedly about the atrocities of the paramilitaries and the Red Berets, but nothing happened. Another officer said, "The Army could not have arrested those [paramilitaries].... It would have been as though it had arrested... its own ally" (*Vreme*, December 9, 1991, March 9, 1992). There were armed confrontations between paramilitaries and regular troops and shouting matches between generals. The leading hard-line general was Adzic, who said that 50 of his relatives had been killed by the Ustasha during World War II. As a small boy he had hidden up in a tree, watching his own father murdered below. He reputedly told the moderate Croat politician Mesic, "You have butchered us once, and I will not allow you to do it again" (*Vreme*, May 11, 1992). Milosevic managed to establish more control over the army in May 1992, purging 38 generals and ending its federal autonomy. The "night and fog" of war allowed him to do this, just as it allowed others to murder. One-quarter of Croatia was seized by November 1991, including most areas with Serb populations. The Croatian part of Greater Serbia had been achieved.

Serb aggression was then launched against Bosnia. By February 1991, Izetbegovic had realized his danger and radicalized, declaring: "I would sacrifice peace for a sovereign Bosnia-Herzegovina, but for that peace in Bosnia, I would not sacrifice sovereignty" (Silber & Little, 1995: 233). Bosnian Serbs voted in December 1991 against Bosnian secession from the Yugoslav Federation, with Muslims and Croats boycotting the election. Karadzic declared an independent Republik Srbska. In March 1992 the Bosnian Muslim and Croat deputies voted overwhelmingly for their own independence. These referenda had effectively asked people to vote for or against their own nation, so few dared organize opposition.

Serb forces repeated their tactics in Bosnia. JNA units began fighting Bosnian forces in April 1992. By May they were 80 percent composed of Bosnian Serbs, fighting the threat on their own territory. The JNA withdrew in June, leaving its equipment to the army of the Republika Srpska and local Serb paramilitaries. Again came army bombardments followed by terrible mopping up. Initially, Serb leaders were again overconfident of a quick victory. They taunted Muslims with weakness and told them to blame "Alia" (Izetbegovic) for provoking a war that would lead to their utter destruction. They besieged Sarajevo while it still contained 50,000 Serbs, who then experienced a year's bombardment by fellow Serbs. Karadzic believed he could take the city and end the war in six days. It was said that when he and his entourage fled Sarajevo for the hills, they took fresh underwear for only three or four days. Indeed, in nine months Serb forces occupied 70 percent of Bosnia. The intention was not usually genocide, but murderous cleansing to terrorize Muslims and Croats to flee.

As the campaign wore on, it became more terrible and more organized. Srebrenica was a majority Muslim city of great strategic value to the Bosnian Serbs. If the Bosniaks held it, this prevented the Serbs from forming a solid bloc of territory adjacent to Serbia. Thus Bosnian Serb President Karadzic issued his ruthless "Directive 7" to his forces in March 1995: "By well thought out combat operations, create an unbearable situation of total insecurity with no hope of further survival or life for the inhabitants of Srebrenica and Zepa." Colonel Ognjenovic, the first commander of the siege, had sent a letter to his officers and men in July 1994. It read: "The enemy's life has to be made unbearable and their temporary stay in the enclave impossible so that they leave the enclave en masse as soon as possible, realising they can not survive there" (ICTY Case IT-98-33/1). After a prolonged siege, on July 11, 1995, Serb forces suddenly overran the enclave. Its Muslim women, children, and the elderly had fled to the nearby UN camp at Potocari, while most of the men (10,000–15,000 of them, including 3,000–5,000 soldiers, not all with arms) were attempting to flee to Bosniak lines. From 7,000 to 8,000 of the men were captured. The decision to kill them all may have emerged only on July 13, when the Serbs discarded in great piles their captives' identity papers, making screening impossible. They were killed over the next three days in mass *Einsatzgruppen*-style executions by the coordinated efforts of the Drina Army Corps, security and military police units, and paramilitaries. The dead included boys and elderly men, not just those of fighting age. Over open telephone lines, officers talked of "distribution of packages," meaning the killing of people and the disposal of their bodies. Colonel Beara became agitated in a conversation with his superior, General Krstic, asking him repeatedly for help:

> BEARA: I don't know what to do. I mean it. There are still three thousand five hundred parcels that I have to distribute and I have no solution.
> KRSTIC: Fuck it, I'll see what I can do.

The Srebenica assault was certainly a genocidal outburst, and General Krstic was later convicted at the Hague of aiding and abetting genocide, for he was in charge of the Drina Corps from July 13 on and was present at meetings when the killings were decided on, and he permitted his own soldiers to participate in the killing. He was sentenced to 46 years in prison, reduced on appeal to 35 years. Though some officers showed distaste for the task, none seem to have refused the murderous orders. Karadzic had initiated all this killing and has been implicated directly in another incident. At the Hague, Bosnian Serb official Deronjic pleaded guilty to launching an attack in May 1992 on Glogova, a Muslim village, in which 60 men were executed in cold blood, scores of homes were burned down, and the women and children were deported. He says he reported what he had done to three Bosnian Serb leaders, including Karadzic and Mladic. They responded with a round of applause (Case IT-02-61).

By the time Kosovo was submitted to cleansing, the Plan was more premeditated. In Milosevic's trial, witness Tanic alleges that by mid-1997 Milosevic was switching from negotiating with Albanian leaders to murderous cleansing. The plan, says Tanic, was to kill a few, burn many homes, and drive abroad enough Albanians to bring their number in Kosovo down from almost 1.5 million to well under 1 million, resettling Serbs in their place. When Army Chief of Staff Persic objected to the preparations, which included supplying army weapons to police forces, Milosevic removed him and created a special chain of command he personally controlled. Several witnesses, including British peacekeepers and Paddy Ashdown, the British politician, testified that villages were being cleansed in 1998 (Drewienkiewicz, Ciaglinki & Ashdown, IT-02-54, March–April 2002). This provoked a KLA rising. Milosevic seems to have now added ruthless exemplary repression to wipe out the KLA. He then backed out of the peace negotiations at Rambouillet, though he was given little incentive to compromise. He had been told that NATO would now bomb Serbia, but believed (not without reason) that NATO countries would not support the bombing once civilian casualties resulted. But he miscalculated when he took the apparent opportunity presented by bombing to launch a policy of politicide in March–April 1999.

Over a dozen witnesses at the Milosevic trial testified to the same pattern of assault on villages. First, the village was surrounded and brief shelling began. Then the mixed army, police, and paramilitary forces entered the village, shooting some men and herding everyone out onto the road while their houses burned. It was highly organized. About 10,000 Albanians, overwhelmingly men, were killed, and between 500,000 and 800,000 Albanians fled into neighboring countries. Virtually all the refugees said they were fleeing from the Serb attacks rather than from the NATO bombings. Systematic statistical analysis also supports the notion that most of the refugee flight and the killings were caused by Serb attacks rather than the bombing (Ball et al., 2002: Ball evidence at the Milosevic trial, IT 02-54, March 13, 2002; Physicians for Human Rights, 1999: 40–2). But this had the effect of stiffening NATO resolve. NATO public opinion was much more appalled by Milosevic's murderous cleansing than by the bombing. He was forced to sue for a humiliating peace. Two years later, this led to his downfall.

ORDINARY SERBS

It is impossible to say how many ordinary Serbs supported these cleansings. One local person estimated that 30 percent of Bosnian Serbs flatly disagreed with it, while 60 percent "agree or are confused enough to go along. They are led by the ten percent who have the guns and who have control of the television towers. That's all they need." His journalist interviewer quotes Edmund Burke: "The only thing necessary for the triumph of evil is for good men to do nothing" (Maas, 1996: 106–8). Mueller (2000) argues that small bands of armed thugs could take over communities, terrorizing them into complicity. In Visegrad, Milan Lukic's gang (see later) comprised only 15–20 people. They were unchallenged after killing the local SDS vice president when he helped Muslims flee. In Vlasenica the imam said the Serb priest had helped Muslims but stopped when he began to fear for his life. Serbs helping Muslim friends were routinely beaten and occasionally killed. Omarska camp also contained some Serb political prisoners, at least one of whom was killed. A Serb woman in Srebeňica said that extremists "keep calling us on the phone at night. They keep telling us if we don't do something to move out, the Muslims will kill us. But I'm not afraid of Muslims, I'm afraid of these Serbs." A Muslim prisoner said that guards who were "good men, honest Serbs" did not last long; they were sent to the front lines, a common practice on all sides. Officers in all the armies were empowered to execute men who refused to obey murderous orders. So dissent went private. Muslim prisoners were quietly told by a Serb guard, "I'd like to let you go, but I don't dare do it. I never wanted this war. I had Muslim neighbors. I told them I didn't want to fight and I was beaten" (Judah, 1997: 237; Scharf, 1997: 129; Sikavica, 1997: 142; Udovicki & Stitkova, 1997: 188, 209; *Vreme*, August 20, 1992; and the ICTY Nikolic and Erdemovic trials).

The journalist Peter Maas came to understand the fear. "I was hardly alone in feeling righteous about Serbs who supported, in their silence, a dirty war. If I was in their shoes, I would speak out. Or so I thought until I was put in their shoes." He was searching for a rumored prison camp with two other journalists. Serb soldiers ordered them away from the area. They ignored the order and tried another route, but their car was stopped by a heavily armed Serb patrol. Fearing the worst, they were escorted to a rundown cafe. The patrol leader, called "Voja Chetnik" by the others, began screaming at a thin, middle-aged Muslim man drinking coffee. "Get out of here, you filth," he bellowed, and started beating him, first with a bottle, then with his fist. He slammed his rifle into the bleeding Bosniak's chest and undid the safety catch. Suddenly the man's wife appeared, running, and threw herself between her husband and Voja. This seemed to interrupt Voja's mounting rage. He kicked the man a bit more but, seemingly bored, then turned away. The man crawled away to safety. But no thanks to Maas and his two companions, who had moved not a muscle to help. Just like Serbs who watched their neighbors shot, Maas grimly concluded (1996: 20–1).

But military power also had more subtler effects. Faced with threat, locals armed themselves. Arms dealers were turning up with looted JNA hardware. An enormous quantity of JNA material went missing – 15,000 rifles, 600 artillery pieces, 500 machine guns, 30,000 hand grenades, and so on (said *Vreme*, June 1, 1992). Patriotic dealers sold only to their own side; pure entrepreneurs sold to anyone. A dealer would turn up in a Serb-dominated village and warn Serbs "in confidence" that nearby Muslims were preparing to attack them. Many Serbs would buy, just in case. Then he would go to the Muslims and repeat the tactic (Udovicki & Stitkovac, 1997: 180). Men who have guns are more likely to use them. Serbs liberating a town would sometimes distribute weapons free to the local Serbs, even women and children, to make them complicit too. New recruits were asked to kill (perhaps to kill a neighbor) to prove their loyalty. Even Muslims sometimes joined a Serb draft, believing that this was the only way they and their families could stay in their homes. Once involved, these people were trapped, and some were inured. It was not then easy to disobey.

Cleansing was sometimes popular. A few crowds bayed for blood. A journalist saw a mob of Serbs following a convoy of Muslim men, women, and children being maltreated by Serb paramilitaries, "streaming across the meadows shouting 'slaughter them, slaughter them'" (Scharf, 1997: 137). Anger grew from a desire for retaliation against atrocities committed against one's friends or family. Here is Sudetic's interrogation of a Serb from Kravica concerning the cold-blooded killing of Muslims at the nearby Bratunac football field (I describe the incident later). Sudetic begins:

> "After the Christmas attack [by Muslims], when the people from Kravica
>   were refugees...the menfolk were bitter, weren't they?"
> "They were angry."

"Everyone in the district was angry?"

"Everyone."

"What did they say?"

"Revenge."

"What did they tell you?"

"They said, '. . . sooner or later our five minutes will come'."

"And after they took back Kravica and found all the bodies and the open graves in the cemetery?"

"Kad tad, kad tad [sooner or later]."

"And the opportunity finally came."

"Yes."

"Vengeance?"

"Yes, blood vengeance."

"Did they come for you?" . . .

"They said 'Grab your gun and come down to the soccer field.'" . . .

"Did guys from Kravica go?"

"They wanted to kill as many of them as they could."

"So they could never come back? So there would not be enough military-age men left to fight their way back?"

"Never."

[This man's father then admitted that he had gone down to the field. Sudetic asked him:]

"Was it honorable to kill them all?"

"Absolutely. It was a fair fight. Absolutely." (Sudetic, 1998: 350–2)

A "fair fight" might seem a perverted description of a mass execution of unarmed civilians, but the old man was really saying that revenge was fair for prior dispossession and humiliation. He is describing a collective rage emerging from a sense of community fear and humiliation, parallel to the escalating individual emotions described by Katz (1988) as characterizing many U.S. homicides. Neither set of murderers knew far in advance that they would be committing murder. They believed they were suddenly provoked.

Thompson (1992: 276) says the Krajina was "a laboratory of provocations." A Canadian UN peacekeeper said that initially "I was convinced that we were facing an ethnic conflict, that the Catholics detested the Muslims and vice-versa." But when an elderly Croat committed suicide in despair over the horrors inflicted on his Muslim friends, he changed his mind:

From that moment, I understood it was not a war of religion . . . but . . . something artificial; an attempt to provoke incidents and violence, hoping that eventually those incidents would encourage hate, revenge, and thus, result in control over people who hated one another, following the atrocities that were committed against their family members or friends. . . . [It was] as if there existed a force from above that made them do what they did not want to do. (Blaskic trial, April 20, 1998)

Radicals also controlled ideological power institutions. On seizing a community, they cut off media links from the outside world. The press, TV, and radio became subject to patriotic censorship and self-censorship. During a war we hear of the enemy's atrocities, not our own. The Yugoslav media placed atrocities within a narrative focused on World War II. Media portrayals were distorted, and some were faked. Videotapes of Serbs cutting the throats of Croatians were presented on Serbian TV as Ustasha atrocities. Ideologists normalized the labels "Chetniks," "Ustashas," "Turks," and "fundamentalists" as descriptions of the enemy (Botica et al., 1992: 197; Thompson, 1994). The radicals did not have magical powers of indoctrination, but this was war. Even cosmopolitan professionals found it hard to remain balanced. A Serb architect tried to get his colleagues to deplore the destruction of Croatia's historic towns and monuments. He failed. One retorted, "Every trace of them should be wiped out. What do they think? That we should look after their monuments while they butcher our children?" The "middle" position was that of an architect who opposed murder and destruction, but asked whether a church full of machine guns was still a church (*Vreme*, May 18, 1992).

Radicals also held local economic power. Armed radicals appropriated resources from the JNA, their victims, aid agencies, and UN soldiers, syphoned off some for themselves, and then distributed the rest to their own community. They controlled businesses, housing, and jobs. Survival became difficult for refugees without access to these resources. Signing up for a paramilitary operation provided subsistence for many men and their families.

These powers brought mixed local emotions. Babic, the Serb leader in Knin, sent armed men to knock on the doors of recalcitrant men at all hours to ask why they had not volunteered. Glenny (1993: 20) says this was "a convincing picture of the general fear which Babic had created to guarantee his order." Yet fear was entwined with shame ("are you a coward or a real Serb?"), since Babic was quite popular in the town. In Serb-dominated Teslic there was no violence until May 1992, though the Serb and Muslim/Croat communities had become segregated. Then a Serb paramilitary group of 23 men, the "Micas," arrived, expelled from Banja Luka by Serb authorities who had found them too wild. The Micas terrorized Teslic, looting, raping, and murdering Croats and Muslims. Then they were kicked out by Serb forces loyal to the Krajina Republic. Things settled down until a buildup of Serb refugees in the town caused more attacks on non-Serbs. Yet many Serbs protected their neighbors, some by marrying them. There were 100 mixed marriages in less than a month, infuriating radicals on all sides.

Life was difficult for those of mixed ethnicity. A Sarajevo university professor had a Montenegrin father and a Croatian mother. She received telephone calls from a colleague cursing her "Ustasha mother." A "bunch of angry and robust" Serbs, including one childhood friend, denounced her for having "Ustasha" contacts. One wanted to kill her, but she was put in jail. She was treated "just like my Muslim fellow prisoners on the other side of the bars, who were beaten by one shift of the guards, and fed by another." A Muslim convict said that when he saw in jail "how well we Serbs, Moslems and Croats are getting along, I figured out that we were better off in jail than those outside. I even thought of bringing my wife and kids here with me, to jail" (*Vreme*, April 13, June 29, August 10, 1992).

Dusko Tadic, a bit player, was the first convicted war criminal. He was a Bosnian Serb born in 1955 in the mainly Muslim town of Kozarac. His father, grandfather, and two uncles had served in World War II with Tito's Partisans. He received a technical secondary education in Belgrade, traveled doing construction jobs, and then moved back to Kozarac, where he gave karate lessons and ran a coffee bar. Solidly built, he was known for violence to a karate pupil and his wife. In 1989 he alleged that his 16-year-old niece had been raped by Muslim boys. Tadic entered their house at 3 AM, seized the girl, beat up the boys, and threw them downstairs. The girl later said her uncle had forced her to make up the rape story. He had lost his head at the sight of his niece enjoying dancing and drinking with Muslims. But the police suggested he was fabricating evidence of the threat local Muslims posed to Serbs. His bar also put him in debt to Muslim creditors. Caught up in the rising political tensions, he joined the local Serb SPS in 1990. It was soon meeting in his house. He banned Muslims from his bar – not very instrumental reasoning, given his financial situation. In May 1992 Serb forces attacked Kozarac. Tadic may have helped direct their shelling. As the Serbs occupied the town, he identified leading Bosnians for execution, became head of the Kozarac SPS, and worked in the Serb police. He admitted denouncing Serbs who were married to Muslims, and he participated in atrocities in the dreadful Omarska prison camp. He killed five Bosniak civilians, accompanied by "egregious violence" (i.e., torture). He was sentenced to 20 years in prison. Tadic was no one special, a working-class man trying to better himself, but also an ethnic bigot of violent disposition and skills (Case IT-94-1; Scharf, 1997).

Drazen Erdemovic was the first man to confess and repent of his crimes. He was a Bosnian Croat, born in 1972 to a Catholic working-class family. He had neither a nationalist background nor a criminal record. He trained to be a locksmith but was unemployed and so joined the federal Bosnia-Herzegovina Army in 1990. Then he switched to the HVO, the Bosnian Croat army, before again switching to the Bosnian Serb army in order to marry his Serb girlfriend and live with her in Serb-held territory. Because he was an experienced soldier, the army was his best chance of employment, and the pay was better with the Serbs. As a Croat in a Serb formation, he felt vulnerable to pressure from his superiors. He was promoted to sergeant but demoted after only one month for disagreeing with his officer. This same officer then asked Erdemovic's unit to kill busloads of unarmed Muslim men at the Bratunac soccer field. He had not killed before and refused, responding,

"Are you normal? Do you know what you are doing?" His officer replied, "If you do not want to, stand with them so that...we can kill you too or give them weapons so that they can shoot you." He says that if he had not been married, with a baby, he would have run away. Instead he obeyed and killed 70 people that day. Near the end, the officer handed Kalashnikovs to the horrified bus drivers, saying, "You must each kill one" so "no one would be tempted to confess later." Erdemovic then refused to kill another batch of Muslims, supported by three others. Four agreed to shoot, aided by 10 soldiers from a Serb unit whose villages had been attacked by Muslims. The officer had enough volunteers, so he left Erdemovic alone. He seems different from Tadic – showing some reluctance, overcome by believable threats. His sentence was 25 years (Honig & Both, 1996: 62–3; IT-96-22; Rohde, 1997).

Goran Jelisic commanded the Luka prison camp. He was born nearby, had left school prematurely, and worked as a farm mechanic. He was sentenced in 1991 to three years' imprisonment for fraud. In May 1992 he returned wearing a police uniform. Witnesses said he was "a man with a mission" "to cleanse the Muslims and create a clean territory for the Serbian people." He said those Muslims who "accidentally survived...could only be slaves." He declared to Muslim prisoners, "I have your lives in my hands, only 5 to 10 percent of you will leave here." "He constantly ran around as if he were mad, he shouted horribly, behaved as if the whole world was his. In order to show us his power, he ordered that one detainee be brought and then he was beaten in front of us." He had killed Muslim SDA members and Bosniaks who had born arms and launched random violence to terrorize the remainder; "he treated us as animals, beasts...he wished to terrorize us." He shot a Serb guard who helped prisoners. Jelisic liked to call himself the "Serb Adolf," unwisely also doing so to the Hague Tribunal. He was sentenced to 40 years' imprisonment as guilty of war crimes and crimes against humanity but not of genocide. Psychiatrists said that he was not mentally ill but had "deep personality disorders, with anti-social and narcissistic tendencies" (IT-95-10-A, Summary Judgment, December 14, 1999). He seems a criminal sadist legitimized by radical wartime nationalism.

Milan Lukic is a Serb from a mainly Bosnian village near Visegrad, on the Bosnian border with Serbia. In World War II his family had been active Chetniks, killing local Muslims in revenge for the Ustasha murder of his grandfather. Born in 1967, Milan at school was athletic, handsome, and popular. He failed to graduate from high school and went to Belgrade. Relatives found him a job in the Serbian police, but he later drifted around Europe and may have robbed a Swiss jewelry store. He was probably a minor player in SDB campaigns against Croat emigres. He was involved in fights, though he once protected a Muslim friend from a knife attack by another Serb. In April 1992 he returned to Visegrad as a Serb paramilitary volunteer. His police connections and his own forcefulness made him the leader of a paramilitary gang, the White Eagles, the most violent of those operating in the town. Its members shot and drowned Muslim men, raped women, and looted and burned homes. With his help, Visegrad passed from being two-thirds Muslim to 96 percent Serb. Lukic acquired a German car and a pizza parlor. Local Serbs are divided about him. "Many people were ashamed, but others said the Muslims got just what they deserved," said one. Lukic later told a doctor that he was proud to have killed so many Muslims, adding that he had an urge to kill again. He has been indicted by the ICTY but is still at large. In 2003 he was sentenced in absentia to 20 years' imprisonment by a Belgrade court that had "irrefutably established" that he and his gang had kidnapped 12 Muslims, "tortured them there, mistreated them and then brought them to the bank of the Drina river and killed them" (Amnesty International, News Service, October 1, 2003; ICTY, Case No. IT-98-32, Lukic and Vasiljevic; Sudetic, 1998: 66, 120–1, 355–6). This was a working-class young man, physically strong, acquiring status and material gain by using his violent talents.

Milan Kovacevic, who weighed 225 lbs., was built like a heavyweight boxer gone flabby. He still acted like one, says Maas (1996: 36–9). As a baby he had lived in Jasenovac, the main Ustasha slaughterhouse camp in World War II. With dreadful irony, in 1992 he was running Omarska camp, declaring, "They had committed war crimes, and now it is the other way round." He was well educated and became an anesthesiologist. He joined the Serb SDS in 1990 and rose quickly. The next year he became the vice president of the SDS Crisis Staff of Prijedor, in charge of the security police and local soldiery. He masterminded the Serb coup in Prijedor in April 1992. Vulliamy describes two interviews with him in 1992 and 1996 after the war. In 1992 Kovacevic, wearing a U.S. Marines T-shirt, had "eyes fiery with enthusiasm" for what he described as "a great moment in the history of the Serbs." In 1996, now director of the town hospital, he was still a "proud nationalist" who "wanted to make this a Serb land, without Muslims." Had the means used been necessary or a moment of madness, asked Vulliamy? He replied, "Both things. A necessary fight and a moment of madness. The houses were burned at the beginning, when people were losing control. People weren't behaving normally." Drinking brandy throughout the interview, his tongue loosened:

What we did was the same as Auschwitz or Dachau, but it was a mistake. It was planned to have been a camp, but not a concentration camp. . . . I cannot explain this loss of control. You could call it a collective madness. . . . I don't know how many were killed in there. God knows, it's a wind tunnel, this part of the world, a hurricane blowing to and fro. . . . It all looks well planned if your view is from New York. But here, when everything is burning, and breaking apart inside people's heads – this was something for the psychiatrists. . . . If someone acquitted me, saying that I was not part of this collective madness, then I would admit that this was not true. . . . If things go wrong in the hospital then I am guilty. If you have to do things by killing people, well – that is my personal secret. Now my hair is white. I don't sleep so well. (ICTY trial, July 13–15, 1998; Vulliamy, 1996)

This seems close to honesty. A radical nationalist, scarred by his own history, he sought to defend Serbs. On the ground, this turned into mass murder he had presumably not initially intended. He was admitting he had done evil deeds that now haunted him. In August 1998, he died in his cell from a massive heart attack induced by stress, an appropriate end for a man who recognized his own evil.

Zeljko Raznatovic became infamous under the alias "Arkan." Born in 1950 in Montenegro close to the Kosovo border, he was the son of a World War II air force colonel who was often drunk and abusive. Arkan ran away from home at age nine and drifted through juvenile delinquency and crime across Europe during the 1970s and 1980s. When he was arrested in Yugoslavia in 1973, his family connections got the charges dropped and arranged for him to be recruited into the secret police. He was assigned to harass and kill Yugoslav political exiles in Europe. At the end of the 1980s he returned and headed the fan club of Yugoslavia's most famous football team, Red Star Belgrade. He was recommended as someone who could discipline football hooligans, and it was said he organized them into an ethnonationalist pro-Milosevic militia. They provided the core of Arkan's Tigers, the most notorious of the paramilitaries, equipped by the SDB. Arkan was elected to Parliament by the Kosovo Serbs in 1992, though he lost his seat the next year. There is no evidence that he directly participated in his men's atrocities. After the wars ended, some of the Tigers were professionally killed, perhaps by the security police eliminating witnesses to atrocities. Arkan lasted longer, a Serb celebrity wearing Armani suits, a war and sanctions profiteer owning six companies, including a football club, married to a celebrity singer. He presented a personable front to the world while uttering menacing threats to his enemies. NATO accorded him the honor of bombing his Belgrade headquarters in May 1999. But it was a former policeman and member of the Tigers (probably paid by the SDB) who gunned him down in Belgrade in December 1999.

Ratko Mladic is a Bosnian Serb born in 1943 in a tiny mountain village near Sarajevo. His father had been killed by the Ustasha, and he talks of his friendship with a woman who had been mutilated as a baby by the Ustasha. Friends said these early experiences scarred him with hatred of Croats. He graduated from the military academy and was an outstanding officer, rising to lieutenant colonel by 1991. Initially a Communist Party member, he switched to fervent Serb nationalism. He was close to Milosevic, who gave him command of the Bosnian Serb Army. Barrel-chested (though going to fat), able to talk, swear, and drink like a peasant, and a hounder of war profiteers, he was popular among his soldiers, who called him "falcon," the symbol of a Serb warrior-hero. He was a very able commander, carving out the territories for a consolidated Bosnian Serb Republic. His motives were strongly ideological. On entering Srebrenica after the bloody siege, he declared on Serbian TV: "We present this city to the Serbian people as a gift. Finally, after the rebellion of the Dahijas, the time has come to take revenge on the Turks in this region." The "rebellion" he mentions was by Serbs against the Ottoman Turks in 1804! When interviewed in 1994 by *Der Spiegel*, Mladic declared, "I am completely indifferent to whether Muslims and Croats would create an Eskimo state... or would fly to the cosmos.... Borders have always been drawn by blood.... Our aim is and remains the unification of all Serb countries." It is alleged that he has also said that Bosnian Serbs can only attain their goals by genocide. Two Serb officers who pleaded guilty at their Hague trials of participating in the massacre of Srebrenica have implicated Mladic. General Obrenovic said he took part after learning that Mladic had personally ordered the killings. He said that at that point there was no point in trying to object to the order. Captain Nikolic described the meeting at which the decision was made. It was at brigade headquarters and involved generals Mladic and Krstic, plus other officers. He said he later asked Mladic what fate actually awaited a crowd of Muslim prisoners to whom Mladic had just promised safety. Mladic flattened his hand and made a slicing gesture, "as if cutting grass," indicating that the 250 prisoners standing behind him were to be killed (Cases IT-98-33/1 and IT-01-43; Glenny, 1993: 23–6, Kovacevic & Dajic, 1995: 216; Rohde, 1997: 167). Mladic remains free.

CROAT ATROCITIES: THE LASVA VALLEY

Croat and Muslim radicals had retaliated against a few exposed Serb villages right from the start. But since they were on the retreat, they initially had less opportunity to commit war crimes. This changed when they acquired arms and counterattacked. Milosevic realized he could not defend all this territory and agreed to an international cease-fire pending negotiations. He began to withdraw support from the overextended *precani* Serbs. Croatia waited for the term limits of international peacekeeping operations to expire, and then attacked and retook western Slavonia. Between May and August 1995 Croatian forces recaptured the whole Krajina. All the Croat parties rejoiced at the great victory (Pusic, 1997). The speaker of the Croat Parliament and the Supreme Court president declared that there could be no Croat war criminals since they had fought only a defensive war. The speaker pronounced himself happy with the cleansing but hoped a few Serbs would stay. If they formed less than 8 percent of the total population "there would be no need for them to obtain a special status" under the Croat Constitution (Kovacevic & Dajic, 1997: 67, 89, 175, 218; Stitkovac, 1997: 168). The UN reported that only 3,000 of the 135,000 Serbs who had lived in the Knin region remained there, a 98 percent rate of cleansing! But by then the world did not care much about oppressed Serbs. It still cared about Bosniaks, however, and by now the alliance between Croats and Bosniaks had broken down in fighting between them. The Vance–Owen Plan of 1992 divided Bosnia into 10 "cantons." Where one ethnic group had managed to capture most of a canton, the Plan recognized its political domination, so radicals tried to consolidate control of cantons and resettle their ethnic refugees there. This involved Croats cleansing Bosniaks and vice versa.

The most detailed evidence of any Yugoslav atrocities – indeed, of any cleansing process anywhere – concerns Croat atrocities against Bosniaks in the Lasva Valley in central Bosnia, about 30 km northwest of Sarajevo. Both sides attempted to cleanse areas they controlled. The ICTY has so far proceeded with five cases against local Croats. Three are senior local officials: the overall military commander in the valley, Colonel Tihomir Blaskic, HDZ party chief Kordic, and local military commander Cerkez. Six lower-ranking men were accused of mass murders in the village of Ahmici (the Kupreskic et al. trial), one man of rapes in the town of Vitez (the Furundzija trial), and a camp commandant, Zlatko Aleksovski, of running a criminal camp regime. Their victims were Muslims. My account is drawn mainly from evidence presented at these trials.

Witnesses agree that there had been no discernible tension between local ethnic communities until the election campaign of late 1990. These were mostly mixed towns and villages in which children went to ethnically mixed schools, the boys then did military service in mixed barracks, and most adults worked and lived together. The communities sometimes even attended each other's Easter, Christmas, or Baijram festivities, the children munching cookies, the teenagers flirting – perhaps higher priorities for them than religious or nationalist identity.

We know most about Visnjica, a mixed Croat/Muslim village studied by the Norwegian anthropologist Tone Bringa in 1988. Her book, *Being Muslim the Bosnian Way* (1995), added comments on later events in the village. These were made more graphic through collaboration with a television team filming the village during January–February and April 1993 (Granada TV, 1993). This amounts to a unique before-and-after snapshot of a single village. Bringa's research was on the Muslim women of the village, though she knew a few Croat women as well.

She found no ambiguity about ethnic identity. The women had a strong sense of their own ethnic/religious identity, which they fitted into "mutually acknowledged and accepted differences between the two village communities." Most socialization occurred within each community, but Croat and Bosniak women chatted together, sometimes had coffee in each other's houses, and even occasionally joined in each other's religious family rituals. Croat and Muslim trial witnesses gave similar accounts of their own villages and towns. Croats sometimes equated "Muslimness" with "lack of culture" and "backwardness," but they saw most Bosnian Muslims as more "modern" and not "very Muslim." Since the village lacked ethnic intermarriage, kinship networks were segregated, and the first stages of the conflict increased segregation. But Bringa, an anthropologist spending 18 months in the village, sensed no ethnic tension. Recognition of difference, not hostility, characterized most ethnic relations across the Lasva Valley.

During the 1990 election ethnic identities acquired an edge, with people "acting and speaking according to their ethnic origin" (Djdic and Mujezinovic, Blaskic trial witnesses). During 1991 the elected municipal assemblies were dominated by the two main Croat and Bosniak parties, the HDZ and the SDA. To counter Serb pressure, they set up joint emergency committees, police forces, patrols, and barricades. Yet tensions were rising between them, and arms and extremism were spreading. Prosecution and defense teams mostly agreed that conflict started locally, with little outside involvement. The Danish UN peacekeeper Major Baggesen said that violence started in April and May 1992 with shootings by drunken soldiers on both sides and a few civilian deaths by snipers and looters (Blaskic trial, August 22, 1997). Repeated provocations by individuals and small groups on both sides followed. Croats formed paramilitaries, and there was increased collective activity by off-duty Bosniak soldiers of the Bosnia-Herzegovina Army. The first flashpoints again concerned sovereignty symbols, guns, and jobs. Armed provocateurs and radical politicians loomed larger in the Croat communities, which were more numerous and better organized and armed. Their pressure, assisted by refugees streaming in from Serb-occupied areas elsewhere, began to split apart the joint authorities.

Outside Croat nationalists then aggravated tensions. The Blaskic prosecutors sought to trace this to Zagreb and President Tudjman. Paddy Ashdown, the then leader of the British Liberal Democrat Party, gave a startling account of his dinner conversation with Tudjman at a VE Day banquet in London in May 1995 (evidence given March 19, 1998). Ashdown asked him how Yugoslavia might look in 10 years' time. Tudjman responded by drawing a map on his menu card (which Ashdown showed the court). The map showed Bosnia largely gobbled up by Croatia. When Ashdown asked about the Muslims, Tudjman replied, "There will be no Muslim area, except as a small element of the Croat state." He then said Izetbegovic was "a fundamentalist and an Algerian," whereas Milosevic was "one of us." Muslims were really Serbs and Croats who had failed to stand up to the Turks. Tudjman later admitted that he had drawn this map, which he said corresponded to the division between "west and east" in Yugoslavia (Kovacevic & Dajic, 1997: 180). Expert witness Bianchi also produced documents suggesting that the new Bosnian Croat Army, the HVO, was controlled from Zagreb by the Croatian Army, the HO. The two were "so tightly linked that, from a political and military point of view, they represented a single army" (Aleksovski trial, May 4–9, 1998). Though no direct orders for ethnic cleansing from Zagreb were produced, the Croatian authorities were seeking to dominate areas in Bosnia where Croats lived.

The Bosnian Croat HDZ Party was divided. Its president, Kljucic, was a nationalist but believed the Croats could attain their goals within Bosnia-Herzegovina. But in October 1991 his vice president, Mate Boban, a supermarket manager, took advantage of Kljucic's absence to proclaim a rival "Croatian Community of Herceg-Bosna," supposedly only a cultural organization but ratified over Kljucic's opposition at a December meeting in Zagreb with Tudjman (Kordic & Cerkez trial, Judgment, para. 472). Mate Boban had better contacts with Zagreb, especially through Susak, the leading Zagreb hard-liner, and through connections with emigre Croats who were funneling arms to him. In February 1992 Kljucic was forced to resign after two closed sessions of the Bosnian HDZ. Control shifted to Boban and his deputy, Kordic. In July Boban declared an independent Republic of Herceg-Bosna centered in Grude. Boban confided to the journalist Vulliamy that Bosnia-Herzegovina was "historically Croatian living space." Though the Constitution of Bosnia-Herzegovina guaranteed individual rights, it did not guarantee the rights of the Croat *narod* (people/race) as a whole. Boban predicted that there would be Croat expansion across Bosnia. Vulliamy commented, "everything predicted by Mate Boban [was later] implemented with great efficiency; it was coherent, everything according to plan. There was only one chain of command and it was working" (Blaskic trial, September 24, 1998). Two states were claiming sovereignty over the same piece of territory (as in my thesis 3). One of them now believed it possessed the military and paramilitary superiority to achieve its goal at relatively little cost (thesis 4b).

The largest town in the Lasva Valley was Vitez. In March 1992 the SDA and the bi-ethnic Crisis Committee were asked by the town's HDZ leader to submit to his authority. Resistance would be futile, he threatened, since "the Bosnian Croats in Vitez are armed 90 percent, and the Bosnian Muslims are armed to the extent of 10 percent." Threats were also made on local TV by local HDZ politicians Valenta and Kordic. They claimed these were all defensive actions against Serb and Bosniak aggression. Now "the Muslims would disappear from Bosnia," for this was "historic Croat land" and "the Croats are ready to correct historical errors, that they had been exploited in these parts, humiliated, and that now they had the power and strength for the Croatian people to win their rights, their historic rights, to assert those rights" (Blaskic trial, evidence of Mujezinovic, August 20, 1998; Kordic/Cerkez trial, Judgment, Paras. 472, 478–9, 522, 525). Here again we see the emotional sequence of threat, humiliation, and supposedly defensive rage.

When the Bosnian Serbs withdrew their forces to more critical sectors, Serbs left en masse. A Serb who stayed said of those who left: "They had more trust in people who described the circumstances under which they were living than the circumstances themselves." They also feared retaliation for what Croat refugees entering the town said that other Serbs had done to them (January 22, 1998). But the Croat and Muslim communities continued to fall out. Aggressive Croat patrols paraded the streets. At road blocks, Bosniaks were beaten and robbed. The Croat currency was declared the only legal tender. Shops and market stalls using other currencies were destroyed. Looting and bombing of Muslim shops and stalls intensified until by March 1993 virtually none were left. Cars were stolen, wealthier Bosniaks robbed and beaten up. Bosniaks were told: "We should go to Iraq, that we should go to Turkey, that this was the Croatian Republic, that we were not a nation, that we would all be killed" (Blaskic trial, evidence of Frustic, September 26, 1997). Then came arrests of men, who were forced to act as human shields or dig trenches under inhumane conditions, while women and children were confined in bad conditions. There were sporadic murders.

Croats were not the only aggressors. On January 25, 1993, Muslim forces killed 14 captured Croat soldiers and several civilians in the village of Dusina, which they then cleansed. There was pressure on Croats in the towns of Zenica and Lasva. Dusina was claimed to be "the first crime that started everything." There followed, they admitted, Croat retaliations in a "spiral of violence" committed by out-of-control paramilitaries and soldiers. They did not attack Muslims in their areas of strength, which was normally where atrocities by Muslims began. Instead, they retaliated against those who were the least likely to have attacked Croats – those living in exposed Muslim neighborhoods. Croat witness Alilovic in the Ahmici massacre case revealed that Croat and Bosniak nationalists might share the same cleansing rationality. Bosniaks did such things, he said, when they gained control of local JNA weapons and when Muslim refugees came flooding in from the Serb-cleansed town of Jajce in late autumn 1992. Now the Bosniaks "felt that they were stronger than we were, and that they had outnumbered us, and it is only logical that they thought that they could take this territory for themselves." Both sides could see the logic in cleansing if on top.

Boban's Herceg-Bosna statelet worsened things. In October several villages were cleansed. Dutch UN Colonel Morsnik told of his fruitless attempts to stop the Croat leaders from broadcasting lies on local TV and radio about assassinations and burnings committed by Muslims. He said they were designed to encourage minority Croat communities to flee: "The purpose of the HVO and the HDZ was to concentrate the Croats in the areas that were under their own domination" (Blaskic trial, June 1, 1998). Croat militias were then brought under HVO orders. The paramilitary "Jokers" and "Vitezi" were absorbed into the HVO military police, alongside a non-local "Convicts Brigade." The HOS militia formed by the near-fascist party of Paraga was also absorbed into the HVO (testimony of Damon, March 25, 1998; Vulliamy, April 24, 1998; Capt. Mcleod, January 26, 1998; Col. Morsnik, June 29, 1998; Col. Bowerbath, June 29, 1998; Capt. Whitworth, July 13, 1998 – all Blaskic trial; Witness "R" 4.10.99 – Kordic/Cerkez trial). These units menacingly brandished their arms, threatened locals, reveled in their power. Some said that letting them have their way was an organized Croat tactic: "the HVO did not fear them, but they let them do the things they were doing... to make it clear to the Muslims... that they should be afraid and they wanted to cause panic" (Kavazovic, August 27, 1997; cf. Zeco, September 26, 1997, both in the Blaskic trial). Vulliamy observed: "this was a war against civilians... the refugees were the raw material of the war, they were its whole point; the removal of populations was what the war was all about."

The town of Busovaca contained three JNA barracks and armories. In late April 1992 the HDZ and the SDA agreed to divide up the armories equally, but in May 1993 HVO units suddenly seized one of them, plus the local post office and the Municipal Assembly. The local Muslim leader was severely beaten. Croat flags flew everywhere, Croat was declared the only official language, and Bosniaks were purged from most official positions and company boards (Kordic & Cerkez trial, Judgment, paras. 494–8). Kiseljak's fate was determined when Serb JNA officers handed over the town's barracks to the HVO at the end of April. In Vitez on June 19, HOS units captured the town and flew the checkered flag. The new chief of police declared, "the Croatian people in Vitez did not have the patience to wait for problems to be solved and they were beginning to take things into their own hands." In November public officials and company managers had to sign a loyalty oath to Herceg-Bosna and the Croatian Defense Council. Even if they signed, many were fired. Beatings, lootings, shootings, and mass expulsions followed in all these towns, a pattern that the judges termed "systematic," "ruthless," and "savage" (Blaskic trial, evidence of Mujesinovic, August 20, 1998; Kordic & Cerkez Judgment, paras. 506–7, 520, 852).

The final escalation started on April 15, 1993, precipitated by the Vance–Owen Plan (evidence of Watters, August 18, 1998). The Herceg-Bosna statelet told the Bosniak government to withdraw all forces from three majority-Croat cantons or the HVO would immediately "enforce its jurisdiction." The next day Croat residents were quietly advised to leave. Then came shelling followed by an infantry assault meeting little resistance, resulting in the expulsion or killing of Muslims and the firing of their houses (Blaskic trial, Witnesses "AA," "B," and "CC," February 16–21, 1998). Blaskic himself wrote to a brigade commander that the ground must be "cleansed," though elsewhere he asked only for "defense" preventing "extremist Muslim forces from openly cleansing the territory and from carrying out a genocide of the Croatian People" (ICTY, Blaskic testimony, February 25, 1999, and Verdict, June 3, 2000). One mosque minaret survived in the entire valley. The offensive included two major atrocities against populations who had resisted most – again, murderous overreaction to a threat, not entirely cold-blooded killing. One was a massive truck explosion in the old town in Vitez, a fortified Muslim ghetto, in which numerous civilians died. The other was the massacre of Ahmici, to be described. After three weeks Blaskic reported to HVO headquarters: "the chain of command functions...with the full coordination and control" (Tribunal Update, 86, July 20–24, 1998).

This escalation had to overcome opposition among Croats. A moderate Croat commander regularly talking to his Muslim opposite number was reined in by a security police unit led by the "most extreme" anti-Muslim officer (Blaskic trial, May 12, 1998). A Colonel Filipovic was a "decent man" seeking conciliation, openly cursing what he called Boban's and Blaskic's policy of aggression (evidence of Vulliamy, May 11, 1998). The HVO commander in Fojnica refused to carry out Blaskic's order to attack a Muslim-controlled village "since we continue to hope for an agreement with the Bosniaks." He told Blaskic that he was "aware of his duties, but he could not carry out orders that would lead to the killings and war." Blaskic relieved him, and he spent 10 months in military prison (evidence of Tuka, November 22–27, 1999, Kordic/Cerkez trial). Witness "D" in the Furundzija trial, one of the paramilitary Jokers, had assisted the family of a Bosniak woman arrested by the Jokers and so was beaten and forced to watch her being raped by his unit. Its commander, Furundzija, was found guilty at the Hague of repeated rapes and sentenced to 10 years in prison. Atrocities resulted because extremist men triumphed over moderates. They did so with help from above and because they were more committed to violence.

Neither Kordic nor Cerkez nor Blaskic had any track record of extreme politics or ethnic prejudice (Judgment, para. 523). But they believed that ethnic cleansing was a necessary defense. A Muslim doctor, Dr. Mujezinovici, whose services were retained by the Croat authorities, gave evidence on politics in Vitez (Blaskic trial, August 20, 1998; Kordic/Cerkez trial, May 10, 1999). He identifies Anto Valenta, a local high school teacher and author of a radical nationalist tract, as the chief Croat ideologist, and Darko Kraljevic, commander of the paramilitary Vitezozi, as brutal, with an "unsettling presence...armed head to toe." Ivan Santic was a graduate technologist and a wavering HDZ politician who felt helpless against extremists and "uncontrollable armed men." Silica, a Croat community leader with "a good reputation in town," proposed conciliation that the HDZ ignored. At least three Croat Socialist Party members who openly criticized radicals were silenced by beatings: "who was not in favour was against, and he would get what was coming to him." Witness "T" (Blaskic trial, January 20, 1998) said that prominent HDZ dissenters were beaten up. Vitez veterinarian Dr. Zeco (Blaskic trial, September 26, 1997) said that the civilian police chief and the mayor both tried to help him. But the police chief gave up when threatened, though the mayor continued to complain and so was sent to the front lines, a potent punishment. Moderate Croat politicians took down the flags in Vitez and restored some guns and jobs to Bosniaks over the summer. Radicals triumphed here only through late October and early November. In Busovaca radicals triumphed earlier, when the moderate HDZ vice president was beaten up (Kordic & Cerkez Judgment, para. 482). Witness "JJ" (Blaskic trial, March 19, 1998) said there was fighting within the Kiseljak HVO. Moderates protected Muslims until their two leaders were killed by radical paramilitaries. Unfortunately, the radicals, not the moderates, specialized in violence.

Mujezinovici says few of his Croat neighbors or colleagues wanted trouble. They warned him "stay out of the streets today" or "don't be alarmed by a coming strong explosion" (i.e., a truck bomb) or suggested that his children "not chant slogans in favor of the B-H army." One, sobbing, said, "You are saved, just be quiet. . . . You keep quiet, you have been saved." He saw a Croat doctor preventing HVO soldiers from removing a wounded patient they intended to kill and Croat nurses sobbing after they had tended the wounded at Ahmici. The veterinarian, Zeco, says that a "sizeable number" of Croats helped Muslims, and a few had keen killed for doing so. So most dared not help. Witness "X" (Blaskic trial, January 27, 1998) had a Croat friend who first refused to don the HVO uniform and was denied alternative employment. In order to eat, he signed up. Prison guards were neighbors and old school friends who declared surprise at seeing Kavazovic there. What had he done? They believed only Muslim extremists were imprisoned. Two guards apologized for his treatment, one giving him cigarettes, saying, "That is how things are, I am sorry; it is neither your fault nor mine" (Blaskic trial, August 26–27, 1997). At Ahmici one young man twice refused an order to kill, so his officer did it itself. The young man did not try to stop him (Witness Ahmic, August 18, 1998). A braver man secretly called UN forces and saved seven men from being executed by the radical Kraljevic, commander of the Jokers (Witness "R," November 4, 1999). Few risked this much.

But many Croats were radicalized. Many materially benefited from cleansing; some are described as enjoying it. Armed Croats would swagger and sing and shoot in the air. At roadblocks they enjoyed the arbitrary power of extorting "tolls," punctuating brutality with gestures of magnanimity. Looting Muslim property was ubiquitous, often by masked men (presumably locals, said witness "JJ"). Others worked themselves up into righteous rage over supposed Muslim atrocities. Radical-controlled media amplified this. Witness "E" (Blaskic trial, September 26, 1997) said she saw on TV an account of the destruction by Muslims of a Croat village and believed it, but went there a month later and found it totally unharmed. There was widespread support for the symbols of sovereignty. Croat primary school teachers were delighted when Croat was declared the sole language of instruction and when Croat flags and pictures of Tudjman appeared in school. Witness "LL," a university-educated Muslim woman, suggested that it was "the more educated people" who "started saying that the Croats and Muslims could no longer live together, that Kiseljak was historically Croatian territory and that it should be ethnically pure, and that Muslims should go to the towns where they were in a majority" (Blaskic trial, May 12, 1998). But refugees were the worst. They needed housing, jobs, and possessions, and took out on others what Serbs or Muslims elsewhere had done to them. Croats displaced from other areas would knock on Bosniak doors proposing a house or apartment "exchange" in return for their abandoned home. Bosniaks took this as a cue for speedy flight. Professor Kajmovic (Blaskic trial, August 27, 1997) said a former student appeared, saying, "You know, director, I feel very awkward but I am here to tell you that you have to leave your apartment." He left.

Tihomir Blaskic had been born in the Lasva Valley in 1960. His father was a miner, then a driver, and the family lacked money for their son's education. So he went to military school (which provided free board and lodging) and became a professional soldier. He showed ability and rose to the rank of captain first class by 1990. He claims he became unhappy about duties he was asked to perform while serving in Kosovo and resented the preference shown there to Serbs. He enrolled part-time for a master's degree in business, intending to leave the army when he qualified. He had almost completed his degree when the troubles started. He left for Austria, for he had married an Austrian girl, but felt a "moral obligation" to return and offer his military expertise to his threatened homeland. He returned in March 1992. Demonstrating his military competence, he was appointed to command the Lasva Valley HVO with the rank of colonel, retaining command until the end of cleansing. Later he became a general. The evidence suggested that he was an ordinary Croat with few military abilities, using them out of seemingly patriotic motives. He had no track record of extreme nationalism or ethnic prejudice, nor did he evince them during his period of command. Yet he efficiently organized the cleansing of the Valley. Though he himself killed no one, he knew what would follow from his orders, the ICTY decided, sentencing him to 45 years in prison. They applied the same reasoning to Kordic, who received 25 years, and to Cerkez, who got 15. They all believed that the protection of the Croat community required ethnic consolidation and saw murderous cleansing as the necessary means. A British officer testified that Ahmici was not of major strategic significance. But the villagers had resisted by setting up a roadblock stopping Croat troop movements in October 1992. Five months later it was selected as the perfect place from which "to send a message . . . to the rest of the Valley that they were no longer welcome and were to leave" (Blaskic trial, testimony of Watters, August 18, 1998 and Blaskic, February 17, 1999).

In the Ahmici massacre 116 Muslim civilians were murdered, including 30 women and 20 children. All 180 Muslim houses and the two mosques in the village – and no Croat buildings – were burned down. The ICTY tried six Croats for this atrocity in the Kupreskic trial. It concluded that this was a

well-planned and well-organized killing of civilian members of an ethnic group. . . . The primary purpose of the massacre was to expel the Muslims from the village, by killing many of them, by burning their houses, slaughtering their livestock, and by illegally detaining and deporting the survivors to another area. The ultimate goal of these acts was to spread terror among the population so as to deter members of that particular ethnic group from ever returning to their homes.

This, said the court, was "only one step away from genocide." The court initially found five of the six defendants guilty, though it noted that they were small fry. The highest placed was Vladimir Santic, a commander of the Jokers unit within the HVO military police in Vitez. The other five defendants were Ahmici villagers, born between 1958 and 1967, all married, most with children, and with working-class occupations (factory worker and foreman, forest ranger, and local police officer). They were in HVO or Joker units. Only one was proved to have had an ethnonationalist record, being from a "Ustasha family." Four others were said to have been previously "decent people" who were "transformed" into Croat nationalists only when the troubles started. One remained active in a multiethnic folklore society into 1993. One had "changed completely" into a "fanatic" during the troubles. In 1991 he praised Hitler, favored "the fascist method of destroying Jews and other nations," and thought "it was necessary to apply this among the Croats." The next year he was strutting around in a variety of uniforms and intimidating people with weapons (Blaskic trial, testimony of Ahmic, August 18, 1998). The accused conceded to having "obeyed orders" as "weak," "pressured," or marginal players. But they were already participating in intimidation and violence against local Muslims. Actions as well as values had been radicalized. On appeal, however, only two of the convictions were upheld. The main prosecution eyewitnesses were a child and a man crawling along the ground, clutching his little child, trying to escape death. Their testimony was discredited since they might have been too distracted to identify the perpetrators properly. Cleansing can be too thorough to leave credible witnesses.

Kaornik was a concentration camp near Busovaca where Muslim prisoners were killed, tortured, and taken out to be used as human shields in Croat advances. Zlatko Aleksovski was the young camp commandant, born in 1960, an ethnic Macedonian but a Croat citizen. He was a sociology graduate, specializing in crime and deviance, who then worked in the Bosnia-Herzegovina prison service. He claimed that his detainees were lucky to have a professional penologist as their warden. He deflected blame for atrocities onto retaliation by guards and HVO soldiers who had lost family members in the war. Inmate testimony confirmed that drunken HVO soldiers could come unhindered into the camp and beat prisoners in supposed revenge for atrocities elsewhere (ICTY Case IT-95-14, especially testimony of Capt. McLeod, January 6, 1998). Aleksovski was sentenced to only seven years.

I return to the village studied by Tone Bringa, now also filmed by a Granada TV crew in February 1993. One villager says hopefully to the camera, "even now relations between neighbors are good. No sane person would commit atrocities. We have to live together." Yet Bringa noticed that previously Catholics and Muslims had used religious forms of greeting – "go with Allah" or "praise Jesus" – only in private within their own ethnic group. In greeting people in public settings, everyone had used secular expressions like "good day." But now Croats were using religious greetings publicly, as if claiming the public space of the village for themselves (Bringa, 1995: 56). The filmmaker Debra Christie noticed "a level of tension, but Muslim and Croat were still going in and out of each other's houses, they were taking teas, they were taking coffee. That changed in the three weeks we were there." A Croat–Muslim village patrol was replaced by a Croat HVO patrol crossing the village every "five or ten minutes." Some poorly armed Muslims tried to patrol at night but were chased off. The HVO began to clear the streets and close the Muslim shops for an hour or so at a time, demonstrating that it was "their" village. Vandalism of Muslim shops started. Croat gun emplacements were built overlooking the village. Refugees arrived, some of them relatives, telling of atrocities committed elsewhere: "My brother was killed by his next-door neighbors." One Muslim said to the camera, "Yes, our Croats. They're out to get us. Neighbors … this is what they're like. Dad went to the shop and those who used to greet him turned their heads and looked the other way. That's what they're like. We always got along. We can't understand how it can happen this way." Two friends of 40 years, the Muslim woman Nasratta, and the Croat Slavka, were now avoiding each other. Said Nasratta, "I'm stopping at home. It's unpleasant to go out visiting now. It's not that you must not. It's just that it's got more difficult. She may think I've come to spy on her and that's not my intention. If they invited me, I'd go."

The film crew left and then returned briefly with UN soldiers on April 23. They found a cleansed, half-destroyed, hostile village. Slavka told them that on April 18 the Muslims had been attacked by Croat soldiers, "foreigners" and "outsiders." "We didn't do it," she says, but then adds that five or six village Croats had helped them. Muslim villagers, now refugees, said that Croat villagers had prior warning of the shelling, but Muslims had been unprepared. About 12 were killed and almost all had fled. Their houses were looted and burned (evidence of Christie, Blaskic trial, April 27, 1998). In her book, Bringa says she is often asked if her prior fieldwork research can explain the seismic shift. She replies:

My answer is no. Neither my material nor this book can or intends to explain the war for the simple reason that the war was not created by those villagers who are the focus of this account. The war has been orchestrated from places where the people I lived and worked among were not represented, and where their voices were not heard. In the end, after resisting for almost a year, these villagers too became a part of the war, initially becoming involved in order to defend their own homes and families. (1995: 5)

Change had come to the village from "above and outside," penetrating the village mainly in the form of "nationalist propaganda." Yet she adds, "war changes people in profound ways. It changes their perceptions of themselves and who they are, and it changes their perceptions of others and who they are" (1995: 5). And in evidence at the Kupreski trial she added, "as Yugoslavia disintegrated, and the national ideology took over, the understanding of neighbors of different faith underwent a gradual change." She also quoted a village woman: "When the clashes approached the village and when someone we knew died, we changed." Bringa comments, "the change means the withdrawal into the safety of one's own national group, since there one does not have to prove to which group one belongs." Mobilization for ethnic war had dragged this village over the abyss.

Bringa may overstate her top-down explanation. Her research was not ideally suited to analyzing the process of ethnic cleansing. As a single woman living with a Muslim family, she was largely confined to the company of Muslim women. She tells us little of Muslim men and nothing of Croat men, some of whom helped the cleansing of the village. Thus she may exaggerate the gulf between the village and the growing nationalism of the outside world. She tells us that the local economy segregated the sexes, confining women to the household and farm while the men worked and did military service in more urban settings elsewhere. Sometimes the men were away for long periods. The women were far more insulated from Yugoslav politics, especially the Muslim women. She quotes a young Muslim cleric as criticizing her choice of this village, since the locals were too insular. They "did not read books and thus did not know anything" (1995: 51–2, 61, 93, 224). Bringa documents that rural Muslim women experienced cleansing as a bombshell. But she cannot prove that the men were passive tools of outside powers. Of course, as we have seen, there were radical pressures coming from the military/party hierarchies in Grude, Zagreb, and Sarajevo, but they were paralleled by radicalization of the local parties – and radicals had more weapons. By now this is a familiar story.

MUSLIM ATROCITIES

Bosnian Muslims and Kosovo Albanians were the weakest ethnic groups involved in these conflicts, and so they were predominantly victims. The Bosnian authorities, originally the most multicultural and the most desirous of gaining intervention by the West, sought to exert more control over their armed men. This restraint is not now so evident among the Kosovo Albanian authorities, and many of their armed men are currently exacting revenge against Serbs remaining in Kosovo – who are presumably the least likely of the Kosovo Serbs to have themselves committed earlier atrocities.

A former JNA facility in the village of Celebici was used by Croat and Muslim forces to imprison Serbs cleansed from the area of Konjic in central

Bosnia in May 1992. The Celebici guards, mostly Muslims, beat, tortured, sexually assaulted, and killed their Serb prisoners. The camp commandant, the Bosnian Croat Zsravko Mucic, was sentenced in 1998 to only seven years for responsibility for nine murders and other inhumane acts. The court agreed that as a Croat commanding Muslims he had felt insecure, unable to impose discipline on them. The Muslim guard Hazim Delic was a local, a locksmith before he became a member of the HVO military police. He had a prior conviction for murder. He was married, with two young children. ICTY gave him 20 years for two murders and many tortures and rapes, saying, "he took a sadistic pleasure in the infliction of pain" and "would laugh in response pleas for mercy." "You have to die anyway" was his favorite phrase. During a rape he declared, "the Chetniks were guilty for everything that was going on. He started to curse my Chetnik mother." The Muslim guard Esad Landzo was sentenced to 15 years for three murders and tortures committed with "imaginative cruelty as well as substantial ferocity." His lesser sentence resulted from his "extreme youth" (he was 19), "poor family background," lack of disciplined training, and his impressionability and immaturity. He wanted to revenge loved ones lost in Serb shelling. A fourth defendant, the Muslim Zejnil Delacic, was acquitted. He was one of the murky "patriotic businessmen" of the war, active in procuring supplies for the Bosniak state and the camp, perhaps also selling supplies to Serbs. Capitalist profit motives might restrain ethnonationalism (Celebici, Case IT-96-21-T).

The war around Konjic had been bitter, since it was strategically important and contained several JNA facilities. The Serbs were the least numerous but the best armed. Bosniaks and Croats were penned into the town itself, reinforced by refugees cleansed from surrounding villages. Serbs started shelling the town but the Bosniak–Croat alliance fought back, occupied some Serb villages, and took prisoners. The victors were thoroughly embittered, seeking revenge. Serbs were beaten even before they reached the camp. Then "severe beatings, torture and humiliations of detainees were the norm" in the Celebici camp. "No one appeared to care whether the detainees survived." Visiting soldiers joined the camp staff in these activities. This was the righteous anger and gratuitous cruelty of revenge, bent on humiliating Serbs as Croat and Bosniak communities had been humiliated earlier.

Naser Oric was born in 1967 in rural Bosnia, near Srebrenica. His grandfather had been a Ustasha fighter. He graduated from high school with a metalworking certificate but found no work. A burly weight lifter and karate fighter, he moved to Belgrade and became a nightclub bouncer. He was recruited to the security police, becoming a Milosevic bodyguard, but as war started, he felt the tug of ethnic loyalty. He returned to Bosnia and became a Sarajevo policeman. The Bosniak authorities recognized his qualities and sent him to organize a militia in his home village. There he rose to become the most effective organizer of paramilitary resistance in Srebrenica, a Muslim hero. Yet he was charged with burning and plundering 50 Serb villages and executing prisoners in reprisal raids. He also violently suppressed Muslims opposing his authority. He and his lieutenants "appeared to the Dutch peacekeepers to be little more than gangsters, who terrorized the refugees and profited greatly from the war." He also tried to provoke the Serbs to fire against the Dutch peacekeepers by firing at them from close to Dutch positions. In 2003 he was captured and formally indicted at the Hague for war crimes (Hakanowicz, 1996: 77; Honig & Both, 1997: 132–3; ICTY Case IT-03-68-I; Sudetic, 1998: 150–1). Those who were good at violence rose to the top in all the communities when ethnic war erupted.

Musan Topalovic, known as "Caco," was born around 1950. He became a Sarajevo nightclub singer and underworld figure. In 1990 a sense of ethnic loyalty led to his cultivating ties with Muslim politicians and policemen. When war threatened in 1991, he helped organize the clandestine Muslim paramilitary Patriotic League and Green Berets. Perhaps 20 men with criminal records led Muslim paramilitary units. After the first weeks of fighting in the spring of 1992 he commanded the Bosnia-Herzegovina's Army's 10th Mountain Brigade. Sarajevo residents acknowledge that but for Caco and his Tigers there would be no city left for Muslims today. But many were also terrified of him. He exercised absolute power over neighborhoods, press-ganged recruits, ran black market smuggling, kidnapped and ransomed rich people, organized rapes, allocated empty houses, and executed Serb fighters and civilians (probably over 400). One former Tiger said, "I have no doubt that Caco would be on The Hague's list of the most wanted war criminals had he survived." But in October 1993 the Bosnian government, prodded by the UN and by the robbery of a funeral parlor, finally turned on him. Special police and army units stormed his headquarters. Caco was killed, either in the firefight or later under torture. In 1996 he was reburied by the Bosnian Union of Veterans. Over 5,000 persons attended the ceremony (Domovina Net, June 10, 1999).

ORDINARY YUGOSLAV PERPETRATORS

The data on perpetrators as a whole are poor and often interpreted by sensational journalism. However, the following characteristics seem to emerge.

1. They were disproportionately from border areas of mixed ethnicity. Most of those indicted by the ICTY committed atrocities in their own home areas. Some observers marvel at the "intimacy" of the carnage: "torturers knew their victims" says Scharf (1997: 216). One-quarter of 123 former Croatian prisoners said they recognized Serbs who had viciously beaten them while in Knin prison, and this is about the proportion found in the Croatian government's list of survivor accounts (Botica et al., 1992). Oberschall (1998) gives a lower estimate. He says Bosnian Muslims could recognize faces and voices in only 2 of 16 Serb assaults on villages in the Prijedor district. Especially active were refugees from these areas. In Kosovo witnesses

said that refugees and local Serbs figured disproportionately among the perpetrators, either as security police or as paramilitaries. Some report being saved from them by policemen or soldiers from Serbia (Judah, 2000: 241–8; *Los Angeles Times*, December 22, 1999). Locals were generally the most radicalized by the process of mutual provocation, retaliation, and withdrawal behind communal barricades. The border areas were also more rural. It is unlikely that the countryside is intrinsically more likely to generate radical nationalists – though some writers on Yugoslav nationalism suggest so. It is more likely that the correlation was due to the threat perceived by border areas, plus their relative poverty, which made them more economically dependent on a strong state and on Milosevic.

2. Practitioners of violence like former army officers and operatives of the police and security forces were overrepresented. Perpetrators came more from paramilitary and secret and other police units than from the regular army. Survivors identified their multicolored camouflage fatigues, rape victims remembered ammunition bandeleros, insignia like skulls or animals dripping blood, and the ubiquitous knives – all paramilitary accoutrements. They had a style and swagger drawn from Hollywood movies, especially from those of mayhem like *Rambo* and the *Terminator* movies. Karadzic's own daughter, stylishly dressed and sporting a Beretta pistol ("as important to me as my make-up"), said, "we got our battle ethics from the movies about Mad Max and Terminator, Rambo and Young Guns" (Rogel, 1998: 132). Vulliamy (1994: 19, 45–9) describes the JNA troopers he saw as "terrified and uncommitted," in contrast to the Serb paramilitaries, who he says were "boozy at their best, wild and sadistic at their worst," full of hatred for Croats and contempt for Muslims. In Kosovo security police seemed the most involved, inured to repressing Albanians. Yet survivors say the paramilitaries were wilder: "The normal police were calm but the paramilitaries were screaming." "We were among wolves," said one witness (Daniszewski, 1999: S2–3). A journalist noted that in one Croat unit "everyone looks as if he had been cast as a thug by a movie director" except for one gentle-looking 24-year-old who said, "I don't really hate Muslims... but because of the situation I want to kill them all" (Block, 1993: 10).

This may be mere journalistic sensationalism. Milicevic (forthcoming) is compiling a sample of paramilitaries who seem more diverse than this. I might add that stereotypes of volunteer paramilitaries have emerged in other contexts and have been shown by research to be false. Hart (1998: chaps. 7, 8) has shown that, contrary to popular wisdom, Irish Republican Army (IRA) paramilitaries fighting the British in the Irish Republic were drawn neither from the highest nor the lowest social classes. They were mostly skilled workers, tradesmen, or white-collar workers. They were mostly urban but, if rural, came from above-average farming families. They were, of course, young unmarried men, and tended to have had closer relations with their mothers than their fathers. The Yugoslav paramilitaries were also volunteers, they were taking risks that JNA soldiers would not take, they were not operating in disciplined secrecy (unlike the IRA), and they were only half-disciplined. That alone might bring more wildness.

3. There was a distinct age and gender structure. Most perpetrators were young men, aged up to 30. A few female leaders encouraged cleansing, like Mirjana Markovic and Biljana Plavsic, but very few women committed atrocities. Equally few were appalled by the behavior of their menfolk. One warned a Muslim of her kinsman: "He's no good. . . . Don't believe anything he says. Don't send anyone to him asking for help. He's always drunk now. They're all drunk. . . . Hide, whatever you do, don't roam around alone. And don't let your daughter-in-law . . . roam around alone" (Sudetic, 1998: 111; cf. Hukanowicz, 1996: 41). Yet in November 1995 a Croat court convicted a Serbian married couple, Dusan and Jagoda Boljevic, of murdering 18 civilians (Kovacevic & Dajic, 1995: 238). In some jeering crowds, women predominated. Men did most of the killing simply because only men did military service and had access to arms.

But the paramilitaries also exuded a macho patriarchal culture. Since they tended to be nationalists, politically opposed by liberals, we would expect them to have generally more conservative values, including on gender issues. A cult of machismo might be expected. Experts in violent sports and occupations may have also been overrepresented, while it is often believed that they came disproportionately from rural backward parts of Yugoslavia. Economic and border resentments may have been more important in their motivations than any rural sexism per se. Yet Ramet (1992: chap. 6) suggests that Serb and Montenegrin patriarchal culture gave lower status to young women and higher status to older mothers. She speculates that Serb nationalist men were rebelling against maternal authority and embracing boastful machismo violence, including maltreatment of young women. Certainly these fighters were accustomed to brandishing arms and shared a drinking culture from which women were excluded. When in their cups, they would boast endlessly, especially to journalists. The story was repeated of one former leader, the bodybuilder Zelko. Wounded by a land mine, Zelko took his own life with a grenade rather than live as a cripple (Block, 1993: 10).

There were also military lures toward macho murder. Since paramilitaries lacked the training to intimidate through a highly disciplined show of force (as the SS did), they resorted to small gang intimidation. The Bassiouni Report said that most Serb rapes were committed by groups of men in front of their comrades in a "gang atmosphere. In the camps and the so-called rape hotels, collective and repeated assault predominated (UN, 1994: 57–60). While the widespread publicizing of rape in these wars is welcome, we do not know whether this was a higher level of rape than occurs in most wars or most civil wars. But it was also *gendercide* in the sense that men formed the vast majority of the victims as well as the perpetrators. Rape was probably not the core of the macho paramilitary culture. Most violent men were more concerned to demonstrate their virility in front of their gang by killing other men.

The indicted perpetrators were mostly leaders, and so they were not especially young. Two generations were overrepresented. Among the top leaders, World War II births predominate. Though in the 1990s men aged 45–50 might be expected to lead most social movements, most of their families had also been activists or victims of the Ustasha or the Chetniks/Partisans. Men born between 1946 and 1957 are few. Then the lower leaders were mostly born between 1958 and 1960, in their early 30s during the troubles. Experiences as children in the cauldron of a murderous war, and as young adults during the rising tensions of the 1980s, seem formative.

4. Some say perpetrators tended to be poor and unemployed, though precise data are unavailable; if so, this might be due to rural backgrounds. There was certainly class resentment displaced onto ethnicity against victims viewed as prosperous and privileged. However, the paramilitaries also contained middle-class "weekend Chetniks," including white-collar workers and high school or university graduates. Moreover, army officers coordinated cleansing operations and desk murderers in the ministries were more middle-class. Most social classes were probably involved, though in different phases of the action. Once again, the dirty work may have been left to the workers.

5. Criminals played a large role in the paramilitaries, using their proficiency in violence. I have instanced Arkan, Beli, Giska, and Caco. The Serb SDB had recruited many of them for its Red Berets, as had Arkan. There were reputed to be about 20 Bosniak gangster-warlords. Among the Croats were Martinovic, nicknamed "Stela," only 24 in 1992, and Naletilic, known as "Tuta," age 46. Stela was later sentenced by a Croatian court to eight years in prison. Both were then handed over to the ICTY, which found them guilty of crimes relating to the unlawful treatment of prisoners. Stela was at first a commander of the neo-fascist paramilitary HOS. Tuta had run clubs, casinos, and protection rackets and in 1992 formed a "Convicts Battalion" – though some of them were former political prisoners (Block, 1993: 9; ICTY Case IT-98-34-T). Vasic (1996) improbably claims that 80 percent of the Serb paramilitaries were common criminals. Mueller (2000), Judah (2000: 245–8), and Human Rights Watch (1999) all exaggerate the role of criminal thugs.

Yet this turbulent, lawless ethnic war also *created* many gangster-thugs. Croatian Minister Ivan Vekic said sarcastically, "There were not enough volunteers among priests and nuns, so we had to accept everyone who offered their help." The war brought them opportunities to smuggle, extort, and rob while defining themselves as patriots, bringing their skills to the defense of their community. More political paramilitary leaders hated them. Savic (also called "Mauser"), a Bosnian Serb who led the Panther paramilitary, waged a long battle against them. He made so many enemies that we cannot tell who had him murdered in 2000. The wars also corrupted the states and statelets as officials got rich quickly. UN official Corwin discovered that the Bosnian regime was just as corrupt and violent as the others, so criticism was dangerous. He himself was threatened with "an accident" by government minister Muratovic, later prime minister and reputedly a war profiteer, for "the war and the economic embargo have raised smuggling and black marketeering to the level of high patriotism. Gangsters have become paramilitary formations in the service of nationalism. It is true all through former Yugoslavia" (Corwin, 1999: ix–xii, 168; Hakanowicz, 1996: 68; Judah, 1997: 254; Peric-Zimonjic, 1998; *Vreme*, November 18, 1991).

Except for Serbia, state administrations were in the process of formation. It was quick and cheap to privatize new state functions. War procurement devolved onto "businessmen" given licenses to provide goods and services without supervision. In protecting convoys and stores, gangsters had useful skills for war procurement. They became patriots, though a Sarajevo TV editor commented sarcastically, "A bunch of fools waving party flags are making money by re-selling arms, food, oil, flour. All that in the name of the Moslems, the Serbs and the Croats.... Well done guys" (*Vreme*, May 11, 1992). Most of them still flaunt their wealth across the states and statelets of Yugoslavia. Economic classes – politically, militarily, and criminally derived – reasserted themselves in the nation. The nation does not trump class for long!

6. Many atrocities were perpetrated by drunken men. Alcohol played its normal roles in murderous cleansing. It inflamed the passions, lessened the perception of the horror perpetrated, and dulled the conscience and memory afterward. The paramilitaries assembled in bars. Senior commanders of the paramilitaries and of the Bosnian Serb Army, like Bobic or Mladic, boasted of their drinking capacity. Rumors abound of Milosevic's alcoholism, though this is not public machismo – more a sleeping pill, I guess. Rank-and-file perpetrators were sometimes paid in alcohol and tobacco. This was a male drinking culture, men often killing and raping while drunk.

7. Finally, material motives sucked in many ordinary men (and indirectly their whole families). The president of Serb Krajina complained, "Theft is flourishing. A tank rolls down the street and liberates it, and the infantry follows since the infantry plunder, and then the volunteers follow with a truck and 'cleanse the area.'" Reserve officers spending more than a month at the front "brought back a fine car filled with everything that would fit inside a car" (Williams & Cigar, 1996: 5). Said a Serb journalist, "The first wave of 'liberators' to enter a town were after 'gold and ready money', the second wave took 'household appliances and other equipment', and they were followed by the 'scavengers' who would take up parquet floors, take down windows, toilets, and practically everything that could be carted off." Serbs could loot more, since they liberated more towns. But others were not far behind when they got the chance (*Vreme*, March 8, 1993). Refugees from Kosovo paid ransoms at every stage of their flight. When Bosnian forces

began to retake territory, they were followed by a horde of ragged, hungry Muslim refugees finishing off wounded Serbs with old guns, knives, and other crude weapons, stuffing sacks with whatever they could find. Angered desperation fired up these "bag people" (Sudetic, 1998: 157). Looting contributed to low morale in the Serb statelets. The leaders looted millions in comfort, the rank-and-file looted consumer durables while risking their lives, the refugees got some property back, and those who remained moderate got nothing.

CONCLUSION: STRUCTURE AND PROCESS IN YUGOSLAV CLEANSING

At the macro level, danger in Yugoslavia was created by democratizing nation-states amid a series of bi-ethnic contexts (my thesis 1c). The nation-state looked attractive compared to a discredited federal Communist regime, and the republics also dispensed economic patronage. Nationalists had a head start over socialists and liberals, channeling class conflict onto ethnicity (thesis 2). The disintegration of the Federation then generated bi-ethnic conflicts over border zones in which minorities believed they were supported by their homeland state next door. Rival nationalists could morally and realistically aspire to their own nation-states over the same territory (theses 3 and 4a). Many Serbs believed they possessed the overwhelming military force to protect Serbs over the border at little risk. Later the Vance–Owen plan emboldened the ethnic majority in each canton to seize possession of it, as in the Lasva Valley. These are examples of thesis 4b. Confronted by a Serbian first strike, the nationalist Croat leadership resisted. Serbia then attacked the easier target of Bosnia (thesis 4b again), which resisted with unexpected vigor. Ethnic civil wars ensued.

The states involved fit only imperfectly into my ethnic thesis 5 of factionalizing and radicalizing states. The disintegration of federal state institutions began the descent, but the military and security institutions of the Serb state were firmly in being, neither destabilized nor much factionalized. Despite dissension in the JNA Army, it was brought under fairly firm control. Croatian "hard" state institutions were in the process of formation, mostly under radicals. This also became true of the Bosniak state and of the Albanian, Croat, and Serb statelets being created from scratch. All these states were destabilized by geopolitical instability leading to war, so this is a mixed picture. Radicalized but consolidating states beset by geopolitical crisis were the main problem.

The two most common explanations for these terrible events invoke ancient ethnic hatreds and "bad, even criminal leadership" (in Ambassador Holbrooke's words). Neither argument is foolish if inserted in a more complex explanation. Old (though not ancient) ethnic hatreds were stirred up among a substantial part of each community. But the perpetrators were not the Serbs, the Croats, the Bosniaks, or the Albanians as whole peoples. Radicalized nationalism spread quite widely among the rival communities, but it was stirred, manipulated, and coerced by elites, armed militants, and core constituencies of radical nationalism – especially threatened border dwellers, emigres, and refugees, and men in violent occupations, legal and illegal. War then made ethnic identity compulsory, triumphant over all other identities. One was forced to be a Serb, a Croat, a Bosniak, or an Albanian, regardless of class, region, and gender.

Only a tiny minority of Serbs, Croats, or Muslims can have actually killed or raped. Even the killing of 100,000 civilians and prisoners across Yugoslavia (a high estimate) might require only 10,000 perpetrators. That sounds like a lot, but it is a very small proportion of Yugoslavs. Many more hung around the fringes, jeering, shouting, full of righteous rage. But we have seen ample evidence (as in other cases) of very varied behavior and attitudes within each community. Sizable dissidence was driven underground or into exile by radical pressures, including many murders; expressions of dismay were driven into muted forms. Lesser forms of participation derived from ordinary human weaknesses. Fear, anger, greed, comradeship, careerism, ignorance, hypocrisy, moral cowardice, and the like allowed many more Serbs, Croats, Bosniaks, and Albanians to jump on the bandwagon of evil. This was mass behavior, but erupting at varying levels of complicity after complex power interactions.

Slobodan Milosevic contributed more than any other person to murderous ethnic cleansing. He did not start out that way. Like many politicians, Milosevic simply wanted power – to lead a noncommunist but somewhat authoritarian regime. I return to the stylized language of Plans identified in my thesis 6. Milosevic's Plan A was a compact Serb-tilting Yugoslav Federation. Socialized in a decaying Communist state, he thought it normal to employ coercion and covert criminality to achieve his plans. Tudjman in Croatia was more sincerely nationalist, scarred by his own persecution and his nationalist view of 20th-century history. His Plan A was steadier: a Croatian nation-state. No more than Milosevic did he intend to preside over mass murder. Neither men, nor most of the lesser men and women around them, blinked when it became clear that to continue their policies would involve murderous ethnic cleansing. Tudjman consistently claimed self-defense, even when he totally cleansed the Krajina of Serbs. Milosevic was pressured by repeated failures first to Plan B of militarily aiding cross-border Serbs to achieve a Greater Serbia, then to Plan C of a swift and overwhelming army invasion. Finally, when the army could not achieve this, he plunged into Plan D, combining army artillery bombardments and wild paramilitary/security police assaults that produced the most murderous cleansing. In Bosnia he moved less far, starting with the Plan C just mentioned, anticipating swift success. Failure then made him escalate quickly to Plan D. In Kosovo he began with Plan D, though unexpected NATO opposition and then bombing made him escalate further than he had intended. He seems to have steadily learned to be more murderous in his cleansing. But he had never imagined that comparisons with Hitler might be considered appropriate.

We again see that even malevolent leaders do not start out that way. Their initial Plan for the defense of their own community encounters resistance and fails. They then escalate. Whatever will prove to be the case for Milosevic – and in May 2004 it seems more likely that he will be convicted of complicity in genocide than of personal intent to commit genocide – the ICTY found that Blaskic, Kordic, and Cerkez were relatively reasonable men whose conception of defense led to terrible atrocities. They seemed to exhibit an elite version of what Katz found among Americans convicted of homicide: a sense of frustration/humiliation at resistance gave them no choice (so they felt) other than to respond with sudden escalation. Since they did not have to personally kill, they exhibited apparently calm, collected decision making, not rage, as they escalated. Nonetheless, they were mass murderers.

But murderous cleansing was not their responsibility alone. Elites, militants, and core constituencies of nationalism were all radicalizing. Few intended or foresaw the full consequences of their actions. Few Yugoslavs imagined they would become murderers. And when they did murder, they still regarded this as necessary defense or revenge. If this accomplished a cleansing that made their ethnic community secure, ordinary people did not define them later as war criminals, but as patriots. Had not Kordic stood unarmed in the path of Serb munitions trucks at the beginning of the conflict, asked witnesses at his trial? To many Serbs, Milosevic still appears as defying the might of the world, and Serb opinion polls still show widespread admiration for this miscreant.

They did not begin as ferocious nationalists, committed to what Max Weber called value rationality, a commitment to values regardless of the means involved. As in other cases, they felt driven to this, to a last desperate defense of the nation, in which bloody measures seemed both grim necessity and release from threat and humiliation. Blood must be spilled to protect the nation, said Mladic and Macura. Criminals must be used, since priests and nuns are not available, said Vekic. Paramilitaries were the only ones who would charge, said the Serb general. Not all nationalists were sucked down. Some drew back. Draskovic did in Serbia and perhaps Plavsic in the Republika Srbska. But most leaders at all levels became committed to an "ethic of values," neglecting what Weber said was the higher task of the political leader, "the ethic of responsibility," the ability to achieve practical goals on behalf of constituents. This made them underestimate their enemy, whom they demonized as Ustasha, Chetniks, and fundamentalists. Leaders and militants neglected to consider how the enemy would respond to their actions. Milosevic spectacularly underestimated his enemies. The result of his defense of Serbs was to destroy most of the Serb *precani* communities, create half a million destitute refugees, and destroy the Serb economy. Tudjman's policies involved massive Croatian deaths and destruction; the leaders of the various statelets and nationalist parties also brought enormous harm to their own constituents; and countless Yugoslavs brought great harm to themselves. Had they been more instrumentally oriented, they might have seen that they could have achieved more of their goals by compromise. Humans like to think they are rational, but the sum of their actions is often irrational – and sometimes it is evil.

Holbrooke's argument implies that change the leaders and all will be well. This became the basis of U.S. policy in the postwar situation: once democratic elections were held, all would be well. Thus the Bosnian Serb and Bosnian Croat statelets would be permitted to keep their own armies. But the elections, as in 1990–1, produced victories for the ethnonationalists who had led the wars. For the next three years these democratically elected governments pursued policies cementing ethnic cleansing. Finally, the United States and other agencies changed course, instituting what Cousens (2002) politely calls a *trusteeship strategy*. In reality this is authoritarian rule with Paddy Ashdown as the current dictator. He is doing much better than ethnic democracy did.

It is not just the fault of the leader, for the same processes affected all three levels of actor simultaneously. Leaders were part-manipulators but also part-hostages of the armed militants and the core constituencies. Milosevic had pledged to bring all Serbs into one state if the other republics prevented a revised Federation. He risked losing power if he did not press for Greater Serbia. But many other Serbs were sucked in by organic nationalist goals and the apparent military power sufficient to achieve them. The strategy of Tudjman and his militants and constituency differed in being more retaliatory than initiating. But Tudjman's regime had also come to power with an organic nationalism program, and it was difficult to backtrack on this when threatened by Serbs. Then a few border radicals provoked, persuaded, and coerced others into expanding chains of defensive, vengeful violence. The outcome at this stage of escalation was decided by paramilitary or military power. Once civil open debate and elections were squarely won by ethnonationalists, the radicals armed themselves the better. In most of the conflicts analyzed, violence from above and outside decided the outcome, sometimes organized by the state, sometimes by the homeland state, sometimes by armed militant bands. Armed Croats from Zagreb killed Osijek's moderate police chief. A passing HVO detachment finished off the Ostociji clan in Medjugorgje. In the Lasva Valley radical Croats were backed by Grude and Zagreb funneling military resources from emigres and through the HVO. Serbs in Croatia, Bosnia, and Kosovo aggressed across broad fronts, armed by Milosevic and the JNA. Each radical victory silenced moderates before the out-group was attacked. The ethnic civil war mobilized both communities, persuading each state and statelet to pour more resources into violence.

Descent over the brink involves the three main actors of my thesis 7: party-state elites, armed militants, and core constituencies of nationalism.

They never constituted a majority for ethnic cleansing, but they did mobilize electoral majorities supporting ethnic defense. Two colliding armed defenses produced ethnic war. Ideological control of the media and superior political and military power could then bring more general compliance when the enemy (under similar pressures) retaliated. But it is striking how complex were the power relations involved. Early on, the democratization of politics made leaders and mass electorates oppose compromise. Then a few radicals and armed militants in the border areas played a disproportionate role in ending a period of stalemate. Then Milosevic's party-state escalated aggression. Then the unexpected inefficiency of its means and the unexpected strength of resistance produced massive escalation. The overall process was not rational, though the actors were trying to calculate means–ends relationships in an instrumentally rational way. They failed, and murderous cleansing ensued.

The killers were much less organized and drilled than had been the Nazis. Their atrocities were wilder – and so less efficient. Of the Nazi era killers, they most resembled the Ustasha – the supreme irony for Serb killers. Motives were typically mixed, as a man in a Seselj paramilitary in Kosovo confessed: "I am a Serbian patriot. I fought for the Serbian cause. And also for the sake of money, money was the main thing. . . . Back then, revenge felt very good. Especially when we killed the KLA. That was back then. Now I can't sleep, I can't eat. It hasn't lasted" (Judah, 2000: 246). Hard-core perpetrators were rather mundane thugs. If in many countries across the world young men are given guns, told to remove the enemies of the people, and licensed to enrich themselves and get drunk, some are likely to commit mayhem and enjoy it. Combine the characteristics of European football hooligans, American gun lovers, and security policemen from across half the world into a single paramilitary unit and license them to pursue ethnic cleansing – especially against people more privileged than themselves – and wild murder and rape might ensue in many countries. Regimes also wished to have thugs do this, for then they could deny responsibility. Again, mundane social structures, processes, and cultures, amid objectively dangerous ethnic/state configurations, led toward murderous cleansing through mainly unintended escalations.

14

Rwanda, I
Into the Danger Zone

Unlike Europe, there has been no long-term trend toward an ethnically cleansed African continent. Not that ethnic violence is lacking. As Horowitz (1985) showed, the building blocks of African politics are almost all ethnic. Parties, and factions of military officers, represent ethnic groups or regional groups that are also substantially ethnic. Most African states are weak, with little infrastructural penetration of their territories, prone to factionalism and some to disintegration. Their weakness often leads to repression and coups involving brutal murders of opponents. Civil wars bring mass killing that often takes ethnic coloration where different regions have majorities and minorities on different sides of the war. This has happened in Biafra, Angola, the Congo, Liberia, and Sierra Leone. Wars between states used to be uncommon, though they have increased in recent years. Particularly destructive wars with ethnic overtones have recently surfaced in Central Africa, triggered by the events described in this chapter.

But a major restraining factor has been the sheer multiethnicity of African states. Tanzania is reputed to have 120 identifiable ethnic groups. Though its parties and factions are often organized along ethnic lines, any wishing to reach power must join in multiethnic coalitions with other parties. Elaborate bargaining then steers politicians into an instrumental view of ethnicity. This typically results in discrimination against ethnic groups denied a share in the patronage system that is so important in developing countries. But it does not encourage value commitment to organic ethnonationalism. As Scarrit (1993) says, most sub-Saharan African politics concern multiethnic coalitions of low ideological intensity. Ethnic groups rarely demand "territorial revisionism," since state boundaries are rarely disputed. Contrary to popular belief, the colonial powers fixed most state boundaries rather sensibly. Some of the few secession movements seek to restore colonial boundaries (as in Eritrea and Somalia). Few ethnic groups seek national independence, and even fewer urge their state to war to aid brethren across the border. The "Minorities in Danger" project data suggest that (at least until the early 1990s) African ethnic conflict was less severe than that of other continents, and that severe discrimination by ethnicity is uncommon (Gurr, 1993).

Things can get worse where macro-ethnic coalitions receive added political or ideological cement. Long dominant regimes can weld together disparate micro-groups into a single macro-ethnic identity, generating collective enmity from out-groups. In Zimbabwe the Shona language of the dominant historic kingdom diffused widely, conferring a macro-identity on the many micro-ethnic groups who spoke it. Shona speakers are about 80 percent of Zimbabwe and have sometimes been in conflict with the minority Ndebele-speaking peoples. The two groups formed the core of the rival ZANU and ZAPU anticolonial liberation movements. Nonetheless, these are less cohesive ethnicities than those of Europe, and they tend to fragment into micro-ethnicities. Having won the armed struggle against both ZAPU and the white settlers, ZANU leader Mugabe played a balancing game between macro- and micro-ethnicities within his single-party state (Schutz, 1990). His rule, like that of Museveni in Uganda in recent years, used to resemble the authoritarian balancing act between ethnicities that Tito practiced so long in Yugoslavia. Unfortunately, he then abandoned this policy for more brutal methods.

In other places, religion has provided ideological macro-cement, especially along the Christian–Muslim "fault line" running across North Africa. There ethnic diversity partially coalesces into Christian and Muslim macro-identities, the latter reinforced by the Arabic language. Religion provides the broadest swathe of ethnic conflict across Africa. Other Nigerian ethnic conflicts are nowadays dwarfed by polarization between the Muslim north and the Christian south, disputing the basic secular constitution of the state (Ibrahim, 1999). Easily the bloodiest case has been the Sudan, home to more than 50 micro-ethnic groups and 114 languages. The diverse ethnicities of the north, 70 percent of the population, have partially merged into a common Arabic-speaking Muslim macro-identity. Overriding opposition from moderate Muslim parties and brotherhoods, northern governments have intermittently tried to create an Islamic state over the whole country in which the Christians and animists of the south and west would play a subordinate role. Resistance was met by policed repression, and then by callous war and politicide. Over three decades, these murderous and famine-inducing conflicts have cost nearly 2 million lives and created 4 million refugees. Most of the victims have been among Christians and animists. Atrocities, including the enslavement of southern children, continue, though increasingly alternating with stuttering peace negotiations (Deng, 1990; Human Rights Watch, 2003; Voll, 1990). Then, in 2003, conflict exploded in the west of the Sudan, in Darfur. It originated as a struggle for land and wells between African agriculturalists and Arab cattle-herders, but then the Sudanese government joined in, forming and arming janjaweed militias of Arabs. Their attacks displaced one million Africans from their homes and involved killings and rapes in the thousands – massive murderous ethnic cleansing. This is not religiously based, since both sides are Muslims (Human Rights Watch, 2004). The Sudan remains one of the two worst cases of ethnic conflict across the continent. They again reveal ethnic conflict escalating into the danger zone of cleansing where two macro-ethnic groups have a plausible and achievable claim to constitute their own state over the same territory. But the only full-fledged case of genocide and the severest case of politicide have both occurred in the other major case, the unusual bi-ethnic environment of two countries in the Central African Great Lakes region.

POLITICIDE AND GENOCIDE IN RWANDA AND BURUNDI

In this chapter, I try to explain the repeated waves of murderous ethnic cleansings in Rwanda and Burundi. In Burundi most estimates of the number killed are somewhat short of 5,000 during 1965, close to 200,000 in 1972–3 (up to 5 percent of the total population), 15,000–20,000 in 1988, 1,000–3,000 in 1991, and close to 100,000 in 1993. Since then killings have continued in irregular waves. Perhaps another 100,000 died during the last six years of the 20th century. After 1993 about 375,000 Burundians fled abroad and about 400,000 fled to other parts of Burundi. The victims have been overwhelmingly Hutus, while the government has remained Tutsi-dominated. The two ethnic groups then retreated into segregated and militarized communities (Laely, 1997: 695–7). By 2003 there were still about 300,000 living in refugee camps in Tanzania and another 300,000 displaced persons within Burundi. But a consociational power-sharing agreement was at last negotiated that year with the main Hutu rebel group, though a second rebel group refused to sign it. If the agreement does stick, then hundreds of thousands of refugees would return to their homes to find others living there. What then?

In Rwanda there were far more dead and they were overwhelmingly Tutsis. Governments were Hutu-dominated until the summer of 1994. Perhaps 1,000 Tutsis were slaughtered in 1959, 20,000 during the mid-1960s, and 2,000–10,000 in 1990–3. The killings culminated in full-scale genocide in 1994. In only 11 weeks beginning April 7, somewhere over 500,000 were murdered, a rate of over 300 murders every hour. This eliminated 75 percent of all Tutsis then living in Rwanda – the most rapid and complete genocide the world has ever seen. It was preceded and accompanied by politicide committed against both Tutsis and Hutus believed to be political opponents of the new regime. These victims may have totaled 10,000. The genocide ended only when an invading Tutsi emigre army, the Rwandan Patriotic Front (RPF), overthrew the perpetrating Hutu government. The RPF retaliated with its own massacres, killing somewhere between 25,000 and 100,000 civilian or POW Hutus (figures from Braeckman, 1994: 312; Des Forges, 1999: 15–16; Dravis and Pitsch, 1995–8; Lemarchand, 1997a; Organization of African Unity [henceforth OAU], 2000: chap. 22; Prunier, 1995; 199, 261–5; Thibon, 1995: 58, 76).

In all these outbursts, masses of victims also fled in pressured emigration, most into primitive refugee camps located over the border. These bred more trouble by organizing guerrilla raids back over the border. There were 2 million refugees from Rwanda and perhaps 300,000 from Burundi there in 1996. Many of their camps were controlled by officials and paramilitaries with prior careers in murderous cleansing, raiding back over the Rwandan border and adapting their murderous skills for the civil wars of Zaire–Congo. They have killed somewhere between 1 and 2 million people in the past seven years. They still rage. Michele Wagner (1998: 25) retains a vivid memory of encountering one young fighter along a road in Zaire:

In military fatigues, it was the determined face of the small boy – the only survivor among his siblings – who now served as a kadogo, or boy-soldier. His AK-47 strapped to his back, he served his officer with the wholehearted faithfulness and the no-holds-barred viciousness of a traumatized orphan who sees his commander as a father – the only "family" left in his world.

Things are not yet over. The current Rwandan Tutsi government charts an uneasy path between conciliation and revenge. In the summer of 2003 it won an overwhelming election victory, but partly because it had banned most Hutu parties. Tutsis dominate the government, the towns, and the monetarized economy; Hutus have been mostly forced back into subsistence agriculture. For Tutsis the motto is "We have our backs to the wall. Unless we maintain absolute control they will finish us next time," while Hutus say, "We only have to wait, numbers will play in our favour" (Prunier, 1997: 9–10). In Burundi there is limited consociational power sharing. The Tutsi government is ceding some entrenched powers to cooperating Hutu parties. However, one of the two main Hutu groups in armed rebellion refused to endorse the agreement or join in power sharing. The situation in both countries remains tense (Human Rights Watch, 2003).

Rwanda and Burundi contain only two significant ethnic groups (Twa pygmies form less than 1 percent of Rwanda), and each is able to form its own state. Before these troubles began, the Hutus comprised about 85 percent of the populations of both countries, the Tutsis about 15 percent. Though about 25 percent of Rwandans have both Hutus and Tutsis among their eight great-grandparents, almost all people readily identify themselves as either Hutu or Tutsi. The two countries are also unusual in Africa in being small and densely settled, with good communications, permitting intensive national mobilization. Both have formed viable states in both countries, the Hutu by weight of numbers, the Tutsi by superior political and military organization. Both have developed the legitimating ideologies seen in other murderous contexts. The Hutu see themselves as an oppressed *proletarian nation*, demand majoritarian democracy, and defend it from all threat. The Tutsis, as a former *imperial nation*, now challenged by democracy, feel threatened and supposedly defend the standards of a more civilized society. They both have rival plausible and achievable claims to their own state over the same territorial area.

Since the Tutsi are such a small minority, they cannot aim at genocide. They prefer the Hutus to remain as a lower class The most radical Tutsis have aimed only at politicide, the extermination of all potential members of a Hutu leadership elite. Thus Burundian events should not strictly be labeled as genocide (despite Lemarchand, 1995b, and Newbury, 1998). It is different for the majority Hutu, whose most radical militants have tried to eliminate the Tutsi, and in Rwanda they almost achieved it. The two groups also live side by side throughout the two countries. This would be normally regarded as a factor encouraging toleration, even multiculturalism. Yet if hostilities do arise between such groups, it becomes impractical to employ regional decentralization and confederation as solutions. Consociationalism might do better, where each group is entrenched within the constitution, parliament, administration, and armed forces. But this is an uncommon political ideal in an age dominated by the nation-state.

RWANDA–BURUNDI BEFORE INDEPENDENCE

As in other cases, such horrors were not the resurfacing of ancient or primitive rivalries. Hutus and Tutsis have not been fighting each other since time immemorial. Though a few journalists have written casually of the genocide as a resurgence of traditional or primordial tribalism, no specialist scholars have done so. Nonetheless, these are old ethnic groups. Indeed, even biology is relevant since there are average genotype and phenotype differences affecting blood groups, sickle cells, and lactose digestion. About half of the Rwandans could nowadays be recognized at sight by each other as being Hutu or Tutsi, these Hutus being shorter and broader (on average there is a 12 cm height difference). The Hutu are generally classified as part of the shorter, broader Bantu peoples, with the Tutsi grouped with other taller, leaner peoples for whom the common labels "Hima" or "Hamitic" are problematic since they originate in the Judeo-Christian Old Testament and were taken up by European racial theory. But the more prominent Tutsi families were cattle herders, while most Hutus were crop growers. Hutus probably descend from older agricultural inhabitants of the region, while Tutsis come from cattle-herding immigrants who by the 15th century had founded kingdoms to which most of the indigenous inhabitants submitted. The Tutsi identity may have been established already, but it soon came to indicate "the rulers." But *Hutu*, meaning "ruled," was probably a later creation of the Tutsi state, formed out of many indigenous peoples (Mamdani, 2001: chap. 2, gives the best account of these matters).

But then history got more complicated. The Tutsi state only ruled the central core of the present territories of Rwanda, alongside smaller independent Hutu polities. But all the states were built on a clan model, and Hutus were admitted to the same clans as Tutsis. The two groups interacted in 400 years of cultural assimilation, developing common customs and a single Kinyarwanda language. But the effects of intermarriage were reduced by social norms whereby the children of mixed marriages have been assigned to the father's ethnicity (Mboinimpa, 1999). By the 20th century Hutus and Tutsis knew who they were, and Tutsis were broadly ranked above Hutus, causing intermittent conflict mixing together class and ethnic grievances. But both ethnicities included rich and poor, powerful and downtrodden. Some Hutus were upwardly mobile, getting classified as Tutsi. So ethnic identities were firmly established but limited by class and of limited political relevance – as Chapter 2 noted was the norm in historical societies.

German (1908–24) and Belgian colonial rule (1924–62) then made ethnic consciousness more racial. Like other colonial regimes, they believed the ethnic groups confronting them were racially distinct. To the Belgians, Tutsis seemed to have some of the qualities of Europeans, yet they were black – so they had to be descended from ancient Hamitic conquerors from the north (Ethiopia or even the Middle East) who had imposed a more advanced "feudalism" on the "primitive" indigenous Hutu. Race added more permanent imputations of superiority/inferiority. The Belgians ruled through Tutsi elites, and the average difference in power resources between the two groups widened. The Belgians reduced the number of clans who could enjoy political office, sidelining Hutu-led clans. Ninety-five percent of the civil service, all but 2 of the 45 chiefs, and all but 10 of the 559 subchiefs were now Tutsis (Des Forges, 1999: 37). Many Tutsis and Hutus internalized this racial model, and Hutus had to try to rid themselves of the sense that Tutsis might be more beautiful than themselves (Malkki, 1995: 82–6). The Belgians also froze racial, political, legal, and educational privileges, reducing ethnic mobility. From 1933 everyone carried an identity card stating that he or she was either Tutsi, Hutu, or Twa. Sixty years later this was a deadly aid to genocide.

Since the Belgians regarded the European–African racial distinction as much more significant than any distinctions among the Africans, both Hutus and Tutsis were ruthlessly subjugated. So as Belgian rule weakened, they joined together in demanding freedom. Their clan and regional groupings became political parties usually led by Tutsis but mobilizing both ethnicities. The Belgians had fewer resources than the French or British to influence African political institutions in the transition period, and they had no valuable minerals to protect there. When pressured, they just quit, with little thought for postcolonial institutions. This was tragic, since Belgium itself had consociationalism: Flemish and Wallonian-French community rights were entrenched in the Constitution and in the central government. This form of constitution might have worked in the two colonies, entrenching Tutsi minority rights collectively amid a political process that (if democratic) would be probably dominated by Hutus.

A second colonial escalation came from a shift in Belgian policy. By the late 1950s Belgium was under pressure to move toward majoritarian democracy in its colonies. "One man, one vote," "majority rule" was the slogan of liberation movements across the continent and the globe. The UN and the Catholic and Protestant churches in both colonies became uncomfortable with the domination by small Belgian and Tutsi minorities over the Hutu majority. Biennial UN inspections of the colony emboldened Hutus, while progressive Social Catholics influenced them through schools and trade unions. As the colonies neared independence, the Belgians in Rwanda – much less in Burundi – began to switch patronage to the majority Hutus. Opening up education and public employment produced younger Hutus with an anticolonial slant on the Belgian view of local history. They viewed Tutsis as being earlier feudal colonialists. In Hutu refugee camps, Malkki heard a new variant of the old anticolonial story: the alien Tutsi had "stolen" the land by "trickery" and violence from the "rightful natives" or the "human beings," whom the Tutsis had renamed "Hutus," a Tutsi word meaning "slave" or "servant" (1995: 58–71). Hutu elites talked of being the "indigenous" and "proletarian" people. They said the *majority people* must now rule what was in effect their own country. This key term, says Prunier (1997a: 403–4), came to have the coded meaning that "one must be Hutu to be allowed to rule and that whoever rules in the name of the 'majority people' is ontologically democratic." This is a version of organic democracy, here potentially generating the demand that the Tutsis, residents but not really natives, should be removed from citizenship. Hutus were devising a plausible and potentially achievable claim to their own state, alternative to the traditional Belgian–Tutsi state.

THE POSTCOLONIAL REGIMES

By 1959 Belgian rule was faltering. Rwandan economic discontent led to a Hutu insurrection. Mbonimpa (1999) terms it a *peasant jacquerie*, like those accompanying the French or Russian Revolutions. Tutsi elites reacted with repression, which made the discontent less economic, more ethnic and political in form. The murder of a Hutu leader by members of a Tutsi youth movement produced an explosion in which hundreds of Tutsis were killed. Newbury (1988: chaps. 9, 10; 1998: 13) says the violence was aimed at educated and politically powerful Tutsi clans, not at Tutsis in general. Liberal Tutsis were also agitating on behalf of the disadvantaged of both ethnicities. Yet the massacres reinforced ethnic polarization, remembered by Hutus as a "gigantic liberation" and by the Tutsis as a "catastrophe" (Mbonimpa, 1999). They panicked 10,000 Tutsis into pressured emigration. In 1961 Hutu nationalists seized the African parts of the Rwandan state, probably with Belgian consent. The Belgians withdrew the next year, leaving Hutus commanding the state and Tutsis resisting the new rules of the political game.

This set up escalating interactions between the two states. The Rwandan coup traumatized Tutsi elites in Burundi. They determined not to relinquish power when independence came. In 1962 riots and murders pitted the JNR, a paramilitary Tutsi youth movement, against Hutu Catholic trade unionists.

In 1965 massacres occurred after the failure of a rising by Hutu soldiers. The Tutsi elite murderously cleansed the army and civil service of Hutus, provoking retaliatory murders by Hutus, which in turn intensified army repression from the Tutsi elite. But some Tutsis claimed to be modern multiculturalists, denying that minority rule involved ethnic discrimination. They asserted (reasonably enough) that a political majority, as opposed to an ethnic majority, was the key to a healthy democracy, and they cultivated Hutu clients who might give them majority support. This led to political conflict between rival Tutsi factions advocating moderation and repression, and between disaffected Hutu nationalists and apolitical Hutus who wanted success through the existing education and occupation structure (Lemarchand, 1995a: 76–105).

The splits among the Tutsis encouraged Hutu nationalists to resist. In the second escalating interaction between the countries, Hutu refugees from Rwanda (and Zaire) provided many armed militants. Their actions shifted power among the Tutsi to factions favoring repression. Since Tutsis monopolized state violence, repression could work in the short term, whereas conciliation was more uncertain. So began a downward spiral culminating in the terrible Burundi massacres of 1972. Amid the complex factionalism, there was also an underlying logic of ethnic polarization, rooted in the mutual provocations of the two sets of radicals, each eliciting a radical response from the other, intensifying each other's mobilizing power in its own ethnic community. The Tutsis monopolized military power (and could also funnel army weapons to paramilitaries); the Hutus had the weight of numbers to dominate any democracy. Thus both sets of radicals had plausible no-compromise strategies.

Burundi also affected Rwanda. Repression by Tutsis in Burundi radicalized Hutus in Rwanda. Though the new Rwandan state of 1962 was dominated by Hutus, its multiparty system was felt by many Hutus to divide the nation. A 1973 military coup led to a single-party dictatorship run by President Habyarimana. His 21-year regime enshrined the slogans "Majority democracy" and "Hutu Power." So during the 1960s and 1970s both countries became locked into severe ethnic discrimination, backed by policed repression and punctuated by bursts of pressured emigration. Since the two countries were mirror images, they exerted "powerful demonstration effects" on each other, increasing mutual distrust between both pairs of ethnic groups (Hintjens, 1999: 279; Lemarchand, 1995b: 407; OAU, 2000: paras. 3.23–3.29). Border areas were often important in fomenting trouble. Their residents felt threatened, and embittered refugees generated more perpetrators of ethnic violence. As we see in Map 14.1, Burundian radicals came especially from northern border zones with Rwanda (exchanging Hutu and Tutsi refugees from each other's troubles) and to a lesser extent from areas adjacent to the Zaire border. The major Burundi massacres of 1988 and 1991 and the main Hutu electoral successes of 1993 occurred there (Lemarchand,

1995a: 120–2, 153–5; Reyntjens, 1994: 55–61, 232–43). We will later see similar patterns in the Rwandan genocide.

The two states were careful not to antagonize each other. Instead, notes Hintjens (1999), there was a vicious cycle of "pre-emptive, internalized retaliation." Rather than aiding their persecuted co-ethnics, each government retaliated inside its own country until 1994, when Tutsis controlled both regimes. The OAU (2000) says, "it remains something of a mystery that the countries have never been willing to go to war with each other." But this reveals that ethnicity is not so salient that it creates value rationality (in Max Weber's sense) or a transcendent ethnic ideology, in which actors are committed to their ethnic group whatever the cost, whatever the means. Undercutting the ideology of ethnic solidarity was the instrumental rationality of political power. Ideologies of Hutu majoritarian democracy or Tutsi civilization have aimed *only* at seizing one's own state. The plight of one's co-ethnics abroad might be deplored, but it was not a reason to go to war. War was to be avoided for good instrumental reasons. As long as the states remained stable, their elites would probably reason thus.

But in developing states like these, political power also brings substantial economic gain. African scholars have noted "patrimonial" or "prebendal" states, dominated by a "state class" sweeping the continent (e.g., Ibrahim, 1999). In the Central Lakes region the Mobutu and Kabyle regimes of Zaire/Congo were the most notorious for the corruption of their state class. But Rwanda and Burundi were also affected. Helped by increasing foreign aid, economic development occurred in both of these very poor countries. In Rwanda foreign aid was only 5 percent of GNP when Habyarimana seized power. It had risen to 22 percent in 1991, constituting 75 percent of the state's capital budget (OAU, 2000: para. 4.20). As in other developing countries, aid and investment were channeled overwhelmingly through state and parastate agencies. "In Rwanda, as elsewhere in Africa, the state was the main if not the sole avenue for rapid wealth accumulation for the new elites" (Uvin, 1998: 21–3, 40). These elites were unusually mono-ethnic – overwhelmingly Tutsi in Burundi, Hutu in Rwanda. Habyarimana's own power base was even narrower, in patronage networks rooted in only 1 of Rwanda's 11 prefectures, Gisenyi, though also spreading to the neighboring northwestern prefecture, Ruhengeri. This can be see in Map 14.1.

This involved a regional shift of power among Hutus. The power base of the previous Hutu regime (of Kayibanda) had been in the center-south, in Gitarama and part of Butare prefectures. But now a northwestern patronage/corruption system distributed state and development aid resources to a favored Hutu minority, rivaling and then outdistancing the commercially based wealth of the Tutsi elite. Since political power was the way to wealth, Rwandan Hutus were no longer really a proletarian nation. But since only a few Hutus managed to swill lavishly at the trough, mainly urban educated northwesterners, the average Hutu remained poorer than the average Tutsi,

MAP 14.1. Prefectures and provinces of Rwanda and Burundi.

and so potentially receptive to proletarian ideology. And in all of Rwanda's *mille collines*, "thousand hills," ordinary policemen, school janitors, nationalized company workers, and others were marginal swillers, owing their jobs to the political class. Though poor, they were better off than those not swilling at all. Patronage networks could mobilize many thousands. Ethnic inequalities were more marked in Burundi, where Tutsi elites still monopolized political, military, and economic power. Economic power relations were to prove key in the buildup and commission of genocide. It is important not to overstate the significance of ethnic ideology in these two cases of cleansing. There was an ethnic economy too. But this was not ethnicity trumping class; it was the blending of the two, so that class interest was hidden behind ethnonationalist ideology.

The murders of 1959 had started the flow of refugees; discrimination and violence kept it flowing. These emigres included many ex-soldiers who formed the core of a Tutsi imperial revisionism, planning to invade Rwanda. The failure of their first two incursions, in 1963 and 1967, led to retaliatory waves of violence against Tutsis in Rwanda. Up to 20,000 Tutsis were killed during these years as supposed accomplices of the invaders. There was another burst of violence in 1973 as Habyarimana's regime purged Tutsis from the public sector. By the late 1970s almost half a million Tutsis had fled the country. But though the public sector was now largely cleansed of Tutsis, there was little killing between 1979 and 1990. If both communities accepted an implicit division of powers – Hutu elite dominating the state and development funds, Tutsis retaining a hold over much of the nonstate private economy – then this might settle into the suspicious coexistence characterizing the division of power between whites and blacks in much of postcolonial Africa. Both communities were now split. Hutu radicals argued that the nonindigenous Tutsis should be excluded altogether from citizenship. But the Habyarimana regime was in power, and it allowed the remaining Tutsis citizenship. It even sponsored ethnic reconciliation as long as Hutus controlled the public realm and the Tutsi emigres were not allowed back. On the Tutsi side, those who remained in Rwanda accepted this *force majeure*. There was as yet little reason to fear genocide.

ESCALATING ETHNIC CONFLICT, 1985–93

Then Rwanda felt three linked sets of external destabilizing pressures – from Burundi, from a Tutsi invasion, and from the international community. In Burundi, the Tutsi regime was clinging determinedly to power by lethal repression while allowing some Hutus into their networks of political clientelism. Few Hutus were allowed into the army, whose guns remained the bastion of Tutsi power. Ethnic consciousness increased among both groups, beginning in the towns, then spreading through the countryside. Unlike Rwanda, killings had a reciprocal logic: bloody Hutu risings were put down even more bloodily, with the Tutsi elite aiming to extirpate educated Hutus down to the secondary school level to end political opposition. This was ethnically aimed politicide, led by the army and the youth movement of the main Tutsi party, with Tutsi refugees from Rwanda, students, and even schoolchildren implicated. The Tutsi elite did not aim to cleanse the land of Hutus. They needed a lower class. Hutu extremists were trying to seize the state and make it their own. Yet in some areas, killings did cause communal riots to spiral into local genocidal bursts. Many Hutus fled into Rwanda. Some organized guerrilla raids back into Burundi; others were incorporated into the lower levels of Rwandan politics and accepted Hutu radicalism (Lemarchand, 1995a, 1995b; Reyntjens, 1994).

The Tutsi invasion of 1990 was the biggest blow to ethnic concilia-tion. It came from Uganda, a country that would face no retaliation and wanted to get rid of its troublesome Tutsis. Tutsi emigres had formed a key part of Musuveni's victorious army in the Ugandan civil war of the late 1970s and early 1980s. They might have settled down in Uganda amid other Kinyarwanda-speaking peoples. But most Ugandans resented them and blocked their advancement in the public sector and their demands for squat-ters' rights over land. The Tutsis were being pressured back to Rwanda. President Musuveni was keen to get rid of these unpopular armed men and offered them help in forming an army, the RPF, to reconquer Rwanda (Mamdani, 2001: chap. 6; Otunnu, 1999). It invaded Rwanda from the northeast in October 1990 (see Map 14.1). This foray was badly organized and quickly defeated, but the RPF regrouped along the Ugandan border throughout 1991 and advanced with more success into Rwanda in 1992 and 1993. Only French military assistance to the Hutu regime turned back the RPF at this stage.

This war made Hutu Power ideology more popular and more racial. The Tutsis were again behaving as alien invaders of the indigenous Hutu people of Rwanda. The war offered "night and fog" opportunities for the Hutu regime, especially for Hutu Power radicals in the northwest, who were most threatened by the invasion. Under the cloak of wartime censorship and mar-tial law, legitimated by wartime patriotism, they rounded up and often killed Tutsis and other accomplices of the RPF. Many young Tutsis fled north to join the invaders. In 1990–2, 200,000 Hutus fled south, 1 million more in the advance of 1993. Up to one-seventh of the population were now home-less and embittered. Bi-ethnicity remained only in the form of Tutsis trapped behind the Hutu lines (Mamdani, 2001: 186–92; Melvern, 2000: 57; OAU, 2000: para. 6.20). Yet the war was fought between two moderately orderly regimes. The RPF was formally multicultural, while Habyarimana remained willing to rule over Tutsis. International pressure – wielding the incentive of development funds – brought them to the bargaining table at Arusha in Tanzania in 1992, and they signed interim power-sharing agreements in 1993.

But there were also disruptive international pressures, first economic, then political. With the collapse of world commodity prices after 1985, coffee prices dropped 50 percent in 1989–90, while tin and tea prices fell more gradually. The economy in tatters, Habyarimana had to accept a rigid Struc-tural Adjustment Program from the International Monetary Fund and the World Bank in 1990 in order to qualify for loans. This neo-liberal "shock therapy" dramatically worsened the situation, ensuring that almost every family suffered a major reduction in income (OAU, 2000: chap. 5; Uvin, 1998: chap. 4). Discontent with the regime intensified. Rural unemployment and indebtedness forced young men to flock to the towns, to hang about the streets desperate for any economic crumbs. The National Revolutionary Movement for Democracy (MRND) regime attempted to keep them occupied with public works projects. Economic hardship increased discontent, but there was no necessary reason why this should be blamed on the Tutsis. Yet there were more indirect links. Economic discontent weakened and destabilized the regime. As we have seen, this is dangerous for ethnic relations in such contexts.

The political pressures came from the collapse of Communism across the world, increasing pressures for Western-style democratization. The Burundian and Rwandan regimes – under domestic pressure anyway – both conceded ground, allowing other parties to organize for elections. As I have emphasized, democracy can encourage ethnic tensions and violence if political parties organize by ethnicity. In Burundi international pressure led the Tutsi regime to risk presidential elections in 1993. A mainly Tutsi party, led by the president, faced a mainly Hutu party. Most Tutsi elites seemed confident that "their Hutus" would resist the "extremists," yet voting was sufficiently along ethnic lines to ensure an easy victory for the Hutu candidate. Though the Tutsi president accepted defeat and stood down, the Tutsi army did not. Composed for the most part of poorer Tutsis who feared the loss of their jobs (and their guns) to Hutus, they murdered the new president, formed their own regime, and systematically murdered both Hutus and Tutsis supporting the new government. This politicide once again fueled pressured emigration by Hutus into Rwanda, where they again provided lower-level Hutu Power militants.

Rwanda had responded in 1991 to international pressures and internal economic discontent by moving toward a multiparty constitution. Rwanda had a highly developed civil society with an associational life capable of generating political alternatives. Associations, parties, journals, and pamphlets flourished everywhere (Nsengimana, 1995). Habyarimana made his own party, the MRND, more election-friendly. Radical Hutu Power parties also emerged, notably the Coalition for Defense of the Republic. These put pressure on the MRND, causing some of its factions to radicalize. Moderate parties emphasized class rather than ethnic inequalities, trying to recruit Tutsis as well as Hutus in order to stop the war. Class appeals were the obvious way to unite Tutsi and Hutu discontent with exploitation by the state class. But this involved moderates in the dangerous game of negotiating with the enemy RPF. But while socialist appeals to class had gone down well in Africa decades before, socialism was now in international retreat. African socialism had declined as political parties became much less class-based than clientelist, mobilizing ethnic-regional coalitions hoping to grab the spoils of office.

In Africa vigorous party competition often generates street violence led by party youth movements. The ruling MRND merged an organization of football clubs among street children with a youth public works program, to generate a youth movement to demonstrate, march, and disrupt meetings. These activities provided an apprenticeship in low-level violence, escalating to physical assaults on opposition groups, denounced as the supposed accomplices of the invaders (Reyntjens, 1995: 57–8; Wagner, 1996: 30–3). Tambiah (1996) and Brass (1997) have perceived a correlation between vigorously contested elections and communal violence in India, Sri Lanka, and Pakistan involving violent "rent-a-crowds" of young men. Rwanda now had a somewhat polarized society, an invasion, a government losing one-party control, and an increase in violence. Electoralism turned virulent, and brawling between youth movements created public disorder in some provinces. Thousands of Rwandans now believed violence was the solution. Habyarimana's authoritarian regime had not been exactly peaceful, but democratization was making things worse, as in thesis 1c.

Under these pressures, the Habyarimana regime began to fragment, as in thesis 5. In 1992 leaders of opposition parties were admitted into a coalition cabinet, and different ministers pursued different policies. The president believed he was staring military defeat in the face, and so made concessions at the international peace negotiations held in Arusha, Tanzania. But his delegation was incoherent. Its "little house" members (see later) knew that any negotiated sharing of power with the enemy would end their rule as a state class; its opposition party members wanted peace; the president dithered between them. Their disagreements led to the fall of the coalition government in July 1993. A temporary rump government, without a clear electoral mandate, signed the Arusha Accords anyway – and survived for only one day into the genocide. The RPF, convinced it was winning the war, had held out for harsh demands. Habyarimana, fearing defeat, finally accepted them.

Yet the Arusha Accords were more than many Hutus could stomach. They excluded the radical Hutu Power parties from power sharing. This was probably a mistake (though it is easy to be wise after the event), since they would lose everything if the Accords worked. The MRND would also lose its control of the cabinet. The worst blow was that the army would become 60 percent Hutu, 40 percent RPF, but with the officer corps split 50/50. This would mean the demobilization into unemployment of over 20,000 Hutus of all ranks, most of them younger, noninheriting sons. Not only Hutu hard-liners rejected that. On more than one occasion, Habyarimana bent toward his radicals by rejecting peace terms to which his own diplomats had just agreed (Jones, 1999). This was now not a stable two-sided struggle, but a fluid three-sided one between a divided regime, an equally factionalized Hutu opposition, and the Tutsi emigre army (Gasana, 1995; OAU, 2000: chap. 8; Prunier, 1995: 99). Implementing the Accords depended on each side being a coherent actor capable of disciplining its own people. The RPF could manage this, since it was an army. But neither the Rwandan government nor the opposition parties could, since they were now all beset by internal radical factions and so were divided over the Accords. The Accords had been built on the premise that a moderate political center could be constructed in Rwanda, but this was fragmenting under the pressures of ethnic mobilization and militarization (Khadiogala, 2002: 492). Nor was the UN Security Council willing to back up the Accords with military muscle. Once again, danger was presented not by a stable, cohesive, or totalitarian state but by a weakening and, in this case, partially democratizing state beset by factionalism and radicalization.

HOW PREMEDITATED WAS GENOCIDE? THE LITTLE HOUSE AND PRIOR PLANNING

Most observers have viewed the genocide that began in April 1994 as highly organized and premeditated by Hutu radical elites. Hintjens (1999) emphasizes careful planning, which she repeatedly compares to the Nazi master plan for the Holocaust. Des Forges (1999: 95–128) believes a coherent master plan was developed over the years 1990–4, being initially hatched soon after the 1990 invasion. Reyntjens (1996) says the formation of "death squads" in 1991–2 was a "dress rehearsal" for genocide. Prunier (1995: 168–9) believes that by mid-1992 "the genocide plan was first put together in outline" by the hard-core conspirators. Longman (1999: 352) identifies a master plan, but dates it later, to around January 1994. A similar view has dominated prosecution cases at the UN War Crimes Tribunal sitting at Arusha. Since we know what eventually transpired, it is tempting to view prior escalations as stages in a single planned process. But this would be mistaken. What more probably happened was that as the regime lost cohesion and then its presidential head, and as it suffered a coup and was then rebuilt, it experienced a radicalization that few had anticipated beforehand, but that was also paralleled by a radicalization of sentiments among ordinary Hutus. Genocide was then improvised by radical elites and militants out of opportunity and threat. It was not long nourished as a Plan A. I am not alone in this view (Mamdani, 2001; Mbonimpa, 1999; OAU, 2000: chap. 7). But we must reconstruct the unfolding of genocide before we can adjudicate this dispute.

Most researchers see genocide as planned beforehand by a clique of leaders within the ruling MRND party-state, conventionally called the *Akazu*, or "little house," later assisted by other Hutu Power factions.[1] A 1998 UN War Crimes Tribunal indictment referred to a conspiracy involving 18 high officials of the president's own party, the MRND. Allegedly, from late 1990 until July 1994, "they conspired ... to work out a plan with the intent to exterminate the civilian Tutsi population and eliminate members of the opposition so

---

[1] I have followed this convention but with some unease. The Akazu was a coherent patronage network, many of whose members were Hutu Power radicals. But I have not seen direct evidence that it actually organized the genocide. My unease is shared by Mamdani (2001).

that they could remain in power" (*Ubutabera*, No. 46, September 28, 1998). The Tutsi invasion led the radicals to press for more extreme measures. A few moved toward urging the elimination of all Tutsis, the accomplices of the invaders: three Tutsi invasions in 15 years required something more than just coerced emigration, since emigres returned, armed. Only mass murder would solve this problem. They recognized the moral taboos they were breaking but felt that killings would be self-defense – the defense of the majoritarian democracy of the indigenous proletarian nation.

Being a state class, the plotters also had economic motives. The little house had first appeared as a patronage network of the clan of Habyarimana's wife. Compliant history professors gave it legitimacy by tracing its lineage back to precolonial Hutu kingships (Hintjens, 1999: 259). The house centered on the prefecture of Gisenyi, which alone provided one-third of the country's top government officeholders, most of the top army and security service officers, and a disproportionate number of university professors and graduates. The neighboring prefecture of Rusengeri was also overrepresented in all these elite positions (Des Forges, 1999: 47, 71). Yet little house power was threatened by looming defeat in the civil war, by Arusha power sharing formulas, and by the multiparty system that would also give patronage to rivals.

Ideological Power

Partly out of ideological conviction, partly to protect their position as a state class, some little house members were radicalizing all four sources of power after the Tutsi invasion of 1990. The most serious radicalizations came after the Arusha Accords of August 1993. Even among the hard-core plotters, Hutu radicalization was a response to real Tutsi threats. In the sphere of ideological power, little house members radicalized in response to the October 1990 invasion. They began to denounce as accomplices of the enemy all Tutsis plus Hutus who opposed the president. Three declarations stand out. Shortly after the 1990 invasion, the newsletter *Kangura*, owned by Habyarimana's private secretary and the army chief of staff, delivered "Ten Commandments" to Hutus. Three of them commanded that Hutus should stop having sex with members of other races, acquire control of "every strategic point" of power, and "stop having mercy on Batutsi." In September 1992 the next chief of staff, also from Gisenyi, aided by Col. Théoneste Bagasora (of whom more later), issued a memorandum to help the army identify its enemies. It equated the RPF with Tutsis in general, who were seeking to "turn public opinion from the ethnic problem to the socio-economic problem between the rich and the poor." The enemies are named as Tutsi refugees, the Ugandan army, Tutsis inside the country, foreigners with Tutsi wives, "the Nilo-hamitic peoples of the region," "Hutu malcontents," the unemployed, and fleeing criminals. The memo did not specify what the army should do to these enemies after they were apprehended. Most Hutu Power rhetoric was still rather windy and vague. But in November 1992 Mugusera, the Gisenyi MRND vice president, made an openly exterminist speech. He denounced Rwandan Tutsis and the opposition parties as "cockroaches talking to other cockroaches." He urged, "exterminate this scum!" "What are we waiting for to execute the sentences? . . . What are we waiting for to decimate these families?" "Destroy them. No matter what you do, do not let them get away." "The fatal mistake we made in 1959 was to let them get out. . . . They belong in Ethiopia and we are going to find them a shortcut to get there by throwing them into the Nyabarongo River. . . . We have to act. Wipe them all out." His speech was distributed throughout Rwanda on cassette. But Mugusera had gone too far. He was threatened with prosecution by the justice minister and fled abroad. He remains in Canada, fighting deportation. Though radical rhetoric was growing within the party-state, it did not dominate it. Nor did any of this cause panic among Tutsis (Braeckman, 1994: 153; Chrétien, 1997: 93; Des Forges, 1999: 62–3, 84–5; Kakwenzire & Kamukama, 1999: 74–7; Melvern, 2000: chap. 6; OAU, 2000: para. 9.9)

Yet the radicals were acquiring control of mass media (Chrétien et al., 1995). Sixty-six percent of Rwandans were literate; 29 percent of households had radios, and more listened in public places. Eleven of the 42 journals founded in 1991 came out of the little house (including *Kangura*). In June 1993 a dynamic and popular radio station, KTLM ("Radio Thousand Hills"), began broadcasting, combining popular music, humor, and radical rhetoric. Two-thirds of its backers were MRND northwesterners, though CDR Hutu Power radicals were also involved. Government-run media were also shedding some moderate journalists. The radical media described the Hutus as "democrats," the "majority people," or the "great majority," attacked by the Tutsi RPF "cockroaches" (occasionally "snakes" or "rats") helped by Tutsi "accomplices" and Hutu "traitors" inside Rwanda – all seeking to reimpose "feudalism" or "slavery" on the Hutu. Those of mixed ethnicity were sometimes described as "hybrids" or "beings with two heads." The Tutsis were part of a "Hima plot" stretching across Africa, so Hutus must lead the whole "Bantu people" against it. From late 1993 radicals urged, "Do not repeat the mistake of 1959"; "this time let us finish the work." Forcing them out was no good, since they kept coming back with armies. "Work," "clearing," or "cleansing" were the euphemisms for murder. Each RPF offensive brought patriotic calumnies down on the heads of Hutu moderates and Rwandan Tutsis.

It is never easy to gauge the effects of mass media in the absence of detailed sociological studies. Many scholars have a tendency to exaggerate the power of this propaganda. People are not cultural dopes: they can make their own judgments about the plausibility of extremist ideology. Since it did not correspond to most people's experience, it did not dominate the country. But the war was making it more plausible.

Political and Economic Power

The multiparty system meant that after 1992 the MRND lost some control of state patronage, especially in the south and center of the country. But since all parties were patronage networks, they contained people of varied ideologies. During 1992–4 almost all the parties split into moderate and Hutu Power factions. Many opposition activists wanted to swill at the MRND-controlled trough, while the MRND was aware that it needed more support in the south (much of the north was in enemy hands) and could offer state patronage to get it. But Tutsis were fleeing north to the RPF, often with helpful intelligence – there really were accomplices. Finally, all Hutu politicians had to consider what might happen should the RPF win the war. Many looked next door to Burundi and saw Tutsi repression of all Hutu politicians. Hutu Power ideology was sweeping across the Hutu community. The little house and the Free Radio and Television of the Thousand Hills (RTLM) encouraged the divisions among their opponents by mobilizing a loose umbrella movement of Hutu Power radicals from several parties, yielding some power to other radicals. The effect of the strategy was to divide all the parties, including the MRND. The party-state was radicalizing and factionalizing. Those tasting economic and political power for the first time were becoming dependent on a radical rather than a conciliatory solution.

Military Power

Military power involved the army and paramilitaries. The war had suddenly expanded the army from 5,000 to 30,000 men, which weakened its cohesion. In mid-1992 radicals, probably led by Bagasora, formed a secret Hutu Power military society called the Amasasu, partly a pressure group for more radical military policy, partly a death squad. But though the radical trend enabled some moderate officers to be purged, the army remained divided. In one revealing incident in August 1993, little house colonels (including Bagasora) tried to kidnap the moderate prime minister but were thwarted by the new chief of staff. In any case, most of the army was at the front, more concerned with the RPF than with enemies in the rear.

The main military radicalization occurred within the party youth groups (Reed, 1996: 496). These had been originally formed to protect party meetings, though the biggest one, the MRND youth group, also engaged in rural self-help work, turning the corvee forced labor traditionally exacted from the Hutu (but not the Tutsi) population to uses that were praised by foreign aid donors. At some point in 1991, first in Gisenyi, the MRND youth group became paramilitarized as the *Interahamwe*, literally "those who stand [or "work"] together." Work was seen as a defining quality of the "Hutu nation." Hutus were "tough," "solid," in contrast to the parasitic Tutsis, whose "delicate constitutions" were unsuited for labor. "They cannot do painful chores" or, in more proletarian ideology, "They eat our sweat" (Malkki, 1995: 78–80). A smaller militia was formed from the youth wing of the CDR Hutu Power party, the *Impuzamugambi,* "those who have only one aim," also calling themselves "the Hutu hard and pure." From 1991 they were given basic military training by sympathetic army officers – sometimes by French military advisers. In the spring of 1993 the *Interahamwe* came under the umbrella of a new civilian self-defense force, which Bagasore and others had pressed for in February. Its units were organized to fight the invaders in their own home area, a reasonable task in an invaded country and first devised in the invasion of 1963. But this one was staffed by radical MRND politicians and army officers. Civil war produces the most intense local mobilization of the civilian population; ethnic civil war mobilizes on an ethnic basis. It was now very difficult for any Hutu, or indeed for any Tutsi in an RPF-occupied zone, to retain a moderate or even an apolitical stance. The nation was finally trumping class, at least among young men.

Wealthy MRND supporters made generous donations to provide pay and arms to the paramilitaries. In 1993 came purchases of large quantities of small arms, machetes, and other sharp agricultural implements abroad. Most of the funds were diverted from foreign aid funds. Over half a million machetes were imported from China in late 1993, one for every third adult Hutu male. This was neither a traditional Rwandan tool nor a useful weapon of war against a well-equipped invading army. It was definitely sinister apparent, preparation for killing unarmed enemies – Melvern (2000: chap. 6) flatly says "for genocide." The regime had also learned from other African experience and preferred to supply the militias with machetes rather than guns (Prunier, 1995: 243). Men so armed would be less of a threat to public order after genocide was accomplished.

Many of the paramilitaries might be considered thugs, but their violence was directed to goals that could be expressed in principled terms. Here is one of their songs:

> We are the MRND Interahamwe.
> We love peace, unity and development.
> We don't attack, we come to the rescue.
> We are not frightened, we frighten others.
> We don't let ourselves get downtrodden,
> On the contrary we trample on others.
> We will silence wrongdoers.
> He [Habyarimana] has brought peace and we sleep safely.
> We are independent and imbued with democratic principles
>
> (*Ubutabera,* No. 38, 1998)

These lovers of peace and democracy would frighten, trample, and silence the wrongdoers!

Organized violence against Tutsis and moderate politicians escalated soon after the RPF invasion in October 1990. In 17 local incidents of ethnic violence between October 1990 and February 1993, well over 2,000 Tutsis died. Fourteen of the incidents were in the little house stronghold provinces of Gisenyi and Ruhengeri. Most were responses to RPF advances. Some were merely local affairs, but at least five were organized from above. In 1991 a Tutsi subgroup, the Bagogwe, was massacred in Gisenyi. This incident started with commune meetings addressed by Kigali officials who were also Gisenyi MRND notables. They told the locals that the Tutsis were aiding the RPF and should be killed as accomplices. MRND paramilitaries then led off the locals to do it. The locals complied, without obvious enthusiasm. This was not systematic wiping out of populations. Yet it was clear that these methods could kill quite efficiently (Des Forges, 1999: 87–91; Prunier, 1995: 136–44; (*Ubutabera*, No. 38, 1998).

Army death squads began in mid-1992. The "Zero Network" was probably organized by the Amasasu to funnel guns to off-duty soldiers and *Interahamwe*. During 1992 and 1993 about 200 political opponents, both Tutsi and Hutu, were killed in this way. Paramilitary and military Hutu Power radicals were now an important pressure group within the party-state, and their violence was going unpunished (Des Forges, 1999: 56–9; Gasana, 1995). But when Braeckman (1994) says they were orchestrating a well-oiled "killing machine," this implies that they were preparing for something much worse – for which there is no evidence. But by the end of 1993 a few insiders certainly were contemplating worse. Kakwenzire and Kamukama (1999: 79) instance three November meetings to discuss how to eliminate all Tutsis and all Hutu opponents – one, they say, was chaired by Habyarimana himself. But they give no sources for these meetings. Plans were certainly being laid soon afterward. In January 1994 a disaffected but credible MRND–*Interahamwe* leader told the UN of a plan to use 1,700 armed men scattered in groups of 40 throughout Kigali to exterminate all the Tutsis in the capital. Lists of hundreds of opponents to be eliminated were shown to foreign diplomats and reporters. Throughout the next months, rumors of projected massacres multiplied amid signs of disunity among the MRND. On the one hand, informants were breaking ranks to alert outsiders; on the other hand, more were urging extermination. Colonel Bagasora, seemingly the key little house plotter, bluntly told UN officials on April 4 that "the only plausible solution for Rwanda would be the elimination of the Tutsi" (OAU, 2000: para. 9.13; Reyntjens, 1995: 662–7). Three days later he was leading it.

We know of no precise plans or conspiracies before April 7, 1994. There are no "smoking gun" documents. In late 1993 radicals were probably preparing, six to eight months before genocide began. But the little house, their plots, and their connections with the paramilitaries and the parties all remain shadowy. Any actual Plan would have been secretive, confined to a few people. A larger group of radicals were shooting their mouths off, and small paramilitaries and death squads were acquiring license to kill. Many ordinary Hutus were implicated in the radicals' patron–client networks. But was genocide being planned? Or were these only loosely connected escalations, generated by an erratic war and by complex interactions within an increasingly factionalized state?

In Kibuye prefecture, Mayor Bagilishema took many of the steps that most commentators see as preparation for genocide. He started military training for the *Interahamwe,* forwarded lists of people suspected of aiding the RPF, and set up local roadblocks. But he thought these were necessary and patriotic steps in a civil war, and he accompanied them with exhortations for Hutus and Tutsis to stick together and not let extremists (including his own Hutu Power deputy) divide them (Case ICTR-95-1A-I; he was acquitted of all charges, and his story was believed by the court). A few Hutus may have seen these as preparations for genocide, but it is unlikely that many did. They were neither publicly known nor widely feared. Neither Tutsis nor moderate Hutus appear to have organized resistance or flight. The victims were as astonished as German Jews had been. Indeed, in this case it was a literal bolt from the blue that sealed their fate.

15

Rwanda, II
Genocide

In the 1994 genocide we can identify six main levels of perpetrator:

1. The Hutu MRND little house clan that seized power on April 7, 1994;
2. Other Hutu Power political factions entering the post-coup regime;
3. Cooperating Hutu officials and army and police officers;
4. Cooperating Hutu local social elites;
5. Hutu paramilitaries;
6. A large number of ordinary Hutus.

The first five of these formed the various levels of a party-state, brandishing an extreme ideology and dispensing economic patronage through public offices, nationalized industries, and aid and development funds. Their ideological, economic, military, and political powers enabled them to mobilize group 6 in a genocidal process. This chapter traces this mobilization process.

Some degree of indirect blame can also be laid on the Great Powers, especially France, allied to the Hutu regime, and the United States, which blocked any UN intervention. General Romeo Dallaire, commanding the small UN force already in Rwanda, asked for reinforcements as soon as the killings began, insisting that 5,500 troops could prevent genocide. Pentagon advisers were later to endorse his assessment, yet the UN did not respond since the Security Council's permanent members, led by the United States, refused to provide troops or money. All this is laid bare by the International Panel of Eminent Personalities (IPEP) Report of the Organization for African Unity and, more bitterly, by Melvern (2000: chap. 14), who believes the Great Powers knew what was happening and still refused to intervene. The OAU is milder, detecting indifference toward Africa but saying that in the comfortable, moralistic atmosphere of the UN, genocide "was literally unthinkable" – "it was simply beyond comprehension that it could be possible" (OAU 2000: paras. 7.13, 9.1). But mistakes, naiveté, even indifference do not constitute criminality. The actual perpetrators were Hutus.

The main sources on the genocide are, firstly, three detailed reports, by African Rights (1994), Human Rights Watch (edited by Des Forges, 1999), and the Organization of African Union (OAU, 2000); then Scott Straus's (2004) unique account of interviews with 210 Hutu perpetrators, backed up by intensive regional and local analyses; and finally the court records of the

UN International Criminal Tribunal for Rwanda, held in Arusha, Tanzania, and available at the UN ICTR website. The full transcripts are not publicly available (unlike those for Yugoslavia – Europe gets more resources than Africa). Nonetheless, its final judgments are long and very detailed, and can be supplemented with the regular case summaries published in the journals *Ubutabera, Tribunal Updates,* and *Hirondelle* (all online). Little information has come out of trials held by the Rwandan government, though its journal *Le Verdict* gives a few details. Currently, 80,000 persons are being detained in the country as genocide suspects (Straus collected his sample from among the detainees who had pleaded guilty), though the government has so far had the resources to try only about 7,000 of them. It is planning mass people's trials, called *gacaca* (literally "justice on the grass"), due to begin on a national scale in 2003 but repeatedly delayed.

THE LITTLE HOUSE CONSPIRACY BEGETS A COUP

On the evening of April 6, 1994, two SAM-16 surface-to-air-missiles destroyed the plane carrying the presidents of Rwanda and Burundi from Arusha as it was about to land at the Rwandan capital, Kigali. All on board were killed. The assassins remain unknown. Most have assumed that they were Hutu Rwandan Army extremists unhappy at the peace accords. Yet there are arguments against this theory. The Rwandan Army does not have SAM-16s, whereas the Ugandan army does. Several prominent Hutu Power radicals on the plane were also killed, and several other radicals on the ground immediately fled for refuge into the French Embassy on hearing of the attack, assuming this would begin a Tutsi coup. In 2000 reports emerged of confessions by Tutsi RPF officers that they had shot down the plane. On March 9, 2004, the French newspaper *Le Monde* reported that a French government judicial investigation into the shooting down of the plane had concluded that the order had been given by Paul Kagame, head of the RPF and now president of Rwanda. This conclusion was reportedly based on the testimony of RPF defectors. There was no official French government confirmation of this, and, of course, Kagame and the Rwandan government denied it.

The sequence of events through April 6–12 point less to a prearranged genocidal plan by Hutu radicals than to their seizing an unexpected chance created by an assassination committed by someone else. The news of the attack broke at 9 PM on April 6. There was confusion in the capital, and the first murders of Hutu moderates and leading Tutsis began over 10 hours later. This time delay does not suggest a prearranged coup and genocide. One of the plotters, Major Ntabakuze, was overheard saying, "They have killed him [Habyarimana], but many people will be buried before him to serve like a bed of straw" (www.hirondelle.org, Feb. 18, 2003). Generalized killing throughout the country did not spread until about April 12. But even if radicals hadn't planned the assassination, they felt they had to move quickly to protect their power position. This factionalized regime was now headless, deprived of the man who had managed to keep minimal control over both the radical and moderate wings of an increasingly divided party. Constitutional succession might pass to the moderate prime minister and national assembly leaders who might move against the radicals. Every level of the army and government was divided. A power vacuum existed in the capital.

It was filled by Col. Théoneste Bagasora, born in 1941 in Gisenyi, close to the president's own birthplace, the son of a wealthy teacher with good connections. Théoneste was an able career soldier whose connections brought him to the center of power. Like his brother, a banker, he was at the center of the little house, close to the president's wife and her brothers. A disaffected member of the Arusha delegation, he purportedly left Arusha declaring that he was returning to Rwanda "to prepare the apocalypse." He had openly stated that if the Arusha Accords were implemented, the result would be the extermination of the Tutsis. It is alleged that in 1993 he wrote a plan for using the civilian self-defense force for mass killing of Tutsis. In February 1993 he had secretly distributed weapons to MRND supporters in Gisenyi. His extreme Hutu Power views had generated distrust within the High Command and he had been denied the position he coveted, chief of the general staff. He was now chief of staff at the Ministry of Defense. His trial at Arusha is now underway (Trial Case Number ICTR-96-7), though at a very slow rate, with numerous adjournments.

In testimony given to the UN Tribunal on January 20, 2003, General Romeo Dallaire, the Canadian who had headed the UN forces in Rwanda at the time of the genocide, said, "It was Bagasora who held the real power. He even overshadowed higher-ranked officers." He described Bagasora as an extremist, resolutely opposed to the Arusha Accords, spoiling for a final crushing of Tutsi power. Throughout the turmoil, he said, Bagasora remained calm and undisturbed. "It was as though everything was going according to plan," or alternatively, "as though he was living on another planet." But, Dallaire added, "The plan aimed at exterminating the opposition," that is, only the political opposition – a politicide, in the terms I have used in this book. Given the extent of the killings, Dallaire said, it was difficult to imagine that someone could have planned them. It was "impossible that a plan to carry out such a holocaust could have existed." Dallaire blamed it on "overspills" adding on to what had been planned "on the political side" (www.hirondelle.org).

Even so, however, Bagasora seemed shocked by the assassination. He did send soldiers to surround the prime minister's house and prevent her from reaching the radio station, but he spent that night and the next morning meeting senior army officers in the capital, trying to talk them into a coup. They refused, and in late morning there were skirmishes between the presidential guard, controlled by Bagasora, and opposed military and gendarmerie forces. Bagasora was aided by seven senior officers, one of whom was now the prefect of Kigali. They were little house men, commanding 1,500 presidential guardsmen (drawn from Habyarimana's own district in Gisenyi), three elite army battalions of 1,000 men each, and 2,000 MRND paramilitaries, plus the prefecture's police and transport. These forces were all outside the ordinary army chain of command, and together they outgunned other forces in the city. Comparable concentrations of military power existed only at the front. The chief of the general staff and the national police chief appealed to UN forces to intervene, in vain.The next evening, hearing of the coup, the RPF broke the Arusha truce and resumed its advance, cutting away the ground from beneath the Hutu moderates.

But on the afternoon of the 7th, Bagasora had overcome the moderate officers in Kigali. UN General Dallaire reported that these "were never able to coalesce because every unit they had under command had been totally infiltrated... they would not risk their lives and the lives of their families. And so they never coalesced within the first few days to build moderate capability to overrun the extremists" (OAU, 2000: para. 14.13). In Bagasora's trial, evidence was presented of a Major Jabo who refused to kill Tutsis. Bagasora spat in his face and had him transferred to the front, to die (www.hirondelle.org, April 20, 2004). The paramilitaries dug up their hidden weapons and manned roadblocks to intercept and kill suspicious persons. Ironically, Hutu relatives of the prefect were killed at roadblocks by paramilitaries who thought they looked Tutsi. By the late afternoon of the 7th the prime minister and other moderate Hutu politicians, civil servants, and businessmen with ties to the opposition were dead. Dissenters were cowed into silence or hiding, but they were gradually rounded up. By mid-May, 26 of the 33 leaders of the moderate PSD (Social Democratic Party) were dead – and so was their class analysis of Rwanda's problems. Politicide preceded genocide.

On April 8 Bagasora abandoned his plan for a military regime, and over the next three days the plotters formed a civilian government. Their cabinet comprised 12 MRND radicals, including 3 of the little house plotters, plus 8 Hutu Power radicals from other parties, most being southerners, an attempt to broaden the base of the regime into opposition-controlled regions. Frodouard Karamira, head of the MRD (Democratic Republican Movement), was the key figure among the Hutu Power allies. On April 8 he broadcast an appeal for all radicals of whatever party to support the new regime; on April 12 he urged them to exterminate all Tutsis (he was executed for genocide by the new Rwandan government in 1999). The driving force inside the cabinet was Karemera, a long-term minister and little house insider, the key figure in MRND–*Interahamwe* links during the early 1990s. As interior minister he now headed the civil service, and so could appoint and dismiss the prefects – a key political power resource. As vice-chairman of the MRND, he was also one of the three top leaders of the *Interahamwe*, who were to prove the main killers.

Army resistance took longer to overcome. Senior military officers met with the new cabinet on April 16, urging them to call off the killings, which they said were damaging morale among the troops, making defeat more likely. But next day the army chief of staff was dismissed and other resisting army and police officers were threatened, arrested, or transferred to the front and replaced by more reliable officers. The rank-and-file soldiers generally did as ordered, some with enthusiasm (African Rights, 1994: 132–49; Des Forges, 1999: 104–9, 187–95, 268–9, 434–46, 462, 500; Melvern, 2000: chap. 12; *Ubutabera*, September 28, 1998).

Many have emphasized the cohesive criminality of the Rwandan state (e.g., Braeckman, 1994; Chrétien et al., 1995: 379; Reyntjens, 1995). After all, this had been "the Switzerland of Africa," neat and well ordered, with a public administration that was, for Africa, unusually efficient, radiating down from the cabinet through 11 regional prefects, their subprefects, and their 145 commune mayors to the councillors and police forces of each *colline*. In a small, densely settled country with good main roads, this had usually provided a relatively tight network of control entwining with dense civil society institutions – churches, rural cooperatives, tontine credit associations, and nongovernmental organizations. But by now this state was divided from top to bottom into various party factions so that the genocide was not statist in the conventional sense. Party and state offices were entwined, and holding them also made one an important notable in local society. State was not clearly separated from society in this hitherto cohesive though now divided country.

The radicals began to replace opposed officials. Three of the 11 prefects were dismissed, and 2 of these were killed. Several dozen subprefects and mayors were also dismissed (Des Forges, 1999: 264–5). Other notables with doubts were frightened by the circulating lists of supposed accomplices. Were their own names on the list? There was considerable confusion, and the killings sometimes seemed quite arbitrary. Thomas Kamilindi, a dissident journalist, was about to be shot when a passing Hutu major shouted "Thomas?" Thomas shouted back, "they're doing me in." The major (whom Thomas did not actually recognize) stopped them. Thomas continued to survive through further strokes of good luck (Gourevitch, 1998: 122). Most reluctant officials and policemen soon felt forced to cooperate out of fear and anxiety to preserve their careers and patronage positions. This went down to the level of the local policeman, the teacher, the janitor.

Straus (2004) shows that killings began on April 7, swelling into mass killings at differing speeds but enveloping the whole country within three weeks. The first prefectures to be engulfed were Habyarimana's core constituencies of Gisenyi and Ruhengeri, plus the capital, Kigali, and then its hinterland. The south lagged. Straus's ecological data show that local MRND and CDR strength was easily the best predictor of the local speed of the genocide. Thus the richer areas of the country tended to be engulfed more quickly, since the party-state had spread its largesse to its local supporters. But other socioeconomic and demographic variables (including the relative proportions of the two ethnic groups in each area) were unrelated to the speed of the genocide.

The tipping point in each area came when the radicals brandished superior physical force. Even a handful of guns or grenades, plus a mob of 50 or so people armed with machetes or sharp farm tools, was usually enough. In areas dominated by the radical MRND–CDR parties, some local officials together with some social elites mobilized such forces and began systematic killing of Tutsis, with little opposition. In more divided areas most local officials and social elites tended to be initially passive, watching to see who won the struggles between a few activist officials and/or elites. In this period some Tutsis were killed, others protected. The tipping point here usually came when the radicals made a determined armed bid for power, often aided by the arrival of a few armed militants from elsewhere. In opposition-dominated areas, passivity lasted longer and few Tutsis were killed until armed outsiders added their weight to a few prominent locals to overwhelm opposition and induce grudging cooperation. Most commonly, paramilitaries provided the decisive force; sometimes soldiers did so. The local police and gendarmes generally dithered or opposed the genocide to begin with. Let us see some examples of how this worked.

In MRND-dominated Gisenyi the radicals immediately cut loose. The prefect and the local military commander were little house members, born locally, while the *Interahamwe* paramilitaries were already experienced in killings in the early 1990s. Here the orders to kill all Tutsis and all remaining Hutu opposition came directly and explicitly from top MRND figures to loyal local clients. The leader of the Gisenyi *Interahamwe* was Omar Serushago, born locally in 1957. His father was a friend of Habyarimana, and he could call on one of the dead president's brothers-in-law to help identify enemies at roadblocks. He testified at Arusha to receiving direct orders from national MRND leaders to begin killing all Tutsis on the morning of April 7. This is the major piece of evidence suggesting that genocide began as soon as the little house seized power. Serushago cooperated with the prosecution and, appearing remorseful at Arusha, was sentenced to only 15 years (Des Forges, 1999: 199; ICTR-98-39; *Ubutabera*, October 12, 1998, February 16, 1999).

The prefect in Kibuye was Clément Kayishema, born there in 1954 into a peasant family. His mother was illiterate; his father rose to become the local schoolteacher. He graduated high school to become clerk of the local court but then won a scholarship to study medicine at the national university. He became a doctor and headed the local hospital. By now a local notable, he was active in the originally moderate Centrist Democratic Party (PDC) in Kibuye. When the power of its Hutu Power faction grew, he was appointed prefect in 1992. Hostile witnesses called him a fanatic, a butcher, yet he says he was intimidated by the violence of Kibuye politics during 1992 and 1993 as the parties squabbled and split and as street fighting and murder of Tutsis intensified. An RPF advance into the prefecture led to massacres of Tutsis. He says the prefecture was paralyzed, lacking elementary resources like petrol, its officials' salaries frozen. The invasion had also convinced him that radical measures were inevitable, for should the RPF share power, his career in Kibuye would be over. Along with five other prefects, he was recalled to Kigali for instructions by the new regime on April 11. They were asked for more action, though he claims he tried to restrain local killings until he was threatened and some of his gendarmes were killed. "We were overwhelmed. The situation was far beyond our capacities." But witnesses said that on the 12th he was urging on the paramilitaries, declaring, "the Tutsis were nothing but filth, and there was cleaning to be done." He told a Canadian nun that butchered victims were "collaborators." On the 15th dissident local gendarmes and their commander were transferred to the front to get them out of the way. The Tutsis retreated to the nearby hills of Bisesero, where at least 10,000 of them were killed in waves of assaults. Kayishema led some of them and also organized a slaughter of Tutsis herded into the Kibuye football stadium on April 18. Found guilty of genocide, he was sentenced to life in 1999. Kayishema seems to have been led into genocide mainly by careerism. Pressures came from above, and he transferred them to his subordinates (ICTR-95-1-T; *Ubutabera*, September 14 and 28, November 25, 1998).

One of his communes was Mabanza. Its mayor, Ignace Bagilishema, was acquitted of all criminal charges (ICTR -95-1A). By 1994 the commune was already riven with dispute. Bagilishema was a relatively moderate and long-serving MRND mayor in a commune with many Tutsis (about 30 percent of the total population). But the RPF invasion increased support for the Hutu Power faction of the MDR. Its local party leader, Laurent Semanza, became his deputy mayor. From 1992 Semanza schemed to replace him, and by 1994 one witness said he was more popular than the mayor. Bagilishema took the routine civil defense measures of the war period, forwarding to Kayishema lists of locals (mostly Tutsis) believed to have arms or to be aiding the RPF. At the beginning of 1994 he arranged for military training of the local *Interahamwe* and resurrected roadblocks originally set up at the beginning of the war and then discontinued during the Arusha negotiations. But he continued to try to damp down local ethnic tensions, using his eight gendarmes to squash violent incidents. The president's assassination produced an explosion of Hutu anger, and some killings began on April 9. Bagilishema appealed for calm and instituted joint Hutu–Tutsi patrols to keep order, but his eight gendarmes were insufficient against Semanza's faction aided by *Interahamwe*. Tutsis fled to the communal compound for protection, and Bagilishema took cautious steps to provide this (some witnesses doubted this) and to issue false identity papers to aid the flight of Tutsis he knew. But on April 13 came a sudden influx of men called *Abakiga*, either refugees from the front areas or militants from the Hutu Power heartland, impoverished young strangers primitively equipped (a few had machetes, most had spears or sticks, and their "uniform" was banana leaves). Somewhere

between 100 and 1,000 strong, they were out for Tutsi blood and possessions. Learning of their approach, Bagilishema urged the Tutsis to leave for
Kibuye, where he said more gendarmes could protect them. An hour after the
main body of Tutsis left, the *Abakiga* arrived, intimidating Bagilishema and
his gendarmes. Under Semanza's direction they killed the remaining Tutsis
and looted Tutsi possessions. At the end of April the *Abakiga* left for fresh
killing fields. Bagilishema remained mayor until June, when he fled abroad.
He was not particularly brave, but the court decided he had tried to maintain
ethnic peace. He had been overwhelmed from below and from outside.

Genocide came slowest in the south, where most officials were moderates.
Butare had the only Tutsi prefect. He kept killings at bay until April 18 by
organizing joint Hutu–Tutsi patrols. Then he was murdered and replaced
by Sylvain Nsabimana, a Hutu agronomist from the hithero moderate PSD,
talked into accepting the post by his party in order to retain its local power
position. He seemed out of his depth and was sucked into participating in
several killings. In late May he began to falter and protected some Tutsis,
appalled at random wild violence by soldiers and paramilitaries. He appealed
to Prime Minister Jean Alphonse Kambanda for protection but got none. He
also had a radical "minder" watching him, Nteziryayo, the Butare chief of
military police, an army colonel seconded to the Ministry of the Interior, well
connected to MRND politicians. He was lodged in a Butare hotel together
with a transferred *Interahamwe* unit, perpetrating numerous murders and
rapes. On June 16 he managed to replace the faltering Nsabimana as prefect.

But the radicals' trump cards in Butare were the two titular heads of the
government, both from Butare. President Théodore Sindikubwabo was a
doctor and professor of pediatrics, a former minister of health and a MRND
deputy, who escaped into the Congo after the genocide. Prime Minister
Kambanda was a commercial engineer, a former official in the National
Bank and leader of the Hutu Power wing of the MDR in Butare. At Arusha,
Kambanda (ICTR-97-23) pleaded guilty to genocide and was sentenced to
life imprisonment. He said that the cabinet had not planned genocide beforehand, but once it began, they had met regularly to discuss its progress.
They organized the distribution of arms, roadblocks, and visits to stiffen the
resolve of laggard prefectures. Kambanda visited at least five, and the two of
them were especially active in Butare. On April 20 they addressed a meeting
of Butare's mayors. The president spoke obliquely:

"the actors who only watch," "those who feel it's not their business" should be
exposed. Let him step aside for us.... Those who are responsible of getting rid of
such a person. Let them do it fast. Other good "workers who want to work" for
their country are there.

"Work" meant kill. If they did not kill, they would be replaced.

Nyakizu commune in Butare had been ruled by a moderate MRND faction, but from 1992 it came into conflict with Kambanda's MDR Hutu Power
faction led by Ladislas Ntaganzwa. He was born there in 1962, a medical

assistant at a local health center and also an athlete, especially proud of his prowess at karate. Leading his party's youth wing, Ntaganzwa embarked on a campaign of violence against the local administration such that the communal officials, including the police officers, dared not go to work for fear of his thugs. Locals now recognized realities and elected Ntaganzwa as mayor in March 1993. In March 1994 he took delivery of arms shipments. Shortly after the president's assassination he called a local meeting, urged those present to kill all local Tutsis, and distributed the arms to local civilians and police. He himself actively participated in the killings. He employed only people he knew and trusted as killers, and he removed local officials who expressed opposition. On May 18, his followers denounced 8 of the 14 local councillors for hiding accomplices and setting Hutu against Hutu. They were replaced by MDR–Hutu Power loyalists, and two were killed. Ntaganzwa overreached himself when he attacked rival Hutu Power notables. They complained to his superiors, and he lost power. But by then, thousands of Tutsis had been killed by his supporters (African Rights, 1994: 232–8; Des Forges, 1999: 370–431; ICTR-96-9; Wagner, 1998).

Most Butare mayors were not radicals. They obeyed from fear or careerism, especially if minders or subordinates seemed prepared to carry on the genocide without them. Joseph Kanyabashi had been a mayor for 20 years. Born in Butare in 1937, he was vulnerable because his wife was a Tutsi and he had contacts with the RPF. But he was a supple opportunist and hastened to cooperate. Most Butare mayors delayed between one and three weeks but then joined in (Des Forges, 1999: 458–69; ICTR-96-15, ICTR-96-8, ICTR-97-29; Straus, 2004: chap. 4).

Gitarama prefecture, north of Butare, was controlled by the opposition. Since the regime lacked local supporters, it had to bring in paramilitaries from neighboring MRND provinces. Prefect Uwizeye responded by organizing joint Hutu–Tutsi resistance, which killed some of the paramilitaries. But on April 12 an RPF offensive forced the government to flee from Kigali into Gitarama, accompanied by presidential guards and paramilitaries. One mayor testified how threatening he found them:

If I continued to protect people I would be killed.... They did in fact shoot at me but I was not struck by a bullet. They prevented me from driving about in the commune, and if I did, they would stop me at the roadblock. (ICTR-94-4-T)

The prefect called a meeting with his mayors on April 18. But Kambanda and other ministers showed up too. The prefect demanded that the government stop distributing arms and close down radio RTML. The ministers responded by denouncing all those who failed to support the patriotic militiamen defending Rwanda against the enemy. One warned, "some of the commune leaders in Gitarama were cockroach accomplices... if these people continued to work in this manner... there will be very serious consequences for them." The writing was on the wall. The Gitarama mayors caved in one by one and abandoned their prefect.

Jaen Paul Akayesu, the mayor of Taba, was one of them. Born locally in 1953, he was a former teacher and inspector of schools. At his trial he described the worsening clashes of the early 1990s between the MRND and the opposition parties. He helped found the local MDR, becoming its president. When the MDR dominated Taba, he was made mayor in April 1993. In the days following the president's assassination Akayesu, aided by the local National Assembly deputy and army colonel, resisted his radical minder, Kubamanda, who had returned to the commune with government money as leader of an *Interahamwe* unit. The villagers initially supported Akayesu. But his nine commune policemen carried only seven guns among them, and the more numerous paramilitaries killed one and wounded another. Akayesu also felt the ideological power of radio RTLM, which denounced him as exterminating the loyal militia. It broadcast a physical description of him that made him sound like a Tutsi. In nearby Kicukiro the mayor had been replaced by an *Interahamwe* leader. He did not want the same fate.

After the April 18 meeting with the ministers, Akayesu said, "the situation was getting extremely dangerous. And I had resisted for a long time. I also had a family, and I thought about abandoning everything and running away." So at the next day's commune meeting he read out a list of persons to be hunted down as accomplices. Three of them were local police officers, his erstwhile allies. Asked at his trial, "you were signing their death warrants, weren't you?" he blurted out, "of course." The massacres in Taba started the following day. By the end of June, over 2,000 Tutsis were dead. Some witnesses said he had tried arguing with Kubamanda in early May, and he had generally just stood around while the *Interahamwe* did the murdering and raping. But others said that he had ordered killings of "intellectuals" (i.e., local notables) and refugees, severely beaten an old woman, and told a group of raping militiamen, "don't ever ask me anymore how a Tutsi woman tastes," adding, "it is tomorrow that they will be killed" – and indeed they were. Not an unduly ideological killer, he was brought into line by political power and its economic payoff. The exact balance of power between the mayor, the *Interahamwe* leader, the local deputy, and the army colonel mattered. He had changed sides mainly to keep the spoils of office. Otherwise, faced with a local rival, lacking support from above, he would be finished. He was convicted of genocide and rape and sentenced to life imprisonment (Des Forges, 1999: 270–8; ICTR-94-4-T; ICTR-96-4; *Ubutabera*, October 27, 1996, February 15 and March 16, 1997).

Another Gitarama mayor, Nyandwi, dragged his feet, but ran into trouble with incoming *Interahamwe* after April 11. He said in an interview with Scott Straus (2004; his story was confirmed by four other locals interviewed):

the population killed an *interahamwe* and that was very expensive for me. One directly said on RTLM that I was killing *interahamwe* and helping the Tutsi. One said that many times. It was the 14th. The population began to be afraid, calling a burgomaster an enemy.... It was grave for me. The population helped me but the police began to be afraid.... We continued all the same, up to the 20th.

On that day he learned that soldiers had arrived and were looking for him. He fled and was replaced by an MRND loyalist. Another Gitarama mayor, Ndagijimana, refused to comply. The *Interahamwe* killed him on April 20. Prefect Uwizeye, a well-connected man, kept up sniping attacks on the genocide for another month, but five of his six subprefects were now opposing him. He could do nothing, and he fled on May 20. One mayor continued giving covert help to Tutsis. But compared to the scale of the local killings under way, he could save pitifully few.

Local businessmen were also heavily involved, since for them also politics mattered. Managers held jobs in nationalized companies; businessmen held licenses and monopolies secured through patronage. There were two economies in Rwanda. The first was subsistence agriculture, involving half of the country. It could support life but generated little surplus. The second economy comprised government employment, foreign development funds, and the export of coffee, tea, and tin. Government ministries and nationalized or licensed companies dominated this economy, which was much more profitable. In tea there were eight nationalized companies and one private one. Almost anyone who wanted more than mere subsistence – for example, who wanted a steady job or health care or education for children – had to be connected by kinship or local residence to ministerial or parastatal patronage networks. Their core had been Habyarimana's men, and they wanted to keep feeding at the trough (OAU, 2000: paras. 14.50–14.51).

Gisovu was the home of the nationalized OCIR-Tea company. Alfred Musema, its boss, was born in 1949 in Byumba prefecture, one of the few directing genocidal operations outside his home area. He made a very good marriage inside the little house. His father-in-law had been an early Hutu Power leader, martyred when killed by Tutsis in 1962, so he got a plum appointment in the Ministry of Agriculture, controlling international aid funds. He was in the Kigali MRND, "a very well-connected young *fonctionnaire*." His reputation fell when his brother-in-law was implicated in a plot to topple Habyarimana in 1980. Though dismissed from the Ministry, he persuaded the minister of industry to appoint him tea company boss in Gisovu. There the locals – even the Kibuye prefect – depended on resources he controlled. He was a councillor to the prefect and was put on various development committees. In 1992 he was radicalized when the RPF occupied his home province, leading demonstrations demanding that the government do more to help the refugees. The 1992 massacres of Tutsis in Kibuye, in which he probably played no role, harmed his chances of retaining his position should the RPF come to power, so he helped found the radical RTLM radio station. Fifty of his employees formed a "Civil Defense" paramilitary trained by the gendarmerie and armed by the local mayor and army brigadier. His trucks and drivers provided transport to the Bisesero hills massacres, and he was active in leading them. The UN Tribunal sentenced him to life. Though not an early Tutsi hater, he was radicalized by concern for his invaded home province, activism in Hutu Power circles, and careerism (ICTR-96-13; *Ubutabera,* November 25, 1998, February 16, March 15, and May 10, 1999).

Obed Ruzindana was born in 1962 in Kibuye. He built up a successful import-export company selling consumer goods in Kibuye and the capital. A leader of the Kibuye CDR, he also helped finance paramilitaries. After 10 years in Kigali improving his business connections, he moved back to Kibuye in 1994. He provided trucks for the slaughter in the Bisesero hills and helped direct activities. He was overheard telling the *Interahamwe,* "Bring me an identity card [of a Tutsi] and I'll pay you." He was convicted of genocide and sentenced to life in May 1999. When local notables like Ruzindana and Musema joined the leading officials and party leaders in urging killings, their imposing collective presence was itself sufficient to incite the local villagers to commit them. The whole local social elite seemed in charge of the killing in the hills of Bisesero (ICTR-96-10, ICTR-96-1, ICTR-96-14-T; *Ubutabera,* October 26, 1998).

The state was first radicalized by a coup at the center supported by sympathizers in the civilian administration, army, and paramilitaries. Local officials and elites complied out of a mixture of ideology, careerism, and fear. Pressures came from superiors above, from minders and roving officials and paramilitaries alongside, and from subordinates below. If the whole state became complicit, it was not through simple top-down bureaucracy. As Wagner (1998: 30) observed:

This was not the hoary face of time immemorial "tribal strife"; it was a modern face – the self-confident face of a rural fonctionnaire projecting himself as an "intellectual" among nonliterate farmers and striving to become a local "patron" in the politics linking his own rural center to Kigali.

MILITARY POWER: SOLDIERS AND PARAMILITARIES

Though the presidential guard and some other army units were implicated in killings, the bulk of the army was at the front, retreating. Suddenly expanded, with rudimentary training, it was ill-disciplined and some radical officers were handing out weapons to the paramilitaries. Wounded men from the front were also prominent in the massacres, seeking revenge on Tutsis.

Survivors interviewed by African Rights (1994) tended to tell similar stories. First, local politicians and policemen said they would protect them. Then soldiers or, more commonly, militiamen arrived and frightened the would-be protectors into abandoning them. Any fighting was now one-sided. Tutsis fleeing with almost no possessions usually had only sticks and stones.

Hutu mobs might have picks, spears, or bows and arrows, but paramilitaries usually had machetes or nailed clubs, and a few had guns. The Rwandan government has estimated that machetes killed about 38 percent of the total victims, clubs 17 percent, and firearms 15 percent (Straus, 2004: chap. 5). Though murdering soldiers were few, their guns, grenades, vehicles, and walkie-talkies went a long way in genocide against an unarmed enemy. Tutsis often managed to repel the initial assaults of locals and local paramilitaries. But then soldiers and more organized paramilitaries were called up, and their guns and grenades broke the Tutsi resistance. The soldiers then left the close-quarters killing to others.

The paramilitaries probably did most of the killing, though survivors have a tendency to describe all armed mobs as *Interahamwe*. In the first week following the coup, the paramilitaries provided about 4,000–5,000 killers (2,000 of them in Kigali), but they soon expanded massively to 20,000–30,000 (some estimates go as high as 50,000). The expansion produced mobs with little prior training and few weapons. Some survivors distinguished between professional paramilitaries – already experienced in interparty fighting, well-organized, and armed – and the mass of expanded ragtag gangs seizing the unexpected chance for loot and power (African Rights, 1994: 229). These were useful to the regime, which wanted Tutsis and moderates dead but could counter international alarm by declaring, "There is no genocide. The people is rising up in righteous, uncontrollable wrath against the enemy." Indeed, the paramilitary thousands – obviously not the whole people – *were* rising up in a murderous mood. Their "professional" core was military or gendarmerie reservists, experienced in street brawling and firearms. Among the officers, physicians, agronomists, and especially teachers were overrepresented (says African Rights, 1994: 121–2). Most were youngish adult men, though survivors identified at least five women leading *Interahamwe* bands.

George Rutaganda was born in 1958 in Gitarama into a strict Seventh Day Adventist family. His father was a well-connected local mayor who rose to be a prefect and ambassador to West Germany. Habyarimana's coup saw him marginalized back to mayor, and he was ousted from this office in 1993 by the local rise of the MDR. All this strengthened his son's resolve to be on the winning side. After university he worked in government development schemes, setting up business activities on the side. In 1991 his father bought him a garage in Kigali, which became a depot for an import-export business, mostly importing foreign beers. He was a big man in every sense, a powerful athlete, a former rugby prop forward, and the financier of a successful soccer team. In 1991 several political parties tried to recruit him. Now a man of the capital, he chose the MRND, which had most economic power. He was elected to its national committee in 1993, was a modest backer of radio RTLM and was chosen to be a vice president of the *Interahamwe* because the combination of wealth, beer, and sports made him popular among young men. He seems to have been sucked into genocide less by political ideology than by desire for connections, reinforced by the culture of athletic, beery masculinity. He ran a roadblock outside his garage and was sentenced to life for genocide, extermination, and crimes against humanity (ICTR-96-3; Internews, December 13, 1999; *Ubutabera*, June 8, 1998, April 12 and 26 1999).

Shalom Ntahobari had been born abroad in 1970. His mother was a Hutu Power cabinet minister, and his father was rector of Butare University. A student dropout, Shalom swaggered around Butare with grenades hanging from his belt, brandishing his gun. He ran several local paramilitaries and a roadblock in front of the family house, committing numerous murders, sometimes for profit. His mother, Pauline Ntahobari, the minister for the family, born in Butare in 1946, was also a regular at this murderous roadblock (no leading Nazi had ever done anything like this). She identified Tutsis, who were then stripped, packed into lorries, and killed and/or raped by the militiamen. She is the first woman to be charged with ordering and assisting rape by a War Crimes Tribunal (Des Forges, 1999: 508–9; tried together in ICTR-97-21). Students dominated the middling militia ranks. The intellectual and state-dependent professions were prominent in the genocide. Most had internalized some Hutu Power ideology, but careerism and looting added important material motives – killers by conviction and connections.

The expanded militias were the loosest of the paramilitaries discussed in this book, being a particularly vicious version of the "African disease," roving bands of armed youths. Their "uniforms" were rags bearing the distinctive colors of their parties or banana, tea, or coffee leaves. With their primitive weapons, they brutally beat and slashed people to death and raped many women. As the genocide developed, they grabbed more guns, which were lovingly displayed and admired as a symbol of power and virility. As among other paramilitaries, songs and chants praising violence and murder, lubricated by alcohol, brought a machismo comradeship to reinforce what little discipline they possessed.

In the south, Hutu refugees from Burundi, thirsting for revenge, were said to be overrepresented in the *Interahamwe*. Looting was ubiquitous among these very poor people. A survivor had played dead under a pile of bodies: "Almost everyone was dead but the *Interahamwe* was climbing over the bodies saying 'whoever is still alive and has money should identify themselves and we will take their money and let them go.' They still killed them" (McGreal, 1999b). The rank-and-file were overwhelmingly lower-class youngish men. One survivor said her group was raped by a gang of 11- to 14-year-old militiamen: "A young man came to take me away. He had a long knife attached to his belt and a little axe in his hand. When we arrived at the primary school ... this child put the axe and the long knife down, close to me. To see a young child rape me, as you can understand, that this is something very difficult" (*Ubutabera*, October 27, 1997). Most were recruited in the towns, among the landless unemployed (Kabirigi, 1994: 10; Willame, 1995: 127). They blamed the Tutsis for their misfortunes rather than the Hutu state class, the real pillagers of the country – but their employers. Guaranteed food, drink, and lodgings, acquiring loot and weapons, and hoping for future employment, they were lured on by the state class.

The paramilitaries were trucked into the countryside by officials in the Ministry of Roads and Bridges (whose minister was a MRND radical) and other nationalized enterprises, given their murderous orders by regional and local officials, and told to implicate locals in the killings. They brought lists of Tutsis and Hutus to be killed, they were the core of most crowd killings, and they manned the ubiquitous roadblocks. They examined faces, checked identity cards (one person per roadblock was supposed to be literate), raped women, and hacked to death anyone they identified as a Tutsi or a Hutu opponent (Keane, 1995). If suspects had no papers, those who looked Tutsi were killed – bad news for some of the 20 percent or so of Hutus who did not resemble the supposed racial stereotype. But the often repeated estimate of the Physicians for Human Rights that each paramilitary killed 200–300 persons cannot be true (e.g., Lemarchand, 1997b: 414). That would only have involved a total of 2,500–4,000 perpetrators, a massive underestimate. Since few of the paramilitaries had guns, more killers than this were required.

ORDINARY HUTUS

Finally, quite ordinary Hutus were drawn into the killings. Des Forges (1999: 395, 770) says one massacre at Cyahinda may have involved up to half of the men of the commune, several thousand people. Mamdani (2001: 5) says that in another big one "everybody participated, at least all men. And not only men, women too: cheering their men, participating in auxiliary roles." Indeed, in 1998, 4,500 children between the ages of 14 and 18 and 1,200 women were imprisoned in Rwanda for participation in genocide (Human Rights Watch, 1999; OAU, 2000: paras. 16.35 and 16.69). Straus (2004: chap. 5) asked his sample (drawn only from prisons for men) about the size of the killing groups in which they were involved. Only one had launched an attack on his own, and just under a quarter participated in groups of up to 10 people, but the average group size was much larger, consisting of 84 people. This was collective behavior by quite large though fluid groups. Straus has made the most careful estimate of the total number of perpetrators: 175,000 to 210,000 of them. This is a very large number, almost 7 percent of the total Hutu population and 15 percent of active adult male Hutus.

Straus (2004) offers the best available evidence on the characteristics of perpetrators. His sample was drawn randomly from among prison inmates who had already pleaded guilty, though, of course, we do not know what biases might have been involved in the detention and conviction process. His sample were not especially young, being mostly adults in their 20s and

30s, much like the national adult population, and they had about the normal number of children for their ages. Their occupations were also representative of the national labor force (overwhelmingly agricultural, though often combined with other casual work), except for some overrepresentation of professionals and administrative cadres, which also meant that they were slightly better educated than the national population. Hutus from all walks of life were involved. Even clerics and nuns betrayed Tutsis taking refuge in their churches (as in the Arusha trial of Pastor Ntakirutimana of the Seventh Day Adventist Church and the Belgian trial of two nuns). Only the small Muslim community seems to have stood aside completely. Teachers and pupils drew up deathlists of Tutsi students. A primary teacher admitted, "I myself killed some of the children.... We had eighty kids in the first year. There are twenty five left. All the others, we killed them or they have run away" (Braeckman, 1994: 229; Gourevitch, 1998: 252; Prunier, 1995: 255). Straus (2004) says that the better-educated and older persons were more likely to have been leaders of the genocide, but they were less likely to have actually killed people – so they said (59 percent said they had not directly killed anyone). Those who admitted killing were mostly young adults of low education and occupation, many trained in firearms. Again, we see that the perpetrators were not marginal to society. They were drawn from all classes and are themselves stratified. Those of higher status gave the orders; the lowest and those experienced in violence did most of the killing. This is all normal to murderous ethnic cleansing.

A few Hutus aided the Tutsis. Survivors acknowledged Hutu help with words like "Not everyone was bad. He was a Hutu but one who cannot harm. Not everyone killed" and "Not all the Hutus had wild hearts. Sometimes I asked food from families, and they gave it me.... There is a difference between Hutus and assassins" (*Ubutabera*, October 27, 1997). A Seventh Day Adventist preacher saved 104 Tutsis, recruiting a network of at least 30 local Hutus who hid them and spied on the *Interahamwe* so as to keep one step ahead of them (McGreal, 1999b). Some survivors attest to the ferocity of their neighbors, others to their reluctance. Ndimbati, the mayor of Gisovu in Kibuye, failed to get the locals to help him kill, so he went to a nearby village to recruit his killers (*Ubutabera*, May 10, 1999). Families often divided. Munyaneza and Turikinkiko say their parents and wives opposed their killings. "Why would I have anything against Tutsis?" Munyaneza's father asked. "They are just like me. We live on the same hill. We have the same houses.... Why should I have anything against them? They should have done something against me for what my son has done. He has brought us shame" (McGreal, 1999a: 11). As in all cases of murderous cleansing, most Hutus neither assisted nor opposed the perpetrators. They stood aside and looked away. "We closed the door and tried not to hear," said one (Des Forges, 1999: 262). Others passed the buck. A Tutsi said, "we realized later that they were not trying to defend us. There was pressure on them to kill us and they did not want to kill us themselves. So they sent us off to be killed to another village" (African Rights, 1994: 344).

The killings were invariably justified as attacks on the accomplices of the wartime enemy, the invaders, the killers of the president. This was resistance, or at worst retaliation or revenge. Straus's (2004) respondents most often gave this as their positive rationale for participating in the killing (i.e., excluding the negative claim that they were coerced). The supporters of Habyarimana were the most incensed, and the most violent perpetrators were also the most incensed by the war and the assassination. Thus male Tutsis of fighting age were the most likely to die. Demographers estimate the male fatality rate as 50 percent higher than the female rate. Of course, among women, rape substituted for slaughter (OAU, 2000: paras. 16.7–16.32). Most observers say that Hutu refugees from fighting in the north and from Burundi were disproportionately involved in the genocide, and Mamdani (2001: 203–6) says that atrocities peaked after refugees moved into an area. Having lost almost everything, they could be induced into righteous revenge – and righteous looting. Straus does not find refugees overrepresented, though as strangers in the areas in which they killed, they may not have been recognized, denounced, and detained later.

By late April the killings were being urged on by the entire government, the radio, and most local social elites as patriotic duty in a civil war. Mobs were killing all the Tutsis they could find, chanting, "Let's exterminate them all." In the hills of Bisesero the chant went up:

Is it a sin to kill the Tutsi? No, let's exterminate them, exterminate them, kill them and bury them in the forests, let's chase them out of the forests and bury them in the caves, let's chase them out of the caves and massacre them. Stop so that we can kill you, don't cause problems because your god fell at Ruhengera, while he was on the way to the market to buy sweet potatoes. Don't even spare the babies, don't spare the old men, nor the old women, even Kagame [the RPF commander] was a baby when he left. (*Ubutabera,* March 2, 1998)

An aid worker caught up in a "hallucinatory" melee of fleeing Tutsis and flailing Hutus says:

always the same thing, a man trying to flee and the others catching him and hitting him, a man on the ground not even trying to protect himself, immobilized by the blows, resigned, and other men crushing his flesh with blows of clubs and machetes, spears, bows and arrows.

Assailants sometimes immobilized the victims by slashing their hamstrings, leaving them helpless on the ground to be finished off later. The aid worker continues:

Not everyone was armed with weapons, but everyone was armed with hate, ready to trip up a Tutsi who was passing, to slap in passing the miserable person who was running, out of breath, out of strength, who exhausted fell flat on the macadam.

Scarcely was he down when the blows fell with twice the force. Children . . . made a game of it, following their older brothers in running after the Tutsi, throwing stones at them, and laughing at each Tutsi who was caught. (Des Forges, 1999: 464–5)

Yet Straus's sample said they had not hated Tutsis beforehand. Ninety-seven percent had had Tutsi neighbors, and two-thirds had a Tutsi relative. Four-fifths said relations with Tutsi neighbors had been good and had only recently changed. However, the worst killers had possessed the most negative views of Tutsis beforehand, and his sample did have a strong sense of the ethnic distinctiveness of the two groups, which the war and the assassination had then converted into hatred. Turikinkiko said:

I had been living with these people all these years. I wasn't afraid of them. They weren't a threat to me. But we were told they were enemies and I believed it. Almost all Tutsis in the village had been my friends. To me it didn't matter. They were relatives of those who killed Habyarimana so they had to pay. We closed our hearts and minds and did the job. . . . When I was killing the young people and women I knew that they weren't necessarily supporting the RPF. But it was a way of discouraging the RPF from fighting because even if they won they would have no one to govern. I didn't hesitate. I found it easy to kill because I knew I was doing it to save the Hutu people.

He added that he had discounted his womenfolk's objections to the killings: "she was a woman so I didn't have to listen to her." Munyaneza also revealed machismo leanings:

It's like a dream. I saw people who were killing treated as heroes so I ventured out. I was convinced I was killing the enemy because of what the radio was saying all the time. Somehow I believed those people whatever their age, could not be trusted, that we had to do it or we would all die. (McGreal, 1999a: 10)

Rumors were planted and spread. There were supposedly hordes of armed Tutsis nearby. Tambiah (1996) and Kishwar (1998a: 29) noted similar fearful rumors of enemy armies massing nearby in Sri Lankan and Indian communal riots. But they had been fictitious, whereas the RPF was real and often nearby. Tambiah (1996) says people have a psychological need to be frightened by the victim. I prefer Katz's (1998) sequence of threat–humiliation–righteous rage. There was a real Tutsi threat from the RPF, and stories of its accomplices were very plausible. The humiliation of a collapsing Hutu army and conquest by a small minority was felt deeply, especially by men. The rage generated was real and righteous. By mid-May it was subsiding when it became clear that there was no Tutsi threat outside the front itself. Hutu violence lost steam, and the killers went straggling back to their homes. Only parts of the ragged expanded paramilitaries remained, still finding employment, food, beer, and shelter in thuggery.

There was also an indirect proletarian motivation. The paramilitary rank-and-file reveled in the reversal of power, humiliating, looting, raping, and killing the rich (Prunier, 1997a: 231–2). Most Tutsis and moderate Hutus who survived told of bribing their way out of difficult situations. Others gave bribes but were still killed. The Arusha Tribunal watched a cameraman's recording of a woman dying on the road. Then the camera closed in on her swollen face, covered with coagulated blood. Through her split lips she was whispering something, but no one could hear the words. She was drowned out by a passerby explaining her murder: "She was a bosses' wife" (*Ubutabera*, June 8, 1998). Years before the genocide, Caroline Newbury (1988: 209) emphasized that Hutu peasants believed they were ground down by Tutsi oppression: "the cohesion of oppression" was the root of Hutu Power. The genocide was legitimized as redistributing Tutsi property. Only 30 percent of Straus's (2004) respondents admitted taking property during the genocide, usually just food, tiles, or other abandoned bits and pieces. But, of course, they might have been lying to allow their families to continue enjoying the fruits of their looting. They also seemed to be excluding bribes and more communally organized redistribution – of "the radio, the couch, the goat, the opportunity to rape a young girl," says Gourevitch (1998: 115). Some radicals feared that locals would just pillage and then go home, so they urged, "Kill first and pillage later." An official remarked, "Those who killed say that the properties of the victims belong to them." Munyaneza says his village officials organized a lucky dip. The victims' properties were listed on pieces of paper and put in a hat. Every Hutu had to draw out a lot so that everyone would be implicated. He won a banana plantation (McGreal, 1999a: 10). Communal councils spent much time discussing property distribution (Des Forges, 1999: 236–7, 299–300). This meant that any prosperous-looking person might be a suspect, denounced as a Tutsi or an accomplice. Economic motives normal in communal violence where the victim is defined as an oppressor (like Jews or Chinese entrepreneurs) can be committed amid war by those bent on mass murder.

The Hutu regime (like the Tutsi regime in Burundi) diverted taxes and international development funds to its own clients. Inequalities widened, mass living standards stagnated, the threat of malnutrition and disease grew. But as in other countries where politics were organized along ethnic and regional lines, class remained rather an abstract conception of exploitation. The Hutu opposition preaching class politics never received much mass support, and they were wiped out in the early days of the genocide, leaving the regime to urge on ethnic conceptions of exploitation. With the rule of law broken, Hutus found it easy to attack Tutsis and other privileged persons within their reach (Gasana, 1995: Reyntjens, 1994: 220–4). Ethnicity trumped and rechanneled class resentments (as in my second thesis).

But considerable social coercion was also exerted within the Hutu community. This was emphasized by over 70 percent of Straus's respondents. Most said they feared the consequences of not participating, though they referred to the lesser social pressures of conformity or of simply obeying officials. Some were told that if they did not participate, they "were no longer considered Hutu." Those citing such pressures tended to be less violent perpetrators than those citing the war and the assassination as their reasons.

Villagers tell of being assembled in the square, lectured by an impressive regional notable or dignitary from the capital, and given lists of victims drawn up from identity card records. In the smaller villages, lists weren't necessary. The local councillor and the schoolteacher knew who was who. Militiamen or soldiers sometimes told them: "Either you kill them or you will be killed." One remembered, "in the end, even those who had hesitations had to kill too. They killed with less zeal, but they killed" (African Rights, 1994: 573; Mamdani, 2001: 219–20). Soldiers were seen "throwing stones at the children to rouse them into killing. Some of them did not want to kill but the army forced them to take part. Everybody must have blood on their hands. Then no one person can be blamed" (Keane, 1995: 134–5). Only accomplices of the enemy would not comply, they said. Some who demurred were murdered. But threats usually sufficed. Wagner (1998: 30) saw beneath "the face of the *fonctionnaire*" "the face of the farmer, turned inward, eyes cast downwards – because looking out was dangerous." One killer said:

I regret what I did...I am ashamed, but what would you have done if you had been in my place? Either you took part in the massacre or else you were massacred yourself. So I took weapons and I defended members of my own tribe against the Tutsi. (Prunier, 1995: 247)

One survivor recounted how his village had first stood firm against the killings.

A few days later, it became apparent that people were becoming demoralized and reluctant to defend the parish. They said they had been discouraged by statements on radio Rwanda by the bourgmestre of [nearby] Runda who had organized the killings in Runda. He accused the victims of being members of the RPF. When our people heard government officials say such things on the radio, they concluded that the killings were being organized from the very top. It had a very bad effect on them. (African Rights, 1994: 621)

A survivor of a massacre explains how reluctant Hutus were pressured by the paramilitaries:

So, OK, he does, and he runs along with the rest but he doesn't kill. They say, "Hey, he might denounce us later. He must kill. Everyone must help to kill at least one person." So this person who is not a killer is made to do it. And the next day it's become a game for him. You don't need to keep pushing him. (Gourevitch, 1998: 24)

Some say that Rwandan culture induced a "cult of obedience" (Des Forges's testimony at the Akeyesu trial; Gourevitch, 1998: 23; Prunier, 1995: 57, 245). But, along with others (Mamdani, 2001: 198–202; Strauss, 2004; OAU, 2000), I am skeptical. The Arusha lawyers were influenced by this view. One asked Akayesu: "Doesn't the farmer find it natural to obey orders 'from above'? Isn't that the tradition?" But Akayesu found such a question difficult to answer. He hesitated and was pressed – "But is it more natural to obey or resist?" – and so (as people in any country would) he chose to obey (*Ubutabera*, March 16, 1998). Farmers – like most people anywhere – would find it easier to obey rather than resist government officials. But this does not mean that the farmers were not mindful of the choices available to them, and of the consequences of making the wrong choice. For officials had menacing powers of enforcement and attractive powers of patronage, while militants could mobilize coercion, conformity, and comradeship. This was not a mass of people passively socialized into a cult of obedience. Particular power structures were mobilized to ensure it.

This was a small, compact country with good communications. The leading genocidaires toured, spoke at meetings, organized the locals. Radio was a potent means of communication, given that secrecy was not the object. Radio Rwanda asked that locals close the borders and stop fleeing Tutsis. Radio Thousand Hills (RTLM) exhorted: "This is the moment to attack the tough fighters [the RTF] simultaneously in the back and the front... our brothers will attack them in the back and exterminate them. The hour of death for the tough fighters has sounded." "No pity for the enemy." "The graves are only half full." "Let 100,000 young people be recruited that they rise up and we kill the tough fighters, we will exterminate them all the more easily since... the proof is that they are a single ethnicity. So look at a person, his height and physical appearance, just look at his pretty little nose and then break it." The "pretty little nose" was supposedly a Tutsi racial characteristic. But, insisted RTLM, extermination was self-defense since "the Tutsi were seeking to exterminate the Hutu." "Look at Burundi" and "remember the assassination of the Hutu chief of state" and others "assassinated by the cockroaches." "It is a war between the Hutu and the Tutsi." Massacres were "inevitable," the product of "righteous popular anger." Multiparty democracy was divisive of the nation; only the Hutus were true Rwandans. The Tutsis were foreign "Hamitic invaders." Hutu Power was the goal – singular, integral, organic. On April 7 RTLM declared, "The graves are not yet quite full. Who is going to do the good work and help us to fill them completely?" (Chrétien et al., 1995: 191–5).

But Straus (2004: chap. 6) is skeptical of the power of the ideology. Only 10–30 percent of his sample appeared to know and approve of the various elements of the Hutu Power ideology. Nonetheless, some killers have said that they were exhorted to particular attacks by radio, and a foreign nun reported she had seen new radios at all 12 roadblocks where she had been stopped (Des Forges, 1999: 67). Gourevitch (1998: 96) says roadblock paramilitaries recited phrases from Mugusera's terrible speech of 1992, quoted in the previous chapter. Keane heard paramilitaries saying "The Tutsis... want us to be their slaves again like in the old days" and comments:

> The words of the men at the roadblock were almost word for word a recitation of the government's line. These men really did believe they were about to be returned to the dark ages of the Tutsi autocracy...the words were old and stale, a script written by the architects of the genocide and repeated endlessly down the line to the most impoverished, illiterate peasant. (Keane, 1995: 165, 174)

The script was repeated five years later. Pinned to the body of a British tourist killed by *Interahamwe* over the border in Uganda in 1999 was a handwritten note (in French) that read:

> Here is punishment for the Anglo Saxons who have sold us out. You protect the minority and oppress us the MAJORITY. (A photograph appeared in *Time* Magazine on March 15, 1999; capitalization as in the original)

But a simple version of this ideology resonated strongly because there *was* an invasion from abroad, fomenting a civil war in which the enemy *was* identifiably Tutsi. The enemy RPF *were* committing massacres of their own, almost all of Hutus, and some Tutsis were collaborating with them. Every part of Rwanda was receiving refugees with believable stories of all this. True, the RPF did not want to impose feudalism or even monarchy, and they said they wanted multiparty democracy. Yet Hutus had reason to suspect that a Burundi-style Tutsi regime would ensue if the RPF were victorious – and indeed, that is now happening in Rwanda. It is not that surprising that a radicalized regime and militants, assisted by incensed but also greedy crowds, could make genocide of the Tutsis and politicide of their accomplices seem like a plausible final solution of the disastrous conflicts plaguing their country. The war had radicalized *all* levels of Hutu perpetrators – the little house, the Hutu Power parties, the army, the civil service, the notables, the paramilitaries, and many of the people. Even many who did not kill seized Tutsi homes and cattle and so became complicit. Few Tutsis returning after the RPF victory could distinguish the killers from the thieves. Indeed, returning Tutsis took the houses and cattle of the fleeing Hutus. Amid the violence, the housing and cattle stock was greatly diminished. If there is a compromise solution of the crisis and both groups come back, who is to have the few remaining houses or cattle? It is difficult not to be seared by the process of murder, dispossession, and flight into a profound ethnic consciousness advocating retaliatory ethnic cleansing, and retribution for the profound humiliation suffered – as the current Tutsi regime is finding.

CONCLUSION: STRUCTURE AND PROCESS
IN THE RWANDAN GENOCIDE

Four conclusions stand out. First, profound bi-ethnic rivalry underlay this genocide, not as constant ancient ethnic hatred but as a series of modern escalations over who was to control the state. The two ethnic identities had been real enough even in precolonial times, and conflict between them had been rising since the late colonial period. The danger zone for murderous ethnic cleansing had probably been reached by the early 1960s. By then powerful factions claiming to represent the two ethnicities were both demanding ideologically plausible and practically achievable rival states over the same territory (as in my third thesis). In Rwanda and Burundi the rivalry followed the form of thesis 4a: the two groups were quite evenly matched, Hutus with weight of numbers, Tutsis with superior military and political organization. Ethnic identity and conflict were not constructed merely in the 1990s. By then they were fairly objectified. One might have other identities as well as ethnicity, but almost everyone knew that he or she was a Hutu or a Tutsi and that a profound conflict was ongoing between the two communities.

Obviously, this did not in itself imply mass murder, but then came regional and international pressures – economic downturn, Ugandan desire to be rid of its armed Tutsis, the Tutsi invasion of 1990, and international pressures for democratization. The four-year civil war radicalized the little house radicals into half-planned politicide and genocide. The war and the assassination of the president legitimized the defensive civilian mobilization plans that were later used for genocide and fired up Hutus for righteous revenge.

Most Hutus did not initially accept the radicals' claim that exploitation by foreign Tutsis constituted the core of their social being. Malkki (1995: 3, 163–70) has studied Hutu refugees in Tanzania. He says those living in multiethnic cosmopolitan cities had "porous identities." They "juggled labels" such as "immigrant," "Tanzanian," "Burundian," and "Rwandan" – rather less often "Hutu." In contrast, those segregated in refugee camps identified themselves as primarily Hutu, even spouting Hutu Power ideology. In Rwanda, Hutu identities began as porous. They might view themselves as farmers and neighbors and Catholics and people from Gitarama, as well as Hutu. But then the salience of Hutu identity and Hutu Power increased. Of course, even in the midst of genocide, Hutus still had other identity options. But Tutsis barely had any. As the killings began, Tutsis discovered that the ethnic label stated on their identity card was the one that mattered. It determined that they would probably die or it led them into desperate stratagems that might bring survival. Tutsis could not now be primarily cattle herders, Catholics, or careerists, only Tutsis. That is why it is so difficult for either of the states they now command, in Burundi and Rwanda, to yield an inch in their defense of Tutsi rights.

Second, genocide resulted from particular forms of power exercised by hundreds of leaders, thousands of militants, and the 200,000 who eventually joined in. Genocide results not from spontaneous masses of people acting identically, but from complex relations of ideological, economic, military, and political power. The Rwandan state class and its clients wielded considerable economic as well as political and military power, which served to rechannel class into ethnic senses of exploitation. Together the party-state elite and paramilitaries coerced and distributed loot, by now important to an impoverished population. Ideological power helped the "moral" accomplishment of genocide, a righteous retaliatory rage buttressed by more mundane sentiments of wartime patriotism, loyalty to one's kin, and masculinity. Through the rechanneling of sentiments of exploitation, ethnicity trumped class (as in my thesis 2). It still does so across the African Great Lakes region.

Third, genocide was again perpetrated not by a cohesive or totalitarian state, but a party-state recently factionalized and radicalized (as in my fifth thesis). This state was seized by the radicals only when the killings commenced, and they started killing their opponents within the state before they turned to kill others. More determination from Hutu moderates or the UN might have aborted this, as both the OAU Report (2000) and Melvern (2000) make clear. The centrality of the party-state and its economic patron–client networks to the country meant that more than any other case, this was slaughter among neighbors. In this small, densely settled country, national notables quickly returned home to activate their patron–client networks into awful tasks. Cabinet ministers personally egged on their laggard home prefectures. In a polarized bi-ethnic civil war context where each group possessed a plausible and achievable claim to the state, a state class reaching from the top to the bottom of society resorted to genocide in righteous defense of its hold on power. There are many state classes ruling across the South of the world, occasionally in polarized bi-ethnic contexts. Such a terrible outcome remains a possible danger elsewhere.

Fourth, this resulted in very mixed perpetrator motives. In Rwanda even top-level perpetrators mixed personal material goals with a strong ideological sense of ethnic identity, justice, and retribution – a little like colonial American leaders but rather unlike most Nazis. Further down the power structure, the mixture was more mundane. Fear of Tutsis generated righteous rage, reinforced by ambition, greed, failure of moral nerve, brown-nosing, a desire to be "a man" or receive approval from one's peers, patriotism, and loyalty to one's kinsfolk. These were the rather ordinary human sentiments dominating most of the 200,000 Rwandan perpetrators, the most popular case of murderous ethnic cleansing we have seen in this book.

We also glimpsed as usual some core constituencies of perpetrators. Since so many finally joined in, in the end these were perhaps not so important as in other cases, but the role of the MRND state class and its key northwestern heartland was clear in the initiation of genocide. Probably embittered refugees from Burundi and the frontline regions and wounded ex-soldiers were also overrepresented. They would have shared more of the emotional sequence of fear–humiliation–rage I have found so generally useful in explaining murdering motives. Also overrepresented were young adults with some prior weapons training and experience in violence. The paramilitaries had provided a setting where inurement to brawling and breaking up meetings softened up members for careers in worse violence (as we saw in the Nazi SA and SS).

Neither Hutus nor Tutsis are intrinsically murderous peoples. Nor were they murderous because they were backward or simple, manipulated by malevolent leaders – the message often subtly conveyed by Western journalists. Rwanda and Burundi are poor but quite effectively organized countries, and the leading perpetrators saw themselves as modernizers. The Hutu Power slogans of "the great majority" and "majoritarian democracy" evoked the dominant ideology and political institution of modern times, and so they evoked mass support. More than any other case, Rwanda exemplifies the first thesis of this book: murderous ethnic cleansing is the dark side of democracy.

16

Counterfactual Cases
India and Indonesia

So far I have studied only cases in which ethnic conflict did murderously escalate. Such sampling on the dependent variable might give a biased as well as an overly pessimistic impression, for many serious ethnic tensions exist but seem to get successfully defused. There are bursts of ethnic violence in which trouble explodes but then seems to die away and communities are spared mass murder. We must also study such cases to see what the differences are between them and cases of mass murder. The large countries of India and Indonesia can serve as "laboratories." Both contain ethnic and religious tensions that explode at widely varying levels of severity. Both countries see recurrent violence, but most of it takes the less serious form of a riot cycle. Yet in a few instances there is escalation into mass murder. Can we explain these varied tensions and outcomes in terms of my ethnic theses? After examining the two countries, I will contrast them to my earlier worst-outcome cases to locate more precisely how trouble either escalates or gets defused. Figure 16.1 will sum up my conclusions, in effect rounding out my general explanation of ethnic cleansing.

INDIA SINCE INDEPENDENCE

India's population of 1 billion people is extremely multiethnic. No one knows how many ethnic groups there are, but they are so numerous that no one could rule the country merely by mobilizing ethnic loyalties. Localities can be split by communal ethnic disputes, but not the nation as a whole. Forty percent of the country does speak a single language, Hindi, but language is not a fundamental cultural divide, partly because so many elites also routinely speak English. Religious differences are more problematic, since over 80 percent of Indians are Hindu but 12 percent are Muslim, which means there are over 100 million Muslims, more than in any country except Indonesia. They are mainly concentrated in the northern states, and there are also Muslim neighboring states there. There are also sizable Sikh, Buddhist, and even Christian minorities. Some Hindu movements have been tempted toward organic nationalism, the ideal of an essential Hindu-ness, *Hindutva*, buttressed by a Hindu state, *rashtra*, granting only second-class citizenship to non-Hindus. Some militants call for actual cleansing of Muslims and others.

This obviously generates hostility among the large Muslim minority, as it does among the regionally concentrated Sikhs in the Punjab. Christians and Buddhists are too few and scattered to provide much resistance. They tend to turn the other cheek when faced with provocations.

In the past, Hinduism did not provide fertile soil for organic nationalism. It has been a tolerant religion, able to absorb rather than resist rivals. It is not monotheistic and over the centuries has incorporated the gods, beliefs, and rituals of other religions into its practices. It has varied so greatly across the regions that many have doubted whether it was really a single faith until quite recently. It still has no single church, priesthood, or orthodox dogma.

Hindu ethnonationalism arose only in the interwar period, and even then it was not the main form of anticolonial ideology. The Indian independence movement was dominated by the secular Congress Party, and the country secured a Constitution under which religion is formally a private matter. Lower castes and tribal peoples were also guaranteed rights and privileges entrenched in the Constitution. The Congress Party was a coalition of fairly secular elites in the civil service, the military, the professions, and business circles together with leaders of lower Hindu castes and religious and ethnic minorities. Congress ruled independent India for its first 40 years, compromising ethnic, religious, and caste/class interests, flanked on its left by socialist/Communist parties, which have also been strong enough to rule in a few of India's states. Hinduism also has caste and caste conflict. Though caste is not identical to class, Hindu politics generate clear left–right political tendencies, and in a way Hinduism assists the Congress and leftist parties' ability to speak for the lower castes, thus weakening potential Hindu ethnonationalism. Indian politics has never been ethnically or religiously blind (especially at the local level), yet it long resisted organic nationalism.

Even today, after the rise of Hindu ethnonationalism throughout the 1980s and 1990s, most Hindus, most Muslims, and most Sikhs do not engage in violence against each other. Violence is not an everyday event anywhere in India, except for Kashmir. Varshney (2002) has calculated that 96 percent of the violence (outside of Kashmir) is urban, though over two-thirds of Indians live in rural areas. Furthermore, he finds that only eight cities provide half of this violence. And only rarely does this violence escalate into seriously murderous cleansing, and even then it is always defused after quite a short period. Quite different have been several other distinct cases of seriously murderous cleansing. The first occurred on the northwest borders immediately after independence in 1947. Then came the violence in East Bengal in 1950, the Sikh outbursts of the 1980s, the intermittent armed conflicts in Kashmir, and some of the small border disputes of northeastern India. I seek to explain these variations in violence between different parts of India.

I start with the less serious form of violence, the urban riot cycle What Jaffrelot (1996), Brass (1997), and Tambiah (1996) describe seems not atypical of riots across the world described by Horowitz (2001). Riot cycles fit some but not all of my first group of ethnic theses seeking to explain movement into the danger zone of conflict. Religious-ethnic conflicts are certainly old in India. The British were confronted by serious riots in the mid-19th century and again during the 1920s, causing them to make concessions to the better-organized Muslims and Sikhs, which Hindus resented. Ethnic-religious riots involve mobs who burn and loot a few houses and shops, rape a few women, and commit a few murders, rarely on a mass scale and rarely with clear intent to cleanse the minority. The vast majority of riots produce no or only a few deaths, mostly rioters shot by the police and army as they suppress them, followed by partly accidental deaths of people burned in torched buildings. Serious riots may generate an orgy of violence, generally lasting only for one to three days in any one place, though it may spread from place to place. Riots mostly start at a time of popular discontent caused either by economic distress, widening or narrowing economic disparities between the communities, or political discontent against the national or local authorities displaced onto religion – all indications of scapegoating of the out-group for other ills.

A very few riots escalate further so that they strain the category. In the Bombay riot of 1992–3 over 1,000 died; in the Gujarat pogrom of 2002 perhaps 2,000 may have died. I discuss this recent case later. But why are almost all these riots/pogroms short-lived, and why don't they lead to worse? Figure 16.1 tries to answer this question and thus summarize the main argument of this book. It compares the sequences of interaction involved in cases that either escalate or do not escalate into murderous cleansing. For the moment, I focus on the riot cycle in the upper part of the figure. It begins by assuming two contending ethnic groups, A and B, living under one government, with a state or states nearby sympathizing with the minority group (in India this does not apply to Hindu–Sikh conflict). It also assumes that there is initially no serious external threat to India. The upper half of the figure concerns outbursts like the Indian riots/pogroms; the lower half concerns the further escalations evident in all the murderous cases described in previous chapters. The processes in the figure assume some history of past disturbances, as in my third thesis. So it assumes that there are some radicals in group A intending to foment violence against group B (and perhaps vice versa). These "ethnic entrepreneurs" mobilize violent militants and core constituencies of support. Brass (1997) stresses the role of malevolent local elites instrumentally furthering their own power goals – an example of the elitist theory discussed in Chapter 1. Tambiah (1996) and Jaffrelot (1996) also note their importance but additionally stress the involvement of more popular forces.

The initial trigger for popular disturbances is usually a rumor of an incident seeming to confirm negative stereotypes of group B. Perhaps a Hindu woman alleges rape by a gang of young Muslims, or a man says he was beaten by a gang drawn from the other community, or Muslims have supposedly stolen a temple idol or a (sacred) cow dies in suspicious circumstances. Hindus have reportedly defiled a mosque, or someone intends building a temple in a provocative site. Poor people are being bribed or coerced to convert. The incident is usually not completely fictional in the sense that something

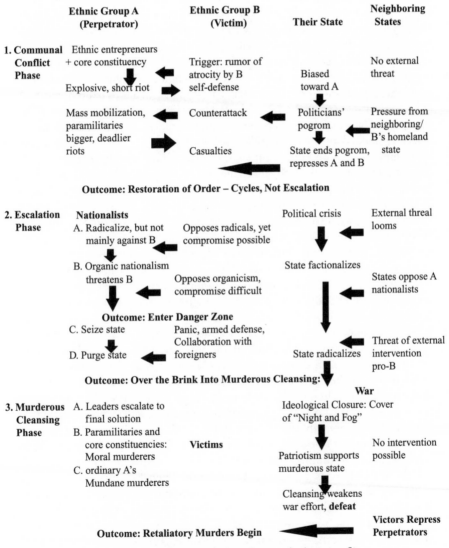

FIGURE 16.1. Three escalating phases of ethnic conflict.

really did occur. But often it is magnified out of all recognition, sometimes by a person with something to hide (e.g., the "raped" woman is a prostitute abetted by a pimp who becomes a "witness" to the rape or the "beaten" man was a pickpocket caught in the act). The rumor then spreads and becomes exaggerated. Many rumors get defused quite quickly by doubts about the veracity of the victim or by the testimony of other witnesses, or community leaders or the police launch prompt investigation or repression of those calling for demonstrations and inciting violence.

Varshney (2002) has offered a powerful explanation of when this happens. Comparing violence-prone cities with peaceful though otherwise comparable cities, he says that the nature of voluntary and professional associations and political parties accounts for the difference. In peaceful cities these span the religious divide; in the riotous cities they are religiously divided. In the former cities these institutions of civil society can step in and act to calm down both sides in coordinated fashion. An *institutionalized peace system*, consisting of trade unions, associations of businessmen, traders, teachers, doctors, and lawyers, backed by local political parties (which they tend to dominate), all organized in both communities, jumps in. They launch, or they get the local government to launch, investigative commissions for the grievances, and they organize peace demonstrations. They nip rumors and small clashes in the bud and defuse the more serious outbursts.

In contrast, where associations are confined inside communal boundaries, either they are internally divided, with some members actually supporting the rioters, or they may deplore the violence but have no powers over the other side and so are ineffectual. Here, a rumor that seems plausible and keeps spreading is an invitation to militants in group A to exact retribution on group B for the supposed outrage. Sometimes this begins spontaneously, but as it grows it is increasingly managed by ethnonationalist elites calling group A to demonstrations. When these are emboldened by a crowd of supporters, they march to the place of the incident or to a weakly defended group B neighborhood to demand with menace that the perpetrators be handed over or the "provocation" ended. They may burn or smash up some property. This is often deliberately provocative. The elites/militants want B to counterattack (though not effectively) since this will confirm what they are telling the crowd about their threat. Group B is not likely to respond with contrition, since it doesn't believe the rumor to be true. Instead it incubates its own paranoid rumors, shouts defiance, and perhaps tries a counterattack, which may only energize group A's violence. Then B residents will retreat to their core neighborhoods, abandoning marginal ones, and prepare to defend themselves. Escalation to a short, explosive riot is now common. This presupposes some segregation between the communities, mutual negative stereotypes, and some communications closure. Rumor gets amplified without being corrected by the other side's version of events – the *information failure* stressed by rational choice theory.

Muslims and Sikhs feel threatened as minorities, but Hindu nationalists also feel threatened. Though it is supposedly their country, they say they have little power. The British, they say, privileged the Muslims out of concern for British rule in other Muslim countries, and the present Constitution also privileges them. The history of the subcontinent placed large mosques in dominating positions in many cities. They say that the Muslims have a global Islamic fundamentalist movement, but the Hindus have no center to their religion; they are divided by multiple castes, regions, and political parties. Thus, in opinion polls, most Hindus in the north (the more vulnerable area) favor assertions of Hindu power like the destruction of the symbolic Alodhya mosque, though they also want to live in peace with their Muslim neighbors (Jaffrelot, 1996: 473, 476–7). Signs of weakness by the national government (especially against Muslims or Pakistan) increase the Hindu nationalist vote. The most radical say that India should be a pure Hindu state, or that Muslims or Sikhs should have far more local political power or be able to build their mosques and temples anywhere they like.

They may loosely command paramilitaries, specialists in communal rioting. Some are quite highly organized, like the Hindu quasi-fascist Rashtriya Swayamsevak Sangh (RSS) and its front organizations, which survived the initially secular era of the Indian state and then revived at the grassroots level from the 1960s and in national politics from the 1980s. It is paralleled by the Muslim Jamaat-i-Islami. In their early anticolonial years in the 1930s and 1940s these movements were influenced by fascism and Nazism. Yet they usually bear less deadly weapons – blades rather than guns – and they contain moderate as well as radical factions. Other Hindu paramilitaries are more loosely organized. The Bajrang Dalis, militants of the Shiv Sena Party, and others rampaged out of control by Hindu nationalist leaders during the 1980s and early 1990s. Some politicians also have client "riot captains" calling out men from particular local villages or subcastes known for their proficiency in thuggery. Many are influenced less by disciplined elite strategies than by the current popular mood, exacerbated by riot processes themselves.

Some riots contain a ritualized repertoire of collective action, with processions, music, chants, flags, holy men or film or rock stars, speeches transmitted at ear-splitting level, caps and T-shirts bearing incendiary logos and slogans, and audio- and videocassettes denouncing supposed atrocities. These make participation enjoyable. Morality is dulled by the collective nature of the action. It cages the participants. Tambiah (1996) emphasizes the expressive side of rioting; militants visibly enjoy the violence, its sense of release, self-expression, and power, buttressed by self-righteous retaliation against a threatening out-group. Demonstrations then characteristically move into looting of abandoned or weakly defended marginal neighborhoods – for few rioters are brave. The sense of power exercised over a hitherto threatening enemy is intoxicating. Looting and torching can be fun, and the mob is in a righteous mood. They are defending themselves, retaliating, teaching the other side a lesson. Liminal boundaries are crossed by collective righteousness. There is a temporary sense of empowerment, of homogeneity, group belongingness, physical intimacy. They would not do it alone, separately, Tambiah says. Afterward no one feels remorse. Alcohol plays less of a role than in Christian countries, though Hindu rioters are sometimes supplied with it.

Rioters are not oblivious of instrumental reason. They keep a wary eye open for police or resistance, and most rioting and looting occur on the edges of the out-group's neighborhood, where resistance is feebler. Thus casualties are low. Horowitz (2001: 527) says of riots over the world, "There is not a single riot...in which rioters miscalculated their own tactics and power, the intentions of the police, or the response of their targets, such that the rioters suffered more casualties than the targets did." Aroused passions do not overwhelm reason. Since these movements are oriented to asserting local control, material motives are involved. Control of the local state involves access to welfare, development, and employment programs, and ethnonationalist elites and rioters are seeking to further their local control – as we saw was also so in far worse incidents in Yugoslavia and Rwanda. Election campaigns are especially feared by the minority, since electoral mobilization enables the majority to reaffirm its control of the local state. Thus martial law tends to damp down riots, while vigorous party competition exacerbates it – one of the counterexamples to democratic peace theory mentioned in Chapter 1.

Those committing serious violence in India – as elsewhere in the world – are overwhelmingly young, unmarried urban males (Horowitz, 2001: 258–66 assembles the global evidence). Some have had paramilitary training. RSS members usually dress to resemble Indian soldiers, though a few are garbed as ancient warriors The more ragtag Shiv Sena paramilitaries mock RSS costumes and marching steps, preferring a more individual, spontaneous, and secular cult of violence. They see themselves as "the hero[es] of a Bombay film in which violence leads to justice" (Heuzé, 1992: 2189; Katzenstein et al., 1998: 227). The militants are not usually drawn from marginal or lumpen elements, but from students, factory and transport workers, bazaar merchants, and artisanal trades (says Tambiah, 1996). Horowitz (2001) says rioters are predominantly working class, but this is belied by the large numbers of students in riots. Jaffrelot (1996) says that the original core of Hindu nationalism was among upper-caste, middle-class groups, but that it then diffused to middle- and lower-middle-class groups, though its leaders remain overwhelmingly Brahmins. Of course, the organizers of large riots are analogous to desk-killers. They give orders but they themselves do not riot/kill. Heuzé (1992) has moved among the Shiv Sena militants, and describes them as being mostly educated or semieducated young men, underemployed in fairly menial and casual jobs, but not a marginal lumpen proletariat, for in Indian cities even such casual employment yields a higher than average income. They claim that they are unemployed and exploited, demanding redress for their exploitation through a transcendent nationalism. Ethnic minorities and caste conflict, they say, are destroying Indian unity, destroying the chances for economic development and full employment.

Some Hindu nationalists believe Muslim men simply cannot be assimilated and so must be driven violently out of India, though they tend to believe that Muslim women can be coercively converted. This type of male chauvinism ensures worse treatment of men. Shiv Sena violence is almost entirely by and against men. But the RSS (like their fellow Hindu Tamil Tigers in neighboring Sri Lanka) also organize a large women's paramilitary movement, the *Samiti*, whose sword-wielding marches through Muslim neighborhoods have been used to provoke riots in various Indian cities. *Samiti* members have an ethnic-feminist paranoia about Muslim men, all of whom they consider to be potential rapists (Bacchetta, 1999). Not all feminism is nice and liberal.

But despite the best efforts of the radicals, riots rarely last long. Tambiah (1996) says a mob's heightened psychic state cannot long endure. People get exhausted by the shouting, the smoke, the rushing. They need food, sleep, family, work. The element of surprise has also gone. Ethnic group B is now defending itself, and more escalation of violence would be risky. Rumors of retaliation from group B or the police frighten the rioters. In any case, retaliation, "teaching them a lesson," has been successfully completed. The ethnic entrepreneurs would like it to continue but have limited powers of manipulation. The crowd was genuinely angry about the rumored incident; they have expressed their anger so that group B will not dare to do it again. They are not much interested in abstract questions of whose state it is, since these do not much impinge on their everyday lives. So riots die away quickly.

A few will escalate further if group A ethnic entrepreneurs can respond to B's counterattack with a higher level of paramilitary violence directed at a threatening and highly politicized target, whose removal will take some time and involve many militants. The destruction of the Alodhya mosque by Hindu mobs in 1992 involved concerted, persistent action by militants already enraged by the government's vacillations over the issue. But when the riots began to spread across the country, Parikh (1998) notes that their incidence also depended on prior Hindu nationalist organizational strength in a locality, conjoined with local politicized grievances against Muslims. She also notes that major intercaste disputes undercut ethnonationalism. Disputes about "job reservations" (quotas) for lower castes are also endemic across India, and where they flare up they generally dwarf anti-Muslim sentiment. In India, not class but caste usually trumps ethnicity (a variant of my second thesis). Once the Alodhya mosque was demolished, says Jaffrelot (1996), Hindu nationalists perceived that they could not mobilize a similar effort for the more mundane task of building a new temple of their own.

Building plans languished, and they began to cast around for a new mobilizing target – but these do not grow on trees. Mass mobilization can be
manipulated only if the supposed threat resonates among the masses.

There is a further precondition of escalation: the absence of political opposition from above. This depends on the degree to which the local authorities
are biased toward ethnic group A. The police may stand aside or even assist the rioters, or local and regional politicians may endorse the righteous
anger of the rioters. The political authorities may encourage the deflection of
discontent onto a minority community, turning a riot into what Figure 16.1
calls a *politicians' pogrom*. Though the Indian state is formally secular, it is
implicitly and increasingly Hindu. Some Hindu politicians are ethnonationalists; many more believe they have to head off ethnonationalist pressure by
voicing some support for it. These are normal elected politicians standing for
reelection. If Hindu nationalism is becoming more popular, or if they themselves are becoming less popular (perhaps for reasons quite unconnected to
nationalism), they often try to play the ethnonationalist card. In this they
resemble democratic politicians anywhere. The local police may be fearful,
biased, or corrupt. They do not like shooting at Hindus, they may favor the
Hindu mob, or they can be bought off to look the other way or induced
to share in the looting. Ordinary Hindus are affected by the same political currents, but official complicity prolongs the rioting and emboldens the
paramilitaries and the crowd. The riot gets bigger and deadlier (Kishwar,
1998a: 20–1; 1998b: 150–4; Parikh, 1998: 54).

The corollary is also true: decisive action by the authorities can stop any
riot or pogrom in its tracks, assuming that their capacities have not been
gravely weakened by some other crisis. Jaffrelot, Tambiah, Brass, and Parikh
all stress this in the case of the Indian subcontinent. Riots continue when the
authorities are inactive or complicit, but are stopped in their tracks when
they are not. We also saw this in the Russian and Ottoman Empires. But
neither the tsar nor the sultan had to stand for reelection. The early regimes
of Jawaharlal Nehru and (at first) Mrs. Indira Gandhi believed ethnonationalism threatened their own secular state. They repressed it. But later regimes,
facing greater ethnonationalist pressures, sometimes bent with the mood of
the riot. This was to be Mrs. Gandhi's fatal mistake against the Sikhs, ending
in her own assassination by her Sikh bodyguard.

But even if the authorities are initially inactive or complicit, they may have
motives for later repressing a riot/pogrom. Scapegoating is an opportunity
for the people to let off steam and anger for a while, to turn an industrial
strike or bread riot or political crisis into an attack on Sikhs or Muslims.
There is no point in its continuing once the deflection has been successful.
Second, the regime becomes more worried about public order than ethnic
solidarity. Continuing disorder reflects badly on it and will evoke opposition among both ethnic groups. Their community leaders and many from
the propertied classes quietly press for action behind the scenes (they may

not care to do this in public). Politicians and administrators are aware that those who cannot keep public order will fall. Third, serious riots bring the threat of international condemnation and intervention. Thus regimes, even somewhat biased ones, normally do step in, end the riot, and repress both sides. These fears even impact on nationalist movements. In the early 1990s the Hindu nationalist Bharatiya Janarta Party (BJP) and even the RSS began to worry about being outflanked by the "lumpen gangsters" of the Bajrang Dal and their strategy of "ethno-nationalist mobilization," so they sought to incorporate, discipline, and moderate them (Jaffrelot, 1996: 478–81). In a stable state, power ultimately and normally brings responsibility.

Hence the normal ultimate outcome in India (and most other countries), even in cities with divided civil societies, is the repression of both sets of troublemakers, perhaps not evenhandedly, but with enough show of force to cow the crowd, the militants, and the ethnonationalist elites into flight. Order is restored, though perhaps temporarily. These are the riot cycles shown in the top part of Figure 16.1, not escalation to the murderous cleansing as depicted in the bottom part.

But the rise of Hindu ethnonationalism threatened Congress Party power, sparking riots from the late 1960s and greater support for Hindu nationalist parties in the 1980s. Mass conversions of low-caste Indians to Islam in the 1980s threatened the ability of the more secular Hindu parties to regulate caste politics as well as the implicit "no conversion" compromise of the Constitution. Under these pressures, Hinduism began to solidify, developing a more cohesive set of rituals, scriptures, and a pantheon of gods; some even see it as straining in the direction of monotheism. The traditional cultural notion of the "angry Hindu" began to be exploited in Hindu ethnonationalism (Jaffrelot, 1996: 388–92) The ruling Congress (I) party of Mrs. Gandhi began for the first time to pander to Hindu nationalism in some regions while conciliating its traditional secular and caste bases elsewhere. This was electoral opportunism – a product of Indian democracy and a polarizing electorate. This inconsistent strategy backfired, making the Hindu BJP Party ideology more acceptable. The BJP vote rose, and then that of the Shiv Sena. Ethnonationalism came to power democratically.

Of course, Hindu ethnonationalism cannot simply transcend caste differences. During the period of Congress decline, intercaste violence *also* grew, especially in the north, intensifying religious–ethnic and caste–class conflict simultaneously. Not even Hindu nationalist parties can ignore this. They must be careful not to be identified as only higher-caste parties – which the background of their leaders suggests. While in government, they had to also keep order, so they tried to damp down disorderly ethnonationalism. On the other side, Muslims are highly dispersed across the north of India. Outside of Kashmir, they are too organizationally weak for aggression to have a plausible chance of success. Fundamentalism needs secure bases and Indian Muslims cannot provide them – except in Kashmir. India's Muslims are fairly secular and politically moderate. There are powerful forces for ethnic–religious compromise.

Yet as the BJP settled into the comforts and corruptions of office, it began to lose popularity among its base. Its radicals denounced corruption and demanded moral and religious purity. They demanded more vigorous action against Muslim Pakistan in the recent border skirmishes between these two nuclear powers. But the radicals have focused their mobilization efforts on the popularity of the project to build a Hindu temple in Ayodha on the site of the now demolished mosque. Very large crowds assemble there to pressure the BJP government into more action.

In February 2002 a large party of supporters was returning home by train to Gujarat, a BJP stronghold, when their train stopped at the town of Godhra. After provocations by the Hindu passengers, the train was stopped outside of the town, right by one of the most militant Muslim suburbs. It was promptly attacked by a crowd of Muslims who stoned and set fire to the train. It went up like a tinder box and 58 Hindus were burned alive, many of them women and children. Hindu retaliation was swift and ferocious. Across the state of Gujarat perhaps 2,000 people, almost all Muslims, were killed by rampaging mobs and 100,000 Muslims fled to relief camps. The killing kept flaring up over several months before the army and police regained control of the state.

Professor Kesharram Shastri was the 96-year-old chairman of the Gujarat branch of the World Hindu Council, a large ethnonationalist association, a scholar of Hindu texts and a respected literary figure. He admitted he had organized the drawing up of a list of Muslim shops for looting in the city of Ahmedabad immediately after the Godhra incident. When asked why, he responded, "it had to be done, it had to be done. We don't like it, but we were terribly angry. Lust and anger are blind." He added that the rioters were "well-bred Hindu boys," as if that also excused it. But what was unprecedented here was the complicity of the BJP-controlled Gujarat state government. A leading BJP state minister took over the police control room and issued orders for the police to disregard Muslim pleas for help. Policemen were seen leading the mobs, while police wanting to intervene to stop the mobs were transferred elsewhere. Narendra Modi, the popular and dynamic chief minister of Gujarat, refused to condemn the riots. In fact he declared that Gujarat's Hindus had shown "remarkable restraint." He fought and won the subsequent state election with rabble-rousing Hindu ethnonationalism. His dramatic electoral victory had repercussions within the BJP. He seemed to present a credible model for election winning by the BJP and pushed Indian Prime Minister Atal Behari Vajpayee toward toughening his nationalist rhetoric.

Many Indians call these Gujarat riots the first state-led pogroms in India. Though 5,000 people were arrested afterward for rioting, most cases have been dismissed and no one has yet been tried. In October 2003 the Indian Supreme Court said it had "no faith left" in the Gujarat government to bring the rioters to book. The court declared, "What is the *rajdharma* of government? You quit if you cannot prosecute guilty. Democracy does not mean you will not prosecute anyone." So it insisted that its officers must approve all prosecutors in future (Human Rights Watch, 2002; http://www.rediff.com/news/godhra.htm). Gujarat in 2002 was a worrying exception to the riot cycles described earlier. It resulted from the 30-year rise in power of Hindu ethnonationalism, followed by a period of instability and factionalism within the ruling party coinciding with a period of Indian–Pakistani conflict. Luckily, national discontent centered on the economic policies of the BJP-led government produced a return to power of Congress and its left allies after the election of May 2004. Gujarat now remains calm.

In general, Indian riots have so far strengthened my thesis 5: no further escalation over the brink into murderous cleansing occurs in the presence of a stable state facing no serious crisis and coping with class (caste) as well as ethnic and religious conflict. Let me now turn to worse Indian cases.

1. *Partition*. The worst incident of all occurred in 1947 at the time of independence and partition of the subcontinent into India and Pakistan. From 200,000 to 400,000 people were killed, thousand of women were raped, and perhaps 10 million people fled in both directions across the Indian–Pakistan border to their new ethnic–religious homeland. This was by far the bloodiest ethnic–religious cleansing ever seen in the subcontinent, occurring almost entirely in the mixed-ethnic Punjab adjacent to the borders between the two new states, in which rival religious communities attempted to secure sovereignty by majority through force. But here, besides Hindus and Muslims, were Sikhs. They lacked the domination over a large enough area to form their own state, but they favored inclusion within India to give them substantial control of local government in the areas of their densest settlement. In advance of partition, their leaders announced that they would force out the local Muslim population to create space for Sikhs fleeing from Pakistan.

The three-way violence that ensued was not committed by states, for there was no effective state. The British state was pulling out and was disinclined to get involved in communal violence, while neither the Indian nor the Pakistani state had started functioning properly. But some local administrators from all three communities were involved, and so were local military formations. The Punjab was highly militarized, having provided about half of the soldiers of the British Indian Army. Local military organizations of ex-servicemen and deserters provided the nuclei of organized bands of killers offering coordinated resistance to the British Punjab Boundary Force, which was half-heartedly attempting to keep the peace. The Sikh *jathas* were probably the most formidable, though the paramilitary Hindu nationalist organization, the RSS, first became prominent here. Murderous ethnic cleansing was also popular, involving substantial numbers of men in all three communities. The atrocities committed against women took a horrific turn. Groups of men, fearing the rape or forcible conversion of their own wives and daughters, killed them. These women and girls are still remembered in Sikh mythology as martyrs, with no blame attached to the male relatives who killed them. After several months, the new military forces of the two states were able to supervise the transfer of populations that "solved" the sovereignty problem. Refugee camps remained predictable nurturers of embittered ethnonationalism in India, Pakistan, and Kashmir, as they do today (Ahmad, 1991: 469; Aiyar, 1995; Brass, 2003; Jaffrelot, 1996; Madhok, 1986: chap. 5).

Such terrible scenes were reenacted in East Bengal in 1950, when anti-Hindu riots led to the deaths of another 100,000, mostly Hindus, with perhaps 2 million more fleeing into India. Yet the carnage resulted in relative ethnic peace, since almost all Hindus fled into India and since India settled into tolerance of its remaining Muslim minority. This concerned rival and achievable sovereignty projects amid a weakening, factionalizing state in which radicals were free to encourage paramilitary violence.

2. *Sikh–Hindu conflict.* This conflict erupted in the 1980s. Sikhs had their own historic political institutions, their own version of Hinduism, and their own language. The British had encouraged Sikh autonomy as part of their divide-and-rule tactics, especially using them as soldiers. In modern India, Sikh dissidents have demanded their own provincial Punjabi state inside India. They had expected that the Indian Constitution would grant it, plus official status for the Punjabi language. Yet this did not happen, and Congress remained unsympathetic. In the early 1980s Sikh armed militants began to take over Punjabi institutions. At first India reacted slowly, which emboldened Sikh terrorism. But India then launched full-scale military repression, and this took over 25,000 lives in the period 1983–92. Large Hindu–Sikh riots also erupted across India, killing about 3,000 people after the Indian president, Indira Gandhi, was killed by Sikh members of her bodyguard in 1984 in revenge for the first wave of repression. These riots were highly organized, instigated by some Congress leaders as part of their policy of exemplary repression. It worked. Although Sikh militants were armed from Pakistan and elsewhere, they suffered severe defeat and the movement has since quieted down, probably to erupt again when the last defeat is forgotten – unless further political concessions are granted (Dhillon, 1998; Kishwar, 1998a).

3. *Jammu and Kashmir.* These states form a disputed border region in the northwest of India, claimed by both India and Pakistan on behalf of rival local Hindu and Muslim communities (Akhtar, 1991; Bhattacharjea, 1994; Evans, 1999; Punjabi, 1984; Rahman, 1996; Schofield, 1996). Kashmir was not part of the 1947 partition since it was still ruled by an independent Hindu maharajah, though its population was mostly Muslim. His repressive rule had been contested since the 1930s by Muslim movements demanding secular forms of democracy. This heightened intercommunal tensions beyond anything previously recorded, assisted by Hindu extremist organizations. During the partition crisis many Muslims were killed and Muslim rebels

retaliated, bolstered by armed tribesmen from Pakistan. Despite aid from the RSS and from embittered Hindu and Sikh refugees from the Punjab, the maharajah was compelled to seek aid from the Indian Army – at the price of signing away his realm to India. At the stroke of a pen, the provinces became Indian. But further trouble led to a new partition in 1972, dividing the provinces between Indian and Pakistani lines of control.

In the Pakistani zone of control the population is overwhelmingly Muslim, and there is little conflict. But in Indian-controlled Kashmir, sovereignty remains disputed. India can continue to rule by force, by right of inheritance from the maharajah, and by a plausible claim to be protecting both Hindus and moderate Muslims. If tensions could be reduced, the moderate Muslims might help produce a majority vote for limited autonomy within India. But the insurgent Muslims can obtain aid from neighboring Pakistan plus the powerful rhetoric of majoritarian democracy. This is sufficient to cause trouble and a degree of ethnic–religious polarization sufficient for them to win any referendum now. The population is majority Muslim – 90 percent in the valley of Kashmir, 60–70 percent in Jammu (the exact figures are disputed and vary according to the large refugee flows). Most Muslims seem to want more political autonomy than India is prepared to grant, while radical Muslims want either independence or union with Pakistan. Increasing dependence on outside armed assistance is driving them toward the Pakistan option. India has rather corrupt elections, and when Indian control seems threatened, the central government steps in with martial law.

Currently, over 100,000 Indian troops are stationed in the region. Though the weaker Muslim rebels cannot face the Indian Army in the field, they can mount guerrilla warfare, bombings, and assassinations, plus local cleansings. The Indians appear to have crushed most resistance in the central valley, but Muslim fighters still dominate along the mountainous borders, supported and supplied by militants and radical state factions in Pakistan. From the late 1980s, "guest militants," or *jihadis* have been flooding in from all over the Islamic world, financed by Islamic states and able to buy sophisticated yet cheap weapons on the world markets. Kashmir and Kashmiri refugees provide one of the main breeding grounds of Islamic fundamentalism armed with the terrorist "weapons of the weak" I identify in the next chapter. On the other hand, as is normal in those confrontations, most casualties are inflicted by the security forces of the state, in this case India.

In this warlike environment Hindu nationalism has also flourished, and both sides have become less secular, more fundamentalist. Between 1988 and 1990 over 100 moderate secular Muslim politicians were assassinated and over 230 secular schools were bombed by Islamic militants. The schools have been replaced by an expanding network of religious schools, *madrassas*, financed from abroad. The world has suddenly learned what locals have known for over a decade: that these schools teach children to fight for their faith. The Indian government now says that the majority of Muslim fighters are from outside the province – though this figure probably includes men from refugee families originally from Kashmir. There are many competing paramilitary groups among them, largely formed of young men aged 15 to 25 or 30. Most leaders are educated teachers and professionals. There is believed to be much sympathy from Muslims within the civil service. The militant core is formed by university students and graduates, though the ability to mobilize youth in both urban and rural settings suggests an ability to cross class boundaries. Access to jobs, especially in the public sector, provides an important economic issue for many militants. Both sides mobilize women's movements, mainly among educated women. Though their rhetoric sometimes urges women to arm themselves, female militants appear to limit themselves to demonstrations and pressure on less devout women. Here, of course, militants on both sides carry firearms and explosives, not merely the blades that dominate ethnonationalist activities in most of India.

This fits my thesis 4a: the weaker side is bolstered in its fight by help from coreligionists and a homeland state abroad, a recipe for continuing, escalating violence and cleansing. Over four decades, somewhat over 50,000 people have been killed, and the killing has been escalating. Evans (1999: 30) estimates that 35,000 were killed in the 1990s alone. The rate of killing in late 2003 and early 2004 was about 300 people per month. More than 300,000 people live as refugees in the provinces, plus many thousands elsewhere. The level of violence is not steady. Sometimes pragmatic politicians and popular war weariness appear to provide a chance of effecting compromise. But so far, radicals on both sides have been able to undermine this. Violence seems here to stay. This is a higher level of ethnic violence because it concerns disputed plausible and achievable claims to sovereignty. The conflict is difficult to settle. The principle of self-determination – majoritarian democracy – will keep Muslim and Pakistani resolution strong, and it will give their cause considerable legitimacy abroad. Indian governments can be accused of perpetrating state terrorism. But Indian governments show no sign of risking giving up what they regard as both an integral and a strategic part of India, and they can claim legitimacy in terms of a struggle on behalf of people coerced by terrorism, which now wields considerable influence in Washington. Yet despite the tensions, the two states remain wary of war. The Indian state is stable, the Pakistani state rather less so. When Pakistan is unstable, trouble in Kashmir tends to escalate, as in 1999. This danger was increased by the U.S. invasion of Afghanistan in 2001 with the aid of the Pakistani military regime and subsequent U.S.–Pakistani operations against militant Muslims in Pakistan.

4. *The northeast borders.* These borders have persistently generated local eruptions of ethnic violence, often taking the "imperial versus proletarian" form. Local ethnic groups claim that they are exploited by imperial India and demand local democracy, while India claims to be bringing modernity and

civilization to a backward area. The "Seven Sisters," comprising the states of Arunachal Pradesh, Assam, Manipur, Maeghalaya, Mizoram, Nagaland, and Tripura, had never been part of India. The kingdom of Assam and the princely states of Manipur and Tripura were formerly independent and then a part of Burma, until annexed by the British in the 19th century. In 1947 the British persuaded them to join India. Some believed they were doing so only for 10 years, and they retain their own political institutions. Most have developed significant autonomy movements. Religion is not usually at issue, since the people are either Hindu or of many faiths. Ethnic divides are stronger but complex. Majorities usually identify themselves as different from Indians, but they are often aggregations of many different ethnic and tribal groups (they are "scheduled tribes" as defined in the Indian Constitution), while some minorities feel ethnically Indian. Ethnic divides also have material bite in everyday life. Local peoples have retained their own languages, creating conflict over whose language is to be recognized in education and employment. These underpopulated areas have also received destabilizing flows of settlers from outside, especially Bangladesh, Myanmar, and elsewhere in India. Indigenous groups claim that the settlers swamp and exploit them. Some groups receive help from abroad. Settlers are aided by their co-ethnics abroad, and dissident paramilitaries have found it easy to obtain arms from neighbors interested in destabilizing India's borders – Pakistan, China, and Myanmar (Dasgupta, 1998; Debbarma, 1998; Gopalakrishnan, 1995; Lainithanga, 1994).

My theses 3 and 4 suggest that these would be dangerous areas. Indeed, many thousands have died in ethnic wars and many hundreds in ethnic election campaigns. Yet since most dissidents demand regional autonomy rather than independence, and since the core ethnic groups of India are rarely involved (it is indigenous peoples against marginal settlers), these disputes seem soluble. Secular and leftist Indian parties are more active in these areas. In Tripura in 2002 a Marxist state government was attacked by armed separatist leftists. As a consequence, Indian governments are more flexible and conciliatory here than in Kashmir. Most offer a dual-track policy: repressing independence movements while conciliating others in ways allowed by the Indian Constitution – that is, confederal and consociational schemes for local state autonomy and jiggling administrative arrangements and economic development funds for governing the tribal peoples, linked to power sharing at higher levels. This has produced several new states with the Indian Republic. Comprehensive solutions remain elusive, but the problems are generally being managed within only moderate though varied levels of violence. Some regional governments have failed to implement agreed-upon compromises, giving new leases of violence to dissident ethnic paramilitaries. Statehood has also sometimes led that state's minorities to make claims of their own, some asserting that they are even more indigenous and "authentic," like the Naga and Bodo in the state of Assam. Some want to redraw state and provincial boundaries around the areas where they predominate. Small ethnic wars and riots continue to smolder in this region. But unless things get really bad in Delhi, the border situation should gradually improve.

Overall, some escalation has been occurring in democratic India as secularism declines in the face of ethnonationalism, as neo-liberalism threatens ethnic compromises based on state-administered positive discrimination, and as the global arms market becomes freer for dissidents' purchases of weapons of the weak. But escalation has not become systematic murderous cleansing. Its secular, liberal, socialist, and especially its caste institutions survive, and its state still channels development funds to backward tribal areas. The worst scenario is that ethnic conflict over Kashmir and Jammu might escalate to war between India and Pakistan (both claiming democratic positions), as it has done four times in the past – but next time with nuclear weapons. Such escalations would shift conflict away from the ethnic terrain to more conventional war and geopolitics. In past outbreaks, rational realist geopolitics served to restrain both powers. We must hope it will do so again, though the emergence of an Islamic regime in Pakistan might tempt India to mount a preemptive strike, behind which massive murderous cleansing of Muslims might occur in Kashmir and elsewhere.

INDONESIA SINCE INDEPENDENCE

Indonesia is also profoundly multiethnic. Supposedly its population of 210 million is dispersed over 13,000 islands, 300 ethnic groups, and 200 languages. But it has seen far less territorial integration than India. The Dutch succeeded in colonizing almost all of the archipelago only in the late 19th and early 20th centuries. Even then their rule was not nearly as centralized as British rule in India, and they were forced to rely more on vicious but erratic repression than on routinized administration. Regional ethnic identities strengthened in the last years of colonial rule, when the Dutch sought to cling to power by dividing and ruling between them (Nordholt, 2001). After 1945 the newly independent Indonesian government expanded outward from its Javanese core, subjugating new islands up to 1975, when East Timor was occupied. So the archipelago saw imperial continuity between Dutch and Javanese imperialism. The main factor of social integration has been Islam, for the country is over 80 percent Muslim. But this has never been an Islamic *state*. In colonial times Islam was kept at a distance from the state, and was slow thereafter to make political demands. Islam is the strongest force in civil society, but it does not run the state. Nowadays the largest political and social movements are in some sense Islamic, but since they are diverse and agree about very little, the state remains quite secular. The largest Muslim population in the world (like the second largest, in India) is not much attracted by fundamentalism. The major ethnic disturbances of the archipelago are not religious ones. As always, they are dominated by disputes over the state, and religion is rarely politicized.

Seventy-five percent of Indonesia's population live in the two core islands of Java and Sumatra, and within these, regional/ethnic differences have been declining. Intensive economic exploitation under the Dutch colonizers undermined local differences, and native elites were then able to mobilize a common sense of a nation in revolt against the Dutch. After independence, mobilizing support from left and center nationalist parties and from the secular, Javanese-dominated armed forces, the Indonesians built up a fairly centralized state. The army also secured physical control of the periphery during the 1950s in highly repressive campaigns. But the state also developed a school system imposing a common national language, Bahasa Indonesia (which was originally from Malaysia). Its acceptance became more voluntary as the locals came to see it as the passport to modernity.

After unification, the country should have moved toward the more decentralized polity implied by the Constitution. But this was thwarted by Sukarno's declaration of martial law in 1959, followed by the appalling massacre of Indonesia's Communists in 1965, and then by intermittent violence and militarism under the Suharto regime. Imperialism continued into the 1970s with the annexation of peripheral territories, while the United States and Australia looked the other way. Thus the nationalists succeeded in creating a broad, partly Javanese but partly nonethnic sense of a nation, but not a state that really represented that nation – especially in the periphery (Hefner, 1991; Horowitz, 1985: 514–16; Liddle, 1999; Malley, 1999). Indonesian nationalists then confronted four difficulties more serious than those confronting their Indian counterparts.

1. They had only weakly institutionalized the state, even in the core territories. Nationalists comprised a loose, uneasy coalition between a fairly secular intelligentsia and army, plus Muslim organizations that did not expect the state to be very Islamic (those that did demand this were repressed). But neither the army nor major Muslim organizations were able to maintain their initial commitment to a democratic, secular nation-state. The state is deeply split between warring mass parties and Muslim organizations. The army is similarly split, containing the added instability provided by large, hard-line special counterinsurgency forces. Political and military instability has resulted.

2. Indonesians did not secure control of the commanding heights of capitalism. About 70 percent of all private economic activity is controlled by resident Chinese, who form only 4 percent of the population. This creates the possibility that class and political resentments might be displaced onto ethnicity. It also makes many Indonesians favor a strong and somewhat ethnic (i.e., Javanese and Muslim) state, since this is their main avenue of social advancement. But the Chinese do not claim any political sovereignty, and so (despite Chua, 2004), anti-Chinese actions have been less murderous than

the cases of disputed sovereignty found around the periphery of Indonesia that I detail later.

3. Indonesia has seen imperialism of the core over the periphery, which has been conquered but is less integrated into an Indonesian identity. It contains significant Christian populations in East Timor, the Moluccas, Sulavesi, and West Papua, and several autonomy or secession movements based on historical legacies of political independence, followed by bitter experience of repression in the 1950s. The lateness of Indonesian consolidation meant that while assimilation into a national identity was occurring in the core territories, military repression dominated some regions of the periphery. Such militarism then acted back on the core, giving the state a decidedly militaristic cast. This was particularly evident when economic development of the great natural resources of the periphery intensified in the 1970s and 1980s, for the profits went back to the center – and often to the army itself – and the periphery remained poor.

4. Imperialism also involved a quasi-colonial settler policy. Indonesian governments have resettled close to 10 million transmigrants from the over-populated central islands to less developed peripheral islands between the early 1970s and the late 1990s. Recent migrants have been workers or traders involved in more intensive economic exploitation of the periphery by international and Chinese logging and mining companies, and by formerly Dutch enterprises run by the Indonesian Army. By seizing and exploiting the land in a ruthless and environmentally disastrous way, these combined foreign forces are often depriving indigenous peoples of their livelihood. From Jakarta this looks like development, modernization, and participation in globalization. Similar conflicts rage in the neighboring southern Philippines, where Christian settlers are favored by the government and multinational corporations, provoking a backlash among the Muslim indigenous population. This dispute lies behind the activities of the Moro Liberation Front and the Abu Sayyaf terrorist movement. This type of economic conflict is dangerous because it acquires a territorial and ethnic base. Ethnic groups begin to contest sovereignty over regions.

So from various parts of the periphery, the attempt to create an Indonesian nation looks like Javanese–foreign imperialism using all four sources of social power – ideological assimilation, economic exploitation and exclusion, and military and political repression. Since Indonesian governments remain divided on such issues, policy is not consistent. Repression, divide-and-rule among locals, and genuine sensitivity to local concerns and autonomies all oscillate uneasily in Indonesian policy. From this brew, five peripheral movements demanding some degree of regional autonomy resurfaced strongly in the late 1980s. All could base their claims on some historical de facto political sovereignty.

1. *East Timor* was not part of Indonesia until it was invaded in 1975, and it had been a Portuguese, not a Dutch, colony. It was predominantly

Christian, and few of its inhabitants spoke Indonesian. In the independence struggle religion was not at issue, since the Portuguese rulers were also Christian. Many Timorese initially viewed Indonesian rule as an improvement on Portuguese rule, preferring some degree of regional autonomy within Indonesia. But the invasion and subsequent repression and starvation killed perhaps 150,000–170,000 of the locals, perhaps 25 percent of the total population (Kiernan, 2003). A minority still sided with the Indonesians, seeing them as modernizers, while others became clients whose way of life depended on the authorities. Since the insurgency movement was also rather violent, some of its minority factions fled to the Indonesian side. So Timorese officials and militias fought alongside the Indonesian Army. Though the divide is in principle both a religious and an ethnic one, not many atrocities have been committed in the name of either religion or ethnicity. Timorese, Hindus, and even Christians were found on both sides. The militias were recruited especially from areas bordering or actually inside Indonesian West Timor (Robinson, 2001b). On their side, the insurgents also received support from abroad, initially from nongovernment organizations and later from the UN and Australia.

In 1999, under international pressure, and in a phase of democratization in Jakarta, the regime suspended repression to prepare for elections. But the local army command, dominated by officers with counterinsurgency backgrounds, with support from high officers in Jakarta, then encouraged its militia clients to up the violence, either to achieve the desired election result by intimidation or to make the elections impossible to hold at all. The violence grew out of control. Many ordinary Indonesians were also opposed to regional secessions. Yet the military overestimated the strength of their local clients. The elections went overwhelmingly in favor of independence, though perhaps 2,000 people were killed and over 200,000 people were forced by the rampaging paramilitaries to flee into neighboring West Timor. International pressure then forced the Indonesian government to let the province go, ceding a UN mandate to supervise the transition to statehood. This was achieved in 2001. Indonesians as well as Timorese are better off as a result (Hainsworth & McCloskey, 2000; Inbaraj, 1995; Robinson, 2001a, 2001b).

2. *Aceh*, on the northern tip of the large island of Sumatra, with a population of 3.6 million, had its own sultanate until the 20th century and has its own rather theocratic Islamic traditions. It is also ethnically fairly homogeneous. Its initial resistance against the new Indonesian state ended in 1962 with the supposed grant of "special region" status involving autonomy in religion, culture, and education. Yet any local dissidence was put down with extreme repression, fueling demands for actual independence.

Timor and Aceh closely approximate danger zones of ethnic violence. They had old ethnic cultures, now making claims to territorial sovereignty, nourished by increasing proletarian resentment of imperial exploitation and settlement. The Aceh insurgent leader Hasan di Tiro declared that "Indonesia is still an unliquidated colonial empire with Javamen replacing Dutchmen as enemies" (Kell, 1995: 62). Aceh insurgents have also received some international support for their aspirations from the global arms market and from Libyan and Malaysian training of their soldiers. This approximates my thesis 4b, where the weaker side is emboldened to fight rather than submit by outside support.

Exemplary repression by the army, helped by local client bosses and militias, doused autonomy claims in the 1980s and early 1990s. Yet this made local politicians and Muslim community leaders more likely to claim independence rather than just regional autonomy (Jones, 1995; Kell, 1995). Religion is only a minor issue, and though economic exploitation helped stir resistance during the early 1990s, this was less important than outrage at the ferocity of Indonesian repression (Robinson, 1998). The army failed to establish a broad base of support. The fall of Suharto in 1998 and the Indonesian withdrawal from East Timor in 1999 encouraged Aceh insurgents to increase their attacks. About 36,000 Javanese settlers were forced to flee during the 1990s. In June 2001 a regional autonomy package was proposed that would allow the Aceh to keep 70 percent of provincial revenues (it was previously 5 percent) and implement aspects of *shari'a* law. But it is still security issues that prevent implementation of any agreement. So many judges, prosecutors, and other legal staff have been forced out that the rule of law no longer operates. In response, the army has intensified repression, and there is no end in sight (Human Rights Watch, 2003). Repression also increases the power of the army in the whole archipelago – and, within the army, of the special forces. The rebels have been careful to disassociate themselves from Muslim international terrorists like Al Qaeda.

3. *The Moluccas* and parts of *Sulawesi* contain large Christian populations. The Dutch used these locals as the core of their colonial army, and their communities tended to Christianize. Moluccan soldiers mostly fought alongside the Dutch against the Indonesian nationalists in the 1940s. They rose up again in 1950, proclaiming an Independent Republic of the South Moluccas. Severe repression followed their defeat. But tensions arose again as Indonesian transmigrants poured in, tending to simplify a multiethnic environment into a two-religion Christian–Muslim divide. Rohde (2001) gives a graphic account of riots in Poso, on Sulawesi, where rival gangs of Christians and Muslims terrorized local minorities. Over 250 people were killed, thousands of homes were destroyed, and 70,000 were made refugees. As in India, small incidents inflamed by rumors sparked the first riots, followed by several stages of escalation in which each side's atrocities were claimed to be self-defense or retaliation against the other's atrocities. But Rohde believes the recent democratization and decentralization of Indonesia contributed to the aggravation of conflicts that Muslim immigration had begun. The gangs were organized by local politicians and businessmen vying for control of the local spoils system, which the central state's ability to repress had weakened.

One Muslim student told Rohde of the influx of refugees from the fighting into his town. They were dangerous, he said, since "They bring their disease here." This remained communal violence, not a struggle for secession, and there is little foreign support. A peace agreement was signed between leaders from both communities in 2002, though small radical groups remain active on both sides. On the Muslim side, Laskar Jihad has become notorious in the U.S. war against Islamic terrorism. This case might resemble the riot cycle scenario more than more serious murderous cleansing.

4. *West Papua/Irian Jaya* is majority Christian and overwhelmingly ethnically Melanesian. Its 1 million people had been essentially stateless, sharing more culture with the rest of the island of Papua New Guinea than with Indonesia. It was invaded by Indonesia in 1963 and integrated into the republic in 1969. Once again, the transmigrant settler program fueled local protests channeled through Papuan nationalist movements demanding autonomy or secession. The relative backwardness of the area and the lack of much foreign support have kept these movements quite weak, and less army repression is needed to maintain Indonesian rule. In 2001 Jakarta promised substantial regional autonomy, including keeping 70–80 percent of the revenue from its natural resources and a council that would administer the province and represent the 250 tribal groups who live there. However, the main Papuan movement initially rejected the offer. Shortly afterward, in November 2001, its leader was found murdered. The Megawati government, like the Habibi government before it, may have conciliatory intentions, but it cannot control other regime elements – the murderers were probably from the special forces. The situation remains uncertain and tense. Over 20,000 people have died there over three decades, 1,500 in 2001 alone.

5. *West Kalimantan's* Dayaks, 3.5 million strong, comprise the majority population of the region. The Dayaks have been threatened by intensive exploitation of their lands by capitalist and army enterprises, accompanied by Madurese transmigrants. Dayaks retaliated against the Madurese in 1997 and 1999, killing several hundred and forcing about 50,000 more to flee the island. Culmination came in 2001, when they killed another 500 Madurese (other sources say 2,000). Their attacks included head-hunting, which made for shock-horror headlines across the world and provoked interpretations in terms of "primitive tribalism." One terrified Madurese recounted to journalists how a Dayak had waved a severed head in his face, saying, "This is the head of the Madurese. If you love your life, you had better flee" (*Los Angeles Times*, March 3, 2001). Terror certainly worked. Over 100,000 Madurese – almost the whole Madurese community – fled back to their own inhospitable island. This was highly successful murderous cleansing.

However, this supposedly primordial head-hunting seems to have been a tactical move to create fear. Violence was organized by modern political parties mobilized in response to the Indonesian government's creation of local political institutions that the Dayaks, the majority group, could capture.

East Kalimantan, in contrast, is less polarized. No ethnic group can form a majority. Bipolarity, not heterogeneity, is the problem. During Suharto's New Order government, local leaders had mobilized patron–client networks to support the ruling party. Suharto had used Dayak allies in his 10-year war against Communist insurgents and their supposed allies, the ethnic Chinese population of the region (Davidson & Kammen, 2002). In return, Dayak leaders were able to share in the centralized spoils system. The development of mining and logging industries had then brought the Madurese in. The spoils system spread to private industry, and jobs were allocated to increasingly ethnic constituencies. The introduction of democracy at the local level politicized these economic conflicts along ethnic lines. Dayak businessmen/politicians used primitive rituals of violence to disguise their role and to feign helplessness before a supposedly surging tide of tribal emotions. The core fighters on both sides were miners and loggers organized into armed gangs controlled by local bigmen. The Madurese could count on some police support, the Dayaks on support from the army. The poor on both sides turned on each other, not on their common class exploiters (van Klinken, 2002). Militias armed and trained by the Indonesian Army have also brandished the heads of insurgents on other islands as a tactic of exemplary repression – this could happen to your head if you cause trouble!

In three of these cases (less so in Aceh and East Timor, where settlers are fewer), the conflicts also pit indigenous peoples against the Indonesian state and Army allied with Indonesian settlers from the core islands. But in all five cases the Indonesian authorities – like the Dutch before them – also enlisted local bosses as their clients in an attempt to divide-and-rule among the local natives, offering employment, government contracts, and the corruptions of office available in inefficient patron–client states. They also followed Dutch examples in using militias raised by local bosses. From the 1970s this became more systematized than under Dutch rule in the Indonesian army strategy of "total people's defense," in which shadowy budgets and special forces formed and trained local militias so that guerrillas could be fought with guerrilla tactics. In the tactic known as *human fences*, lines of local people were forced to walk as a screen in front of militias or soldiers while they advanced into rebel villages. The specialized counterinsurgency units, the militias, the youth gangs of recent Islamic parties, and the violent and often criminal gangs hired by local bosses tended to escape control by the state. Violence became larger, more chaotic, and yet often more ethnically targeted as local clans and peoples were defined as friend or foe (Nordholt, 2001; Robinson, 1998, 2001b).

The Indonesian state that precipitated and then had to cope with all this violence is less securely institutionalized than the Indian one. Under the pressure of a reviving, mass-mobilizing, but factionalized Islam, of crises on the periphery, and of economic cycles unevenly impacting upon the population, the regime has repeatedly fragmented. This has usually increased the violence. In 1965, an attempted military coup led to the elimination of the Indonesian Communist Party by right-wing army elements and hired Islamic militants – not natural allies! As van Langenberg (1990: 53) concludes of this terrible *politicide*, which killed over 500,000 people (easily the most murderous conflict Indonesia has witnessed), this was not a bureaucratic or totalitarian atrocity, for there was no "efficient, centralized government to issue a coherent policy of genocide or mass extermination of political enemies." Says Hefner (2000: 65), "Rather than reducing the likelihood of gratuitous violence, this volatile fragmentation of the state apparatus only increased it. State and society were in segmental turmoil . . . rival political factions created extra-constitutional alliances that linked forces in the state with those in society against rival syndicates organized in an equally segmentary manner." The rise of Islamic modernizing movements increased sacred–secular divisions among the political parties, inside the civil administration, and even inside the armed forces. Thus most ethnic–religious violence is exacerbated by state factionalism and radicalization, as in other cases. Political leaders cannot control the crowds and militias they recruit to do their dirty work. This raises the specter of further disintegration and chaos. Recent democratic decentralization seems to have worsened the problem.

But there is in Indonesia no simple relationship between cleansing and democracy. As Chua (2004) notes, elected parties sometimes play the ethnic card, inciting hatred against the Chinese populations. Yet, since authoritarian governments depend more on the army, and since the army is the bastion of integral nationalism, relatively democratic regimes in Jakarta have recently been more likely to seek resolution through compromise involving regional autonomy. As we saw in Kalimantan, this can worsen things. Unfortunately, stable democratic institutions have never existed in Indonesia. Danger might result when any regime weakens, though so far it has been weakening authoritarian ones that have been more dangerous. Then it or some of its factions have often played the integral-nationalist and religious-nationalist cards.

Most large anti-Chinese riots have also been assisted by regime factions seeking to deflect blame for economic and political crises. There were major riot/pogroms in 1959, after which about 100,000 Chinese were expelled from the country, and again in 1965–6, 1973, 1980, and 1998. Anti-Christian and anti-Chinese pogroms in 1996 and 1998 (in which upward of 1,200 Chinese died) were generally interpreted as a last-ditch attempt by President Suharto to deflect widespread economic discontent onto Chinese entrepreneurs and political discontent onto the Muslim opposition (Chua, 2004: 43–5, dissents from this view, instead blaming democratization). On both occasions the police were mysteriously absent from the riot areas, while the initial rioters were organized black-garbed paramilitaries trucked in from outside (probably disguised policemen or soldiers). Then a large number of ordinary Indonesians joined in, looting, killing, and raping. In 1996 these appear to have been mainly Madurese transmigrants settled into coastal northeastern Java, normally supporters of the moderate Nahdlatul Ulama (NU) Islamic movement, seemingly subverted by the regime to discredit the movement. The Moluccas Christian–Muslim riots occurring since 1998, in which perhaps 2,500 people have been killed, may also have been fomented by rogue army elements; this time it seems to discredit both Christians and Islamic hard-liners (Hefner, 2000: 190–3, 205–12). The effect of these riots was to force substantial parts of each community behind its own armed men, intensifying the popular elements of the ethnoreligious conflict. It is estimated that tens of thousands of the Muslim transmigrants have fled the islands to return to Java and Sulawesi, and that tens of thousands of Chinese have fled the country since 1998.

So the Indonesian core and periphery once again push us toward a contested sovereignty and a disorderly statist explanation. Murderous cleansing does not occur where there is no contest over sovereignty or where firm, stable state institutions exist that are not beset by internal economic or political crisis or external geopolitical crisis; it might occur when these conditions are not met. Threats of violence are also greater where imperial and proletarian liberation movements collide, the one claiming to represent civilization and the global economy against backwardness, the other representing democracy – and both of them purporting to represent modernity. Yet whereas in India majoritarian governments have become more dangerous, in Indonesia it is weakening authoritarianism that seems more dangerous. There is no simple relationship in these two countries between democracy and ethnic cleansing.

We should not exaggerate the significance of these Indonesian conflicts. The international media focus on bad Indonesian news, mostly from the periphery of this sprawling archipelago. This is often horrific, part of the tendency I note in the final chapter toward the creation of ethnonationalist "black holes" on the peripheries of larger imperial states of the poorer, ex-colonial South of the world, largely shunned and ignored by the world's North. In the Indonesian core, as in the Indian core, ethnic and religious tensions simmer, but rarely do they boil over. It is different on their exploited peripheries.

Indonesia's future seems rather uncertain. It combines all three worsening trends I identify in the next chapter. Liberal and socialist influences have both declined, while secularism has become more embattled by increasing Islamicization of politics. This has not taken fundamentalist paths and probably will not do so, since there is no dominant secular elite in alliance with foreign imperialism. But the state is weakening and some political factions are radicalizing – as in my fifth ethnic thesis. The level of economic and political crisis has worsened to the point where capital is fleeing the country, deepening the crisis and emboldening radicals on all sides of the archipelago's complex ethnic–religious divides. There are greater reasons for pessimism in Indonesia than in India.

IS THERE A LOGIC OF ESCALATION FROM RIOTS TO MURDEROUS ETHNIC CLEANSING?

I can now attempt an overall explanation of the contrast between these two counterfactual cases and my earlier cases involving mass murder. The lower two parts of Figure 16.1 chart interactive processes that are generally absent in India and Indonesia but present in the worst cases. The essential question is: did these worst-case scenarios begin as repetitive communal riots and pogroms such as we find in India? Did they escalate through the first to the second and third phases of Figure 16.1 or did they follow some other route? I very briefly review my worst cases of recent ethnic cleansing (i.e., excluding the colonial and Communist cases).

The Armenian Genocide

Several large pogroms of Armenians had preceded the genocide of 1915 and the last two had been massive, much bigger than anything in India or Indonesia. In 1894–6 50,000 were killed and in 1909 20,000. They were also much bigger than any earlier incidents. They represented two new features of Ottoman society: a modernizing organic political project amid a more threatening geopolitical situation. These earlier pogroms had been committed not by Turkish ethnonationalists, but by their opponents. We can also trace back Turkish hatreds of Christians to the massive ethnic cleansing occurring from the 1820s to 1913 in the Balkans. Here Turkish Muslims had been the main victims. Yet Armenians were not at all involved. There had been some earlier three-way ethnic conflict between Russians, Turkic groups, and Armenians, but this had occurred in the Russian, not the Ottoman Empire. Though the pogroms of 1894–6 and 1909 obviously greatly worsened Turkish–Armenian relations and increased the possibility of something much worse happening, they were repressed. Something else was needed between 1909 and 1915 that focused ethnic tensions directly on the issue of sovereignty, which was not at issue in the earlier atrocities. We saw that this was a succession of wars, losses of territory, and the possibility of looming Armenian–Russian collaboration to destroy the Ottoman Empire. These new and predominantly external and geopolitical crises destabilized and radicalized the Ottoman state in the way suggested in the lower parts of Figure 16.1. The pressures came from the right-hand column of that figure.

The Nazi Final Solution

There had been many pogroms of Jews over the centuries in Europe. But there had been no significant ones in Germany for over a century before the Final Solution. The tradition of German anti-Semitism had been at a level that was about average for Europe. In the preceding century German Jews were assimilating, largely voluntarily. Austria saw more political anti-Semitism, but the main pogrom areas had been much farther east, in Russia and Poland, and they were getting worse in the late 19th and early 20th centuries. But it was Germans who initiated the Final Solution. Again, various processes intervened to politicize German–Slav–Jewish relations and to destabilize and radicalize the German state. Again, a world war transformed a policy of ethnic cleansing into genocide. This involved much less continuity than in the Armenian case, but again, the new pressures were mostly external.

The Rwandan Genocide

There were bursts of pogroms and murderous cleansings in the period from 1962 to 1979. But then there was a gap until 1990, after the RPF invasion, when a series of murderous incidents were closely connected to the genocide of 1994. Some see an essential continuity to this final period of escalation. Nonetheless, genocide would have been highly unlikely without the political destabilizations provided first by the Tutsi invasion and the consequent four-year civil war (which was a direct armed struggle over sovereignty), then by the Arusha Accords (which especially destabilized Hutu politics), and finally by a bolt from the blue, the assassination by missile of the two presidents. Much had to intervene, from the "Neighboring States" column in the lower parts of Figure 16.1, before pogroms became genocide.

Yugoslavia

The ethnic wars of the 1990s had been preceded by wartime murderous cleansing during 1941–5, mainly of Serbs by Croats, with revenge coming in 1945. Yet all of this had been set in motion by an external force, a German invasion, and had not been preceded by many 20th-century riots or pogroms. There had been significant communal riots/pogroms in Kosovo between Serbs and Albanians over much of the 20th century, but these had not occurred elsewhere in the post–World War II period. Murderous cleansing in the 1990s did not begin in Kosovo. It began quite suddenly in Croatia and Bosnia, with no prior riots or pogroms. Again, to explain this requires that we add a struggle over sovereignty amid destabilized, radicalized states.

All these cases involved old ethnic tensions and conflict – as in India and Indonesia. Yet murderous cleansing seems to need additional causes beyond those embedded in mere intercommunal ethnic or religious violence. Those causes are listed in my cumulative ethnic theses. Hence there is a fundamental discontinuity within Figure 16.1 between the Communal Conflict Phase and the Escalation Phase. Escalation is not endogenous to bi-ethnic societies. Instead, it results from political and geopolitical crises destabilizing the state, preventing decisive state repression of communal conflict – except by those radicalized by the crises to seek murderous cleansing to attain organic sovereignty. Sovereignty is the issue, and political and geopolitical instability is the process in which things can get really nasty. Without their combination, riot cycles ensue, not truly murderous cleansing. That at least offers some degree of comfort. Escalation is not endemic to the existence of ethnic rivalries and tensions. It needs the transposition of these to rival nation-states, both domestically and geopolitically. For murderous ethnic cleansing is the dark side of the would-be democratic nation-state.

17

Combating Ethnic Cleansing
in the World Today

EIGHT THESES RECONSIDERED

1. Murderous cleansing has been modern. In earlier times it sometimes resulted when conquerors seized the land but did not require the labor of the natives, while monotheistic salvation religions later attempted forced conversions. But the pace of murderous ethnic cleansing quickened greatly when modern people sought to establish rule by the people in bi-ethnic environments. "The people" came to have a dual meaning – as the *demos* of democracy and as the *ethnos* or ethnic group. Modern ethnic cleansing is the dark side of democracy when ethnonationalist movements claim the state for their own *ethnos*, which they initially intend to constitute as a democracy, but then they seek to exclude and cleanse others. There was also a dark side of socialist versions of democracy. The people was equated with the proletariat, and after the revolution cleansing of classes and other enemies might begin.

Yet the relationship with democracy has been a dynamic process, not a static correlation. Definitionally, perpetrating regimes cannot be democracies. Some were ethnocracies, democratic only within the *ethnos*, like settler regimes. Some began the slide into murderous cleansing by attempting to democratize, but then became authoritarian party-states, as in Yugoslavia, Rwanda, and Bolshevik Russia. The Young Turks began with democratic aspirations but slid simultaneously into authoritarianism and ethnic cleansing. Some began the slide as authoritarian party-states, with democratic processes already subverted during the preceding years, as in the Nazi, Chinese, and Cambodian cases. Except for most Nazis and a few individuals like Milosevic, my perpetrators moved from being democrats, to then advocating more dubious "organic" conceptions of democracy, and then acting in ways that were obviously fundamentally incompatible with any conception of democracy. The perversion of democracy was found most concretely in thousands of individual life trajectories. This is not democracy itself, but its perverted dark side.

2. Where successful, these movements trump class divisions, displacing class feelings of exploitation onto ethnic groups. Murderous cleansing does not result merely from differences. There must also be hierarchy: a plausible tale of exploitation and defense of democracy by one group, and defense of

privilege as civilization or survival by the other – ideologies of imperial versus proletarian nations. This was also evident among the Khmer Rouge, though most Communists made the reverse connection, giving national-ethnic coloration to class. But mere market or occupational economic differences seem insufficient. It is where monopolies arise, either through rival claims to land ownership or through statist monopolies, that ethnic economic conflict becomes most serious.

3. Things got more dangerous where two ethnic groups that were old (never newly constructed) made political claims to the same territory, both of which had some legitimacy and a plausible chance of being implemented. Even in Bosnia and the Punjab three rival groups arranged themselves into bipolar confrontations. This thesis did not fit one of the very worst cases – the Nazi genocide against the Jews. Nonetheless, Hitler himself believed in it, with his paranoia about the threat presented by a Judeo-Bolshevik enemy, which supposedly connected Jews to Slav enemies, and these enemies were indeed contesting sovereignty with Germans, especially those who were most likely to be perpetrators of genocide. However, the Holocaust had too many peculiarities to fit easily into any general model. All general explanations of murderous ethnic cleansing have suffered from taking this case as the model.

4. Actual mass murder required one of two further scenarios. In (a) the less powerful rival was bolstered to fight rather than submit (which does not produce mass murder), believing that help would be forthcoming from coethnics or allies abroad. In (b) a stronger group fears its power is declining in the long run, but can use its present strength to create its own cleansed state without much physical or moral risk to itself. Scenario (a) produces mass murder as an ethnic civil war begins and escalates; (b) produces genocidal preemptive strikes. Yet settler cases are distinct here, since settlers tended to embark on murderous cleansing only when much weaker native populations loom as violent irritants rather than major threats.

5. These scenarios require the state to have lost its normal repertoire mixing conciliation with repression. It becomes faction-ridden, and some factions radicalize and triumph, almost always as a result of external geopolitical pressures, usually including war. Though radicalization occurs in the name of the (ethnic) people, the state is by now not democratic. Yet we saw different kinds of factionalism: colonial frontiers with fluid states; states divided in different ways across the republics of Yugoslavia; and the Nazi state factionalized only in the limited sense of different institutions vying for the fuhrer's favor through genocidal zeal. Political fragmentation was often caused by the breakup of empire or the onset of a difficult war. Yet neither were present in the colonial or Communist cases, while in the Nazi case, imperial breakup was not a factor and mass cleansing and some mass murder (of mental patients) had started before the war.

6. Murderous cleansing is rarely initially intended by the perpetrators. They feel themselves forced into what is in effect a Plan C by the frustration of

earlier Plans A and B, which may involve repression but not mass murder. In scenario 4a the switch of plans is often unpredictable and contingent. It could easily have gone otherwise, and indeed, pragmatic political scheming does often prevent further escalation. The escalating Plans in 4b seem more logical outgrowths of initial intentions – the most obvious being Hitler's escalations against the Jews, followed by Milosevic's against his enemies. Though at first not even Hitler probably intended genocide, it was predictable (had we possessed intimate knowledge of him and of the Nazi movement) that when his "milder" plans were frustrated, genocide would be the consequence. Colonial cleansings tended to fall more into 4a but were distinctive in that the overall process involved a rolling series of cleansings, each with different perpetrators as the frontier expanded.

7. The perpetrators are neither coherent state elites nor entire peoples. Escalation occurs in complex interactions between leaders, militants, and masses, with majorities standing indifferently or fearfully by, with key perpetrators drawn disproportionately from core constituencies favoring violent ethnonationalism. This often includes elections giving victory to the radicals – though no elections have been won by openly inciting mass murder. Leaders are always the most important agents. Better or more moderate leadership could have headed off all the murderous outcomes I have discussed. But leaders do not act alone, and democracy is no protection against escalation – if the *demos* and *ethnos* (or the proletariat) are being confused. But as escalation proceeds, violence takes over from the hustings, and each *ethnos* is forced within its own barricades under the protection of its radical leaders and militants. By now they are also ideologically well armed, believing in the justice of their cause, defining it as self-defense. Self-defense is, of course, legally and morally legitimate. Rather appallingly, they pose as moral murderers.

8. The entire group of perpetrators is driven by the many motives that are normally found among ordinary people participating in more mundane social movements. Ordinary people are brought by normal social processes behind the ethnic barricades and then into committing murderous ethnic cleansing. By now, leaders can easily authorize this. As with leaders organizing the bombing of civilians in wartime, death is an abstraction that they do not have to confront directly. They are merely desk-killers. They believe in their cause, so the end justifies the means. Radicals at all levels are helped to kill by their sense of righteousness. But even you or I could do it, for reasons of career, comradeship, patriotism, work routines, and other mundane human motives. We are humans, capable of evil.

My theses run the gamut from broad background conditions to local processes. They also contain tension between broad comparative generalizations and the uniqueness of each case. There are two distinct subgroups, colonial and Communist cases. Exact prediction is not possible, and statistical analysis of cases will soon run out of the necessary numbers to control all the factors involved. Social science has its limitations, especially when dealing with macrophenomena where there are few cases and they interact. Actors in the colonial and Communist cases were learning from predecessors in other countries, while some Nazis knew of the Herero or Armenian genocides. Hitler and Himmler learned lessons from the extermination of native Americans. These were processes, not single events, and processes can develop in myriad ways.

So I take only limited comfort from the fact that the overall drift of my argument is broadly supported by the statistical data collected by political scientists on ethnic wars and civil wars throughout the world today. My argument is that ethnic cleansing diffuses along with the process of democratization. Gurr (1993, 2000) shows that ethnic rebellions have risen in the South of the world ever since the 1960s or 1970s, the period of its ostensible democratization. They remain low in the North, dominated by institutionalized democracies and the politics of class. During the 1950s they declined greatly in the Communist states, authoritarian and dominated by the politics of class. They fluctuated in the Middle East and North Africa, increased steeply in sub-Saharan Africa after 1960 amid democratizing states, rose after 1965 in Asia, and rose after 1975 in South and Central America. After 1975 all the southern regional trends rose until about 1995. The curve rose as a result of the collapse of the Soviet Union and Yugoslavia. After 1995 the trend may have declined a little, except in sub-Saharan Africa, though the overall trend is not yet back to pre-1991 levels (Gurr, 1994; 2000: Figures 2.2–2.9; Sollenberg & Wallensteen, 2001). This is some support for theses 1 and 2, though obviously some of these regional fluctuations have other causes too. I would expect the trend to decline once democracies are safely institutionalized without the *ethnos*.

Outside interventions might also force the trends down. Two of my theses concern external and therefore more contingent pressures. Outside aid for the weaker side and international instability leading to war were both aggravating geopolitical factors in my cases. But this does not have to be so. In Rwanda and Yugoslavia the international community might have intervened to try to stop the murderous cleansing, yet did not do so (except at the very end in Yugoslavia). This contrasted with the Cambodian case, where the Vietnamese Army overthrew the perpetrating regime and ended the killing. It is difficult to see how outside intervention might have prevented the Holocaust of the Jews and the genocide of the Armenians because of the wartime situations. But the international community could act more forcefully in relation to less powerful and protected perpetrators. I will explore this possibility in this chapter.

I had most difficulty evidencing thesis 7. Though all social movement have core constituencies of support, and this is presumably also true of extreme ethnonationalists, data on the social backgrounds of perpetrators have been sparse. We know most about elites, then militants, and least of all about rank-and-file perpetrators. Refugees are well documented as overrepresented among perpetrators; so are those from threatened border regions. Among dominant ethnic groups, statists – those socialized in or economically dependent on the state – are usually overrepresented. Once violence is seen as a possible solution to ethnic conflicts, specialists in violence, like policemen, ex-soldiers, and (in the more fluid cases) athletes, criminals, and juvenile gangs also seem to figure disproportionately. Ethnonationalists also arise from economic sectors lying outside the main arenas of class conflict in society (for the latter are drawn more into class than ethnic conflict). Fascists certainly were drawn from such backgrounds (see Mann, 2004). Cleansers seem to have been drawn from professional subcultures that at the time were scientifically and technically supportive of racialism, like biology and medicine. But solid evidence has sometimes come only from the best-evidenced Nazi case.

Nor is it easy to distinguish among three ideological components involved in perpetrators' worldviews: extreme nationalism, extreme statism, and endorsement of violence. For example, security policemen almost always figure prominently, but is this because they are statist, nationalist, or professionally inured to violence? Are athletes prone to nationalism, to deferring to older, more experienced authority and team leaders, or just to valuing physical solutions to social problems? I cannot really tell. We need more data, but data are exceedingly hard to find. When perpetrators talk, they usually lie – for *their* lives are now usually at stake.

Gender and age present distinctive problems. Murderous ethnic cleansing is gendered in the obvious sense that almost all perpetrators have been male – the clearest core constituency of all. But men have also been the overwhelming majority of victims. Young men predominate among the killers, and men of fighting age dominate among the victims. Murderous ethnic cleansing primarily concerns relations among young and early middle-aged men. But is this due to their greater commitment to nationalism or statism? These disproportions may merely reflect the dominance of men in most forms of public behavior, and especially of the dominance of younger men in military organizations. Whether ethnonationalism is peculiarly likely to attract men or young men – as some feminist writers have argued – has not yet been demonstrated. In the case of Yugoslavia, I doubted interpretations of the violence of Serb nationalism in terms of gender patriarchy rather than of more obvious causes like the possession of guns by Serb men in threatened border districts and a specific first-strike incentive for Serbs, given that they then had far more weapons. In the Yugoslav case, much attention has been paid to rape, because for the first time we had plenty of evidence. Rape may be a perennial behavior by armed men in contexts where normal moral taboos are breaking down – wars and civil wars. It may not be especially encouraged by nationalism. Such uncertainties can only be settled by further research.

THE DECLINE OF ETHNIC CLEANSING IN THE NORTH

Europe is nearing the end of the centuries'-long drive I have charted toward ethnically cleansed and democratic nation-states. Yugoslavia's wars are almost over, with Macedonia remaining as the one substantially bi-ethnic state there, its ethnonationalists weakened by horrific events just over its borders and by pressure from Europe and the United States. Though Europe and America had horrific histories of ethnic cleansing, they now ironically endorse multiculturalism, at least in theory. They do not support ethnonationalism, and in areas where they have influence, this is now a powerful restraint. The North can affect outcomes in the South.

There are only a few exceptions of remaining multiethnicity across the whole of Greater Europe. First, four older Western European states remain multiethnic – the United Kingdom, Belgium, Switzerland, and Spain. Their multiethnicity was acquired in the pre–nation-state era, when ethnicity mattered much less than class. Their ethnic groups squabble, but they do not kill – except in small and declining numbers in Northern Ireland and the Basque country. All other European Union (EU) countries are now at least 80 percent mono-ethnic, and so are almost all Eastern European countries. Emigration within the EU has declined over the past 40 years, as Italians, Portuguese, and Spaniards increasingly stay at home. The EU provides a federal level of coordination between mono-ethnic nation-states, but it is not a state.

Immigrants to the EU from outside its borders now form around 10 percent of most national populations, and this percentage will rise as aging creates labor shortages. Immigration from Eastern Europe will further grow as their countries are admitted into the EU. Yet such immigrants do not claim their own state. Indeed, they make few political claims and cannot be plausibly linked by nationalists to some external threat to the nation. Muslim immigrants can be linked to Christian fears of Islam, and they raise political difficulties in areas such as education and family law. But most immigrants are resented for more direct material reasons – employment, education, and housing competition – while employers welcome them. There are intermittent riots and some support for far-right parties, but little danger of murderous cleansing. In Europe the politics of class, region, and gender dominate, and my thesis 2 no longer operates. Of course, as long as the American "war against terrorism" continues along its counterproductive path, generating further terrorist backlash, the greater the chances of an anti-Muslim reaction occurring in the northern countries. Then ethnic–religious conflicts might rise to new levels there.

The second part of the North comprises the advanced economies of East Asia, especially Japan, South Korea, Singapore, and Taiwan. These are substantially monoethnic countries (except perhaps for Taiwan), none containing major ethnic tensions. The third part of the North comprises the former white colonies. In past centuries Europeans here launched their most murderous ethnic cleansings. But once North America and Australia were 95 percent cleansed, impeccably liberal nation-states could bloom above the massed graves of the natives. The ex-settler colonies can flaunt multiculturalism because immigrants, as in Europe, are not *politically* threatening. They may occupy distinct niches in the local economy and maintain their own culture. Ethnic tensions periodically surface, which on occasion escalate to riots, though these became much less violent and frequent throughout the 20th century. However important these tensions may seem to the countries involved, they are trivial compared to the terrible atrocities discussed in this book.

Since immigrants tend to come from many countries and cultures, the capacity of any group to make collective claims is limited, while immigrants as a whole have little basis for collective action. They seek voluntary partial assimilation into the host community, which in turn has developed institutions for facilitating this through labor markets, schooling, and legal statuses on the way to full citizenship. Where immigrants seek citizenship, they seek it as individuals. They seek neither confederal nor consociational collective rights. They wish to retain some of their original culture, but their maximal political strategy tends to involve local machine politics, aimed at capturing local political office and patronage for their ethnic group. In the United States, St. Patrick's Day and the Cinquo de Mayo are cultural, not political, festivals – even in territories that used to belong to Mexico! Their tricolors are paraded alongside the stars and stripes. No immigrant group since the first white settlers has made sovereign claims on the territories of the United States, Canada, Australia, or New Zealand. Though the host state may seem to belong to a dominant ethnicity – Anglos in these cases – this has been able to absorb new ethnic groups like the Irish and Jews.

My theory predicts that these rather apolitical conflicts will be quite mild. Recent mass immigration of Latinos and Asians into the United States has produced virtually no riots. That is also true of Japan, which retains rather more racism in its view of Korean and other immigrants. But since none of these immigrants make political demands, the host nations do not react with organic nationalism. The main goal of nativist movements is to get the borders tightened, not to cleanse the land of its present immigrants. Americans and Canadians often seem smug about their multiculturalism (Australians are less smug, aware of aboriginal maltreatment and anti-Asian hostility). They often regard ethnic strife as produced by a less civilized world elsewhere, but they do not confront rival groups claiming their own state over the same territory. Yet a world modeled on the United States and Australia might be as close to multiculturalism as we are likely to get. They are preferable to Europe's two main historical traditions: forcible assimilation and murderous cleansing. But perhaps the South of the world can do better than the North did.

A few problem areas remain around the European periphery. Ethnic cleansing in Yugoslavia is virtually complete, with Kosovo nearing its de facto cleansed solution (as was revealed by a further burst of cleansing of Serbs by Albanians in March 2004) and Macedonia remaining the one uncertain case. So Russians now remain as the only substantial minorities in many others' states, while some parts of the Russian Federation remain multiethnic.

There is much discrimination against minorities, yet relatively little violence between Russians and others. Chechnya is the massive exception. This is a very old case of ethnic conflict in which a long-established minority of Russian settlers are aided by the occupying Russian state. Both Russians and Chechen rebels believe they have a legitimate and achievable claim to their own sovereign state in the same territory. Chechnya fits well into my theses. The ferocity of Russian exemplary repression has recently forced the rebels into the arms of foreign Islamist allies. Though this lessens their popularity among Chechens, the desire for independence is probably too widespread to suppress. In early 2004, both sides continue to kill enemy combatants and non-combatants alike. This remains a murderous, unsolved case.

Yet elsewhere, Russian minorities choose emigration or they accept discrimination over resistance. The weaker side does not fight. Russians' settler immigration to the Baltic states and the Asian-stan states has been recent, and settlers have never claimed their own state, independently of Russia. Any such claim would have no historic or international legitimacy. In some of the -stans, Russians are tending to emigrate back to Russia, as they are being forced out of employment in central Asia. Some could in theory choose irredentism, union of their border areas with Russia, but Russia is not interested in supporting them. The westerly cases (especially the Baltic republics) differ, since many Russians believe they are materially better off there than in Russia. Additionally, the geopolitical environment is not supportive of murderous cleansing by either side. All the westerly successor states of the former Soviet Union want entry into the EU and NATO. They also seek economic aid, mainly from the EU, though also from the United States. They will get none of these things if they precipitate ethnonationalist violence. Europe is now a powerful restraining force on its own periphery. Moreover, Russia has enough problems of its own and does not want to provoke its neighbors. The geopolitical environment of the northern peripheries is no longer supportive of murderous cleansing.

THE REVIVAL OF ETHNICITY AND RELIGION ACROSS THE SOUTH

Today, almost all murderous cleansing occurs in the less developed South of the world, in countries where immigration is not the main problem and assimilation is not the main solution. The greatest threat is the spread into the South of the ideal of the nation-state, where this confuses the *demos* and the *ethnos*, the mass electorate and the ethnic group. This is overwhelmingly so of ethnonationalist conflict, and in slightly modified fashion it also applies to religious conflict. However, all is not gloom and doom.

Until 1945 the colonial empires blocked the globalization of the nation-state ideal. They were fundamentally racist and operated by divide-and-rule. Of course, among native ethnic groups, Europeans used particular

ethnic groups as their client rulers, increasing tribal consciousness the better
to preserve their own rule. But after the collapse of colonialism, all countries
of the world acquired anthems, flags, official languages, and education systems to encourage a single national identity – and all 191 of them sit together
in a body called the United Nations. They are in a formal sense nation-states,
and they claim (often spuriously) to be ruled by the people.

Decolonization produced high hopes of development, democracy, and the
transcendence of ethnic rivalries. Aware of their multiethnicity, most colonial
liberation movements carefully steered away from ethnic definitions of the
people, except to define it as distinct from the colonialists.

Southerners blended their own traditions with three northern ideologies:
liberalism, socialism, and secularism. Liberalism idealized a democracy representing the diverse economic, and not ethnic, interest groups of society.
Socialism stressed class, not ethnic conflict, and provided much material
support for anticolonial movements. Secularism accepted the separation of
church and state, and many liberation movements viewed their own religion
as backward, traditionalist, and antimodern, to be kept well away from the
state. A religion-centered sense of ethnicity would not dominate anticolonial struggles, except that a minority of Muslims were tempted by a broader
anti-imperialism represented by the ideal of a single Islamic caliphate. But we
saw that the Indian National Congress Party of Gandhi and Nehru sought
a modern secular state, not a Hindu state, and that was more typical of
anticolonial struggles.

This trend was strengthened by the victory of the liberal, socialist, and
secular allies over the fascists in World War II. In the interwar period, fascism and Nazism had influenced numerous anticolonial movements, opening
up an alternative route to modernity for those blending fascism with local
religion. Fascist-leaning Hindu and Muslim nationalists had sought states
cultivating the racial/religious purity of the nation. After 1945, however,
secularism or apolitical religious sensibilities pervaded political parties and
officer corps. Socialism now blended into Third World nationalism. African,
Arab, Indian, and other forms of socialism saw the oppressed peoples of the
colonies as a proletarian people, while the colonial power constituted an exploiting imperialist class. There were no significant class divisions within the
peoples of the Third World, so they said. But though organic, this was not an
ethnic conception of the people. Class was trumping ethnicity in anticolonial
struggles and in the early postcolonial years.

And so statistical data reveal no significant growth in ethnic or religious
violence and war in the world in the first two decades after World War II
(Gurr, 1993; Singer & Small, 1982). As in India and Indonesia, the infrastructures of the modern state would carry education, health, and taxation
systems across their territories, developing a rather secular and civic notion
of nationality across elites and then down to the masses. The achievements
of this period remain, in the form of some political parties, officer corps, and

professional and business classes still committed to such ideals. But their three imported ideological props then began to weaken. Socialism declined, political liberalism hollowed out into imperial neo-liberalism, and secularism was assailed by fundamentalism.

1. *The decline of socialism* reduced the influence of class models of collective action. As we saw, Communist states mostly damped down ethnic conflict except on their imperial fringes, where they perpetrated atrocities against ethnic secession movements – as in the Caucasus and Tibet. Their collapse led to an explosion of ethnic conflict in the 1990s. But socialist influence had begun to decline earlier across most of the postcolonial South. Once the colonial power left, class rhetoric no longer suited either dominant political interests or economic realities. The new elites controlled the state, economy, and media and used their power to deny the truth that they were now a ruling class. They were helped by the fact that in relatively backward countries disparities between regions usually outweighed those between the classes, and ethnic groups tended to be regionally concentrated. Many states focused more on regulating ethnic than class shares of the pie.

So, though postcolonial political parties may have started out as socialist or liberal (and occasionally as conservative), and as ethnically blind or multiethnic, most became regionally and/ or ethnically bound (Horowitz, 1985: 298–332). A socialist party would become a party representing the socialist aspirations of only one regional or ethnic group. Or socialist aspirations would collapse altogether as parties claimed to represent the common interests of an entire ethnic group against other ethnic groups. Often at the national level, and almost everywhere at the local/regional level, elections became ethnic censuses, with party votes highly correlated with the ethnic composition of the population. Ethnicity was beginning to trump class (thesis 2).

The Cold War obscured the breadth of this trend. Some Third World socialist movements were strengthened by aid from the Soviet Union, China, or Cuba, while others were crushed by U.S. intervention. Both sides saw conflicts in left–right terms, not as ethnic or religious. As the United States began to win this war, the left declined. Southern movements defining themselves as socialist were forced into the Soviet corner, and the Soviets had less to offer them. Southern socialist regimes became less able to provide economic development, and they became less popular. In some cases, religious solidarity encouraged resistance to U.S. and Soviet imperialism. In Iran the United States vigorously supported the shah's regime against the threat of Communism. But Iranians then turned to Islam rather than socialism to overthrow the shah. Ayatollah Ruhollah Khomeini's revolution was the first major demonstration of the fundamentalist upsurge, which was to pit it against the United States.

The end of the Cold War ushered in more general socialist decline. It was not universal. Socialist parties and Naxalite guerrillas remain significant in

India and Maoists in Nepal. Communist influence on the African National Congress (ANC) in South Africa helped ensure that African rule would not be initially racist. There are still Latin American leftist insurrectionaries like the Colombian FARC and the Zapatistas in Mexico. In Guatemala between 1960 and 1996 politicide was committed against the left, killing perhaps 150,000 and displacing millions from their homes. This case also contained ethnic overtones, as military regimes (allies of the United States) also wiped out several Mayan indigenous peoples in what were effectively local genocides. But most cases involving leftists as perpetrators or victims have become rather localized. Socialism has become more an ideology of warring localities than of global change. Where is African socialism or Ba'athist Arab socialism today? In politics, ethnicity and religion are now trumping class in many countries across the South.

2. *The hollowing out of liberalism into neo-liberalism* has weakened the appeal of liberalism and liberal democracy in less successful parts of the South. As we saw in Europe, classical liberalism had a strong political theory. This focused not only on the virtues of free markets, but also, more importantly, on the virtues of institutionalizing interest group conflict through multiparty elections and parliaments. Liberal democracy proved capable of compromising class conflict through the development of national citizenship, welfare states, and Keynsian economics.

Liberalism today remains secular and tolerant, and it opposes most ethnonationalisms and formal empires. Yet it is more American-defined and puts much more stress on free enterprise and free markets as the preconditions of democracy. It recognizes individual liberties, but not class and interest-group conflict. American-centered neo-liberalism focuses on exporting to the world laissez-faire economics aimed specifically against the kinds of state interventions that have historically embodied class compromise (welfare states, regulated labor markets, etc.). Neo-liberalism also tends to subordinate Southern states to an American-dominated political economy. It is avowedly antisocialist, and is often perceived in the South as masking economic imperialism. Fluctuations in interest rates, mostly generated within the Northern economies, have also impacted harshly on the South. In the 1970s, low interest rates encouraged Southern countries to borrow heavily to finance economic development. Then interest rates shot up, generating a Southern debt crisis. The combination of these two crises led to American-led neo-liberal interventions to solve the debt crisis of depressed Southern economies. The structural adjustment programs of the IMF, World Bank, and Northern banking consortia have meant disruptive cutbacks in Southern state expenditures, welfare programs, and labor market regulation. Their net economic effect has usually widened inequalities and social conflict in the South, increasing the plausibility of denunciations of the Washington consensus as imperialism (see Mann, 2003: chap. 2). As Chua (2004) notes, where inequality is linked to ethnicity, this increases ethnic hatreds.

Thus the world has polarized. On the one hand, successful capitalist development has widened the North. Southern Europe and Japan joined the North in the 1960s, soon followed by the "Little Tigers" of East Asia. They enlarged a *zone of peace* in which war and ethnic war seem a thing of the past. But much of the South is being shunned by capitalism amid widening international and domestic inequality. Trade with and investment in the South are declining. Economic crises weaken the power and legitimacy of the poorer states, worsening local discontent. If ethnic or other forms of disorder stir there, capital will shun them even more, increasing the disorder. Zones of peace are paralleled by *zones of turmoil* increasingly containing ethnic conflict. The greater the infant mortality rate of a country and the less its international trade, the greater the chance of civil war, including ethnic war (Esty et al., 1998; Goldstone et al., 2002; Harff, 2003). The Marxist nightmare of being exploited by capitalism is not nearly as bad as the postmodern nightmare of being excluded from it! Since the globalization of capitalism has also shifted some power from labor to capital, it further weakens socialist movements in the South, aiding the surge in ethnonationalist and religious movements.

3. *The rise of fundamentalism* weakened secularism, liberalism, and socialism. Salvation religions claim a unique revealed truth. Monotheistic religions (Christianity, Judaism, and Islam, but not Buddhism or Hinduism) claim the one true God. One cannot belong to two such religions. Religions are deeply implanted in everyday family and community rituals, generating intense emotional and moralistic commitment. Those who follow different faiths may be intolerant and seek to impose their truth on the other. In earlier centuries this often produced attempts at forced conversion, severer where it coincided with attempts at colonization (as in Ireland or Lithuania) or at imposing imperial political rule over other territories (as in Spain). The politicization of religion produced the most problems, and so eventually Christianity, the least tolerant religion, solved its problems by moving to the secular state. Shintoism, Buddhism, and Hinduism had been far more tolerant and so fought each other rarely. Nor did Jews or Muslims in the past seek to cleanse or forcibly convert. Even today, most religious believers across the world tolerate other religions. Like Christ, religions have learned to yield up to Caesar what is Caesar's and to keep what is theirs. Yet in some parts of the world there is increasing religious violence. Why?

My answer will rest on a variant form of my first ethnic thesis: contemporary religious violence results primarily from the rise of claims to *theodemocracy* – claims to political rule by "we, the religious people." Muslim fundamentalism centers on the notion of self-government by a religious community adhering to the prescriptions of the Qur'an and applying the *shari'a*, Islamic law. The *shari'a* is not state law. Historically, it was more akin to Western civil law, with most of its cases being brought by individuals against other individuals and not by the state. Then in the 19th century the modernizing Ottoman state began to attempt to codify *shari'a* law (Keddie, 1998: 708). Today's fundamentalists remain ambiguous on the issue. Though basing their claims on the Qur'an, they combine the statism and populism of the 19th and 20th centuries into a religious version of rule by we, the people. At first they idealized theo-democracy, the term coined by Maulana Maududi, the leading Islamicist of the Indian subcontinent in the 1940s, to indicate a "divinely-directed democratic government" (Saulat, 1979: 134). So fundamentalists initially mobilized as populists, stirring popular and implicitly classlike sentiments against authoritarian rulers (either the colonial powers or postcolonial secular rulers accused of imbibing Western culture). Comparable Hindu nationalists (pursuing *dharma yuddha*, a holy or righteous war) and even Sri Lankan Buddhist nationalists also arose. Hindu fundamentalists wish to impose a Hindu conception of religious purity derived from sacred texts like the Hindi Ramayana.

As these fundamentalist movements grew, however, they became less democratic. When they seized power, as in Iran or Afghanistan, they became dictatorial and theocratic, embodying rule by religious imams or mullahs. So we tend to think of fundamentalists as having nothing to do with democracy. Yet their mass appeal is a democratic one, aimed against local authoritarian rulers and foreign imperial powers. Indeed, in the contrast between ideals and practices, revolutionary Islam resembled revolutionary socialism. Both movements generated alternative versions of the ideal of rule by the people against ruling classes and imperial powers – and both then betrayed them by endorsing a powerful state.

This state is supposed to express the religious purity of the people – a religious variant of an organic nation-state. This is curious since the religions are in their doctrines neither statist nor nationalist. They argue that states should be subordinate to the religious community, and the community is seen as transnational, not national, spreading right across nation-state boundaries (except in Nepal, which is constitutionally a Hindu state). Yet Hindu and Islamic theo-democrats have unintentionally become nationalists and statists (as Juergensmeyer, 1993, notes). By requiring that each state enforce the *shari'a* or Hindutva, they become trapped de facto into statism and nationalism. Since Pakistan should belong to true Muslims alone, its state should enforce the *shari'a*. Since Hinduism centers on one very large state, its organicists distinguish between a transnational Hindu nation, a kind of Greater India, stretching right across South Asia, and the national core of motherland India itself. Islam has no such core state. Both sets of theo-democrats assert that religious minorities are to be forcibly assimilated or allowed to maintain only a private religious life, as second-class citizens or noncitizens. "The foreign races must lose their separate existence... or may stay in the country, wholly subordinated to the Hindu Nation, claiming, deserving no privileges... not even citizens' rights," said Gowalkar, the leader of the radical Hindu nationalist movement, the RSS (Gold, 1991: 566).

WHERE DO ETHNONATIONALIST BLACK HOLES APPEAR?

These three trends set the stage for a rise of ethnic–religious conflict across parts of the South. Of course, the South is very varied. Some countries are already nearly mono-ethnic, having earlier developed a single national culture. This is true of Korea, most of the other Asian Little Tigers, and China, except for its far western peripheries. It is mostly true of the core territories of India and Indonesia. Their relative cultural homogeneity has clearly contributed considerably to their rapid economic development. They continue the main tradition of ethnic cleansing in the North, mainly assimilating and culturally suppressing minorities over quite a long period of time, with more serious trouble occurring only in peripheral colonized territories.

Some other ethnic configurations are not conducive to rival ethnonationalist struggle either. Some nations contain a hierarchy of ethnic color existing amid a broader and rather secular national culture. In Latin America groups are often stratified according to degrees of European, indigenous, or black slave blood. Their *mestizo* cultures produce a rather weak sense of both nation and ethnicity (Centeno, 2001). Ethnic differences are tied closely to class, resulting in stronger left–right than ethnic politics. The exceptions here are again peripheral struggles over land between settlers (usually *mestizos*) and indigenous peoples, as in Chiapas, the Guatemalan highlands, and parts of Colombia and Amazonia. In these peripheries serious ethnic cleansing does occur, if weakened by the reluctance of the indigenous peoples to claim their own state.

But the culture of these countries is often also transnational. Latin America has a shared *mestizo* and Catholic heritage cutting across the states' boundaries, and Arabic and Islamic countries are integrated by the Arabic language and/or Islam. Even the great ethnic divides of Pakistan are lessened by a shared Muslim culture. Again, there are exceptions on the peripheries of such states – Berber regionalist demands in Algeria and Kurdish separatism in several countries. Elsewhere, however, these countries have been likewise spared much murderous ethnic conflict.

At the other extreme are nations containing many ethnicities. Across much of Africa politics are dominated by ethnicity, but no single ethnic group can seize and control the state as its own. The more successful countries embody multiethnic compromises, inscribed between political parties or within officer corps. In the long run some might develop a core national macroethnicity gradually assimilating and culturally suppressing many other small ethnic groups, as India and Indonesia have done and as most European countries did before them.

This may require states with quite developed integrative capacities, but these are often lacking across the poorer parts of the South. Colonialism destroyed their traditional infrastructures and forms of property ownership, replacing them with alien Western institutions that the postcolonial regimes have been unable to maintain. Under the strain of regional–ethnic conflict, these states are increasingly breaking up in the face of civil wars, most of them taking an ethnic form. Fearon and Laitin (2003) attribute the increasing frequency of civil wars in poorer countries to weak or failed states. In this context, they argue, no particular ethnic or religious configuration determines the onset or duration of civil wars. More decisive are conditions directly favoring insurgency against weak states – rough and mountainous terrain, political instability, local economic spoils that insurgents can seize to finance themselves, a large population offering concealment, and poverty itself, which starves the state of adequate repressive resources. There is indeed an increasing tendency to see insurgents as bringing a new form of warfare in which loot-seeking, Kalashnikov-wielding thugs without any serious political ideology massacre local populations (Collier & Hoeffler, 2002; Kaldor, 1999). Along with Kalyvas (2001), I have doubts about this since it seems yet another version of the ethnocentric conflict between "we, the civilized" and "they, the primitives." It minimizes both the criminality of old wars and the ideology of new ones. Most African insurgent movements begin with genuine organic nationalist ideologies; only later do they degenerate under conditions of civil war stalemate into criminality. These black holes differ from the cases I have analyzed in having no victor. Both sides murderously cleanse, but they are unable to create their own stable state or eliminate the enemy.

States with fewer ethnicities offer conflicts more in line with those I have analyzed. However, only some of these involve rival claims to sovereignty. Ethnic niche economies do not usually do so. Here an ethnic minority is concentrated in certain sectors and occupations, fueling claims from others of unfair competition and exploitation. As in my second thesis, economic grievances are displaced onto the minority. Conflict is generally less severe where the minority clusters among lower-level occupations. Immigrant laborers usually experience discrimination and a few riot cycles, but not murderous cleansing. They provide scarce low-wage labor, and so are regarded as useful by capitalists and governments. The troubles of immigrant workers in the Gulf States (or those in eastern Germany or the French industrial suburbs) are serious. But they pale beside the events discussed in this book, because they do not claim the state for themselves.

Worse treatment is sometimes meted out to *middlemen ethnicities* – entrepreneurial merchant and trading groups like Jews in Europe, Asians in East Africa, and Chinese across Southeast Asia. These groups are typically accused of economic exploitation by radicals from the host community. At their worst, these accusations fuel pogroms and deportations, displacing class tensions onto easy targets whom the regime is willing to sacrifice in order to appease popular discontent. Of course, the targets are ultimately ethnic – all Chinese in Indonesia, not just capitalists, are vulnerable to attack. Pressured by popular violence, East African governments deported their Asian populations – long seen as stooges of the white colonialists. In Malaysia and Indonesia, Chinese communities have suffered many assaults involving deaths, vividly and acutely analyzed by Chua (2004). However, the regime and the upper classes find middlemen ethnicities too useful to be eliminated, and they ultimately move in to protect them. Unlike Chua, I do not believe that such conflicts underlie the most murderous cases of ethnic cleansing.

Though rival bi-ethnic claims to the state are more dangerous, escalation rarely materializes where power sharing has long involved both ethnic groups. Usually, the minority dominates the economy, while the majority possesses the state, as in Malaysia, Fiji, or Guyana. Their postcolonial states then develop entrenched power sharing. These arrangements may break down, sometimes amid dangerous riots, but they rarely descend further. Each side's sense of exploitation is only partial, and neither generates the whole imperial versus proletarian ideology. They also usually live among each other and so cannot easily detach themselves. Specifically, the minority cannot claim regional autonomy, still less its own state, especially if neither is supported by a homeland or neighboring state. Power sharing has already brought some benefits to both sides. Alternatives seem abstract and risky.

Rwanda was a partial exception. Hutus and Tutsis did live among each other, and for a short time the minority Tutsis dominated the private economy, while the majority Hutus formed the large state sector. But this power sharing had never been institutionalized. The Rwandan Tutsis had traditionally dominated both power sources, and they still do so in neighboring Burundi. There was also an actual invasion by emigre Tutsis aided by Uganda. These factors made Hutu Power radicals escalate into genocide. This then spilled over into the Congo in the form of enraged Hutu refugees and enraged Tutsi punitive raids – aided by opportunistic neighboring powers seeking mineral wealth. These converted Congo from a scenario of African multiethnic disintegration (as described earlier) into one of massively murderous cleansing. I can think of no other closely analogous case to Rwanda/Burundi anywhere else in the world. Perhaps this was the last of the world's genocides.

The more dangerous cases today conforming most closely to my theses mostly exist around the fringes of bigger imperial countries – as was also the case in the 19th and early 20th centuries across Greater Europe. The previous chapter discussed the fringes of India and Indonesia. There are also cases around the former Soviet fringe in Chechnya, Abkhazia, Nagorno-Karabakh, and the Fergana Valley. China's southwestern fringe generates ethnonationalist conflict in Tibet and Xinjiang. Kurdish ethnonationalists agitate across the peripheral territories of Turkey, Iran, and Iraq. Burma's fringe territories are tinderboxes; so are parts of the southern Philippines. Ethiopia, Somalia, and Eritrea have all contained ethnic minority secession movements aided from across the border. In such contexts insurgents denounce Turkish, Iraqi, Indian, Burmese, Indonesian, Mexican, Guatemalan, Brazilian, and other imperialisms. Imperialism is now also Southern, and resistance to it may involve claims to ethnic democracy similar to those we saw revealed earlier in Europe.

Most of these conflicts also occur in some of the poorest, most isolated parts of the world, and so they become only local black holes. Armenia and Azerbaijan, Abkhazia and Georgia, are wasted, but their conflict does not spread. The very worst case, Rwanda, does spread its deadly virus to the African Great Lakes region as a whole, but the rest of the world then consigns the entire region to its peripheral vision, accepting that its precious metals will come north through more circuitous warlord- and mercenary-ridden routes. Turkey, Russia, China, India, Indonesia, and so on are also given a free hand. Most choose repression, and so ethnic conflict and cleansing worsen, making international capitalists less interested in trading or investing in these trouble spots. Their economic crisis deepens and local conflict escalates.

WHERE DO RELIGIOUS WARRIORS APPEAR?

Most fundamentalists are not very violent. They focus on making their own community doctrinally purer, seeking to overcome the opposition of either local infidels or corrupt, authoritarian, and usually rather secular Muslim rulers. This, say the Islamists, is part of the broader injunction of *jihad*, meaning "struggle/striving in the name of Allah." *Jihad* does not necessarily imply violence and should not be translated as "holy war," for Christians understand by that term actual war. Fundamentalists do threaten second-class citizenship for religious minorities, displace women from the public sphere, and impose a high level of cultural censorship on all. But (in the categories of my Table 1.1) this takes them only as far as discrimination, cultural suppression, and some policed repression. We might add that most secular regimes in the Muslim world are not much better.

But some Islamic fundamentalists take the notion of struggle much further, into *qital*, or "combat," against the enemies of Islam. They become religious warriors and are generally referred to by Muslims as *jihadis*. All religions can find among their holy texts some phrases appearing to endorse combat, since religions articulate norms governing all aspects of human life. Islamic warriors quote the repeated injunctions in the Qur'an to resist oppression – "for oppression is even worse than killing" (2:191), so "fight against them until there is no more oppression and all worship is devoted to Allah alone" (2:193). Oppression helps define some secular or authoritarian conservative rulers in the Muslim world as no longer Muslims, thus setting aside the normal Qur'anic injunction against overthrowing a Muslim ruler. Religious warriors enjoin armed struggle in the name of the one true faith. Hindu warriors denounce Gandhi's nonviolence as weakness, and they applaud his Hindu nationalist assassin for restoring militant violence as one of the "four pillars" of Hinduism. Then Islamic and Hindu movements embrace paramilitarism, the occupation of an inner, purer elite

(Juergensmeyer, 1993; Keddie, 1998; for India and Pakistan, see Ahmad, 1991; Gold, 1991; Jaffrelot, 1996; Katzenstein et al., 1998: 226; Saulat, 1979: 132–5).

When local enemies seem entwined with infidel imperialists, the resonance of a religious call to combat is much greater. So Muslims denounce global imperialism, Hindus and Buddhists denounce only a local Southern version. Declining terms of trade, debt crises, and neo-liberal restructurings reinforce the resonance. Where the United States props up Southern regimes for its own geopolitical purposes, arming them against their local enemies and domestic dissidents, discontent against them is also turned against the United States. This has particularly affected the Muslim world. The United States gives large military support to oppressive and corrupt regimes like those of Egypt and Saudi Arabia. It is even clearer where the United States appears to take sides in regional conflicts. Its two invasions of Iraq and its support for Israel give Arabs and Muslims a clear-cut sense of a dual local/imperial enemy.

Israel is the main contemporary example of settler-conquerors. For half a century, Israelis have been cleansing the occupied territories of native Arabs, most murderously in the late 1940s, renewed again in the Jewish land-grabbing of the past few years. Israelis have mainly cleansed within their own occupied territories, devising the typical settler state: democracy for the settlers, lesser rights for the natives – what Yiftachel (1999) accurately terms an *ethnocracy*, a *demos* only for the *ethnos*. A few Jews have even been drawn into their own theo-democratic vision of the state in which the Jews are entitled to occupy the Land of Israel only if they follow the laws of the Torah, a covenant between God and the ancient Israelites, so that they must impose Jewish law on the land, regardless of other faiths. Though both sides began this conflict with fairly secular materialist goals, they have been drawn toward more fundamentalist views as the situation has worsened. The United States has become embroiled on the imperial Israeli side of the war. After all, its tanks are the ones driving into the West Bank, and Israel receives far more U.S. military and economic assistance than any other country in the world (see Mann, 2003: chap. 2).

Huntington (1996) claims that broad religiously based conflict flares up today along the fault lines between religious civilizations, though he shows only that it does along one fault line across Africa and Asia where Islam meets Christianity, Buddhism, or Hinduism. As he notes, most interreligious conflict is between Muslims and others, from northern Nigeria through the Sudan to Armenia/Azerbaijan, to Kashmir, to the southern Philippines, to the Moluccas. As I noted in Chapter 1, religion is particularly effective at creating larger macro-ethnic aggregations out of diverse ethnic groups. So the ethnic diversity of the Sudan becomes polarized into a single principal division, a Muslim/Arabic North against a somewhat less cohesive Christian and animist South.

But Huntington ignores the fact that this is also conflict *about* religion as well as between religions. It involves intense struggles *within* each faith. The Sunni–Shia divide is particularly difficult within Islam, as Iraq reveals. But in the 20th century, Islam was also rent by the same sacred–secular debate that rent Christendom in the previous century. Now, as then, the dispute ranges fundamentalists, believing that the state must enforce religious truth, against those favoring some degree of separation between religion and state – secularists, mystics, and most minority sects. Yet since the latter usually control the military, they are not very tolerant either. In a sense, two fundamentalisms oppose each other within each faith, one sacred, one more secular, disputing the nature of democracy. Both sides claim exceptions to rule by the people. Fundamentalists do so only if the people is pure, while secularists abandon democracy, claiming that fundamentalists will ditch democracy if elected. Neither side is much disposed to let elections decide the issue. Within Islam this conflict dominates Algeria and threatens all the relatively secular states in Muslim countries, from Egypt and Turkey through the new Central Asian republics to Indonesia. The struggle is often bloody. It occasionally acquires local ethnic coloration, though its main issues involves broader religious matters.

Some of these fault lines are also where Northern imperialism meets Southern dependency. Religious warriors can mobilize powerful religious sentiments against local oppressors, but their cosmology will resonate more if the enemy is also identified as a global, infidel oppressor. Islamic *jihadis* attacking the West must be understood as anti-imperialists, the word that neither Huntington nor American foreign-policy makers will let cross their lips, though it is essential to understand the phenomenon. This is a new form of anti-imperialism, very different from the old socialist variety because religious warriors denounce materialism. They denounce not economic exploitation, but the political imperialism of a North seen ideologically as both Christian and irreligious. Anti-imperialism rejects materialism as part of the hated secularism of Northern conceptions of modernity. However, no one should doubt that it also thrives on a real sense of economic and political oppression among Muslims: restore Palestinian lands, remove the U.S./Israeli tanks, and establish a genuine Palestinian as well as an Israeli state and the appeal of *jihadis* to Palestinians would be cut to near zero. Remove U.S. bases from Arab lands, and the same effect would be felt more generally.

Do these struggles involve cleansing? They involve possible forcible conversion, though the imposition of fundamentalism within each faith is unlikely to involve much killing. Fundamentalist rule in Iran and Afghanistan has also involved cultural cleansing, discrimination, and pressured emigration of minorities. The most extreme Hindu fundamentalists favor the forcible deportation of Muslim men and the conversion of Muslim women. And in escalating confrontations, as in Kashmir or Palestine or Chechnya, murderous ethnic–religious cleansing is launched by both sides, involving as much killing and intimidation as is necessary to force the other community into flight. Greater callousness is also shown to civilians caught up in this war – the residents of Moscow tower blocks, the shoppers in Israeli malls, the workers of the World Trade Center, the commuters of Madrid, and tens of thousands of Chechens, Palestinians, Afghans, Iraqis, and others assaulted in retaliation. As we have seen throughout this book, retaliation mostly hits not the initial perpetrators but their coethnics or coreligionists. One side is denounced as terrorists, the other as state terrorists. All their actions have moved modern ethnic–religious conflicts into the shaded murderous cleansing areas of my Table 1.1. These religious–ethnic rivalries do present very serious danger, and the counterproductive American, Israeli, Russian, and Indian retaliatory measures worsen the danger (see Mann, 2003).

I have argued that this global swathe of religious–ethnic conflict is largely explicable in terms of a religious version of my first ethnic thesis: a claim that the modern state should essentially represent we, the holy people, and not the people of other or lesser faiths. As in my earlier case studies, the politicization of religion into rival claims to sovereignty over the same territory increases the danger of mass violence – making military power relations also crucial.

My thesis 4a states that murderous ethnic conflict usually requires the weaker group to become emboldened to resist and fight, rather than to submit to discrimination and coercive assimilation. Emboldening usually comes from outside sympathizers. Transnational capitalism also assists insurgents. The end of the Cold War liberated many arms producers from control by the superpowers, and they became freer to supply the small arms that are the weapons of choice for groups of ethnic or ethnic–religious warriors. This industry is the most global of all, since it does not shun the poorer parts of the South. A Russian inventor became its household name. Kalashnikov simplified the mass-produced, hand-held automatic rifle, the AK-47. At a conference, after I had outlined an early version of my views on ethnic conflict, Archbishop Walter Makhulu, then the Anglican archbishop of Central Africa, turned to me and said in criticism: "The African problem is simple – the Kalashnikov." He had a point. Armed gangs across many countries can acquire the low-level weaponry to make paramilitary warfare into a way of life, extorting their subsistence from the local population. This is now perhaps the main reason weak, destabilized governments generate the most ethnic violence. September 11, 2001, revealed a more spectacular example of such weapons of the weak. Tens of terrorists armed with knives boarded civilian airliners and killed almost 3,000 people amid the buildings symbolizing American power. This atrocity continues the trend of 20th-century warfare toward the increasing targeting of civilians as the enemy. It also means that high-tech military power alone will not eliminate the threat of religious warriors or ethnonationalists – as we see clearly in both Afghanistan and Iraq today. What will?

POLICY IMPLICATIONS

Can we identify antidotes to ethnic conflict? My theses identify the circumstances in which murderous cleansing occurs and the processes whereby it unfolds. Murderous ethnic cleansing derives from a broad developmental tendency of modernity. It is pointless to stand on the sidelines, morally deploring this trend or blaming malevolent elites, primitive peoples, or the evil in human nature. We must accept that ethnic cleansing arises amid bi-ethnic conflict that is real and obdurate. We in the North must show more realism in our views of ethnic cleansing. We must abandon the complacency conferred by the notion that the emergence of liberal, tolerant democracy is the inevitable outcome of modernity, sidetracked only by primitive or malevolent in peoples and their leaders. The ideal of democracy, rule by the people, is diffused by modernity, but this can become organic and exclusionary, creating danger for ethnic and religious minorities. We must be realistic about this tendency, be prepared for it to show itself, and help head it off. We must engage with the world as it is, not as it appears in our dreams.

Ethnic cleansing was central to the modernization of the Old and New Worlds. Though not invented by our civilization, it was perfected by us. Our liberal democracy did not emerge by the simple granting of universal human rights amid social harmony, but through serious social conflict, mostly between social classes. Ethnic conflict was most often dealt with through cultural suppression of minorities. Nowadays this would be considered a breach of fundamental human rights, though with the perspective of time it does not seem too bad. Liberalism and then social democracy deepened through realistic acceptance of the inevitability of class and interest group conflict, which was then institutionalized and compromised. Conflict did not disappear but was managed through common citizen rights. Any solution to ethnic (and class) conflict today requires that we recognize its normalcy. We evade recognizing this by pious denunciations of evil leaders. Unaccompanied by more comprehensive action, mere threats to extremist leaders may actually increase their local popularity. Since we ourselves live in ethnically cleansed countries, our denunciations also smack of hypocrisy.

My ethnic theses detail where organic conceptions of democracy emerge, become dangerous, and go over the brink into murderous cleansing. Thus we can identify what other researchers have called the early warning signals of ethnic conflict (Davies & Gurr, 1998; Goldstone et al., 2002; Gurr, 1993, 2000). Their quantitative data drawn from many countries produces conclusions parallel to mine. They strive to predict where conflict will arise, not without success, though they admit to both false positives, predictions of impending catastrophes that do not materialize, and false negatives of seemingly little danger that suddenly erupts into violence. They sometimes imply that their predictive failures are a product of poor data, improvable through more intensive research. I doubt this. Though I have mainly studied the few most serious cases, I have demonstrated that things rarely go according to anyone's plan; murderous cleansing is rarely intended from the outset but instead emerges out of unpredictable interactions. We can identify danger zones and cases approaching the brink, but exact prediction of murderous cleansing seems impossible – as is a rational choice theory of perpetrators.

But I draw from my first and third ethnic theses to make a fairly general prediction. Where a significant minority movement is already making collective political demands on a state dominated by another ethnic or religious group, these demands will neither wither away nor be repressed, once aired and organized. The nation-state ideal is too strongly entrenched in the modern world for them to be simply repressed or ignored. Many governments, from Russia, to India, to Israel, to the United States, still do not recognize this. They should. The less developed the country, the more likely the demand will grow as the country moves into a world that adores nation-states. The ideal will doubtless spread to some ethnic groups at present largely uninfected by it.

But not to all ethnic groups. Most ethnic groups in the world are much too small to achieve their own states. They are already assimilating into the nation-states of others, mostly with relatively little violence. One index of this is the continuing decline in the number of languages spoken in the world, halved to around 5,000 over the past 50 years and likely to swiftly decline further. Aspirations to collective political rights are not universal. As my third thesis emphasizes, it is rival *plausible* and *achievable* claims to political sovereignty that spell difficulties, that is, some past history of sovereignty and some recent continuity of claim. As I have emphasized, serious ethnic conflicts generally occur between old, not newly constructed groups. This limits the claim to around 50 ethnic groups at present lacking their own collective political rights. These will be difficult to stop.

Thus I predict that Indonesia will be unable to assimilate or repress Aceh or West Papuan autonomy movements; India will be unable to assimilate or repress Muslim Kashmiris or several of its small border peoples; Sri Lanka will be unable to assimilate or repress Tamils; Macedonia will be unable to assimilate or repress Albanians; Turkey, Iran, and Iraq will be unable to assimilate or repress Kurdish movements; China will be unable to assimilate or repress Tibetans or Central Asian Muslims; Russia will be unable to repress Chechens; the Khartoum regime will be unable to contain South Sudanese movements. Israel will be unable to repress Palestinians. None of these regimes should draw much confidence from the fact that the autonomy (or terrorist) movements confronting them may mobilize only a minority among the ethnic out-group, most of whom would rather live quietly under their dominance without causing any political trouble. Silent majorities remain silent; they do not come to the aid of alien imperial regimes. The Indonesian government made serious attempts to arm local clients among the ethnic out-groups but failed to embed them deeply enough within local populations. Nor should the regimes delude themselves that their next military offensive will finally defeat the autonomy movements. It might repress them into quietude for a time, but they will reemerge, supported by the nation-state ideals, the arms trade, and the weapons of the weak of the modern world.

Only some minority movements demand states of their own. Most autonomy aspirations could be satisfied within present state boundaries. This requires that the regime make real concessions of either a confederal or a consociational form: the minority would secure some regional self-government or new entrenched collective rights at the center. Consociational arrangements involve combinations of guaranteed quotas for minorities in the cabinet, the parliament, the civil service, and the army, plus veto powers over policy held by the dominant ethnic groups. In the extreme, a consociational government might be a "Grand Coalition" of parties representing all the main ethnic groups. Majority ethnic groups are rarely attracted by this prospect, since they can win elections on their own; and even if the Grand Coalition works, it tends to reduce the vitality of political opposition, which is usually considered a precondition of democracy. But such schemes may be usefully diluted by electoral incentives whereby parties are in practice rewarded with more seats if they draw votes and candidates from across the ethnic divide. Incentive schemes rarely refer directly to ethnicity. Instead they balance regions or devise alternative or transferable vote systems that are in practice tailored to favor moderate second-choice parties appealing across the ethnic divide.

Confederal and consociational regime elements are no panaceas. They work better in some places than others. Sometimes they actually strengthen minority ethnic identity and even discontent. Giving a national minority power at the regional level may make it oppress its own regional minorities – including the local minority that is the majority in the central state. In practice, no country will suddenly change its constitution wholesale to a design considered confederally or consociationally ideal. When new constitutions are added to traditional political practices, the mix may produce unintended consequences (see Horowitz, 1999, for a skeptical view of recent attempts at constitutional design). Regional autonomy may not assuage but encourage demands for independence – a point often made by organic nationalists attached to the integral unity of the state, from Indonesia to the United Kingdom. But mere liberal guarantees of individual rights are inadequate to appease autonomy demands. In these contexts most persons identify with their own ethnic community, so that free first-past-the-post elections produce ethnic domination, since they are ethnic censuses – as in Northern Ireland, which has had a genuinely liberal polity for 100 years. Individual and group-based conceptions of rights are both necessary (as Rothschild, 2002, shows).

Effective constitutions must vary case by case, and they must not be set in stone. Any constitution has unintended consequences, some good, others bad. But once majority and minority communities are locked into institutionalized power-sharing arrangements and become used to the compromises they embody, the situation eases. Does it finally matter whether Quebec remains part of Canada, or Scotland part of the United Kingdom, or Catalonia part of Spain? It matters only at a much lower level of troubles than those discussed in this book. If Quebec, Scotland, or Catalonia separate from their imperial ruler, people will not die or be driven from their homes. Rather, they will worry about the consequences for investment and unemployment, what languages they will learn, and whether a tiny country would ever qualify for the World Cup finals. Hopefully, settling down into the mundane will also occur in cases that are more troublesome at present. Eventually, after Kurds have secured and enjoyed some degree of regional autonomy within Turkey, Iran, and Iraq, they will perhaps seek their own nation-state. But by then Kurds, Turks, Iranians, and Iraqis may not care very much either way. For the past decade the Québecois, Scots, and Catalans have been dithering at election time, unable to decide whether they really do want independence. It doesn't matter much, one way or the other, either for them or for their supposed exploiters.

In extreme cases, realism suggests that separation into two nation-states may be the least bad immediate solution. This may be so where past violence has created too much distrust for power sharing to emerge peaceably. That is so in Kosovo, and probably in Aceh and Tibet, but probably not yet in the South Sudan, with little history of its own sovereignty and where the rival identities are weaker. Of course, separation brings its own problems. Now conflict might be warfare between separate states, while it is difficult to protect those who are made minorities within the new state. Collective guarantees of minority rights are required, policed by international agencies. In some cases it may be better to deflect hatreds onto milder stages of cleansing achieved by mutual negotiation through agreed-upon population and property exchanges, border alterations, and so on than to risk further cleansing by force – as in Kosovo and perhaps Bosnia. This is not now the preferred policy of the UN, NATO, or the United States. But how much longer must their forces continue repressing Croats and Serbs who demand their own statelets and continue harassing the few returning refugees? Might it not be preferable to assist population exchanges and recognize those nation-statelets – even allow them to merge with Croatia and Serbia if they wish (with minority rights guarantees, of course)? After all, we have our nation-states. But solutions must vary according to the type and level of threat. There are no general antidotes.

Can we in the North help the countries of the South avoid the worst scenarios, which are, after all, those of our own past? Yes, since we have seen that geopolitical contexts matter considerably, in terms of both outside aid and international conflict. In the case of the European periphery, we have seen powerful geopolitical restraining influences currently operating against ethnic violence. Unfortunately, these are rarely exercised elsewhere. It is easy to see what some of them should be. We should exercise much greater control over our arms sales, both of the heavy weapons of repression by state terrorism and the small-arms weapons of the weak on which paramilitarism and terrorism thrives.We should seek an international regime more sensitive to regional conflicts and to our own imperialist tendencies. We should help reduce inequality in the South; we should not subordinate ethnic conflicts or dissidence against authoritarian regimes to our geopolitical games; we should encourage the institutionalization of conflict of both ethnicity and class. This would imply, for example, more sensitivity to sub-Saharan African poverty, to Arab/Islamic fears of Israel, to indigenous peoples being expropriated by big capital allied to incoming settlers, and so on. This is pie in the sky, of course. Imperialists, international capitalists, arms smugglers, religious warriors and ethnonationalists are not motivated primarily by noble sentiments. Little of this is at present on the international agenda.

One problem is the United States. There is a lamentable contrast between the recent performance of American neo-liberal imperialism compared to American policy in Europe and Japan immediately after World War II. Then the U.S. government sought to encourage both the center–right and the center–left of Europe and Japan to establish conciliatory labor relations and parliamentary coalitions, isolating extremists outside viable institutions of class compromise and cutting the ground from under their feet (Maier, 1981). Now, in contrast, international institutions seek to free capital from the "dead hand" of regulation and economies are given the "shock therapy" of market freedom, almost regardless of the consequences in terms of unemployment, wage levels, worker protections, and political reactions. Where inequalities acquire ethnic overtones, they encourage ethnic conflict between proletarian and imperial ethnic groups. The IMF, World Bank, and other lending institutions should examine a new kind of conditionality, attaching to loans conditions that require steps toward greater equality of class and region, and toward protection of both individual and collective human rights. Moreover, the U.S. "war against terrorism" is extremely unbalanced. It aims only at terrorists and not at state terrorists (except for the few rogue states otherwise opposing U.S. foreign policy). This means the United States is currently intervening on the side of dominant states against their ethnic–religious insurgents. From Palestine to Georgia, to Chechnya, to Kashmir, to the southern Philippines, to Colombia, U.S. policy favors state terrorists. It even gives most of them military aid useful for suppression.

U.S. policy today might be thought of as farsighted, since it aims right at my thesis 4a. The United States seeks to end cross-border aid to terrorists (i.e., rebels) by sympathizers abroad and by aiding state terrorists. Thus it seeks to sap the will to resist of the weaker party. Can it succeed, forcing rebels into submission or to agree to paltry gains at the negotiating table? In a few cases it might if a rebel movement is not well entrenched among a dissident people. The Abu Sayyaf movement of the southern Philippines now seems to have little support among the local Muslim minority. Perhaps the United States can assist the Filipino government to suppress it. But it is doubtful that this can work more generally where the demand for rule by the people is deeply entrenched. Ethnonationalism has grown ever stronger in the world. It is now universally regarded as legitimate for a people (in both senses) to rule itself. Self-determination has become global since President Woodrow Wilson enunciated it in 1917. Even in the Philippines, the new policy has so far failed to weaken the more deeply rooted Muslim insurgent group, the Moro Liberation Front; indeed, the Filipino government has been forced to adopt a conciliation strategy. I have argued elsewhere that U.S. biases actually increase the flow of terrorists – as well as increasing their propensity to also attack the United States (Mann, 2003). The policy of supporting state terrorists against terrorists is doomed to failure. The disastrous current state of Iraq and Afghanistan also confirm the failure of such policies.

Ethnic and other civil wars are currently getting larger and more difficult to solve. More peace agreements fail than succeed. Stedman et al. (2002) see three obstacles thwarting them – local spoilers (power actors who do not want the agreement to work), neighboring states also acting as spoilers, and local valuable commodities that allow combatants to sustain themselves in the war. Stedman and his coauthors suggest that the international community should provide economic and military resources to counteract all three. The fighters must be helped to find civilian employment, the economy must be jump-started, the neighbors must be appeased, and so on. But they also note that the international community is a very long way from committing such resources. Rwanda in 1994 showed how far we are from effective intervention even against quite puny perpetrators of genocide. General Dallaire, the commander of the small UN monitoring force on the ground in Rwanda, wired his superiors in New York that the prompt dispatch of 5,000 UN troops would stop what he correctly identified as an unfolding genocide. A subsequent military commission of inquiry in the United States supported his estimate. The UN did nothing, mainly because the Great Powers of the Security Council, especially the United States, France, and Britain, blocked any intervention. They did not want to spend their money or risk their soldiers' lives in an obscure African country, especially if foreigners commanded the operation (Melvern, 2000). In contrast, we intervene to protect oil or our allies, and now we pressure the European periphery. The UN is useful in policing borders between enemies that want to be policed, but it cannot police those that do not. The United States pursues its own interests in choosing when to consult multilateral agencies and when to bomb or invade. We are a long way from an international regime capable of enforcing global norms.

There is also judicial intervention, prosecution after an ethnic war for crimes already committed. Two ad hoc UN War Crimes Tribunals already operate. They are an advance on any previous war crimes tribunals since they do not simply represent the victors' definition of justice – as the Nuremberg trials did. Both tribunals move slowly, and the Rwandan Tribunal is painfully short of resources. The Yugoslav, though not the Rwandan, Tribunal has prosecuted offenders from all perpetrating sides. A projected Cambodian court stalled after protracted negotiations. Some countries changed their laws to allow prosecution of resident foreigners who committed their crimes elsewhere. This permitted the trial and conviction of four Rwandans in Belgium in June 2001. The hounding of General Augustin Pinochet in 2000 and 2001 failed to bring him to justice but furthered international cooperation in future efforts to capture perpetrators. Indeed, a permanent International Criminal Court has been endorsed by most UN members and is in principle ready to hold trials.

These courts can mete out retribution for past deeds and make judgments laying down international norms beyond which no one should go. These are useful roles. Yet my case studies suggest two limitations. First, the courts presuppose an elite theory of crimes. They can deal with only a few offenders unless given enormous resources. Yet my cases involved thousands of offenders. The courts are forced to be highly selective, but selection is based on who falls easily into their hands and whose actions were so public as to create many witnesses. Selectivity creates the sentiment among the perpetrating community that prosecution is unfair, which makes reconciliation more difficult. International trials send signals and punish a few, but they cannot administer justice more generally. National courts can act more swiftly and cheaply against many offenders, but their justice may appear summary and the trials are conducted by the victors over the vanquished, threatening reconciliation. Rwanda's mass *gacaca* trials, though not kangaroo courts, raise unease. Truth and Reconciliation Commissions, as in South Africa, are better at reconciliation, but few believe that mass murderers should be forgiven, even if they appear contrite.

My case studies suggest that trials are unlikely to deter radicals from atrocities. The threat of prosecution would not have seemed real to ideologically driven leaders like Hitler or Pol Pot, while those more driven by contingencies, like Milosevic or the Young Turks, feel that they are not the masters of their own fate and are already playing for high stakes. If they lose, they may die anyway; if they win, the risk of future prosecution pales beside being hailed as the savior of the nation. The rank-and-file add the reasoning of the common criminal: they have to catch me first; if I wear a mask or kill all witnesses, I am safe. Rape may now be more easily prosecuted, since most victims remain alive, retaining vivid memories of their violators. But the Arusha and Rwandan courts deter no one. The core Hutu perpetrators fled over the Congo border and have been continuing murderous rampages there ever since. The warring factions in the Congo have caused the deaths of between 3 and 4 1/2 million civilians in the decade in which the court has been sitting.

The two goals involved often conflict. Justice should be blind to politics; reconciliation *is* politics. True justice would involve long jail sentences for thousands of murderers and rapists, plus the mass restitution of property and financial reparations. Quite apart from its impracticality, this does not seem the way to reconciliation. Reparations have not happened in South Africa, despite the charter of the Truth and Reconciliation Commission, nor are they practical in the aftermath of large-scale ethnic cleansing. In Yugoslavia 100,000 people occupy each other's houses, and all the ethnic communities have been greatly impoverished. In this context, reparations and restitution may not even be desirable, for more deaths might flow from an attempt to impose them. In Rwanda reparations are impractical, given the poverty of the country. Most Hutus have nothing to give. Since the politics necessary for reconciliation vary from case to case, this also means that there are no absolute standards of achievable justice.

U.S. governments also oppose the World Criminal Court. They fear that Americans might be indicted for their numerous interventions across the world. Indeed, the bombing of neutral Cambodia or the treatment of prisoners in Guantanamo Bay and Iraq seem potentially indictable war crimes. Yet if the world relies on the United States as its global sheriff, it must accept that the sheriff sometimes intervenes with guns blazing. Since the court could be effective only with U.S. participation, compromise is required on this and other issues. But while realistically achievable international intervention forces and criminal courts achieve little now, once expanded and routinized, they could lead toward a broader interventionist regime. They could provide the supportive geopolitical environment to bring ethnic conflicts back from the brink, at least into the zones of more moderate cleansing specified in Table 1.1. But in the meantime we should prepare for more of the worst.

This book may seem depressing. Not only have I argued that ethnic cleansing is essentially modern, a part of our own civilization, the dark side of democracy. I have also suggested that it is quite popular, not produced merely by manipulative elites. It is widespread among modern peoples. Yet I have argued *against* the notion that murderous cleansing is a necessary feature of the human condition or that ethnicity generally triumphs over less violent bases of social organization. Ethnicity is not (as many argue) generically more powerful or more mobilizing than class or other bases of collective action. Nor is extremism more generally powerful in the world than moderation. Ethnic cleansing results from one secular trend of modern societies; that is all. The dark side of democracy is passing through modern societies. It has finished passing through the North and is now engulfing parts of the South. But it will end before long, when democracy is securely institutionalized in forms appropriate to multiethnic, and especially bi-ethnic, populations. It will hopefully end during the 21st century. By now we can recognize the circumstances in which ethnic cleansing threatens danger and then goes over the brink into mass murder. From recognition comes the ability to formulate solutions. But at present we lack the will to commit resources to those solutions in the South of the world. The South may be forced to repeat our own doleful history of ethnic cleansing.

Works Cited

Aaronsohn, A. 1916. *With the Turks in Palestine*. London: Constable.

Abbott, W. (ed.) 1939. *The Writings and Speeches of Oliver Cromwell. Vol. II: The Commonwealth 1649–1653*. Cambridge, Mass.: Harvard University Press.

Adanir, F. 1998. "Nicht-muslimische Eliten im Osmanischen Reich," in W. Höpken & H. Sundhaussen (eds.), *Eliten in Südosteuropa. Südosteuropa Jahrbuch*, Vol. 29. Munich: Südosteuropa-Gesellschaft.

———. 2001. "Armenian Deportations and Massacres in 1915," in Chirot and Seligman (eds.), *Ethnopolitical Warfare*.

Adanir, F., & Kaiser, H. 2000. "Migration, Deportation and Nation-Building: The Case of the Ottoman Empire," in R. Leboutte (ed.), *Migrations et migrants dans une perspective historique*. Brussels: Peter Lang.

Adelman, H., & Suhrke, A. (eds.) 1999. *The Path of a Genocide: The Rwanda Crisis from Uganda to Zaire*. New Brunswick, N.J.: Transaction.

African Rights. 1994. *Rwanda: Death, Despair and Defiance*. London: African Rights.

Ahmad, F. 1982. "Unionist Relations with the Greek, Armenian and Jewish Communities of the Ottoman Empire," in B. Braude & B. Lewis (eds.), *Christians and Jews in the Ottoman Empire*. London: Holmes & Meier.

———. 1993. "War and Society Under the Young Turks, 1909–18," in A. Hourani (ed.), *The Modern Middle East*. New York: Taurus.

Ahmad, M. 1991. "Islamic Fundamentalism in South Asia: The Jamaat-i-Islami and the Tablighi Jamaat of South Asia," in Marty & Appleby (eds.), *Fundamentalisms Observed*.

Aiyar, S. 1995. "'August Anarchy': The Partition Massacres in Punjab. 1947." *South Asia*, vol. 28.

Akcam, T. 1992. *Turk Ulusal Kimligi ve Ermeni Sorunu* [Turkish National Identity and the Armenian Issue]. Istanbul: Iletisim Yaynlari.

———. 1997. "The Genocide of the Armenians and the Silence of the Turks," in *Proceedings of the International Conference on "Problems of Genocide."* Cambridge, Mass.: Zoryan Institute.

Akhtar, S. 1991. "Uprising in Indian-Held Jammu and Kashmir." *Regional Studies*, vol. 9.

Alexander, S. 1987. *The Triple Myth: A Life of Archbishop Alojzije Stepinac*. New York: Columbia University Press.

Allen, B. 1996. *Rape Warfare: The Hidden Genocide in Bosnia-Herzogovina and Croatia*. Minneapolis: University of Minnesota Press.

Allen, M. 2002. *The Business of Genocide: The SS, Slave Labor, and the Concentration Camps*. Chapel Hill: University of North Carolina Press.

Almaguer, T. 1994. *Racial Fault Lines: The Historical Origins of White Supremacy in California*. Berkeley & Los Angeles: University of California Press.

Altshuler, M. 1990. "Ukrainian–Jewish Relations in the Soviet Milieu in the Interwar Period," in Potichnyj & Aster (eds.), *Ukrainian–Jewish Relations*.

Ancel, J. 1989. "The Romanian 'Christian' Regimes from 1940 to 1944 and Their Attitude Toward Jews, the Church, the Clergy, the Press," in Y. Bauer et al. (eds.), *Remembering for the Future: Working Papers and Addenda*, 3 vols. Oxford: Pergamon.

Ancel, J. 1993. "Antonescu and the Jews." *Yad Vashem Studies*, vol. 23.

1994. "German–Romanian Relations During the Second World War," in R. Braham (ed.), *The Tragedy of Romanian Jewry*. New York: Columbia University Press.

Anderson, B. 1983. *Imagined Communities: Reflections on the Origin and Spread of Nationalism*. London: Verso.

Andonian, A. 1920. *Documents officiels concernant les massacres arméniens*. Paris: Turabian.

Andreopoulos, G. 1994. *Genocide: Conceptual and Historical Dimensions*. Philadelphia: University of Pennsylvania Press.

Arad, Y. 1987. *Belzec, Sobibor, Treblinka: The Operation Reinhard Deathcamps*. Bloomington: University of Indiana Press.

1989. "The 'Final Solution' in Lithuania in the Light of German Documentation," in Marrus (ed.), *The Nazi Holocaust*, 4, part 2.

Arad, Y., et al. 1989. *The Einsatzgruppen Reports*. New York: Holocaust Library.

Arai, M. 1992. *Turkish Nationalism in the Young Turk Era*. Leiden: Brill.

Arendt, H. 1965. *Eichmann in Jerusalem: A Report on the Banality of Evil*. New York: Viking Press.

Armenian Political Trials, Proceedings 1. 1985. *The Case of Soghomon Tehlirian*. Los Angeles: Varantian Gomideh.

Armstrong, J. 1963. *Ukrainian Nationalism*. New York: Columbia University Press.

1982. *Nations Before Nationalism*. Chapel Hill: University of North Carolina Press.

Ashman, C., & Wagman, R. 1988 *The Nazi Hunters*. New York: Pharos.

Astourian, S. 1995. *The Armenian Genocide: An Interpretation*. Glendale, Calif.: ARF Shant Publications.

Avakumovic, I. 1971. "Yugoslavia's Fascist Movements," in P. F. Sugar (ed.), *Native Fascism in the Successor States, 1918–1945*. Santa Barbara, Calif.: ABC-Clio.

Bacchetta, P. 1999. "Militant Hindu Nationalist Women Reimagine Themselves." *Journal of Women's History*, vol. 10.

Baghdjian, K. 1987. *La confiscation, par le gouvernement turc, des biens armeniens... dits abandonnés*. Montreal: no publisher stated.

Ball, P., et al. 2002. *Killings and Refugee Flow in Kosovo, March–June 1999*. Washington, D.C.: American Association for the Advancement of Science.

Banach, J. 1998. *Heydrichs Elite: das Führerkorps der Sichesheitspolizei und des SD 1936–45*. Paderborn: Schöningh.

Bankier, D. 1996. *The Germans and the Final Solution*. Oxford: Blackwell.

Barber, M. 2000. *The Cathars*. London: Longman.

Barkai, R. (ed.) 1994. *Chrétiens, musulmans et juifs dans l'Espagne mediévale*. Paris: Editions du Cerf.

Barkawi, T., & Laffey, M. (eds.) 2001. *Democracy, Liberalism and War: Rethinking the Democratic Peace Debates*. Boulder, Colo.: Lynne Rienner.

Barnett, A. 1983. "Democratic Kampuchea: A Highly Centralized Dictatorship," in Chandler & Kiernan (eds.), *Revolution and Its Aftermath*.

Barton, J. 1998. *"Turkish Atrocities": Statements of American Missionaries on the Destruction of Christian Communities in Ottoman Turkey, 1915–1917*. Ann Arbor, Mich.: Gomida Institute.

Bartov, O. 1985. *The Eastern Front, 1941–45, German Troops and the Barbarisation of Warfare*. London: Macmillan.

1991. *Hitler's Army: Soldiers, Nazis and War in the Third Reich*. New York: Oxford University Press.

1996. *Murder in Our Midst: The Holocaust, Industrial Killing, and Representation*. New York: Oxford University Press.

Basu, A., & Kohli, A. (eds.) 1998. *Community Conflicts and the State in India*. Delhi: Oxford University Press.

Bauer, F. (ed) 1968–81. *Justiz und N-S Verbrechen*, 22 vols. Amsterdam: University Press.

Baumann, Z. 1989. *Modernity and the Holocaust*. Ithaca, N.Y.: Cornell University Press.

Bax, M. 1995. *Medjugorje: Religion, Politics and Violence in Rural Bosnia*. Amsterdam: VU Uitgeverij.

Bebler, A. 1993. "Political Pluralism and the Yugoslav Professional Military," in Seroka & Pavlovic (eds.), *The Tragedy of Yugoslavia*.

Becker, E. 1998. *When the War Was Over: Cambodia and the Khmer Rouge Revolution*. New York: Public Affairs.

Becker, J. 1996. *Hungry Ghosts: Mao's Secret Famine*. New York: Free Press.

Becking, B. 1992. *The Fall of Samaria*. Leiden: Brill.

Bedoukian, K. 1978. *Some of Us Survived: The Story of an Armenian Boy*. New York: Farrar.

Bedrossyan, M. (ed.) 1983. *The First Genocide of the 20th Century: The Perpetrators and their Victims*. N.p.: Voskedar Publishing.

Beissinger, M. 1998. "Nationalist Violence and the State: Political Authority and Contentious Repertoires in the Former USSR." *Comparative Politics*, vol. 30.

2002. *Nationalist Mobilization and the Collapse of the Soviet State*. Cambridge: Cambridge University Press.

Bell-Fialkoff, A. 1996. *Ethnic Cleansing*. New York: St. Martin's.

Berenbaum, M. (ed.) *A Mosaic of Victims: Non–Jews Persecuted and Murdered by the Nazis*. New York: New York University Press.

Bernardini, G. 1989. "The Origins and Development of Racial Anti-Semitism in Fascist Italy," in Marrus (ed.), *The Nazi Holocaust*.

Bhattacharjea, A. 1994. *Kashmir: The Wounded Valley*. New Delhi: UBS Publishers Distributors.

Bilinsky, Y. 1990. "Methodological Problems and Philosophical Issues in the Study of Jewish–Ukrainian Relations During the Second World War," in Potichnyj & Aster (eds.), *Ukrainian–Jewish Relations*.

Birn, R. 1986. *Die Höheren SS- und Polizeiführer*. Düsseldorf: Droste.

1991. "Austrian Higher SS and Police Leaders and Their Participation in the Holocaust in the Balkans." *Holocaust and Genocide Studies*, vol. 6.

1998. "Revising the Holocaust," in Finkelstein & Birn (eds.), *A Nation on Trial*.

Black, P. 1984. *Ernst Kaltenbrunner: Ideological Soldier of the Third Reich*. Princeton, N.J.: Princeton University Press.

Blau, T. 1993. "Psychological Perspectives on the Perpetrators of the Holocaust." *Holocaust and Genocide Studies*, vol. 7.

Bley, H. 1971. *South-West Africa Under German Rule 1894–1914*. Evanston, Ill.: Northwestern University Press.

Block, R. 1993. "Killers." *New York Review of Books*, November 18.

Boehnert, G. 1981. "The Third Reich and the Problem of Social Revolution: German Officers and the SS," in V. Berghahn (ed.), *Germany in the Age of Total War*. London: Croom Helm.

Bogosavljevic, S. 1995. "Statistical Picture of Serbia, Montenegro and Parts of the Former Yugoslavia with a Serbian Majority," in Janjic (ed.), *Serbia Between the Past and the Future*.

Bond, D. 1998. "Timely Conflict Risk Assessments and the PANDA Project," in J. Davies & T. Gurr (eds.), *Preventive Measures: Building Risk Assessment and Crisis Early Warning Systems*. Lanham, Md.: Rowman & Littlefield.

Botica, S., et al. 1992. *Mass Killing and Genocide in Croatia 1991/92: A Book of Evidence*. Zagreb: Hrvatska sveucilisna naklada.

Braeckman, P. 1994. *Rwanda: Histoire d'un génocide*. Paris: Fayard.

Braham, R. 1981. *The Politics of Genocide: The Holocaust in Hungary*, 2 vols. New York: Columbia University Press.

　1983. *Genocide and Retribution: The Holocaust in Hungarian-Ruled Northern Transylvania.* Boston: Kluwer-Nijhoff.

　1989a. "The Kamenets Podolsk and Delvidek Massacres: Prelude to the Holocaust in Hungary," in Marrus (ed.), *The Nazi Holocaust.*

　1989b. "The Holocaust in Hungary: An Historical Interpretation of the Role of the Hungarian Radical Right," in Marrus (ed.), *The Nazi Holocaust.*

Braham, R., & Pok, A. (eds.) 1997. *The Holocaust in Hungary: Fifty Years Later.* New York: Columbia University Press.

Brass, P. 1997. *Theft of an Idol.* Princeton, N.J.: Princeton University Press.

　2003. "The Partition of India and Retributive Genocide in the Punjab, 1946–47." *Journal of Genocide Research*, vol. 5.

Breitman, R. 1991. *The Architect of Genocide: Himmler and the Final Solution.* New York: Knopf.

Bridgman, J. 1981. *The Revolt of the Hereros.* Berkeley & Los Angeles: University of California Press.

Bringa, T. 1995. *Being Muslim the Bosnian Way.* Princeton, N.J.: Princeton University Press.

British Broadcasting Corporation. 1998. *Death of a Nation.* BBC documentary film.

Broszat, M. 1981. *The Hitler State.* London: Longman.

Browder, G. 1996. *Hitler's Enforcers.* New York: Oxford University Press.

Brown, D. 1970. *Bury My Heart at Wounded Knee: An Indian History of the American West.* London: Barrie & Jenkins.

Brown, P. 1996. *The Rise of Western Christendom.* Oxford: Blackwell.

Browning, C. 1978. *The Final Solution and the German Foreign Office.* New York: Holmes & Meier.

　1985. *Fateful Months: Essays on the Emergence of the Final Solution.* New York: Holmes & Meier.

　1992. *The Path to Genocide: Essays on Launching the Final Solution.* Cambridge: Cambridge University Press.

　1993. *Ordinary Men: Reserve Police Battalion 101 and the Final Solution in Poland.* New York: HarperCollins.

Brubaker, R. 1992. *Citizenship and Nationhood in France and Germany.* Cambridge, Mass: Harvard University Press.

　1996. *Nationalism Reframed: Nationhood and the National Question in the New Europe.* Cambridge: Cambridge University Press.

Brubaker, R., & Laitin, D. 1998. "Ethnic and Nationalist Violence." *American Review of Sociology*, vol. 24.

Bryce, Viscount. 1972. *The Treatment of Armenians in the Ottoman Empire 1915–1916: Documents Presented to the Secretary of State for Foreign Affairs*, 2nd ed. (first ed. 1919). Beirut: Donuigan & Sons.

Buchheim, H., et al. 1968. *Anatomy of the SS State.* New York: Walker.

Budreckis, A. M. 1968. *The Lithuanian National Revolt of 1941.* Boston: Lithuanian Encyclopedia Press.

Bukey, E. 1992. "Nazi Rule in Austria,"in *Austria History Yearbook*, Vol. 23.

Bunce, V. 1999. *The Design and Destruction of Socialism and the State.* Cambridge: Cambridge University Press.

Burke, P. 1978. *Popular Culture in Early Modern Europe.* London: Temple Smith.

Burleigh, M. 1988. *Germany Turns Eastwards: A Study of Ostforschung in the Third Reich.* Cambridge: Cambridge University Press, 1988.

　1994. *Death and Deliverance: 'Euthanasia' in Germany, 1900–1945.* Cambridge: Cambridge University Press.

　2000. *The Third Reich: A New History.* London: Macmillan.

Butnaru, I. 1992. *The Silent Holocaust: Romania and Its Jews.* New York: Greenwood Press.

Campbell, B. 1998. *The SA Generals and the Rise of Nazism.* Lexington: University of Kentucky Press.

Campbell, J. 1995. "The United Kingdom of England: The Anglo-Saxon Achievement," in A. Grant & K. Stringer (eds.), *Uniting the Kingdom? The Making of British History.* London: Routledge.

Caplan, J. 1988. *Government without Administration: State and Civil Service in Weimar and Nazi Germany.* Oxford: Clarendon Press.

Carnegie Endowment. 1914. *Report of the International Commission to Inquire into the Causes and Conduct of the Balkan Wars.* Washington, D.C.: Carnegie Endowment. Re-issued by the Endowment in 1993 under the title *The Other Balkan Wars,* with an Introduction by George Kennan.

Centeno, M. 2001. *Blood and Debt: War and the Nation-State in Latin America.* Princeton, N.J.: Princeton University Press.

de Certeau, M., et al. 1975. *Une politique de la langue. La révolution française et les patois: L'enquête de Gregoire.* Paris: Gallimard.

Chalabian, A. 1988. *General Andranik and the Armenian Revolutionary Movement.* No place: no publisher.

Chalk, F., & Jonassohn, K. 1990. *The History and Sociology of Genocide.* New Haven, Conn.: Yale University Press.

Champagne, D. 1992. *Social Order and Political Change: Constitutional Governments under the Cherokee, the Choctaw, the Chickasaw and the Creek.* Stanford, Calif: Stanford University Press.

Chandler, D. 1991. *The Tragedy of Cambodian History: Politics, War and Revolution since 1945.* New Haven, Conn.: Yale University Press.

1992. *Brother Number One: A Political Biography of Pol Pot.* Sydney: Allen & Unwin.

1999. *Voices from S-21: Terror and History in Pol Pot's Secret Prison.* Berkeley & Los Angeles: University of California Press.

Chandler, D., & Kiernan, B. (eds.). 1983. *Revolution and Its Aftermath in Kampuchea: Eight Essays.* New Haven, Conn.: Yale University South East Asian Studies.

Charny, I. 1986. "Genocide and Mass Destruction: Doing Harm to Others as a Missing Dimension in Psychopathology." *Psychiatry,* vol. 49.

Chen, Y.-T. 1980. *The Dragon's Village.* New York: Pantheon.

Chesterman, S. (ed.) 2001. *Civilians in Wars.* Boulder, Colo.: Lynne Rienner.

1997. *Le défi de l'ethnisme: Rwanda et Burundi: 1990–1996.* Paris: Karthala.

Chirot, D., & Seligman, M., (eds.). 2001. *Ethnopolitical Warfare: Causes, Consequences, and Possible Solutions.* Washington, D.C.: American Psychological Association.

Chrétien, J.-P., et al. 1995. *Rwanda: Les médias du génocide.* Paris: Karthala.

Chua, A. 2004. *World On Fire: How Exporting Free Market Democracy Breeds Ethnic Hatred and Global Instability.* New York: Anchor Books.

Churchill, Winston. 1937. *Great Contemporaries.* New York: Putnam.

Churchill, Ward. 1997. *A Little Matter of Genocide: Holocaust and Denial in the Americas, 1492 to the Present.* San Francisco: City Light Books.

Cigar, N. 1995. *Genocide in Bosnia.* College Station: Texas A&M University Press.

1995. *Genocide in Bosnia: The Policy of Ethnic Cleansing.* College Station, Tex.: Texas A&M Press.

1996. "The Serbo-Croatian War, 1991," in S. Mestrovic (ed.), *Genocide After Emotion.*

Clifton, R. 1999. "'An Indiscrimate Blackness'? Massacre, Counter-Massacre and Ethnic Cleansing in Ireland, 1640–1660," in Levene & Roberts (eds.), *The Massacre in History.*

Cocker, M. 1998. *Rivers of Blood, Rivers of Gold.* London: Jonathan Cape.

Cohen, L. 1995. *Broken Bonds: Yugoslavia's Disintegration and Balkan Politics in Transition.* Boulder, Colo.: Westview.

Colley, L. 1992. *Britons: Forging the Nation 1707–1837*. New Haven, Conn.: Yale University Press.

Collier, P., & Hoeffler, A. 2002. "Greed and Grievance in Civil War." World Bank paper, www.econ.worldbank.org.

Collins, R. 1974. "Three Faces of Cruelty: Towards a Comparative Sociology of Violence." *Theory and Society*, vol. 1.

Connolly, S. 1992. *Religion, Law and Power: The Making of Protestant Ireland 1660–1760*. Oxford: Clarendon Press.

Connor, W. 1994. *Ethnonationalism: The Quest for Understanding*. Princeton, N.J.: Princeton University Press.

Conquest, R. 1986. *Harvest of Sorrow: Soviet Collectivization and the Terror Famine*. London: Hutchinson.

1990. *The Great Terror: A Reassessment*. New York: Oxford University Press.

Corwin, P. 1999. *Dubious Mandate: A Memoir of the U.N. in Bosnia, Summer 1995*. Durham, N.C.: Duke University Press.

Coster, W. 1999. "Massacre and Codes of Conduct in the English Civil War," in Levene & Roberts (eds.), *The Massacre in History*.

Courtois, A., et al. (eds.). *The Black Book of Communism: Crimes, Terror, Repression*. Cambridge, Mass.: Harvard University Press.

Cousens, E. 2002. "From Missed Opportunities to Overcompensation: Implementing the Dayton Agreements on Bosnia," in Stedman et al. (eds.), *Ending Civil Wars*.

Crnobrnja, M. 1994. *The Yugoslav Drama*. Montreal: McGill-Queen's University Press.

Crook, I., & Crook, D. 1979. *Mass Movement in a Chinese Village: Ten Mile Inn*. London: Routledge.

Crosby, A. 1986. *Ecological Imperialism: The Biological Expansion of Europe, 900–1900*. Cambridge: Cambridge University Press.

Crowe, D. 1996. *A History of the Gypsies of Eastern Europe and Russia*. New York: St. Martin's.

Dabag, M. 1994. "Le traumatisme des bourreaux: àpropos du livre de Taner Akcam." *Revue du Monde Arménien*, vol. 1.

Dadrian, V., 1986a. "The Naim-Andonian Documents on World War I Destruction of Ottoman Armenians: The Anatomy of a Genocide." *International Journal of Middle East Studies*, vol. 18.

1986b. "The Role of Turkish Physicians in the World War I Genocide of Ottoman Armenians." *Holocaust and Genocide Studies*, vol. 1.

1992. "The Role of the Turkish Military in the Destruction of Ottoman Armenians: A Study in Historical Continuities." *Journal of Political and Military Sociology*, vol. 20.

1993. "The Role of the Special Organisation in the Armenian Genocide in the First World War," in P. Panayi (ed.), *Minorities in Wartime*. Oxford: Berg.

1994a. "Documentation of the Armenian Genocide in German and Austrian Sources," in I. Charny (ed.), *The Widening Circle of Genocide. Genocide: A Critical Biographic Review*, vol. 3. New Brunswick, N.J.: Transaction.

1994b. "Party Allegiance as a Determinant in the Turkish Military's Involvement in the World War I Armenian Genocide." *Revue du monde Arménien*, vol. 1.

1995. *The History of the Armenian Genocide*. Providence, R.I.: Berghahn Books.

1997a. "The Turkish Military Tribunal's Prosecution of the Authors of the Armenian Genocide: Four Major Court-Martial Series." *Holocaust and Genocide Studies*, vol. 11.

1997b. "The Convergent Roles of the State and a Governmental Party in the Armenian Genocide," in *Proceedings of the International Conference*.

Daniszewski, J. 1999. "The Death of Belanica." *Los Angeles Times*, Special Supplement, April 25.

Dasgupta, J. 1998. "Community, Authenticity and Autonomy: Insurgence and Institutional Development in India's North-East," in Basu & Kohli (eds.), *Community Conflicts*.

Davidson, K. 1985. *Odyssey of an Armenian of Zeitoun.* New York: Vantage Press.

Davidson, J., & Kammen, D. 2002. "Indonesia's Unknown War and the Lineages of Violence in West Kalimantan." *Indonesia,* vol. 73.

Davies, J., & Gurr, T. R. (eds.) 1998. *Preventive Measures: Building Risk Assessment and Crisis Early Warning Systems.* Lanham, Md.: Rowman & Littlefield.

Davies, L. 1989. *The Slaughterhouse Province: An American Diplomat's Report on the Armenian Genocide, 1915–1917.* New Rochelle, N.Y.: Caratzas.

Davis, M. 2001. *Late Victorian Holocausts: El Niño Famines and the Making of the Third World.* London: Verso.

De Nogales, R. 1926. *Four Years Beneath the Crescent.* New York: Scribner's.

Dean, M. 1996. "The German Gendarmerie, the Ukrainian Schutzmannschaft and the 'Second Wave' of Jewish Killings in Occupied Ukraine." *German History,* vol. 14.

2000. *Collaboration in the Holocaust: Crimes of the Local Police in Belorussia and the Ukraine, 1941–1944.* New York: St. Martin's.

Debbarma, K. 1998. "Insurgency and Counter Insurgency in Tripura," in N. Malla (ed.), *Nationalism, Regionalism and Philosophy of National Integration.* New Delhi: Regency.

Del Boca, A. 1969. *The Ethiopian War 1935–1941.* Chicago: University of Chicago Press.

Deng, F. 1990. "The Identity Factor in the Sudanese Conflict," in Montville (ed.), *Conflict and Peacemaking.*

Derogy, J. 1986. *Opération Némésis.* Paris: Fayard.

Des Forges, A. 1999. *Leave None to Tell the Story.* New York: Human Rights Watch.

Dhillon, K. 1998. "A Decade of Violence, 1983–1992," in J. Grewal & I. Banga (eds.), *Punjab in Prosperity and Violence.* Chandigargh: K. K. Publishers.

Dicks, H. 1972. *Licensed Mass Murder: A Socio-Psychological Study of Some SS Killers.* London: Chatto Heinemann.

Djemal Pasha, 1922. *Memories of a Turkish Statesman.* New York: George Doran.

Djordjevic, D. 1971. "Fascism in Yugoslavia, 1918–1941," in Sugar (ed.), *Eastern European Nationalism in the Twentieth Century.*

Documents on Ottoman-Armenians, 2 vols. 1983. Ankara: Prime Ministry Directorate General of Press and Information.

Dolukhanov, P. 1994. *Environment and Ethnicity in the Middle East.* Aldershot: Avebury.

Dominguez Ortiz, A., & Vincent, B. 1994. "La tragédie se répète: le bannissement des morisques," in Barkai (ed.), *Chrétiens, musulmans et juifs.*

Domovina Net. 1999. "From Thug to Hero." Available at http://w.w.w.xs4all.nl/frankti/Warcrimes/caco.html

Don, Y. 1989. "The Economic Effect of Anti-Semitic Discrimination: Hungarian Anti-Jewish Legislation, 1938–1944," in Marrus (ed.), *The Nazi Holocaust.*

Dorian, E. 1982. *The Quality of Witness: A Romanian Diary 1937–1944.* Philadelphia: Jewish Publication Society of America.

Dower, J. 1986. *War without Mercy: Race and Power in the Pacific War.* New York: Pantheon.

Doyle, M. 1983. "Kant, Liberal Legacies and Foreign Affairs, Parts 1 and 2." *Philosophy and Public Affairs,* vol. 12.

Dravis, M., & Pitsch, A. 1995–8. "Burundi Chronology" (with updates). Available at http://www.bsos.umd.edu/cidcm/mar/burundi.htm

Drechsler, H. 1980. *"Let Us Die Fighting": The Struggle of the Herrero and the Nama Against German Imperialism.* London: Zed.

Du Preez, P. 1994. *Genocide: The Psychology of Mass Murder.* London: Boyars/Bowerdean.

Edwards, J. 1999. *The Spanish Inquisition.* Stroud, Gloucestershire: Tempus.

El Mallakh, D. 1979. *The Slovak Autonomy Movement, 1935–1939: A Study in Unrelenting Nationalism.* New York: Columbia University Press.

Elias, N. 1996. *The Germans.* New York: Columbia University Press.

Emerson, D. (ed.) 1999. *Indonesia Beyond Suharto.* Armonk, N.Y.: M. E. Sharpe.

Erez, Z. 1989. "The Jews of Budapest and the Plans of Admiral Horthy August–October 1944," in Marrus (ed.), *The Nazi Holocaust*.

Esty, D., et al. 1998. "The State Failure Project: Early Warning Research for U.S. Foreign Policy Planning," in J. Davis & T. Gurr (eds.), *Crisis Early Warning Systems*. Boulder, Colo.: Rowman & Littlefield.

Etcheson, C. 2000. "The Number" – Quantifying Crimes Against Humanity in Cambodia. Documentation Center of Cambodia. Available at www.mekong.net/cambodia/toll.htm.

Evans, A. 1999. "Kashmir: The Past Ten Years." *Asian Affairs*, vol. 30.

Ezergailis, A. 1996. *The Holocaust in Latvia, 1941–1944: The Missing Center*. Washington, D.C.: United States Holocaust Memorial Museum.

Fargion, L. 1989. "The Anti-Jewish Policy of the Italian Social Republic (1943–1945)," in Marrus (ed.), *The Nazi Holocaust*.

Farris, N. 1984. *Maya Society Under Colonial Rule*. Princeton, N.J.: Princeton University Press.

Fearon, J. 1995. "Rationalist Explanations for War." *International Organization*, vol. 49.

Fearon, J., & Laitin, D. 1996. "Explaining Interethnic Cooperation." *American Political Science Review*, vol. 90.

2000. "Violence and the Social Construction of Ethnic Identity." *International Organization*, vol. 54.

2003. "Ethnicity, Insurgency and Civil War." *American Political Science Review*, vol. 97.

Fein, H. 1979. *Accounting for Genocide*. New York: Free Press.

Feingold, H. 1983. "How Unique Is the Holocaust?" in A. Grobman & D. Landes (eds.), *Genocide: Critical Issues of the Holocaust*. Los Angeles: Simon Wiesenthal Center.

Fejes, J. 1997. "Carpatho-Ruthenia in 1941," in Braham & A. Pók (eds.), *The Holocaust in Hungary*.

Felak, J. 1994. *"At the Price of the Republic." Hlinka's Slovak People's Party, 1929–1938*. Pittsburgh: University of Pittsburgh Press.

Fieldhouse, D. 1965. *The Colonial Empires from the Eighteenth Century*. New York: Weidenfeld & Nicolson.

Finkelstein, N., & Birn, R. (eds.). 1998. *A Nation on Trial: The Goldhagen Thesis and Historical Truth*. New York: Owl Books.

Fischer, C. 1995. *The Rise of the Nazis*. Manchester: Manchester University Press.

Fitzpatrick, S. 1978. "Cultural Revolution as Class War," in Fitzpatrick (ed.), *Cultural Revolution in Russia, 1928–1931*. Bloomington: Indiana University Press.

1994. *Stalin's Peasants*. Oxford: Oxford University Press.

Frame, G. 1992. *Babylonia 689–627 B.C.: A Political History*. Istanbul: Nederlands Historisch-Archaeologisch Instituut.

Fredrickson, G. 1988. "Colonialism and Racism: The United States and South Africa in Comparative Perspective," in his *The Arrogance of Race*. Middletown, Conn.: Wesleyan University Press.

Freeman, M. 1995. "Genocide, Civilization and Modernity." *British Journal of Sociology*, vol. 46.

Friedgut, T. 1987. "Labor Violence and Regime Brutality in Tsarist Russia: The Ivzovka Cholera Riots of 1892." *Slavic Review*, vol. 46.

Friedländer, H. 1995. *The Origins of Nazi Genocide: From Euthanasia to the Final Solution*. Chapel Hill: University of North Carolina Press.

Friedländer, S. 1997. *Nazi Germany and the Jews. Vol. I: The Years of Persecution, 1933–1939*. New York: HarperCollins.

Friedman, E., et al. 1991. *Chinese Village, Socialist State*. New Haven, Conn.: Yale University Press.

Friedman, J. 1994. "New Christian Religious Alternatives," in Waddington & Williamson (eds.), *The Expulsion of the Jews*.

Gagnon, V. 1997. "Ethnic Nationalism and International Conflict: The Case of Serbia," in M. Brown et al. (eds.), *Nationalism and Ethnic Conflict*. Cambridge, Mass.: MIT Press.

Gallagher, W. 1999. *Sennacherib's Campaign to Judah*. Leiden: Brill.

Gasana, J. 1995. "La guerre, la paix et la démocratie au Rwanda," in Guichaoua (ed.), *Les crises politiques*.

Gellately, R. 1990. *The Gestapo and German Society*. Oxford: Clarendon Press.

Gellner, E. 1983. *Nations and Nationalism*. Oxford: Blackwell.

Gerlach, C. 1999. *Kalkulierte Morde. Die deutsche Wirtschafts- und Vernichtungspolitik in Weissrussland 1941 bis 1944*. Hamburg: Hamburger edition.

Getty, J. A. 1985. *Origins of the Great Purges*. Cambridge: Cambridge University Press.

Getty, J. A., & Chase, W. 1993. "Patterns of Repression Among the Soviet Elite in the Late 1930s: A Biographical Approach," in Getty & Manning (eds.), *Stalinist Terror*.

Getty, J. A., & Manning, R. (eds.) (1993). *Stalinist Terror: New Perspectives*. Cambridge: Cambridge University Press.

Gibson, R. 1994. "The Intensification of National Consciousness in Modern Europe," in C. Bjorn et al. (eds.), *Nations, Nationalism and Patriotism in the European Past*. Copenhagen: Academic Press.

Gisevius, W. 1947. *To the Bitter End*. Boston: Houghton Mifflin.

Glenny, M. 1993. *The Fall of Yugoslavia*. Harmondsworth, Middlesex: Penguin.

Goati, V. 1995. "Serbian Parties and Party System," in Janjic (ed.), *Serbia Between the Past and the Future*.

Goebbels, J. 1948. *The Goebbels Diaries 1942–1943*. Garden City, N.Y.: Doubleday.

Gold, D. 1991. "Organized Hinduisms: From Vedic Truth to Hindu Nation," in Marty & Appleby (eds.), *Fundamentalisms Observed*.

Goldhagen, D. 1996. *Hitler's Willing Executioners: Ordinary Germans and the Holocaust*. London: Little, Brown.

Goldstone, J., et al. 2002. "State Failure Task Force Report. Phase III Findings." www.cidcm.umd.edu/inser/stfail

Gopalakrishnan, R. 1995. *Insurgent North-eastern India*. New Delhi: Vikas.

Gordon, F. 1990. *Latvians and Jews Between Germany and Russia*. Stockholm: Memento.

Gordon, S. 1984. *Hitler, Germans, and the "Jewish Question."* Princeton, N.J.: Princeton University Press.

Gordy, E. 1999. *The Culture of Power in Serbia*. University Park: University of Pennsylvania Press.

Gorski, P. 2000. "The Mosaic Moment: An Early Modernist Critique of Modernist Theories of Nationalism." *American Journal of Sociology*, vol. 105.

Gourevitch, P. 1998. *We Wish to Inform You That Tomorrow We Will Be Killed with Our Families*. New York: Farrar, Strauss & Giroux.

Graber, G. 1996. *Caravans to Oblivion: The Armenian Genocide, 1915*. New York: John Wiley.

Granada Television. 1993. *We Are All Neighbours*. Granada TV "Disappearing World" documentary series.

Grayson, A. K. 1982. "Assyria," in J. Boardman et al. (eds.), *Cambridge Ancient History, Vol. II, Part 1: Prehistory of the Balkans and the Middle East and the Aegean World, Tenth to Eighth Centuries B.C.*, 3rd ed. Cambridge: Cambridge University Press.

Greenfeld, L. 1992. *Nationalism: Five Roads to Modernity*. Cambridge, Mass.: Harvard University Press.

Grmek, M., et al. 1993. *Le nettoyage ethnique: Documents historiques sur une idéologie serbe*. Paris: Fayard.

Gross, J. 2000. "A Tangled Web: Confronting Stereotypes Concerning Relations Between Poles, Germans, Jews and Communists," in I. Deak et al. (eds.), *The Politics of Retribution in Europe: World War II and Its Aftermath*. Princeton, N.J.: Princeton University Press.

2001. *Neighbors: The Destruction of the Jewish Community in Jedwabne*. Princeton, N.J.: Princeton University Press.

Guichaoua, A. (ed.). 1995. *Les crises politiques au Burundi et au Rwanda (1993–1994)*. Lille: Universite de Lille.

Gurr, T. 1993. *Minorities at Risk. A Global View of Ethnopolitical Conflicts*. Washington, D.C.: United States Institute of Peace.

1998. "A Risk Assessment Model of Ethnopolitical Rebellion," in Davies & Gurr (eds.), *Preventive Measures*.

2000. *People versus States: Minorities at Risk in the New Century*. Washington, D.C.: United States Institute of Peace.

Gutman, I. 1990. "The Victimization of the Poles," in M. Berenbaum (ed.), *A Mosaic of Victims: Non-Jews Persecuted and Murdered by the Nazis*. New York: New York University Press.

Gutman, R. 1993. *A Witness to Genocide*. New York: Macmillan.

Haberer, E. 2001."The German Police and Genocide in Belorussia, 1941–1944," *Journal of Genocide Research*, vol. 3, in three parts.

Haebich, A. 1988. *For Their Own Good: Aborigines and Government in the Southwest of Western Australia 1900–1940*. Perth: University of Western Australia Press.

Hagen, W. 1996. "Before the 'Final Solution': Toward a Comparative Analysis of Political Anti-Semitism in Interwar Germany and Poland." *Journal of Modern History*, vol. 68.

Hagtvet, B. 1980. "The Theory of Mass Society and Weimar," in S. Larsen et al. (eds.), *Who Were the Fascists? Social Roots of European Fascism*. Oslo: Universitetsforlaget.

Hainsworth, P., & McCloskey, S. 2000. *The East Timor Question*. London: I. B. Taurus

Hancock, I. 1996. "Responses to the Porrajmos: The Romani Holocaust," in A. Rosenbaum (ed.), *Is the Holocaust Unique?* Boulder, Colo.: Westview.

Haney, C., et al. 1973. "Interpersonal Dynamics in a Simulated Prison." *International Journal of Criminology and Penology*, vol. 1.

Harding, N. 1984. "Socialism, Society and the Organic Labour State," in Harding (ed.), *The State in Socialist Society*. London: Macmillan.

Harff, B. 1998. "Early Warning of Humanitarian Crises: Sequential Models and the Role of Accelerators," in Davies & Gurr (eds.), *Preventive Measures*.

2003. "No Lessons Learned from the Holocaust? Assessing Risks of Genocide and Political Mass Murder since 1955." *American Political Science Review*, vol. 97.

Harff, B., & Gurr, T. 1988. "Toward an Empirical Theory of Genocides and Politicides: Identification and Measurement of Cases Since 1945." *International Studies Quarterly*, vol. 32.

Hart, P. 1998. *The I.R.A. and Its Enemies*. Oxford: Oxford University Press.

Hartunian, A. 1986. *Neither to Laugh Nor to Weep: A Memoir of the Armenian Genocide*, 2nd ed. Cambridge, Mass: Armenian Heritage Press.

Hastings, A. 1997. *The Construction of Nationhood*. Cambridge: Cambridge University Press.

Havranek, J. 1971. "Fascism in Czechoslovakia," in Sugar (ed.), *Eastern European Nationalism in the Twentieth Century*.

Hayden, R. 1996. "Imagined Communities and Real Victims: Self-Determination and Ethnic Cleansing in Yugoslavia." *American Ethnologist*, vol. 23.

Headland, R. 1992. *Messages of Murder: A Study of the Reports of the Einsatzgruppen of the Security Police and the Security Service, 1941–1943*. London: Associated Universities Press.

Heer, H. 1997. "Killing Fields: The Wehrmacht and the Holocaust in Belorussia, 1941–1942." *Holocaust and Genocide Studies*, vol. 7.

Hefner, R. 1991. "Ethicity, Nation, and Nationalism in Modern Indonesia," in U. Ra'anan (ed.), *State and Nation in Multiethnic Societies*. Manchester: Manchester University Press.

2000. *Civil Islam: Muslims and Democratization in Indonesia*. Princeton, N.J.: Princeton University Press.

Heizer, R. 1993. *The Destruction of California Indians. A Collection of Documents*. Lincoln: University of Nebraska Press.

Helsinki Watch. 1992, 1993. *War Crimes in Bosnia-Hercogovina*, Vols. I & II. New York: Human Rights Watch.

Heng, L., & Demeure, F. 1994. *Cambodge: Le sourire baillonne*. Xonrupt-Longemer: Anako.

von Hentig, H. 1977. "Beiträge zu einer Sozialgeschichte des Dritten Reich." *Vierteljahrshefte für Zeitgeschichte*, vol. 16.

Herbert, U. (ed.) 2000. *National Socialist Extermination Policies*. New York: Berghahn.

Herczl, M. 1993. *Christianity and the Holocaust of Hungarian Jewry*. New York: New York University Press.

Heuveline, P. 2001. "Approaches to Measuring Genocide: Excess Mortality during The Khmer Rouge Period," in Chirot and Seligman (eds.), *Ethnopolitical Warfare*.

Heuzé, G. 1992. "Shiv Sena and 'National' Hinduism." *Economic and Political Weekly* (Delhi), October 3 and 10.

Hilberg, R. 1978. *The Destruction of the European Jews*. New York: Octagon.

  1980. "The Significance of the Holocaust," in H. Friedländer & S. Milton (eds), *The Holocaust: Ideology, Bureaucracy and Genocide*. Millwood, N.Y.: Kraus International.

  1993. *Perpetrators, Victims, Bystanders: The Jewish Catastrophe 1933–1945*. London: Lime Tree.

Hintjens, H. 1999. "Explaining the 1994 Genocide in Rwanda." *Journal of Modern African Studies*, vol. 37.

Hinton, W. 1966. *Fanshen: A Documentary of Revolution in a Chinese Village*. New York: Monthly Review.

Höffkes, K. 1986. *Hitlers Politische Generale*. Tuebingen: Grabert.

Hoffman, D. 1993. "The Great Terror on the Local Level: Purges in Moscow Factories, 1936–1938," in Getty & Manning (eds.), *Stalinist Terror*.

Hoffman, P. 1988. *German Resistance to Hitler*. Cambridge, Mass.: Harvard University Press.

Holbrooke, R. 1998. *To End a War*. New York: Random House.

Holquist, P. 2003. "The Russian Empire as a 'Civilized Nation': International Law as Principle and Practice in Imperial Russia, 1874–1917." Unpublished paper presented at the Sawyer Seminar on the Dynamics of Mass Killing, Palo Alto, Calif., March 2003.

Honig, J., & Both, N. 1996. *Srebrenica: Record of a Warcrime*. Harmondsworth, Middlesex: Penguin.

Horowitz, D. 1985. *Ethnic Groups in Conflict*. Berkeley & Los Angeles: University of California Press.

  1999. "Constitutional Design: An Oxymoron?" *Nomos*, vol. 41s.

  2001. *The Deadly Ethnic Riot*. Berkeley & Los Angeles: University of California Press.

Horowitz, I. 1982. *Taking Lives: Genocide and State Power*. New Brunswick, N.J.: Transaction.

Horwitz, G. 1990. *In The Shadow of Death*. New York: Free Press.

Höss, R., et al. 1978. *KL Auschwitz Seen By the SS*. Cracow: Panstwowe Muzeum.

Hovannisian, R. (ed.) 1986. *The Armenian Genocide in Perspective*. New Brunswick, N.J.: Transaction.

  1994. "Etiology and Sequence of the Armenian Genocide," in his *Genocide: Conceptual and Historical Dimensions*. Philadelphia: University of Pennsylvania Press.

Hoxie, F. 1984. *A Final Promise: The Campaign to Assimilate the Indians, 1880–1920*. Lincoln: University of Nebraska Press.

Hughes, R. 1987. *The Fatal Shore*. New York: Knopf.

Hukanowicz, R. 1996. *The Tenth Circle of Hell: A Memoir of Life in the Death Camps of Bosnia*. New York: Basic Books.

Hull, I. 2004. *Going to Extremes: Military Culture and Wars of Annihilation in Imperial Germany* (provisional title). Ithaca, N.Y.: Cornell University Press.

Human Rights Watch. 1999 and 2003. "World Reports: Burundi, Rwanda, Sudan." Available at http: //www.hrw.org/hrw/wr2k/Africa

Human Rights Watch. World Report 1999. Yugoslavia. www.hrw.org/hrw2k

2002. "We Have No Orders to Save You." State Participation and Complicity in Communal Violence in Gujarat. Available at www.hrw.org

2004. "Ethnic Cleansing in Darfur." Available at www.hrw.org/reports/2004/Sudan.

Hunczak, T. 1990. "The Ukrainian Losses during World War II," in Berenbaum (ed.), *A Mosaic of Victims*.

Hunter, E. 1993. *Aboriginal Health and History*. Cambridge: Cambridge University Press.

Huntington, S. 1996. *The Clash of Civilizations and the Remaking of World Order*. New York: Simon & Schuster.

Hurtado, A. 1988. *Indian Survival on the California Frontier*. New Haven, Conn.: Yale University Press.

1994. "Indian and White Households on the Californian Frontier, 1860," in his *Indian Survival on the California Frontier*.

Hutchinson, J. 1994. *Modern Nationalism*. London: Fontana.

Ibrahim, J. 1999. "Ethno-Religious Mobilisation and the Sappings of Democracy in Nigeria," in J. Hyslop (ed.), *African Democracy in the Era of Globalisation*. Johannesburg: Witwatersrand University Press.

in't Veld, N. 1976. *De SS en Nederland: documenten uit SS-archieven 1935–1945*. 's-Gravenhage: Nijhoff.

Inbaraj, S. 1995. *East Timor: Blood and Tears in Asean*. Chiang Mi, Thailand: Silkworm Books.

Institut Für Armenische Frage. 1988. *The Armenian Genocide, Vol. 2: Documentation*. Munich: author (in German).

Institute for War and Peace Reporting. 1998–2000. Tribunal Updates & Press Releases. Available at http://www.iwpr.net

Institute of National Remembrance. 2002. *The Jedwabne Case, Vol. I: Analyses* (English Summary 1). Warsaw: author.

Internews. 2000. "Reports." http://interneews.org/projects/ ICTR

Ioanid, R. 1990. *The Sword of the Archangel*. New York: Columbia University Press.

1991. "The Pogrom of Bucharest 21–23 January 1941." *Holocaust and Genocide Studies*, vol. 6.

1994. "The Antonescu Era," in Braham (ed.), *The Tragedy of Romanian Jewry*. New York: Columbia University Press.

2000. *The Holocaust in Romania*. Chicago: Ivan Dee.

Izzet Pasa, A. 1992. *Feryadim [My Crying Out]*, Vol. I. Istanbul: Nehir Yayinlari.

Jacobsen, H.-A.: 1968. "The Commissar Order and Mass Executions of Soviet Prisoners of War," in: Buchheim et al. (eds.), *Anatomy of the SS-State*.

Jafarian, B. 1989. *Farewell Kharpert*. Madison, Wis.: Mangasarian.

Jaffrelot, C. 1996. *The Hindu Nationalist Movement in India*. New York: Columbia University Press.

Jamin, M. 1984. *Zwischen den Klassen: Zur Sozialstruktur der SA-Fuhrerschaft*. Wuppertal: Hammer.

Janjic, D. (ed.). 1995. *Serbia Between the Past and the Future*. Belgrade: Institute of Social Sciences and Forum for Ethnic Relations.

Jansen, C., & Weckbecker, A. 1992. "'Der Volksdeutcher Selbschutz' in Polen 1939/40," in *Schriftenreihe der Vierteljahrseschefte für Zeitgeschichte*, Vol. 14. Munich: Oldenbourg.

Jarausch, K. 1990. *The Unfree Professions: German Lawyers, Teachers and Engineers, 1900–1950*. Oxford: Oxford University Press.

Jelinek, Y. 1976. *The Parish Republic: Hlinka's Slovak People's Party, 1931–1945*. New York: Columbia University Press.

1989. "The 'Final Solution' – the Slovak Version," in Marrus (ed.), *The Nazi Holocaust*.

Jenkins, G. (ed.) 1997. *The Welsh Language Before the Industrial Revolution.* Cardiff: University of Wales Press.

Jenkins, G., et al. 1997. "The Welsh Language in Early Modern Wales," in Jenkins (ed.), *The Welsh Language.*

Jonassohn, K., with Björnson, K. 1998. *Genocide and Gross Human Rights Violations in Comparative Perspective.* New Brunswick, N.J.: Transaction.

Jones, B. 1999. "The Arusha Peace Process," in Adelman & Suhrke (eds.), *The Path of a Genocide.*

Jones, S. 1995. "The Pattern of Human Rights Violations," in K. Coates (ed.), *Timor: Twenty Years On.* Nottingham: Bertrand Russell Foundation.

Judah, T. 1997. *The Serbs.* New Haven, Conn.: Yale University Press.

2000. *Kosovo: War and Revenge.* New Haven, Conn.: Yale University Press.

Juergensmeyer, M. 1993. *The New Cold War? Religious Nationalism Confronts the Secular State.* Berkeley: University of California Press.

Kabirigi, L. 1994. *Génocide au Rwanda: Honte pour l'humanité.* Kigali, Rwanda: PREFED.

Kaiser, H. 1996. "Denying the Armenian Genocide: The German Connection." *Journal of the Society for Armenian Studies*, vol. 9.

1997. *Imperialism, Racism and Development Theories: The Construction of a Dominant Paradigm on Ottoman Armenians.* Ann Arbor, Mich.: Gomidas Institute.

1999a. *Marsovan 1915: The Diaries of Bertha Morley.* Ann Arbor, Mich.: Gomidas Institute.

1999b. "The Baghdad Railway and the Armenian Genocide, 1915–1916," in R. Hovannisian (ed.), *Remembrance and Denial: The Case of the Armenian Genocide.* Detroit: Wayne State University Press.

2000a. "From Empire to Republic: The Continuities of Turkish Denial." Unpublished paper.

2000b. "Armenian Property, Ottoman Law and Nationality Policies during the Armenian Genocide, 1915–1918." Unpublished paper.

2001a. "The Armenian Genocide: Governing Myths Revisited." Paper presented at the European University Institute, Robert Schuman Centre for Advanced Studies, Second Mediterranean Social and Political Research Meeting, Florence, March 21–25.

2001b. *Eberhard Count Wolffskeel Von Reichenberg, Zeitoun, Mousa Dagh, Ourfa: Letters on the Armenian Genocide.* Princeton, N.J.: Gomidas Institute.

Kakwenzire, J., & Kamukama, D. 1999. "The Development and Consolidation of Extremist Forces in Rwanda," in Adelman & Suhrke (eds.), *The Path of a Genocide.*

Kaldor, M. 1999. *New and Old War.* Stanford, Calif.: Stanford University Press.

Kalyvas, S. 1999. "Wanton and Senseless? The Logic of Massacres in Algeria." *Rationality and Society*, vol. 11.

2001 "'New' and 'Old' Civil War. A Valid Distinction?" *World Politics*, vol. 54.

Kamen, H. 1993a. "The Mediterranean and the Expulsion of Spanish Jews in 1492," in his *Crisis and Change in Early Modern Spain.* Aldershot, Hants: Variorum.

1993b. "A Crisis of Conscience in Golden Age Spain: The Inquisition Against 'Limpieza de Sangre,'" in *Crisis and Change in Early Modern Spain.*

Kangeris, F. 1998. "The Former Soviet Union, Fascism and the Baltic Question: The Question of Collaboration and War Criminals in the Baltic Countries," in S. Larsen & B. Hagtvet (eds.), *Modern Europe After Fascism, 1943–1980s.* New York: Columbia University Press.

Kansu, A. 1997. *The Revolution of 1908 in Turkey.* Leiden: Brill.

Kaplan, R. 1993. *Balkan Ghosts: A Journey Through History.* New York: St. Martin's.

Karay, F. 1996. *Death Comes in Yellow: Skarzysko-Kamienna Slave Labor Camp.* Amsterdam: Harwood.

Karpat, K. 1975. "The Memoirs of N. Batzaria: The Young Turks and Nationalism." *International Journal of Middle East Studies*, vol. 6.

Karsai, L. 1998. "The Last Phase of the Hungarian Holocaust: The Szalasi Regime and the Jews," in R. Braham & S. Miller (eds.), *The Nazis' Last Victims: The Holocaust in Hungary.* Detroit: Wayne State University Press.

Karsh, E., & Karsh, I. 1999. *Empires of the Sand.* Cambridge, Mass.: Harvard University Press.

Katz, F. 1993. *Ordinary People and Extraordinary Evil.* Albany: State University of New York Press.

Katz, J. 1988. *Seductions of Crime: Moral and Sensual Attractions in Doing Evil.* New York: Basic Books.

Katzenstein, M., et al. 1998. "The Rebirth of the Shiv Sena in Maharastra," in Basu & Kohli (eds.), *Community Conflicts.*

Kazanjian, P. (ed.) 1989. *The Cilician Armenian Ordeal.* Boston: HYE Intentions, Inc.

Keane, F. 1995. *Season of Blood: A Rwandan Journey.* London: Viking.

Keddie, N. 1998. "The New Religious Politics: Where, When and Why Do 'Fundamentalisms' Appear?" *Comparative Studies in Society and History,* vol. 40.

Kell, T. 1995. *The Roots of Acehnese Rebellion, 1989–1992.* Ithaca, N.Y.: Cornell Modern Indonesia Project, Publication No. 74.

Kelly, D. 1995. *The Czech Fascist Movement 1922–1942.* New York: Columbia University Press.

Kenez, P. 1992. "Pogroms and White Ideology in the Russian Civil War," in J. Klier & S. Lambroza (eds.), *Pogroms: Anti-Jewish Violence in Modern Russian History.* Cambridge: Cambridge University Press.

Kenrick, D., & Puxon, G. 1972. *The Destiny of Europe's Gypsies.* London: Heinemann.

Kershaw, I. 1984. *Popular Opinion and Political Dissent in the Third Reich.* Oxford: Clarendon Press.

1997. "'Working Towards the Führer': Reflections on the Nature of the Hitler Dictatorship," in Kershaw & Lewin (eds.), *Stalinism and Nazism.*

1998. *Hitler: 1889–1936: Hubris.* New York: Norton.

2000. *Hitler: 1936–45: Nemesis.* New York: Norton.

Kershaw, I., & Lewin, M. (eds.) *Stalinism and Nazism: Dictatorship in Comparison.* Cambridge: Cambridge University Press.

Kersten, F. 1956. *The Kersten Memoirs 1940–45.* London: Hutchinson.

Kévorkian, R. 1998. "L'extermination des déportés arméniens ottomans dans les camps de concentration de Syrie-Mésopotamie (1915–1916): La deuxième phase du génocide." *Revue d'histoire arménienne contemporaine,* vol. 2.

1999. "La Cilicie (1909–1921): Des Massacres d'Adana au Mandat Français." *Revue d'Histoire Armenienne Contemporaine,* vol. 3, numero special.

Keyder, C. 1987. *State and Class in Turkey: A Study in Capitalist Development.* London: Verso.

Keyder, C., et al. 1993. "Port-Cities in the Ottoman Empire: Some Theoretical and Historical Perspectives." *Review,* vol. 16.

Khadiogala, G. 2002. "Implementing the Arusha Peace Agreement in Rwanda," in S. Stedman et al. (eds.), *Ending Civil Wars: The Implementation of Peace Agreements.* Boulder, Colo.: Lynne Rienner.

Kiernan, B. 1983. "Wild Chickens, Farm Chickens and Cormorants: Kampuchea's Eastern Zone Under Pol Pot," in Chandler & Kiernan (eds.), *Revolution and Its Aftermath.*

1996. *The Pol Pot Regime.* New Haven, Conn.: Yale University Press.

1997. "Enver Pasha and Pol Pot: A Comparison of the Armenian and Cambodian Genocides," in *Proceedings of the International Conference on "Problems of Genocide."* Cambridge, Mass.: Zoryan Institute.

2001. "The Ethnic Element in the Cambodian Genocide," in Chirot and Seligman (eds.), *Ethnopolitical Warfare.*

2003. "The Demography of Genocide in Southeast Asia." *Critical Asian Studies,* vol. 35.

Kirk, T. 1996. *Nazism and the Working Class in Austria.* Cambridge: Cambridge University Press.

Kishwar, M., 1998a. "Gangster Rule: The Massacre of the Sikhs," in his *Religion at the Service of Nationalism and Other Essays.* Delhi: Oxford University Press.

1998b. "Safety Is Indivisible: The Warning from Bombay Riots," in ibid.

Klee, E. 1983. *"Euthanasie" im NS-Staat*. Frankfurt: Fischer.

"The Good Old Days": The Holocaust as Seen by Perpetrators and Bystanders. London: Hamilton.

Klee, E., et al. 1989. *"Gott mit Uns": Der deutsche Vernichtungskrieg im Osten 1939–1945*. Frankfurt: Fischer.

Klier, J. 1993. "Unravelling of the Conspiracy Theory: A New Look at the Pogroms." *East European Jewish Affairs*, vol. 23.

van Klinken, G. 2002. "Indonesia's New Ethnic Elites," in H. Schulte Nordholt (ed.), *Indonesia: In Search of Transition*. Yogyakarta: Pustaka Pelajar.

Knezevic, A., & Tufegdzic, V. 1995. *Kriminal koji je izmenio Srbiju (Crime that Changed Serbia)*. Belgrade: Radio B-92.

Koehl, R. 1983. *The Black Corps: The Structure and Power Struggles of the Nazi SS*. Madison: University of Wisconsin Press.

Komjathy, A., & Stockwell, R. 1980. *German Minorities and the Third Reich*. New York: Holmes & Meier.

Koshar, R. 1986. *Social Life, Local Politics and Nazism: Marburg, 1880–1935*. Chapel Hill: University of North Carolina Press.

Kosyk, W. 1986. *L'Allemagne national-socialiste et l'Ukraine*. Paris: Publications de l'Est Europeen.

Kovacevic, S., & Dajic, P. 1995. *Chronology of the Yugoslav Crisis 1994*. Belgrade: Institute for European Studies.

1997. *Chronology of the Yugoslav Crisis 1995*. Belgrade: Institute of European Studies.

Krausnick, H. 1993 *Hitlers Einsatzgruppen*. Stuttgart: Taschenbuch.

Kumanev, G. 1990. "The German Occupation Regime on Occupied Territory in the USSR (1941–1944)," in Berenbaum (ed.), *A Mosaic of Victims*.

Kuo-Chun, C. 1960. *Agrarian Policy of the Chinese Communist Party 1921–1959*. Bombay: Asia Publishing House.

Kuzmanovic, B. 1995. "Social Distance Towards Individual Nations," in M. Lazic et al. (eds.), *Society in Crisis: Yugoslavia in the Early 90s*. Belgrade: Filip Visnjic.

La Pérousse, J.-F. 1989. *Monterey in 1786: Life in a California Mission: The Journals of Jean Francois de la Pérousse*, ed. M. Margolin. Berkeley: Heyday Books.

Laely, T. 1997. "Peasants, Local Communities and Central Power in Burundi." *Journal of Modern African Studies*, vol. 35.

Lainithanga, P. 1994. "Mizo National Front Movement," in Prasad (ed.), *Autonomy Movements*.

Laitin, D. 1998. *Identity in Formation*. Ithaca, N.Y.: Cornell University Press.

1999. "Language Conflict and Violence: The Straw That Strengthens the Camel's Back." Unpublished paper, Department of Political Science, Stanford University.

Landau, J. 1995. *Pan-Turkism: From Irredentism to Cooperation*, 2nd ed. London: Hurst.

van Langenberg, M. 1990. "The New Order State: Language, Ideology, Hegemony," in A. Budiman (ed.), *State and Civil Society in Indonesia*. Clayton, Victoria, Australia: Monash University Press.

Lasik, A. 1994a. "Historical-Sociological Profile of the Auschwitz SS," in Gutman & Berenbaum (eds.), *Anatomy of the Auschwitz Death Camp*. Bloomington, Ind.: Indiana University Press and the United States Holocaust Memorial Museum.

1994b. "Rudolf Hoess: Manager of Crime," in Gutman & Berenbaum (eds.), in ibid.

Laurière, H. 1951. *Assassins au nom de Dieu*. Paris: La Vigie.

Leboutte, R. (ed.). 2000. *Migrations et migrants dans une perspective historique*. Brussels: Peter Lang.

Ledeen, M. 1989. "The Evolution of Italian Fascist Anti-Semitism," in Marrus (ed.), *The Nazi Holocaust*.

Lee, H. Y. 1978. *The Politics of the Chinese Cultural Revolution*. Berkeley & Los Angeles: University of California Press.

Leff, C. 1988. *National Conflict in Czechoslovakia*. Princeton, N.J.: Princeton University Press.

Legters, L. 1997. "Soviet Deportations of Whole Nations: A Genocidal Process," in S. Totten et al. (eds.), *Century of Genocide: Eyewitness Accounts and Critical Views*. New York: Garland.

Lemarchand, R. 1995. *Burundi: Ethnic Conflict and Genocide*. New York: Cambridge University Press.

1997a. "The Burundi Genocide," in S. Totten et al. (eds.), *Century of Genocide: Eyewitness Accounts and Critical Views*. New York: Garland.

1997b. "The Rwanda Genocide" in ibid.

Letica, S. 1996. "The Genesis of the Current Balkan War," in Mestrovic (ed.), *Genocide After Emotion*.

Levai, E. 1948. *Black Book on the Martyrdom of Hungarian Jewry*. Zurich & Vienna:

Levene, M. 1993. "Frontiers of Genocide: Jews in the Eastern War Zones, 1914–20 and 1941," in Panayi (ed.), *Minorities in Wartime*.

Levene, M., & Roberts, P. (eds.) 1999. *The Massacre in History*. New York: Berghan Books.

Lewin, M. 1985. *The Making of the Soviet System*. New York: Pantheon.

Lichtenstein, H. 1990. *Himmlers grüne Helfer*. Köln: Bund-Verlag.

Liddle, R. W. 1999. "Regime: The New Order," in Emmerson (ed.), *Indonesia Beyond Suharto*.

Lieven, D. 2000. *Empire: The Russian Empire and Its Rivals*. New Haven, Conn.: Yale University Press.

Lifton, R. 1986. *The Nazi Doctors*. New York: Basic Books.

Linklater, M., et al. 1984. *The Fourth Reich: Klaus Barbie and the Neo-Fascist Connection*. London: Hodder & Stoughton.

Littman, S. 1983. *War Criminal on Trial: The Rauca Case*. Toronto: Lester & Orpen Dennys.

Locard, H. 1996. "Le goulag Khmer rouge." *Communisme*, nos. 47–8.

2000a. "Réflexions sur *Le Livre noir*: le cas du Kampuchea démocratique." *Communisme*, nos. 59–60.

2000b. "Ben Kiernan, Le génocide au Cambodge, 1975–1979: Race, idéologie et pouvoir." *Communisme*, nos. 59–60.

Loewenberg, P. 1983. "The Psychohistorical Origins of the Nazi Youth Cohort," in his *Decoding the Past*. New York: Knopf.

Loftus, J. 1982. *The Belarus Secret*. New York: Knopf.

Longman, T. 1999. "State, Civil Society and Genocide in Rwanda," in R. Joseph (ed.), *State Conflict and Democracy in Africa*. Boulder, Colo.: Lynne Reinner.

López Castro, 1995. *Hispania Poena. Los Fenicios en la Hispania Romana*. Barcelona: Crítica Grijalbo Mondadori.

Losowick, Y. 2000. *Hitler's Bureaucrats: The Nazi Security Police and the Banality of Evil*. London: Continuum.

Lower, W. 2002. "'Anticipatory Obedience' and the Nazi Implementation of the Holocaust in the Ukraine." *Holocaust and Genocide Studies*, Vol. 16.

Lumans, V. 1993. *Himmler's Auxiliaries*. Chapel Hill: University of North Carolina Press.

Lupher, M. 1996. *Power Restructuring in China and Russia*. Boulder, Colo.: Westview.

Maas, P. 1996. *Love Thy Neighbor: A Story of War*. New York: Knopf.

Mace, J. 1984. "The Man-Made Famine of 1933 in the Soviet Ukraine: What Happened and Why?" in I. Charny (ed.), *Toward the Understanding and Prevention of Genocide*. Boulder, Colo.: Westview.

1997. "Soviet Man-Made Famine in Ukraine," in S. Totten et al. (eds.), *Century of Genocide: Eyewitness Accounts and Critical Views*. New York: Garland.

MacFarquhar, R. 1974, 1983. *The Origins of the Cultural Revolution*, Vols. I & II. Oxford: Oxford University Press.

MacFie, A. 1998. *The End of the Ottoman Empire 1908–1923*. London: Longman.

Madhok, B. 1986. *The RSS and Politics*. New Delhi: Hindu World Publications.

Madsen, B. 1994. "Mormons, Forty-Niners, and the Invasion of Shoshone County," in Hurtado & Iverson (eds.), *Major Problems in American Indian History*.

Maier, C. 1981. "The Two Postwar Eras and the Conditions for Stability in Twentieth-Century Western Europe." *American Historical Review*, vol. 86.

Maksudov, S. 1993. "The Jewish Population Losses of the USSR from the Holocaust," in Dobroszycki & Gurock (eds.), *The Holocaust in the Occupied Soviet Union*. London: M. E. Sharpe.

Malaparte, C. 1946. *Kaputt*. New York: Dutton.

Malcolm, N. 1994. *Bosnia: A Short History*. New York: New York University Press.

Malkki, L. 1995. *Purity and Exile: Violence, Memory and National Cosmology among Hutu Refugees in Tanzania*. Chicago: University of Chicago Press.

Malley, M. 1999. "Regions: Centralization and Resistance," in Emmerson (ed.), *Indonesia Beyond Suharto*.

Mamdani, M. 2001. *When Victims Become Killers: Colonialism, Nativism and the Genocide in Rwanda*. Princeton, N.J.: Princeton University Press.

Mann, M. 1986. *The Sources of Social Power. Vol I: A History of Power from the Beginning to 1760 A.D.* Cambridge: Cambridge University Press.

　1993. *The Sources of Social Power. Vol II: The Rise of Classes and Nation-States, 1760–1914*. Cambridge: Cambridge University Press.

　1995. "Sources of Variation in Working Class Movements in Twentieth-Century Europe." *New Left Review*, no. 212.

　1997. "The Contradictions of Continuous Revolution," in I. Kershaw & M. Lewin (eds.), *Stalinism and Nazism*.

　2000. "Were the Perpetrators of Genocide 'Ordinary Men' or 'Real Nazis'? Results from Fifteen Hundred Biographies." *Holocaust and Genocide Studies*, vol. 14.

　2003. *Incoherent Empire*. London: Verso.

　2004. *Fascists*. Cambridge: Cambridge University Press.

Manning, R. 1993. "The Great Purges in a Rural District: Belyi Raion Revisited," in Getty & Manning (eds.), *Stalinist Terror*.

Marashlian, L. 1999. "Finishing the Genocide: Cleansing Turkey of Armenian Survivors, 1920–1923," in Hovannisian (ed.), *The Armenian Genocide in Perspective*.

Mardin, S. 1971. "Ideology and Religion in the Turkish Revolution." *International Journal of Middle Eastern Studies*, vol. 2.

Margolin, J.-L. 1999a. "China: A Long March into Night," in Courtois et al. (eds.), *The Black Book of Communism*.

　2000. "Du cas cambodgien comme enjeu et comme révélateur." *Communisme*, nos. 59–60.

Markus, A. 1994. *Australian Race Relations 1788–1993*. St. Leonard's, N.S.W.: Allen & Unwin.

Markusen, E., & Kopf, D. 1995. *The Holocaust and Strategic Bombing: Genocide and Total War in the Twentieth Century*. Boulder, Colo.: Westview.

Marrus, M. (ed.) 1989. *The Nazi Holocaust 4. The "Final Solution" Outside Germany*, Vol. I. Westport, Conn.: Meckler.

Marrus, M. 1985. *The Unwanted: European Refugees in the Twentieth Century*. New York: Oxford University Press.

　1987. *The Holocaust in History*. Harmondsworth, Middlesex, England: Penguin.

Marty, M., & Appleby, R. (eds.) 1991. *Fundamentalisms Observed*. Chicago: University of Chicago Press.

Matthäus, J. 1996. "What About the 'Ordinary Men'? The German Order Police and the Holocaust in the Occupied Soviet Union." *Holocaust and Genocide Studies*, vol. 10.

Mayer, A. 2000. *The Furies: Violence and Terror in the French and Russian Revolutions*. Princeton, N.J.: Princeton University Press.

Mayer, A. J. 1990. *Why Did the Heavens Not Darken?* London: Verso.

Mazower, M. 1993. *Inside Hitler's Greece*. New Haven, Conn.: Yale University Press.

Mbonimpa, M. 1999. "Le Rwanda n'est pas une île," expert evidence given at the Rutaganda trial. *Ubutabera*, no. 59, April 12.

McCarthy, J. 1983. *Muslims and Minorities: The Population of Ottoman Anatolia and the End of Empire.* New York: New York University Press.

1995. *Death and Exile: The Ethnic Cleansing of Ottoman Muslims, 1821–1922.* Princeton, N.J.: Darwin Press.

McGreal, C. 1999a. "We Saw Killers Treated as Heroes." *The Observer* (London), March 7.

1999b. "Lives Discarded to Save Face." *The Observer* (London), April 4.

McKenzie, J. 1995. *War Criminals in Canada.* Calgary: Detselig Enterprises.

McQueen, M. 1998. "The Context of Mass Destruction: Agents and Prerequisites of the Holocaust in Lithuania." *Holocaust and Genocide Studies*, vol. 12.

Melson, R. 1992. *Revolution and Genocide: On the Origins of the Armenian Genocide and the Holocaust.* Chicago: University of Chicago Press.

Melvern, L. 2000. *A People Betrayed: The Role of the West in Rwanda's Genocide.* London: Zed Books.

Mendelsohn, E. 1983. *The Jews of East Central Europe Between the World Wars.* Bloomington: University of Indiana Press.

1920. *Les Arméniens d'Angora déportés et massacrés.* Le Caire: Hindié.

Merdjimékian, P. 1919. *Les Mémoires de ma vie de déporté.* Aleppo: As-sabat J. Adjami.

Merkl, P. 1975 *Political Violence Under the Swastika.* Princeton, N.J.: Princeton University Press.

Mestrovic, S. (ed.). (1996). *Genocide After Emotion: The Postemotional Balkan War.* London: Routledge.

Michaelis, M. 1995. "The Current Debate Over Fascist Racial Policy," in R. Wistrich & S. DellaPergola (eds.), *Fascist Antisemitism and the Italian Jews.* Jerusalem: Vidal Sassoon International Center.

Mihajlovic, S., et al. 1991. *Of izbornih rituala do slobonih izbora (From Electoral Rituals to Free Elections).* Belgrade: University of Belgrade, Center for Political Research and Public Opinion.

de Mildt, D. 1996. *In the Name of the People: Perpetrators of Genocide in the Reflection of their Post-War Prosecution in West Germany: The 'Euthanasia' and 'Aktion Reinhard' Trial Cases.* The Hague: Nijhoff.

Milgram, S. 1974. *Obedience to Authority: An Experimental View.* New York: Harper & Row.

Milicevic, A. Forthcoming "Joining Serbia's Wars: Volunteers and Draft-Dodgers." Ph.D. dissertation, UCLA.

Miller, D., & Miller, L. 1993 *Survivors: An Oral History of the Armenian Genocide.* Berkeley & Los Angeles: University of California Press.

Mirkovic, D. 1993. "Victims and Perpetrators in the Yugoslav Genocide 1941–1945." *Holocaust and Genocide Studies*, vol. 7.

Misiunas, R., & Taagepera, R. 1993. *The Baltic States: Years of Dependence*, 2nd ed. London: Hurst.

Molnar, J. 1997. "Local Administration and the Holocaust in 5th Szeged Gendarmerie District" (in Magyar), in Braham & Pok (eds.), *The Holocaust in Hungary.*

Mommsen, H. 1991. *From Weimar to Auschwitz.* Princeton, N.J.: Princeton University Press.

1997. "Cumulative Radicalisation and Progressive Self-Destruction as Structural Determinants of the Nazi Dictatorship," in Kershaw & Lewin (eds.), *Stalinism and Nazism.*

Montville, J. (ed.) 1990. *Conflict and Peacemaking in Multiethnic Societies.* Lexington, Mass.: Lexington.

Moore, B., Jr. 2000. *Moral Purity and Persecution in History.* Princeton, N.J.: Princeton University Press.

Morgenthau, H. 1918. *Ambassador Morgenthau's Story.* Garden City, N.Y.: Doubleday, Page & Co.

Motyl, A. 1980. *The Turn to the Right: The Ideological Origins and Development of Ukrainian Nationalism, 1919–1929.* New York: Columbia University Press.

Mueller, J. 2000. "The Banality of 'ethnic war.'" *International Security*, vol. 25.

Müller-Hill, B. 1988. *Murderous Science: Elimination by Scientific Selection of Jews, Gypsies and Others, Germany 1933–1945.* Oxford: Oxford University Press.

Musial, B. 1999. *Deutsche Zivilverwaltung und Judenverfolgung im Generalgouvernement.* Wiesbaden: Harrassowitz.

Nagy-Talavera, N. 1997. "Laszlo Endre: The Frontrunner of the Final Solution in Hungary," in Braham & Pok (eds.), *The Holocaust in Hungary.*

Naimark, N. 2001. *Fires of Hatred: Ethnic Cleansing in Twentieth-Century Europe.* Cambridge, Mass.: Harvard University Press.

Nardini, L. 1983. "The Political Programme of President Tiso," in S. Kirschbaum (ed.), *Slovak Politics.* Cleveland: The Slovak Institute.

Nash, G. 1992. *Red, White and Black: The Peoples of Early North America*, 3rd ed. Englewood Cliffs, N.J.: Prentice Hall.

Nedelsky, N. 2001. "The Wartime Slovak State: A Case Study in the Relationship Between Ethnic Nationalism and Authoritarian Patterns of Governance." *Nations and Nationalism*, vol. 7.

Neshamit, S. 1977. "Rescue in Lithuania Under the Nazi Occupation, June 1941–August 1944," in *Rescue Attempts During the Holocaust. Proceedings of the Second Yad Vashem International Historical Conference.* Jerusalem: Yad Vashem.

Newbury, C. 1988. *The Cohesion of Oppression: Clientship and Ethnicity in Rwanda, 1860–1960.* New York: Columbia University Press.

1998. "Ethnicity and the Politics of History in Rwanda." *Africa Today*, vol. 45.

Ngor, H. 1988. *Surviving the Killing Fields.* London: Chatto & Windus.

Nichols, D. 1978. *Lincoln and the Indians: Civil War Policy and Politics.* Columbia: University of Missouri Press.

Nirenberg, D. 1996. *Communities of Violence: Persecution of Minorities in the Middle Ages.* Princeton, N.J.: Princeton University Press.

Nordholt, H. 2001. "A Genealogy of Violence." Unpublished paper, Univerity of Amsterdam/ Erasmus University, Rotterdam.

Nove, A. 1993. "Victims of Stalinism: How Many?" in Getty & Manning (eds.), *Stalinist Terror.*

Nsengimina, N. 1995. "Qu'en est-il de la société civile rwandaise?" in Guichaoua (ed.), *Les crises politiques.*

O'Shea, S. 2001. *The Perfect Heresy: The Revolutionary Life and Death of the Albigensians* London: Profile Books.

Oberschall, A. 1998. "From Ethnic Cooperation to Violence and War in Yugoslavia." Unpublished paper.

Oded, B. 1979. *Mass Deportations and Deportess in the Neo-Assyrian Empire.* Wiesbaden: Dr. Ludwig Reichert.

Oren, N. 1989. "The Bulgarian Exception: A Re-assessment of the Salvation of the Jewish Community," in Marrus (ed.), *The Nazi Holocaust.*

Organization of African Unity IPEP Report. 2000. Http: //www.oau-org/document/ipep/report/ Rwanda-e

Orth, K. 2000. *Die Konzentrationslager – SS. Sozial strukturelle Analysen und biographische studien.* Göttigen: Wallstein.

Otunnu, O. 1999. "A Historical Analysis of the Invasion by the Rwandan Patriotic Army (RPA)," in Adelman & Suhrke (eds.), *The Path of a Genocide.*

Paddison, J. 1999. *A World Transformed: Firsthand Accounts of California Before the Gold Rush.* Berkeley, Calif.: Heyday Books.

Panayi, P. (ed.). 1993. *Minorities in Wartime.* Oxford: Berg.

Parikh, S. 1998. "Religion, Reservations and Riots: The Politics of Ethnic Violence in India," in Basu & Kohli (eds.), *Community Conflicts*.

Paris, E. 1961. *Genocide in Satellite Croatia, 1941–1945*. Chicago: American Institute for Balkan Affairs.

Parker, G. 1984. *The Thirty Years War*. London: Routledge & Kegan Paul.

Pearson, R. 1983. *National Minorities in Eastern Europe, 1848–1945*. London: Macmillan.

Perez Diaz, V. 1993. *The Return of Civil Society*. Cambridge, Mass.: Harvard University Press.

Peric-Zimonjic, V. 1998. "Criminals given a free hand in the Balkans." Available at http://www.oneworld.org/ips2/mar98/balkans.html

Phillips, G. 1975. *Chiefs and Challengers: Indian Resistance and Cooperation in Southern California*. Berkeley & Los Angeles: University of California Press.

Physicians for Human Rights. 1999. *War Crimes in Kosovo*. Boston: author.

Picq, L. 1989. *Beyond the Horizon: Five Years with the Khmer Rouge*. New York: St. Martin's.

Piotrowski, T. 1998. *Poland's Holocaust*. London: McFarland.

Pipes, R. 1991. *The Russian Revolution*. New York: Vintage Books.

Pohl, D. 1996. *Nationalsozialistische Judenverfolgung in Ostgalizien, 1941–1944*. München: Oldenbourg.

　1997. "Die Holocaust-Forschung und Goldhagens Thesen." *Vierteljahrshefte für Zeitgeschichte*, vol. 47.

Polichnyj, P., & Aster, H. (eds.). 1990. *Ukrainian–Jewish Relations in Historical Perspective*. Edmonton, Alberta: Canadian Institute of Ukrainian Studies.

Porat, D. 1994. "The Holocaust in Lithuania: Some Unique Aspects," in Cesarani (ed.), *The Final Solution*. London: Routledge.

Posen, B. 1993. "The Security Dilemma and Ethnic Conflict." *Survival*, vol. 35.

Poulton, H. 1997. *Top Hat, Grey Wolf and Crescent: Turkish Nationalism and the Turkish Republic*. New York: New York University Press.

Pran, D. 1997. *Children of Cambodia's Killing Fields: Memoirs by Survivors*. New Haven, Conn.: Yale University Press.

Prasad, R. (ed.) *Autonomy Movements in Mizoram*. Delhi: Vikas.

Preti, L. 1974. "Fascist Imperialism and Racism," in R. Sarti (ed.), *The Ax Within: Italian Fascism in Action*. New York: New Viewpoints.

Proctor, R. 1988. *Racial Hygiene*. Cambridge, Mass.: Harvard University Press.

Prucha, F. 1994. "Andrew Jackson's Indian Policy: A Reassessment," in Hurtado & Iverson (eds.), *Major Problems in American Indian History*.

Prunier, G. 1995. *The Rwanda Crisis: History of a Genocide*. London: Hurst.

　1997. "Rwanda: The Social, Political and Economic Situation." http://www.africanews.org/specials/glakes/prunier.html

Pryor, Z. 1973. "Czechoslovak Economic Development in the Interwar Period," in V. Mamatey & L. Radomir (eds.), *A History of the Czechoslovak Republic, 1918–1948*. Princeton, N.J.: Princeton University Press.

Punjabi, R. 1984. "Communal Politics in Jammu and Kashmir State," in A. Engineer (ed.), *Communal Riots in Post-Independence India*. Bombay: Sangam Books.

Pusic, V. 1997. "Croatia's Struggle for Democracy." *Revija za socioloogiju*, vol. 28.

Putnam, R. 1993. *Making Democracy Work: Civic Traditions in Modern Italy*. Princeton, N.J.: Princeton University Press.

　2000. *Bowling Alone: The Collapse and Revival of American Community*. New York: Simon & Schuster.

Rabb, T. (ed.) 1964. *The Thirty Years War: Problems of Motive, Extent and Effect*. Boston: D. C. Heath.

Rabushka, A., & Shepsle, K. 1972. *Politics in Plural Societies*. Columbus, Ohio: Merrill.

Rahman, M. 1996. *Divided Kashmir: Old Problems, New Opportunities for India*. Boulder, Colo.: Lynne Rienner.

Ramet, S. P. 1992. *Balkan Babel: Politics, Culture and Religion in Yugoslavia.* Boulder, Colo.: Westview.

Reed, W. C. 1996. "Exile, Reform and the Rise of the Rwandan Patriotic Front." *Journal of Mosdern African Studies,* vol. 34.

Reitlinger, G. 1968. *The SS: Alibi of a Nation 1922–1945.* New York: Viking Press.

Renfrew, C. 1992. *Archeology and Language.* London: Cape.

Reyntjens, F. 1994. *L'Afrique des Grands Lacs en crise.* Paris: Karthala.

——— 1995. "Akazu, 'Escadrons de la mort' et autres 'Réseau Zero': Un historique des résistances au changement politique depuis 1990," in Guichaoua (ed.), *Les crises politiques.*

——— 1996. "Rwanda: Genocide and Beyond." *Journal of Refugee Studies,* vol. 9.

Riggs, H. 1997. *Days of Tragedy in Armenia: Personal Experiences in Harpoot, 1915–1917.* Ann Arbor, Mich.: Gomidas Institute.

Roberts, P. 1997. "Tudor Legislation and the Political Status of 'the British Tongue,'" in Jenkins (ed.), *The Welsh Language.*

Robinson, G. 1998. "*Rawan* Is as *Rawan* Does: The Origins of Disorder in New Order Aceh," *Indonesia,* vol. 66.

——— 2001a. "The Fruitless Search for a Smoking Gun: Tracing the Origins of Violence in East Timor." Unpublished paper, Department of History, UCLA.

——— 2001b. "People's War: Militias in East Timor and Indonesia." Unpublished paper, Department of History, UCLA.

Rogel, C. 1998. *The Breakup of Yugoslavia and the War in Bosnia.* Westport, Conn.: Greenwood.

Rogowski, R. 1977. "The Gauleiter and the Social Origins of Fascism." *Comparative Studies in Society and History,* vol. 19.

Rohde, D. 1997. *Endgame: The Betrayal and Fall of Srebrenica, Europe's Worst Massacre Since World War II.* New York: Farrar, Straus & Giroux.

Rohde, D. 2001. "Indonesia Unravelling?" *Foreign Affairs,* vol. 80.

Ron, J. 2000. "Territoriality and Plausible Deniability: Serbian Paramilitaries in the Bosnian War," in B. Campbell & A. Brenner (eds.), *Death Squads in Global Perspective.* New York: St. Martin's.

Rossino, A. 1997. "Destructive Impulses: German Soldiers and the Conquest of Poland." *Holocaust and Genocide Studies,* vol. 11.

Roth, N. 1995. *Conversos, Inquisition and the Expulsion of the Jews from Spain.* Madison: University of Wisconsin Press.

Rothkirchen, L. 1989. "Vatican Policy and the 'Jewish Problem' in 'Independent' Slovakia (1939–1945)," in M. Marrus (ed.), *The Nazi Holocaust, 4: The "Final Solution" Outside Germany.* Westport, Conn.: Meckler.

Rothschild, D. 2002. "Settlement Terror and Post-Agreement Stability," in Stedman et al. (eds.), *Ending Civil War.*

Rowley, C. 1970. *The Destruction of Aboriginal Society.* Canberra: Australian National University Press.

Rummel, R. 1992. *Democide: Nazi Genocide and Mass Murder.* New Brunswick, N.J.: Transaction.

——— 1994. *Death by Government.* New Brunswick, N.J.: Transaction.

——— 1998. *Statistics of Democide: Genocide and Mass Murder Since 1900.* Muenster: LIT.

Sabrin, B. (ed.) 1991. *Alliance for Murder: The Nazi–Ukrainian Nationalist Partnership in Genocide.* New York: Sarpedon.

Safrian, H. 1993. *Die Eichmann-Männer.* Wien: Europaverlag.

Sagvari, A. 1997. "Did They Do It Under Orders? Public Administration, Change of Guard and Law-Abiding Citizens in 1944" (in Magyar), in Braham & Pok (eds.), *The Holocaust in Hungary.*

Sandkühler, T. 1996. *"Endlösung" in Galizien.* Bonn: Dietz.

Sarafian, A. 1994. "The Paper Trail: The American State Department and the Report of Committee on Armenian Atrocities." *Revue du Monde Arménien*, vol. 1.

Saulat, S. 1979. *Maulana Maududi*. Karachi: International Islamic Publishers.

Scarritt, J. 1993. "Communal Conflict and Contention for Power in Africa South of the Sahara," in T. Gurr (ed.), *Minorities at Risk: A Global View of Ethnopolitical Conflict*. Washington, D.C.: U.S. Institute of Peace.

Scharf, M. 1997. *Balkan Justice*. Durham, N.C.: Carolina Academic Press.

Schechtman, J. 1989. "The Transnistria Reservation," in Marrus (ed.), *The Nazi Holocaust*.

Schectman, B. 1962. *Postwar Population Transfers in Europe, 1945–1955*. Philadelphia: University of Pennsylvania Press.

Schellenberg, W. 1956. *The Schellenberg Memoirs*, ed. L. Hagen. London: Andre Deutsch.

Schmidt-Hartmann, E. 1988. "People's Democracy: The Emergence of a Czech Political Concept in the Late Nineteenth Century," in S. Kirschbaum (ed.), *East European History*. Columbus, Ohio: Slavica.

Schmidt, K. 1983. "The Constitution of the Slovak Republic, 1939–1945," in S. Kirschbaum (ed.), *Slovak Politics*. Cleveland: The Slovak Institute.

Schofield, V. 1996. *Kashmir in the Crossfire*. London: L. B. Taurus.

Schutz, B. 1990. "Political Change and the Management of Ethnic Conflict in Zimbabwe," in Montville (ed.), *Conflict and Peacemaking*.

Schwarz, G. 1994. "SS-Aufseherinnen in nationalsozialistischen Konzentrationslagern (1933–1945)." *Dachauer Hefte*, vol. 10.

Segev, T. 1987. *Soldiers of Evil*. New York: McGraw-Hill.

Seifert, R. 1994. "War and Rape: A Preliminary Analysis," in A. Stiglmayer (ed.), *Mass Rape: The War Against Women in Bosnia-Herzegovina*. Omaha: University of Nebraska Press.

Sekulic, D., & Sporer, Z. 1997. "Regime support in Croatia." *Revija za sociologiju*, vol. 28.

Sells, M. 1996. *The Bridge Betrayed: Religion and Genocide in Bosnia*. Berkeley & Los Angeles: University of California Press.

Serbian Academy of Sciences & Arts. 1986 (1999 English ed.). *Memorandum*. Belgrade: author/GIP "Kultura."

Sereny, G. 1974. *Into That Darkness: From Mercy Killing to Mass Murder*. New York: Random House.

Seroka, J., & Pavlovic, V. (eds.). 1993. *The Tragedy of Yugoslavia*. New York: M. E. Sharpe.

Shaw, S., & E. 1977. *History of the Ottoman Empire and Modern Turkey, Vol. II: Reform, Revolution, and Republic: The Rise of Modern Turkey, 1808–1975*. Cambridge: Cambridge University Press.

Sheehan, B. 1973. *Seeds of Extinction: Jeffersonian Philanthropy and the American Indian*. Chapel Hill: University of North Carolina Press.

Shelah, M. 1990. "Genocide in Satellite Croatia," in Berenbaum (ed.), *A Mosaic of Victims*.

Shenfield, S. 1999. "The Circassians: A Forgotten Genocide?" in M. Levene & P. Roberts (eds.), *The Massacre in History*. Oxford: Berghahn.

Shiragian, A. 1976. *The Legacy: Memoirs of an Armenian Patriot*. Boston: Hairenik Press.

Shissler, H. 2003. *Between Two Empires: Ahmet Agaoglu and the New Turkey*. London: Tauris.

Siber, I. 1993. "The Impact of Nationalism, Values and Ideological Orientation on Multi-Party Elections in Croatia," in Seroka & Pavlovic (eds.), *The Tragedy of Yugoslavia*.

Sikavica, S. 1997. "The Army's Collapse," in Udovicki & Ridgeway (eds.), *Burn This House*.

Silber, L., & Little, A. 1995. *The Death of Yugoslavia*. London: BBC Books.

Singer, J., & Small, M. 1982. *Wages of War, 1816–1965*. Ann Arbor, MI: Inter-University Consortium for Political and Social Research.

Sliwinski, M. 1995. *Le Génocide Khmer Rouge: Une analyse démographique*. Paris: L'Harmattan.

Smedley, A. 1993. *Race in North America*. Boulder, Colo.: Westview.

Smelser, R. 1975. *The Sudeten Problem: 1933–1938*. Folkeston: Dawson.

Smith, A. 1986. *The Ethnic Origins of Nations*. Oxford: Blackwell.

2000. *The Nation in History: Historiographical Debates About Ethnicity and Nationalism*. Cambridge: Polity Press.

2001. *Nationalism*. Oxford: Polity.

Smith, L. 1980. *The Aboriginal Population of Australia*. Canberra: Australian National University Press.

Smith, R. 1987. "Human Destructiveness and Politics: The Twentieth Century as an Age of Genocide," in I. Walliman & Dobkowski (eds.), *Genocide in the Modern Age*. New York: Greenwood.

1997. "State Power and Genocidal Intent," in *Proceedings of the International Conference*.

Snyder, J. 2000. *From Voting to Violence: Democratization and National Conflict*. New York: Norton.

Sochat, A. 1974. "Jews, Lithuanians and Russians, 1939–1941," in B. Vago & G. Mosse (eds.), *Jews and Non-Jews in Eastern Europe 1918–1945*. New Brunswick, N.J.: Transaction.

Sofsky, W. 1997. *The Order of Terror: The Concentration Camp*. Princeton, N.J.: Princeton University Press.

Sollenberg, M., & Wallensteen, P. 2001. "Patterns of Major Armed Conflicts, 1990–2000," in *Stockholm Institute of Peace Research Yearbook*, Appendix 1A. Stockholm: Authors.

Spector, S. 1990. *The Holocaust of Volhynian Jews 1941–1944*. Jerusalem: Yad Vashem.

Stannard, D. 1992. *American Holocaust: The Conquest of the New World*. New York: Oxford University Press.

Statische Reichsamt. 1935. *Volkzählung die Bevolkerung, 1933*. Berlin: author.

Staub, E. 1992. *The Roots of Evil: The Origins of Genocide and Other Group Violence*. Cambridge: Cambridge University Press.

Stedman, S. 2002. "Introduction," in S. Stedman et al. (eds.), *Ending Civil Wars: The Implementation of Peace Agreements*. Boulder, Colo.: Lynne Rienner.

Stedman, S., et al. (eds.) 2002. *Ending Civil War: The Implementation of Peace Agreements*. Boulder, Colo.: Lynne Rienner.

Stein, G. 1966. *The Waffen-SS: Hitler's Elite Guard at War, 1939–1945*. Ithaca, N.Y.: Cornell University Press.

Steinberg, J. 1990. *All or Nothing: The Axis and the Holocaust 1941–43*. London: Routledge.

1994. "Types of Genocide? Croatians, Serbs and Jews, 1941–45," in Cesarani (ed.), *The Final Solution: Origins and Implementation*. London: Routledge.

Stiglmayer, A. 1994. *Mass Rape: The War Against Women in Bosnia-Herzogovina*. Lincoln: University of Nebraska Press.

Stitkovac, E. 1997. "Croatia: The First War," in Udovicki & Ridgeway (eds.), *Burn This House*.

Stoddart, P. 1963, *The Ottoman Government and the Arabs, 1922–1918*. PhD. dissertation, Princeton University.

Straede, T. 1999. "Jewish Slave Labor in Nazi German Industry: The Case of Volkswagen." Paper presented to the Center for European and Russian Studies, UCLA, January 28, 1999.

Straus, S. 2004. "The Order of Genocide: Race, Power and War in Rwanda." Ph.D. dissertation, University of California at Berkeley.

Streit, C. 1978. *Keine Kamaraden. Die Wehrmacht und die sowjetischen Kriegsgefangenen 1941–1945*. Stuttgart: Deutsche Verlags-Anstalt.

Stuermer, H. 1917. *Two War Years in Constantinople*. New York: George H. Doran Co.

Sudetic, C. 1998. *Blood and Vengeance: One Family's Story of the War in Bosnia*. New York: Norton.

Sugar, P. 1971a. "Conclusion," in Sugar (ed.), *Eastern European Nationalism in the Twentieth Century*.

Sugar, P. (ed.) 1971b. *Eastern European Nationalism in the Twentieth Century*. Washington, D.C.: American University Press.

Sunstein, C. 2000. "Deliberative Trouble? Why Groups Go to Extremes." *Yale Law Journal*, vol. 109.

Suny, R. 1998. "Empire and Nation: Armenians, Turks and the End of the Ottoman Empire." *Armenian Forum*, Vol. 1.

Sydnor, C. 1977. *Soldiers of Destruction: The SS Death's Head Division, 1933–1945*. Princeton, N.J.: Princeton University Press.

Szinai, M. 1997. "The Politics of Hungarian Governments on the Jewish Question, 1936–1944" (in Magyar), in Braham & Pok (eds.), *The Holocaust in Hungary*.

Szita, S. 1990. "The Forced Labor of Hungarian Jews at the Fortification of the Western Border Regions of Hungary, 1944–45," in R. Braham (ed.), *Studies on the Holocaust in Hungary*. New York: Columbia University Press.

Sznajder, M. 1995. "The Fascist Regime, Anti-Semitism and the Racial Laws in Italy," in Wistrich & DellaPergola (eds.), *Fascist Antisemitism and the Italian Jews*. Jerusalem: Vidal Sassoon International Center.

Tambiah, S. 1996. *Leveling Crowds: Ethnonationalist Conflict and Collective Violence in South Asia*. Berkeley & Los Angeles: University of California Press.

Tec, N. 1990. *In the Lion's Den: The Life of Oswald Rufeison*. New York: Oxford University Press.

Teiwes, F. 1987. "Establishment and Consolidation of the New Regime," in R. McFarquar & J. Fairbank (eds.), *The Cambridge History of China, Vol 14: The People's Republic*. Cambridge: Cambridge University Press.

Thibon, C. 1995. "Les origines historique de la violence," in Guichaoua (ed.), *Les crises politiques*.

Thion, S. 1983. "Chronology of Khmer Communism, 1940–1982," in Chandler & Kiernan (eds.), *Revolution and Its Aftermath*.

  1993. *Watching Cambodia*. Bangkok: White Lotus.

Thomas, H. 1993. *Conquest: Montezuma, Cortes and the Fall of Old Mexico*. New York: Simon & Schuster.

Thompson, M. 1992. *A Paper House: The Ending of Yugoslavia*. London: Hutchinson.

  1994. *Forging War: The Media in Serbia, Croatia and Bosnia-Herceogovina*. Article 19. London: International Centre Against Censorship.

Thompson, T. 1992. *Early History of the Israelite People*. Leiden: Brill.

Thornton, R. 1997. *American Indian Holocaust and Survival: A Population History Since 1492*. Norman: University of Oklahoma Press.

Thurston, R. 1993. "The Stakhanovite Movement: The Background to the Great Terror in the Factories, 1935–1938," in Getty & Manning (eds.), *Stalinist Terror*.

Tomasic, D. 1946. "Nationality Problems in Yugoslavia." *Journal of Central European Affairs*, vol. 6.

Trials of the War Criminals Before the Nuremberg Military Tribunals, 15 vols. 1946–9.

Trigger, B. 1994. "Early Native North American Responses to European Contact," in Hurtado & Iverson (eds.), *Major Problems in American Indian History*.

Trumpener, U. 1968. *Germany and the Ottoman Empire 1914–1918*. Princeton, N.J.: Princeton University Press.

Tucker, R. 1990. *Stalin in Power: The Revolution From Above, 1928–1941*. New York: Norton.

Tudjman, F. 1981. *Nationalism and Contemporary Europe*. New York: Columbia University Press.

Udovicki, J. 1997. "The Bonds and the Faultlines," in Udovicki & Ridgeway (eds.), *Burn This House*.

Udovicki, J., & Ridgeway, J. (eds.). 1997. *Burn This House: The Making and Unmaking of Yugoslavia*. Durham, N.C.: Duke University Press.

Udovicki, J., & Stitkovac, E. 1997. "Bosnia and Hercegovina: The Second War," in Udovicki & Ridgeway (eds.), *Burn This House*.

Udovicki, J., & Torov, I. 1997. "The Interlude: 1980–1990," in Udovicki & Ridgeway (eds.), *Burn This House.*

United Nations Security Council. 1994. *Final Report of the Commission of Experts* (The Bassiouni Report), S/1994/674. New York: United Nations.

United Nations, International Criminal Tribunal for Yugoslavia. 1996–2000. www.un.org/icty/cases-te.htm. Transcripts of these cases: Aleksovski (IT-95-14/1), Blaskic (IT-95-14), Delacic et al. (IT-96-21), Erdemovic (IT-96-22), Furundzija (IT-95-17/1-PT), Kovacevic (IT-97-24), Kordic & Cerkez (IT-95-14/2), Krstic (IT-98-33), Kupreskic et al. (IT-95-16), Mrksic et al. (IT-95-13a), Milosevic (IT-02-54), Naletilic & Martinovic (IT-98-34-T), Nikolic (IT-95-3), Tadic (IT-94-1), and Vasiljevic (IT-98-32-T).

United States Official Documents on the Armenian Genocide, reprinted 1993–5. Vol I: *The Lower Euphrates.* Vol II: *The Peripheries.* Vol III: *The Central Lands.* Watertown, Mass.: Armenian Review.

Uttley, R. 1994. "Wars of the Peace Policy, 1869–1886," in Hurtado & Iverson (eds.), *Major Problems in American Indian History.*

Uvin, P. 1998. *Aiding Violence: The Development Enterprise in Rwanda.* West Hartford, Conn.: Kumarian Press.

Vago, R. (ed.). 1987. "Eastern Europe," in D. Mühlberger (ed.), *The Social Basis of European Fascist Movements.* London: Croom Helm.

Varshney, A. 2002. *Ethnic Conflict and Civic Life: Hindus and Muslims in India.* New Haven, Conn.: Yale University Press.

Vasic, M. 1996. "The Yugoslav Army and the Post-Yugoslav Armies," in D. Dykeer & I. Vejvoda (eds.), *Yugoslavia and After: A Study in Fragmentation, Despair and Rebirth.* London: Longman.

Vestermanis, M. 1992. "Der Holocaust in Lettland: Zur "Postkommunistischen" Aufarbeitung des Themas in Osteuropa," in A. Herzig & I. Lorenz (eds.), *Verdrängung und Vernichtung der Juden unter dem Nationalsozialismus.* Hamburg: Hans Christians.

Vickery, M. 1983. "Democratic Kampuchea: Themes and Variations," in Chandler & Kiernan (eds.), *Revolution and Its Aftermath.*

1984. *Cambodia 1975–1982.* Boston: South End Press.

Viola, L. 1993. "The Second Coming: Class Enemies in the Soviet Countryside, 1927–1935," in Getty & Manning (eds.), *Stalinist Terror.*

1996. *Peasant Rebels Under Stalin.* New York: Oxford University Press.

Vivitsky, B. 1990. "Slavs and Jews: Consistent and Inconsistent Perspectives on the Holocaust," in Berenbaum (ed.), *A Mosaic of Victims.*

Völkl, E. 1998. "Spirals of Violence, Mass Executions and Wars within Wars: Settling Accounts with Fascism in Croatia," in Larsen & Hagtvet (eds.), *Modern Europe After Fascism 1943–1980s.* New York: Columbia University Press.

Voll, J. 1990. "Northern Muslim Perspectives," in Montville (ed.), *Conflict and Peacemaking.*

Vreme News Digest Agency. 1990–9. Belgrade: Vreme.

Vujacic, M. 1995. "Communism and Nationalism in Russia and Serbia." Ph.D. dissertation, University of California at Berkeley.

Vukomanovic, D. 1995. "The Creation of Political Parties – a Chronological Review," in Janjic (ed.), *Serbia Between the Past and the Future.*

Vulliamy, E. 1994. *Seasons in Hell: Understanding Bosnia's War.* New York: St. Martin's.

1996. "Middle Managers of Genocide." *The Nation* (Washington), June 10.

Waddington, R., & Williamson, A. (eds.) 1994. *The Expulsion of the Jews: 1492 and After.* New York: Garland.

Wagner, M. 1998. "All the Bourgmestre's Men: Making Sense of Genocide in Rwanda." *Africa Today*, vol. 45.

Wallace, A. 1999. *Jefferson and the Indians: The Tragic Fate of the First Americans.* Cambridge, Mass.: Belknap Press.

Watkins, S. 1991. *From Provinces into Nations. Demographic Integration in Western Europe, 1870–1960.* Princeton, N.J.: Princeton University Press.

Watts, L. 1993. *Romanian Cassandra: Ion Antonescu and the Struggle for Reform, 1916–1941.* New York: Columbia University Press.

Weber, E. 1976. *Peasants into Frenchmen.* Stanford, Calif.: Stanford University Press.

Weber, M. 1958. "The Economic Foundations of 'Imperialism,'" in H. Gerth & C. Wright Mills (eds.), *From Max Weber: Essays in Sociology.* New York: Galaxy Books.

  1978. *Economy and Society,* Vol. I, 2nd English ed. Berkeley & Los Angeles: University of California Press.

Wegner, B. 1990. *The Waffen-SS.* Oxford: Blackwell.

Weiner, A. 2001. *Making Sense of War: The Second World War and the Fate of the Bolshevik Revolution.* Princeton, N.J.: Princeton University Press.

Weingast, B. 1989. "The Rationality of Fear," in J. Snyder & B. Walker (eds.), *Military Intervention in Civil Wars.* New York: Columbia University Press.

Weiss, A. 1990a. "Jewish–Ukrainian Relations in Western Ukraine During the Holocaust," in Potichnyj & Aster (eds.), *Ukrainian–Jewish Relations.*

  1990b. "The Holocaust and the Ukrainian victims," in Berenbaum (ed.), *A Mosaic of Victims.*

Weiss-Wendt, A. 1998. "The Soviet Occupation of Estonia in 1940–41 and the Jews." *Holocaust and Genocide Studies,* vol. 12.

Werth, N. 1999a. "A State Against Its People: Violence, Repression and Terror in the Soviet Union," in Courtois et al. (eds.), *The Black Book of Communism.*

  1999b. "Logiques de violence dans l'URSS stalinienne," in H. Rousso (ed.), *Stalinisme et nazisme: Histoire et mémoire comparées.* Paris: Editions Complexe.

Wheatcroft, S. 1993. "More Light on the Scale of Repression and Excess Mortality in the Soviet Union in the 1930s," in Gettty & Manning (eds.), *Stalinist Terror.*

Wheeler, J. 1999. *Cromwell in Ireland.* Dublin: Gill & Macmillan.

Wildt, M. 2002. *Generation des Unbedingten.* Hamburg: Hamburger edition.

Willame, J.-C. 1995. "Aux sources de l'hetacombe rwandaise." *Cahiers Africains,* vol. 14.

Williams, P., & Cigar, N. 1996. *War Crimes and Individual Responsibility: A Prima Facie Case for the Indictment of Slobodan Milosevic.* Washington, D.C.: Balkan Institute.

Wimmer, A. 2002. *Nationalist Exclusion and Ethnic Conflict: Shadows of Modernity.* Cambridge: Cambridge University Press.

Winter, J. 1988. "Some Paradoxes of the First World War," in R. Wall & J. Winter (eds.), *The Upheaval of War.* Cambridge: Cambridge University Press.

Wistrich, R. 1982. *Who's Who in Nazi Germany.* London: Weidenfeld & Nicolson.

Woodward, S. 1995. *Balkan Tragedy.* Washington, D.C.: The Brookings Institution.

Wynn, C. 1992. *Workers, Strikes and Pogroms: The Dombass-Dnepr Bend in Late Imperial Russia, 1870–1905.* Princeton, N.J.: Princeton University Press.

Yalman, A. E. 1970. *Yakin Tarihte Gorduklerim ve Gecirdiklerim [What I have Seen and Experienced in the Near Past],* Vol. I. Istanbul: Yenilik Basimevi.

Yamada, S. 2000. *The Construction of the Assyrian Empire.* Leiden: Brill.

Yang, C. K. 1959. *A Chinese Village in Early Communist Transition.* Cambridge, Mass.: Harvard University Press.

Yang, D. 1996. *Calamity and Reform in China.* Stanford, Calif.: Stanford University Press.

Yathay, P. 1987. *Staying Alive, My Son.* New York: Free Press, 1987.

Yeghiayan, V. 1990. *The Armenian Genocide and the Trials of the Young Turks.* La Verne, Calif.: American Armenian International College.

  1991. *British Foreign Office Dossiers on Turkish War Criminals.* Pasadena, Calif.: Doctorian Productions.

Yiftachel, O. 1999. "Ethnocracy: The Politics of Judaizing Israel/Palestine." *Constellation: An International Journal of Critical and Democratic Theory,* vol. 6.

Zabka, A. 1994. "Analyses of the Conflict in Former Yugoslavia." *National Defence Academy Series, Vienna, Studies and Reports*, no. 2

Zacek, J. 1971. "Czechoslovak Fascisms," in Sugar (ed.), *Eastern European Nationalism in the Twentieth Century*.

Zbikowski, A. 1993. "Local Anti-Jewish Pogroms in the Occupied Territories of Eastern Poland, June–July 1941," in L. Dobroszycki & J. Gurock (eds.), *The Holocaust in the Soviet Union*. London: M. E. Sharpe.

Zürcher, E. 1998. *Turkey: A Modern History*. London: Tauris.

Zuccotti, S. 1987. *The Italians and the Holocaust*. New York: Basic Books.

Index

Aaronsohn, A.
  (1916), 146
Abakiga, 455–6
Abdulhamit II, Sultan, 118–19, 125, 130
Abu Sayyaf movement, 526
abuse, gender, 89, 152, 171. *See also*
  rape
Accounting for Genocide (Fein), 279
Aceh, 493–4
Acquitainians, 14
Act of Settlement (1652), 52
Act of Union (1536), 58
actor
  ideological, 100
  in interwar ethnic relations, 68
  settler, in South West Africa, 102–6
  in South West Africa, 100
Adana, 127–8
Addis Ababa, 309
Adler, 63
Adzic, General, 394
affectual action, 26
Africa, 11, 428–9
Agaoglu, 122
Agayev. *See* Agaoglu
age, 56–7
agriculture, collectivization of, in Soviet
  Union, 323
Ahmici, 357, 406, 409, 410, 413–14
AK-47. *See* Kalashnikov
Akayesu, Mayor Jean Paul, 458, 469
Akazu. See "little house"
Akcam, J.
  (1992), 172
Akcam, Taner, 154
Akcura, 131
Aktion Reinhard (death camps), 213, 251,
  259–62, 291
Alai Bey, 160
Albania, 112

Albanians
  in Kosovo, 356, 359, 363, 386, 416
  and religion, 10
Albigensians, 42
alcohol, 65, 242, 262, 266, 271, 278, 287,
  419, 420, 422, 462, 480
Aleksovski, Zlatko, 406, 414
Aleksynas, 285
Aleppo, 161
Alexander II, Tsar, 64
Alexander, King, 294
Alexander the Great, 38
Ali Muenif Bey, 160, 161
"Alia." *See* Izetbegovic
Alilovic, 409
Allen, M.
  (2002), 215
Allers, Dietrich, 260
Alodhya mosque, 481
Alp, Tekin, 131
Amasasu, 445
Amdja, Hassan, 158
America
  Indians, 505. *See also* specific tribes
  Indians, perception of, 84
  Indians, Plan A for, 89–90, 96
  Indians, Plan B for, 90, 96
  Indians, Plan C for, 92, 96–7
  Indians, rationales for extermination of,
    vii
  native population in, 76
  peoples of, 9
  Spanish incursions into, 71
Anatolia, 112
And Quiet Flows the Don (Sholokhov), 324
Anderson, B.
  (1983), 30
"Angel of Death," 218
Angka, 344, 345, 346, 348, 349, 350
Ankor Vat, 340

Anschluss, 194
anti-Semitism, 47, 183, 184, 190–1, 193
anti-Slav sentiments, 184
Antonescu, Marshal, 303, 304–7
Aosta, Duke of, 309
Apache Indians, 91, 96
Arad, Y.
    (1987), 213
Arajs, Major Viktor, 283, 284, 292
Arapaho Indians, 98
Arendt, H.
    (1965), 244
    (1983), 29, 189
Arkan. *See* Raznatovic, Zeljko
Arkan's Tigers, 392, 404
Armenia
    Armenian Problem, 6, 8
    "the Armenian Question," 141
    genocide in, 140–79
    peoples of, 8
Armenians, 115, 116, 117–18
arms sales, 526
Arrow Cross, 302
Artamen League, 213
Arunachal Pradesh, 489
Arusha Accords (1993), 441–2, 443, 451, 500
Ashdown, Paddy, 396, 407
Asia, 71
Asiatic-Bolshevism, 273
Assam, 489
assimilation, 72
    in America, 87
    aristocratic lateral, 72, 78
    civic definition of, 181
    coercive, in America, 88
    coercive, in Ireland, 49, 53
    coercive, in Ottoman Empire, 131
    cultural, in Bulgaria, 307
    forced, in Greater Serbia, 357–8
    under Hapsburgs, 182
    institutional, in South West Africa, 100
    institutional, in Spain, 47
    lateral, 35, 41
    lateral aristocratic, 60
    lateral aristocratic, in Australia, 79
    lateral aristocratic, in South West Africa, 101
    partial, in America, 89
    voluntary, 13–14
    voluntary, in America, 86
    voluntary, in Germany, 181
    voluntary, partial, 508
Assyrians, 34, 39, 40–1
Ataturk, 130, 163
atrocities
    "bottom-up," 22
    Bulgarian, 113
    Croatian, in the Laska Valley, 405–16
    four types of, in Yugoslavia, 356–7
    Muslim, 416–18
Augustus, 38
Aumeier, Hans, 252
Auschwitz, 212, 216, 240
Ausrottung, 191
Australia, 13, 79–83
    Aboriginal population in, 76, 79–80, 83
    peoples of, 9
    Plan A in, 79
    Plan B in, 79
    Plan C in, 80
    Plan D in, 82
    Plan E in, 82
Austria, 63–4
    Austrian Germans, and Slavic threat, 182
    Austrian Germans, and Jewish threat, 182
    and Slavic threat, 183
"Austrian Legion," 216
Auxiliary Police Battalion 101, 215, 266–72
Auxiliary Police Battalion 309, 271
Ayodha, 484
Azeris, 9

Babic, 384, 387–8, 393, 400
Babylonian rebellion, 40
Bach-Zalewski, General von dem Erich, 199, 246–7, 268
Baer, Richard, 252
Bagasora, Colonel Theoneste, 443, 445, 447, 451
Baggesen, Mayor Ignace, 407
Baghdjian, K.
    (1987), 170
Bagilishema, Mayor, 448, 455–6
Bagogwe, 447
Bajrang Dal, 479, 483
Baky, 300
Balkan states
    Plan A in, 281
    Plan B in, 282
    Plan C in, 282
Balkan wars, 131

Baltic states, 16, 19, 113, 281–6, 353
Banach, J.
  (1998), 214
Bandwagon Nazis, 235
Bantu, 432
Barbie, Klaus, 218, 222
Barnett, A.
  (1983), 349
Bartov, O.
  (1985), 273
  (1996), 29
Bassiouni Report, 420
Battle of Kosovo Field (1389), 19–20, 358, 361
Bauchenwald, 200
Baumann, Z.
  (1989), 21, 29, 240
Beara, Colonel, 396
"Beast of Belsen," 218. *See* Kramer
Becker, E.
  (1998), 349
Being Muslim the Bosnian Way (1995), 406
Beissinger, M.
  (2002), 25, 355
Bekir Sami Bey, 161
Belarus, 286–8
Belgium, 60
Bell-Fialkoff, A.
  (1993), 69
Belzec, 259, 292
Benes, President, 353
Berger, General, 199
Berktay, Halil, 154
Bernau, Mr., 111, 153
Best, Werner, 202
Beziers, 42
Bianchi, 407–8
Bigler, Governor, 91
Bilinsky, Y.
  (1990), 291
biological-racial reasoning, 185
Birn, R.
  (1998), 189, 271
Bisesero, 455, 460, 465
"Bitch of Buchenwald," 218
BJP, 483
Black-and-Tans, 15
Black Hawk War, 93
Blaskic, Colonel Tihomir, 406, 410, 411, 413
"bloodlines" and mass murder, 342–3
"Bloody Brygida." *See* Lachert, Hildegard

Blume, Walter, 264
Bluttkit, 263
Boban, Mate, 378, 384, 408
Bodo, 489
Böhme, General Franz, 274
Boljevic, Dusan and Jagoda, 420
Bolshevik Revolution, 183
Bolshevism, 5, 273, 321
Bond, D.
  (1998), 20
Book of the Courtier, The (Guicciardini), 43
border disputes, 355
  between Armenians and Azeris, 355
  between Georgians and Ossetians, 355
  in India, 488
  between Jammu and Kashmir, 486–8
  between Tajikhistan and Uzbekhistan, 355
Boris, Czar, 307
Bosnia, 368–9, 381
  Bosniaks in, 10, 369
  Bosnian Serb Party (SDS), 369
  Bosnian state, 7
  cantons of, 406
  Muslims, 416
  population in, 366
  Serb aggression against, 395–6
Bosnia-Herzegovina, 356
  ethnic self-identification in, 363
  population in, 366
Bosnian Croat army (HVO), 407, 409
Bosnian Croat party (HDZ), 408
Bosnian refugees, 116
Brack, 210
Bradford, William, 85
Braeckman, P.
  (1994), 447
Braham, R.
  (1981), 301
Brandt, Karl, 257
Brass, P.
  (1997), 22, 441, 475, 476
Bratunac, 385
Braunsteiner, Hermine, 253
Bridgman, J.
  (1981), 107
Bringa, Tone, 406–7, 414–16
Britain, 13
Broad, Corporal Perry, 254, 292
Broszat, M.
  (1981), 190
Browder, G.
  (1996), 214–15, 231

Brown, P.
  (1996), 35
Browning, C.
  (1978), 215
  (1978, 1985, 1993, 1994), 247–8
  (1983), 248
  (1993), 189, 215, 267, 270
Brubaker, R.
  (1996), 68, 360
Bryce Report, 136, 150, 151, 153, 169
Buchheim, H.
  (1968), 270
Buddhism, 42
Bulgaria, 112, 307–8
Bulow, Reich Chancellor von, 104,
  105
Bürckel, Josef, 246
Burke, P.
  (1978), 43–4, 58
Burleigh, M.
  (1994), 260
  (2000), 183, 259
Burnett, Governor, 91
Burundi, 430, 431–2, 435, 438
Busovaca, 410, 411
Butare, 456

"Caco." *See* Topalovic, Musan
Cahit, Huseyin, 144
California Indians, 76, 87–8. *See also*
  America, native population; America,
  Indians
callous class warfare, 324
callous policies, 16
callous warfare
  and Albigensians, 42
  in China, 337
  in Holy Roman Empire, 48
  in Ireland, 51
  in Ottoman Empire, 113
  against Poles, 185
Cambodia, 339–42, 350
  Plan A in, 341
  Plan B in, 341
Campbell, B.
  (1998), 196
Canaris, Admiral, 273
Canby, General, 92
Caribbean islands, 16
Carthage, 34, 36
Casas, Bartolome de las, 77
Castillo, Bernal Diaz del, 77

Cathar heresy, 42
Caucasus, the, 98, 112, 114
CCP, 337, 338–9
Cefalonia, 274
Celebici, 416–17
Cerkez, Commander, 406, 411, 413
Chandler, D.
  (1999), 346, 347, 348
"Chaos Thesis," 264
Charny, I.
  (1986), 9
Chechia, 6, 99, 329
Chechnya, 329, 355
Cheka secret police, 65, 321
Cherokee Indians, 86–7, 93, 94, 108
Chetniks, 362, 392, 421
Cheyenne Indians, 98
Chickasaw Indians, 108
China, 330–9
  bureaucracy, 39
  famine in, 336
  "five black categories" in, 337
  "five red categories" in, 337
  inflation in, 334–5
  land distribution in, 332
  Plan A in, 333
  Plan B in, 333–4
  Plan C in, 334, 335, 337
  Plan D in, 337
  Red Guards in, 337
Chinese Communist Party (CPP), 330–1, 332,
  333
chistka. See purge
Chivington, Colonel, 98
Choctaw Indians, 93, 108
Christendom, 16th-century Western, 48
Christian Greeks, 115
Christian Socialists, 63
Christianity, 42, 75
Christie, Debra, 415
Chumash Indians, 18. *See also* American
  Indians
Churchill, Winston, 190, 353
Ciano, 308
Cigar, N.
  (1995), 20, 360
Cilicia, 127
Circassians, 99–100
citizenship, 56
Citizenship Law, 193
Civil Service Academy, 122
civil society theory, 21

Civil War
  in England, 51
  in Ireland, 50
  Soviet, 321
civilian deaths, 2
Civilization and Its Discontents (Freud), 18
class, 56, 57, 58, 59
  "class-divided societies," 36
  and ethnicity, 60–1
classicide, 17, 320
  in Cambodia, 340, 342
  in China, 337
cleansing
  biological, 15
  colonial, 70–6, 107–8
  ethnic, 522. *See also* power, networks
  ethnic, defined, 11
  ethnic, five steps of, in Yugoslavia, 361
  ethnic, in Northern Europe, 506–9
  ethnic, Plan A for, 7
  ethnic, Plan B for, 7
  murderous, 97
  murderous, alternative scenarios for, 6–7
  murderous, as Plan C, 7–8
  murderous, danger zone of, 6
  murderous, modernity of, 2–3, 502
  murderous, perpetuation of, 7
Clifton, R.
  (1999), 50
coercion, institutional, 14
  in Germany, 181
  on Iberian Peninsula, 45
  during Thirty Years War, 49
Cohen, L.
  (1995), 360
Cohen, Moses. *See* Alp, Tekin
Cold War, 511
"collective conscience" (Durkheim), 121
"collective madness," 403
colony
  economy, types of colonial, 71–2
  expansion, Russian, 99–100
  mixed, 71
  occupation, 71
  plantation, 71
  pure settlement, 72
  settler cases, 22
Commanche Indians, 97
Commissar Order, 187
"commitment problem," 24
Committee of the Committee of Union and
  Progress (CUP), 123, 126–7

common law (English), 43
Communist
  deaths under regimes, 319
  perceived enemies of, 318–21
"comprador capitalist," 342
concentration camps, 200–2
confederal methodology, 13
confederalism, multicultural, under
  Hapsburgs, 182
Conference of the Undersecretaries, 248
Congo, 7
Connolly, S.
  (1992), 53
Connor, W.
  (1994), 31, 59, 365
consociationalism, 13, 114, 118, 524
Constitution of 1850, 90
constructivism, 21
"contradictions of continuous revolution,"
  197
conversion
  forced, 16
  forced, and Albigensians, 42
  forced, of Serbs, 296
conversos, 45–6
Convicts Brigade, 409
convivencia, 45
Conwy, 58
Coote, Charles, 52
core constituencies, 20, 505–6
Corradini, 62, 309
Cortes, 76–7
Corwin, P.
  (1999), 422
Cossacks, 15
Coster, W.
  (1999), 52
CPP, 336, 337. *See* Chinese Communist
  Party
CRD, 440
Creek Indians, 85, 92, 93, 108
Croatia, 294–8, 367, 376, 379
  Chetniks, 295
  Croatian army (HVO), 407
  Croatian Community of Herceg-Bosna,
    408
  Croatian Democratic Party, 385
  Croatian Party of Rights, 379
  Croatian state, 7
  Croats in, 10
  ethnic self-identification in, 363
  Tito's Partisans, 295

Crocker, M.
  (1998), 98
Cromwell, Oliver, 50–2
Crook, General, 96
Crosby, A.
  (1986), 76
CUP. *See* Committee of the Committee of Union and Progress
Custer, General George Armstrong, 92
Cyahinda, 463
Czechoslovakia, 353

Dachau, 200, 201, 213, 216, 252
Dadrian, V.
  (1992), 127, 128
  (1993), 174
  (1996), 20
  (1997), 133
Dahijas, 405
Dallaire, General Romeo, 449, 452, 527
Davidson, K.
  (1985), 172
Davies, Consul, 152, 153, 162, 171
Dayaks, 5, 495–6
Dayton Agreement (1995), 387
Dean, M.
  (2000), 271
death camps, 242
Death of a Nation (BBC documentary), 370
Declaration on the Sovereignity and Autonomy of the Serbian People, 387
Deir Zor, 146, 148
Del Boca, A.
  (1969), 309–10
Delacic, Zejnil, 417
Delic, Hazim, 417
democracy, 3. *See also* demos
  conceptions of, 68–9
  liberal, 55
  majoritarian, 22
  settler, 4, 73, 88, 90
Democratic League of Kosovo, 387
democratic peace theory, 21–2, 108
demos, i, 3–4, 55, 184, 502. *See also* democracy
Deng, Xiaoping, 336
Department of Jewish Affairs, 307
Deportation Order, 158
deportations, 87, 90
  Assyrian, 41
  coerced, Jewish, 66
  forcible, in America, 90

forcible, in Spain, 47
forcible, in the Ottoman Empire, 141
limited, in America, 89–90
in the Ottoman Empire, 131, 156
policed, 15
policed, Assyrian, 41
policed, in America, 87, 96
policed, in Australia, 79, 83
policed, in Cambodia, 341
policed, in Hungary, 299
policed, in Ottoman Empire, 113, 143
policed, in Poland, 281
policed, in Romania, 303
policed, in Russia, 282
policed, in South West Africa, 101
policed, in Spain, 47
policed, under Stalinism, 321, 323
violent, in Ottoman Empire, 144
violent, of Jews, 208
violent, of Poles, 208
wild, 15
wild, in Greater Serbia, 359
wild, in Hungary, 299
wild, in Ottoman Empire, 113
wild, in Yugoslavia, 357
wild, of Jews, 194
wild, of Poles, 182
wild, of Serbs, 296
wild, of Soviet Slavs, 186
Deronjic, 396
Des Forges, A.
  (1999), 442, 463
Deutsche Volkspartei (German People's Party), 63
di Tiro, Hasan, 493
direct rule, 73
"Directive 7," 395
discrimination, 14, 67, 509
  and the anti-Catholic Penal Laws, 52
  in Australia, 82
  under Hapsburgs, 183
  in Ireland, 53
  in Macedonia, 368
  in Romania, 303
  in Rwanda, 435
  in South West Africa, 100
  under Stalinism, 322
  in Yugoslavia, 355
disease, 74, 75–80, 85, 89
dispersal, 81
Dittrich, Erich, 249
Djemal Bey, 159–60

Djemal Effendi, 160
Djemal Pasha, 118, 123, 129, 132, 144,
    158–9, 164
Djevdet Bey, 147
Dolukhanov, P.
    (1994), 35, 37
"Domovnica," 382
Dorian, 305–6
Dortyol, 145–6
Draskovic, Vuk, 367, 371, 372, 374
Drina Army Corps, 396
"Driving while Black," 14
Drogheda, 50–1, 52
Durkheim, Emil, 25
Duruy, 59
Dusan the Mighty, 392
Dusina, 409
Dutch, 44
dynastic empires
    Hapsburg (Austria), 62
    multiethnic, 62
    Ottoman (Islamic, Turkey), 62
    Romanov (Russia), 62

Eberl, Irmfried, 260
ecological imperialism, 76
Edip, Halide, 162–3
Ehlers, Ernst-Boje, 268
Eichmann, Adolf, 199, 208, 209, 218,
    244–5, 260, 300
Eicke, Theodor, 201, 216, 252
Einsatzgruppen, 215, 263–6
elections
    German, 1928–32, 183–4
    Serbia, 1990–91, 184
Elias, N.
    (1996), 195
elites, 39–40
Emancipation of 1826, 88
emigration
    coerced, 67
    pressured, in Rwanda, 430, 434, 435,
        440
    pressured, in Yugoslavia, 357
    pressured, of Jews, 193, 208
encomienda, 77
Endre, 300
Entfernung, 191, 240
Entress, Friedrich, 255
Enver Pasha, 123, 124, 125, 129, 131, 132,
    135, 144, 155
Erdemovic, Drazen, 401–2

Eremija, Lieutenant Colonel, 394
Erzindjan, 171–2
escalation, 504
Essad Bey, 161
ethic of responsibility, 425
Ethiopia, 309–10
ethnic
    confederalism, 321
    conflict, antidotes to, 522–9
    conflict, development of, 6
    enemies, 328
    hostility, 5–6
    imperial revisionism, 183
    "niche," 31
    niche economies, 516
    revisionism, 227
    victims, 328–9
    wars, obstacles to thwarting, 527
ethnicity, 37, 79, 324–5, 383
    and class, 60–1
    defined, 11
    German, 181, 214
    revival of, in Southern Europe, 509–14
    in Yugoslav republics, 362–6
ethnocide, 36, 72, 75
    in America, 84, 88
    in Australia, 80
    defined, 16
    in Mexico, 76, 78
    in Ottoman Empire, 144
ethnocracy, 39, 502, 519
ethnonationalism, i, 5, 20, 515–18
    Hindu, 482, 483–4
ethnos, i, 3, 4, 55, 184, 502
ethnosymbolism, 19
EU, 507
Europe, 57–8, 61–2
"Euthanasia" project. *See* T4
Evans, A.
    (1999), 488
Evans, Governor, 98
expulsion, forcible, 354
    of Greeks and Turks from Cyprus, 354
    of Greeks from Abkhazia, 354
    of Greeks from Turkey, 354
    of Turks from Bulgaria, 354
extraterritoriality, 72–3
Ezergailis, 284

factionalism, 503
Fanslau, Heinz-Karl, 235
fascism, defined, 180

Fascist Union of Christian Romanian
    Students, 303–4
Fascists (Mann, 2004), 65
Fearon, J.
    (1995), 24
Fearon, J., and D. Laitin
    (2000), 21
    (2003), 4, 11, 516
fedais, 124, 129
Fein, H.
    (1984), 21, 279, 298
Feingold, H.
    (1983), 240
Fetterman Massacre, 108
Fieldhouse, D.
    (1965), 71, 72
Filbert, Dr. Alfred, 264, 269
Filipovic, Colonel, 411
"Final Solution," 8, 18, 107, 187, 188, 195,
    208–11, 240, 305, 499–500
Fischböck, Hans, 249
Fisher, Harriet, 162–3
Five Year Plan (1928), 322
Flick, Friedrich, 249
Florstedt, Hermann, 235
Flossenburg, 200
Four Year Plan (1976), 343
France, 13
    minorities in, 59
Franciscan Missions, 87–8
Frank, Hans, 246
Franz, Kurt, 261
fratricide, 320, 337, 340, 345
Frederickson, G.
    (1988), 71, 72, 185
Freikorps, 195–6, 203, 213, 234, 235, 237
French Revolution, 61
Frenzel, Karl, 262
Friedländer, H.
    (1995), 259
Friedländer, S.
    (1997), 192
Fritzsche, Karl, 252
Fuchs, Sergeant, 274
fundamentalism, 513–14
Furundzija, Commander, 411

Gagauz, 307
"Galahad of National Socialism." *See*
    Ohlendorf, Otto
Gandhi, Indira, 486
Gecas, Antanas, 285

Gellately, R.
    (1990), 214
Gellner, E.
    (1983), 36–7
genocide, 34
    in America, 85, 91, 94, 98
    Armenian, 499
    attempted, of Gypsies, 181
    in Australia, 83
    "banality" of, 240–1
    complicity of non-Nazi institutions in, 247
    defined, 17
    escalation of, in South West Africa, 106
    of Jews, 185, 188
    in Lithuania, 285
    in the main Nazi camps, 251–6
    Nazi, institutionalized, 240–78
    in the Ottoman Empire, 149
    partial, 17
    in Rwanda, 430, 500
    scale of Nazi, 184–91
    scenarios required for, 503
    statist, in the Ottoman Empire, 156
    Yugoslav, 358, 500–1
Gerlach, C.
    (1999), 209
German Ideology, The (Marx), 347
"German Question, the," 180
Germans
    "ethnic," 353–4
    Sudetan, 353
Germany. *See also* Iberian peninsula;
        Deutsche Volkspartei
    Germans in, 6, 10
Gerstein, Kurt, 250
Gestapo, 202
Getty, J.A.
    (1985), 330
Ghalib Bey, General, 164
"Ghengizism," 132
Gisenyi, 436, 443, 447, 451, 453, 454
Gisovu, 459, 464
Gitarama, 436, 457
Glavas, 388
Glenny, M.
    (1992), 359, 380
    (1993), 400
Glina, 385
Globocnik, Odilo, 247
Glogova, 396
Glücks, Major-General Richard, 217, 243
Godhra, 484–5

Goebbels, Joseph, 195, 208, 211
Goeth, Amon, 253
Gökalp, 120–2, 131, 132, 144
Goldhagen, D.
  (1996), 20, 189, 190, 215, 267, 282
Gordy, E.
  (1999), 374
Gorgass, Dr., 204–5
Goring, Herman, 193, 194, 195, 209
Gorski, P.
  (2000), 44
Gourevitch, P.
  (1998), 467, 469
grain expropriations, in Soviet Union, 324
Granada, 46, 47
Grant, Ulysses, 91
Graziani, General, 309
Great Famine, 324, 329
"Great Leap Forward" (China), 15–16, 334, 336, 339
Great Purge, 327
Great Terror (1937–38), 326–7
"Greater Serbia," 365, 369, 372, 389
Greece, 112
  Greek polis, 39
  Greeks, 116, 117
Grese, Irma, 256
Grosscurth, Lt. Col., 250
Grude, 408
Guatemala, 512
Gujarat pogrom (2002), 484–5
Gurr, T.
  (1993), 505
  (2000), 20
gypsies, 185, 305, 307

Haberer, E.
  (2002), 267
habitual action, 25
Habyarimana, President, 435, 436, 439, 440, 441
Hadjin, Mufti of, 172
Hagen, Dr. Wilhelm, 250
Halder, Army Chief of Staff, 209
Halil Bey, 158, 163, 166
Halim, Grand Vizier Said, 158
Hantl, Emil, 255
Hapsburg, 181, 182
Hapsburg Empire, 112
Harff, B.
  (1998), 20
Harster, Wilhelm, 203

Hartl, Lieutenant Albert, 250, 269, 270
HDZ, 377, 379–80, 407, 409. *See also* Bosnian Croat party
Headland, R.
  (1992), 187
Hefner, R.
  (2000), 497
Heissmeyer, Kurt, 235
Henry VII, King, 58
Henry VIII, King, 58
Herero, 102, 103–6, 108
Hetmans, 66
Heuze, G.
  (1992), 480
Heyde, Werner, 258
Heydrich, Reinhard, 187, 195, 198, 202, 209, 210, 242
Hezekial, King, 40–1
Highland Clearances, 61
Hilberg, R.
  (1978), 187, 213, 263, 303
Hill people, 342
Hima, 432
Himmler, Heinrich, vii, 66, 195, 198, 199, 201, 202, 209, 211, 215, 246
Hinduism, 42
Hindutva, 474
Hintjens, H.
  (1999), 436, 442
Hinze, Günther, 254
Hitler, Adolf, vii, 183, 184, 185, 190, 191, 204, 206–7, 211, 272, 307–8
  and the Poles, 209
Hlinka Slovak Populist Party, 293–4
HO. *See* Croatia, Croatian army
Höcker, Karl, 252
hodja, 171
Hoffman, Franz, 201–2, 252
Holbrooke, Richard, 360
Hollweg, Chancellor Bethmann, 173–4
Holocaust. *See* "Final Solution"
homeland states, 68
Horowitz, D.
  (1983), 428
  (2001), 476, 480
Horthy, Admiral, 298–300, 302, 306
HOS militia, 409
Höss, Major Rudolf, 175, 201, 212, 252
Hoss, R.
  (1978), 244
Hoxie, F.
  (1984), 87

Huber, Irmgard, 258
human action, types of (Weber), 25–6
"Human Beast, The." *See* Wagner
Hungary, 298–302
  the "Jewish Question" in, 300
  Plan A in, 298
  Plan B in, 299
Huntington, S.
  (1996), 519
Huron, 84
Hutu, 5, 7, 10, 17, 18, 430, 431,
  443
HVO. *See* Bosnian Croat army

Iberian peninsula, 45–53
ICTR. *See* Rwanda, UN International
  Criminal Tribunal for
IG Farben, 249
Ilias, Hodja, 166
"imperial nation," 133, 431
Impuzamugambi, 446
Independent Republic of the South
  Moluccas, 494
Independent State of Croatia, 295
India, 474–90
  Bombay riot of 1992–93, 476
  Congress Party in, 475, 483
  East Bengal riots (1950), 486
  Gujarat pogrom (2002), 476
  intercaste violence in, 483–4
  languages of, 474, 486
  multiethnicity of, 474–5
  partition of, 485–6
  religions of, 474–5
  "seven sisters" of, 489
  Sikh/Hindu conflict in, 486
Indian Bureau, 90
Indians, 108
indios, 78
indirect rule, 73
individualism, 55
Indo-Europeans, 35
Indonesia, 490–8
  anti-Chinese riots in, 497
  difficulties faced by nationalists in, 491–2
  Dutch in, 490, 496
  East Timor, 492–3
  Irian Jaya, 495
  martial law declared (1959) in, 491
  massacre of Communists (1965) in, 491
  the Moluccas, 494–5
  Sulawesi, 494–5

  West Kalimantan, 495–6
  West Papua, 495
Industrial Revolution, 79
in-group policing, 21
information failure, 25
Ingushi, 329
Innocentists, 305
Institute of National Remembrance, 281
instrumentally rational action, 25
Interahamwe, 445, 446, 448, 452, 454, 455,
  460, 461, 462, 464, 470
International Criminal Court, 528
Ioanid, R.
  (1990), 303
  (1991), 304
  (2000), 302
Iran, 511
Ireland, 49–53, 58, 61
  1845 famine, 336
Ireton, 52
"Iron George." *See* Sorge, Gustav
Iron Guard, 304. *See also* Legion of the
  Archangel Michael
Iron Wolf, 283, 285
Iroquois Indians, 84, 85
Islam, 42
Italian Socialist Republic. *See* Salo
Italy, 308–11
Ittihadist, 125, 172
Izetbegovic, 367, 368, 388, 395

JA, 393
Jackson, Andrew, 93
Jackson, Consul, 153, 171
Jaeger, Emil, 276
Jaffrelot, C.
  (1996), 475, 476, 480
Jamaat-i-Islami, 479
Jarolin, Josef, 252
Jasenovac, 377
Jassy, 304
Java, 491
Jedwabne, 281
Jefferson, Thomas, vii, 70, 92–3
Jelisic, Goran, 402
Jesenovac, 296
Jevdet, Tahir, 160
"Jew, the," 207
Jews, 310–11. *See also* Judeo-Bolshevism
  Judaism
  atrocities by, 9
  and Auxiliary Police Battalion 101, 266

and the Bolshevik Revolution, 183
in Bulgaria, 307–8
and *conversos*, 46–7
in Croatia, 297
in death camps, 262
in Estonia, 282, 283
exterminated because of foreign
    entanglements, 184
genocide of, 8, 263
in Germany, 25
in the Hapsburg Empire, 182
in Hungary, 302
in Italy, 308
"Jewish Question" and population
    transfers, 69
"Jewish subhumanity," 273
in the *Kaiserreich*, 181
in Latvia, 282, 283
linked to Bolshevik uprisings, 192–3
in Lithuania, 282, 283
oppression of, by Roman Empire, 19
perceptions of, 254, 256, 316–17
and perpetrators, 231
in Poland, 280
and Poles, 208–9
as "privileged" victims, 184
rationales for extermination, 265, 267
in Romania, 302–7
in Russia, 64–6, 209–10
and salvation religions, 42, 43
shooting of, 272
in the Soviet Union, 187
in Spain, 45, 46–7
as targets of resentment, 64–6
in the Ukraine, 66, 289, 290
as *Untermenschen*, 272
variables in killing of, 279
Jihad, 171, 518
JNA, 380–1. *See* Yugolavia, Yugoslav army
JNR, 434
Jokers, 409
Jovic, State Council President, 376, 381
Judah, T.
    (2000), 386–7
Judaism, 38, 187. *See also* Jews
Judeo-Bolshevism, 9, 65, 66, 183, 191, 196,
    207, 209, 210, 211, 273, 280, 281, 290,
    301, 305, 306
Justiz und NS-Verbrechen, 218

Kadets, 66
Kadir, Hilme Abdul, 161–2

Kaiser, H.
    (1999a), 150, 153
    (1999b), 174
    (2001a), 145
Kaiserreich, 62
Kajmovic, Professor, 413
Kakwenzire, J. and D. Kumukama
    (1999), 447
Kalashnikov, 521
Kallay, Prime Minister, 299
Kaltenbrunner, Ernst, 243–4
Kalyvas, S.
    (1999), 24
Kambanda, Prime Minister Jean Alphonse,
    456
Kamil, General, 147, 168
Kamilindi, Thomas, 453
Kangura, 443
Kanyabashi, Mayor Joseph, 457
Kaornik, 414
Karadzic, Radovan, 384, 388–9, 393, 395–6,
    517
Karamira, 452
Karay, F.
    (1996), 291
Karemera, 452
Kashmir, 6, 475, 487
Kashubians, 185
Katschenka, Anna, 259
Katz, J.
    (1988), 28, 383, 399
    (1993), 29, 212–13, 466
Katzmann, Friedrich, 247
Kavazovic, 412
Kayishema, Clément, 454–5
Kazakhs, 99–100
Kazakhstan, Russian minority in, 23–4
Keane, F.
    (1995), 469
Keitel, Field Marshal Wilhelm, 274
Kemal, Mustapha. *See* Ataturk
Kershaw, I.
    (1984), 206
    (1997), 194
Kevorkian, 127, 128, 158
Khairi, Shaikh-ul-Islam, 158
Khmer Rouge, 17, 339–47
Kiazim, Musa, 158
Kiebach, 266
Kiernan, B.
    (1996), 343, 346, 349
Kigali, 453

killer. *See also* perpetrator
  bigoted, 27, 189
  bigoted, in Cambodia, 349
  bigoted, in death camps, 202
  bigoted, in Germany, 198
  bureaucratic, 29
  bureaucratic, in Germany, 189
  careerist, 28
  careerist, in death camps, 202
  careerist, in Germany, 189, 194
  comradely, 28–33
  comradely, in death camps, 202
  comradely, in Germany, 189, 198
  disciplined, 28
  disciplined, in death camps, 202
  disciplined, in Germany, 189, 194
  elite desk, 242–51
  fearful, 28
  fearful, in Germany, 189
  ideological, 27, 239
  ideological desk-, 243
  materialist, 28
  materialist, in Germany, 189
  violent, 28
  violent, in Cambodia, 349
  violent, in Germany, 198
Kinyarwanda language, 432, 439
Kirschbaum, 64
Kiseljak, 410, 412
Kishwar, M.
  (1998a), 466
KL officers, 1945, 217
KLA, 387
Klehr, Josef, 253
Kljucic, President, 408
Klujic, 384
Kneissler, Pauline, 205
Knights of Serbia, 392
Knin, 385, 387, 418
Koch, Ernst, 246
Koch, Karl, 252
Koehl, R.
  (1983), 214
Koljevic, 384
Komeno, 276
Konia, 146, 148
Kordic, 408, 411, 413
Kosiy, Bohdan, 290
Kosovo, 1, 357, 359, 363, 364, 386, 393, 418
Kovacevic, Milan, 403–4
Krahner, Josef, 265

Krajina, 379, 382, 384, 393, 399, 405
Kraljevic, Darko, 411, 412
Kramer, Josef, 253
Kremenets, 289
Kremer, Johann Paul, 255
Kretschmer, Lieutenant Karl, 265
Kripo, 202
Kristallnacht, 194, 198, 201, 206
Kritzinger, 248
Krstic, General, 358, 396
Krumey, 245
Krupp, Gustav, 249
Kubamanda, 458
Kube, Wilhelm, 250–1
kulak, 323, 325
Kurds, 114
Kuzmanovic, B.
  (1995), 360

labor
  concentrated, 71–2
  disbursed, 71
  nonnative, 72
Lachert, Hildegard, 255
Lahousan, General, 185, 273
Laitin, D.
  (1999a, 1999b), 23–4
Lakota Indians, 92
LANC, 303
land, 31, 72, 79, 84, 92, 95
Landau, Sergeant-Major Felix, 265
Landzo, Esad, 417
Langenberg
  (1990), 497
language, 37, 43, 57, 58–9, 123, 328
Lasik, A.
  (1994), 213, 214
Laska Valey. *See* atrocities, Croatian
Laskar Jihad, 495
Lasuen, Father Fermin, 87
Lasva, 409
Latin America, 515
Latvia
  Plan B in, 284
  Plan C in, 284
Latvian Auxiliary Police battalions, 283
Law on Croatian Citizenship (1991), 379
Lazar, Prince, 361–2
Leadership Principle, 194, 199
Lechthaler, Major Franz, 266
Legion of the Archangel Michael, 302. *See also* Iron Guard

Lemkin, Raphael, 17
Lenin, 322
Lepanto, battle of (1572), 53
Letica, S.
  (1996), 360
Leutwein, Major Theodor, 102, 105
liberal representative states, 5
liberalism, and neo-liberalism, 119–20, 510,
  512–13
Libya, 309, 310
Liebenhenschel, Arthur, 252
Lieven, D.
  (1998), 329
  (2000), 112, 113
Lifton, R.
  (1986), 256
Likic, Milan, 397
Liman von Sanders, General, 171
limited property franchise, 61–2
limpieza se sangre, 47
Lincoln, Abraham, 93–4
List, Field Marshal Wilhelm, 274
List, Friedrich, 123
Lithuanian Activist Front, 283, 284
Lithuanian 2nd Battalion, 285
"little house," 442–7, 450–70
Litzmann, Karl-Siegmund, 250
Liu, Shaoqi, 333, 336
Loewenberg, P.
  (1983), 222
Lolling, Enno, 255
Lon Nol, General, 339
Longman, T.
  (1999), 442
Losowick, Y.
  (2000), 245
lost territories, 194, 195–6
Loughridge, Stella, 157
Lüdke, Corporal, 269
Luger, 63
Lukic, Milan, 402–3
Lupher, M.
  (1996), 333
Luther, 247
Ly, Heng, 346

Maas, Peter, 398
Macartney, Charles, 67
Macedonia, 356, 363, 368
macroethnicity, 10–11, 37, 515
Macura, Deputy Mayor, 387
madrassas, 487

Madurese, 495–6
Maeghalaya, 489
Magdeburg, 48–9
Magill, Sergeant, 265
Maharaja, 486–7
Mahareru, Samuel, 103
"majority people," 434
Makhullo, Archbishop, 521
Maksudov, S.
  (1993), 187
Malaga, 46
Malaparte, C., 186, 304
Malkki, L.
  (1995), 471
Mamdani, M.
  (2001), 463, 465
Manipur, 489
Manstein, General von, 273
Mao, 334, 335, 337
Maoists, 5, 17
Markovic, Mirjana, 391, 420
Maronite Christian community, 118
Marsovan, 150–1, 168
Martic, 384, 387–8
Marticevci, 385
Martinovic, 421
Marxian theory, and social transformation,
  318–19
Mathausen, 200
Maududi, Maulana, 514
Maurer, Gerhard, 243
Maurer, Wilhelm and Johann, 265
"Mauser." *See* Savic, Dinko
Mbonimpa, M.
  (1999), 434
McCarthy, J.
  (1995), 113
McDougall, Governor, 91
McElroy, 95
Medjugorje, 386
Melson, R.
  (1992), 174
Memoir (Höss), 212
*Memorandum, Serb Academy of Sciences
  and Arts* (1986), 364–5, 366
Mengele, Josef, 218, 256
Mennecke, Friedrich, 256
Mentz, Willi, 261
Mesic, 394
Mesopotamia, 37
mestizo, 78, 515
Mexico, 76–8

Micas, 400
microethnicity, 10, 37
middlemen ethnicities, 516
Migonis, Motiejus-Pranus, 285
migrants, European, 59
Mildt, D. de
  (1996), 214, 259
Milgram, Stanley, 26–7
militants, Islamic, in India, 487
"Military Line, the." *See* Milosevic,
    Slobodan, plan B for Serbia
"military Keynesianism," 206
Military Medical College, 122
Miliutin, General, 99, 109
millet, 114, 135, 136
Milosevic, Slobodan, 184, 369–76, 381, 387,
    390, 396–7, 424, 425, 426
  core constitutiences of, 391–2
  Plan A for Serbia, 370, 371, 373, 390,
    424
  Plan B for Serbia, 371, 372, 373, 390,
    424
  Plan C for Serbia, 390, 424
  Plan D for Serbia, 391, 424
minorities, 64, 67
"Minorities in Danger," 428
Mirkovic, D.
  (1993), 295, 297
Mizoram, 489
Mladic, Ratko, 396, 404–5
Modi, Narendra, 484
Modoc Indians, 92
mohadjis, 114, 172
Moluccas Christian/Muslim riots,
    498
Mommsen, H.
  (1991, 1997), 190
monotheism, 42
Montenegro, 363, 368
Moorehead, B.D., 82
Morgenthau, Ambassador, 129,
    154–5
Morley, Bertha, 150–1
Moro Liberation Front, 527
Morsnik, Colonel, 409
Moser, Lieutenant-General, 250
Mostar, 385
MRND, 440, 441, 442, 445
MSVN, 311
Mucic, Zsravko, 417
Mueller, J.
  (2000), 360, 397

Mugabe, 429
Mugesera, 444
Mujezinovici, Dr., 411, 412
Mulkieye. See Civil Service Academy
Muller-Claudius, Michael, 194
Müller, Heinrich, 203
multiculturalism, 11–13
Munster, 51
Munyaneza, 464, 466, 467
Münzberger, Gustav, 261
Muratovic, 422
Muscovy, 112
Musema, Alfred, 459–60
Musial, B.
  (1999), 249
Musiuveni, President, 439
Muslim Chams, 342
Muslim refugees. *See mohadjis*
Muslim Skanserbeg SS regiment, 362
Muslims, 42, 45, 47, 113–16, 483, 490
Mussolini, Benito, 308–9, 310
mustard gas, 309

Naga, 489
Nagaland, 489
Naimark, N.
  (2001), 21
Naletilic, 421
Nama, 105–6
narodi, 362
narodny, 328
Nash, G.
  (1992), 84, 89
Nastorian Christian villages, 136
nation
  defined, 11
  national minorities, 68
  national self-determination, 67
  nationalizing states, 68
  -state, 11, 45, 525
  -statism, 188
  statism, 233, 320
nationalism
  civic, 180
  ethnic, 180
  German, in the late 19th century, 181
  leftist version of, 62
  organic, 180
  organic, potential vices of, 63–4
  types of, 180–1
Nationalism and Contemporary Europe
    (Jasenovac), 377

Nazi, 17, 180–211, 212–39
core constituencies of, 206, 214, 219,
223–8
genocide, 9
hierarchical comradeship, 191
hierarchical radicalization, 191–5
paramilitary comradeship, 191,
200
paramilitary radicalization, 195–208
and Plan A, 191, 193, 210
and Plan B, 191, 194
and Plan C, 208
and Plan D, 210, 211
radicalization, 189–1
state, 7
violence, career in, 234–9
Nazim, Dr., 127, 132, 144
Ndagijimana, Mayor,
Ndimbati, Mayor, 464
Neolithic revolution, 37
NEP. *See* New Economic Policy
Netherlands, 44
Neuengamme, 200
Neurath, Otto von, 248
New Economic Policy (NEP), 322
New Liberals (Great Britian), 62
Newbury, C.
(1988), 434
(1998), 467
Ngor, H.
(1988), 347
Nikolic, Captain, 405
NKVD, 289
Nogales, Major Rafael de, 136, 147, 154,
163, 170
noncolonial regimes, 4
non-Nazi elites, 193
North African colonies, 308–10
Nouri Bey, 161
Nsabimana, Sylvain, 456
Ntaganzwa, Ladislas, 456–7
Ntahobari, Pauline, 462
Ntahobari, Shalom, 462
Ntakirutimana, Pastor, 464
Nteziryayo, 456
Numantia, 34, 36
Nuremberg Laws, 193, 206
Nyandwi, Mayor, 458–9

Oberschall, A.
(1998), 418
Obrenovic, General, 405

Oded, B.
(1979), 41
Ognjenovic, Colonel, 395
Ohlendorf, Otto von, 30, 263
Old Nazis, 235, 237–9
Omarska, 397
ONU, 288, 289
Operation Barbarossa, 209, 210
Opium Wars, 73
Oric, Naser, 417–18
Osijek, 384, 385, 388
Ostojici, 386
Ottoman Empire, 113–15
descent to murderous cleansing, 137–9
and the Entente Powers, 173
ethnicity in, 177
and Germany, 173–5
mono-religiousness of, 114–16
Plan A in, 127, 134, 177
Plan B in, 130, 131, 143, 145, 178
Plan C in, 141, 145
Plan D in, 144–5, 149
Ottoman Turkish state, 111. *See also*
Ottoman Empire

Palestine
cause, proletarian tone of, 5
Palestinians in, 5
Pan-German Party, 63
Paraga, 367, 409
Paragraph 47, German Army Code, 268
paramilitaries, 8–9, 164–7, 391–5, 419–20,
421–2, 460–3, 468, 479, 493, 497,
521
German, postwar, 195–6
pariah states, 68
Parikh, S.
(1998), 481
Paris, E.
(1961), 297
Partisans, 421
party-states, 22
Pasa, Ahmet Izzet, 147
Peace Treaties of 1918, 66
Peasants into Frenchmen (Weber, 1976), 59
peasants, under Stalinism, 329
Peng, Dehuai, 335–6
"people, the," 3, 502
and the American Constitution, 55–69
liberal version of, 55–61
organic, 55
stratified, 55

Pequot War, 84
Perez-Diaz, V.
  (1993), 62
perpetrator, 213–15. *See also* killer; named
    individual perpetrators
  backgrounds, in Ottoman Empire,
    172–3
  core constituencies of, 8–9
  elite, in the Ottoman Empire, 156–72
  factionalized official, in the Ottoman
    Empire, 158–63
  factionalized soldier, in the Ottoman
    Empire, 163–4
  levels of, 8–9
  levels of, in Rwanda, 449
  ministerial elite, in the Ottoman Empire,
    156–63
  motives, in the Ukraine, 290
  motives of, 27–9, 504
  motives of Nazi, 188–95
  ordinary, in the Ottoman Empire, 167
  ordinary, in Yugoslavia, 418–23
  paramilitary, 164–7
  samples of, 216–39
  statist view of, 320–21
persecution, 527–9
Philippines, 526–7
Phleve, 64
Plains Indians, 97
Plan C, 503
Plavsic, Biljana, 388–9, 420
plunder (and tribute taking), 71
pogroms, 15, 36, 43, 64–6, 194, 284
  in Byelorussia, 286
  Polish, 280–1
Pohl, D.
  (1996), 243, 289
Pol Pot, 340, 343, 344, 345, 346, 349
Poland, 185–6, 280–1
  Poles, Hitler's justification for killing,
    175
  Poles in, 17, 272
  Poles in the *Kaiserreich*, 181
  politicide against Poles, 186
political
  enforcement, types of, 72–3
  instability, forms of, 7
  power relations, 6
"political soldier," 163
politicide, 16–17, 71, 186
  Assyrian, 40–1

  in Burundi, 438
  in Cambodia, 340, 341
  in China, 337
  in Ethiopia, 309, 310
  in Indonesia, 497
  in Ottoman Empire, 144, 148
  in Rwanda, 430, 431, 440
  of Serbs, 296
  in Tibet, 338
  in Yugoslavia, 357
Pomaks, 307
Pomiankowski, Vice-Marshal, 133
"populace, the," 56
population
  exchanges, 15
  exchanges, in Greater Serbia, 359
  in the Holy Roman Empire, 48
  transfers, 354
Porsche, 249
Portugese, 71
Potocari, 395
power
  biological, 74, 75
  economic, 30–2, 38–9, 71–2
  ideological, 30, 37–8, 74
  military, 32, 39, 74, 96
  networks, and ethnic cleansing, 30
  political, 32, 39–40, 72–4
  social, sources of, 6, 37–40
pre-Columbian Indians, 76
Prijedor, 403, 418
Proctor, R.
  (1988), 215
professional ideologists, 75
"proletarian nation," 62
  Hutu as a, 431
proletariat, 4
protectorates, 73, 80
Protestant Scots, 15. *See also* Scots
Protocols of the Elders of Zion, 66
Provencals, 14
Prucha, F.
  (1994), 93
Prunier, G.
  (1995), 442
  (1997a), 434
Prussian Germany, 181
  expansion in, 182
"psychology of hard times," 219,
    223
"psychosis of disappearance," 133

Punjab, 485
"purge," 325–6

qital, 518
Quakers, 86
Qur'an, 513–14

Rabushka A., and K. Shepsle
  (1972), 24
race, 85
racial-genetic notions of human progress,
  180
Rademacher, Franz, 248
radical elites, 8–9
Radical Republicans (France), 62
radicalization, 503
  of "ordinary Germans," 206–8
Rahmi Bey, 159
"RAM." *See* Milosevic, Slobodan, Plan C for
  Serbia
Ramet, S.P.
  (1992), 420
Ramsey, Governor, 91, 94
rape, 80, 102, 136, 152, 166, 287, 357–8,
  420–1, 422, 462, 463, 481, 528. *See
  also* abuse, gender
Ras-ul-Ain, 171
Rasch, Otto, 268
rashtra, 474
Raskovic, Jovan, 380, 384, 387, 388
"ratio of representation," 223
rational choice theory, 23, 24, 26
rationality
  instrumental, 188
  value, 188
Rauca, Sergeant Helmut, 265
Ravenbruch, 200
Ravens, 287
Raw Nazis, 235, 237–9
Raznatovic, Zeljko, 404
Red Berets, 390, 394
"redemptive anti-Semitism," 192
Refi, Kerim, 160
refugee camps/associations, 196–7
refugees, 67–8, 223–8
Regat, 305, 306
Reichenau, General, 273
Reichl-Kir, 384, 388
Reichleitner, Franz, 260
Reichstag, 62
Reinecke, General, 273

Reitlinger, G.
  (1968), 263
religion, 37–8
  salvation religions, 42–5, 57
religious warriors, 518–21
Removal Act of 1830, 93
Renfrew, C.
  (1972), 35
Renno, Georg, Dr., 205
repression
  exemplary, 16, 77, 99, 509
  exemplary, in America, 94, 96, 98
  exemplary, in the Caucasus, 113
  exemplary, in Ethiopia, 309
  exemplary, in Indonesia, 494
  exemplary, in Ireland, 50, 51
  exemplary, in the Ottoman Empire, 113,
    147, 148
  exemplary, in Yugoslavia, 357
  policed, 15
  policed, in Rwanda, 435
  policed, total cultural, 15
  selective, in the Ottoman Empire, 130, 131
  selective, of Jews, 185
  selective policed, 15
  selective policed, in Cambodia, 341
  selective policed, in China, 337
  selective policed, under Stalinism, 323
Republic of Herceg-Bosna, 408, 409, 410
Republika Srbska, 393, 395
Resid, Dr., 172
Reuter, Paul, 205
"Revenge Operations," 275
"revenge-people," 347
Revolutionary Fascist Party, 311
revolutionary projects
  callous, 320
  mistaken, 15, 88, 319, 320, 336
Reyntjens, F.
  (1996), 442
Reza, Atif, 144
Rhineland Missionary Society, 100
Riggs, Reverend, 168
"riot circle," 475–81
riots, escalating, 481–2, 499–501
Ritz, Lieutenant Hans, 266
Robinson, George, 83
Röhm, Ernest, 197, 201
Rohde, D.
  (2001), 494–5
Rohrbach, Dr. Paul, 101–2, 105, 107

Roman Senate, 39
Romania, 112, 302–7
  Iron Guard in, 282
  Plan A in, 303
Romanov Empire, 112
Romans, 16
Rome, 36, 39
Ron, J.
  (2000), 393
Roosevelt, Theodore, vii, 94
Rosenberg, 198
Ross, 51
Roth, N.
  (1995), 45
Rowley, C.
  (1972), 81, 83
RPF, 440, 441, 443, 466, 470
RSHA, 243
RSK. *See* Serb Republic of Krajina
RSS, 480, 481, 483, 485
RTLM, 469
Rugova, Ibrahim, 387
Ruhengeri, 436, 447, 453
Rummel, R.
  (1994), 22
Rupert, Prince, 52
Rusengeri, 443
Russians, 273
Rutaganda, George, 461–2
Ruzindana, Obed, 460
Rwanda, 6, 430, 473
  African Rights (1994) report on, 449
  army death squads in, 447
  Belgian colonial rule in, 433
  casualties in, 430
  and the "cult of obedience," 468–9
  destabilizing pressures in, 438–42
  French influence in, 449
  Human Rights Watch (1999) report on,
    449
  international pressures on, 439–42
  mass media in, 444
  massacre of 1959, 438
  Organization of African Union (2000)
    report on, 449
  paramilitaries in, 446
  Plan A in, 442
  premeditated genocide in, 442–8
  refugees from, 430
  sources documenting genocide in, 449
  Structural Adjustment Programme for, 439
  Tutsi invasion of 1990, 439
    two economies in, 459
    UN International Criminal Tribunal for,
      450
    U.S. influence in, 449
    youth groups in, 445–6

S-21, 346–7, 348–9
SA, the, 197–8
Sabrin, B.
  (1991), 189, 290
Sachsenhausen, 200
Safa, Ismael, 161
Safrian, H.
  (1993), 215
Sakir, Dr. Bahaeddin, 144
Salo, 311
Salonika, 127
salvation religions, 513
Samiti, 481
Sanborn, General, 97
Sand Creek, 98
Sandberger, Dr. Martin, 269
Santee Sioux Indians, 91
Santic, Ivan, 411
Santic, Vladimir, 414
Sarajevo, 385
Savic, Dinko, 296–7, 421
Scarrit, J.
  (1993),
Schacht, 193
Scharf, M.
  (1997), 418
Schechtman, J.
  (1962), 354
Schellenberg, Walter, 203–4
Scherpe, Herbert, 253
Schlieffen, Chief of Staff von, 104, 106
Schönerer, 63
Schroeder, Kurt, 249
Schulz, Erwin, 268
Schwammberger, Josef, 254
Scots, 11. *See also* Protestant Scots
Scott, Winfield, 94
SD, the, 202–4
  officers in 1945, 217–18
SDA, 407
SDB. *See* Serb Security Police
SDP, 380
secularism, 510
security dilemma, 24
Segev, T.
  (1987), 215

segregation, 14, 72
  in America, 88, 90, 96
  in Australia, 82
  in Ethiopia, 310
  of Germans, 185
  of Jews, 193
  of Poles,
  in South West Africa, 100
  of Soviet Slavs, 186
Self-Defense Force, 283
Semanza, Laurent, 455
Semites, Middle Eastern, 35
Sennacherib, 40
September 11, 2001, 3
Serafinowicz, Szymon, 287
"Serb Adolf, the." *See* Jelisic, Goran
Serb nationalist parties, 389
Serb Radical Party, 392
Serb Republic of Krajina (RSK), 387
Serb Security Police (SDB), 374
Serbia, 112, 363, 366, 376, 379,
    390–405
  ethnic self-identification in, 363
Serbian Guard, 392
Serbian National Council, 387
Serbian Renewal Party, 388
Serbian Volunteer Guard, 392
Serbs, 10, 16, 18, 19–20, 274
  precani, 363–4, 365
Serushago, Omar, 454
Seselj, 367, 380, 391, 392
settler, democracy, 107, 108–10
Shakir, Dr., 160
shari'a, 513–14
Shastri, Professor Kesharram, 484
Sheridan, General, 96, 97
Sherman, General William Tecumseh, 92,
    96–7, 109
Shiragian, 171
Shiv Sena, 480, 481, 483
"Shoah." *See* "Final Solution"
Sholokhov, Mikhail, 324
Shukru, 157
Shukru Bey, 161
Shulgin, 66
Siber, I.
  (1993), 367
Sibley, General, 91
Sikavica, 392
Sikh *jathas*, 485
Silica, 411
Simpson, Sir George, 88

Sindikubwabo, President Théodore, 456
Sioux Indians, 91, 94
slaves, American, 89
Slavka, 415
Slavonia, 357
Slavs, 185
  and the Bolshevik Revolution, 183
  in the Soviet Union, 187
Sliwinski, M.
  (1995), 342–3
Slovakia, 293–4
  1938 Manifesto, 294
  Plan A in, 294
Slovenia, 367, 374, 376
  ethnic self-identification in, 363
Smircina, Lieutenant, 353
Smith, A.
  (1986), 19
Smith, L.
  (1997), 34, 36, 40, 71
Snyder, J.
  (2000), 22
Sobibor, 259
Social Darwinism, 79, 81, 98, 180, 181
Social Democrats (Germany), 63
socialism, 510, 511–12
Socialist Party (SPS), 370, 371, 372–3, 389,
    391
Socialists of the Chair (Germany), 62
"societal paranoia," 133
societies, stages of historical development in,
    121
Sofsky, W.
  (1997), 216
Sonderweg, 176
Sorbians, 185
Sorge, Gustav, 196–7
South Africa, 6, 14
South West Africa, 100
  Plan A in, 106
  Plan B in, 106
  Plan C in, 106
sovereign claims, 382–3
Soviet Union, 186–8
  Plan A in, 322, 324
  Plan B in, 323
  Plan C in, 323
  Plan D in, 324
  Plan E in, 324
Spain. *See* Iberian peninsula
  during the Inquisition, 46, 47
  and Plan A, 77

Spain (*cont.*)
  and Plan B, 78
  unification of, 45–6
"Special Organization." *See Teskilat-I Mahsusa*
Spenser, Edmund, 50
SPS. *See* Socialist Party
Srebrenica, 356, 358, 395, 405, 417
SRS, 391
SS, The, 198–200
  Galician Division, 290
Stahlecker, 269, 283, 284
Stalinism, 321–30
  phases of, 322
Stalinists, 17
Stange, General, 165
Stangl, Franz, 260–1, 262
Stark, Johannes, 254
state elites, 21
statists, 6
Statute of Kilkenny (1366), 49
Staub, E.
  (1992), 219
Stauffenberg family, 250
Stedman, S.
  (2002), 527
Steinberg, J.
  (1990), 311
"Stela." *See* Martinovic
Strauch, Colonel, 251
Straus, S.
  (2004), 449, 453, 463–4, 465, 466, 467, 469
structural adjustment programs, 512
Student, General, 275
Stuermer, H.
  (1917), 123, 172, 174
Suad, Ali, 160
Suchomel, Franz, 262
Sudan, 429
Sudetenland, 227–8
Sudetic, 398–9
"Sugerfoot Jack," 98
Sukru, Midhat, 144
Sultania, 146
Sumatra, 491
Sunstein, C.
  (2000), 25
superiority, ideologies of, 74–5
suppression
  cultural, 14, 17

cultural, in America, 87
cultural, in Romania, 303
Susak, 386, 408
Switzerland, 60
syncretic religion, 37
Szalasi, 302
Szeged Idea, 300

T4, 185, 204–5, 214, 241, 256–60
Tadic, Dusko, 401
Tahsin Pasha, 147
taifa, 114
Talaat Pasha, 123, 129, 132, 141, 144, 148, 149–50, 154–5
Tambiah, S.
  (1996), 22, 466, 476, 477, 479, 481
  (1998), 441
Tamil Tigers, 481
Tanic, 396
Tanzania, 428
Tartars, 329
Tasmania, 82–3
Taylor, Zachary, 94
Tekinalp, 131
Tenochtitlan, 77
Tepeaca, 77
terra nullius, 84
Teskilat-I Mahsusa, 144, 164–7
Teslic, 400
theo-democracy, 513, 514
Theodoric, King, 35
Theresianstadt, 293
Thion, S.
  (1983), 349
  (1993), 341
Third Spanish Republic (1930s), 60
Thirty Years War (1618–48), 48, 49
Thompson, T.
  (1992), 380, 399
"Three Mountains, the," 348
Thunder Cross, 282
Tibet, 338–9
  "cultural genocide" in, 338
  Plan A in, 339
  Plan C in, 339
Tiso, 63
Tito, Marshall, 366
toleration, 13
Tomasic, Professor, 354
Topalovic, Musan, 418
Torkildsen, 391
Torquemada, 46

Tothill, Colonel, 52
trade, 71
Trail of Tears, 93
Trapp, Major, 267, 270
Trawnicki training camp, 291
Treaty of San Stefano (1878), 117
Treblinka, 259
triangle of tension, 81
tribute taking. *See* plunder
Trieste, in Italy, 310
Trifan, Valerian, 303–4
Trigger, B.
  (1994), 74
Tripura, 489
Trotha, General von, 104, 106, 107, 109
Trumpener, U.
  (1968), 158
Tudjman, 367, 377–8, 379, 380, 388, 390,
  407, 425, 426
"Tula." *See* Naletilic
Tuol-Sleng. *See* S-21
Turan, 132
Turikinkiko, 464, 466
Turkish nationalism, 119–24
Turkish refugees, 116
Turks, 6, 114–15, 307
Turner, Colonel, 275
Tutsis, 8, 10, 17, 430, 431, 432–48

Udovicki, J.
  (1997), 359
Uganda, 439
Ukraine, 288–93, 327
  Plan A in, 288
  Plan B in, 288
  Plan C in, 289
Ukrainian Auxiliary Police Battalions, 290
UN War Crimes Tribunals, 527–8
United States, 13, 83–98. *See also*
  America
UNO, 305
Untermenschen, 187, 272
Ustasha, 16, 294–8, 362, 363, 377, 379, 380,
  386, 394, 404, 421
utilitarian genocide, 71
Uwizeye, Prefect, 457, 459

vacuum domicilium, 84
Vajpayee, Prime Minister Atal Behari, 484
Valencia, 47
Valenta, Anto, 408, 411
value-rational action, 26, 88

Van, 147
Vance-Owen Plan (1992), 391, 406, 410,
  423
Vaps, 282
Varshney, A.
  (2002), 475, 478
Vasiljevic, General, 394
Veesenmayer, Edmund, 245
Vekic, Ivan, 421
Verbannung, 191
Vernictung, 191
Versailles, 67
Vickery, M.
  (1983), 349
  (1984), 347
Virginia, 84
Visnjica, 406
Visogoths, 35
Vitez, 385, 406, 408, 410
Vitezi, 409
Vivitsky, B.
  (1990), 291
"Voja Chetnik," 398
Vojvodina, 354, 363
Vucevik, 385, 388
Vukcevic, 388
Vukovar, 356
Vulliamy, E.
  (1994), 359, 408, 410
  (1996), 403–4

Waffen-SS, 271, 279
Wagner, Gustav, 261
Wagner, M.
  (1998), 431, 460, 468
Waldheim, Kurt, 275
Wales, 57–9
Wallace, A.
  (1999), 98
Walter, Bernhard, 254
War Academy, 122
"war communism," 321
war criminals
  and disrupted employment, 222
  economic data on, 232–4
  and life traumas, 222–3
  and prewar criminal marginality, 223
  renegade Catholics as, 228–32
  samples of, 218–39
  from threatened border regions, 223–8,
    232
wartime Nazis, 237–9

wartime patriotism, 194
Washington, George, 92
Watkins, S.
  (1991), 59
Weber, Eugene, 59
Weber, Max, 25–6, 72, 188, 425
"weekend Chetniks," 421
Wegner, B.
  (1990), 200
Wehrmacht, 272–6
Wehrverbande, 195
Weingast, B.
  (1998), 24
Weinman, Ernst, 235, 264
Weinman, Erwin, 264
Welsh people, 14
Werner, Hans-Ulrich, 266
Werth, N.
  (1999), 330
Western Slavonia, 405
Wexford, 51
White Eagles, 392, 403
Whitlam, Gough, 82
Wilson, Woodrow, 67
Wimmer, A.
  (2002), 3
Windhoek, 102
Winkelman, Lieutenant-General Otto,
  245
Winthrop, John, 85
Wirth, Christian, 260, 269
Wirths, Eduard, 256
Wisliceny, Dieter, 244, 245
World War I, 134, 135–6, 138
World War I, changes to Germany as a
  result of, 182–3
WVHA, 243

Xinyiang, 338

Yalcin. *See* Cahit, Huseyin
Yalman, A.E.
  (1972), 159
Yathay, P.
  (1987), 341, 345
Yevdokimov, Count, 100
Yiftachel, O.
  (1999), 22, 519
Young Nazis, 235, 237–9
"Young Turks," 111–20, 124–31, 139
Young Turks Congress (1902), 120
Yozgat Special Forces, 166
Yugoslavia, 6, 353, 356, 423
  casualties in, 356
  economic conflict in, 364
  elections of 1990, 367–9, 384
  organic nationalism in, 376–81
  Yugoslav army (JNA), 376, 377, 389, 390,
    393–4, 395

Zagreb, 379
ZANU, 429
ZAPU, 429
Zeco, Dr., 411, 412
Zeitun, 146
Zeki, Salh, 160
Zelko, 420
zemstvo, 62
Zenica, 409
"Zero Network," 447
Zimbabwe, language in, 429
Zionism, 65
Zucotti, S.
  (1987), 311
Zyklon B gas, 187, 241